Marketing
Volume I

KV-648-761

The International Library of Critical Writings in Business History

Series Editor: Geoffrey Jones
Professor of Business History,
University of Reading

1. The Growth of Multinationals
    Mira Wilkins

2. Government and Business
    Steven W. Tolliday

3. Mergers and Acquisitions
    Gregory P. Marchildon

4. Antitrust and Regulation
    Giles H. Burgess Jr

5. The Rise of Big Business
    Barry E. Supple

6. Marketing (Volumes I and II)
    Stanley C. Hollander and Kathleen M. Rassuli

Future titles will include:

Coalitions and Collaborations in International Business
Geoffrey Jones

Business Elites
Youssef Cassis

Technology Transfer and Business Enterprise
David J. Jeremy

Organizational Capability and Competitive Advantage
William Lazonick

Women in Business
Mary A. Yeager and Lisa Jacobsen

Entrepreneurship and the Growth of Firms
Harold C. Livesay

Human Resources and the Firm in International Perspective
Bernard Elbaum

Marketing
Volume I

Edited by

Stanley C. Hollander

Emeritus and Adjunct Professor
Michigan State University, US

and

Kathleen M. Rassuli

Assistant Professor of Marketing
Indiana–Purdue University at Fort Wayne, US

An Elgar Reference Collection

© Stanley C. Hollander and Kathleen M. Rassuli 1993. For copyright of individual articles please refer to the Acknowledgements.

All rights reserved. No part of this publication may be reproduced, stored in a retrieval system, or transmitted in any form or by any means, electronic, mechanical, photocopying, recording, or otherwise without the prior permission of the publisher.

Published by
Edward Elgar Publishing Limited
Gower House
Croft Road
Aldershot
Hants GU11 3HR
England

Edward Elgar Publishing Company
Old Post Road
Brookfield
Vermont 05036
USA

A CIP catalogue record for this book is available from the British Library

ISBN 1 85278 601 9 (2 volume set)

Printed in Great Britain at the University Press, Cambridge

To Selma D. J. Hollander
and Ali Rassuli

QM LIBRARY
(MILE END)

Contents

Acknowledgements

The editors and publishers wish to thank the following who have kindly given permission for the use of copyright material.

Academy of Marketing Science for articles: Mary Ellen Zuckerman and Mary L. Carsky (1990), 'Contribution of Women to US Marketing Thought: The Consumers' Perspective 1900–1940', *Journal of the Academy of Marketing Science*, **18** (4), Fall, 313–18; Donald F. Dixon (1990), 'Marketing as Production: The Development of a Concept', *Journal of the Academy of Marketing Science*, **18** (4), Fall, 337–43; D.G. Brian Jones and David D. Monieson (1990), 'Historical Research in Marketing: Retrospect and Prospect', *Journal of the Academy of Marketing Science*, **18** (4), Fall, 269–78; Ronald A. Fullerton (1990), 'The Art of Marketing Research: Selections from Paul F. Lazarsfeld's "Shoe Buying in Zurich" (1933)', *Journal of the Academy of Marketing Science*, **18** (4), Fall, 319–27; Robert A. Mittelstaedt (1990), 'Economics, Psychology, and the Literature of the Subdiscipline of Consumer Behavior', *Journal of the Academy of Marketing Science*, **18** (4), Fall, 303–11.

American Academy of Political and Social Science for article: Ewald T. Grether (1940), 'Marketing Legislation', *The Annals of the American Academy of Political and Social Science*, May, 165–75.

American Marketing Association for articles: Robert Bartels (1951), 'Influences on the Development of Marketing Thought, 1900–1923', *Journal of Marketing*, **XVI** (1), July, 1–17; D.G. Brian Jones and David D. Monieson (1990), 'Early Development of the Philosophy of Marketing Thought', *Journal of Marketing*, **54**, January, 102–13; Ronald Savitt (1980), 'Historical Research in Marketing', *Journal of Marketing*, **44**, Fall, 52–8; (1991), 'Alfred Politz, the Man', in Hugh. S. Hardy (ed.), *The Politz Papers: Science and Truth in Marketing Research*, 1–14; Wolfgang Schaefer (1991), 'The Influence of Politz on European Research' in Hugh S. Hardy (ed.), *The Politz Papers: Science and Truth in Marketing Research*, 291–301; Hugh S. Hardy (1991), 'Epilogue: The Legacy of a Research Legend', in Hugh S. Hardy (ed.), *The Politz Papers: Science and Truth in Marketing Research*, 302–6.

AMS Press, Inc. for excerpts: Ruth Prince Mack (1936, reprinted 1968), 'The National Industrial Recovery Act,' and 'Administrative Machinery and the Public Interest', *Controlling Retailers: A Study of Cooperation and Control in the Retail Trade with Special Reference to the NRA*, 135–49 and 304–16.

Lucy Black Creighton for extract: Lucy Black Creighton (1976) 'Advocacy and Education', *Pretenders to the Throne*, 69–82 and notes.

Michael Bliss for excerpt: (1974), 'The Flight from Competition', *A Living Profit: Studies in the Social History of Canadian Business, 1833–1911*, McClelland and Stewart, 33–54 and notes.

Business Research Division, University of Colorado at Boulder, USA for articles: Van R. Wood and Scott J. Vitell (1986), 'Marketing and Economic Development: Review, Synthesis and Evaluation', *Journal of Macromarketing*, **6** (1), Spring, 28–48; Kathleen M. Rassuli and Stanley C. Hollander (1986), 'Desire – Induced, Innate, Insatiable?', *Journal of Macromarketing*, **6** (2), Fall, 4–24.

Cambridge University Press for article: Charles W. McCurdy (1978), 'American Law and the Marketing Structure of the Large Corporation, 1875–1890', *Journal of Economic History*, **XXXVIII** (3), September, 631–49.

Free Press, a Division of Macmillan, Inc. for extracts: Marshall I. Goldman (1963), *Soviet Marketing: Distribution in a Controlled Economy*, 1–6, 12, 203–7.

Harvard Business School, the President and Fellows of Harvard College for articles: Quentin J. Schultze (1982), ' "An Honorable Place": The Quest for Professional Advertising Education, 1900–1917', *Business History Review*, **LVI** (1), Spring, 16–32; Stanley C. Hollander (1964), 'Nineteenth Century Anti-Drummer Legislation in the United States', *Business History Review*, **38**, 479–500; Robert Griffith (1983), 'The Selling of America: The Advertising Council and American Politics, 1942–1960', *Business History Review*, **LVII** (3), Autumn, 388–412.

Journal of International Business Studies (JIBS) for article: Jean J. Boddewyn (1981), 'Comparative Marketing: The First Twenty-Five Years', *Journal of International Business Studies*, Spring/Summer, 61–79.

Macmillan Publishing Company, New York, USA for article: Charles Gide (1931), 'Consumers' Cooperation', in Edwin R.A. Seligman (ed.), *Encyclopaedia of the Social Sciences*, **4**, 285–91 (copyright renewed 1959); Jagdish N. Sheth and Barbara L. Gross (1988), 'Parallel Development of Marketing and Consumer Behavior: A Historical Perspective', in Terence Nevett and Ronald A. Fullerton (eds), *Historical Perspectives in Marketing: Essays in Honor of Stanley C. Hollander*, 9–33.

Charles E. Magoon for excerpt: Charles E. Magoon (1981), 'Introduction', *Photos at the Archives: A Descriptive Listing of 800 Historic Photographs on Food Marketing at the National Archives*, Santa Barbara: McNally and Loftin, West, 12–19.

Marketing Science Institute, Cambridge, Massachusetts, for excerpts: Paul N. Bloom and Stephen A. Greyser (1981), ' "The Co-ops" and "The Corporates" ', *Exploring the Future of Consumerism*, Report No. 81–102, July, 25–8.

McClelland and Stewart, Toronto, Canada for article: Douglas McCalla (1984), 'An Introduction to the Nineteenth-Century Business World', in Tom Traves (ed), *Essays in Canadian Business History*, 13–23 and notes.

Michigan State University for articles: Don R. Webb and Donald L. Shawver (1989), 'A Critical Examination of the Influence of Institutional Economics on the Development of Early Marketing Thought', in Terence Nevett, Kathleen R. Whitney and Stanley C. Hollander (eds), *Marketing History: The Emerging Discipline*, Proceedings of the Fourth Conference on Historical Research in Marketing and Marketing Thought, 22–39; D.G. Brian Jones (1991), 'Historiographic Paradigms in Marketing', in Charles R. Taylor, Steven W. Kopp, Terence Nevett and Stanley C. Hollander (eds), *Marketing History – Its Many Dimensions*, Proceedings of the Fifth Conference on Historical Research in Marketing and Marketing Thought, 3–12; Terrence H. Witkowski (1991), 'A Writer's Guide to Historical Research in Marketing', in Charles R. Taylor, Steven W. Kopp, Terence Nevett and Stanley C. Hollander (eds), *Marketing History – Its Many Dimensions*, Proceedings of the Fifth Conference on Historical Research in Marketing and Marketing Thought, 13–22; Noel J. Stowe (1983), 'Periodization of the History of Marketing Thought', in Stanley C. Hollander and Ronald Savitt (eds), *Proceedings: First North American Workshop on Historical Research in Marketing*, June, 1–2; Richard Germain (1989), 'The Adoption of Statistical Methods in Market Research: 1915–1937', in Terence Nevett, Kathleen Whitney and Stanley C. Hollander (eds), *Marketing History – The Emerging Discipline*, Proceedings of the Fourth Conference on Historical Research in Marketing and Marketing Thought, 317–30.

Carole Scott for article: Carole E. Scott (1991), 'Were Freight Rates Used to Keep the South and West Down?' in Edwin J. Perkins (ed.), *Essays in Economic and Business History*, **IX**, 51–68.

Jagdish N. Sheth and Tan Chin Tiong for article: Grant McCracken (1985), 'Clio in the Marketplace: Theoretical and Methodological Issues in the History of Consumption', in Tan Chin Tiong and Jagdish N. Sheth (eds), *Historical Perspectives in Consumer Research: National and International Perspectives*, 151–4.

University of Wisconsin Press for article: Marilyn A. Chase (1991), 'Review of: *The Credit Card Industry: A History*,' *Journal of Consumer Affairs*, **25** (2), Winter, 415–18.

Every effort has been made to trace all the copyright holders but if any have been inadvertently overlooked the publishers will be pleased to make the necessary arrangement at the first opportunity.

The publishers wish to thank the library of the London School of Economics and Political Science, The Alfred Marshall Library, Cambridge University, and the library of the City University Business School for their assistance in obtaining these articles.

Introduction

Over the past decade, scholars in many fields have demonstrated a burgeoning interest in marketing history.[1] More importantly, the field of marketing history has undergone both growth and transformation. We have attempted to pull together a set of essays that demonstrates both the diversity of recent interest in marketing history and the rich, if somewhat untapped, array of vintage scholarship that preceded it. We worked within the parameters of a time frame – the history of the past one hundred or so years – and subject to the availability of material.

The last century or century and a half holds a great deal of interest for marketing history. These volumes focus on a time when major technological advances facilitated an expansion of marketing activities, and when the discipline of marketing grew to hold a place of prominence within universities. Given the focus of this collection (the last hundred or so years), the volumes do not explore many interesting aspects of the history of marketing, such as trade routes of antiquity, the bustle of retail activity in the agora, the domestic and international commerce of the medieval era, the rise of mercantilism, or even the onset of *laissez-faire* capitalism and industrialism. We hope that the materials presented here will help graduate students and other scholars in marketing to understand and to review the recent roots of modern marketing. We also hope that historically-minded scholars and researchers in related fields will find this a useful introduction to the new marketing history.[2]

The Rise of the 'New' Marketing History

Marketing history has enjoyed a stunning growth of interest and development of content during the past ten to 15 years. Things are really improving for marketers with a historical bent; marketing history is becoming a very respectable means of adding to one's bibliography.[3] This was not always the case. Much of what would seem to be the natural audience for marketing historians, in both the marketing professorate and among marketing practitioners, is ahistorical, if not anti-historical. In spite of this prevailing sentiment, there have always been pockets of interest in marketing history. When one examines academic research in the history of marketing, it becomes apparent that the interests of academicians have changed over time.

In the 1930s and 1940s, as some of the pioneer American teachers of marketing and their students began to look back, they responded to requests to record their recollections of the origins of the formal marketing professorate (see Hagerty, 1936*; Maynard, 1941*; Weld, 1941*. Note that complete citations for books/articles cited in the introductory material which are not found in our anthology, denoted with an asterisk, may be found in the reference section). Thus, these early marketing historians preserved for later generations their impressions of the early history of our discipline. To some extent, they and their colleagues also recorded the history of marketing (as opposed to marketing thought), especially retailing and advertising history (for example, Clarke (1892*), Nystrom (1932), Hotchkiss (1938*), Converse (1945*), Atherton (1948*)).

After 1950, the main thrust in marketing history was a detailed review of the growth of marketing teaching. This thrust was based almost entirely on the energy and enthusiasm of the late Professor Robert Bartels of The Ohio State University and his students. Bartels' *History of Marketing Thought* went through three editions (1962*, 1976*, 1988*). His approach is represented in this collection by an early article he published in the *Journal of Marketing* (1951). His historical work, which in part was organized around rather arbitrarily designated decennial periods, provided a rich, full picture of the texts used by the marketing professorate from the second decade of the 20th century to very recent times.

What we refer to as the 'new' marketing history has sought to enlarge this body of thought and, apparently to a much greater degree, reach out for substantive marketing history. The great majority of the papers given at marketing history conferences between 1981 and 1991 deal with marketing practice rather than marketing teaching. The same is true of the larger body of work from which this collection is drawn. The collection we have built attempts to capture and expand on the spirit of the new thrust in marketing history.

Of course, the advocates of any submerged discipline are likely to take great delight in even the smallest of triumphs. Each conference held, each journal article accepted, each book published, even every kind word from an outsider, is likely to be seen as an achievement. Yet, we believe significant strides have been made in the last decade.

Starting in 1981, Michigan State University in cooperation with, first, the American Marketing Association (AMA), and then the Academy of Marketing Science, has sponsored five biennial Conferences on Historical Research in Marketing and Marketing Thought. These Conferences have drawn a steadily increasing number of paper submissions and attendees. Proceedings volumes have been published for all five Conferences. A sixth Conference is planned for May 1993, to be held at Emory University, with Professor Jagdish Sheth as local chair. A marketing history conference was held in England in 1991 at the University of Reading under the leadership of Professor Geoffrey Jones (a publication from the conference, edited by Tedlow and Jones, will appear in 1993*); a second conference is scheduled for 1993. In recent years, at least one annual or semi-annual meeting of the American Marketing Association, Business History Conference and Fuji Conference (Japan) has had marketing history as a major theme. Tan and Sheth (1985) chaired a conference on international historical research in consumer behaviour in Singapore.

Furthermore, a number of marketing journals have begun to show an interest in historically-oriented articles. The *Journal of the Academy of Marketing Science*, the *Journal of Retailing* and the *Journal of Public Relations*, have published special historical issues. The *Journal of Macromarketing* has decided that it will be especially hospitable to historical work, and the *Journal of Nonprofit and Public Marketing* plans to establish a special historical section that will accommodate one or more articles per issue. After one or two abortive starts, the *Journal of Advertising History*, a British publication, did perish, although that seems to have been more because of difficulty in arranging non-academic financing than due to a lack of scholarly interest. We now understand efforts to revive it are underway. Besides those rather highly focused efforts, more historically-oriented articles have appeared in the major general marketing journals, such as the *Journal of Marketing* and the *Journal of Consumer Research*.

The bookshelves have also gained numerous works on the history of advertising from both within and outside the marketing professorate. These include Schudson (1984*), Marchand (1985*) and Daniel Pope (1983*). Two major studies of the general development of American marketing have come from Richard Tedlow (*New and Improved*, 1990) and Susan Strasser (*Satisfaction Guaranteed*, 1989*). Tedlow organizes his study of marketing development in several industries around a three-stage process: an original condition of fragmented markets bounded by distance and transportation costs; the growth of large-scale mass marketing to achieve scale economies; and the development of large enough markets to permit subdivision into profitable segments. This collection includes a chapter from Tedlow's (1990) book. The AMA has published the *Politz Papers* (1991) edited by Hugh Hardy, a discussion of Politz's contribution to European and American marketing research. The AMA, through its new co-publisher, NTC Business Group, has also published Hollander and Germain's *Was There a Pepsi Generation Before Pepsi Discovered It?* (1992*), a history of marketing to, and on the basis of, youth. In 1988, Terence Nevett and Ronald Fullerton edited a collection of contributed papers entitled *Historical Perspectives in Marketing: Essays in Honor of Stanley C. Hollander*.*

Susan Benson, a labour historian, has published *Counter Cultures* (1986*), a very interesting study of retail, particularly department store, labour relations over time. Rosenberg has also written a history of Sanger-Harris (1978*) and Dillard's Department Store (1988*). Two well-received British retail company histories have dealt with W.H. Smith, the news vending chain, (Wilson, 1985*) and Victoria Wine & Spirits, the wine merchants (Briggs, 1985*). Recently, Stephen Brown (1992*) has pointed out that several current British commentaries see an historic retail revolution that was comparable to the Industrial Revolution. In this connection he particularly cites John Dawson and D. Kirby (1980*) 'Urban Retailing and Consumer Behavior: Some Examples from Western Society', in Herbert and Johnson, eds; Dawson (1982*); and Gardner and Sheppard (1989*).

Perhaps the strongest burst of work in the new marketing history has been concerned with consumer behaviour and consumption patterns. This has developed outside the marketing professorate, primarily among social historians, although some of the writers have varying degrees of familiarity with the marketing literature and use it in equally varying degree. The leading work (although its own roots may lie in Fernand Braudel's emphasis on the details of daily life) is McKendrick, Brewer and Plumb's *The Birth of a Consumer Society* (1982*), a British study of the way in which 18th century marketing (and other factors) stimulated 18th century consumption, and thus empowered the Industrial Revolution. The Canadian social historian, Grant McCracken, has published numerous articles on historical aspects of consumption and fashion. Some of those have been reprinted in his *Culture and Consumption* (1988*). He is well acquainted in marketing circles and has collaborated with some well-known marketing professors. We have included one of his methodological works in the collection (McCracken, 1985). Other major writers in this area include Richard Wightman Fox and T. J. Jackson Lears (1983*), Mary Douglas and Baron Isherwood (1978*), Rosalind Williams (1982*), and Chambre Mukerji (1983*). Lears' keynote address from the Second Historical Conference is included in these volumes. Notation of all of the marketing anecdotes and insights tucked away in numerous histories of housing, recreation, cuisine, education and other such topics is beyond the scope of this article, but a marketing historian could easily and happily fill a sabbatical purusing such material in a major research library.

Advertising archives and museums have grown substantially during the last decade or so. Major advertising archival collections have been added at the National Museum of American History (Smithsonian Institution) and the Center for Sales, Advertising and Marketing History at Duke University. Advertising museums and broadcasting museums with archival collections have been established in New York, Chicago and Portland, Oregon. These considerably extend archival resources available at the Universities of Illinois, Wisconsin and British Columbia.

To return to the work of marketing historians (meaning thereby people who feel that their primary professional affiliation is with the marketing discipline), the question arises as to what has fuelled this recent historical drive. We believe that new interest is partially a response to opportunity, partially to need.

Newly minted marketing PhDs may be recognizing opportunities to publish in an, as yet, uncrowded field. The 'publish or perish' syndrome that characterizes most major research universities and would-be research universities may be a contributing factor. While historical work is not the easiest way to get published, if an opportunity presents itself, one does not turn it away. Many American doctoral marketing students take a course in 'History of Marketing Thought' or a course in 'Marketing Theory' that contains a major historical component. The term paper from that course goes, along with its counterparts from other courses, into the student's file of 'potential articles'. A call for papers for a conference or a journal special issue induces completion of a submissable manuscript. Thus, a market engenders its own supply.

The economics of the teaching profession have played a second role. The relative per capita opportunities have been much greater during the last ten or 20 years for academics who work in the applied and vocational fields than for those who want to teach the liberal arts. This has induced some who originally trained in humanities, including history, at undergraduate and graduate levels, to pursue additional training in business administration and join marketing or other business faculties. Doing marketing history allows those individuals to exploit the full range of their talents.

But there is much more to the blossoming of marketing history than response to opportunity. There is also response to need. Formal instruction in marketing, at the university level, has existed for at least 80 years. Although that means that marketing is still a relatively young discipline, this has been a long enough time to build a history. Reasonably curious people, such as marketing professors, cannot help but wonder what happened during that time span. Perhaps, and this is all speculation, a deep suspicion of the historical naïvete of the profession has arisen among enough of those entering the professorate in the 1950s, 1960s, and even the 1970s, who subsequently heard the ideas that they learned in those years presented as novel contributions of later decades. Those whose innate attitude is congenial or receptive to historical reasoning may wonder how long this process of continuous reinvention has been going on. Some inconsistencies in the received doctrine must (or, at least, should) stimulate this reaction. The standard textbook presentation describes the existence of: (1) a production era in which industry struggled to fill demand, until (2) the Stock Market Crash/Great Depression of 1929 spawned a sales era in which industry used high pressure tactics to force its products on consumers, until (3) the birth of a marketing era in 1950 when industry became concerned with studying consumer desires. Although the production/sales/marketing triad is widely accepted, almost as a religious incantation, it simply does not square with the facts. For one thing, it does not explain the growth of marketing faculty prior to World War II; for another thing, it includes the World War II period with all of its shortages and rationing in the supposedly high pressure sales era. Three articles in Volume II on marketing management deal with the controversial issue of the history of the marketing concept: a vintage article by Beckman (1958) which provides some insights into the time when the marketing concept was purportedly born, and two contemporary articles by Hollander (1986) and Fullerton (1988), which debunk the notion.

Add a desire for roots, for a knowledge of origins (common as a discipline matures), a belief that one can learn from the past, and some antiquarian tastes that say history is interesting, and the nucleus of a marketing history boom comes into being.

The new marketing history does not yet, and may never be completely able to, answer such questions as: 'Is marketing change evolutionary or revolutionary?'; 'Is it logical and predictable or is it random?', 'How marked has change been over how long a period of time?'; 'To what extent is marketing change a function of, or a cause of, environmental change?'; 'Are there observable patterns in the marketing change process and, if so, how do they relate to accepted theories of innovation, diffusion, and paradigmatic shift, and so on?'; 'What has been the relative role of individual marketers in effecting change?'; 'How have marketing practitioners, academics, consultants and commentators, critics and regulators related to each other and to marketing within whatever change process has occurred?'; and 'What has the economy or society gained or lost by virtue of the change process?'. But if the new history has not yet resolved such questions, it is providing an experience base that should help develop useful insights into these basic issues. The definitive works have not yet appeared and are probably a long way off. In the meantime, however, much has been accomplished.

General Comments on the Collection

In commenting on the collection and the recent growth of marketing history it seeks to represent, we must begin with a few remarks regarding our choices. Given the existence of so much good recent work in marketing history, as well as the supply of fine older studies, we want to tell our readers and our colleagues why we selected these particular materials out of so many possible worthwhile choices.

We believe the readings in this anthology are all first-rate, and that each deserves to be read on its own merit.[4] An anthology is similar to a collage or assemblage in the visual arts. One must work with 'found objects', of the right shapes, colours and textures. The individual components are important, but the overall impression – the relationships among these components and the total impact that results from those relationships – are what matters. It was the overall impression which dictated our choice of readings. Therefore, taken as a whole, we believe the articles included in this collection make a statement about the history of marketing and marketing thought in this century.

Although seeking to represent the entire literature, we have imposed a number of decision rules on these selections. One aim has been to present as wide a variety of authors and sources as practicable. Consequently, all other things being equal, we have generally preferred an additional author to an additional selection by an author already in the mix. The more obscure, esoteric source has generally been preferred to the more familiar one. One natural source of contributions was the five Conferences on Historical Research in Marketing and Marketing Thought sponsored by Michigan State University, mentioned earlier. Six papers have been drawn from the proceedings of these conferences, and many of the leading figures at those meetings are otherwise represented in our volumes.

There was a special desire to include as much of an international dimension to the assemblage as possible. About one-quarter of the readings are either written by non-US authors or deal with marketing history in non-US environments. A higher percentage would have been desirable, but several limitations controlled the mixture. Some were personal to us and to many of our readers, in that we were limited to English language publications and, of course, American sources were more accessible than non-US ones in our case. A very considerable amount of work is being done on European consumption history and some current marketing history is beginning to demonstrate the deep roots of non-US marketing practices. In time, a much stronger comparative historical literature should develop.

About one-fifth of the items in the collection were published prior to 1975 and about one-half of those antedate 1950. The reasons for including these older items were four-fold. First is the sheer merit and long-term value of some of the earlier writings. Secondly, some of that writing, such as that by Professor Robert Bartels, represents important contributions to the building of our understanding of the history of marketing and marketing thought. Third is an attempt to call attention to some neglected sources that marketing historians might well want to use. The *Encyclopaedia of the Social Sciences* (*circa* 1931) and its successor, the *International Encyclopaedia of Social Sciences* (*circa* 1968) are treasure houses of very well-written essays by outstanding scholars on topics that, in many instances, are very relevant to marketing. There once was a tradition of elegance and depth to encyclopaedia presentation. The two social science publications fit in that tradition. Similarly, the *Annals of the American Academy of Political and Social Sciences* is a journal published every other month that contains requested articles on one specific topic of interest to the intelligent lay reader. It has not published any marketing issues since 1950, but during the first half of the century there were several issues devoted to consumption, credit and the cost of distribution. This all culminated in the special marketing edition (1940) from which a selection has been included in our collection. Finally, some pieces are here to demonstrate how long important marketing historical questions have been of concern. Many current students of marketing behaviour will have difficulty in believing that Levett actually wrote a history of consumption that was published in 1929. It may appear as remarkable as the fact that one of the early advertising books was Sampson's *A History of Advertising from the Earliest Times* issued in 1874*, or that an early article (by Sherman) on the history and current status of advertising practices appeared in the *Journal of the American Statistical Society* in 1900*.

The distinction between marketing history, business history and economic history becomes blurred at the margins. Some ambivalence marks the selections here in this connection. We attempt to demonstrate the depth and range of marketing history, so we have tended in some degree to prefer pieces prepared by people who are clearly identified as marketing scholars or practitioners. At the same time, there is a desire to show how marketing history can be enriched by the insights of people who do not see themselves as attached to the marketing discipline.[5] Note that these remarks tend to define the parameters of marketing history by reference to the professional affiliation of the historian. That is a traditional approach to the field, although it is a rather odd one, and we at least partially reject it in favour of considering subject matter as the determinant. In the remarks that immediately follow, we note some differences in subject interest between business and marketing historians. Later in this article, we note some methodological and stylistic ones.

There are also some rather marked differences in orientation between marketing and business historians. Subject to some very notable exceptions (Chandler (1977*), Hower (1943*), Stalson (1969*) and Tedlow (1990)), business historians generally have had little interest in marketing. They have preferred to concentrate on the history of transportation (particularly the history of carriers), finance and general management. Very few of the members of The Business History Conference or the Economic and Business Historical Society (the two major business history organizations in the US) have listed marketing or advertising as a major interest in those organizations' rosters. Although, again, we include some notable exceptions, both the American *Business History Review* and the British *Business History* contain disproportionately few marketing-related articles. Notable exceptions are R. P. T. Davenport-Hines (ed.) (1986*) *Markets and Bagmen: Studies in the History of Marketing and British Industrial Performance 1830–1939*, which was a pioneering attempt to generate interest in UK marketing history, and T. A. B. Corley (1987*) 'Consumer Marketing in Britain 1914–60'. In the US, business historians, strongly influenced by the Harvard case study tradition and the seminal work of N. S. B. Gras, have – at least until recently – emphasized individual company studies. This has given them access to rich data sources. It has also been consistent with the emphasis upon diversity and individuality. It has, however, hindered generalization.

Since the formal study of marketing is an outgrowth of the formal study of economics (see Webb and Shawver (1989) and Mittelstaedt (1990) in this collection), and since a core of marketing interest is business activity, the closeness of marketing history to business and economic history should be a matter of no surprise. After wrestling with the question of just what is the distinction between the three fields at several sessions of the Marketing History Conference, the group reached the decision that whatever interests marketers is marketing. We hope that definition applies to the contents of these volumes.

Ultimately, the relationship between the material and the collagist is a two-way street. Although the artist seeks to impose his or her concepts on the material, the found objects themselves also shape those concepts. The availability of material imposed some limitations on us.

Comments on the Articles in the Collection

Marketing Thought

The last century was a time when the body of marketing thought was formalized into a curriculum for business colleges. Our collection seeks to represent that development. As is the case with the phrase 'history of economic thought', the 'history of marketing thought' can denote the development of the body of ideas that marketing students study. More broadly defined, it can and should include the ideas that practitioners, public administrators and others also embrace. Ideally, the two definitions should coincide, but the emphasis in courses and formal publications in marketing thought *per se*, at least in America, has stressed the academic. The first section of Volume I deals with this area.

The new history has done many things in dealing with the area of marketing thought. It has deepened our understanding of the acknowledged pioneer marketing professors. It has done this by providing additional important details of their lives and by examining their journal articles as well as their textbooks. It has given detailed consideration to the training that shaped their thinking. A lively debate has flowered over the relative influence on the German Historical School and the British Neoclassical School of Economics on early marketing teachers and teaching. The Jones and Monieson (1990) article deals with this issue. Some new names have been added to the list of pioneers (Jones and Monieson, 1990) and scholars who were stimulated by thought of geography, space and location have been placed alongside the members of the standard commodity, institutional and functional schools (Sheth, Gardner and Garrett, 1988*). Dixon (1990) discusses how many leading marketing writers dealt with the familiar economic concept of value.

Zuckerman and Carsky (1990), in this collection provide an introduction to the role of female faculty, particularly those in the field of consumer economics, in building marketing thought. Additional work should be forthcoming from these authors, and perhaps others, on female professors of retailing and advertising. Both in academe and in 'the real world', these three areas were the most receptive, within marketing, to females before the women's liberation movement. However, the degree of acceptance substantially decreased as one moved from consumer economics through retailing to advertising.

The new history of thought has also begun to pay much more attention to non-US sources, a trend that we hope this collection will help accelerate. We have included an article by Kjaer-Hansen (1966) on Danish marketing. Also, reviews of two important international areas, that of comparative marketing and marketing and economic development, have been included in Volume I (Boddewyn, 1981; and Wood and Vitell, 1986, respectively).

In examining the work of such prominent consultants as Politz, Lazersfeld, Alderson and Drucker, the new marketing history has also begun to incorporate the influence of that type of practitioner. Hopefully, that trend will continue and attention will also go to the ideas of managerial practitioners beyond Wedgwood, and writers/journalists beyond Daniel Defoe and Arch W. Shaw. Fullerton's (1990) article on Lazersfeld and the two readings from Hardy's (1991) book on Politz, all included in Volume I of this collection, provide an introduction to the contribution of professional consultants. In addition, Schultze (1982), argues that professionalization of our discipline went hand in hand with education.

Historical Methods in Marketing

Since we anticipate that one of the uses of this anthology will be for doctoral seminars, we have included a section on historical methods. When people who have trained primarily as historians look at marketing history (and probably at many other varieties of applied professional and business history), they will be struck by some of the differences in philosophy, theory, methodology and style between such work and what they might regard as 'pure' history. Marketers want to shave with Occam's razor. Parsimony is a watchword and they seek the single, most powerful, law or theorem that will govern the greatest number and variety of phenomena. Many historians are suspicious of broad generalizations. They are attracted to the complexity and diversity of phenomena and their relationships to their environments. They tend to be less positivistic, more relativistic than marketers.

Savitt (1980) addresses the importance of history to marketers. For us, and we suspect the same holds for many historians, his work is an exercise in preaching to the converted. However, given the ahistorical, and even anti-historical, bias of the marketing discipline, Savitt's work was an important first step in preparing the discipline for the arrival of more historical work. Witkowski's (1991) article takes a pragmatic approach. Given the marketing disciplines' general lack of receptivity to history, Witkowski gives some advice on how to move a historical manuscript through the review process. He notes the stylistic as well as the substantive differences with typical historical journals. Articles in marketing journals tend to be shorter, less descriptive, less supported by case data, more general, precise, scientific and impersonal (or at least written in such a way as to try to seem to have those characteristics) than articles in the more humanistic historical journals. To cite just one stylistic indication, marketing writers appear very comfortable with avoiding the use of pronouns. Few would be troubled by the sentence: 'A survey of 142 Ford sedan owners revealed that 47 per cent of the Ford sedan owners thought that Ford sedan owners were more conservative than non-Ford sedan owners'. Such a style avoids any ambiguity about pronoun antecedents, and so it contributes to precision – but not to literary elegance. Reading marketing journals is like eating olives, an acquired taste, but you cannot dip the articles in martini cocktails to improve their flavour.

The differences between current marketing history (at least as explicated by some of its exponents) and traditional history are more than stylistic. Savitt (1980), Witkowski (1991) and Jones (1991) emphasize deductive paradigms while many traditional historians probably find induction more comfortable. No scholar is ever totally deductive or inductive; even the most inductive historian starts off with *a priori* assumptions about what to look at and what to look for. Nevertheless, many traditional historians (and, in practice at least, some marketing historians) want to go where the data lead them. Jones (1991), in fact, classifies marketing historians on the basis of whether they use explicit hypothesis testing – the predominant approach in non-historical marketing studies.

Since 1970, interest in the marketing of services (as a distinct area from the marketing of goods) has flowered. The distinction and the interest have strong historical roots but have taken on new intensity and a new search for a theoretical foundation in the last 20 years. Professor Leonard Berry (of Texas A&M University) and A. Parasuraman are currently preparing a history of the recent flowering, through a survey of people who have participated in or have been interested in the process. They have asked them to evaluate a list of conceivable stimulating and inhibiting factors and contributions. While surveys of professional opinion are not unknown to historians *per se*, the technique is obviously one with which marketing specialists are more comfortable.

As a final entry in the section of Volume I on methods, Stowe (1983) discusses the pitfalls of periodization, a topic which we mentioned in an earlier section.

Macromarketing

A balance has been sought between micromarketing (the study and practices of individual firms and consumers), and macromarketing (the study of marketing's relationship to the total social, political, economic and physical environment). Nevertheless, we found more work on the macro side. A large portion of Volume I deals with macromarketing. One definition of macromarketing, attributable to George Fisk, is that 'macromarketing is the study of how societies provision themselves'. Most business practitioners, and most of the marketing professorate, concentrate on micromarketing. After all, it is their job (or the job of the people they are training). Marketing scholars with historical orientations tend to be more interested in macromarketing. When the Conferences on Historical Research in Marketing and Marketing Thought recently concluded an informal agreement with the *Journal of Macromarketing* to facilitate the *Journals* republication of selected conference papers, an analysis of the five completed conference contents indicated that between 80 and 90 per cent of the presentations would qualify as macromarketing under some definition of the term. This, as was also noted earlier, is quite different from the orientation of many American business historians, who have been trained and focused on individual firm case studies. Those who, in a sense, are marketing practitioners through their roles as regulators and analysts, often have more of a macro orientation than the individual firm practitioner. Of course, in societies where an individual organization is the national or regional marketer of a particular commodity or set of commodities, as is true in some branches of agricultural marketing in capitalist societies as well as in collective ones, the distinction between macro and micro becomes blurred. (Bateman (1976) provides an introduction to the relationship between agricultural and non-agricultural marketing.) The definition also becomes blurred for individual firm practitioners who are concerned either with the impact of their activities upon the society or with how societal conditions may be altered to fit their strategic needs.

Over the past century, governments as well as individuals have proposed alternative methods of accomplishing marketing activities which directly impacted the marketing operations of individual firms and entire marketing institutions. McCalla (1984) discusses the Canadian approach, given Canada's unique characteristics. Goldman (1963) provides an introduction to a Soviet solution to distribution involving elimination of middlemen. Ruth Mack (1936) provides an overview of the National Industrial Recovery Act (NIRA), the United States' attempt at institutionalizing 'fair' pricing during the Great Depression. Critics of the syndicalist NIRA have, only half-jokingly, called it 'America's greatest conspiracy in restraint of trade'. Bloom and Greyser (1981) and Gide (1931) introduce the consumer cooperative movement, with its emphasis on putting the operation of and profit from distribution in the hands of the ultimate consumer. Gide, a well-known French economist, was one of the outstanding early 20th century philosophers of the 'Cooperative Commonwealth' movement. Readers may want to compare his style and way of thinking with that of the more recent and more pragmatic British economist, P. Sargant Florence. The differences are typical of changes among European consumer cooperative leadership during the century.

Grether(1940) and Keller (1990) give an introduction to American legal structures as they impact marketing practice. Tedlow (1981) discusses federal regulations of the advertising industry in the United States, and Miracle and Nevett (1988) compare American regulations to their United Kingdom counterparts. Magoon (1981) and Chase (1991) review food markets and credit cards (respectively), both partially regulated institutional structures which facilitate marketing activities. Finally, Scott (1991) takes up the controversial issue of whether freight rate structures were designed to keep the southern and western regions of the United States from developing.

Firms, in turn, have attempted to structure societal institutions to facilitate their operations. In our section, 'The Fight for Protection', McCurdy (1978), Hollander (1964), and Griffith (1983) discuss American marketing organizations' attempts to gain protection through legal remedies. Bliss (1974) discusses Canadian firms' solutions.

Consumer Behaviour

The major theme that has run through the social history of consumption has been the development of a consumer culture. The article by Rassuli and Hollander (1986), included in this collection, reviews this literature extensively and provides insights into the history of consumption. The dawn of the culture of consumption has been variously dated as occurring in the 15th to the 18th century and has been attributed to religious, political, scientific, economic and commercial influences. All are probably involved and interrelated. It has been accompanied by a rise in individualism and has been nurtured by a tendency towards increasing urbanization. Participation or existence in large communities has meant that people are increasingly involved in more or less anonymous contacts in which only their consumption demonstrates their status. As noted earlier, the literature on this aspect of marketing is both very rich and steadily growing.

Micromarketing-related consumer research has also grown steadily in this century.

Sheth and Gross (1988), in this collection, review the development of the consumer behaviour subdiscipline and compare it to the development of marketing thought. We include several selections that deal with this topic (see the marketing research section), but marketing historians still have many opportunities to work in this realm.

Marketing Management

Our collection covers the area of marketing management, having broken it down into the typical marketing functional areas: promotion, product, price, distribution, overall marketing management coordination and marketing research.

The main picture of mid-19th and 20th century marketing management practice that is emerging from the new marketing history is one of technical change and conceptual continuity, although certainly not rigidity. We have included the discussion of marketing from the *Encyclopaedia of the Social Sciences* (1933), as well as a classic Alderson (1958) article on a framework for marketing. Alderson is widely viewed as the outstanding marketing theorist of the post-World War II era. To provide a useful comparison with the usual discussion of marketing evolution in the Western industrial democracies, Lim (1981) discusses the development of marketing during the industrialization of Korea.

Marketing technology has changed very rapidly in recent decades, with the development of new communication devices, analytical methods, research techniques and logistical and materials handling approaches. Yet much of the strategy and tactics remain remarkably similar. If we stand back from the excitement of immediate technical changes and look at them in long-run perspective, some technical advances seem less precipitous than commonly believed. The fax machine and the satellite disc have speeded communication, but they have not provided the degree of improvement over their predecessors that the telegraph and then the telephone provided over more physical means of moving messages and messengers. While many histories of the telegraph exist, we need a good analysis of its impact on marketing. It permitted centralized management of dispersed operations, was a vital link to the control and support of travelling salesmen, and it often became an effective selling tool. It was an essential factor in the operation of modern railways. The steam-powered railroad locomotive and ship, in turn, had greater impact on the movement of goods and people than any 'miracle' of modern jet aircraft. Probably the invention of the wheel and writing must be seen as the most fundamental steps in permitting modern marketing. None of this gainsays the fact that marketers of the 1990s can draw upon an array of tools and techniques that simply were not available to their 1890s counterparts. Germain (1989) discusses the adoption of statistical methods in marketing research between 1915 and 1937. To Chandler (1988), however, marketing technology is much more than a matter of machinery, communication methods and research techniques. He is especially interested in organization structure in the large firm, where he has seen marketing functions and responsibilities become interestingly specialized, professionalized and hierarchical. A counter-tendency has emerged in the past few years, so that the future pattern is unclear. Past experience suggests that, over the long run, organizations do tend to become more complex. Increasing technical development of many marketing planning and control tasks has, and probably will continue to contribute to the growth of both internal and consulting specialists. This is another reason why some people think modern marketing started in the 1950s, when many corporate marketing departments expanded to accommodate specialization of these functions.

Products and Markets

The basic problems and tasks to which marketing techniques are applied, and the types of approaches that are made towards reaching solutions, have exhibited much less change. Marketers, for years or for centuries, have faced the problems of identifying markets or creating them. Sapir (1931) provides an introduction to the creation of fashions and their markets. Kirby (1988) discusses product diversity in the British locomotive industry. And Hollander (1984) discusses product proliferation and the simplification campaigns of the 1920s.

Even if, as some historians wish, we confine the concept of modern marketing to the large bureaucratic corporations, we have to note how strategists in the early American transcontinental railroad companies induced immigration and western settlement to provide farm markets for freight services; or how the major electric power equipment companies created markets for their machinery by financing municipal power plants and domestic electrification (Field, 1990*). Making a market is even more strategic than adapting to a market. Techniques of price discrimination and market segmentation are very old. Again, transportation provides good examples. Bonavia (1936*) describes the methods the early British railroads used to sort customers into appropriate fare categories. One line made certain that no one who could afford better rode third class by removing all light and heat from the carriages and drilling ankle-high holes in the carriage walls.

Pricing

Philips (1953) and Burns (1953) provide background history of pricing in the United States. Yamey's (1966) book looks at the issue of resale price maintenance worldwide. Dickinson (1988) discusses retailers' pricing strategies and experiences in the 1950s in the United States.

Advertising

The present work does give somewhat disproportionate attention to advertising and retailing. That reflects the availability of selections. The strong concentration on advertising in marketing history is readily explainable. Advertising is highly public. Not only is it so very visible, but in the case of print media (for so long the major medium), advertising is preserved and readily available in the historian's natural habitats, the library and the archive. Rick Pollay has called advertising 'the archaeology of marketing'.

Reyer (1927) introduces us to some antiquarian foreign (that is, from an American perspective) books on advertising. Gross and Sheth (1989) and Belk and Pollay (1985) analyse advertisements' contents, the former for the United States, the latter authors for the impact of America on Japanese advertising. Kreshel (1990) looks at the culture within an American advertising agency between 1915 and 1925. Hiley (1987) looks at the influence of Sir Hedley LeBas in British propaganda. Finally, both Pollay (1986) and Lears (1985) reflect on the societal consequences of advertising.

Information

The term 'information' is a troublesome word in the marketing literature. In a denotive sense, it designates something almost physiological – an external stimulus (or perhaps also a bit of memory) that affects some part of a cognitive (or also perhaps a subcognitive) process. Its connotation, however, goes much further and implies some notion of accuracy, completeness and objectivity. The information clerk in the railway terminal simply *informs* that the next train for X is scheduled to leave on track 10 at 11:42 a.m. He does not suggest that we need a vacation or that we will mingle with a specially glamorous group of people if we go to the dining car for the Chef's Special Lunch.

Many marketing theorists, for example, Alderson (1958), discuss advertising and selling messages as information. They are absolutely correct so long as they, and the readers, stick to the denotation. But it becomes very easy to slip and to draw conclusions about the social value of promotional work based upon the connotation of the term. Please note that the point raised here is not a condemnation of sales promotion, but only a criticism of its justification on the basis of semantic manipulation.

Whatever we consider the word 'information' denotes or connotes, and whether we look at marketing to consumers or to businesses, we can note an enormous increase. Creighton (1976) criticizes the choice that many consumeristic agencies make to supply 'better buymanship' information. Myers' (1960) article provides an interesting perspective on the growth of ABC (Audit Bureau of Circulation) and SRDS (Standard Rate and Data Service) – two informational agencies that serve the advertising industry. However, we need many more studies of such informational specialists.

Retailing and Wholesaling

The case of the abundance of historical research in retailing is a little more difficult to explain than is the similar concentration in advertising. Retailing, however, is also public in the sense that it forms part of nearly everyone's conscious daily experience (including historians) in a way that, say, wholesale establishments and market research agencies do not. Moreover, the opportunity to 'play store' vicariously seems to have great appeal. People appear to like to read about the operation of stores, hotels and hospitals. Becker and Larson (1987*) have provided an extensive bibliography of US merchant history. Much of this, of course, consists of glossy puff volumes, commissioned and designed only to please 'The Founder' and his family. However, an impressive number of critical and analytical works does exist in the retail field. (An expanded, privately reproduced list is available from Professor Boris Becker at the University of Washington, Seattle.)

Nystrom (1932) explores the development of retailing in America; Jefferys and Knee (1962) do the same for Europe, and Maeda (1981) explores the evolution of Japanese retailing. While Samson's (1981) article is somewhat dated, it still provides a good review of the department store. Benson (1981) looks at the role of saleswomen in department stores. Brown (1990) shows how the literature on the 'wheel of retailing' concept has grown since the 1950s.

The relative power of wholesalers and retailers has fluctuated over the past century. Barger (1955) provides a vintage look at the channel of distribution. Porter and Livesay (1971) and Bucklin (1972) also chronicle this history. Marx (1985) discusses the development of a distribution channel. And Shaw (1990) takes a fresh look at the old question of the costs and productivity of marketing activities in the United States.

Whatever the fluctuation in marketing activity, several long-term secular growth trends can be noted, although some of these observations could benefit from fuller historical documentation. If we distinguish between what might be called 'backroom boys', that is, planners, analysts and similar desk-based technicians and 'front-line workers', that is, wholesale sales representatives and retail store workers, it is clear that the number, role and specialization of these professionals has greatly increased. This is, in part, a manifestation of the great bureaucratization and hierarchy-heightening of the modern corporation. Whether retail and wholesale firms have become more or less specialized over time is a question whose answer, at least in part, seems to depend upon the time period under consideration.

Marketing Research

Marketing research is an area where there has been steady technical progress. The Fullerton (1990) article on Lazersfeld, the Hardy (1991) articles on Politz and the Germain (1989) article on the adoption of statistical methods in marketing research, represent our selections on this topic in the anthology.

Agenda

We have already noted particular opportunities and needs for marketing historical work on the nature of marketing change. More good micromarketing history is needed, both for its own sake and as data for macro work. We need to know more about the roles of women as both marketing teachers and practitioners. Relatively little marketing labour history exists. Benson's (1981) study (included in this collection) of department store labour is a notable exception. So is Rancher's (1991*) excellent article on variety chain store management training programmes. We have also noted the tendency of consumption history to concentrate on the upscale consumer. Fraser (1981*) is an important and valuable exception to that observation. A more mass market orientation would be welcome, as would more comparative work. But the shopping list of marketing history needs goes well beyond what we have already mentioned. For example:

1. Several areas of marketing management are under-represented in the current historical literature:
   - selling and sales management are very important aspects of marketing

management and marketing employment, but they are seldom examined in an historical context;

- although logistics has only recently been formalized as an academic discipline, it was preceded by traffic management and inventory control. There could be much benefit in long-run histories that would, in part, re-interpret the large body of transportation history into a user-oriented perspective.
- modern decision-making, facilitating technologies and research techniques have a long enough record by now to support historical analysis. Such analysis must explore practitioner utilization as well as academic popularity.

2. We need to know more about how marketing actually worked in the past. As we move away from the outmoded concept of a pre-1930 production era, a 1930–1950 sales era, and a post-1950 marketing era, we want more understanding of just who was charged with marketing responsibility (whether top management or hierarchical specialists interpreted these tasks). Just how did they interact with colleagues, competitors, customers, and suppliers? What were their strategies?

- For example, quite possibly, litigation and the threat of litigation, were more important to the 19th century firm than is the case today. Grocery trade magazines carried a substantial volume of advertising that claimed patent and brand name infringement and threatened dire consequences for any merchant who handled the offending goods.
- How have marketing ethics changed over time? Have such changes matched any growth in the information- and power-gap between buyers and sellers?

3. Turning to the supply side, there are rich, although perhaps not easily accessible, untapped data sources.

- An enormous number of newsletters circulate regularly in marketing and all other business fields. They range from promotional pieces issued by consulting and advertising agencies and other would-be business suppliers, to expert executive-directed news digests. They contain expositive and exhortatory essays, industry news and trade personnel gossip. Librarians classify these as ephemera, but one period's ephemera is the next decade's historians' ore. The main problem is to find holdings, since no institution appears to act as a newsletter depository.
- Marketing historians have made relatively little use of regulatory agency archives and court documents. In the United States, the Bureau of Corporations, which preceded the Federal Trade Commission (FTC), the FTC itself and the wartime regulatory agencies accumulated vast bundles of detailed depositories on such matters as channel, pricing and promotion practices. Some thoughtful works on grocery retailing (Morris Adelman, 1959*, *A&P*), motion picture marketing (Ralph Cassady Jr, 1964*) and gasoline distribution (Fred Allvine and Patterson, 1972*) have resulted from the study of antitrust cases, but again there are numerous waiting opportunities. When the W. T. Grant variety chain closed in what was then one of America's largest failures, the bankruptcy court proceedings were complex enought to support the publication of a newsletter for interested parties, but the case history really went unrecorded for marketing scholars.

- Marketing is a process that reaches out to all sectors of society. As noted, marketing historians have had a mid- to upper-class bias. The fashion historians have been especially concerned with elites. The more general marketing historians have claimed to be interested in mass culture, but have often interpreted this as focusing on such icons of middle class respectability as *The Saturday Evening Post*, the *Ladies Home Journal* and the *Readers Digest*. We suggest some attention to really lowbrow materials. Marketing historians have some obligation to read comic books, movie fan magazines and pulp periodicals (although we should be careful to classify that activity as working, rather than recreational, time).

4. Finally, much work can be done on the role of marketing in society. The question is very broad and it can accommodate a wide range of studies. We propose just two very different endeavours:
   - how have the dominant or more popular literary works of various periods depicted (or ignored) marketing? This 'Marketing in Shakespeare' approach may provide some clues to the popular comprehension of marketing;
   - what has been the role of marketing in economic development? There was a very self-conscious movement to export American and other marketing techniques to the Third World during the 1950s and 1960s. Enough time has elapsed to permit a good assessment of that effort. Certainly, though, that was not the first attempt to use marketing to lever economic growth. For example, as noted earlier, 19th century transport media that wanted new customers and shippers along their routes, and other land developers often used aggressive marketing techniques to attract settlers. When and how did this work?

Hopefully this will not be the last marketing history anthology to appear in print. Perhaps this present work will go into further editions, but that is for the readers, not us, to say. Also, we cannot say whether any subsequent volumes will contain articles that deal with the specific subjects that we have outlined above. But given the talent and energy that is currently being devoted to marketing history, we are certain that there will be new contributions, new insights and new questions.

S.C.H.
K.M.R.

Notes

1. The authors would like to express their gratitude to Mrs. Linda Cooley for her valuable research assistance and to Ms. Jane Lott for word processing assistance.
2. Those who want more information about earlier times can turn to good economic histories or, for a brief marketing-oriented view, to a book that may seem quite simplistic but that contains some very useful insights—G.B. Hotchkiss's *Milestones of Marketing* [1938]. Stanley Shapiro and Alton Doody (1968) have also provided a very interesting set of documents of American marketing history from the Colonial period to the Civil War.
3. The course of empires has not changed. In the United States at least, all other things being equal, the marketing doctoral student who writes an historical dissertation will still face less receptivity on the part of faculty recruitment committees than his or her colleagues who write

on strategic decision making, consumer behaviour, international marketing or marketing research methodology.

4. We will only sulk in silence, and not protest vigorously, if anyone says that that laudatory statement does not apply to our own contributions to the collection.

5. The question of defining the borders of marketing is an old and unsettled one. There are those who believe that any exchange is a marketing activity and they would extend the scope of marketing to include all sorts of social and personal interaction. Many contemporary marketing professors give lip service to that definition, but the bulk of the articles that appear in the marketing journals are devoted to the activities of business or business-like organizations and consumers seeking satisfaction from goods and services offered through what is generally understood to be the marketplace.

References*

*[Only sources not presented in the anthology are included here.]

Adelman, Morris (1959), *A&P: A Study in Price-Cost Behavior and Public Policy*, Cambridge: Harvard University Press.

Allvine, Fred C. and James M. Patterson (1972), *Competition Ltd: The Marketing of Gasoline*, Bloomington: Indiana University Press.

Atherton, Lewis E. (1948), *The Southern Country Store, 1800–1860*, New York: Greenwood Press.

Bartels, Robert (1962; 1976; 1988), *History of Marketing Thought*, Columbus, OH: Grid Inc.

Becker, Boris and Carl Larson (1987), 'Lives in Retailing: A Bibliography of American Retail Merchants in Books', *Journal of Marketing Education*, Fall, 64–71.

Benson, Susan Porter (1986), *Counter Cultures: Saleswomen, Managers and Customers in American Department Stores, 1890–1940*, Urbana: University of Illinois Press.

Bonavia, Michael R. (1936), *The Economics of Transport*, London: Nisbet Co. Limited.

Briggs, Asa (1985), *Wine for Sale: Victoria Wine and Liquor Trade, 1860–1984*, London: Botsford; Chicago: University of Chicago Press.

Brown, Stephen (1992), 'Wheel Meat Again', *International Journal of Retail and Distribution Management*, **20** (2), 39–40.

Cassady, Ralph Jr (1964), *The Private Antitrust Suit in American Business Competition: A Motion-Picture Industry Case Analysis*, Los Angeles, CA: University of California, Bureau of Business and Economic Research.

Chandler, Alfred (1977), *The Visible Hand: The Managerial Revolution in American Business*, Cambridge, MA: Belknap Press of Harvard University Press.

Clarke, Isaac Edwards (1892), *Industrial and Manual Training in Public Schools*, Washington: US Bureau of Education.

Converse, Paul D. (1945), 'The Development of the Science of Marketing – An Exploratory Survey', *Journal of Marketing*, **X**, July, 14–23.

Corley, T.A.B. (1987), 'Consumer Marketing in Britain 1914–60', *Business History*, **XXIX**, (4), October.

Davenport-Hines, R.P.T. (ed.) (1986), *Markets and Bagmen: Studies in the History of Marketing and British Industrial Performance 1830–1939*, Aldershot and Vermont: Gower.

Dawson, John (1982), *Commercial Distribution in Europe*, London: Croon Helm.

Dawson, John and D. Kirby (1980), 'Urban Retailing and Consumer Behaviour: Some Examples from Western Society', in D. T. Herbert and R. J. Johnson (eds), *Geography and the Urban Environment: Progress in Research and Application*, London: John Wiley, pp. 87–132.

Douglas, Mary and Baron Isherwood (1978), *The World of Goods*, Harmondsworth, Middlesex, England: Penguin Books Ltd.

Field, Gregory B. (1990), 'Electricity for All': The Electric Home and Farm Authority and the Politics of Mass Consumption, 1932–1935', *Business History Review*, **64** (1), 32–61.

Fox, Richard Wightman and T. J. Jackson Lears (eds), (1983), *The Culture of Consumption*, New York: Pantheon Books.

Fraser, W. Hamish (1981), *The Coming of the Mass Market in 1850–1914*, Hamdon: Archon Books.

Gardner, C. and J. Sheppard (1989), *Consuming Passion: The Rise of Retail Culture*, London: Unwin Hyman.

Hagerty, James E. (1936), 'Experiences of Our Early Marketing Teachers', *Journal of Marketing*, **I**, July, 20.

Hollander, Stanley C. and Richard Germain (1992), *Was There a Pepsi Generation Before Pepsi Discovered It?*, Linwood, IL: NTC Business Group for the American Marketing Association.

Hotchkiss, George B. (1938), *Milestones in Marketing*, New York: MacMillan Company.

Hower, Ralph (1943), *History of Macy's of New York, 1858–1919*, Cambridge, MA: Harvard University Press.

Marchand, Roland (1985), *Advertising the American Dream*, Berkeley: University of California Press.

Maynard, H. H. (1941), 'Marketing Courses Prior to 1910', *Journal of Marketing*, **V**, April, 382.

McCracken, Grant (1988), *Culture and Consumption*, Bloomington: Indiana University Press.

McKendrick, Neil, John Brewer and J. H. Plumb (1982), *The Birth of a Consumer Society*, Bloomington: Indiana University Press.

Mukerji, Chambre (1983), *From Graven Images: Patterns of Materialism*, New York: Columbia University Press.

Pope, Daniel (1983), *The Making of Modern Advertising*, New York: Basic Books.

Rancher, Alan R. (1991), 'Dime Store Chains: The Making of Organization Men: 1880–1940', *Business History Review*, **65**, Spring, 130–63.

Rosenberg, Leon Joseph (1978), *Sangers', Pioneer Texas Merchants*, Austin: Texas State Historical Association.

Rosenberg, Leon Joseph (1988), *Dillard's, The First Fifty Years*, Fayetteville: University of Arkansas Press.

Sampson, Henry (1874), *A History of Advertising from the Earliest Times*, London: Chatto and Windus.

Schudson, Michael (1984), *Advertising, the Uneasy Persuasion*, New York: Basic Books.

Shapiro, Stanley J. and Alton F. Doody (eds) (1968), *Readings in the History of American Marketing: Settlement to Civil War*, Homewood, ILL: Richard D. Irwin, Inc.

Sherman, Sidney A. (1900), 'Advertising in the United States', *Journal of the American Statistical Society*, No. 52, December, 119–62.

Sheth, Jagdish N., David M. Gardner and Dennis E. Garrett (1988), *Marketing Theory: Evaluation and Evolution*, New York: Wiley.

Stalson, J. Owen (1969), *Marketing Life Insurance*, Byrn Mawr, PA: Richard D. Irwin.

Strasser, Susan (1989), *Satisfaction Guaranteed*, New York: Pantheon Books.

Tedlow, Richard and Geoffrey Jones (eds) (1993), *The Rise and Fall of Mass Marketing*, London and New York: Routledge.

Weld, L. D. H. (1941), 'Early Experiences in Teaching Courses in Marketing', *Journal of Marketing*, **V** (April), 380.

Williams, Rosalind (1982), *Dream Worlds: Mass Consumption in the 18th Century*, Berkeley: University of California Press.

Wilson, Charles (1985), *First with News: The History of W.H. Smith 1792–1972*, London: Cape.

Part I
History of Thought

[1]

THE Journal of

Marketing

Volume XVI   JULY, 1951   Number 1

INFLUENCES ON THE DEVELOPMENT OF MARKETING THOUGHT, 1900-1923

ROBERT BARTELS
The Ohio State University

As THE study of marketing approaches the half-century mark, it is both interesting and profitable to review its development and to observe some of the early influences which helped to shape its course.

Such influences were varied and were both objective and subjective in nature. Evidence of the more objective factors is found in the fact that the form and content of marketing thought have usually reflected the nature of the predominant marketing problems. They have mirrored also the growing need for a body of instructional material for academic use. Subjective factors were equally influential in the development of marketing thought, for in many instances the attention of early students was drawn to marketing mainly because of characteristics of their own make-up.

Between 1902 and 1905, four men, simultaneously and independently in different parts of the country, so crystallized their knowledge of marketing that they began to teach it. Not only was the environment ripe for investigation owing to the increasing concern of businessmen with distributive activities but also men had by then begun to see the potential benefits of a research approach to the solution of marketing problems. Subsequently, as scientifically trained minds sifted the known and discoverable facts about marketing, writers produced a literature useful for both business and educational purposes. Thus there developed during the years prior to the early 1920's a substantial and rather uniform body of marketing thought.

1

From that starting point have evolved broader and more specialized studies of marketing.

This paper is concerned with those subjective influences which inspired the first students of marketing. A study of the initial group of student-writers, active before the middle 1920's, reveals some of the basic influences which have promoted and shaped contemporary marketing thought.

TYPES OF SUBJECTIVE INFLUENCES

The initial interest of pioneering students in the subject of marketing was generally the result of three types of influences: youthful experiences, academic stimulus, and occupational demands. Youthful experiences planted, and academic stimulus cultivated, seeds of interest in marketing activity; occupational demands shaped the growing thought until it yielded a harvest of writings.

Youthful Experiences

Youthful experiences most often included contacts with marketing made through family and friends and through part-time and after-school clerking and selling in retail stores. By such means many youths were made aware of problems of marketing and were attracted to marketing as an interesting field of economic activity.

Youthful experiences did not produce immediate marketing thought, but they did have a remote influence upon it. They furnished food for thought and also helped to shape the frames of reference through which individuals later viewed marketing activity. Thus they not only stimulated interest in marketing but also they molded to some extent the forms in which inquiry would take shape.

Academic Stimulus

The second influence upon the development of marketing thought and literature was academic in nature, stimulated not by first-hand marketing experiences of students but by their contacts with teachers and textbooks. Youthful experiences, involving mainly physical perceptions rather than intellectual conceptions, tended to raise questions rather than answer them. It was necessary, therefore, that the casual observer become a student before a science of marketing could be born.

Teachers constituted one important source of such influence; books, another. At first, the influential teachers were those in the fields of economics, sociology, psychology, and the like; marketing teachers later constituted a more direct and stronger influence. Through books, too, some students discovered their interest in marketing. Such influences sometimes brought sudden illumination. In other cases they worked more slowly, first providing information, next arousing interest and intellectual curiosity, and finally stimulating original marketing research.

Occupational Demands

Professional necessities constituted the third, and possibly the most important, influence upon the development of marketing thought. They usually provided the occasion for research and for the expression of the thought which was developed.

In order to learn the facts of their subject, early teachers of marketing had to trace the course of products to the market, observe the operation of marketing institutions, and analyze the costs incurred by middlemen. They explained and interpreted marketing phenomena, created concepts, coined phrases, and defined terms. They wrote textbooks and articles to provide material for their students. They talked to civic and business groups, engaged in professional consultation, and pooled their information for mutual benefit. Such demands on them had direct bearing upon the development of marketing thought and literature.

INFLUENCES UPON EARLIEST TEACHERS OF MARKETING

Four of the earliest contributors to marketing thought were Edward D. Jones, Simon Litman, George M. Fisk, and James E. Hagerty, who, between the years of 1902 and 1905, offered marketing courses in Michigan, California, Illinois, and Ohio, respectively. Their interest in marketing grew mainly out of their occupational environment.

Edward D. Jones. Jones was a product of the University of Wisconsin, where he taught from 1895 until 1902 and where he undoubtedly came into contact with the prominent liberal economists of that campus. He went to the University of Michigan in 1902, at a time when Henry C. Adams, head of the economics department at Ann Arbor, was extending the field to "more practical activities of men." Both Adams and Fred M. Taylor encouraged him to give a course entitled "The Distributive and Regulative Industries of the U. S.," described in the University Bulletin of 1902 as follows: "This course will include a description of the various methods of marketing goods, of classification, grades, brands employed, and of wholesale and retail trade. Attention will also be given to those private organizations, not connected with money and banking, which guide and control the industrial process, such as trade associations, boards of trade and chambers of commerce, etc."

This was presumably the first marketing course taught in this country. Jones very soon devoted himself entirely to the field of management, and neither Ralph Starr Butler nor Hugh E. Agnew, both of whom were at Michigan when he introduced his course, had direct contact with him. Nor did any other subsequent marketing writers, so far as is known.

Simon Litman. Litman studied at the School of Political Science, Paris, and also in Munich and Zurich before going to Berkeley. At the suggestion of Adolph C. Miller, chairman of the newly organized department of economics, he offered at the University of California, beginning in January 1903, a marketing course described in the Bulletin of 1902–1903 as follows: "Technique of Trade and Commerce: A study of the organization and institutions of commerce; commercial forms and practices." Faced with the problem of developing content for such a course, Litman interviewed San Francisco merchants and studied outlines of related material in two German books written by Cohn and Grunzel. With these aids he organized the course which he presented there from 1902 until 1908 and which he developed thereafter at the University of Illinois, where he replaced George M. Fisk. Litman continued to teach marketing at Illinois until 1921, when the work was taken over by Berhrens and, two years later, by Paul D. Converse. His writings were in the field of international trade. He retired in 1946.

George M. Fisk. In 1903, Fisk introduced marketing instruction at the University of Illinois, where he taught five years. Shortly after he left Illinois' for another school, his career was terminated by an untimely death. He, too, wrote in the field of foreign commerce, his main contribution being entitled *International Commercial Policies.*

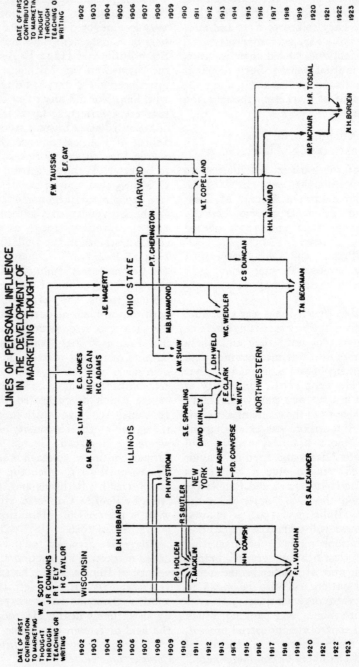

LINES OF PERSONAL INFLUENCE
IN THE DEVELOPMENT OF
MARKETING THOUGHT

James E. Hagerty. The first marketing course at The Ohio State University was offered by Hagerty in 1905. Originally entitled "The Distribution of Products," it was renamed in the following year "The Distributive and Regulative Industries." Hagerty's interest in marketing evidently was first felt about 1900 when, as a graduate student of sociology at the University of Pennsylvania, he undertook for his dissertation a study of mercantile institutions. He, too, had studied at the University of Wisconsin, as well as elsewhere at home and abroad, but his early investigation of marketing occurred in Philadelphia. By questionnaire and interview, he interrogated merchants concerning their practices, and familiarized himself with the scant writings on the subject then appearing. They consisted mainly of articles in trade journals, filed at The Philadelphia Commercial Museum. After 1901, when he went to Columbus, his thinking was shaped also by such books as *Credits and Collections*, edited by T. J. Zimmerman (1902); *The History of the Standard Oil Company*, by Ida M. Tarbell (1904); and reports of the Bureau of Corporations and of the Industrial Commission, Volume VI of which he used as a text for the marketing course which he introduced in the spring of 1905. Hagerty continued to develop the subject of marketing for many years and retained an interest in it until his retirement in 1940.

CENTERS OF INFLUENCE UPON MARKETING THOUGHT

Although the first marketing courses were offered at the four above-mentioned schools, the principal contributions to early marketing thought were made elsewhere. The eminent marketing writers of the first two decades of this century were not the product of instruc-

tion by those teachers, nor did the more marketing-minded students become connected with those institutions. Interest in marketing germinated not so much in specific courses in that subject as in progressive study of economics. Consequently, individuals receptive to a career in the study of marketing found a natural attraction to universities renowned for their advanced economic thought, and the majority of the earliest marketing writers were sooner or later associated with such schools. Foremost among such institutions were the University of Wisconsin and Harvard University.

The Wisconsin Group

At the turn of the century the University of Wisconsin was a seat of progressive and liberal economic thinking, for on her campus were W. A. Scott, John R. Commons, Richard T. Ely, and H. C. Taylor. It was natural, therefore, that Wisconsin should play a leading role in the evolution of marketing thought. To her campus were attracted such pioneer students of marketing as Jones, Hagerty, Hibbard, Macklin, Nystrom, Butler, Converse, Comish, and Vaughan. Since the residence of some of these men at Madison overlapped, they were a stimulating influence upon one another.

Benjamin H. Hibbard. The impulsion to study marketing came to Hibbard gradually, almost accidentally, growing for the most part out of conditions of his work. While living in northern Iowa, he had noticed for years that farmers sold their produce at a very low figure, whereas the same products were resold later at a much augmented price. In 1902, therefore, when he began teaching at Iowa State College in a small department of agricultural economics which aspired to do some research work but which had no funds for such activity, he undertook a modest study of grain marketing, the novelty of which gained for him attention out of proportion to his findings.

A few years later, in 1913, Hibbard was invited to the University of Wisconsin to take charge of marketing studies and research. There he gave what was probably the first organized course in cooperative marketing of agricultural products, and he wrote a number of bulletins, particularly on the subject of marketing dairy products. In 1921, he published the book, *Marketing Agricultural Products*, for which he is perhaps best known as a marketing writer.

Theodore Macklin. During the latter years of Hibbard's teaching at Iowa State College, Macklin, a student there, became interested in marketing. Immediately following his graduation in 1911, and while serving as a lecturer at the college, he assisted P. G. Holden, Director of Extension, in work which took him on observation trips throughout the state. Like Hibbard, Macklin was strongly impressed with the fact that while farmers did a fine job of producing, they did not perform the marketing task with equal effectiveness. His conviction that he should learn more about marketing led him in 1913 to the University of Wisconsin, where he studied the subject and received his Ph.D. in 1917. Macklin's selection of Wisconsin may have been influenced by Hibbard's transfer there in the same year.

Before completing his doctoral requirements, Macklin observed, studied, and taught agricultural marketing at Kansas State Agricultural College (1915–1916, 1918–1919). He became associated in 1919 with the University of Wisconsin in a professorship which continued until 1930, when he departed for California

to become Chief of the State's Division of Markets. During the early years after his return to Wisconsin he wrote his principal contribution to marketing literature, a book entitled *Efficient Marketing for Agriculture*, published in 1921.

Paul H. Nystrom. The Wisconsin terms of Nystrom, Hibbard, and Macklin overlapped by one year. Nystrom left Madison for Minnesota in 1914. During his stay at Wisconsin, he was instrumental in advancing marketing as a subject of economics; Hibbard was teaching the subject in the agricultural division of the University.

The marketing interests of Nystrom apparently were a by-product of other academic pursuits. His interest in the subject appeared relatively late in his scholastic development, arising out of his earlier experiences as a worker on farms and in retail stores until 1897, as a teacher and principal in Wisconsin schools until 1908, and as special investigator for the Wisconsin Tax Commission during the summers of 1906, 1907, and 1908. Contrary to common procedure, it was after most of those varied activities that he proceeded to take his college training, receiving his Ph.B. in 1909, M.Ph. in 1910, and Ph.D. in 1914, all from Wisconsin. During that period of study he was also employed in the extension division of the University.

Nystrom's principal interest during those years was in economics, particularly in taxation. His interest in marketing reputedly grew partly from a study of taxation of retail establishments. In 1913, while yet an Assistant Professor of Political Economy at the University of Wisconsin, he published a book entitled *Retail Selling and Store Management*. The manuscript had been in circulation in mimeographed form as early as 1911, when it was used by extension classes of the University. He completed his graduate studies in 1914, and his doctoral dissertation was published the following year as his second book, *Economics of Retailing*.

After teaching for one year at the University of Minnesota, Nystrom interrupted his academic career with several years in business practice. From 1921–1927, he was director of the Retail Research Association and the Associated Merchandising Corporation. His writings were likewise interrupted, and not until after his return to teaching did he, in 1928, publish *The Economics of Fashion*. The contents of this book were drawn in large measure from his practical experience. Upon returning to teaching, he offered a course in the economics of consumption, and that too found ultimate expression in *The Economics of Consumption*, published in 1929.

Ralph Starr Butler. Butler joined the staff of the University of Wisconsin in 1910 as an Assistant Professor of Business Administration, with responsibility for developing correspondence study courses in business for the University Extension Division. He went there fresh from a stimulating experience in Cincinnati as assistant to the Eastern Sales Manager of the Procter & Gamble Company, his first work in the field of marketing. He had been impressed with the fact that a manufacturer seeking to market a product had to consider and solve a large number of problems before he ever gave expression to the selling idea through salesmen or advertising. This recollection was vividly with him when he went to Wisconsin with responsibility for preparing the correspondence course.

When Butler arrived at Wisconsin, the curriculum included mostly courses which dealt with such specific business activities as bookkeeping, retail salesmanship, advertising, commercial law, courses which had prior to that time also been taught in other schools and colleges. Upon surveying the meager literature of business then available, he was astonished to find that none of it dealt with the broader considerations which lie behind the final expression of the sales idea. Since the subject had never been treated by any writer, he decided to prepare a correspondence course covering those marketing functions a manufacturer must perform before making actual use of salesmen and advertising.

After experiencing considerable difficulty in finding a name for this field of business activity, Butler finally decided upon "Marketing Methods." A course consisting of six printed pamphlets was published under that title by the University in the fall of 1910. The following year, Butler revised the same material for publication by the Alexander Hamilton Institute under the title *Selling and Buying*, as part of the 14th Volume of its first series of textbooks. The title was changed to *Marketing* after a year or two, with further revision of the material. The only such book on the subject, it was widely used in schools and colleges for several years.

In 1911 also, Butler expanded the material and offered his course to resident students of commerce at the University. Although courses of similar content were then offered elsewhere, it is possible that Butler's was the first to use the title of "Marketing," even as his text was the first to appear with that term in the title. He later wrote some articles on marketing subjects, but his major contributions to the field have perhaps been made in his practice of marketing, during his many years as a distinguished business executive.

Newel H. Comish and *Floyd L. Vaughan.* Newell H. Comish was another marketing writer who also came under the Wisconsin influence. He took his Master's degree at Madison in 1915 and his Ph.D. in 1929. His work brought him into contact with Hibbard and Macklin, both of whom contributed to his training in the field. Very likely the influences of that environment, as well as of his own direct farm experience induced Comish later to write *The Cooperative Marketing of Agricultural Products,* published in 1929.

Floyd L. Vaughan was another early student of marketing at the University of Wisconsin where he received his Ph.D. in 1923. Before that time he had had considerable teaching experience and had worked with the Federal Trade Commision. In 1920, with W. H. S. Stevens, he wrote on country grain marketing for *The Grain Trade,* Vol. 1. Following his work at Wisconsin, he published *Marketing and Advertising* in 1928.

Contribution of the Wisconsin Group

Thus the men who studied, taught, and wrote of marketing at the University of Wisconsin were responsible for taking several of the initial steps in the establishment of marketing science. Attracted from different sections of the country and from both academic and practical pursuits, nurtured by the progressive atmosphere of the campus to which they gravitated, and mutually stimulated by their associations with one another, they are credited with several innovations. They crystallized the conception of this field of activity as *marketing* and were perhaps the first to use this term in the title of a course or book on the subject. They are credited with offering the first course in cooperative marketing of agricultural products, with spreading the knowledge of marketing through university extension correspondence and resident courses, and with the promotion of research in institutional as well as agricultural marketing. From that university, therefore, emanated during the early years of the century a strong influence upon the development of marketing thought and literature.

The Harvard Group

Another center of influence in the development of early marketing thought was at Cambridge, with Harvard University's Graduate School of Business Administration and its Department of Economics. The marketing contribution there has been distinguished and unique. In addition to producing much of its own marketing talent, Harvard has played a generous part in the intellectual development of other students whose residence there has been only temporary. Among the earlier contributors to marketing thought and literature who have either taught or studied at Harvard are the following: Cherington, Shaw, Copeland, Tosdal, Weidler, Maynard, McNair, Borden and Vaile.

Paul T. Cherington. An example of the nature and importance of personal influence is found in the case of Cherington, whose interest in marketing was stimulated in part by his association with James E. Hagerty. The contact was made at the University of Pennsylvania, where Cherington was a student and Hagerty, while teaching, was assembling the material on marketing channels and institutions which constituted his Ph.D. dissertation in sociology. Cherington probably had commercial interests prior to his meeting with Hagerty, but it is understood that he acknowledged that personal contact and influence to be instrumental in molding his thought and interest in marketing.

Cherington received his B.S. in 1902

INFLUENCES ON DEVELOPMENT OF MARKETING THOUGHT   9

and, while carrying on graduate studies for which he received his A.M. in 1908, served also as Editor of Publications of The Philadelphia Commercial Museum. Upon leaving Philadelphia in that year, he went to Harvard University, where he taught marketing through 1935. For a number of years after that he devoted his efforts entirely to professional marketing research. As an early marketing writer, he is best known for *Advertising as a Business Force,* published in 1912, and for *The Elements of Marketing,* published in 1920.

A. W. Shaw. Shaw contributed to and partook of the Harvard influence when, about 1910, he went to Cambridge to help reorganize the new Graduate School of Business Administration. While there, he also lectured on business policy. He wrote "Some Problems in Market Distribution" for the *Quarterly Journal of Economics* in 1912, the year of publication of the advertising book by Cherington, with whom he had close contact. His book, *An Approach to Business Problems,* was published in 1916.

Shaw's interest in marketing evidently developed after he had made notable contributions to general business practice. From the early 1900's, while in business with L. D. Walker, manufacturing office equipment, he widely observed business procedures as a means of devising improved systems and methods. Everywhere the uniformity of business needs and functions impressed him more forcibly than the diversity of circumstances in which the basic practices were found. He devoted himself, therefore, particularly through his magazine called *System,* to advancing the interchange of ideas among businessmen, who, he felt, were retarding business progress by the narrow isolation of their individual interests and experiences. This effort to emphasize the order and uniformity of

business also colored his later writings on marketing.

When he was at Harvard, other factors contributed to his thinking which resulted in the above-mentioned article entitled "Some Problems in Market Distribution." Having become more conscious of marketing activity, he was aware of the need for a name to identify the distributive activity, as Butler also had been. A German professor had made him aware of the fact that a science must have a concept. While seeking the concept for the unformulated and undescribed activity in which he was interested, his thinking was further influenced by an awareness of the constant change which pervades all things, an idea which he gained from a lecture on the religion of pure experience. Thus he began to conceive marketing as the process of "matter in motion" and to discern therein the uniformity and order which he had found in other business practice.

At that same time he was influenced also by Dean Gay, whose lectures emphasizing the merchant in the economic history of England challenged Shaw to trace the activity of trade and its functions. At Gay's suggestion, Shaw later lectured to the former's class on what he had found out about the functions of the British merchant. The substance of the lecture became the content of the article published in the *Quarterly Journal of Economics.*

Melvin T. Copeland. The weight of personal influence is clearly evident in the marketing career of Copeland, both as regards the factors which led him to become a specialist in knowledge of the cotton industry and those which stimulated his contribution to marketing literature in the form of a problems book.

His interest in the cotton industry was an outgrowth of a study made in 1906 as a graduate student in economics under the direction of Professor F. W. Taussig. The usual library research and field investigation familiarized him with the industry and its marketing activities. During the next six years, he taught economic history and economic resources of Europe at Harvard, spent a year abroad as a Traveling Fellow giving particular attention to cotton manufacturing, and returned to teach for two years at New York University. In 1912, the year of publication of his *Cotton Manufacturing Industry of The United States*, he returned to Harvard to the Graduate School of Business Administration with a specific assignment to start a course known as "Commercial Organization." Two years later the name of the course was changed to "Marketing."

Upon his return to Cambridge, his development was further influenced by his contact with Dean Gay, who, according to Copeland, had brought to the Graduate School the idea of teaching by "cases" and who required that instruction, insofar as possible, should be by discussion of problems rather than by lecturing. Copeland started to teach by this method in 1912. The following summer, as field agent of the newly established Bureau of Business Research, he gathered figures on the cost of doing business in retail shoe stores. The next year he was put in charge of a similar study of the retail grocery trade. In 1916 he was appointed Director of the Bureau of Business Research, in charge of the studies of operating expenses in various retail and wholesale trades. Thus, throughout the early years of his teaching career Copeland was not only indoctrinated with the method of teaching from problems, but also by his experience prepared himself for the development and presentation of courses in that manner.

In 1919, when Wallace B. Donham became Dean of the Graduate School of Business Administration and when Copeland returned to teaching from his wartime service, one of Dean Donham's first requests was that he undertake the preparation of a problems book. This resulted in the publication of the first edition of Copeland's *Problems in Marketing*, published in 1920. In that same year, again at Dean Donham's request, the Bureau of Business Research undertook to organize a collection of problems for other courses. Copeland's continued research and contacts with business led ultimately to the publication in 1924 of his *Principles of Merchandising*.

Harry R. Tosdal. Tosdal, like a number of other marketing writers, entered the field by way of the department of economics. Upon completion of his doctorate in 1915 at Harvard University, he taught economics at Massachusetts Institute of Technology (1915–1916), at Boston University (1916–1920), and at Harvard, as a lecturer on economics, from 1918–1920. In 1920, he became affiliated with the Graduate School of Business Administration on a full-time basis as an Associate Professor of Marketing and Director of Student Research. The following year, he published *Problems in Sales Management*.

Malcolm P. McNair. McNair was one of the men whose training and experience were both gained at Harvard. He received two degrees there and has taught there since 1917. For the first three years, however, he instructed in government and English. In 1920, like Tosdal, he began to teach marketing. Five years later he published *Retail Method of Inventory* and, in 1926, *Problems in Retailing*.

Neil H. Borden. The thinking of Borden concerning marketing as well as the character of some of his contributions to the field have been in some measure the product of his associations as a student and member of the staff at the Harvard Graduate School of Business Administration. Going there from the University of Colorado, where in 1919 he received his A.B. degree, he was exposed to the case method of teaching which Copeland and others had been developing for several years. Thus not only the substance of his marketing thought but his convictions as to the method by which the subject should be taught were firmly molded by the guiding influence of his associates.

Following the completion of his M.B.A. work in 1922, he served as a case collector in the Harvard Bureau of Business Research. The following year he taught marketing under Professor Copeland, from the latter's newly published *Problems in Marketing*. He also assisted Daniel Starch in the latter's advertising course. Starch's interest in advertising came from his training as a psychologist, and, although he made some use of problems, his teaching method differed from that being developed at Harvard. When Starch left the school, Borden was put in charge of the advertising course and immediately put it on a problems basis. Out of that effort came his original edition of *Problems in Advertising*, published in 1927.

Contribution of the Harvard Group

In contrast to the University of Wisconsin, which early marketing writers left after their student days to teach elsewhere, the Harvard Graduate School retained on its teaching staff a large proportion of the early writers who studied there. Members of the Harvard staff were participants in the early development of principles of marketing, but their principal contribution throughout the years has been the compilation of marketing problems, both general and specialized.

The Middle Western Group

Notwithstanding the fact that the earliest marketing courses were offered mainly in the Middle West, the universities of that area, with the exception of Wisconsin, did not make major contributions to marketing thought and literature during the early years. That seeming paradox may have resulted, not from the character of the marketing taught but from the nature of the offerings in economics. While these institutions had some notable economists on their faculties, none of them had such an aggregation of prominent economists as there were at Wisconsin and Harvard. Nevertheless, as interest in marketing grew, valuable contributions to the growing body of marketing thought were made by men working and teaching in Minnesota, Michigan, Illinois, and Ohio. Among the men of that group were Weld, Clark, Ivey, C. S. Duncan, Converse, Weidler, Maynard, and Beckman.

L. D. H. Weld. Weld was another early writer whose interest in marketing grew out of the demands of his working environment. Going to the University of Minnesota in 1912, he spent one year in the Economics Department before moving to the College of Agriculture, which was eager to develop knowledge of how Minnesota products were marketed. Farmers were particularly interested in the practice of cooperative marketing. Accordingly, Weld spent much of his time in finding out what became of products after they left the farms. He also taught one course in agricultural marketing. It is possible that the word "marketing" in the title was the first such use of the term in connection with a course on the marketing of farm products, notwithstanding the fact that Taylor and Hibbard were simultaneously covering similar ground in their course in farm management at Wisconsin.

Since there was practically no literature on the subject when Weld began to teach marketing in the fall of 1913, he had to develop his knowledge of it largely by his own resourcefulness. He studied at first hand the movement of grain through the Minneapolis Chamber of Commerce, and the use of future trading. His findings were reported to the Bureau of Markets of the U. S. Department of Agriculture, but were not published, reputedly because they put future trading and its economic functions in too favorable a light. Furthermore, he was called before a Minnesota legislative investigating committee which tried to prove that he had been instructed by the trustees of the University to teach his dangerous doctrines about the efficiency of grain marketing through the Minneapolis Chamber of Commerce and about the beneficial functions of future trading.

In gathering information on marketing processes, Weld actually accompanied shipments of butter and eggs to the market in order to trace their course through the wholesalers, jobbers, and retailers in New York, Chicago, and other cities. He also studied pricing methods, commodity exchanges, auction markets, and the cooperative shipping associations of Minnesota.

The results of his investigations were twofold. First, he increased his knowledge of marketing for teaching purposes; second, he developed in his own mind some fundamental principles about marketing. After two years of this activity, he finished writing in 1915 *The Marketing of Farm Products*, which was published the following year, after Weld had gone to Yale. He remained at the Sheffield Scientific School for the two more

years that he continued in the teaching profession. During his tenure there he continued in marketing research, with his interests mainly in the field of manufactured goods.

Another significant event of those years was perhaps the first associative effort among men interested in teaching marketing. In 1914, Weld had an opportunity to read before the American Economic Association a paper on "Market Distribution," thus making the first scientific presentation of the subject of marketing before that group. Four years later, at a meeting of the same Association in Richmond, Weld assembled five or six men who were interested in marketing for a discussion of their work. That small group, meeting annually and growing fairly rapidly, was the nucleus out of which later developed the National Association of Teachers of Marketing.

Fred E. Clark. A variety of factors contributed to the interest which Clark found in marketing. As a young man he sold house-to-house such commodities as Rand McNally Atlases, Wearever Aluminum Ware, and ironing boards. His first intellectual contact with marketing, however, was made during his graduate study, and the major influences upon his writing occurred after he had begun to teach.

Reared on a farm and schooled at Albion College, Clark went for graduate training in economics to the University of Illinois, where he was influenced by David Kinley, head of the Department of Economics and of the School of Commerce, to the end that his interests in practical economics and private business were enlarged. For his Master's thesis he chose a marketing subject, "The Cooperative Grain Elevator Movement in Illinois." Like all early students of marketing, he was much influenced by the works of such pioneers as Weld, Nystrom, Butler, Shaw, and Samuel E. Sparling of the University of Wisconsin.

From 1914 to 1919, following his academic training, Clark had a succession of one-year teaching appointments, the demands of which evidently caused him to shift his major interest from economics to marketing. By 1918 he had prepared in mimeographed form the first draft of his text, *Principles of Marketing*, which was used that year at the University of Michigan, where he was teaching. Henry C. Adams, head of the Economics Department there, gave him strong encouragement to write, as did Dean Heilman at Northwestern University, to which Clark moved in 1919. The book finally was published in 1922, after the first draft had been used as a text at Michigan, Minnesota, and Northwestern.

Paul W. Ivey. Ivey's professional path closely paralleled that of Clark. Having taken his A.B. at Lawrence College, he did his Master's work concurrently with Clark at the University of Illinois. Each earned his degree there in 1913. Ivey, too, had a succession of teaching assignments which took him consecutively to Dakota Wesleyan, to the Universities of Michigan, Iowa, and Nebraska, and, in 1923, to Northwestern University, where by that time Clark had been for four years. After some years, he went to teach at the University of Southern California.

During his years of teaching, Ivey, like Clark, was evidently distilling from his experiences and business contacts the essence which he presented in his book, *Principles of Marketing*, published in 1921. The influences of his subsequent years evoked from him a series of publications specially related to the field of retail salesmanship.

Paul D. Converse. The marketing interests and viewpoint of Converse were shaped significantly during his youth and college years by intellectual influences both parental and academic, which gave him a social consciousness as well as a high regard for practicality. In his father, a well-educated Presbyterian minister with interests in social reform, Converse saw, sometimes by contrast, the importance of practical applicability of theory. From his economics teachers, trained at Wisconsin, he gained a healthy respect for private property, profit, and individual initiative. From experience as an examiner for the Federal Trade Commission, he gained convictions of the soundness of "progressive" liberalism, the partiality of pressure groups, and the basic soundness of individual self-interests in the private enterprise system.

His first course in marketing was taken during a brief enrollment at the University of Wisconsin in 1915, where he studied under Ralph Starr Butler the material which appeared in the latter's book, *Marketing*. There he received the benefit of Butler's practical experience, a viewpoint which was valuable to him when, following three years of teaching at Washington and Lee, his Alma Mater, he began to teach marketing in 1915 at the University of Pittsburgh, a school characterized by a strong vocational emphasis. Because no general marketing textbooks were available, Converse had his students read Nystrom's *Economics of Retailing*. All of these influences led him to use mainly the middleman or institutional approach in his first book, *Marketing Methods and Policies*, published in 1921 while he was still teaching at Pittsburgh.

Moving to the University of Illinois in 1924, where the marketing work had been developed by Litman and Behrens, Converse came under two other influences of location. In that area he saw more clearly the importance of agricultural marketing. Away from a large metropolitan center, he de-emphasized vocational training and gave more attention to sound training in the fundamentals of marketing.

Walter C. Weidler. One of the early students of James E. Hagerty who made a career in marketing, Weidler was enrolled during 1911–1912 in the course which Hagerty had started in 1905. As a graduate student at The Ohio State University, he briefly assisted both Hagerty and M. B. Hammond, labor economist, of whom he was also a protégé. He was faced with the decision as to whether he would specialize in marketing or in labor. On the one hand, he was the better acquainted with marketing, having served an apprenticeship during earlier years in a wholesale dry goods company. He also had friends and relatives engaged in distribution. On the other hand, his intellectual interests seemed to lie in broader economic problems.

Continuing doctoral work at Harvard University, Weidler elected to take a course in marketing and applied for, but did not gain admission to, the section taught by Cherington. While taking the course with another professor, he also audited a labor course in the event that he should later wish to continue in that field. Upon his return to Ohio, however, the way opened for him to specialize in marketing rather than in labor, and ultimately he became co-author of a text entitled *Principles of Marketing*.

C. S. Duncan. The entrance of Duncan into the marketing field illustrates the influence of intellectual curiosity in encouraging, and the impotence of other occupational demands in preventing, the development of a genuine interest in a subject. His attention had first been drawn to marketing activity in the early 1890's while he was clerking in a general

merchandise store in a small town. His many questions concerning marketing went mainly unanswered until, while teaching English at The Ohio State University and after reading a stimulating book by J. D. Whelpley entitled *Trade of the World*, he enrolled in a summer course in marketing being taught at the University of Chicago by a visiting professor, Paul Cherington. Duncan was on leave at the time to complete his doctoral requirements. That course, according to Duncan, had marked influence upon what he later thought and wrote on the subject, and showed him the possibilities of study in this field with which he had been so dimly acquainted and about which he had much curiosity. Following that course with Cherington, Duncan remained at Chicago for several years teaching marketing. His books, *Commercial Research* and *Marketing—Its Problems and Methods*, were published in 1919 and 1920, respectively.

Harold H. Maynard. Like others whose predilection for marketing did not appear during their undergraduate years, Maynard became interested in marketing gradually, and evidently through fortuitous circumstances. As an undergraduate at Iowa State Teachers College, he was interested mainly in political science and collegiate debating. As a graduate student at the University of Iowa from 1914 to 1916, he became interested in economics and economic history. For his Master's thesis he studied credit unions, under the direction of Harvard-trained Eliot Jones. Marketing was not then taught at Iowa but, through his work in economic history, Maynard became familiar with the names and activities of prominent business leaders and developed receptivity to an interest in marketing.

Behind those intellectual influences

and in line with his interest in debating, were other experiences which contributed to this receptivity. At an early age he had done house-to-house and farm-to-farm selling. During summers of his college years he had been business manager of a traveling Chautauqua unit and thus had not only excellent selling experience but also repeated opportunities to hear a lecture on the problems of small town merchants faced with growing chain store competition.

In 1916, Maynard enrolled in the marketing course offered at Harvard by M. T. Copeland and studied in mimeographed form some of the material which Copeland published in 1920 under the title, *Problems in Marketing*. There, too, he came under the tutelage of Cherington, who replaced Copeland for the last sixty days of the term when the latter was called to Washington in connection with war work. The influence of contact with those two men was great enough to lead Maynard into the teaching of marketing after the war.

Following the war, he taught for one year at Vanderbilt University and for three years at Washington State College, before going to Ohio State in 1923 to initiate a course in Introduction to Business. Constantly he availed himself of opportunities to learn of marketing, writing a dissertation on "Marketing Northwestern Apples" while teaching retailing at Washington State College, and working in the established course in Marketing Problems at Ohio State. Having met Weidler at Harvard and having been brought to Columbus by his invitation, Maynard collaborated with him and T. N. Beckman in preparing *Principles of Marketing*, published in 1927.

Theodore N. Beckman. Beckman's discovery and pursuit of marketing interest was largely the result of an intellectual challenge. While awaiting accept-

ance of his application for admission to a diplomatic school with the idea of pursuing a career in the consular service, Beckman found interest in economics and business subjects at The Ohio State University, where he was doing undergraduate work during the years prior to 1920. Hagerty's marketing course and the writings by Weld and Cherington helped him to see opportunities for expanding the knowledge of marketing and for correcting misconceptions therein. He renounced his diplomatic aspirations and began his career in marketing.

The inclination of his special marketing interests toward credit and wholesaling was the result of influences in his university environment. While teaching a general marketing course, and upon encouragement by Hagerty, who was also interested in the subject of credit, Beckman taught a short course in credit administration for the Columbus chapter of the Institute on Credit of the National Association of Credit Men. In preparing for this, he spent much time in credit offices of Columbus business concerns talking with credit managers. When the course was offered at the University in 1922, the inadequacy and incompleteness of the available literature and readings impelled the writing of his textbook, *Credits and Collections in Theory and Practice*, published in 1924. That book was accepted in fulfillment of the requirement for his doctoral dissertation, although for that purpose he had for a considerable period been making a special study of wholesaling. Encouragement in the wholesaling study was given by C. S. Duncan, when others saw little or no profit in such an endeavor, and it too was ultimately published in book form.

Contribution of the Middle Western Group

The literary contributions of early

Middle Western teachers of marketing appeared within the space of a few years around 1920 like the second of a succession of waves, the first of which had broken eight to ten years earlier in the writings of Butler, Cherington, Shaw, and Nystrom. During the decade from 1910 to 1920 the early explorative concepts of marketing were refined, established, and augmented, and the study attained an integration which effectually terminated the pioneeer stage of the development of marketing thought. Whereas at the beginning of the decade the field of study was delineated by the new concept and term "marketing," by the end of the decade the *principles* of marketing were being widely postulated. Students at the beginning of the century explored the marketing practices of businesses in general. Those who developed the subject ten years later, particularly at Wisconsin, specialized in the commodity analysis of marketing. Those whose contributions appeared following the first World War concentrated primarily on the functional aspects of marketing. Thus the Middle Western group of writers contributed mainly an integration to the study of marketing, emphasizing functions and principles and treating the subject with a form and fullness which has since characterized the central body of marketing literature.

The New York Group

Although neither Columbia nor New York University made prominent contributions to marketing literature during the early years, they are deserving of mention in this review of influences. About 1920, toward the end of the period with which we are presently concerned, Hugh Agnew, whose teaching experience extended back a number of years and who was to become perhaps the first of the leading contributors to mar-

keting thought in that area during the later years went to New York University. Nystrom and R. S. Alexander also began teaching in the New York area during the decade of the 1920's. They and others in that area who have been associated with marketing are distinguished primarily by their contributions to marketing thought developed from the institutional approach.

Hugh E. Agnew. Employment factors were instrumental in shaping the thinking and writing of Agnew, giving emphasis to advertising and journalism. He had done typesetting on the campus paper at Hillsdale (Michigan) College, which he attended from 1893 to 1896. With this and other college publication experiences behind him, upon graduation from the University of Michigan in 1902 he bought a country newspaper. Successful direct mail advertising stimulated his interest in that means of selling and gave him a glimpse of what could be done with it.

In 1912, he took over the management of a newspaper business in Canton, Illinois. There he wrote several articles on advertising, and controversies incited by them led him to write more. In 1913, he joined the faculty of the University of Washington for a short period. He then went into the advertising business until 1920, in which year he accepted simultaneously a professorship at New York University and an editorial position on *Printers' Ink*.

SUMMARY AND CONCLUSIONS

At the end of the first half-century of study of marketing, a review of its progress and status reveals certain significant facts:

1. That the study was originally an outgrowth or extension of the field of economics rather than an inductive theorization of business experience,

2. That inductive research into business activity developed early and furnished the substantial basis for a marketing science,
3. That students of the subject were drawn from academic and business fields alike and were motivated by a variety of subjective as well as objective influences,
4. That the structural outlines of the study were fairly well crystallized by 1920 when the principles of marketing were the subject of many writings,
5. That the majority of the principal contributors to marketing thought during the first two decades of this century have continued to be prominent in the ranks of marketing scientists, and
6. That the early analysis and statement of marketing have remained sound and tenable and for the most part have been only refined and elaborated by subsequent writings.

Drawn from diverse academic and business experiences and working in a variety of places, the early contributors to marketing thought nevertheless constituted a homogeneous group, unified by their common interest and by the influence which they had upon one another. There were fewer than a dozen university centers at which, during the period of 1902–1920, the early contributors to marketing thought were found, and still fewer to which the majority of them were attracted for study and research. The predominant characteristics of the respective institutions inevitably influenced the students whom they touched, and ideas and attitudes were carried throughout the country from those centers.

The principal stimulus to marketing study at first appears to have been an environment of progressive economic thought, as illustrated by the impetus given the study of marketing at Wisconsin and Harvard. The character of the contribution made to marketing thought, however, was less an outgrowth of the economics taught at a given school than of other environmental factors. Students working in agricultural areas devoted themselves largely to study of agricultural marketing. Those in urban and metropolitan centers specialized more in the marketing of manufactured goods and in institutional and technical aspects of marketing. The earliest students developed primarily the commodity approach to marketing study while those of slightly later years developed the functional and institutional approaches and the literature of marketing problems.

Early marketing literature was the product of academicians, notwithstanding the fact that original thinking on the subject was not confined to academic centers. The nature and demands of teaching have inevitably stimulated writing. While indulging their individual interests in marketing research, teachers of marketing, almost exclusively, have been the compilers, writers, and often the originators of marketing thought.

[2]

Contribution of Women to U.S. Marketing Thought: The Consumers' Perspective, 1900–1940

Mary Ellen Zuckerman
Columbia University

Mary L. Carsky
The University of Hartford

This paper examines the early contributions of women to marketing thought with particular emphasis on marketing's evolving interest in the consumer. The emergence of marketing and home economics in the beginning of the present century provides a background for development of consumer theory and the relationships between these two disciplines. In addition, the contributions of women more closely aligned with mainstream marketing thought in the first half of the century are described and the significance of the "feminine perspective" and unique understanding of the consumer is demonstrated.

INTRODUCTION

Women made an important but neglected contribution to marketing thought in the early part of this century: a focus on the centrality of the consumer. Home economists such as Christine Frederick, Hazel Kyrk, and Elizabeth Hoyt pioneered the study of consumption and the development of consumer behavior theory. The discipline of home economics was closely aligned to marketing in its questions and concerns. Women in marketing research such as Pauline Arnold emphasized the necessity of understanding consumers to build sales (Arnold 1937). Adelaide Benedict-Roche (1914), Lucille Eaves (1920), Ruth Leigh (1921), and sev-

Journal of the Academy of Marketing Science
Volume 18, Number 4, pages 313-318.
Copyright © 1990 by Academy of Marketing Science.
All rights of reproduction in any form reserved.
ISSN 0092-0703.

eral others published books on salesmanship aimed at women in retail sales with specific emphasis on customer interaction.

Sources

This paper examines early contributions of women to marketing thought with particular emphasis on marketing's evolving interest in the consumer. In its preparation, archival materials and oral histories were used in conjunction with the traditional sources of books and journal publications. The papers of Christine Frederick and Dorothy Dignam housed at the Schlesinger Library at Radcliffe College were examined, along with published works of these women. Oral histories were obtained by interviewing former students of Hazel Kyrk, Margaret Reid (Charters 1989; Morse 1989, 1990), and Paul Nystrom (McCabe 1988).

EMERGENCE OF THE DISCIPLINE OF HOME ECONOMICS

The disciplines of home economics and marketing emerged around the same time period—the beginning of the present century. Both were born of the Industrial Revolution. These two disciplines, along with scientific management, attempted to answer the fundamental problems of production, distribution, and consumption. Scientific management, established earlier than the other two, turned its attention to problems of production. The newer fields of marketing and home economics sought to solve the problems of distribution and consumption respectively.

The beginnings of the home economics profession were rooted in the changes in *consumption* at the turn of the

CONTRIBUTION OF WOMEN TO U.S. MARKETING THOUGHT: ZUCKERMAN AND CARSKY
THE CONSUMERS' PERSPECTIVE, 1900–1940

century. Values and living standards in the American home were affected by the number of new goods being produced, the problems of consumer choice, and perhaps most importantly, the lack of awareness among homemakers of ways to improve the quality of life through the use of new "devices," scientific advances in sanitation and nutrition, and methods for improving efficiency in the home (Andrews 1941; Frederick 1923; Hunt 1908; Van Horn 1941). The dominant focus centered on the interaction of the household with the marketplace; home economists, from the beginning believed that maximizing customer or household satisfaction would benefit both the consumer and the business.

In the development of concepts, home economics and marketing drew on common theoretical disciplines. Both were heavily steeped in economics, particularly agricultural economics. Both drew from sociology and psychology, as well as from the earlier "applied field" of scientific management (Converse 1945; Frederick 1923). Before the turn of the century, home economics programs were developed at the University of Illinois and the University of Wisconsin, both of which shortly thereafter became early centers of marketing thought (Bartels, 1962).

There is evidence that marketing courses were offered early as part of the home economics curriculum, and that marketing programs may have originated within home economics colleges. In 1910 home economics curricula across the country included a "selling course" (Baldwin 1949), and in 1923 the home economists in business (HEIB) section of the American Home Economics Association suggested that women needed training in business administration including courses in the psychology of advertising, and journalism (Sellers 1923). A 1922 *Journal of Home Economics* article (Bailey 1922) describes a marketing course offered at the Iowa State University, and the first marketing course at the University of Connecticut was initiated within the school of home economics in the 1920's (Palmer 1981).

Founders of both marketing and home economics were members of the American Economics Association, and home economists such as Hazel Kyrk, Margaret Reid, Elizabeth Hoyt and Isabel Wingate participated in early marketing conferences (Hollander 1988) and published articles in the *Journal of Marketing*.

Despite these interactions, differences in point of view existed between the two disciplines. For home economics, consumer satisfaction with the marketplace was the end; for marketing, it was the means to an end. Home economics has always focused on the consumer; marketing's academic interest developed much later.

CONTRIBUTIONS OF HOME ECONOMISTS

We focus here on the work of three home economists. Hazel Kyrk and Elizabeth Hoyt pioneered the study of consumption through the development of theory, and the delineation of areas for research. Christine Frederick did pioneering and widely-known work in both educating the consumer and assisting marketers to understand consumers.

The Development of Consumer Theory: Hazel Kyrk and Elizabeth Hoyt

In 1923, Hazel Kyrk published a seminal work entitled *A Theory of Consumption*. Kyrk took on this study because of a direct interest in the consuming process as a phase of human behavior, and because of a belief that an understanding of this process was essential to deal with some of the most fundamental economic problems. Although a trained economist herself, Kyrk was highly critical of the discipline in its treatment of consumption. She said they (economists) concentrated their attention upon the consumer while engaged in the process of utilization, and portrayed consumption as "practically timeless and spaceless. There is no suggestion that the motives, interests, and impulses behind it are of infinite variety, and are molded, shaped and organized by the whole environment in which the individual is placed" (Kyrk 1923, p.19). This book, then, departs from traditional economic treatment of the consumer by viewing consumption as human behavior rather than as passive participation in the economic system.

Kyrk's rationale for writing her theory of consumption reflected the normative perspective and educational orientation of the home economist rather than the business perspective of the marketer, even as it spelled out areas that came to concern theorists in marketing. She proposed the need to solve three problems of human behavior and institutions: (1) the problem of control and guidance of the economy, (2) the problem of choice—of values and valuation, and (3) the problem of human welfare as a function of wealth (p. 5).

The major problem among these three, according to Kyrk, was choice and selection among values. To understand choice, it was necessary to chart the desires, and purposes that "move men to action." The study of consumption therefore involves (1) observation of people's behavior as consumers, (2) asking whether it follows a standard type of pattern, and (3) attempting to explain why it takes the form it does (p. 9).

Kyrk viewed standards of living as "scales of preference" that direct expenditures and are manifested in the choice of goods. She said that the standards could serve as a starting point for the analysis of consumption. Factors external to the individual, including social class differences, environmental differences, effects of cultural contacts, and the value of certain goods beyond that of mere function, were discussed in terms of their effect on standards. Kyrk spoke of the expressive value of goods, their symbolism and meaning to consumers (pp, 182–183) and how and why the meaning of goods change over time (pp. 234–278). On these issues, Kyrk raised questions whose answers would, in part, define the theory of consumption. For example, she asked: "How does the group select from the material at hand the approved norms of conduct which it then passes on to the individual? How can the formation of specific consumer habits and conventions be explained?" (p. 212). "What determines the choice of luxuries or goods which for any reason are deemed non-essential?" (p. 235).

These factors of consumption for which Kyrk sought answers in 1923 include those which innovative consumer behavior scholars have rediscovered in recent years. The works of McCracken on culture and consumption (McCracken 1986, 1988) address many of these same issues. Belk (1988), Holbrook (1985), and Hirschman (1985), among others, have examined the symbolism and expressive value of goods both cross-culturally and within our society.

Elizabeth Hoyt's 1928 book *The Consumption of Wealth* viewed the study of consumption from a theoretical perspective, as did Kyrk, but its analysis was more narrowly focused. Early in the work Hoyt offered an explanation for the late start of the study of consumption:

> . . . so long as wealth was small and the variety of goods was meager, and so long as men knew little about other peoples' ways of living, there was slight reason for considering alternative ways of spending money, and certainly not much practical incentive to do so. As wealth and knowledge increased, the inertia of customary consumption, like all inertias, lifted but slowly (Hoyt 1928, p. 5).

Hoyt went on to say that after discovering what is actually consumed, we need to look at what causes it to be consumed, and how consumption differs in populations around the world (p. 10). Ultimately, consumption should be evaluated in terms of achieving maximum satisfaction. If answers are found to all these, Hoyt believed that generalizations could be made about the effect of consumption according to the nature (durability) of the satisfactions it produces (p. 11), an area which consumer behavior scholars have gone on to explore.

Hoyt and Kyrk were active figures in their own time. Their continuing involvement in consumer theory and their influence on marketing thought and that of other women in the 1930's is evident from articles and book reviews in the earliest issues of the *Journal of Marketing* and citations by marketing scholars. In a review of the field of consumption, Kyrk (1939) stated that nearly all the books labeled 'consumption' had appeared after 1927. Prior to the publication of her book in 1923, Kyrk believed there were only two books (written in English) on the subject, while by 1930 the number had grown to five. These included Paul Nystrom's *Economic Principles of Consumption* (1929).

Nystrom, a major figure in academic marketing thought, was clearly familiar with the work of Kyrk and Hoyt. His bibliography in *Economic Principles of Consumption* included entries by Kyrk, Hoyt, and five other home economists, including Christine Frederick. Nystrom's interaction with home economists probably began at the University of Wisconsin, where he was affiliated with the College of Agriculture Extension Division until 1914 (Bartels 1951). This would have continued during his years at Columbia University, where he mentored home economists from Teachers College who studied in the areas of clothing and textiles, and who were interested in retailing and fashion (see A. Edwards 1940).

Educating Consumers and Marketers: Christine Frederick

Perhaps the best example of a home economist who carried on the twin missions of educating the consumer and assisting the marketer is Christine Frederick. She was the first woman to address Congressional hearings on distribution and home buying problems, a frequent speaker before advertising and sales conventions, and author of a comprehensive book on female consumers. Frederick's initial work (before 1920) centered on testing products and scientific homemaking ideas, writing about these in women's magazines, and, eventually, in manufacturers' promotional pamphlets (Frederick Papers). Her early books dealt with scientific housekeeping (e.g., Frederick 1923), but by the 1920s she had turned her attention to the female consumer, her needs and habits, and the best way to reach and inform her (Frederick 1925, 1929).

Frederick's major contribution to marketing thought came through her 1929 book, *Selling Mrs. Consumer*. In contrast to the other home economist works referenced by Nystrom (1929), this book is targeted to marketers and marketing educators. Its purpose was to inform them of the importance of meeting the consumer's needs and to provide guidelines on methods of reaching her. The book's three parts describe "Mrs. Consumer," explicate her interactions to different product markets, and delineate her views on advertising, pricing, and retailing strategy.

In the first section of the book, Frederick emphasizes the necessity of listening to the consumer and looking to her for guidance in product development and promotional strategy; numerous examples of success and failure attributable to the presence or absence of consumer consciousness on the part of the businessmen are cited. Frederick stresses the virtues of consumer marketing research and provides cost justification along with a list of uses for the results. Throughout the book, she uses an abundance of empirical data to back up her statements and recommendations to marketers. For example, in demonstrating the importance of the female consumer to marketers, she cites a research study which found that the only purchase of consumer products which men made themselves, without consulting women, was their own shirt collars, and another which found that the only product categories for which men made more purchases than women were automobiles and hardware. She provides systematic guidelines for successful business practices. For each product category (food, clothing, appliances, drugs and cosmetics, home furnishings) under consideration, the author details the manner in which consumers buy, the features/benefits which are important, and the marketing appeals that will be successful.

Having been a contributing editor to *Ladies' Home Journal* and *Delineator*, Frederick utilized her magazine experience to advise marketers on magazine and newspaper advertising to "Mrs. Consumer," as well as the need for consumer marketing research. She called for research to identify customers and to test advertising copy. Being influenced by the infusion of psychology in advertising, Frederick emphasized the importance of "appeals" in advertising, including the effective use of color to stimulate mood (p. 364).

Although the book was targeted to practitioners, Frederick's frequent references to research studies conducted by business schools in the 1920s provide evidence of interaction with marketing academicians. Frederick herself worked on such studies at Columbia during the decade.

CONTRIBUTIONS OF WOMEN IN MARKETING

In addition to the home economists, women engaged in advertising, marketing research, and retailing contributed to marketing thought during the early part of the century. Within each of these specialties, women's emphasis lay primarily in understanding the perspectives and problems of the consumer, and in enabling the marketing profession (both men and women) to incorporate these into marketing strategy.

Advertising and Marketing Research

Their perspective on the consumer's needs and wants led women into marketing research in its formative years (Fox 1984). Pauline Arnold, a marketing researcher who directed her own firm, emphasized (1937) that there was only one purpose to marketing research and that was to build sales. To build sales, however, it was necessary to understand the customers' motives. She cites cases of industrial and consumer buyers, and in all cases the message is the same: Find out what the customer wants and then produce it!

Women in advertising were more likely to be practitioners than scholars or academicians and, consequently, most of their writings were found in trade journals such as *Printer's Ink* (Dignam Papers). However, this is not to say that they did not influence thought on the topic. In a 1945 survey of marketing academicians on the importance of materials for teaching and research, *Printer's Ink* was ranked second after *Journal of Marketing* in the periodicals listing (Converse 1945).

Retailing and Retail Selling

Women were especially active in analyzing retailing and retail selling. In Bartel's extensive bibliography, seven of the twenty books authored by women deal with retailing or retail sales. This association of women with retailing in the formative years of the marketing discipline is not surprising when one considers that as early as 1880 women were disproportionally represented in retail sales jobs. After 1900 it was a rare department store that did not have a clear majority of female salespeople (Benson 1981, pp. 179, 231; Waller-Zuckerman 1989). By the teens and twenties women had risen to positions of advertising manager, buyers, department store managers, and training directors (Leach 1984). Several translated their experiences into publications such as training manuals, and books on general retailing and retail selling (Kennard 1917, 1918; Leigh 1921, 1936). Women were also teaching retailing and retail selling in high schools and colleges.

The greatest proportion of retailing books authored by women were in the area of salesmanship. Ten books on retail selling by women have been identified (Baer 1923; Benedict-Roche 1914; Butler 1912; Eaves 1920; Hayter 1939; Kennard 1918; Leigh 1921; Norton 1919; O'Leary 1916; Prince 1918). An examination of several of these shows a marked contrast to those written by men during the same time period. Books authored by women (e.g., Hayter

1939; Kennard 1918; Leigh 1921) generally had a stronger emphasis on meeting and greeting the consumer and on the presentation of merchandise. This subject matter was presented at the beginning of the books. By comparison, books authored by men (e.g. Nystrom 1936; Ivey 1921) placed greater emphasis on retail business operations. Nystrom, for example, does not discuss selling techniques and customer interaction until Chapter 12, and Ivey relegates "The Selling Process" to chapter eight of his nine chapter text.

One female author, Lucinda Prince, pioneered courses on retail salesmanship and in the training of store education directors. She opened the Prince School of Education for Store Services in 1905 in Boston, which later became part of Simmons College. In a nine-month course of study at the Prince School, high school teachers of distributive education along with aspiring retail executives and training directors were instructed in educational theory and practice, store operations and economics, along with the merchandise characteristics, particularly that of textiles. These areas of study were elaborated on in her detailed guide, *Retail Selling* (1918).

CONCLUSION

It is not surprising that women's contributions to marketing thought should have been most evident in their contributions of the consumer perspective. From the late nineteenth throughout much of the twentieth century, women were THE purchasing agents of the household, its expert consumers. Thus, when women, both in the field of marketing and in related disciplines such as home economics, began exploring marketing problems, they were predisposed toward placing the consumer at the center of their analysis. As Pauline Arnold stated, "our experiential background is helpful in the profession" (1937).

For home economists, this focus on the consumer came primarily from the orientation and mission of their profession. While home economists, like marketers, addressed problems caused by increased production attendant on the Industrial Revolution, home economists' analysis centered on changes in consumption patterns, by households and by individuals. From its beginnings at the turn of the century, its focus was on the consumers' dilemma.

While some marketers such as Nystrom were influenced by the work of Kyrk, Hoyt, and Frederick, this cross-influence did not immediately result in attention to the consumer on the part of most marketing theorists. In fact, such pervasive attention came only two or three decades later.

The research presented here raises the question of why marketing theory came so late to its focus on the consumer. Marketing practitioners knew early on that they must pay attention to consumer needs, must investigate and learn about those needs. Theorists in home economics had presented major works on this topic, and practitioners wrote about it in *Printer's Ink* and other publications utilized by marketing academicians in the earlier part of the century. Recognition of marketing theory's slow response to this concept forms an interesting addition to marketing history.

CONTRIBUTION OF WOMEN TO U.S. MARKETING THOUGHT: ZUCKERMAN AND CARSKY
THE CONSUMERS' PERSPECTIVE, 1900–1940

The overview of the contributions and accomplishments of the women cited here opens the door to additional studies on the topic. Potentially fruitful areas of research include: (1) Contributions from women in other related disciplines; (2) Detailed research on the exact effect of women marketing to women, and how this has differed, if at all, from men marketing to women; (3) Gender analysis of the history of marketing.

Further inquiry into women in related disciplines of economics, psychology, and sociology would be a particularly fruitful line of inquiry for scholars in consumer behavior. The descriptions of the early works of women presented here provide a "mere glimpse" of early understandings of the consumer. These understandings lend both an honorable past and a rich context for contemporary consumer behaviorists.

NOTE

1. Authorship of this article is equal. Name order was determined by the authors.

REFERENCES

Andrews, Benjamin R.D. 1941. "Home Economics Date Lines in Consumer Education." *Practical Home Economics* (June): 202–205.

Arnold, Pauline. 1937. "How Research Builds Sales." *Journal of Marketing* 2 (July): 134–140.

Baer, Laura. 1923. *Retail Selling Methods*. New York: McGraw-Hill.

Bailey, N. Beth. 1922. "A Course in Marketing." *Journal of Home Economics* 14 (May): 220–222.

Baldwin, Keturah E. 1949. *The AHEA Saga*. Washington, DC: The American Home Economics Association.

Bartels, Robert. 1962. *Development of Marketing Thought*. Homewood, IL: Richard D. Irwin.

———. 1951. "Influences on the Development of Marketing Thought, 1900–1923." *Journal of Marketing* 16(2) (September): 139–168.

Belk, Russell W. 1988. "Possessions and the Extended Self." *Journal of Consumer Research* 15(2) (September): 139–168.

Benedicte-Roche, Adelaide. 1914. *Salesmanship for Women*. New York: The Ronald Press.

Benson, Susan P. 1986. *Counter Cultures. Saleswomen, Managers, and Customers in American Department Stores, 1890–1940*. Urbana, IL: University of Illinois Press.

Butler, Elizabeth B. 1912. *Saleswomen in Mercantile Stores, Baltimore, 1909*. New York: Russell Sage Foundation.

Charters, Margaret A. Personal Interview with Mary Carsky on Hazel Kyrk and Margaret Reid. Baltimore, MD : March 30, 1989.

Converse, Paul. 1945. "The Development of the Science of Marketing: An Exploratory Review." *Journal of Marketing* 10 (July): 54–57.

Dignam, Dorothy. *Papers*. Schlesinger Library, Radclife College, Cambridge, Massachusetts.

Eaves, Lucile. 1920. *Training for Store Service*. Boston: Richard G. Badger.

Edwards, Alice L. 1940. *Product Standards and Labeling for Consumers*. New York: The Ronald Press.

Fox, Stephen. 1984. *The Mirror Makers*. New York: Random House.

Frederick, Christine. 1925. "Advertising Copy and the So-Called 'Average Woman'," in *Masters of Advertising Copy—Principles and Practice of Copywriting According to its Leading Practitioners*, George J. Frederick, ed., New York: Frank-Maurice, Inc.

———. 1923. *Household Engineering: Scientific Management in the Home*. Chicago: American School of Home Economics.

———. *Papers*. Schlesinger Library, Radcliffe College, Cambridge, Massachusetts.

———. 1929. *Selling Mrs. Consumer*. New York: The Business Borse.

Hayter, Edith F. 1939. *Retail Selling Simplified*. New York: Harper & Brothers.

Hirschman, Elizabeth C. 1985. "Primitive Aspects of Consumption in Modern American Societies." *Journal of Consumer Research* 12(2) (September): 142–154.

Holbrook, Morris B. 1985. "Aims, Concepts, and Methods for the Presentation of Individual Differences in Aesthetic Responses to Design Features." *Journal of Consumer Research* 13(3) (December): 337–347.

Hollander, Stanley C. 1988. "Where Is Consumption History Going?" Paper presented at the Conference on Macromarketing, San Jose, California.

Hoyt, Elizabeth Ellis. 1928. *The Consumption of Wealth*. New York: The Macmillan Company.

Hunt, Caroline. 1908. *Home Problems from a New Standpoint*. Washington, DC: The American Home Economics Association.

Ivey, Paul W. 1920. *Elements of Retail Salesmanship*. New York: The Macmillan Company.

Kennard, Beulah. 1917–1918. *Department Store Merchandise Manuals*, Vols. 1–10. New York: The Ronald Press.

———. 1918. *The Educational Director*. New York: The Ronald Press.

Kyrk, Hazel. 1929. *Economic Problems of the Family*. New York: Harper & Brothers.

———. 1940. "The Consumer and the Economic Order." *Journal of Marketing* 4 (Proceedings Issue): 111–116.

———. 1939. "The Development of the Field of Consumption." *Journal of Marketing* 4(1) (January): 16–19.

———. 1923. *A Theory of Consumption*. Boston: Houghton-Mifflin.

Leach, William R. "Transformation in a Culture of Consumption: Women and Department Stores, 1890–1925." *Journal of American History* 71(2) (September): 319–342.

Leigh, Ruth. 1936. *Elements of Retailing*, rev. ed. New York: D. Appleton-Century.

———. 1921. *The Human Side of Retail Selling*. New York: D. Appleton-Century.

McCabe, Esther M. Personal Interview with Mary Carsky on Paul Nystrom. Storrs, CT: July 16, 1988.

McCracken, Grant. 1986. "Culture and Consumption: A Theoretical Account of the Structure and Movement of the Cultural Meaning of Consumer Goods." *Journal of Consumer Research* 13(1) (June): 71–84.

———. 1988. *Culture and Consumption*. Bloomington, IN: Indiana Press.

McMahon, Theresa. 1925. *Social and Economic Standards of Living*. Boston: D.C. Heath.

Morse, Richard L.D. Personal Interview with Mary Carsky on Margaret Reid. Baltimore, MD: March 31, 1989.

———. Personal Interview with Mary Carsky on Hazel Kyrk. Vernon, CT: February 8, 1990.

Norton, Helen Rich. 1919. *A Text Book on Retail Selling*. Boston: Ginn and Company.

Nystrom, Paul. 1929. *The Economics of Consumption*. New York: The Ronald Press.

———. 1936. *Elements of Retail Selling*. New York: The Ronald Press

O'Leary, Iris Prouty. 1916. *Department Store Occupations: Cleveland Foundation Education Survey*. New York: Russell Sage Foundation.

Palmer, Michele. 1981. *Decades of Pride: School of Home Economics and Family Studies*. The University of Connecticut. Storrs, CT: Parousia Press.

Prince, Lucinda. 1918. *Retail Selling*. Washington, DC: Government Printing Office.

Sellers, Marie. 1923. "Home Economics Women in Business." *Journal of Home Economics* 15 (June): 297–300.

Van Horn, Edna. 1941. "Forty Years of Consumer Education." *Journal of Home Economics* 33 (June): 377–381.

Waller-Zuckerman, Mary Ellen. 1989. "Women in Marketing and Marketing to Women." Paper presented at the AMA Educators' Meeting. St. Petersburg, FL: February 16.

ABOUT THE AUTHORS

Mary Ellen Zuckerman is a Research Fellow at the Gannett Center for Media Studies at Columbia University, on leave from her position as Associate Professor of Marketing at

CONTRIBUTION OF WOMEN TO U.S. MARKETING THOUGHT:
THE CONSUMERS' PERSPECTIVE, 1900–1940

ZUCKERMAN AND CARSKY

SUNY Geneseo. She holds a doctorate in history and an MBA, both from Columbia University. Her publications include articles on marketing and advertising history, on women in marketing, and *The Magazine in America* (in press, Oxford University Press), co-authored with John Tebbel. She is currently finishing a book on U.S. women's magazines.

Mary L. Carsky is Assistant Professor of Marketing at the

University of Hartford. She received her Ph.D. from Virginia Polytechnic Institute and State University in 1985. Dr. Carsky's teaching and research expertise lie in the consumer interaction in the marketplace. Past research has focused on consumer education/information and consumer satisfaction. Recent articles have appeared in the *Journal of CS/D & CB*, *Journal of Food Distribution Research*, and in proceedings of marketing educators' conferences, including AMA, AMS, and marketing specialty conferences.

[3]

A CRITICAL EXAMINATION OF THE INFLUENCE OF INSTITUTIONAL ECONOMICS
ON THE DEVELOPMENT OF EARLY MARKETING THOUGHT

by
Don R. Webb
University of Missouri--Columbia
and
Donald L. Shawver
Eastern Illinois University

ABSTRACT

The most direct link to early marketing thought and
institutional economics stems from the fact that Professor
Paul D. Converse was a student under John R. Commons at
the University of Wisconsin. The authors contend that
Commons influenced Converse's thinking on such matters as
marketing functions, value added, and time, place, and
possession utility.

Most of the impact of institutional economic thought
on early marketing writers was indirect and round-about.
The impact is associated with both methodology and
concepts. Institutional economics was in large part a
rebellion against the then accepted and revered method of
the theoretical approach. Institutional economics
embraced the empirical approach eagerly. And the early
marketing pioneers were empiricists through and through.

*   *   *   *

"There is going to be a rebirth of interest in
history and literature in American education. As
marketing educators we should endeavor to nudge along this
predicted trend. General history in my view, is a topical
subject for the 1990s." (Wright, 1988)

The purpose of this paper is to explore the influence of institutional
economics on early marketing thought. Specifically, the influence of two
well-known institutionalists--Thorstein Veblen and John R. Commons will be
examined.

FOREWORD ON INSTITUTIONAL ECONOMICS

Institutional Economics is a phenomenon of the twentieth century. The
seed for a new crop of "institutional" ideas was planted by Thorstein Veblen
in 1899 when his Theory of the Leisure Class first appeared. It was nurtured
by John R. Commons during the 1910s and 1920s, and culminated by his
publication of Institutional Economics in 1934. The "Institutional Approach"
reached full flower in 1933 when Franklin Delano Roosevelt became president of
the United States and summoned numerous institutional economists to Washington
as his advisors and architects of the New Deal.

Basic Concepts of Institutionalist Thought

The Institutionalists:

1. Believed that group "behavior," not price, should be the central theme of economics.

2. Recognized that human behavior is constantly changing, and that economic generalizations should be relative to time and place.

3. Emphasized custom, habit, and law, as modes of organizing economic life.

4. Held that the important motives that influence individuals cannot be measured.

5. Asserted that maladjustments in economic life are not to be regarded as departures from a normal equilibrium, but are themselves normal--at least under existing institutions. (Haney 1948, pp.741-2.)

The surprising thing about institutional economics is its ability to survive. In 1947 a noted economic historian wrote that the institutionalist school was almost completely dead, and intermittent attempts to revive it had "invariably failed to arouse much interest." (Roll 1947, p. 498) Today, as the 1980s draw to a close, there is increasing interest in re-examining the concepts and economic philosophy of institutional economics.

Control and Conflict

While some institutionalists were content to describe and analyze economic activity, the predominant school of thought always emphasized the "problem of control."

Institutional economists claimed human motives were largely instinctive; they criticized economists who assumed rational self-interest as the dominant motive. They focused attention upon institutions, their origin, evolution, and their reactions on man, i.e., upon actual economic arrangements, habits, customs, property, technological methods, and legal forms. They regarded these arrangements to be the dominant factors in governing human behavior.

Institutionalists point out that such social institutions as the "rights" of private property, contract, and inheritance, and the changing forces of custom and government activity in their development, have consistently modified economic theories. Thus the notion of conflict also evolves as a core concept in institutional economies, analogous to the central concept of equilibrium for classical economics. For example, Veblen theorized that institutions failed to keep in adjustment with current experience; thus a "cultural lag" was the result, accompanied by strains and clashes of interests. (Veblen, 1899, p. 363).

The chief economic institutions for Veblen were (1) the price system that tied together the complex of interdependent units in modern industry and adjusted their relations, (2) property (which he associated with acquisitive and predatory activities) and (3) technological methods--the profit motive balanced against the workmanship ethic.

Some institutionalists, e.g., Mitchell, stressed the irrationality of human action, and accepted "instincts" (perhaps habits), as the prime and determinant of human ends. W. C. Mitchell, who knew Veblen well, also stressed the apparent irrationality of human action.

Vulnerabilities of Institutional Theory

Institutional thought can be criticized because of the set of assumptions made. Institutionalists do not and cannot prove that their kind of "economic man" is real. Their claim that people have habits, and are lead by the "unseen hand of instinct" to prefer the common good, is vulnerable. Institutionalists base their thought, either upon a behavioristic psychology and instincts, thus rejecting value economics and its traces of hedonism; or upon a study of legal institutions and doctrines; or upon the authority of the state and the duties of individuals thereto.

Institutionalists often tacitly assume that present conditions are undesirable or bad and can be better. They assume institutions are the cause of any malaise, and that by changing them, conditions can be remedied. (In a sense, this contemplates a kind of "benign optimism" about what the future could hold.) Institutionalist thought conceives of economics as dealing with ever-moving bodies ungoverned by any causal forces and tending toward no equilibrium.

Opposing Notions in Institutionalist and Classical Theory

A common thread that links institutionalist and classical theory are notions of opposition between an ethical idea of utility, (which characterizes the main stream of institutionalist thought) and the Classicists' non-ethical concept of exchange value.   Some of these opposing notions of Institutional and Classical Theory were:

	DISSENTING THOUGHTS	
Institutional School		Classical School
Limited needs	vs.	Indefinite expansion
Leisure necessary	vs.	Continuous striving to produce
Consumption emphasized	vs.	Production emphasized
Perceived Utility	vs.	Marginal Utility
Overproduction possible	vs.	No overproduction possible
Public wealth (People)	vs.	Private riches (Entrepreneurs)
"Societism"	vs.	Individualism
(Socialism or Nationalism)		

VEBLEN'S VIEWS AND INSTITUTIONAL ECONOMICS

The Theory of the Leisure Class

Thorstein Veblen (1857-1929) was born in Wisconsin, but grew up in Minnesota. His The theory of the Leisure Class first appeared in 1899. The book was very well-written. Veblen chose his words carefully and today's reader cannot help but contrast his style with much of the prose cranked out on word processors by today's would-be scholars.

Veblen was a keen observer of the real world in which he lived. Much of what he had to say about the role of women in society sounds biased when read today. His judgments should be evaluated in light of the times in which he wrote. Similarly,, Veblen's observations on the intertwining of religion and college athletics should be judged by conditions existing at the time rather than by today's standards.

Veblen's observations on conspicuous leisure, conspicuous consumption, and conspicuous waste may have indirectly influenced much of today's marketing thought on fashion, spending patterns, the hierarchy of needs, private property, and varying consumption patterns by social classes. For example, Veblen explained the shifting fashions by observing that leisure class "dress should show wasteful expenditure." (Veblen 1899, p. 176). But, if the principle of conspicuous waste required an obviously futile expenditure, the resulting style of conspicuous expensiveness of dress would be intrinsically ugly. Hence, all innovations in dress attempted to show some ostensible intrinsic purpose. But each new style must conform to the requirement of wastefulness. The result was an essential ugliness and an unceasing change of fashionable attire. (Veblen 1899, p. 177). (Oscar Wilde once wrote: "Style is a form of fashion so ugly that it has to be changed every six months.")

Veblen wrote that the "motive that lies at the root of ownership is emulation." (Veblen 1899, p. 25). Again, he wrote: "The motive is emulation--the stimulus of an invidious comparison which prompts us to outdo those with whom we are in the habit of classing ourselves." (Veblen 1899, p. 103). Again, Veblen stated: "With the exception of the instinct of self-preservation, the propensity for emulation is probably the strongest and most alert and persistent of the economic motives proper." (Veblen 1899, p. 110).

Turning the labor theory of value on its head, Veblen wrote that "Conspicuous abstention from labour therefore becomes the conventional mark of superior pecuniary achievement and the conventional index of reputability. (Veblen 1899, p. 38).

Veblen understood well the economic concept of value. He used the example of a hand-wrought silver spoon compared with a machine-made silver spoon. He observed that the utility of articles valued for their beauty depends closely upon the expensiveness of the articles. For example, Veblen stated that a hand-wrought silver spoon, of a commercial value of about twenty dollars, is not necessarily more serviceable, and very likely even less serviceable, than a machine-made silver spoon selling for about twenty cents. Each spoon possesses beauty and has some measure of serviceability. Yet one is worth 100 times the other. Veblen explained that the hand-wrought feature gratifies our taste and our sense of the beautiful, while the machine-made is not useful for anything except "brute" efficiency. (Veblen, pp. 125-127).

Veblen observed that a well-kept lawn appealed especially to the tastes of Western peoples, and while a "lawn unquestionably" has an element of sensuous beauty, its chief claim to being functional was use as a cow pasture. (Veblen 1899, pp. 133-4).

Ever ready to draw supporting analogies from human attire and custom,

Veblen quoted with approval the phrase: "A cheap coat makes a cheap man."
(Veblen 1899, p. 156).

Veblen compared the binding of women's feet in Japan with the wearing of
corsets in America. Both customs served as evidence of honorific leisure by
symbolizing physical disability. Veblen found that "mutilations and
contrivances for decreasing the visible efficiency of the individual" were
endorsed by the higher social classes, but such things as corsets and high-
heeled shoes were likely to be rejected by the lower classes. (Veblen 1899,
p. 186).

Throughout his writings Veblen gave evidence that he believed in an
evolutionary process. For example, he wrote: "institutions are not only
themselves the result of a selective and adaptive process. . .they are at the
same time special methods of life and of human relations, and are therefore in
their turn efficient factors of selection." (Veblen 1899, p. 188).

Veblen observed that people have a strong aversion to change, that people
offer up an instinctive resistance to making any readjustment to changes. He
believed leisure classes would make changes first and argued that it was in
the interest of the leisure classes to keep the lower classes "conservative".
(Veblen 1899, pp. 203-4).

Veblen pointed out that merchandisers ranked low on the hierarchy of
reputability. Owners of enterprises ranked first, followed by bankers and
lawyers. But Veblen wrote: "Mercantile pursuits are only half-way reputable,
unless they involve a large element of ownership and a small element of
usefulness." (Veblen 1899, p. 232).

Veblen wrote: "In its positive discipline, by prescription and by
selective elimination, the leisure-class scheme favours the all-pervading and
all-dominating primacy of the canons of waste and invidious comparison at
every conjuncture of life." (Veblen 1899, p. 334). He continued that the
leisure-class canon requires withdrawal from the industrial process--
especially "as regards the upper-class and upper-middle-class women of
advanced industrial communities.

Veblen's general postulate was that the present level of man and his
institutions was but one stage in cultural development. (Bell 1967, p. 545)
His basic thesis was that all institutions developed by man represent
processes of cumulative change in which the only stable elements are certain
human traits. Veblen examined anthropology, psychology, and indeed most
elements of the cultures of many peoples to support his contentions.

To Veblen, the price system was the leading economic institution. He
argued that modern industry was a complex, interdependent series of units,
each of which was a potential profit-making unit, controlled by the
businessman. The price system tied these units together and adjusted their
interrelationships.

Veblen argued that the price for which goods are sold is not determined
by the forces of competition but by "what the traffic will bear." He rejected
the theory that competition was an effective force in leveling profits to a
minimum. Instead he suggested that over the years the tendency was for small

concerns to be eliminated by merger with larger firms which finally combined into great trusts exerting monopolistic power.

Veblen believed that not only could prices be controlled by corporate management, but that output, production costs, and final prices could all be controlled for maximizing net profits. He believed that technological advances made it possible to turn out virtually unlimited quantities of goods that would have a lowering effect on net profits. In so doing, he likely ignored the influence of the patent system on technological change. In any event, he argued that a "business equilibrium" would be disturbed by increased productivity and subsequent lowering of prices.

Veblen was a pessimist. He did not believe that an economy ever tended toward equilibrium. Rather he argued that it was inevitable that boom periods were followed by depressions, and that the conflict between technological advances and absentee capitalists would simply create an impasse. However, Veblen rejected the idea of Marx that constant warfare between the vested interests would lead to the end of capitalism and the establishment of a new society. He neither predicted a decay of the capitalistic system nor did he visualize what form economic society would ultimately take.

COMMONS' VIEWS ABOUT INSTITUTIONAL ECONOMICS

John Rogers Commons (1862-1945) was a founding father of institutional theory. Commons' The Distribution of Wealth appeared in 1893. The book was not especially well received—either as a reform vehicle or as an academic accomplishment. Commons was a long-time professor of economics at the University of Wisconsin and was a teacher of some of the early contributors to marketing thought, e.g. Paul D. Converse.

Commons was not only a gifted scholar, but a successful practitioner as well. He promoted research in such new vital areas of study as industrial relations and administrative economics. He grew up in the wake of America's great industrial revolution. He was a product of the turmoil-ridden Middle West. He was keenly aware of the transfer of dominance from the agricultural-commercial economy of pre-Civil War days to that of the powerful industrial state.

It would be Common's role to help accelerate this process of adjustment. through his analysis of the collective behavior of man-made institutions as they functioned around the institution of private property, codified laws, and court decisions.

Commons' Contributions to Institutionalist' Thought

John R. Commons devoted his entire life to studying the conflict of economic, political, and social interests. Commons emphasized behavior with stress upon negotiation as a key element in marketing activity and behavior. He also gave emphasis to the distinction between routine and strategic activities in economic operations, which was characterized by the extent of negotiations which pertained to a given market transaction.

Common's insight was well depicted in his phrase "The Going Concern."

(Commons 1934, pp. 52-55) His emphasis on the firm as a continuously
functioning entity contributed to institutionalist thought. His observations
on the parallelism of the movement of goods, with that of productive efforts
in agriculture and manufacturing, also added further robustness to
institutional theory.

Commons pointed out one difficulty in defining the so-called
institutional economics as a field of thought was the "uncertainty" of the
word institutions. (Commons 1934, p. 69). He observed that institutions
sometimes refers to buildings. At other times institutions refers to a
framework of laws and regulations within which individuals act like inmates.
Also at times, anything critical of the classical or hedonic economics was
conveniently called institutional. Then too, anything that is "dynamic" as
opposed to "static" seemed to be institutional economics. (Commons 1934),
p.69). After wrestling with the notions above, Commons defined an institution
as "Collective Action in Control of Individual Action." (Commons 1934, p. 69)

Commons observed (with approval) that "Ricardo and afterwards Marx viewed
a market as a part of the whole process of production. The market consisted
in a labor process, all the way from extraction of raw material, manufacturing
it in new forms, transporting, delivering it physically to the wholesaler in
exchange for another physical delivery, until finally the finished goods are
delivered physically by the grocery boy to the ultimate consumer." (Commons
1934, p. 364).

Commons wrote: "In more modern terminology, this meaning of marketing as
transportation, is the creation of place utility' by labor not different from
labor's creation of form utility.' But utility, in this meaning, is physical
use-value. Labor is not really creating' anything. It is only changing the
form and place into use-values of the elementary materials furnished by
nature." (Commons, 1934, p. 365). Your authors conclude that Commons, while
recognizing form and place utility was slow to recognize time utility and
perhaps didn't even think of possession utility. But, perhaps early marketing
scholars extended Commons' notions. Converse's favorite definition of
marketing was the creation of time, place, and possession utility.

EARLY 20TH CENTURY MARKETING THOUGHT

Emergence of Marketing as a Discipline

The discipline of marketing grew from the rib of economics. Marketing
was originally an outgrowth or extension of the field of economics, rather
than an inductive theorization of business experience. Bartels claims that
economic theory has provided more concepts for the development of marketing
thought than has any other social discipline. (Bartels 1988, p. 186)
Paradoxically, Bartels contended: "The debt of early students of marketing to
economic theory for guidance of their thinking should not be underestimated;
yet the significance of departure from theoretical economics that marketing
thought represented cannot be overemphasized." (Bartels 1988, p. 9)

The influence of economic concepts is evident throughout the marketing
literature. In general, marketing writers have articulated the consumer
viewpoint, the justification of institutional specialization, the concept of

the productivity of marketing, a theory of integration and specialization in institutional management, a role of price in theory and practice, the bases of competition, and a philosophy of the relation of government to business. (Bartels 1988, p. 188)

Unlike earlier economic theorists, who brought forth divergent theories,while remaining in the ranks of theoretical economists, early marketing scholars evolved a body of thought that, by its nature, scope, and application, set them apart from contemporary economists. Marketing studies were more empirical than theoretical, more practical than abstract, more descriptive than philosophical. Marketing writers were concerned with social and economic problems of the day, but more from the standpoint of the business firm than from that of public administration.

Early contributors to marketing thought, although having diverse backgrounds and academic and business experiences, constituted a homogenous group. They knew and influenced each other. (Converse, 1959, p.3) Many of them had common backgrounds and training. For example, Bartels wrote that early marketing scholars such as Jones, Butler, Macklin, Nystrom, Hagerty, and Converse, among others, attended the University of Wisconsin and were influenced by liberal economists, e.g., John R. Commons and Richard T. Ely, then teaching at the University of Wisconsin. (Bartels 1951, p. 5).

Bartels claimed the principal stimulus to early marketing study took place within an environment of progressive economic thought. (Bartels 1951, p. 3). The early marketing scholars at Wisconsin and Harvard studied economics. However, Bartels concluded that the character of their contributions to marketing thought was less an outgrowth of the economics taught a given school than of other environmental factors. (Bartels, 1970, p. 126). Scholars working in agricultural areas devoted themselves largely to the study of agricultural marketing--especially the cooperative marketing of farm products. Scholars in urban areas specialized more in the marketing aspects of manufactured goods. The earliest students developed primarily the commodity approach to marketing study, while those in slightly later years developed the functional and institutional approaches.

Early College Marketing Courses

The senior author remembers that Converse lectured about the great increase in the incidence of higher education beginning around 1900. Prior to this time college education had been largely for those preparing for the learned professions of theology, medicine, and law. At about this time also, the idea of higher education for businessmen gained popularity. For example, transportation was taught at the Wharton School in 1893-94. The New York University School of Commerce, Accounts, and Finance was established in 1902. By 1908 schools of commerce or business had been established at Denver, Harvard, Pittsburgh, and Northwestern.

According to Converse, the first marketing courses at the college level were offered at the Universities of Illinois and Michigan in 1902 and at the University of California a few months later. This was confirmed by Litman who in 1950 wrote a short article at the urging of P.D. Converse and published by the Journal of Marketing. Litman contended the first teachers in the field were George M. Fisk at Illinois, E. D. Jones at Michigan, and Simon Litman at

California, all of whom taught marketing courses during academic year 1902-3.(Litman 1950, pp. 222-223).   Bartels mentioned these three, and credited
James E. Hagerty of Ohio State as one of the first marketing teachers.
(Bartels, 1951, p. 3. Fisk left Illinois for Wisconsin in 1908, and Litman
left California for Illinois at the same year. J. E. Hagerty started teaching
a marketing course at Ohio State University in 1905. These early teachers
secured most of their information by interviewing businessmen. They also used
government reports and material gained from books on economics.   A
considerable amount of material was available by 1920 when Clark's
bibliography included references to Ralph Starr Butler, and Melvin T.
Copeland, among others. (Converse 1945, pp. 54-57).

     The senior author remembers Walter Dill Scott speaking about the first
course in advertising research at the collegiate level which Scott taught in
1908 at Northwestern University. Scott also talked about the first meeting of
the National Association of Advertising Teachers which eventually became the
National Association of Marketing Teachers, and finally the American Marketing
Association. Arch Shaw (1916) called attention to the existence of market
countours (segments) and the use of "market plus" pricing that reflected the
psychic value of branding and promotion. These early courses were obviously
quite different from present-day courses. Early marketing literature was
scarce. So early marketing teachers wrote books and articles so that classes
could be taught. They focused largely on the buying and selling of
agricultural commodities. Transportation was viewed as a necessary function.
Gradually, marketing came to mean a study of the performance of a set of
business activities. And even as late as 1960, the American Marketing
Association's official definition of marketing was "the performance of
business activities that direct the flow of goods and services from producer
to consumer or user."

     During the 1930s and the 1940s there was a vast expansion of texts,
courses, and enrollments in marketing. C. C. Parlin generally credited as the
"Father of Marketing Research" laid down the substance of that discipline in
1911. Percival White's Market Analysis: Its Principles and Methods was
published in 1920. College courses in marketing research became extremely
popular after Lyndon O. Brown's Market Research and Analysis published in
1937.

     By 1940 courses were offered in transportation, in selling, in retailing,
in marketing research, in advertising, in industrial marketing, and in both
sales management and marketing management. The late Samuel G. Wennberg
introduced a course called "Marketing Management" at the University of
Missouri in 1937. The authors submit that this was the first college course
to be titled "Marketing Management."   During the 1940s and well into the
1950s such courses were still termed "Sales Management" at most colleges.

Early College Marketing Texts

     After 1910 published information on marketing increased sharply.
Cherington's Advertising as a Business Force appeared in 1913. Paul Nystrom's
Economics of Retailing first appeared in 1915. L.D.H. Weld's The Marketing of
Farm Products was first published in 1916. Ralph Starr Butler's Marketing
Methods appeared in 1917 and was an elaboration of previous monographs. The
structural outlines of the discipline of marketing were fairly well

crystallized by 1920 when books emphasizing the principles of marketing began appearing.

An assortment of marketing texts appeared in the 1920s. Duncan published his Marketing in 1920. Cherington's The Elements of Marketing appeared in 1920. Copeland's Marketing Problems was first published in 1920; the second edition appeared in 1923. Converse's Marketing Methods and Policies was first published in 1921 with a revised edition appearing in 1924. Converse published his Selling Policies in 1927. Fred Clark published his Principles of Marketing in 1921, and Ivey's book Principles of Marketing appeared in the same year. Russell started teaching sales management at the University of Illinois in 1919 and published his The Management of the Sales Organization in 1922. Norris Brisco's Fundamentals of Salesmanship first appeared in 1916.

As the discipline of marketing matured, more textbooks were published and more courses were offered. Converse's Marketing Methods and Policies, (1921) was likely the forerunner of the numerous excellent texts on marketing management that exist today. Beckman's Credits and Collections In Theory and Practice was first published in 1924.

The now dusty black and white marketing texts of the 1920s seem vastly different than the bright multi-colored texts of today. However, these works should be judged by the conditions of the time. And what marketing text writer of today, does not owe a debt, although he may not be aware of it, to someone who before him tried to put his thoughts on paper?

THE IMPACT OF INSTITUTIONAL ECONOMICS

One must struggle a bit to fix the impact of institutional economics on early marketing thought. Some concepts found in the early marketing literature could have stemmed from institutional economics. In retailing, for example, concepts relating to location, rent, pricing, integration, and scale of operation were known to institutional economists. In advertising, product differentiation, scale of operation, and substitution costs may relate to institutional economics. The concepts of specialization, price behavior, business cycles, purchasing power, patterns of consumer spending, and terms of sale can perhaps be traced to institutional economics. Certainly, institutional economics anticipated the concepts of evolution, expressed by early marketing writers when they wrote of the development of marketing institutions.

The Evolving Philosophy of Competition

The authors contend that the early marketing writers' general philosophy of doing business stemmed from institutional economic thought. They had a general philosophy of optimism, a vision of new frontiers of progress, a businessman's viewpoint of confidence in free play in the market, and widespread agreement that consumers acted rationally in the market. (Bartels 1988, p. 18).

Throughout the 19th Century, businessmen largely shaped the philosophical atmosphere in which business operated. To be sure, it can be considered a self-serving philosophy. Most 19th Century businessmen believed strongly in

31

individualism, in a dominating class of business aristocracy, in social
Darwinism (competitive success goes to the strong), and in minimum
governmental regulation, but with maximum governmental assistance to business.
Market competition would protect the consumer and reward the efficient firm.
It was generally believed that thrift and hard work would be rewarded and that
poverty stemmed from laziness and shiftlessness. (Bartels 1988, p. 18)

Notions about Demand

Economists, especially institutional economists have had a considerable
influence on marketing scholars on the notions of demand. Gilboy (1932, p.
621) pointed up that the creation of demand by conscious efforts was an
essential element in the development of modern industrialized economies, even
as early as the latter part of the 18th Century. For example, in this period
Josiah Wedgewood was practicing effectively the use of product
differentiation, style, obsolescence, and testimonials in the development of
increased demand for his wares. (McKendrick, Brewer, and Plumb 1982). Alfred
Marshall later generalized it in the concept of elasticity. His
interpretation of demand has long been used by marketing writers as a
theoretical basis for selling, advertising, and the promotional work of
marketing in general. (Bartels 1988, p. 11).

Other Direct Impacts

While most of the impact of institutional economic thought was indirect
and round-about, there were some direct linkages. One direct link concerned
the senior author's mentor--Paul D. Converse and his ideas on marketing
functions. "P.D." as he was known affectionately by all who knew him, studied
at the University of Wisconsin under John R. Commons.

Converse wrote in 1940: "My teachings of economics were largely of the
Wisconsin School trained under Ely, Commons, etc., in the day when Wisconsin
was considered radical. They taught sound money, were very critical of the
ethics of business, perhaps did not believe that the profit motive always
produced the most desirable ends, but they were not socialists. They believed
in private property, profit, and individual initiative. (Bartels 1988, p.
297).

Commons wrote that historically the term "marketing" had a double
meaning, a meaning that persisted in modern,(i.e., 1934), economics.
Economists view marketing as the last step in the production of wealth by
physical delivery and physical exchange. On the other hand, marketing is used
to describe the first step of bargaining by agreeing upon the prices that
would result in an ownership change of wealth. (Commons 1934, p. 366). The
authors speculate that Converse was influenced by Commons on this point.

The charts in Commons' Institutional Economics remind the authors of
those in Converse's Elements of Marketing. For example, Commons'
"Manufacturing Corporations, Rations of the Specified Items," (Commons 1934,
p. 565) is more than vaguely familiar to those conversant with Converse's
writing on value added by distribution and perhaps was the forerunner of his
much quoted estimate of the "cost of marketing."

Commons wrote of bargaining transactions, managerial transactions, and rationing transactions. (Commons 1934, pp. 59-68). While he distinguished carefully among these, and used them for other purposes, the notion of "marketing functions" comes to mind. Could it be that the Converse's notion of marketing functions stemmed directly from his interaction with Commons?

Perhaps the best known concept of consumer behavior - Veblen's "Conspicuous Consumption" came straight away from his Theory of the Leisure Class. In addition Veblen may have pioneered the idea of making a detailed analysis of a given culture as it relates to a market. While institutional economists' concepts of the consumer may not have aided much in making a real-world market analysis, their concepts may have paved the way for early marketing scholars writing on the subject.

Concepts of pricing and price behavior had also to be altered with the advent of new factors in pricing. The concepts of price as market or natural price, and of price comprising the cost of factors of production, were insufficient to explain managed price in a distributive system. Price became less a matter of accountable costs entering into production and more a managed phenomenon.

Thus, while economists' concepts of the consumer may not have aided much in making market analyses, their concepts of marginal utility, opportunity costs, subjective and objective value, abstinence, hedonism, "the marginal man," and rationalism were useful tools of thought available when students of marketing began their research into this new area of thought.

Notions on Lack of Equilibrium

Classical economic theory assumed that producers, at least in the long run, adjusted their activities to the market and reasoned that the market was always tending towards an equilibrium. In the real world however, producers of the early 20th Century increasingly attempted, at least, to adjust the market to their production capacities and ambitions. Production was no longer carried on for an immediately available and known market, but in advance for unknown markets at great distances. Early marketing scholars viewed the real world and rejected the notion of automatic equilibrium.

Early marketing scholars rejected the classical economic theories of pricing and price behavior. The concepts of price as market or natural price, and of an equilibrium price equating the cost of factors of production, were insufficient to explain managed price in a distributive system. Price became less a matter of accountable costs entering into production and more a managed phenomenon.

Notions About General Welfare

Classical economists assumed that general welfare was best served by complete freedom in the marketplace. Institutional economists tended to assume the opposite, that the general welfare was not served automatically by the workings of the marketplace. This assumption gained considerable acceptance as a description of the real world at the beginning of the 20th Century. At the same time, the notion, postulated by economic liberals, that problems created by new practices in the market were a result of natural law, was refuted.

In 1901 Theodore Roosevelt was elected on a tide of movement for
economic, social, and political reform of the evils which had grown out of
advanced industrialism. The Progressive Party demanded government control of
large industry and of financial and transportation companies and the enactment
of pure food and drug legislation. Pools, trusts, mergers, and combinations
were under continual legislative and judicial fire, indicating that the long-
held belief that competition would regulate the market efficiently was being
abandoned. There was growing opposition to private monopoly, even as after
the Civil War there was opposition to government-granted monopoly. The
opposition expressed in the antagonism of agriculturists and labor groups to
business and of the South to the industrial North.   (Bartels 1988, p. 19).

    Among leading thinkers of the period there was much disagreement on these
issues. Richard. T. Ely and others interested in reforms established the
American Economic Association in 1885 as a protest against their conservative
colleagues, who in general espoused the principles of laissez faire. And
Oliver Wendell Holmes and Louis Brandeis at the same time introduced economic
and sociological data into court decisions. (Bartels 1988, p. 19)

    Various economists have distinguished different types of utilities, and in
due course marketing students identified time, place, and possession utilities
as three for which marketing activities were directly responsible. It was not
until after many years, however, that the concept of "value added by
marketing" was set forth.

    Economists distinguish between value-in-use and value-in-exchange
theories. Value-in-use consists of the general total utility inherent in an
item; value-in-exchange is the power to command another good in exchange. The
influence of institutional economics has been strong here.

Indirect Impacts

    The indirect impact of institutional economic thought on early marketing
thought is associated with both methodology and concepts. Institutional
economics was in large part a rebellion against the then accepted and revered
method of the "theoretical approach." Institutional economics embraced the
"empirical approach" eagerly. The early marketing pioneers were "empiricists"
through and through.

    Marketing thought in the 1920s and 1930s was pragmatic and empirical.
Traditional economists viewed the empirical approach as inferior—they
especially viewed marketing scholars as also inferior, for using the empirical
method and perhaps for other reasons. It is ironic that in more recent times,
economists have "rediscovered" the empirical approach, and that would-be
marketing scholars are complaining about the lack of theoretical foundations
into the discipline of marketing?

    The concept of marketing evolution and development can, with some
imagination, be traced to institutional economics. The early concepts of
consumer behavior were rooted in institutional economic thought. The concept
of consumption patterns and the fashion cycle were found in Veblen's seminal
work, The Theory of the Leisure Class. Nystrom's ideas on the subject have a
distinct institutional flavor. The authors submit that he likely was inspired
by institutional economic thought while at the University of Wisconsin.

34

Of course, marketing teachers of the 1920s and 1930s did not offer separate courses in consumer behavior--nor did they specialize in consumer behavior. They were specialists in the sense that they specialized in teaching marketing--this distinguished them from those who specialized in accounting, in economics,in management, or in finance. But the marketing professors of that time were generalists relatively within the field of marketing.

SOME CONCLUDING OBSERVATIONS

The Key Contribution of Institutional Thought to Economic Theory

The inherent vulnerability of an institution to becoming anachronistic is a theme that rings throughout the works of both Veblen and Commons. Thus the signal contribution to economic theory that could be attributed to institutional thought is in its centering on <u>present</u> institutional structure as a <u>harbinger</u>--as a compelling rationale for <u>forecasting</u> needed structural changes in a dynamic economic system.

The Laws of Economics: Caveats for Institutionalists

The discipline of economics developed as a body of laws that can be definitely and positively formulated. But these laws are mostly "provisional" and subject to the assumption of "given conditions." Nonetheless, many economic laws are scientifically valid, and practically useful.

Economists should never forget that economics should not be a defense of prevailing institutions. Nor is it a defense of any set of institutions. Economics deals with human desires, and the factors and functions of production and consumption. It continues to seek a definite criterion of "economic value." In seeking such answers, economics invariably finds important physical limitations and costs that differ according to individuals and locations.

Thus while institutionalists describe our institutions, and even attempt to change them; institutionalists cannot in so doing repeal the laws of supply and demand, the law of diminishing utility, or the law of diminishing returns. Still the evidence is strong that the laws of economics work through institutions, but that they are more fundamental than institutions. However, institutionalists make a valid case for refinements in these principles.

REFERENCES

Institutional Economics References

Commons, John R. (1893), <u>The Distribution of Wealth,</u> New York: Augustus M. Kelley, Bookseller, 1963.

Commons, John R. (1924a), "The Delivered Price System in the Steel Market," <u>American Economic Review</u>, XIV, 505.

Commons, John R. (1934), <u>Institutional Economics--Its Place in Political Economy</u>. New York: The Macmillan Company.

Mitchell, W. C. (1927), Business Cycles, The Problem and Its Setting, New
    York: National Bureau of Economic Research, Inc.

Veblen, Thorstein (1899), The Theory of the Leisure Class. New York:
    Augustus M. Kelley, Bookseller, Reprints of Economic Classes, 1965.

Veblen, T. (1904), The Theory of Business Enterprise. New York: Mentor
    Books, 1958.

Veblen, Thorstein (1914), Instinct of Workmanship, and the State of the
    Industrial Arts, New York: B. W. Huebsch.

Veblen, Thorstein (1921), The Engineers and the Price System. New York: The
    Viking Press, Inc., 1968.

Veblen, Thorstein (1923), Absentee Ownership--The Case of America. Boston:
    Beacon Press, 1967.

History of Economic Thought References

Bell, John Fred (1967), A History of Economic Thought, 2nd ed., New York: The
    Ronald Press Company.

Dowd, Douglas (1978), "Introduction to the Transaction Edition of Veblen's The
    Theory of Business Enterprise. New Brunswick, New Jersey: Transaction
    Books.

Dorfman, Joseph et al. (1963), Institutional Elements in Contemporary
    Economics, Berkeley: University of California Press.

Dorfman, Joseph (1934), Thorstein Veblen and His America. New York: Augustus
    M. Kelley, Publisher, Reprints of Economic Classics, 1966.

Dorfman, Joseph (1963), "The Foundations of Commons' Economics," in Commons'
    The Distribution of Wealth, New York: Augustus M. Kelley, Bookseller.

Gilboy, Elizabeth W. (1932), "Demand as a Factor in the Industrial
    Revolution," Facts and Factors in Economic History, Cambridge: Harvard
    University Press, pp. 620-39.

Haney, Lewis H. (1936), 3rd ed., History of Economic Thought, New York: The
    Macmillan Company.

McKendrick, Neil, John Brewer, and J. H. Plumb (1982), The Birth of a Consumer
    Society, Bloomington: Indiana University Press.

Mitchell, Wesley C. (1936), What Veblen Taught, New York: The Viking
    Press.

Roll, Eric (1947), A History of Economic Thought, New York: Prentice-Hall,
    Inc.

Whittaker, Edmund (1940), A History of Economic Ideas, New York:
        Longmans, Green and Co.

36

History of Marketing Thought References

Bartels, Robert (1951), "Influences on the Development of Marketing Thought, 1900-1923," Journal of Marketing, XVI (July), pp. 1-17.

Bartels, Robert (1970), Marketing Theory and Metatheory, Homewood, Illiniois: Richard D. Irwin, Inc.

Bartels, Robert (1988), The History of Marketing Thought, 3rd ed., Columbus, Ohio: Publishing Horizons, Inc.

Converse, Paul D. (1945), "Fred Clark's Bibliography as of the Early 1920's," Journal of Marketing, X, (July), pp. 54-57.

Converse, Paul D. (1952), "Notes on Origin of the American Marketing Association," Journal of Marketing, XVII, (June), pp. 65-67.

Converse, Paul D. (1959), The Beginning of Marketing Thought in the United States, with Reminiscences of Some of the Pioneer Scholars. Bureau of Business Research Studies in Marketing, No. 3. Austin, Texas: University of Texas.

Coolsen, Frank G. (1960), Marketing Thought in the United States in the Late Nineteenth Century. Lubbock, Texas: Texas Tech Press.

Dixon, D. F. (1981), "Role of Marketing in Early Theories of Economic Development," Journal of Macromarketing 1, (Fall), 19-27.

Litman, Simon (1950), "The Beginnings of Teaching Marketing in American Universities," Journal of Marketing, XV (October), pp.220-223.

Maynard, H.H. (1941), "Marketing Courses Prior to 1910," Journal of Marketing, V, (April), pp. 382-4.

Wright, John S. (1988), "Can an Understanding of General History Broaden Our Understanding of Marketing?" a paper delivered at the 1988 Winter Marketing Educators Conference, San Diego, California, February 8.

Early College Marketing Texts

Beckman, Theodore N. (1924), Credits and Collections in Theory and Practice, New York: Ronald Press Company.

Beckman, Theodore N. (1926), Wholesaling, New York: Ronald Press Company.

Brisco, N. A. (1916), Fundamentals of Salesmanship, New York: D. Appleton-Century Co., Inc.

Brown, Lyndon O. (1937), Market Research and Analysis, New York: The Ronald Press Company.

Butler, Ralph Starr (1911), Selling, Buying, and Shipping Methods, New York: Alexander Hamilton Institute.

Butler, Ralph Starr (1917, Marketing Methods and Policies, New York:
    Alexander Hamilton Institute.

Cherington, Paul (1913), Advertising as a Business Force, Garden City,
    New York: Doubleday, Page & Co.

Cherington, Paul (1920), The Elements of Marketing, New York: Macmillan
    Co.

Clark, Fred E. (1922), Principles of Marketing, New York: Macmillan Co.

Clark, Fred E. (1936), Principles of Marketing, New York: The Macmillan
    Company.

Collins, V. D. (1935), World Marketing, Philadelphia: J. B. Lippincott
    Co.

Converse, Paul D. (1921), Marketing: Methods and Policies, New York:
    Prentice-Hall, Inc.

Converse, Paul D. (1927), Selling Policies, New York: Prentice-Hall, Inc.

Converse, Paul D. (1930), Elements of Marketing, New York: Prentice-Hall
    Inc.

Copeland, Melvin (1920), Marketing Problems, New York: A. W. Shaw Co.

Duncan, C. S., (1919), Commercial Research, New York: Macmillan Co.

Duncan, C. S. (1921), Marketing: Its Problems and Methods, New York: D.
    Appleton and Company.

Estabrook, P. L. (1904), Science of Salesmanship, Dallas: University
    Textbook Co.

Goodard, Frederick B. (1899), The Art of Selling (New York: Baker and Taylor)

Hamilton, Walton and Associates (1938), Price and Price Policies, New York:
    McGraw-Hill Book Company, Inc.

Ivey, Paul Wesley (1921), Principles of Marketing: A Textbook for Colleges
    and Schools of Business Administration, New York: The Ronald Press
    Company.

Maynard, H. H., W. C. Weidler, and T. N. Beckman (1927), Principles of
    Marketing, New York: The Ronald Press Co.

Moriarity, W. D. (1923), The Economics of Marketing and Advertising, New York:
    Harper & Bros.

Nystrom, Paul H. (1913), Retail Selling and Store Management, New York:
    The Ronald Press Company.

Nystrom, Paul H. (1930), 3rd. ed., Economics of Retailing, Volume I: Retail

Institutions and Trends: A Critical Analysis of the Retail Business as the Central Factor in Present-Day Distribution of Goods, New York: The Ronald Press Company.

Nystrom, Paul H. (1930), 3rd. ed., Economics of Retailing, Volume II: Principles of Retail Store Operation--Retail Methods Described and Appraised, New York: The Ronald Press Company.

Phillips, Charles F. (1938), Marketing, Boston: Houghton Mifflin Company.

Russell, Fred A. (1922), The Management of the Sales Organization, New York: McGraw Hill Book Co., Inc.

Russell, Fred A. (1924), The Texbook of Salesmanship, New York: McGraw Hill Book Co., Inc.

Scott, Walter Dill (1903), The Theory of Advertising, Boston: Small, Maynard & Co.

Shaw, A. W. (1912), "Some Problems in Market Distribution," Quarterly Journal of Economics.

Shaw, A. W. (1915), Some Problems in Marketing Distribulion, Cambridge, Mass.: Harvard University Press.

Shaw, A. W. (1916), An Approach to Business Problems, Cambridge, Mass., Harvard University Press.

Tosdal, Harry R. (1921), Problems in Sales Management, Chicago: A. W. Shaw Company.

White, Percival (1920), Market Analysis: Its Principles and Methods, New York: McGraw-Hill Book Co., Inc.

Weld, L. D. H. (1910), Practical Salesmanship, New York: Universal Business Institute.

[4]

D. G. Brian Jones & David D. Monieson

Early Development of the Philosophy of Marketing Thought

An extensive study of archival materials is used to examine the philosophic origins of marketing thought at two centers of early development, the University of Wisconsin and the Harvard Business School. Evidence suggests that the German Historical school of economics provided much of the philosophic foundation of the discipline.

IN this article, we attempt to examine some of the currents from which twentieth century marketing thought emerged in order to provide a correct account of its philosophic origins. Marketing historians have identified the first associations, books, and articles pertaining to marketing as we know it today (Bartels 1962). However, these elements reflect marketing once it had been labeled as such. We do not take issue with the accepted wisdom about who the first marketing scholars were, what constitutes the earliest marketing literature, or which university courses were the first in the field of marketing. Nor do we attempt to redefine marketing as it was conceived initially. These facts about the early history of marketing ideas were certainly considered. However, ideas do not develop in a vacuum. We therefore look beyond this patchwork of surface facts and identify some common threads. More precisely, the purpose of our article is to identify and describe some of the philosophic underpinnings of marketing.

Method

Significant historical research involves the collection, analysis, and reporting of primary data (Savitt 1983, p. 30). Therefore, archival research was an essential part of our study. Previous historical research in marketing has identified the significant contributors to the discipline (Bartels 1951, p. 4; Converse 1959; Wright and Dimsdale 1974), the earliest published literature (Converse 1933; Hagerty 1936), and the first university courses (Maynard 1941; Monieson 1981, p. 14). This literature provided many potential sources of primary data.

Inasmuch as the University of Wisconsin and Harvard University were the original centers of influence on the development of marketing thought (Bartels 1962, p. 34), those two institutions were chosen as the major sites of primary research. The collections of Edwin Francis Gay, first dean of the Harvard Business School, and of Richard T. Ely, first director of the School of Economics at the University of Wisconsin, were ma-

D. G. Brian Jones is Assistant Professor of Marketing, School of Business Administration, University of Prince Edward Island, Charlottetown. David D. Monieson is Nabisco Professor of Marketing, School of Business, Queen's University, Kingston, Ontario. The authors thank Ronald Savitt, Stanley Shapiro, George Fisk, Stanley Hollander, Thomas Kinnear, and two anonymous JM reviewers for constructive comments, and the Summer Research Program of the School of Business, Queen's University, for funding in connection with the research.

Journal of Marketing
Vol. 54 (January 1990), 102–113

jor sources of data, as were the collections of several other scholars associated with those institutions (see References section). Specifically, data sources included diaries, journals, correspondence, autobiographies, school essays, research notes, and unpublished papers and books.

We do not compare the influences derived from economics with those possible from other social sciences. Such a task is beyond the scope of our study. Instead, we limit our focus to the major influences apparent through economics at two original centers of development of marketing thought.

Origins of the Institutional Approach

During the nineteenth century many American students seeking higher education were attracted to Germany. Various estimates place the number of American students there between 1820 and 1920 at approximately 10,000 (Herbst 1965, p. 1; Thwing 1928, p. 40). This academic migration was impressive, not only in absolute numbers, but also in relation to the American attendance at other European institutions (Thwing 1928, p. 76).

In American colleges the emphasis was on uniformity and discipline. Instruction followed the lecture-and-recitation method. By contrast, the German universities were professional schools. They provided an atmosphere of academic freedom and equality between students and professors. When the first business school associated with the University of Berlin began classes in 1906, seminars rather than lectures were thought to be a partial answer to the unique educational needs of business students (Redlich 1957, p. 62). During the 1890s and perhaps even earlier, students in economics often went on excursions to various industrial establishments to study firsthand the institutional forces in the economy (Brooks 1906). The academic atmosphere in Germany created in American students a "craftsman's regard for technical expertise, an unfailing respect for accuracy, and a concern for the application of knowledge and skills to social ends" (Herbst 1965, p. 19).

In the latter part of the nineteenth century, a scientific model of historicism, which became identified with the Historical school, began to dominate the social sciences in Germany (Herbst 1965). The Historical school of economics emerged during the middle of the nineteenth century as a reaction to classical economic thinking (Myles 1956). The founders of the Historical school were dissatisfied with the inability of classical economics to resolve the problems associated with the rapid growth of the German economy at that time, such as poverty, industrial development,

and development of a banking system (Hildebrand 1848). This preoccupation with solving real economic problems was to reinforce a unique and consistent set of philosophic assumptions about teaching as well as studying economics. The Historical school was distinctive for its historical, statistical methodology (e.g., Roscher 1843), its pragmatism (e.g., Conrad 1868), and its ideals (Herbst 1965, p. 145), rather than for theoretical or conceptual ideas.

A steady stream of German-trained economists began returning to North America during the 1870s. Columbia University hired J. B. Clark, R. Mayo-Smith, and E. R. A. Seligman. To the University of Pennsylvania went S. N. Patten, J. F. Johnson, E. J. James, R. P. Falkner, and E. R. Johnson. This movement also included F. W. Taussig and Edwin Francis Gay, who both went to Harvard, and Richard T. Ely and Henry C. Adams, appointed to positions at Johns Hopkins University. Later, Ely and Adams moved to the University of Wisconsin and University of Michigan, respectively. These individuals were among the most influential Americans to train under the German Historical school. Others followed until the onset of World War I, but the influence was probably strongest during the 1870s and 1880s (Dorfman 1955, p. 24). There are no estimates of the number of economists who trained in Germany during that period, but the total appears to have been substantial (Farnam 1908; Myles 1956, Appendix 2).

Richard T. Ely was a vocal and enduring disciple of the Historical school. On returning from Germany, he accepted a position at Johns Hopkins University and established a reputation as one of America's most reform-minded economists. Ely led an attack on orthodox economic doctrine, ideology, and methodology. In "The Past and Present of Political Economy," Ely proclaimed the succession of the "New School," the German Historical school, over the old school of orthodox, classical economics (1884). He criticized the rigidity and determinism of classical economics as well as its oversimplified notion of economic man (1884, p. 10–12). Ely claimed enthusiastically that "the younger men in America are clearly abandoning the dry bones of orthodox English political economy for the methods of the German school" (1884, p. 64).

In 1885 Ely led a group of German-trained economists in forming the American Economic Association (AEA). In its founding statement of principles and in its early publications, the AEA revealed the influence of the German Historical school (Ely 1936, p. 144). According to Ely, the formation of the AEA represented both a protest against the system of *laissez-faire* economics and an emphasis on historical and statistical study (Ely 1931, Appendix B).

In 1892 Ely became the first director of the new School of Economics at the University of Wisconsin.

Ely's belief in a strong role for the state in certain spheres of industrial activity fit well with the unique philosophy of education at the University of Wisconsin. That philosophy was represented by the term "Wisconsin Idea," which stood essentially for better government through better education. It involved a close working relation between the university and the state government whereby academic experts gave advice on matters of administration. More generally, the Wisconsin Idea was part of the Progressive Movement for which the state became noted during the late nineteenth century. Ely, later described as a "barometer of Wisconsin Progressivism" (Rader 1966, ch. 7), seemed to have been a perfect choice to head the new School of Economics at Wisconsin.

In 1904 Ely invited John R. Commons, who had been his student at Johns Hopkins, to join the faculty at Wisconsin. Commons was to become one of America's most notable institutional economists and his work became a legendary part of the Wisconsin Idea. Commons also was known for his pragmatic approach to teaching. He often brought civil servants, union officials, and other practitioners into his classroom to speak to students. Ely, too, followed this principle of pedagogical pragmatism by employing the seminar method, with which he had become familiar in his course work in Germany. He cited his German education for the realization that book knowledge and practical experience must be combined, especially for business education (Ely, undated). He also liked to quote Commons that "academic teaching . . . is merely brains without experience; the practical extreme [however] is experience without brains; one is half-baked philosophy, the other is rule of thumb" (Ely 1938, p. 186).

For graduate research, Ely felt the most appropriate topics were ones that were historical and descriptive. Theses supervised by Ely certainly reflected this notion—for example, B. H. Hibbard's (1902) "The History of Agriculture in Dane County, Wisconsin," Paul Nystrom's (1914) "Retail Distribution of Goods," and Theodore Macklin's (1917) "A History of the Organization of Creameries and Cheese Factories in the U.S." In addition, for one of his graduate courses in economics offered in 1899, Ely kept a book that listed suitable topics for student papers. These topics included "The Economic Effects of Changes in Fashion," "Advertising Considered From an Economic Standpoint," and "Competition in Advertising and Effects of Trademarks." Graduate students carried out these studies by applying an inductive method, adopting a historical perspective, and maintaining a concern for the general welfare of society in their search for solutions to economic (often marketing) problems. In this way, many of Ely's students were applying the institutional approach to the study of marketing.

Applying the Institutional Approach to Marketing

Among the first students in economics at Wisconsin were David Kinley (later head of the Economics Department at Illinois), E. D. Jones, Samuel Sparling, James Hagerty (later head of the Economics Department at Ohio State), M. B. Hammond (who later taught under Hagerty at Ohio State), H. C. Taylor, and B. H. Hibbard. These individuals also were among the first noted contributors to the development of marketing thought (Bartels 1951, p. 4).[1] Each had spent some time studying in Germany, as it became Ely's habit to encourage his students to do so whenever possible. In this way a direct link was formed between the German Historical school and many of the earliest contributors to marketing thought.

In 1894, for example, Jones, Sparling, and Hammond traveled together to Germany to study economics. Edward David Jones, though recognized for teaching the first university course in marketing (Bartels 1951, p. 3; Maynard 1941, p. 382), has been curiously overlooked by marketing historians. A recent biographical sketch of Jones describes his considerable contributions to the marketing literature and to teaching (Jones 1987). For example, Jones wrote about the evolution of marketing methods (Ely 1903), the efficiency of the marketing process (1912a), distributive justice (1911b), and the functional approach to marketing (1911c, 1912b, 1913a). He believed that marketing courses were basic to an education in business, along with instruction in administration and accounting/finance. To teach business, however, he believed that scientific investigation was necessary to discover the general principles of those subjects. He added that the appropriate methodology for such study is "the inductive form of the scientific method" (1913b, p. 188). Jones used that method in his own research in marketing, gathering historical, descriptive case studies of marketing processes.

Between 1911 and 1914 Jones published a series of articles in *Mill Supplies* that were remarkable for the tone in which they were presented as well as for the principles and concepts of marketing they identified. In the opening piece, "The Larger Aspects of

---

[1]We do not discuss L. D. H. Weld because no strong, direct links could be demonstrated between Weld and either of the two American institutions used as data collection sites. However, we can speculate on Weld's indirect connection with the German Historical school by virtue of his having studied economics at the University of Illinois (MA Economics 1907) and Columbia (PhD 1908) and having taught at Wharton (1909–1910). Both Columbia and Pennsylvania were popular with German-trained economists during the late nineteenth century. The University of Illinois also had the potential for such influence through George Fisk, Simon Litman, and David Kinley (Figure 1). An institutionalist and prominent early marketing scholar, Weld may have been influenced through his association with these institutions.

Private Business," Jones stated that his purpose in presenting the work was to examine "some marketing problems," the most general of which, in Jones' estimation, was the apparent inefficiency of the marketing process (1911a, p. 2). For example, in the retail trade Jones had determined that marketing activity added 50% to the cost of goods and he felt that much of the added cost was waste due to advertising and an overabundance of retail stores (1912c, p. 461).

Jones believed that a philosophy or science of business, and similarly of distribution or marketing, could be developed. It would require the development of principles based on empirical data and would be practiced by professionals whose objective would be to promote the general welfare (Ely 1918). This vision of science was similar to that held by his mentor, Richard T. Ely, and by the German Historical school under which Jones had also studied.

Samuel Sparling returned from Germany with Jones to complete a thesis on public administration. He then taught that subject at Wisconsin until 1909. In 1906 Sparling published *Introduction to Business Organization*. In that volume (p. 3–4) he described how he believed a science of business could be developed:

> Science is based upon accumulated experience. Classification is the result of a comparison of differences and similarities. . . . We may describe and classify the facts of business in such a way as to indicate their underlying tendencies and principles.

Sparling classified all business activity as extractive, manufacturing, or distributive. Distribution was divided further into marketing activities that facilitate exchange. Marketing proper was defined as "those commercial processes which are concerned with the distribution of raw materials of production and the finished output of the factory. . . . Their function is to give additional value to these commodities through exchange" (p. 17).

In the section of Sparling's book covering "Organization of Distributive Industries" are chapters on the evolution of the market, exchanges, direct selling, wholesaling and retailing, traveling salesmanship, the mail-order business, advertising, and credits and collections. Sparling clearly viewed marketing as part of a science of business that would be developed by following the methodology of the German Historical school, that is, by using an inductive, comparative, historical approach. With its extensive discussion of marketing-related topics, Sparling's book later was credited by James Hagerty (1936, p. 22) as one of the earliest contributions to the literature of marketing.

Hagerty himself was a student of Ely's and also studied in Germany. Of this training he later commented, "I believe that I have been influenced as much by American as by German teachers in the methods of the German economists. I make to mention Pro-

fessor Ely especially whose influence has been in that direction" (1906).

Another of Ely's students, Henry C. Taylor, was even clearer on the influence of Ely and the German Historical school. Following Ely's advice, Taylor went to England in 1899, then to Germany where he studied under Johannes Conrad at the University of Halle and Max Sering at the University of Berlin. Conrad's courses in agricultural economics were described by Taylor as "historical and descriptive in character," concentrating on the political economy of agriculture rather than on the technical aspects of farming. At Berlin he also took courses from Wagner and Schmoller of the Historical school.

When Taylor returned from Germany to Wisconsin in 1901, he began teaching economic history and economic geography. One of Taylor's first moves was to give the course in economic geography more emphasis on agriculture and marketing. As he later described it (1941, p. 23):

> From two-thirds to three-quarters of the time in the course in economic geography was spent in describing where each of the important agricultural products was grown, where it was consumed, and the transportion, merchandising, and processing which it underwent as it passed from producer to consumer.

The text used in this course was Volume VI of the Report of the United States Industrial Commission of 1900, entitled, "Distribution and Marketing of Farm Products" (Taylor 1941, p. 23). It provided descriptions of the distribution of cereals, cotton, and dairy products and of the marketing of livestock, as well as a discussion of the significance of cold storage and refrigeration in the marketing of perishable products. In Taylor's opinion (Taylor and Taylor 1974, p. 517), Volume VI of the Industrial Commission Report was:

> . . . by all odds the bet book on agricultural marketing available to students of agricultural economics at the beginning of the twentieth century. . . . The facts assembled and the methods of presentation made it possible for the reader to develop in his mind a fairly clear picture of marketing processes and price-making forces.

In presenting statistical facts from original and official sources in a descriptive way, the approach used in that report was consistent with the general approach to the study of economics at Wisconsin.

In 1906, as the interest of Wisconsin farmers in the activities of middlemen grew, Taylor began studying the cooperative creameries and cheese factories in southern Wisconsin. In 1910 he published an article on the prices of farm products. Taylor's conclusions about the prices of eggs, butter, and cheese were consistent with the notion that middlemen serve an essential function for which a price must be paid. Nevertheless, there was continued skepticism and the state legislature wanted further investigation.

As part of those investigations, two senior students in agricultural economics were given the task of studying the marketing of Wisconsin cheese. Together with Taylor, in 1913, they published the results of their investigations as "The Marketing of Wisconsin Cheese" (Taylor, Schoenfeld, and Wehrwein 1913). Using extensive descriptive statistics and maps, they illustrated where cheese was produced and where it was consumed. Most of the study, however, described the middleman processes: the advantages and disadvantages of a cheesemaker versus a sales agent in carrying out the selling function, the various types of retailers and wholesalers, the operation of dairy boards, retail prices, and the services rendered by various middlemen. Taylor commented that "while our findings tended to sober those persons who had been speaking excitedly about the marketing problem, they made it perfectly clear that, in certain stages in the marketing of Wisconsin cheese, the agencies were not functioning satisfactorily" (1941, p. 16).

This early research on the marketing of Wisconsin cheese was significant in several ways. It signified the beginning of a specialization by the Department of Agricultural Economics in marketing and cooperatives, which is considered to be its single most important contribution to the study of agriculture (Pulver 1984, p. 7). Also, a flurry of graduate research inspired by this initial study led to numerous theses in agricultural marketing, including G. S. Wehrwein's (1913) "The Dairy Boards of Wisconsin," W. A. Schoenfeld's (1914) "Seasonal and Geographical Distribution of Wisconsin Cheddar Cheese for the Year 1911," H. R. Walker's (1915) "The Cooperative Marketing of Livestock in Wisconsin," E. T. Cusick's (1916) "The Raising and Marketing of Wisconsin Tobacco," and P. A. C. Eke's (1920) "Marketing Wisconsin Potatoes."

This research led to the return to Wisconsin of B. H. Hibbard (from the University of Iowa) in 1913 and Theodore Macklin (from Kansas State College) in 1917 as faculty members in agricultural economics to specialize in cooperation and marketing (Taylor 1941, p. 19). Hibbard, Taylor, and several of the graduate students in the department published a series of studies including "Agricultural Cooperation" (1914), "Markets and Prices of Wisconsin Cheese" (1915), "The Marketing of Wisconsin Butter" (1915), "Cooperation in Wisconsin" (1917), and "Marketing Wisconsin Milk" (1917). The latter study led to a thesis and subsequent book entitled *The Marketing of Whole Milk* (1921), by H. E. Erdman. That book, as well as Hibbard's (1921) *The Marketing of Agricultural Products* and Macklin's (1921) *Efficient Marketing for Agriculture*, were seminal contributions to the marketing literature.

Taylor observed that the series of articles published between 1913 and 1917 all followed a common pattern. Each study was designed "to picture the marketing process clearly in order that the true character of the problems of marketing might be discovered" (1941, p. 22). Each study proceeded from a perceived marketing problem and the method was always the same: to observe the facts, to look and see, and then formulate principles and recommendations.

From its inception in 1892, the School of Economics at the University of Wisconsin developed an institutional approach to the study of economics. This approach included an inductive, statistical methodology with a historical perspective and a concern for the application of knowledge and skills to social ends. Directly and indirectly this approach was derived from the German Historical school of economics. Therefore, as a center of the early development of marketing thought, the University of Wisconsin provided the emerging discipline with a distinctive and well-developed philosophic foundation.

Origins of Scientific Marketing Management

Harvard University, and in particular the Graduate School of Business, was the other center of early influence on the development of marketing thought. Founded in 1908, the School was based on a vision of business as a profession, an art, and a science. As such, it became one of the first truly academic, professional business schools in the world.

As at Wisconsin, the seeds of teaching and research in marketing at Harvard were planted by the Economics Department. For example, the Harvard economists Frank W. Taussig and Edwin Francis Gay have been recognized for their contribution to the development of marketing thought (Bartels 1951, p. 4). Both were instrumental in the planning of the Harvard Business School and Gay became the School's first dean. As dean of the Business School, Gay was the major instigator of research and teaching in marketing.

Taussig studied at the University of Berlin in 1879 and 1880. He was less enthusiastic than some, however, about the ideas of his German teachers, claiming (1906) to have been influenced more by Alfred Marshall. During the early twentieth century many American marketing scholars turned to the more deductive approach of the neoclassical economists such as Marshall in their attempts to develop marketing theory (Sheth and Gross 1988, p. 10). The most popular sources of these ideas were Marshall's *Principles of Economics* (1890) and *Industry and Trade* (1919).

In 1911 Taussig published his own *Principles of Economics*. Nonetheless, he was an economic historian, as demonstrated in his first book, *Tariff History of the United States* (1886). Though he may have been influenced more by Alfred Marshall, he would at least have appreciated the positive contributions of the Historical school. As Marshall himself stated (Pigou 1956, p. 165):

> It would be difficult to overrate the importance of the work that has been done by the great leaders of this school in tracing the history of economic habits and institutions.

Taussig was also a friend and colleague of Ignaz Jastrow, who became the first Rector of the business school founded at Berlin in 1906. Under Jastrow the Berlin Handelshochschule shared an educational philosophy with Harvard that "focused on the real world of business and at the same time was truly academic in nature" (Redlich 1957, p. 35).

As a member of the committee formed in 1906 by Harvard President Charles W. Eliot to plan the Harvard Business School, Taussig singled out the German business schools for comparison with existing American ones. He wrote the following comments to Gay in 1907:

> The movement for advanced instruction of this kind is active throughout the world, most so in Germany and in the U.S. In Germany it has resulted in at least two large institutions of high grade, liberally supported at Berlin and Cologne. In this country, the Universities of Pennsylvania, Michigan, Wisconsin, Illinois, California and Dartmouth College.

Undoubtedly, Taussig's opinions about the formation of the Business School were influenced by his familiarity with developments in Germany and by his own training there.

Much more profound was the impact of the School's first dean, Edwin Francis Gay, on the development of marketing thought. Like Taussig, Gay was very familiar with developments in Germany. He had studied history at the University of Leipzig during 1890–91, then political economy at the University of Berlin from 1891 to 1893 under Wagner and Schmoller of the Historical school. He later studied in Zurich during 1894 before returning to Berlin to finish his doctoral degree under Schmoller in 1901–02. According to Heaton (1949, p. 12–13):

> It was Schmoller who really fired Gay's enthusiasm: first by belief that economics could be made into a real social science by being brought into close relation with psychology, ethics, history and political science; second, by his faith, accompanied by hope, charity and hard work—that economics could be converted into an inductive science through the patient study of economic phenomena past and present. . . . Private conversations with Schmoller were among Gay's treasured memories of his Berlin days; the phrase "Schmoller says" appears occasionally in letters when Gay was interpreting some part of the European scene; and when Gay began to have graduate students of his own he tried to model his treat-

ment of them on the example of his German master.

Indeed, Gay once commented, "If I could only transfer some of Schmoller's qualities into my work as a teacher I would be happy" (Heaton 1949, p. 61). That wish apparently was realized. One of Gay's students in economic history later observed that "he was not given to vague theorizing . . . hardly ever paused to generalize" (Cole 1970, p. 34).

Gay credited the German Historical school for founding the discipline of economic history (1941). He singled out Wilhelm Roscher as the "original formulator" of the Historical school and cited Karl Knies' principle of historical relativity as well as the use of a comparative method as highlights of the school's contribution to research methodology. He also recognized the intense struggle of the Historical economists, especially Schmoller, with the manner in which generalizations could be developed from the mass of economic facts being collected, summarized, and synthesized. The reason for that struggle was the inherent complexity of economic events. Gay commented (1923, p. 2) that:

> . . . the longer I live, the more inclined I am to agree with the late Professor Schmoller of Berlin that the world of political, social-psychological, and economic phenomena is a terribly complicated business.

Nevertheless Gay maintained, as the Historical school had, that the ultimate objective of inductive research is to produce generalizations and principles. Consistent with his German training, Gay believed that the scientific principles and generalizations of business should be "built up by observation and induction from widely gathered and carefully sifted facts" (1927a).

In Gay's words, the Harvard Business School was to become a "simple scientific endeavor" (Cruikshank 1987, ch. 2). This modest objective, however, was to lead to some fundamental achievements that became Harvard's principal contributions to the development of marketing thought. First, Gay had to determine what was essential to be taught; he had to define the subject matter of business. Second, he had to determine how that subject matter would be taught.

Gay's answer to the first of these challenges was to divide business into "two fundamental functions of industrial management [production] and commercial organization or marketing" (Gay quoted by Hanford 1954, p. 7). During the time when the Business School was being planned, Frederick W. Taylor and his associates were developing a body of knowledge about the industrial management aspect of business and Gay adopted it enthusiastically for the School. Taylor used time and motion studies of work activity and the detailed observation and measurement of work to develop his principles of scientific management. Those principles were considered scientific because they were "generalized rules of conduct based on law . . . a summary statement of fact or a description of a tendency common to a class of things" (Thompson 1917, p. 5). Apparently, as a member of a committee drafting a detailed plan of programs, courses, and arrangements, Gay was searching for and identifying materials for the Business School's courses. Taylor's seminal articles on the "Art of Cutting Metals" (1906) and "Shop Management" (1903) were among the first to be noted in that connection (Gay 1907).

Industrial management was only one of the two basic functions of business. The other, as Gay defined it, was distribution or marketing. When the School opened in 1908, there were three required courses: Principles of Accounting, Commercial Contracts, and Economic Resources of the United States. According to Copeland (1958, p. 3), the general idea for the latter course was developed by Gay on the basis of his background in economic history and his interest in marketing methods. The course first was taught by Paul Cherington and later (in 1914) evolved into the course titled "Marketing."

The distinctive philosophy of marketing science being developed at Harvard was manifested in three specific forms: the case method of teaching, the Bureau of Business Research, and Arch W. Shaw's description of the basic functions of marketing.

The Case Method

The case method often is cited as a significant and distinctive contribution of Harvard to the development of marketing thought. On the basis of his 1945 survey of marketing scholars, Converse reported that the case method was voted one of the most important concepts or techniques in marketing (1945, p. 20). Bartels also concluded that the case method was Harvard's "principal contribution throughout the years to the development of marketing thought" (1951, p. 11) and cited Copeland (1920), Tosdal (1921), McNair and David (1925), and Borden (1927) as examples.

Consistent with his vision of business as a profession, a science, and an art, Gay recognized from the outset the need for a unique means of teaching business (1908, p. 161):

> The teacher of business . . . must discover the fundamental principles of business system, and then, in a scientific spirit, teach not only those principles, but the art of applying them after investigation, to any given enterprise. This means, then, that new courses of study must be organized and that a laboratory-system of instruction must, as far as possible, be introduced.

The term "laboratory method" was derived from the method of teaching in the natural sciences on which the seminar method, used so successfully in Germany, was modeled. In a 1927 speech about the

founding of the Business School, Gay further described this conception of the laboratory method as an "experimental laboratory studying genetically and theoretically the institutions and processes of our economic organization and practically [applying] the new insights for the continued betterment of our business practise" (1927b, p. 400).

Another emphasis in Gay's early thinking about business training was the role of historical study. Certainly here his training under the Historical school was influential. The following reflections were jotted down in Gay's personal journal in 1910 shortly after the School opened.

> For most business men do not know enough history to make analogies, those who do, know enough to make analogies. . . . Some influence of the historical method in spirit. Gaining of perspective, realization of changing character of institutions apparently stable . . . sense of proportion . . . relation to principles . . . realization of complexity and interrelations and their modification of too rigid and simple standards of judgement.

Though these notes are only fragments of Gay's thinking on the matter, they indicate the importance he attributed to historical study in a business school. Therein lay the foundation of the case method at the Harvard Business School. As Harvard business historian Alfred Chandler recently observed, "Don't forget, the heart of this school's curriculum has always been the case study, and the case study is precisely what a historian does, what a historian is trained to do" (Kantrow 1986, p. 82).

Research in Marketing

Gay's training as an economic historian probably influenced his views on research methodology even more than those on pedagogy. Much of that methodological perspective is described in the preceding section. The first clear example of its application to the field of marketing, however, was probably the Bureau of Business Research. The Bureau was formed in 1911 with the financial assistance and urging of Arch W. Shaw.

In 1911 Gay remarked to Shaw, "What is needed is a quantitative measurement for the marketing side of distribution," to which Shaw replied in writing, "I wish to give for use in this School a fund which shall be applied for the purpose of investigation of business problems, primarily for the problem of distribution of products" (Cruikshank 1987, p. 59). The result of Shaw's initiative was the establishment of the Bureau of Business Research under the direction of staff members of the Business School.

The first director of the Bureau was Seldin O. Martin and the first studies carried out were of the shoe industry. As Martin explained (1916, p. 266):

The field of marketing seemed especially promising for research. It has apparently received less scientific attention than production in the field of manufacturing at least. Why was there such a variety of methods of selling and in channels of distribution? The concrete fact that from one-fourth to one-half of the retail selling price of an article is consumed in getting the article from the producer to the consumer seemed of itself worthy of study without prejudice for or against the existing order.

In the more industrialized economy of the eastern United States, the distribution or marketing problems being studied were different from those of the Midwest. Whereas agriculture provided most of the subject matter for research on marketing problems at the University of Wisconsin, retailing and manufacturing were the focus of similar work at Harvard. Hence, studies of the shoe industry were the first to be carried out and were followed by the study of grocery retailing. Following from this research, classroom discussion in marketing courses often centered on such topics as the department store, retailers' work and methods, and marketing problems as factors in industrial development.

The problems studied at Harvard were also different from those studied at Wisconsin in that they were the problems faced by individual marketing managers. In Arch W. Shaw's words, they were concerned with the "how to" of marketing. Marketing scholars at Wisconsin tended to be more concerned with whether the entire system was working "properly." At Harvard the emphasis was on the marketing policies of business firms.

In commenting on the research being carried out by the Bureau, Gay drew a parallel between the research methodology of the School and its pedagogy (1912a, p. 1215–17):

> There are laboratories for the natural sciences both pure and applied; there are agricultural experiment stations for the farmer; why not a laboratory for business? The primary object of this research is the development of instruction in the school. But it should also give to the business man a partial basis for judgement in meeting his particular problems.

This use of an inductive, historical method was not confined to the Bureau of Business Research, though. One of the earliest student research papers to apply the historical approach was one that identified the basic functions of marketing.

Basic Functions of Marketing

The concept of "marketing functions" has been hailed as one of the most significant theoretical developments of early contemporary marketing thought (Hunt and Goolsby 1988). Indeed, it has been compared with the discovery of atomic theory (Converse 1945, p. 19). There is some consensus that Arch W. Shaw originated the functional approach in his 1912 article, "Some

Problems in Market Distribution (Converse 1945, p. 18; Faria 1983, p. 162; Hunt and Goolsby 1988, p. 36). Shaw used the term "functions" to refer to acts or services performed by middlemen (1912, p. 731). In describing these as "general" functions, Shaw clearly had in mind that they were universal, that the performance of such functions was a principle or law-like generalization of marketing. To study such marketing problems, Shaw advocated what he called the "laboratory method," which included the use of observation, statistics, comparison, and an historical perspective (1912, p. 754). The product of such a scientific method, in Shaw's view, would be general principles, exemplified by the functions of middlemen.

On the surface Shaw's 1912 statement of marketing functions appears to be a series of simple assertions. In fact, Shaw had used the laboratory method in the form of a historical, statistical study of the role of merchants in the British economy. The findings of that study led to the writing of "Some Problems in Market Distribution." As a student of Gay's in 1910, Shaw undertook a research project that led directly to his seminal 1912 article. Shaw (1950) described that sequence of events in the following way:

> Dean Gay of Harvard had the knack of challenging the energies of students. In one of his lectures on the economic history of England he put special emphasis on the contribution of the merchant in the extension of the British economy both at home and around the world. The emphasis to me was, in effect, a challenge to trace the development of distribution stage by stage starting with the role of the British merchant as the handicraft period came to a close. . . . So it seemed of significance also to trace through the functions supplementing those of the merchant, which together with his functions made up the compound of the British economy and then to search for some simple concept by means of which these functions would fall naturally into definite classifications and their interdependence disclosed.

At about the same time as Shaw's 1912 article was published, Gay presented an address to the American Historical Association in which he stated (1912b, p. 7):

> One of the most interesting problems which the historian of domestic trade will face is that of the organization of the domestic market, and with this goes the study of the middleman, the morphology of the merchant. . . . It is of importance to know how this orthodox system of market distribution came into existence, what needs it met, how far and in what industries those needs have persisted. We ought to know more definitely what has been the evolution of the merchant and his various functions.

Gay's research agenda apparently had been accepted by Shaw, as was evident in the latter's description of the evolution of distribution in England and in his seminal article on the basic functions of marketing.

Gay's use of the term "morphology" in his address is especially interesting as it reflects a tendency to anthropomorphize the phenomena of economics, a tendency very characteristic of the German Historical school. For example, in his lecture notes on the Historical school, Gay often referred to their "organic conception of society" (undated). In fact, Wilhelm Roscher referred to the historical method as yielding the anatomy and physiology of the economy (1878, p. 111):

> Our aim is simply to describe man's economic nature and economic wants, to investigate the laws and the character of the institutions which are adapted to the satisfaction of these wants, and the greater or less amount of success by which they have been attended. Our task is, therefore, so to speak, the anatomy and physiology of social or national economy.

But for the last sentence, that quotation could have appeared in any modern-day marketing text. Similarly, Gay saw the task of marketing scholars to be the description of the morphology of the merchant. Shaw's contribution in that area was the basic functions of middlemen.

Conclusion

During the early part of the twentieth century, when marketing thought began to emerge in its contempo-

rary form, North American economics was divided fairly clearly into neoclassical and institutional schools of thought (Arndt 1981, p. 38). Neoclassical economics was the offspring of English classical economics. Institutionalism has been traced to the German Historical school of economics (Dorfman 1955; Myles 1956).

The German Historical school developed a particular version of a positivistic philosophy of science. Their approach to economics might well be considered a paradigm or a research tradition. That research tradition was an inductive-statistical version of positivism. It combined the exploratory, descriptive, process orientation of nineteenth century German Idealism with a faith in the objectivity of facts and a concern with problem solving. Together, these intellectual threads were woven into a relatively sophisticated vision of science, one that was used by scholars at the University of Wisconsin and at Harvard to intellectualize marketing practice.

The courses taught and literature written by many of the earliest marketing scholars at the University of Wisconsin and the Harvard Business School reflected

FIGURE 1
The Intellectual Genealogy of Marketing

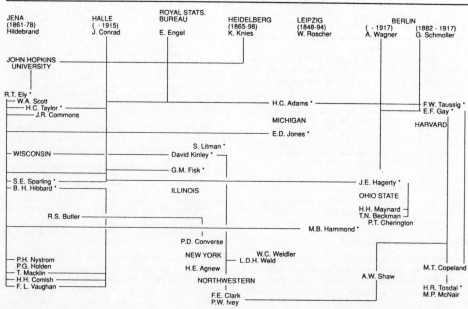

* Studied in Germany.

the philosophic assumptions and ideals we have described. This evidence, combined with the fact that many of the early marketing scholars actually studied in Germany under the Historical school or under American economists who had studied there and who had adopted that philosophic position, would be enough to suggest that the German Historical school provided a philosophic foundation for many of our early marketing scholars (Figure 1). In addition, several scholars clearly identified with the field of marketing, as well as economists with a major interest in marketing, explicitly acknowledged that the German Historical school influenced their thinking.[2]

We do not suggest that scholars at these two institutions were not influenced by other individuals or ideas not associated with the Historical school. The Progressive Movement and the relatively large German population in Wisconsin at the turn of the century provided a receptive environment for Ely's German-inspired institutionalism. Also, the relatively well-developed doctrine of scientific management, together with the popular philosophic movement of Pragmatism at Harvard, undoubtedly reinforced the philosophy followed by Taussig and especially by Gay. The extent of other such influences and the nature of philosophic underpinnings at other institutions in North America are topics for further research. We examine only the major sources of philosophic influence at the two recognized centers of early development of marketing thought.

Many marketing scholars today believe that the discipline only recently has become aware of its underlying philosophy of science and, hence, to debate the status of marketing as a science. Most date the beginning of this discussion to Converse's 1945 article. However, we now can see more clearly that the earliest scholars of this century believed marketing could be developed into a science—one based largely on the philosophy of the German Historical school.

---

[2]We speculate that marketing courses may actually have been offered in Germany before those offered at American institutions around the turn of the century. A report sent to Benjamin Hibbard at the University of Wisconsin from the American Consulate-General in Berlin indicates that courses in agricultural marketing were offered as early as 1912 and possibly earlier (Thakara 1913). A course description in the 1912/13 catalogue for the University of Berlin read (Thakara 1913, p. 5):

General course in business management. Includes credit, competition, speculation, the methods and psychology of advertising, selling methods and organization tariff technique. Organization of commercial establishments in particular branches. The grain trade and the marketing of grain.

The report concluded, ". . . in most, if not all, of the universities there are opportunities for the study of various phases of economics bearing in a broad way on the subject of marketing" (Thakara 1913, p. 2).

REFERENCES

Arndt, Johan (1981), "The Political Economy of Marketing Systems: Reviving the Institutional Approach," *Journal of Macromarketing*, 1 (Fall), 36–47.
Bartels, Robert (1951), "Influences on the Development of Marketing Thought, 1900–1923," *Journal of Marketing*, 16 (1), 1–17.
————— (1962), *The Development of Marketing Thought*. Homewood, IL: Irwin Press.
Borden, Neil H. (1927), *Problems in Advertising*. New York: A. W. Shaw Co.
Brooks, Robert (1906), Brooks to Henry W. Farnam, unpublished correspondence, *Farnam Family Papers*. New Haven, CT: Yale University Library Archives.
Cole, Arthur (1970), "The First Dean: A Wondrous Choice," *Harvard Business School Bulletin* (May–June), 32–34.
Conrad, Johannes (1868), "Die Statistik der Landwirthschaftlichen Production," *Jahrbucher fur Nationalokonomie und Statistik*, 10, 81.
Converse, Paul D. (1933), "The First Decade of Marketing Literature," *NATMA Bulletin* (November), 1–4.
————— (1945), "The Development of the Science of Marketing," *Journal of Marketing*, 10 (July), 14–23.
————— (1959), *The Beginning of Marketing Thought in the United States*. Austin: Bureau of Business Research, University of Texas.
Copeland, Melvin T. (1920), *Marketing Problems*. New York: A. W. Shaw Co.
————— (1958), *And Mark an Era: The Story of the Harvard Business School*. Boston: Little, Brown & Co.
Cruikshank, Jeffrey L. (1987), *A Delicate Experiment: The Harvard Business School 1908–1945*. Cambridge, MA: Harvard Business School Press.
Dorfman, Joseph (1955), "The Role of the German Historical School in American Economic Growth," *American Economic Review*, 45 (May Supplement), 17–39.
Ely, Richard T. (1884), "The Past and Present of Political Economy," in *Johns Hopkins University Studies in Political Science*. Baltimore: Johns Hopkins University, 1–64.
————— (undated), "Economics and Social Science in Relation to Business Education," unpublished manuscript, *Ely Papers*. Madison: State Historical Society of Wisconsin.
————— (1891), Ely to E. A. Ross, June 23, unpublished correspondence, *Ely Papers*. Madison: State Historical Society of Wisconsin.
————— (1903), E. D. Jones to Ely, March 18, unpublished correspondence, *Ely Papers*. Madison: State Historical Society of Wisconsin.
————— (1906), Ely to Henry W. Farnam, unpublished correspondence, *Farnam Family Papers*. New Haven, CT: Yale University Library Archives.

——— (1918), E. D. Jones to Ely, February 3, unpublished correspondence, *Ely Papers*. Madison: State Historical Society of Wisconsin.

——— (1931), Remarks of Richard T. Ely at the Annual Meeting of the AEA, unpublished manuscript, *Ely Papers*. Madison: State Historical Society of Wisconsin.

——— (1936), "The Founding and Early History of the American Economic Association," *Proceedings of the American Economic Association*, 26 (December), 141–50.

——— (1938), *Ground Under Our Feet*. New York: Macmillan Publishing Co.

Faria, A. J. (1983), "The Development of the Functional Approach to the Study of Marketing to 1940," in *First North American Workshop on Historical Research in Marketing*, Stanley Hollander and Ronald Savitt, eds. East Lansing: Michigan State University, 160–9.

Farnam, Henry W. (1908), "Deutsche-amerikanische Beziehungen in der Volkswirtschaftslehre," in *Die Entwicklung der Deutschen Volkswirtschaftslehre im Neunzehnten Jahrundert*, Gustav Schmoller, ed., Leipzig, 25–9.

Fullerton, Ronald A. (1987), "The Poverty of Ahistorical Analysis: Present Weakness and Future Cure in U.S. Marketing Thought, in *Philosophical and Radical Thought in Marketing*, F. Firat, N. Dholakia, and Richard Bagozzi, eds. Lexington, MA: Lexington Books.

Gay, Edwin Francis (1907), Diaries 1907–1914, unpublished diaries, *Edwin Francis Gay Collection*. San Marino, CA: The Huntington Library.

——— (1908), "The New Graduate School of Business Administration," *Harvard Illustrated Magazine*, 9, 159–61.

——— (1912a), "The Scientific Study of Retailing," *Hardware Dealer's Magazine* (December), 1215–17.

——— (1912b), "The History of Modern Commerce as a Field of Investigation," unpublished address to Historical Association, *Edwin Francis Gay Collection*. San Marino, CA: The Huntington Library.

——— (1923), "The Rhythm of History," *Harvard Graduate Magazine*, 2.

——— (1927a), "Social Progress and Business Education," Gay's Addresses, Address delivered at the Dedication of Weiboldt Hall, Northwestern University, June 16, *Edwin Francis Gay Collection*. San Marino, CA: The Huntington Library.

——— (1927b), "The Founding of the Harvard Business School," *Harvard Business Review*, 5 (July), 397–400.

——— (1941), "The Tasks of Economic History," *Journal of Economic History*, 1.

Hagerty, James E. (1906), "Hagerty to Henry W. Farnam," unpublished correspondence, *Farnam Family Papers*. New Haven, CT: Yale University Library Archives.

——— (1936), "Experiences of Our Early Marketing Teachers," *Journal of Marketing*, 1 (July), 20–7.

Hanford, G. H. (1954), "About the Formative Years," *Harvard Business School Bulletin*, 219–24.

Heaton, Herbert A. (1949), "The Making of an Economic Historian," *Journal of Economic History*, Supplement 9, 1–18.

Herbst, Jurgen (1965), *The German Historical School in American Scholarship*. New York: Cornell University Press.

Hildebrand, Bruno (1848), *Die National Okonomie der Gegenwart and Zukunst*. Frankfurt: J. Rutten.

Hunt, Shelby D. and Jerry Goolsby (1988), "The Rise and Fall of the Functional Approach to Marketing: A Paradigm Displacement Perspective," in *Historical Perspectives in Marketing: Essays in Honor of Stanley Hollander*, Terence Nevett and Ronald Fullerton, eds. Lexington, MA: Lexington Books, 35–51.

Jones, D. G. Brian (1987), "Edward David Jones: A Pioneer in Marketing," in *Marketing in Three Eras*, Stanley Hollander and Terence Nevett, eds. East Lansing: Michigan State University, 126–34.

Jones, Edward David (1911a), "The Larger Aspects of Private Business," *Mill Supplies*, 1, 2–4.

——— (1911b), "Quantity Prices Versus Classified Lists," *Mill Supplies*, 1, 245.

——— (1911c), "Functions of a System of Grades," *Mill Supplies*, 1, 529–30.

——— (1912a), "Cost of Living and the Retail Trade," *Mill Supplies*, 2, 577.

——— (1912b), "Functions of the Merchant," *Mill Supplies*, 2, 575–7.

——— (1912c), "Principles of Modern Retail Merchandising," *Mill Supplies*, 2, 461–2.

——— (1913a), "Function of Trade Marks," *Mill Supplies*, 3, 69–70.

——— (1913b), "Some Propositions Concerning University Instruction in Business Administration," *Journal of Political Economy*, 21, 185–95.

Kantrow, Alan M. (1986), "Why History Matters to Managers," *Harvard Business Review*, 64 (January–February), 81–8.

Knies, Karl (1853), *Die Politische Oekonomie vom Standpunkte der Geschichtlichen Methode*. Braunschweig: C. A. Schwetschke.

Marshall, Alfred (1890), *Principles of Economics*. London: Macmillan & Co.

——— (1919), *Industry and Trade*, 2nd ed. London: Macmillan & Co.

Martin, Seldin O. (1916), "The Bureau of Business Research," *Harvard Alumni Bulletin*, 266–9.

Maynard, Harold H. (1941), "Marketing Courses Prior to 1910," *Journal of Marketing*, 5 (April), 382–4.

McNair, Malcolm P. and D. K. David (1925), *Problems in Retailing*. Chicago: A. W. Shaw Co.

Monieson, David D. (1981), "What Constitutes Usable Knowledge in Marketing?" *Journal of Macromarketing*, 1 (Spring), 14–22.

Myles, Jack C. (1956), "German Historicism and American Economics—A Study of the Influence of the German Historical School on American Economic Thought," PhD dissertation, Princeton University.

Pigou, A. C., ed. (1956), *Memorials of Alfred Marshall*. New York: Kelley & Millman Inc.

Pulver, Glen C. (1984), "Improving Agriculture and Rural Life," in *Achievements in Agricultural Economics 1909–1984*. Madison: University of Wisconsin.

Rader, Benjamin (1966), *The Academic Mind and Reform: The Influence of Richard T. Ely in American Life*. Lexington: University of Kentucky Press.

Redlich, Fritz (1957), "Academic Education for Business: Its Development and the Contribution of Ignaz Jastrow (1856–1937)," *Business History Review*, 31 (Spring), 35–93.

Roscher, Wilhelm (1843), *Grundriss zu Vorlesungen uber die Staatswirthschaft nach Geschichtlichen Methode*. Gottingen: Dieterich.

——— (1878), *Principles of Political Economy*, translated by John J. Lalor, Vol. 1. Chicago: Callaghan & Co.

Savitt, Ronald (1980), "Historical Research in Marketing," *Journal of Marketing*, 44 (Fall), 52–8.

——— (1983), "A Note on the Varieties and Vagaries of Historical Data," *First North American Workshop on Historical Research in Marketing*, Stanley Hollander and Ronald Savitt, eds. East Lansing: Michigan State University, 30–4.

Shaw, Arch W. (1912), "Some Problems in Market Distribution," *Quarterly Journal of Economics*, 26, 703–65.

———— (1950), "Acceptance Speech at the 1950 Converse Award," unpublished manuscript, *Edwin Francis Gay Collection*. San Marino, CA: The Huntington Library.

Sheth, Jagdish N. and Barbara L. Gross (1988), "Parallel Development of Marketing and Consumer Behavior: A Historical Perspective," in *Historical Perspectives in Marketing*, Terence Nevett and Ronald Fullerton, eds. Lexington, MA: Lexington Books, 9–33.

Sparling, Samuel E. (1906), *Introduction to Business Organization*. New York: Macmillan Publishing Co.

Taussig, Frank (1906), Taussig to Henry W. Farnam, unpublished correspondence, *Farnam Family Papers*. New Haven, CT: Yale University Library Archives.

———— (1907), Taussig to Gay, unpublished correspondence, *C. W. Eliot Papers*. Cambridge, MA: Harvard University Archives, Pusey Library.

Taylor, Henry C. (1908), Taylor to B. H. Hibbard, unpublished correspondence, *Henry Charles Taylor Papers*. Madison: State Historical Society of Wisconsin.

———— (1910), "The Prices of Farm Products," *University of Wisconsin Agricultural Experiment Station Bulletins*, 209 (May), 1–29.

———— (1920), "The Development of Research and Education in Agricultural Cooperation and Marketing at the University of Wisconsin 1910–1920," unpublished manuscript, *Henry Charles Taylor Papers*. Madison: State Historical Society of Wisconsin.

———— (1922), "What's Back of Marketing?" unpublished manuscript, *Henry Charles Taylor Papers*. Madison: State Historical Society of Wisconsin.

———— (1941), "Plus Ultra," unpublished autobiography, *Henry Charles Taylor Papers*. Madison: State Historical Society of Wisconsin.

————, W. A. Schoenfeld, and G. S. Wehrwein (1913), "The Marketing of Wisconsin Cheese," *Agricultural Experiment Station Bulletins*, 231 (April), 1–36.

———— and Ann Dewees Taylor (1974), *The Story of Agricultural Economics in the U.S. 1840–1932*. Westport, CT: Greenwood Press.

Thakara, A. M. (1913), "German Educational Courses in Co-operation and Marketing," unpublished report, *Benjamin Hibbard Papers*. Madison: University of Wisconsin Library Archives.

Thompson, Clarence B. (1917), *The Theory and Practice of Scientific Management*. Boston: Houghton-Mifflin Company.

Thwing, Charles F. (1928), *The American and the German University*. New York: The Macmillan Co.

Tosdal, H. R. (1921), *Problems in Sales Management*. New York: A. W. Shaw Co.

Wright, John and P. B. Dimsdale (1974), *Pioneers in Marketing*. Atlanta: Georgia State University.

Reprint No. JM541106

[5]

Marketing as Production: The Development of a Concept

Donald F. Dixon
Penn State Great Valley

The conventional view of marketing as somehow adding to the work of manufacturing is rooted in the concept of production as the creation of material attributes. A view of marketing as an integral part of a productive process generating "bundles of utilities" has a long history in economic analysis. This approach offers several advantages for marketing thought.

INTRODUCTION

In economic theory production is "The process of increasing the capacity of goods to satisfy human desires or of rendering services capable of satisfying human desires" (Sloan and Zurcher 1970, p. 348). Marketing activity falls within this definition. However, the way that marketing textbooks have differentiated marketing from other productive activity has created theoretical difficulties. For example, a generation of marketing students have been told that "Stated simply, the job of manufacturing is to create form utility, while marketing's job is to provide time, place, and possession utility" (McCarthy 1981, p. 5).

Cox identifies a significant problem arising from this approach:

> By a long-established convention, what manufacturers and farmers do results in "production," or "value added." What "distributors" do is more likely to be counted as a "margin," a "bill," or simply a "cost." The bias inherent in this usage undoubtedly makes much more difficult a disinterested evaluation of what marketing is and does (Cox 1965, p. 26).

Journal of the Academy of Marketing Science
Volume 18, Number 4, pages 337-343.
Copyright © 1990 by Academy of Marketing Science.
All rights of reproduction in any form reserved.
ISSN 0092-0703.

The definition of marketing in terms of types of value or utility generated has been criticized in the marketing literature. Alderson argues that "It is a highly arbitrary procedure to divide the utility to the consumer into two parts and to say that one part is created by production and the other by marketing" (1957, p. 68). In referring to the distinction drawn between form and other aspects of utility, Alderson remarks: "There is only one kind of utility—namely the value which a product contributes to the potency of an assortment . . . All economic activities create a single form of utility" (1957, p. 198).

Beckman also argues against any distinction between marketing and manufacturing: "The best current economic thinking" is that "values are created through the addition of utilities, which are capacities in goods or services to satisfy human wants." Moreover:

> It is now generally recognized among economists and other students of the subject that the creation of these utilities spells the creation of economic values and that this is the essence of production. This means that whoever creates these utilities is engaged in production, so that a wholesaler or a retailer who normally creates place, time, and possession utilities is as much a producer as is a processor who changes a product from one form to another (1957, p. 8).

Beckman concludes that "It is high time that we all get in line with sound economic thinking and stop the silly argument" about who is engaged in production and who is not (1957, p. 9).

Although Beckman's conclusion is similar to Alderson's, the conceptual foundations underlying the two discussions are different; each writer uses a different concept of value. Beckman is arguing in terms of *value-in-exchange*, basing his calculation of value added upon "the selling value" of products (1957, p. 7). On the other hand, Alderson is reasoning in terms of *value-in-use*. Because the exchange transaction increases the utility of the assortment held, "It creates value in the sense that there is greater value in use after the exchange" (1957, p. 198). Clearly Alderson's concept of utility as "increasing the potency of an assortment" differs from Beckman's "selling value."

The failure to recognize different meanings of "value" leads to conflicting interpretations of economic theory. In McCarthy, the distinction between marketing and other productive activities lies in "what economists believe" (McCarthy 1981, p. 665), while "the best current economic thinking" leads Beckman to consider such a distinction to be "silly." Such confusion also leads to a misunderstanding of the influence of economic theory upon the analysis of marketing as a productive process. Bartels asserts that "In 1900 there was no clear concept of marketing as a productive activity or as a contribution to economic production" (1962, p. 16). This situation is said to have obtained because "economists" were mainly concerned with "value in tangible goods created in the process of physical production." Consequently, "New concepts of value were required after 1900" (1962, p. 15). The inference seems to be that marketing writers in the United States developed these new concepts.

This paper demonstrates that there was a clear concept of marketing as a productive process at the turn of the century. The discussion traces two streams in the development of value and utility theory in the literature of economics. Value as usefulness or utility, underlying Alderson's work, is examined first, and then the focus shifts to exchange value, that underlies Beckman's position. Finally, the treatment of marketing in the context of utility by some early marketing writers are examined.

USE VALUE

Aristotle distinguishes between use value or utility, and exchange value (4th c. B.C., I, iii, 10). However, it is the Medieval Schoolmen who give utility its primacy of position in economic analysis, arguing that the origin of economic value lies in the needs of consumers. St. Augustine (d. 604), the first archbishop of Canterbury, holds that the price of marketable goods depends upon their usefulness or utility to men (5th c., 70.13).

The originator of the concept of subjective utility is the Franciscan, Pierre de Jean Olivi (1248–1298), who asserts that one aspect of the value of a commodity is "according to how it is more or less pleasing to our will to have it in our possession," and "In this way one person considers a commodity, which appears inferior to another, very much to be appreciated." Thus value will vary "within some suitable range, with respect to times, places and persons" (13th c., f. 295c).

And the times and places that influence value are recognized as contributions made by marketing activity. St. Thomas Aquinas (c. 1225–1275), the best known of the Schoolmen, confirms that "The price of saleable things . . . depends upon the usefulness to man" (13th c., 77.2). This "usefulness" created by altering commodities, generates income; if a man "sells at a higher price something that he has changed for the better, he would receive the reward

of his labor." And this "changing for the better" can occur in several ways:

> Either because he has bettered the thing, or because the value of the thing has changed with the change of place, or time, or on account of the dangers he incurs in transferring the item from one place to another, or again in having it carried by another (13th c., 77.4).

By the close of the Middle Ages the Schoolmen understood that value arises from the creation of form, time and place utility, and risk bearing. The analytical similarity between the contribution to a product's usefulness made by merchants and other economic agents was generally acknowledged.

A Seventeenth Century secular work written by Nicholas Barbon (d. 1698), who Schumpeter considers "one of the top half dozen English seventeenth century economists" (1954, p. 294), gives the impression that the contribution of marketing activities is so obvious that it does not require elaboration: "The Value of all Wares arises from their Use. . . .The Use of Things are to supply the Wants and Necessities of Man." Two types of wants are identified, those of the body and of the mind. The wants of the mind are infinite: "Man naturally Aspires, and as his Mind is elevated, his Senses grow more refined, and more capable of Delight; his Desires are inlarged, and his Wants increase with his Wishes."

What is the role of marketing in this process? Barbon states simply that "The Use of Trade is to make, and provide things Necessary, or useful for the Support, Defence, Ease, Pleasure, and Pomp of Life." In the event that this statement is not sufficiently clear, many participants in the productive process are listed, among whom appear various types of manufacturers and retailers (Barbon 1690, p. 21).

In the following century the concept of subjective utility was carried to its logical conclusion by Ferdinando Galiani (1728–1787), the Italian economist who Schumpeter considers "one of the ablest minds that ever became active" in economics (1954, p. 292). Galiani asserts that "It is certain that nothing has a price among men except pleasure, and that only satisfactions are purchased" (1751, p. 304). This view makes it possible to develop the precise mechanism by which marketing activities create use value.

An early effort to accomplish this is found in the work of Etienne B. de Condillac (1715–1780), the noted French philosopher and associate of Rousseau. The discussion begins with the statement that the value of goods is based upon the use made of them, and this is based upon men's needs. Two types of needs are identified: those that are "a consequence of our makeup," such as food, and those "born out of our practice of choosing to satisfy our natural needs by particular methods." It is especially interesting that social needs, which "are a consequence of civilized societies," are as "natural" as the need for food, for example (1776, p. 6).

The demonstration of the significance of marketing activities begins in the chapter titled "How Commerce Increases the Stock of Wealth":

> We have seen that commerce, which consists of the exchange of one thing for another, is carried on

principally by merchants, traffickers and wholesalers. We now try to understand the utility which society derives from all these men who have established themselves between producers and consumers.

There are two steps in the argument. First, the transaction itself creates wealth. Each party gains something that they prefer to that given in exchange.

This idea that the transaction itself creates value is not often stated explicitly, but it survived until the end of the nineteenth century. Henry George (1839–1897), the American economist noted for his view that land values represented monopoly power and should bear the entire tax burden, argues:

> In itself exchange brings about a perceptible increase in the sum of wealth, . . . Each of the two parties to an exchange aims to get, and as a rule does get, something that is more valuable to him than what he gives. . . . Thus there is in the transaction an actual increase in the sum of wealth, an actual production of wealth (1898, p. 33 1).

Besides the direct creation of value by the completion of a transaction, marketing activity also makes an indirect contribution. It makes it possible for transactions to take place: "Exchange gives value to the abundance of production, which without exchange would not have any value." Specialists must conduct this exchange because "it would be uneconomic for the producer to go to the market rather than remaining at work in his fields." The contribution of marketers is shown by analogy:

> A spring that disappears in the rocks and sand is not wealth for me; but it becomes wealth if I build an aqueduct to carry it to my fields. This spring represents the surplus production of the farmers, and the aqueduct represents the merchants.

In conclusion, "exchange is also, in the last analysis, a source of wealth" (1776, p. 50).

This result is accepted by J.B. Say (1769–1832), the French economist whose treatise offered the first popular treatment of economic principles. However, Say objects to Condillac's argument that the contribution of marketing is indirect: "The value added by commerce to the things exchanged is not operated by the act of exchange, but by the commercial operations that precede it." The activities of marketing create utility directly, and in a manner that is no different than other types of productive activities. Transport, for example, increases value because a good is more useful in one place than another: "Transportation is a modification that the trader gives to the commodity, whereby he adapts to our use what was not before available." All branches of industry increase value in this manner, that is, by the "approximation to the customer . . . by fitting them [resources] for the use of mankind" (1803, Vol. I, p. 9).

Other nineteenth century writers did little more than repeat Say's argument. John R. McCulloch (1789–1864), whose

textbook dominated English economics in the early nineteenth century, states:

> It is plain that the capital and labour employed in carrying commodities from where they are produced to where they are to be consumed, and in dividing them into minute proportions, so as to suit the wants of consumers, are really as productive as if they were employed in agriculture or manufacturing. . . . We do not owe our fires exclusively to the miner, or exclusively to the coal-merchant. They are the result of the conjoined operations of both (1825, p. 177).

Toward the end of the century the argument was cast in more modern terms. A work coauthored by John Hobson (1858–1940), "an archeretic in the heyday of Marshallian supremacy" (Schumpeter 1954, p. 832), held that "logically, and in the last resort . . . 'utilities and conveniences' are non-material; that is to say, they consist of the 'services' rendered by instruments" (Mummery and Hobson 1889, p. 16). Moreover, these writers carry the analysis through an entire marketing channel. The process of producing a pair of shoes is traced from the animal providing the hide to the ultimate consumer, to show that raw material gathers value continuously "by change of form or change of place."

The modern form of this line of reasoning was introduced by the Austrian School. W. Stanley Jevons (1835–1882), "one of the most genuinely original economists who ever lived" (Schumpeter 1954, p. 826), is considered a member of the Austrian School despite his English birth because he independently discovered concepts associated with the School. Jevons holds that value depends entirely upon utility. "The keystone of the whole Theory of Exchange" is the concept of marginal utility (1871, p. 95). He notes that one limitation of this proposition is that quantities are not infinitely divisible: "There is always, in retail trade, a convenient unit below which we do not descend in purchases. Paper may be bought inquires, or even in packets, which it may not be desirable to break up" (1871, p. 125). A corollary is that marketing activity, which enables purchasers to match more closely the size of the unit purchased to the amount required, results in exchange being more perfectly adjusted.

From his general proposition Jevons derives a result that counters the "fallacious tendency to believe that the whole benefit of trade depends upon the difference in prices" (1871, p. 142). That is, "he who pays a high price must have a great need of that which he buys, or very little need of that which he pays for it; on either supposition there is gain by exchange." The rule is that "no one will buy a thing unless he expects advantage from the purchase" (1871, p. 145).

Karl Menger (1840–1921), the founder of the Austrian School, develops a similar argument in his chapter on "The Theory of Exchange." Two individuals are seen adjusting their assortments of goods by exchange, and thereby increasing their joint utility. In his concluding paragraph Menger clearly states that the work of marketing contributes to the well-being of individuals in the same way as other productive activities:

> An economic exchange contributes, as we have seen, to the better satisfaction of human needs . . .

just as effectively as a physical increase of economic goods. All persons who mediate exchange are therefore—provided always that the exchange operations are economic—just as productive as the farmer or manufacturer. For the end of economy is not the physical augmentation of goods, but always the fullest satisfaction of human needs (1871, p. 190).

Thus, during the nineteenth century writers in Austria, England, and France, offered a clear conception of the productive contribution of marketing to the usefulness of commodities. Moreover, these writers unequivocally demonstrate that there is no analytical distinction between the contribution of marketing and other types of productive activity.

EXCHANGE VALUE

A parallel stream of thought, focusing upon exchange value rather than use value, can be traced to Adam Smith (1723–1790). Although Smith is aware of use value, as "expressing the utility of some particular object" (1776, p. 28), he devotes his attention to exchange value. Wealth consists of tangible goods, not the use made of them.

But even in the context of exchange value, Smith shows that merchants are productive, just as manufacturers are, because their labor "fixes and realizes itself in some particular object or vendible commodity, which lasts for some time at least after that labor is past" (1776, p. 314).

Additional arguments also are presented. Where Smith speaks of retail activity as breaking and dividing goods into small parcels, he argues that this enables the workman who purchases from the retailer to reduce inventory costs. As a result the workman can earn a greater profit, which more than compensates for the higher price he pays. The wholesaler also makes a contribution, by affording a ready market to the manufacturer, by taking his goods off his hands as fast as he can make them, and by sometimes even advancing funds. Thus the manufacturer may produce "a much greater quantity of goods than if he was obliged to dispose of them himself to the immediate consumers, or even to the retailers" (1776, p. 342).

Here, as in Condillac's analysis, the contribution of marketing is indirect. But in Smith's scheme the nature of this indirect contribution has immense significance, because it has to do with the division of labor. The division of labor plays a dominant role in *The Wealth of Nations* because it leads to increased output. There are two ways in which marketing activity contributes to the division of labor. First, if a workman must perform marketing activities rather than doing his own work, then the potential gains from his specialization cannot be enjoyed. In addition, since the marketer is also a specialist, this means that the work of marketing is carried out at the lowest possible price.

The second way in which marketing makes a contribution arises because the extent to which specialization is possible depends upon the amount of work to be done. That is, "The division of labor is limited by the extent of the market." By lowering costs and prices, marketing activity increases market size. Increased market size leads to increased specialization, which further increases economic efficiency.

Robert Torrens (1780–1864), English soldier and economist, sees marketing as the transport and exchange of "articles of wealth" acquired from other sectors of the economy. The first marketing activity, transport, makes a direct contribution to wealth: "Many articles which possess utility in one place, do not possess it in another place; and therefore, the industry which conveys such articles is instrumental in conferring utility" (1821, p. 153). To this extent, Torrens agrees with the utility approach and departs from Smith's position.

The second marketing activity, exchange, which has "an indirect operation in the formation of riches," is divided into two parts. First, it makes possible the division of labor: "The divisions of employment to which the exchange of commodities gives occasion, augment, to an astonishing degree, the productive power of human industry." The second role of exchange is to make a continuous market by setting up warehouses and shops for the "collection and vending of commodities." As a result, each producer, "knowing where he can at all times be supplied . . . is enabled to devote his whole time and labor to his proper calling." In short, exchange gives "a more continued and uninterrupted motion to the cultivator and the manufacturer" (1821, p. 177).

The position taken by Torrens is equivocal at best. No conceptual scheme is introduced to justify a different treatment of the two types of marketing activity. If utility is produced by movement in space, why is there not a similar effect from movement in time? Alternatively, there is a spatial aspect to exchange activity since it involves "setting up warehouses and shops." Why then is it that transport does not also contribute to the division of labor?

Such analytical inconsistencies were resolved as an understanding of the direct contribution of marketing to exchange value emerged during the remainder of the nineteenth century. The foundation of this subsequent work was provided by James Mill (1773–1836), Scottish philosopher and economist, and father of John Stuart Mill. Mill's *Elements of Political Economy* is unique in its organization into four chapters: Production, Distribution, Interchange, and Consumption. This is the first time that the treatment of exchange, Mill's "interchange," is identified as a separate topic, and it established the pattern for the next generation of writers. This pattern focused attention upon marketing activities because it was necessary to assign them to one of the categories in the quadripartite arrangement. Various writers argued for the placement of marketing into one or another of the categories, but agreement was finally reached that marketing activity was part of the production process.

The relevant discussion Mill's *Elements* consists of little more than the argument that "The agency of man can be traced to very simple elements. He does nothing but produce motion. He can move things toward one another, and he can separate them from one another" (1821, p. 5). This brief statement is of the utmost significance, for it removes completely the possibility of any conceptual distinction between the work of marketing and that of any other productive activity. Indeed, it leads to the same conclusion as the utility, or use value approach.

John Stuart Mill (1806–1873), the classical economist whose textbook dominated English economics for two generations, restated the argument of the *Elements*:

> Putting things into fit places for being acted upon by their own internal forces, and by those residing in other natural objects, is all that man does, or can do, with matter. He only moves one thing to or from another . . . He has no other means of acting on matter than moving it.

This proposition inevitably brought J.S. Mill to accept Say's view of the significance of utility:

> All the labour of all the human beings in the world could not produce one particle of matter. . . . Though we cannot create matter, we can cause it to assume properties, by which, from having been useless to us, it becomes useful. What we produce, or desire to produce, is always, as M. Say rightly terms it, an utility. Labour is not creative of objects but of utilities (1848, p. 24).

Yet even John Stuart Mill is trapped by the weight of tradition. Despite his recognition of utility, he argues that the term "production" must refer not to utility but wealth. And wealth can be created only by utilities "fixed or embodied in any object." Marketing activity adds properties to objects: "It adds the property of being in the place where they are wanted, instead of being in some other place; which is a very useful property, and the utility it confers is embodied in the things themselves" (1848, p. 47).

This definition of production as adding properties to matter was widely accepted by later writers. But, although the process of production was a unitary one, it nevertheless was subdivided according to the types of "properties" added to matter. For example, Henry Sidgwick (1838–1900), English philosopher and economist, offers a tripartite arrangement of agriculture, manufacturing, and commerce distinguished by "the nature of the utility produced" (1883, p. 91).

The American economist Francis A. Walker (1840–1897), identifies time, place, and form value, "in respect of their origin," but denies any analytical distinction between form and other aspects of utility. Walker emphasizes that the creation of value does not imply any change in form: "However little the material may be wrought, and by whatever agencies that little may be effected, we may say that wealth is produced whenever value is added or acquired through any act or process" (1888, p. 33).

Another list of values, offered in a textbook by Richard T. Ely (1854–1943), American economist, includes elementary, form, place, and time value. Marketing produces time and place value by adding properties to goods, "namely the property of being in the right place and of being there at the right time" (1889, p. 177). But the connection with utility is made explicit, so that marketing is productive in the same sense as other branches of industry:

> Man creates no new matter. Neither the farmer nor the merchant adds one atom to the existing material of the earth. Yet they are both properly called producers. What do they produce? Simply quantities of utility. And how do they produce quantities of utility? Simply by putting things in their proper places. Man can only move things, and when he moves them in a suitable manner he creates utilities (1889, p. 143).

Thus, although the Classical writers emphasized exchange value, it was seen that production resulted not in the creation, but modification of matter, so that there could be no analytical distinction drawn between marketing and other productive activities. This point is restated by Alfred Marshall (1842–1924), whose *Principles* was the most influential economics textbook in the late nineteenth and early twentieth centuries:

> Man cannot create material things . . . He really only produces utilities; or in other words, his efforts and sacrifices result in changing the form or arrangement of matter to adapt it better for the satisfaction of wants. . . . It is sometimes said that traders do not produce; that while the cabinet-maker produces furniture, the furniture dealer merely sells what is already produced. But there is no scientific foundation for this distinction. They both produce utilities, and neither of them can do more (1890, p. 63).

DEVELOPMENTS IN THE EARLY TWENTIETH CENTURY

American economics textbooks published in the early twentieth century, and thus contemporary with some early U.S. marketing literature, continued to present the arguments that had developed in the nineteenth century. For example, Irving Fisher (1867–1947) postulates two attributes of wealth, "materiality" and "ownership." He then divides the process of production into three categories. The first two of these, "transformation," which changes form, and "transportation," which changes position, are viewed as so closely related that the distinction is "merely one of convenience" (1910, p. 80). Both include marketing activities. The third category of production is "exchange," which alters ownership. Fisher's contribution to marketing theory is his demonstration of the unity of the production process by including marketing activity in each of this three categories of production.

John Bates Clark (1847–1938), classifying labor "according to the particular result which it accomplishes," refers to various types of utility. His discussion of form utility, explicitly includes marketing activity:

> A form utility is created when a raw material is fashioned into a new shape, subdivided, or combined with other materials, as is done in manufacturing, and, in a certain way, in commerce. Buying goods in bulk and selling them in small quantities is the creating of form utilities and makes an addition to total wealth.

After offering two examples of this, Clark concludes that "Merchants are not mere exchangers, for they make positive additions to the utility of goods" (1907, p. 17).

These examples have a common theme, but perhaps the best generalization is that of Frank Taussig (1859–1940), who states that economic theory "is often brought to unity and consistency by the analysis of production as ending in utilities" and adds that "no conclusions of importance for economics flows from the distinction between those who shape material wealth and those who bring about utilities of other kinds" (1911, p. 17).

Some early marketing writers in the U.S. were familiar with contemporary economic theory, and incorporated the analysis of production in their textbooks. Ralph Starr Butler, for example, begins his discussion by defining a producer as "one who creates utility," and notes that "The definition says nothing about the kind of utility created." Reference is made to Ely's work to justify the position that "A producer is one who creates any kind of utility." It is concluded that the middleman is a producer (1923, p. 22).

Ralph Breyer reaches the same conclusion in the following decade. Specific citations are no longer provided; Breyer simply reviews "a few fundamentals of economics." The reader is informed that "the economist . . . defines 'production' as the creation of utilities, and 'utility' as the capacity to satisfy a want." From a description of marketing functions it becomes clear that marketing creates all types of utilities, and "It is evident, then, that marketing is a productive activity" (1934, p. 13).

The stream of economic thought, as well as the work of some early marketing writers in the U.S. provides a justification for Alderson's rejection of the notion that different aspects of utility can be attributed to production and marketing (1957, p. 68). But Alderson seems unaware of his precursors. First, he views his position as unique, commenting that "It may appear to stretch the meaning of marketing to imply that it is concerned with changes in form utility" (1965, p. 27). Moreover, he has difficulty in reconciling his argument with the "conventional view," for he admits that "The choice of methods for changing the form is indeed within the realm of production technology." Ultimately, he is forced into an indirect justification of his position: "The decision to change the form at all is explicitly or implicitly a marketing decision" (1965, p. 27).

IMPLICATIONS FOR MARKETING THEORY

The "conventional view" of marketing as adding properties to matter, caused a problem for Alderson and "makes more difficult a disinterested evaluation of what marketing is and does" (Cox 1965). This view also underlies the dissatisfaction with marketing theory that led to the services marketing literature. If marketing is the process that adds properties to matter, then it cannot contribute to the production of "immaterial" goods. These problems do not arise once the contribution of the two streams of thought examined above are recognized.

Since marketing has to do with satisfying needs, the emphasis of the Schoolmen and other early writers on system output suggests the starting point. A market offering must be perceived as meeting the needs of a purchaser. That is, the purpose of marketing activity is to supply output "Necessary, or useful for the Support, Defence, Ease, Pleasure, and Pomp of Life" (Barbon 1690). Emphasis must be placed on the concept of "useful," since "only satisfactions are purchased" (Galiani 1751).

Usefulness is increased by the "approximation to the customer" (Say 1803). When this process results in a market transaction, usefulness is increased directly, because each party gains more than is given up in exchange (Condillac 1776; George 1898; Jevons 1871). Most of the sources reviewed held that usefulness is indirectly increased by activities such as breaking and dividing, transport, storage, and "nonmaterial" elements, such as information.

Marketing systems also contribute to usefulness by reducing the cost of its production. When markets are expanded, specialization increases, so that costs fall. The Classical School also understood that the emergence of specialized marketing organizations reduce cost by reducing uncertainty; that is, it gives "a more continued and undisturbed motion" (Torrens 1821).

Alderson called for "a marketing interpretation of the whole process of creating utility" (1957, p. 69). The elements of such an interpretation were available early in the Twentieth Century. The task of responding to Alderson's challenge remains.

REFERENCES

Alderson, Wroe. 1957. *Marketing Behavior and Executive Action.* Homewood, IL: Richard D. Irwin.

Aquinas, Sancti Thomae. 13th c. *Summa Theologica.* Parmae: Petri Fiaccadori [1855].

Aristotle. 4th c. B.C. *Politics.* H. Rackman, tr. London: Wm. Heinemann [1959].

Augustini, Sancti. 5th c. *Enarratio in Psalmum.* Migne: Patrologiae Latinae.

Barbon, Nicholas. 1690. *A Discourse of Trade.* Baltimore: The John Hopkins Press [1903].

Bartels, Robert. 1962. *The Development of Marketing Thought.* Homewood, IL: Richard D. Irwin.

Beckman, Theodore N. 1957. "The Value Added Concept As A Measurement of Output." *Advanced Management* (April): 6–9.

Breyer, Ralph F. 1934. *The Marketing Institution.* New York: McGraw-Hill.

Butler, Ralph Starr. 1923. *Marketing and Merchandising.* New York: Alexander Hamilton Institute.

Clark, John Bates. 1907. *Essentials of Economic Theory.* New York: The Macmillan Company [1924].

Condillac, Etienne B. de. 1776. *Le Commerce et le Gouvernement.* Paris: Lecointe et Durey [1821].

Cox, Reavis. 1965. *Distribution in a High-Level Economy.* Englewood Cliffs, NJ: Prentice Hall.

Ely, Richard T. 1889. *An Introduction to Political Economy.* New York: The Chautauqua Press.

Fisher, Irving. 1910. *Elementary Principles of Economics.* New York: The Macmillan Company.

Galiani, Ferdinando. 1751. *Della Moneta.* In: *Early Economic Thought.* Arthur E. Monroe, ed. Cambridge: Harvard University Press.

George, Henry. 1898. *The Science of Political Economy.* New York: Schalekenbach Foundation [1941].

Jevons, W. Stanley. 1871. *The Theory of Political Economy.* New York: Kelley and Millman [1957].

MARKETING AS PRODUCTION:
THE DEVELOPMENT OF A CONCEPT   DIXON

McCarthy, E. Jerome, 1981. *Basic Marketing.* Homewood, IL: Richard D. Irwin.

McCulloch, John R. 1825. *Principles of Political Economy.* Edinburgh: Adam and Charles Black [1844].

Marsh all, Alfred. 1890. *Principles of Economics.* New York: The Macmillan Company [1920].

Menger, Carl. 1871. *Principles of Economics.* Glencoe, IL: The Free Press [1950].

Mill, James. 1821. *Elements of Political Economy.* London: Henry G. Bohn [1844].

Mill, John Stuart. 1848. *Principles of Political Economy.* London: Longmans Green [1871].

Mummery, A.F., and J.A. Hobson. 1889. *The Physiology of Industry.* New York: Kelley and Millman [1956].

Olivi, Pierre de Jean. 13th c. *Quaestiones de permutatione rerum, de emptionibus et venditionibus.* Manuscript.

Say, Jean Baptiste. 1803. *Le Traite d'economie politique.* Boston: Wells and Lilly [1821].

Schumpeter, Joseph A. 1954. *History of Economic Analysis.* New York: Oxford University Press.

Shaw, Arch. 1915. *Some Problems in Market Distribution.* Cambridge: Harvard University Press.

Sidgwick, Henry. 1883. *The Principles of Political Economy.* London: Macmillan and Company [1887].

Sloan, Harold S., and Arnold J. Zurcher. 1970. *Dictionary of Economics.* New York: Barnes & Noble.

Smith, Adam. 1776. *An Inquiry into the Nature and Causes of the Wealth of Nations.* New York: Modern Library [1937].

Taussig, Frank. 1911. *Principles of Economics.* New York: The Macmillan Company.

Torrens, Robert. 1821. *An Essay on the Production of Wealth.* New York: Augustus M. Kelley [1965].

Walker, Francis A. 1888. *Political Economy.* New York: Henry Holt.

ABOUT THE AUTHOR

Donald F. Dixon is a Professor of Marketing in the Graduate Management Program at Penn State Great Valley, near Philadelphia. He received a B.A. in economics from Brown University (1951), and M.B.A. in marketing from Wharton (1952), and a Ph.D. in economics from the London School of Economics (1961). His area of specialization is marketing. He has published articles in economics, buyer behavior, channels of distribution, marketing theory, multinational marketing, and the history of marketing thought, and (with I.F. Wilkinson) a textbook, *The Marketing System.*

[6]

Historical Research in Marketing: Retrospect and Prospect

D.G. Brian Jones
University of Prince Edward Island

David D. Monieson
Queen's University, Kingston, Ontario

The history of historical research in marketing is reviewed as background to an examination of the state of the art. We focus on the major current contributors to historical research in marketing, their recent works, and opinions about future prospects for this field.

INTRODUCTION

In 1976 E.T. Grether examined four decades of publication in the *Journal of Marketing* dividing the literature into twelve categories, one of which was "historical." At that point in time as a percent of articles published, historical research in marketing represented the category of lowest relative interest. Furthermore, Grether's analysis pointed out the fairly consistent decline in interest (and hence publication) since the late 1940s. Of course, the *Journal of Marketing* was not the only outlet for historical research in marketing, although few would disagree with Grether that it has "played an integral role in the development of marketing as a discipline" (1976, p.63). Even fewer could have predicted the explosion of activity in this field during the 1980s. Indeed, the quantity and quality of historical research in marketing is now such that a review of this work would be useful.

The purpose of this article is to review historical research in marketing. The editors of the first Marketing History Conference Proceedings expressed the need for "amplification, synthesis, and promotion" (Hollander and Savitt 1983, p. v)

Journal of the Academy of Marketing Science
Volume 18, Number 4, pages 269-278.
Copyright © 1990 by Academy of Marketing Science.
All rights of reproduction in any form reserved.
ISSN 0092-0703.

of the substantially growing literature in marketing history. This article attempts to address that need. We begin with a history of the history, so to speak, focus on recent activity in the field, and then speculate on its future directions.

CLASSIFICATION OF THE LITERATURE

For the purposes of this paper historical research in marketing refers to research which deals with marketing exclusively or almost exclusively from an historical perspective as well as publications on doing historical research in marketing (e.g., methodological). As Savitt (1980) has pointed out, historical research in *marketing* includes marketing content (the activities, practices, and processes of marketing) as well as marketing thought (the ideas about marketing content). In either case, historical research in marketing is defined by the content of marketing (1980, p. 52). Therefore, any or all events or activities generally understood to be part of marketing (e.g., advertising, marketing research) at the time such research was carried out could be included. Because of space restrictions, however, a few exceptions have been made here.

First, many company and industry histories include much discussion of marketing practice, especially those of retailing institutions (e.g., Hower's *History of Macy's of New York, 1858–1919*). However, such histories seldom have as their primary purpose an examination of marketing. Therefore, except for some recent examples from conference proceedings and the periodic literature these have been excluded from this review. Also, although not that recent, Hidy (1970) presented an excellent review of books covering this area. A second (qualified) exception is advertising. Again, a somewhat dated bibliography and review of this area has been published (Pollay 1979). Since then several books on advertising history have been written, although most by historians outside the marketing discipline (Pollay 1988, p. 195). Therefore, we will restrict our attention here primarily to the advertising history which has appeared more recently in the marketing and marketing-related literature. Finally, the history of consumption (McCracken 1987; Rassuli and Hollander 1986) has also been reviewed very recently. Therefore, these areas will not be given the attention otherwise warranted in a complete review of the history of historical research in marketing.

Again, this review includes research which deals with marketing exclusively or almost exclusively from an *historical* perspective. An historical perspective involves the description, analysis, or explanation of events through time (Savitt 1980, p. 53); even more so, it involves a thorough, systematic, and sophisticated awareness of change—or lack of it—over time, and of the contexts of place, situation, and time in which change—or continuity—occurs (Fullert on 1987, p. 98). That perspective characterizes most of the research reviewed here. In some instances it was difficult to assess the extent to which a publication dealt with change or explained events through time since they essentially described marketing at some point in history (rather than through time) and only implicitly compared to some other era.

Again, however, an exception is noteworthy. A good deal of the earliest research by marketing scholars in this century, for example, Nystrom's (1915) *The Economics of Retailing* followed an historical perspective. However, since this research appeared before there were well recognized traditions of business and marketing history, and has been reviewed elsewhere (Jones 1987; Jones and Monieson 1990) it has also been excluded from this survey.

Our search included all of the major marketing journals, business and economics history periodicals, a computerized bibliographic search, and a survey of participants at the first three Marketing History Conferences. This produced a bibliography of 318 publications including 172 conference proceedings[1], 101 journal articles, 26 articles in books of readings, and 19 books, not including the exceptions mentioned above. It was a thorough, but not exhaustive, review of the literature. Without the relatively narrow definition of historical research in marketing given above we undoubtedly could have added to this list. Nevertheless, we believe our more restricted set accurately represents the mainstream of historical research in marketing.

Three broad categories of research were identified including the two suggested by Savitt (1980)—"history of marketing thought" and "history of marketing content". To this we added a third category represented by Savitt's article cited above—"methodology." Further, a variety of subcategories were developed to produce the classification shown in the Table. Each publication reviewed was classified according to its major thrust. Of course, some of the works dealt with more than one topic and were classified accordingly. We were interested in identifying any patterns or changes over time. Therefore, the number of publications was summed by subcategory for each decade starting with the 1930s. There was no reason to group the literature by decade other than for convenience. Each decade/column indicates the

number of publications dealing with each topic or subcategory as well as the relative proportion of total publications for the decade. For example, between 1930 and 1939 one publication [Converse's (1933) "The First Decade of Marketing Literature"] dealt with "history of marketing thought—literature." That article represents 17 percent of all publications for the decade.

Admittedly this taxonomy is subjective. We can only echo the sentiment expressed by the editors of the second Marketing History Conference Proceedings, "taxonomy is in the eyes of the [authors] and readers are cordially invited to consider other ways of classifying" (Hollander and Nevett 1985, p. xvii). There is not sufficient space here to adequately define all of the subcategories employed. However, a brief discussion of the ones most heavily represented is useful.

The category "marketing thought—theory/schools of thought" included research which dealt with ideas in their various forms and levels of aggregation—concepts (e.g., marketing management concept), theories (e.g., wheel of retailing), and schools of thought (e.g., functional approach). "Marketing content—activities/functions" included marketing practices such as advertising (the most heavily represented in this category), pricing, and product innovation strategies. While subcategories such as retailing, wholesaling, and market research could certainly be considered as marketing practices they were considered separately in this review.

RETROSPECT

As illustrated in the Table, a steady increase in publication through the 1960s was followed by a sharp drop during the subsequent decade. Thus, Grether's observation in 1976, cited above, was not surprising. However, an explosion of interest in historical research during the 1980s is evident in the dramatic increase in the number of publications during that decade. Along with the increase in scope there has been a change in the nature of historical research in marketing. Recently there has been a relative shift towards researching the history of marketing practices and writing about historiography. However, there has always been a consistent interest in the history of marketing thought.

Recording the Facts: 1930–1959

From 1930 to 1959 historical research in marketing was dominated by interest in the development of marketing thought. The earliest example reviewed for this study was Converse's (1933) "The First Decade of Marketing Literature" published in the *NATMA Bulletin*. During this period attention was focused on tracing the earliest literature (Applebaum 1947; 1952; Bartels 1951; Converse 1945; Coolsen 1947; Maynard 1951) and the teaching of marketing (Bartels 1951; Hagerty 1936; Hardy 1954; Litman 1950; Maynard 1941; Weld 1941). A few publications focused on individuals and organizations that pioneered in the development of the discipline (Agnew 1941; Bartels 1951; Converse

TABLE 1
Classification of Historical Research in Marketing

Category	Sub-category	←1930–39→ Number	(%)	←1940–49→ Number	(%)	←1950–59→ Number	(%)	←1960–69→ Number	(%)	←1970–79→ Number	(%)	←1980–89→ Number	(%)
		Number of publications[1] by decade/Percent of decade total											
Marketing thought	Literature	1	(17)	4	(44)	3	(14)	4	(11)	4	(15)	15	(6)
	Organizations	—	—	1	(11)	1	(5)	1	(3)	—	—	1	—
	Teaching	1	(17)	2	(22)	4	(18)	1	(3)	—	—	2	(1)
	Biography	—	—	—	—	1	(5)	2	(6)	1	(4)	4	(2)
	Theory/ Schools of thought	1	(17)	—	—	4	(18)	9	(25)	6	(22)	51	(20)
Marketing content	Activities/ Functions	—	—	2	(22)	—	—	5	(14)	2	(7)	57	(22)
	Company/ Industry	—	—	—	—	—	—	1	(3)	3	(11)	31	(12)
	Retailing	1	(17)	—	—	3	(14)	4	(11)	3	(11)	15	(6)
	Wholesaling	—	—	—	—	3	(14)	2	(6)	—	—	1	—
	Biography	—	—	—	—	—	—	—	—	1	(4)	3	(1)
	Marketing systems	1	(17)	—	—	1	(5)	1	(3)	—	—	17	(7)
	Marketing research	—	—	—	—	1	(5)	—	—	1	(4)	4	(2)
	Other	—	—	—	—	—	—	—	—	1	(4)	11	(4)
Methodology	Justification of history	1	(17)	—	—	1	(5)	5	(14)	3	(11)	15	(6)
	Data sources	—	—	—	—	—	—	—	—	1	(4)	8	(3)
	Method	—	—	—	—	—	—	1	(3)	1	(4)	16	(6)
	Philosophy of science	—	—	—	—	—	—	—	—	—	—	10	(4)
	Total	6	(100)	9	(100)	22	(100)	36	(100)	27	(100)	261	(100)

[1] Some publications, especially books, dealt with multiple topics. Totals may differ from 100% due to rounding.

1959b), and a series of biographical sketches published in the *Journal of Marketing* between 1956 and 1961 was later compiled in book form (Wright and Dimsdale 1974).[2] During the 1950s, however, a trend began towards focusing on the history of major marketing concepts (Breen 1959; Kelley 1956), theories (McGarry 1953), and schools of thought (Brown 1951; Cassels 1936).

There was less historical research done between 1930 and 1959 on marketing content. Most of this focused on the history of retailing and wholesaling (Barger 1955; Jones 1936; Marburg 1951: Nystrom 1951). A more general history of marketing content which was distinctive in its scope of subject matter and historical perspective was Hotchkiss's (1938) *Milestones of Marketing*. Using the American Marketing Association's definition of marketing to guide his choice of topics Hotchkiss traced "the most important steps in the evolution of marketing" (p. vii) back to ancient Rome and Greece through medieval England to modern North American practices (mostly retailing, advertising, and merchandising). Since the book drew heavily from published sources on economic history one reviewer described it as an "economic history of marketing" (Larson 1938, p. 13).

Barger's (1955) book examined the changing role of wholesale and retail sectors in the American economy from 1869 to 1950. It was a unique statistical study of the cost and output of distribution, and of the relative importance of wholesale and retail sectors as measured by the proportion of the labor force engaged in each.

A history of marketing content which complements the Hotchkiss book by focusing on marketing practices of the twentieth century is Converse's (1959b) *Fifty Years of Marketing in Retrospect*. This was written as a companion to his (1959a) study of the beginnings of marketing thought. Converse described it as "the story of business and particularly of market distribution as I have seen it and as I have studied it" (p. vi). In addition to marketing practices such as advertising and promotion, pricing, merchandising, and others, Converse describes the changing economic conditions and technological developments which influenced such practices.

Throughout this early period historical research was mostly descriptive as marketers focused on recording the facts of marketing history and the history of marketing thought.

Integration of Practice and Thought: 1960–1968

The 1960s were a transition period for historical research in marketing. A number of significant works and events laid the foundation for the growth in interest evident today. During the early 1960s successive conferences of the American Marketing Association featured tracks on historical research (Greyser 1963; Smith 1964). Most of the papers published from those sessions presented justifications for doing historical research. Four books in succession were published on the history of marketing thought. Converse (1959a) presented a biographical and literature survey of the development of the discipline. Coolsen (1960) described the contributions to marketing thought representative of liberal economics in the late nineteenth century. Essentially, this was an expansion of some of the material in Converse's book (no surprise, since Converse was part of the committee for Coolsen's thesis on which the book was based). Two books which complemented each other were Bartels' (1962) *The Development of Marketing Thought*, which focused on a chronology of published literature, courses, and events since 1900, and Schwartz's (1963) *Development of Marketing Theory*, a summary of the development of major theoretical approaches in the discipline. In fact, historical research on concepts, theories, and schools of thought was the largest subcategory of publication during the 1960s. Other examples include Hollander (1960; 1963a; 1966), Keith (1960), Lazer (1965), and LaLonde and Morrison (1967).

A distinctive quality of some research during the 1960s was the integration of marketing content with marketing thought. Such work went beyond the descriptive character of earlier writings by using the history of marketing practice to analyze the history of marketing thought. An example of this was, and continues to be, Hollander's work (cited above, and more recently 1986b). His distinctive approach to historical research has recently been explicated by Rassuli (1988). This approach also helped to raise the popularity of historical research on marketing content close to that of marketing thought.

The history of marketing activities or functions emerged as a strong subcategory of marketing content. This included research in advertising and promotion (McKendrick 1960), product innovation (Silk and Stern 1963), and personal selling (Hollander 1963b; 1964). And a broad range of marketing content, especially in corporate/industry and activities/functions,³ was covered in Shapiro and Doody (1968), *Readings in the History of American Marketing, Settlement to Civil War*.

Shapiro and Doody stated that their objective was to "awaken the interest of students of marketing in history and historical analysis" (1968, p. 12). Judging from the drop in historical research during the early 1970s the book's impact was not immediate. However, it contributed to the critical mass of historical research in marketing during the 1960s and undoubtedly inspired marketing historians of the 1980s.

Expanding the Scope of Marketing History: 1969–1979

There is no obvious or simple explanation for the paucity of historical research during the 1970s. Indeed, most of the research appeared in conference proceedings and even then, not until the end of the decade. An exception was the second edition of Bartels (1976) *The History of Marketing Thought*. However, two developments which carried on strongly into the 1980s are noteworthy.

The first was an attempt to push back the history of marketing thought past the turn of the century (Dixon 1978; 1979; 1981; 1982; Lazer 1979). Of course, this carried with it a refocusing of attention beyond North American concepts of marketing to those in other parts of the world.

A second development of the late 1970s was the integration of advertising history into the marketing literature. At that time Pollay observed that there were very few significant sources on advertising history (1979, p. 8) and those had been written outside the marketing discipline. To correct that situation, an ambitious research program for advertising history was detailed, including the justification, research method, and data sources for such work (Pollay 1977; 1978; 1979). The continuation of that program contributed to a stream of research on advertising history during the 1980s.

THE STATE OF THE ART

The quantity and quality of historical research in marketing have grown enormously in recent years. Returning to the Table—the 261 topic/publications during the 1980s represent a substantial body of literature. Of course, much of this work is accounted for by the Marketing History Conferences. In 1983 Michigan State University began hosting the Marketing History Conference to provide a regular platform for the critical mass of scholars interested in marketing history. Even if we exclude the 111 papers published in the Proceedings of the four Marketing History Conferences from 1983 through 1989 the increase in publication remains significant. And there is a breadth to this interest evident in developments across all three categories of historical research in marketing.

Methodology

If one were looking for a single publication or event which signalled the emergence (or rather, the revival) of history as a 'legitimate' field within the marketing discipline, it could be Ronald Savitt's (1980) "Historical Research in Marketing." In substance it was a statement of the rationale and method for historical research, although in the latter, only one of a range of possible methodological perspectives. In spirit, however, it was both a symbol of the legitimacy of doing historical research by marketing scholars, and a challenge to them to do so. As a statement on method, Savitt's article initiated a much needed discussion in the marketing literature about the theory and methods of historical scholarship.

There are a number of different traditions within historiography, ranging from positivistic (e.g., Hempel 1959) to hermeneutic ones (e.g., Collingwood 1974). These have recently been summarized in the marketing literature by Firat (1987). Savitt proposed what was essentially a positivistic method of historical research based on hypothesis testing (1980; 1982; 1984) and a search for causal relations (1988, p. 119). Kumcu (1987) has also outlined an historical method close to Savitt's in its concern with probable causes, hypothesis testing, and relative validity of laws. On the other hand, Firat (1987) suggests going beyond such methods— that explanation and understanding of marketing history requires the interpretation and reflection characteristic of a hermeneutic approach. Fullerton (1987) distinguishes between the philosophy of history, which is concerned with epistemological and ontological issues, and historical method, which follows from the philosophy of history one believes in. Fullerton's approach to history is based on the philosophy of German historicism (1986), a distinctive philosophy of social science, and as such, is based on assumptions very different from those of a positivistic historical method. For Fullerton, the basic elements of historical method include systematic doubt, flexible use of analytical tools, use of multiple data sources, creative and critical synthesis, and a narrative form of description (1987, p.112).

In the echoes of discussions about the philosophy and method of marketing history there have also been voices calling for more historical research and providing rationales and justifications for marketing history in teaching (Peterson 1987; Witkowski 1989) as well as research (Fullerton 1987; Savitt 1980; 1982). Finally, rounding out the discussion of methodology are descriptions of various data sources for historical research in marketing (Pollay 1988a; Rassuli and Hollander 1986a).

Marketing Content

The 1980s mark the first period in which marketing content has accounted for the largest relative proportion of publications among the three major categories of research identified here. Within this category some fifty publications dealt with marketing activities or functions, for example, product simplification strategy (Hollander 1984a), market segmentation (Fullerton 1985), channel relations (Marx 1985) and retailers' pricing strategies (Dickinson 1988). Among the marketing activities studied, however, advertising has become a leading topic of interest.

There are two major themes in the advertising history published during this decade. One of these is the examination of British advertising history. One prominent contributor here has been Terence Nevett, whose work includes a book (1982) on the subject. Much of Nevett's work is comparative and cross cultural, for example, a study of societal perceptions of advertising in Britain and Germany (Fullerton and Nevett 1986), American influences on British advertising (Nevett 1988a), and vice versa (1988c). At times his work has taken on a macromarketing perspective (1988b; Fullerton and Nevett 1986) by looking at the impact of advertising on society.

Others have contributed to the recent popularity of British advertising history while focusing on specific companies (Ferrier 1986; Seaton 1986), professional sales promotion organizations (Legh 1986), and self-regulation in the advertising industry (Miracle and Nevett 1988).

A second major theme in advertising history this decade was the analysis of American print advertising over the last century. During the late 1970s Richard Pollay established the requirements for, and outlined a program of, research in advertising history. Having identified and contributed to extensive archival sources (Pollay 1979; 1988a), Pollay followed with the content analysis of American print advertising since the turn of the century to identify the values portrayed (Belk and Pollay 1985; Pollay 1984a; 1988b), the extent of informativeness (1984b), and creative aspects of advertising strategy (1985). More recently, his work had taken on a macromarketing perspective (Pollay 1988c; Pollay and Lysanski forthcoming).

Pollay's use of quantification, content analysis, and hypothesis testing is representative of the positivistic approach to historical research. Similarly, Gross and Sheth (1989) performed content analysis of advertisements spanning 100 years in the *Ladies Home Journal* to investigate the use of time-oriented appeals. However, a diversity of methodologies is evident in recent work by others in advertising history. For example, Stern (1988) uses a descriptive approach in examining the medieval tradition of allegory and relating it to contemporary advertising strategy.

In addition to "activities and functions" three other subcategories of marketing content have attracted considerable attention. Corporate and industry marketing practices emerged as a popular field of study (Clark 1986; Erb 1985), although most of this work has appeared in the Proceedings of Marketing History Conferences. Marketing systems—the study of whole economies or systems of marketing—has also emerged during the 1980s as a significant topic for historical research (Corley 1987; Fisk 1988; Fullerton 1988b; Kaufman 1987) and is also undoubtedly related to the rising interest in macromarketing. Of course, an essential aspect of the history of marketing systems is the relationship between marketing and economic development (Dixon 1981; Savitt 1988; McCarthy 1988). The fundamental importance of marketing history to the study of economic development has been used as a justification for more historical research in marketing since the late 1950s (Myers and Smalley 1959).

A third category of marketing content which continues to hold interest for marketing historians is retailing. Next to marketing thought, retailing may have the longest consistent tradition of historical research in marketing. What we know about retailing history, however, remains largely as scattered threads, focusing on selected firms and specific individuals. In a proposal for American retailing history Savitt (1989) agrees with Hollander's (1983) assessment of the need for a synthetic history of retailing, one which goes beyond simple, descriptive chronology, identifying patterns and integrating marketing practice with marketing thought.

Examples of such an approach include Hollander's study of the effects of industrialization on retailing in the twentieth century (1980c) and his evaluation of hypothesized patterns of retail institutional evolution (1980a). The testing of hypotheses about retail institutional evolution has also been a focus in Savitt's work on retailing history. Having developed specific hypotheses from McNair's wheel of retailing theory, Savitt (1984) used single-firm, total-product line data for a ten year period to test them. Recent work by others has also contributed to the tracing of retail institutional evolution (Cundiff 1988; Kotler 1988).

Marketing Thought

It is probably a natural progression for a discipline to move from isolated writings and courses to widely accepted theories and schools of thought. This is evident in looking at the progress of the history of marketing thought. With only a handful of publications during the 1980s on the history of marketing literature (Bartels 1988; Lichtenthal and Beik 1984) and teaching (Lazer and Shaw 1988; Schultze 1982), the history of *ideas* now dominates this category. Consistently over the past forty years about one quarter of the published history of marketing thought has dealt with concepts, theories, and schools of thought. Furthermore, within this subcategory there has been a progression of interest towards schools of thought, although we continue to examine the historical accuracy of key concepts.

Among the recent historical examinations of major marketing concepts or theories are Hollander's (1986b) discussion of the marketing concept and Fullerton's (1988a) related study of the production era. Both scholars concluded that serious and sophisticated marketing has been practised much longer than the received doctrine suggests. Taken together these studies point to the value of historical research in evaluating existing theory. More importantly, perhaps, they have contributed to a rewriting of the history of marketing thought. This has included an extensive reevaluation of the schools of thought from which marketing emerged as a discipline (Jones 1987; Jones and Monieson 1990).

Schools of thought within the discipline have attracted increasing attention from marketing historians. Discussions of the so-called classical schools such as the institutional (Hollander 1980) and functional (Hunt and Goolsby 1988) have been complemented by studies of more contemporary schools of thought (Mittelsteadt 1989; Savitt 1989; Sheth and Gardner 1982; Sheth and Gross 1988; Sheth et al. 1988). The most extensive among the latter studies is the recent book by Sheth, Gardner, and Garrett (1988) which identifies, classifies, and evaluates twelve schools of marketing thought that have emerged during the twentieth century. Interestingly, given the criteria they used for identifying a school of thought—a distinct focus, a perspective on why marketing activities are carried out, and, association with a pioneer thinker and significant number of scholars—one might speculate on the status of marketing history itself as a school of thought.

PROSPECT

The recent growth of interest in marketing history is surely a natural development in a maturing discipline. Parallel debates and discussions about philosophies of science have

focused the attention of marketing scholars on their identity as a discipline and have increased their tolerance of different methodologies and perspectives. A more mature marketing discipline has recognized the legitimacy of—as well as the need for—historical research.

It is also no accident that those active in marketing history tend to overlap with the group of scholars working in macromarketing. Macromarketing issues, for example economic-development, tend to demand a longer time perspective. Therefore, the institutionalization of macromarketing during the late 1970s through an annual Seminar and subsequent publication of the *Journal of Macromarketing* helped to justify and stimulate historical research in marketing as well.

At the conference level there has been widespread acceptance by the academic associations. During 1988 the AMA, AMS, and ACR all devoted significant portions of conferences to historical perspectives. In addition to being the major outlet for historical research in marketing, the Marketing History Conferences have been a catalyst and promoter of research in the field and have served to institutionalize historical research in marketing. The success of the History Conferences (held every two years since 1983), the invisible college of marketing historians (becoming more and more visible), a regularly published newsletter ("Retrospectives in Marketing"), and a special issue in a primary journal, are all convincing evidence of the pattern Ziman (1984) has identified for the development of an academic specialty (p.94). The time may have come for a formal association and even a journal of historical research in marketing.

As for the nature of future work, this review seems to suggest trends in some key directions. For example, we have seen a synthesis of marketing practice and thought which, hopefully, will continue. As Nevett, Whitney, and Hollander (1989) recently described, "Practice is not entirely thoughtless and thought is often practice-driven" (p. xx). One natural and desirable outcome of this synthesis of practice and thought is an increase in theory development and testing. Many marketing concepts and theories are inherently historical in nature and *must* be tested with historical evidence. It is worth noting that such theory testing and development has been carried out convincingly with both a positivistic method of historical research (e.g. Savitt 1984) as well as a hermeneutic approach (e.g., Fullerton 1988).

Another recent trend has been that of identifying and describing sources of historical data and various methodologies of historical research. A better understanding is needed of the various philosophies of history, historical methods, types of primary historical data and how to use them. Continued efforts in this direction will help improve the quality of historical research in marketing.

In connection with this review several major contributors to historical research in marketing offered their views on the current state of interest in the field and likely future directions. There was a general recognition that the level of interest has risen during the past decade, but that much of the work being done was "superficial," "repetitive," and based solely on secondary sources. One response to that condition has been an attempt to raise the acceptance standards for the Marketing History Conferences. As a result, there has been consistent improvement in the depth and quality of the papers presented there. Some feel that the editors of many marketing journals still do not appreciate the value of historical research. However, the number of recent articles published in major journals, indeed this special issue of the *Journal of the Academy of Marketing Science*, seems to signify a shift in the quality of historical research being done as well as its acceptance by the gatekeepers of the discipline.

When asked which topics will generate interest in the near future, the personal interests of those surveyed undoubtedly played a role. Nevertheless, they expected that the history of marketing thought will continue to be a focus of interest, as will marketing practices such as advertising and retailing. Notwithstanding new developments in the field, these are hot topics at this time. There has also been a recent trend to focusing on marketing in corporate and industry history. Finally, macromarketing historians have been expanding the work on the history of marketing systems.

One observation was that the discipline has defined its history too narrowly, suggesting that a broadening of historical inquiry may be in order. In this connection Stanley Hollander offered the following comments.

> There is need for much effort to wean the profession away from the feeling that marketing is something that has only been thought about by male professors of marketing in the United States. There must be increasing recognition of the way in which marketing was shaped by practitioners, critics, regulators, scholars, and publicists in many fields. We are reaching out pretty well to many; we are now working in consumer behavior history. We need to do the same to those working in legal and political history. We probably also need much more dialogue with economic and business historians (1989).

In many ways our expectations for historical research in marketing are accurately portrayed by the title given to the 1989 Marketing History Conference—"Marketing History: The Emerging Discipline."

NOTES

1. This includes the Proceedings of all four Marketing History Conferences. Because of space limitations we have omitted all but key citations of conference proceedings and many of journal articles. A complete bibliography is available from the authors on request.
2. For classification in the table this book was counted once in the category "marketing thought—biography." The series of sketches in the *Journal of Marketing* were not included.
3. For classification in the table this book was counted once each in the following subcategories: activities/functions, company/industry, retailing, wholesaling, and marketing systems.

ACKNOWLEDGMENTS

The authors thank Alan J. Richardson and anonymous JAMS reviewers for comments on earlier drafts of this paper. They would also like to acknowledge the financial assistance of the Summer Scholar-In-Residence Program, School of Business, Queen's University, and the Senate Research Council, University of P.E.I.

REFERENCES

Agnew, Hugh E. 1941. "The History of the American Marketing Association." *Journal of Marketing* 5(4): 374–379.

Applebaum, W. 1947. "The Journal of Marketing: The First Ten Years." *Journal of Marketing* 11: 355–363.

——. 1952. "The Journal of Marketing: Post War." *Journal of Marketing* 16(3): 294–300.

Barger, Harold. 1955. *Distribution's Place in the American Economy since 1869*. Princeton, NJ: Princeton University Press.

Bartels, Robert. 1951. "Influences on the Development of Marketing Thought, 1900–1923." *Journal of Marketing* 16 (July): 1–17.

——. 1962. *The Development of Marketing Thought*. Homewood, IL: Irwin.

——. 1976. *The History of Marketing Thought*. Second Edition. Columbus, OH: Grid.

——. 1988. *The History of Marketing Thought*. Third Edition. Columbus, OH: Publishing Horizens.

Belk, Russell W., and Richard W. Pollay. 1985. "Images of Ourselves: The Good Life in Twentieth Century Advertising." *Journal of Consumer Research* 11(4) (March): 887–897.

Bermays, Edward L. 1984. "Father of PR Analyzes Its History." *Communication World* 1(6): 38–39.

Blankenship, A.B., C. Chakrapani, and W. Harold Poole. 1985. *A History of Marketing Research in Canada*. Toronto, Ontario: Professional Marketing Research Society.

Breen, John. 1959. "History of the Marketing Management Concept." In: *Advancing Marketing Efficiency*. Lynn Stockman, ed. Chicago: American Marketing Association, pp. 458–461.

Brown, George H. 1951. "What Economists Should Know About Marketing." *Journal of Marketing* 16(1): 60–66.

Cassels, J.M. 1936. "The Significance of Early Economic Thought on Marketing." *Journal of Marketing* 1 (October): 129–133.

Chapman, Stanley D. 1979. "British Marketing Enterprise: The Changing Roles of Merchants, Manufacturers and Financiers 1700–1860." *Business History Review* 53(2): 205–233.

Collingwood, R.G. 1974. "Human Nature and Human History." in *The Philosophy of History*. Ed. Patrick Gardiner. London.

Converse, Paul, D. 1933. "The First Decade of Marketing Literature." *Natma Bulletin Supplement* (November), pp. 1–4.

——. 1945. "The Development of the Science of Marketing—An Exploratory Survey." *Journal of Marketing* 10(1) (July): 14–23.

——. 1959a. *Fifty Years of Marketing in Retrospect*. Texas: Bureau of Business Research, The University of Texas.

——. 1959b. *The Beginning of Marketing Thought in the United States*. Texas: Bureau of Business Research, University of Texas.

Coolsen, Frank. 1947. "Pioneers in the Development of Advertising." *Journal of Marketing* 12(1) (July): 80–86.

——. 1960. *Marketing Thought in the United States in the Late Nineteenth Century*. Texas Technical Press.

Corley, T.A.B. 1987. "Consumer Marketing in Britain, 1914–1960." *Business History* 29(4) (October): 65–83.

Cundiff, Edward. 1988. "The Evolution of Retailing Institutions Across Cultures." In: *Historical Perspectives in Marketing: Essays in Honor of Stanley C. Hollander*. Terence Nevett and Ronald Fullerton, eds. Lexington, MA: Lexington Books, pp. 149–162.

Curti, Merle. 1967. "The Changing Concept of Human Nature in the History of American Advertising." *Business History Review* 41(4): 355–357.

Dickinson, Roger. 1988. "Lessons from Retailers' Price Experiences of the 1950s." In: *Historical Perspectives in Marketing: Essays in Honor of Stanley C. Hollander*. Terence Nevett and Ronald Fullerton, eds. Lexington, MA: Lexington Books, pp. 177–192.

Dixon, Donald F. 1978. "The Origins of Macro-Marketing Thought." In: *Macromarketing: New Steps on the Learning Curve*. George Fisk and Robert W. Nason, eds. Boulder: University of Colorado, Business Research Division, pp. 9–28.

———. 1979. "Medieval Macromarketing Thought." In: *Macromarketing: Evolution of Thought*. George Fisk and Phillip D. White, eds. Boulder: University of Colorado, Business Research Division, pp. 59–69.

———. 1981. "The Role of Marketing in Early Theories of Economic Development." *Journal of Macromarketing* (Fall): 19–27.

———. 1982. "The Ethical Component of Marketing: An Eighteenth Century View." *Journal of Macromarketing* 1 (Spring): 38–46.

Erb, Lyle C. 1985. "The Marketing of Christmas: A History." *Public Relations Quarterly*: 24–28.

Ferrier, R.W. 1986. "Petroleum Advertising in the Twenties and Thirties: The Case of the British Petroleum Company." *European Journal of Marketing* 205: 29–51.

Firat, A. Fuat. 1987. "Historiography, Scientific Method and Exceptional Historical Events." *Advances in Consumer Research*. Melanie Wallendorf and Paul Anderson, eds. Provo, Utah: ACR, Vol. 14, pp. 435–438.

Fisk, George. 1988. "Interactive Systems Frameworks for Analyzing Spacetime Changes in Marketing Organization and Processes." In: *Historical Perspectives in Marketing: Essays in Honor of Stanley C. Hollander*. Terence Nevett and Ronald Fullerton, eds. Lexington, MA: Lexington Books, pp. 55–70.

Friedman, H.H. 1984. "Ancient Marketing Practices: The View from Talmudic Times." *Journal of Public Policy and Marketing* 3: 194–204.

Fullerton, Ronald A. 1985. "Segmentation Strategies and Practices in the 19th Century German Book Trade: A Case Study in the Development of a Major Marketing Technique." In: *Historical Perspective in Consumer Research: National and International Perspectives*. C.T. Tan and Jagdish N. Sheth, eds., Singapore: National University of Singapore, pp. 135–139.

———. 1986. "Historicism: What It Is, and What It Means for Consumer Research." In: *Advances in Consumer Research*. Melanie Wallendorf and Paul Anderson, eds. Association for Consumer Research, pp. 431–434.

———. 1987. "The Poverty of A Historical Analysis: Present Weakness and Future Cure in U.S. Marketing Thought." In: *Philosophical and Radical Thought in Marketing*. A. Fuat Firat, Nikhilesh Dholakia, and Richard P. Bagozzi, eds. Lexington, MA: Lexington Books, pp. 97–116.

———. 1988a. "How Modern Is Modern Marketing? Marketing's Evolution and the Myth of the 'Production Era.'" *Journal of Marketing* 52 (January): 108–125.

———. 1988b. "Modern Western Marketing as a Historical Phenomenon: Theory and Illustration." In: *Historical Perspectives in Marketing: Essays in Honor of Stanley C. Hollander*. Terence Nevett and Ronald Fullerton, eds. Lexington, MA: Lexington Books, pp. 71–89.

Fullerton, Ronald A., and Terence R. Nevett. 1986. "Advertising and Society: A Comparative Analysis of the Roots of Distrust in Germany and Great Britain." *International Journal of Marketing* 5: 225–241.

Grether, E.T. 1976. "The First Forty Years." *Journal of Marketing* 40(3) (July): 63–69.

Greyser, Stephen, ed. 1963. *Toward Scientific Marketing*. American Marketing Association Proceedings Series. Chicago: American Marketing Association.

Gross, Barbara L., and Sheth, Jagdish N. 1989. "Time Oriented Advertising and 20th Century Economic Development: A Content Analysis of United States Magazine Advertising, 1890–1988." *Journal of Marketing* 53(4): 76–83.

Hagerty, J.E. 1936. "Experiences of an Early Marketing Teacher." *Journal of Marketing* 1: 20–27.

Hardy, Harold. 1954. "Collegiate Marketing Education Since 1930." *Journal of Marketing* 19(2): 325–330.

Hempel, Carl G. 1959. "The Function of General Laws in History." In: *Theories of History*. Patrick Gardiner, ed. Glencoe, IL: The Free Press, pp. 344–355.

Hidy, Ralph W. 1970. "Business History: Present Status and Future Needs." *Business History Review* 44(4) (Winter): 483–497.

Hoagland, William, and William Lazer. 1960. "The Retailers Manual of 1869." *Journal of Marketing* 24(3) (January). 59–60.

Hollander, Stanley C. 1960. "The Wheel of Retailing." *Journal of Marketing* 25 (July): 37–42.

———. 1963a. "A Note on Fashion Leadership." *Business History Review* (Winter): 448–451.

———. 1963b. "Anti-Salesman Ordinances of the Mid-Nineteenth Century." In: *Toward Scientific Marketing*. Stephen Greyser, ed. American Marketing Association, pp. 344–351.

———. 1964. "Nineteenth Century Anti-Drummer Legislation in the United States." *Business History Review* 38 (Winter): 479–500.

———. 1966. "Notes on the Retail Accordion." *Journal of Retailing* 42 (Summer): 29–40.

———. 1972. "Consumerism and Retailing: A Historical Perspective." *Journal of Retailing* 48 (Winter): 6–21.

———. 1978. "Can We Go Back—The Case of Farmer's Stall Markets." In: *Research Frontiers in Marketing: Dialogues and Directions*. S.C. Jain, ed. Chicago: American Marketing Association, pp. 301–303.

———. 1980a. "Oddities, Nostalgia, Wheels and Other Patterns in Retail Evolution." In: *Competitive Structure in Retail Marketing: The Department Store Perspective*. R.W. Stampfl and E. Hirschman, eds. Chicago: American Marketing Association, pp. 78–87.

———. 1980b. "Some Notes on the Difficulty of Identifying the Marketing Thought Contributions of the Early Institutionalists." In: *Theoretical Developments in Marketing*. Proceedings Series. C.W. Lamb and P.M. Dunn, eds. Chicago: American Marketing Association, pp. 45–46.

———. 1980c. "The Effects of Industrialization on Small Retailing in the United States in the Twentieth Century." In: *Small Business in American Life*. S. Bruchey, ed. New York: Columbia University Press, pp. 212–239.

———. 1983. "Who and What Are Important in Retailing and Marketing History: A Basis for Discussion." In: *First North American Workshop on Historical Research in Marketing*. Stanley Hollander and Ronald Savitt, eds. Lansing: Michigan State University Press, pp. 35–40.

———. 1984a. "Herbert Hoover, Professor Levitt, Simplification and the Marketing Concept." In: *Scientific Method in Marketing*. Paul Anderson and Michael Ryan, eds. Chicago: American Marketing Association, pp. 260–263.

———. 1984b. "Sumptuary Laws: Demarketing by Edict." *Journal of Macromarketing* 4 (Spring): 3–16.

———. 1985. "A Historical Perspective on the Service Encounter." In: *The Service Encounter*. J. Caepiel, M. Solomon and C. Surprenant, eds. Lexington: Lexington Books, pp. 49–64.

———. 1986a. "A Rearview-Mirror Might Help Us Drive Forward: A Call for More Historical Studies in Retailing." *Journal of Retailing* 62 (Spring): 7–10.

———. 1986b. "The Marketing Concept: A Deja-Vu." In: *Marketing Management Technology as a Social Process*. George Fisk, ed. New York: Praeger, pp. 3–26.

———. 1988. "Dimensions of Marketing Reform." In: *Marketing: A Return to the Broader Dimensions*. Proceedings of the Winter Educators' Conference. Stanley Shapiro and A.H. Walle, eds. Chicago: American Marketing Association, pp. 142–146.

———. 1989. Correspondence with the authors. August 9.

Hollander, Stanley C., and Terence Nevett, eds. 1985. *Marketing in the Long Run*. Proceedings of the Second Marketing History Conference. East Lansing: Michigan State University.

Hollander, Stanley C., and Ronald Savitt, eds. 1983. *First North American Workshop on Historical Research in Marketing*. Proceedings of a Conference. East Lansing: Michigan State University Press.

Hotchkiss, George Burton. 1938. *Milestones of Marketing*. New York: MacMillan.

Hower, Ralph M. 1946. *History of Macy's of New York, 1858–1919*. Cambridge: Harvard University Press.

Hunt, Shelby D., and Jerry Goolsby. 1988. "The Rise and Fall of the Functional Approach to Marketing: A Paradigm Displacement Perspective." In: *Historical Perspectives in Marketing: Essays in Honor of Stanley C. Hollander*. Terence Nevett and Ronald Fullerton, eds. Lexington, MA: Lexington Books, pp. 35–52.

Johnson, Scott D., and Stanley C. Hollander. 1988. "An Attempt at Agricultural Marketing Reform: Volume 6 of the Report of the United States Industrial Commission, 1901." In: *Marketing: A Return to the Broader Dimensions*. Proceedings of the 1988 Winter Educators' Conference. Stanley Shapiro and A.H. Walle, eds. Chicago: American Marketing Association, pp. 129–136.

Jones, D.G. Brian. 1987. "Origins of Marketing Thought." PhD. Dissertation. Queen's University, Kingston, Ontario.

Jones, D.G. Brian, and David D. Monieson. 1990. "Early Development of the Philosophy of Marketing Thought." *Journal of Marketing* 54(1): 102–113.

Jones, Fred. 1936. "Retail Stores in the United States, 1800–1860." *Journal of Marketing* 1 (October): 135–140.

Kaufman, Carol J. 1987. "The Evaluation of Marketing in a Society: The Han Dynasty of Ancient China." *Journal of Macromarketing* 7(2): 52–64.

HISTORICAL RESEARCH IN MARKETING:
RETROSPECT AND PROSPECT

Keith, Robert J. 1960. "The Marketing Revolution." *Journal of Marketing* 24 (January): 35–38.

Kelley, William T. 1956. "The Development of Early Thought in Marketing and Promotion." *Journal of Marketing* 21 (July): 62–76.

Kotler, Philip. 1988. "The Convenience Store: Past Developments and Future Prospects." In: *Historical Perspectives in Marketing: Essays in Honor of Stanley C. Hollander*. Terence Nevett and Ronald Fullerton, eds. Lexington, MA: Lexington Books, pp. 163–176.

Kumcu, Erdogan. 1987. "Historical Method: Toward a Relevant Analysis of Marketing Systems." In: *Philosophical and Radical Thought in Marketing*. A. Fuat Firat, N. Dholakia, and R. Bagozzi, eds. Lexington, MA: Lexington Books, pp. 117–133.

La Londe, Bernard J., and Edward J. Morrison. 1967. "Marketing Management Concepts, Yesterday and Today." *Journal of Marketing* 31(1): 9–13.

Larson, Henrietta. 1938. "Review of *Milestones of Marketing*." *Bulletin of the Business Historical Society*: 12: 12–13.

Lazer, William. 1965. "Marketing Theory and the Marketing Literature." In: *The Meaning and Sources of Marketing Theory*. Michael Halburt, ed. New York: McGraw-Hill, pp. 58–94.

———. 1979. "Some Observations on the Development Marketing Thought." In: *Conceptual and Theoretical Developments in Marketing*. Proceedings Series. O.C. Ferrell, Stephen Brown, and Charles W. Lamb Jr., eds. Chicago: American Marketing Association, pp. 652–664.

Lazer, William, and Shaw, Eric. 1988. "The Development of Collegiate Business and Marketing Education in America: Historical Perspectives." In: *Marketing: A Return to the Broader Dimensions*. Proceedings of the Winter Educators' Conference. Stanley Shapiro and A.H. Walle, eds. Chicago: American Marketing Association, pp. 147–152.

Legh, Faith. 1986. "Half a Century of Professional Bodies in Sales Promotions." *European Journal of Marketing* 20(9): 27–40.

Lichtenthal, David J., and Leland L. Belk. 1984. "A History of the Definition of Marketing." *Research in Marketing* 7: 133–163.

Litman, Simon. 1950. "The Beginnings of Teaching Marketing in American Universities." *Journal of Marketing* 15(7) (October): 220–223.

Lockley, Lawrence. 1950. "Notes on the History of Marketing Research." *Journal of Marketing* 14 (April): 733–773.

Marburg, Theodore. 1951. "Domestic Trade and Marketing." In: *The Growth of the American Economy*. H.F. Williamson. pp. 551–553.

Marx, Thomas G. 1985. "The Development of the Franchise Distributive System in the United States Auto Industry." *British History Review* 59(3) (August): 465–474.

Maynard, H.H. 1941. "Marketing Courses Prior to 1910." *Journal of Marketing* (April): 5.4: 382–384.

———. 1951. "Developments of Science in Selling and Sales Management." In: *Changing Perspectives in Marketing*. Hugh G. Wales, ed. Urbana: University of Illinois Press, pp. 169–184.

McCracken, Grant. 1987. "The History of Consumption: A Literature Review and Consumer Guide." *Journal of Consumer Policy* 10(2) (June): 139–166.

McCarthy, E. Jerome. 1988. "Marketing Orientedness and Economic Development." In: *Historical Perspectives in Marketing: Essays in Honor of Stanley C. Hollander*. Terence Nevett and Ronald Fullerton, eds. Lexington, MA: Lexington Books, pp. 133–146.

McGarry, E.D. 1953. "Some New Viewpoints In Marketing." *Journal of Marketing* 18(1): 33–40.

McKendrick, N. 1960. "Josiah Wedgwood: An Eighteenth Century Entrepreneur in Salesmanship and Marketing Techniques." *Economic History Review* 12: 408–431.

Mittelstaedt, Robert. 1989. "Economics and the Development of the Subdiscipline of Consumer Behaviour in Marketing." In: *Marketing History: The Emerging Discipline*. Proceedings of the Fourth Marketing History Conference. Lansing: Michigan State University Press, pp. 3–21.

Miracle, Gordon E., and Terence Nevett. 1988. "A Comparative History of Advertising Self-Regulation in the United Kingdom and the United States." *European Journal of Marketing* 22(4): 7–23.

Myers, K., and D. Smalley. 1959. "Marketing History and Economic Development." *Business History Review* 33 (Autumn): 387–401.

Nevett, Terence. 1982. *Advertising in Britain, A History*. London: Heinemann.

———. 1983. "Blood, Sweat, Tears and Biography." In: *First North American Workshop on Historical Research in Marketing*. Proceedings

of a Conference held at Michigan State University. Stanley Hollander and Ronald Savitt, eds. Lansing: Michigan State University Press, pp. 20–29.

———. 1985. "The Ethics of Advertising: F.P. Bishop Reconsidered." *International Journal of Advertising* 4: 4.

———. 1988a. "American Influences in British Advertising Before 1920." In: *Historical Perspectives in Marketing: Essays in Honor of Stanley C. Hollander*. Terence Nevett and Ronald Fullerton, eds. Lexington, MA: Lexington Books, pp. 223–240.

———. 1988b. "Reform in Great Britain—The Scapa Society." In: *Marketing: A Return to the Broader Dimensions*. Proceedings of the Winter Educators' Conference. Stanley Shapiro and A.H. Walle, eds. Chicago: American Marketing Association, pp. 120–124.

———. 1988c. "The Early Development of Marketing Thought: Some Contributions From British Advertising." In: *Marketing: A Return to the Broader Dimensions*. Proceedings of the Winter Educators' Conference. Stanley Shapiro and A.H. Walle, eds. Chigago: American Marketing Association, pp. 137–141.

———. 1988d. "Thomas Barratt and the Development of British Advertising." *International Journal of Advertising* 7: 267–276.

Nevett, Terence, Kathleen Whitney, and Stanley C. Hollander, eds. 1989. *Marketing History: The Emerging Discipline*. Proceedings of the Fourth Conference on Historical Research in Marketing. East Lansing: Michigan State University Press.

Nystrom, Paul H. 1915. *The Economics of Retailing*. New York: Ronald Press.

———. 1951. "Retailing in Retrospect and Prospect." In: *Changing Historical Perspectives in Marketing: Essays in Honor of Stanley C. Hollander*. Terence Nevett and Ronald Fullerton, eds. Lexington, MA: Lexington Press, pp. 91–108.

Pollay, Richard W. 1977. "The Importance, and the Problems of Writing the History of Advertising." *Journal of Advertising History* 1(1): 3–5.

———. 1978. "Maintaining Archives for the History of Advertising." *Special Libraries* 69(4): 145–154.

———. 1979. *Information Sources in Advertising History*. Riverside Connecticut: Greenwood Press.

———. 1984a. "The Identification and Distribution of Values Manifest in Print Advertising 1900–1980." In *Personal Values and Consumer Behavior*. Eds. E. Pitts Jr. and A.G. Woodsides. Lexington: Lexington Press, pp. 111–135.

———. 1984b. "Twentieth Century Magazine Advertising: "Determinants of Informativeness." *Written Communication* 1(1): 56–57.

———. 1985. "The Subsiding Sizzle: A Descriptive History of Print Advertising, 1900–1980." *Journal of Marketing* 49 (Summer): 24–37.

———. 1988a. "Current Events That are Making Advertising History." In *Historical Perspectives in Marketing: Essays in Honor of Stanley C. Hollander*. Eds. Terence Nevett and Ronald Fullerton. Lexington: Lexington Books, pp. 195–222.

———. 1988b. "Keeping Advertising From Going Down in History—Unfairly." *Journal of Advertising History* 11(2): (Autumn).

———. 1988c. "Promotion and Policy for a Pandemic Product: Notes of the History of Cigarette Advertising." Unpublished Paper. History of Advertising Archives.

——— and Steven Lysonski. Forthcoming. "Advertising Sexism is Forgiven, But Not Forgotten: Historical, Cross Cultural and Individual Differences in Criticism and Purchase Boycott Intentions." *International Journal of Advertising*.

Rassuli, Kathleen M. and Stanley C. Hollander. 1986a. "Comparative History as a Research Tool in Consumer Behaviour." *Advances in Consumer Research* Eds. Melanie Wallendorff and Paul Anderson, pp. 442–446.

——— and Stanley C. Hollander. 1986b. "Desire—Induced, Innate, Insatiable?" *Journal of Macromarketing* 6(3) (Fall): 4–24.

———. 1988. "Evidence of Marketing Strategy in the Early Printed Book Trade: An Application of Hollander's Historical Approach." in *Historical Perspectives in Marketing: Essays In Honor of Stanley C. Hollander*. Eds. Terence Nevett and Ronald Fullerton. Lexington: Lexington Press, pp. 91–108.

Robins, George W. 1947. "Notions About the Origins of Trading." *Journal of Marketing* 11(3): 228–236.

Savitt, Ronald. 1980. "Historical Research in Marketing." *Journal of Marketing* 44: 52–58.

————. 1982. "A Historical Approach to Comparative Retailing." *Management Decision* 20(4): 16–23.

————. 1984. "The Wheel of Retailing and Retail Product Management." *European Journal of Marketing* 18: 43–54.

————. 1988. "A Personal View of Historical Explanation in Marketing and Economic Development." In: *Historical Perspectives in Marketing: Essays in Honor of Stanley C. Hollander.* Terence Nevett and Ronald Fullerton, eds. Lexington: Lexington Books, pp. 113–132.

————. 1989. "Some Antecedents of Macromarketing." Unpublished Paper.

————. 1989. "Looking Back to See Ahead: Writing the History of American Retailing." *Journal of Retailing* 65(3): 326–355.

Schultz, Quentin J. 1982. "An Honourable Place: The Quest for Professional Advertising Education 1900–1917." *Business History Review* 56(1): 16–32.

Schwartz, George. 1963. *Development of Marketing Theory.* Cincinnati, OH: South-Western Publishing.

Seaton, A.V. 1986. "Cope's and the Promotion of Tobacco in Victorian England." *European Journal of Marketing* 20(9): 5–26.

Shapiro, Stanley, and Alton F. Doody. 1968. *Readings in the History of American Marketing, Settlement to Civil War.* Homewood, IL: Irwin.

Sheth, Jagdish N., and David M. Gardner. 1982. "History of Marketing Thought: An Update." In: *Marketing Theory: Philosophy of Science Perspectives.* Proceedings Series. Ronald F. Bush and Shelby D. Hunt, eds. Chicago: American Marketing Association, pp. 52–58.

Sheth, Jagdish N., D.M. Gardner, and D. Garrett. 1988. *Marketing Theory: Evolution and Evaluation.* New York: Wiley and Sons.

Sheth, Jagdish N., and Barbara L. Gross. 1988. "Parallel Development of Marketing and Consumer Behaviour: A Historical Perspective." In: *Historical Perspectives in Marketing: Essays in Honor of Stanley C. Hollander.* Lexington, MA: Lexington Books. 9–34.

Silk, A., and Louis Stern. 1963. "The Changing Nature of Innovation in Marketing: A Study of Selected Business Leaders, 1852–1958." *Business History Review* 37: 182–199.

Smith, George L. Ed. 1965. *Reflections on Progress in Marketing.* Proceedings Series. Chicago: American Marketing Association.

Stern, Barbara B. 1988. "Medieval Allegory: Roots of Advertising Strategy for the Mass Market." *Journal of Marketing* 52(3) (July): 84–94.

Tedlow, Richard. 1981. "From Competitor to Consumer: The Changing Focus of Federal Regulation of Advertising, 1914–1938." *Business History Review* 55(1) (Spring): 35–58.

Weld, L.D.H. 1941. "Early Experience in Teaching Courses in Marketing." *Journal of Marketing* 5(4) (April): 380–381.

Witkowski, Terrence H. 1989. "History's Place in the Marketing Curriculum." *Journal of Marketing Education* (Summer):

Wright, John S., and Parks B. Dimsdale Jr. 1974. *Pioneers in Marketing.* Atlanta, GA: Georgia State University.

Ziman, John. 1984. *An Introduction to Science Studies: The Philosophical and Social Aspects of Science and Technology.* Cambridge: Cambridge University Press.

ABOUT THE AUTHORS

D.G. Brian Jones received his Ph.D. in Management at Queen's University, Kingston, Ontario, in 1987, and is currently Assistant Professor of Marketing at the School of Business, University of Prince Edward Island.

David D. Monieson received his Ph.D. at Ohio State University in 1957 and is currently the Nabisco Professor of Marketing at Queen's University, Kingston, Ontario.

[7]

Main Features of Danish Research in Marketing*

By MAX KJÆR-HANSEN**

1. The Origin of Theoretical Studies of Marketing Problems in Denmark

In all spheres of science there is a close connection between research and academic education. Almost always the development of each depends on the development of the other. This has also been the case with the theoretical marketing studies in Denmark. These studies originated in the Copenhagen School of Economics and Business Administration, founded in 1917 with the object of providing various specialized courses in business economics. In 1924 the School was expanded, and both general and specialized courses in business economics were organized. The first chair of marketing was established in 1925, when the writer was appointed associate professor, with the task of lecturing on general business economics as well as on advertising and market analysis.

In 1930 an independent degree course in marketing was organized, and since then the marketing activities carried on at the School have undergone a steadily expanding development. Today the marketing departement is one of the most important departments of the School. In addition, this department is considered one of the most developed marketing departments in Europe. From 1930 the first chair was principally concerned with marketing. Since then the teaching and research staff continued to increase. Today, the staff comprises fifteen persons, including full professors, associate professors, assistant professors and lecturers.

The University of Aarhus, founded in 1935, immediately appointed two professors of business economics. Since then the University has organized both courses and research in marketing. In 1953 Denmark's second School of Economics and Business Administration was established at Aarhus. There, too, research into marketing problems has been conducted to an increasing extent. Finally, education in marketing has in recent years been organized at two Danish colleges of business administration providing higher commercial education.

In Denmark the pioneer work in marketing was performed by the Copenhagen School of Economics and Business Administration, and today the School is still the institution which devotes most time to

---

* The article has not previously been published, but was written as an introduction to "Readings in Danish Theory of Marketing".

** Professor at the Copenhagen School of Economics and Business Administration.

the marketing problems and has most persons engaged on research in marketing. In support of these activities the Marketing Institute at the Copenhagen School of Economics and Business Administration was established in 1932. Three tasks were assigned to the Institute: (1) to be the administrative centre of the organization and development of the education in marketing provided by the School, (2) to contribute to the international theoretical research into marketing problems, and (3) to conduct investigations illustrating practical marketing conditions in Denmark.

These objects of the Institute's activities comprise a two-sided research programme, since the Institute is to take part in international fundamental and methodological research as well as currently to carry out practical Danish analyses in marketing. Research has now been conducted for more than thirty years. The results have chiefly been published through two channels, viz. "Det Danske Marked" (The Danish Market), a periodical created towards the end of 1941, which appears four times a year as organ of the Institute, and "Skriftrække F – Skrifter fra Instituttet for Salgsorganisation og Reklame" (Publications F – Writings of the Marketing Institute), which were established in 1942. Before the creation of the Institute's own series of writings, which up to now have comprised 37 publications, eight books from the marketing department were published in the School's general series of writings. Over the years about a dozen books written by the Marketing Institute staff have been published elsewhere. Thus, the marketing theorists at the Copenhagen School of Economics and Business Administration have so far published approximately sixty works. These publications include both general and specialized textbooks and research results.

2. Practical Market Analyses

Most of the publications fall within the third task of the Institute, i. e. the majority of the books contain analyses and evaluations of conditions and procedures in major Danish industries.

Moreover, in 1947 the Institute set itself the task of determining the advertising expenditure of Danish trades and industries. At that time national advertising expenditure surveys had only been made in the United States (for years 1935, 1939 and 1940, published in 1942 and 1945 respectively). Besides, an investigation of British advertising expenditure had been started in 1945.

In 1947 it seemed natural to carry out the Danish survey on the same fundamental basis as that of the first analyses published in English. However, as the latter were also pioneer work, and as the possibilities of determining the relevant figures in the individual countries were essentially different, the first Danish investigations varied somewhat in respect of methods from the models taken. Retail shop advertising was not included in the American surveys and only partially in the British investigation, and, consequently, the picture of these expenditures was not complete. This became clear to us after finishing the Danish survey, and, therefore, an independent analysis of the expenditure of total Danish retail shop advertising was made in 1950. The figures of the latter investigation were later converted to the relevant level and inserted in the advertising expenditure survey.

Our survey dealt with two years, 1948 and 1935. Although the figures for the latter year could only be outlined summarily, they were included by way of comparison to show the situation between the First World War and Second World War. The attempt was received with interest. Our analyses were continued, and since then the Institute has surveyed Danish advertising expenditure every five years. Thus, besides the figures for 1935 and 1948, results for 1953, 1958 and 1963 have also been published.

The world-wide accelerating economic expansion which characterized economic developments in the 1950's led to a heavy increase in advertising expenditure. This trend made it important to determine the cost of advertising in an increasing number of countries and to watch developments in national expenditures. In consequence of the growth of international trade and the intergration of both the national and the private economy the determination of the cost of advertising and the distribution of advertising expenditure by media and industries in the different countries have become of importance not only for the individual society, but for everybody interested in selling goods in these markets. Accordingly, the last decade has seen the publication of national reports for an increasing number of countries all over the world.

Once a problem becomes of world-wide importance, it has to be solved on a uniform basis by the individual countries. Otherwise, results will not be comparable, and their international effect will be misleading rather than guiding. Consequently, in 1956 the *International Chamber of Commerce* took the initiative in laying down uniform lines of direction for national advertising expenditure surveys. In 1958 the results of the Chamber's deliberations were published in the form of a list comprising thirteen specified categories of costs which should be determined in national advertising expenditure surveys, a list which was largely based on the principles underlying the Danish investigations made by the Marketing Institute for 1935, 1948 and 1953 as well as an over-all survey of advertising expenditures in Denmark, Finland, Norway and Sweden made by the Institute for the year 1953.

Owing to the great difficulties involved in determining retail shop advertising expenditure the international list includes only a very limited proportion of total costs. The category concerned is group VIII, "Display and Point of Sale". From this category are excluded, among other items, all indirect retail shop advertising costs and rent of shop windows. If the same principle was applied to the cost of press advertising, the result would be that the fee charged for inserting advertisements in papers was left out of account.

13

What is important is not only the fundamental error made, but also the fact that the picture of total advertising expenditure is distorted. Retail shop advertising must, in the nature of things, be one of the largest items of a country's advertising bill. In our survey for the four Scandinavian countries for 1953 we found that retail shop advertising constituted the following proportions of the total national advertising expenditures: Denmark 38.0 per cent, Finland 41.3 per cent, Norway 32.4 per cent and Sweden 32.3 per cent. Roughly, it appears that retail shop advertising constituted some 36 per cent, or more than one-third, of total advertising expenditures in these four countries. If we look at the international reports which provide figures for group VIII, we note that on the average the costs in this category amount to 5 per cent of total advertising expenditures. In this connection it should be noted that American reports give no figures for retail shop advertising. In comparing the figures for the Scandinavian countries with those of other countries it will be observed that, in the case of an analysis of national advertising expenditure and a breakdown of this expenditure by individual media, the inclusion or exclusion of retail shop advertising costs gives two entirely different pictures of the total national expenditure as well as of the distribution on media. Consequently, the Marketing Institute holds that if an item as heavy as retail shop advertising is excluded from the overall advertising expenditure, the cost estimate will be relevant neither for the individual country nor in the case of international comparisons. For this reason the total cost of retail shop advertising has been included in all our advertising expenditure surveys.

The four reports of Danish advertising expenditure published in 1949, 1957, 1963 and 1965 were based on detailed analyses of the expenditure on each individual advertising medium. For instance, as far as press advertising in daily newspapers is concerned the expenditure was ascertained by means of a chartered accountant's report on the receipts from commercial advertising in all circulation-audited daily newspapers (95 per cent of total newspapers circulation). The advantage of determining developments in a small country is firstly that total analyses can be made. Secondly, in conducting sample surveys it is possile to find some concrete measures of the uncertainties that appear.

Even at the time when Danish advertising expenditure surveys were first made the trend of developments was such that advertising could not be taken as an all-inclusive expression of national promotional activities. This holds good today with even greater force: the tendency to use the advertising parameter alone is declining. Advertising is a factor used in combination with other parameters; between them these parameters make up the increasingly comprehensive marketing function. Consequently, when we planned our analyses of advertising expenditures in the four Scandinavian countries for the year 1953, we deemed it essential to determine the total Scandinavian marketing costs, and therefore our analyses became an attempt in this direction. This was pioneer work, but we continued to deal with the methodological problems involved in such estimates. Finally, in 1963 a comprehensive analysis was made of total Danish marketing costs. This analysis was published in English in "Cost Problems in Modern Marketing", 1965. Apart from the primitive American survey "Does Distribution Cost too Mush?" published in 1939, our analysis seems to be the first detailed estimate of the total marketing costs of a national economy.

In the Danish survey total costs are determined first; these costs are then broken down into administrative distribution costs and promotional costs. Then an attempt is made to distribute costs by principal trades and industries, and, additionally, a distribution is made on cost categories. This leads to an absolute and relative distribution by major groups such as direct selling activities, advertising, service, merchandising and other promotional activities.

As an element of the research conducted to determine the concrete marketing conditions in Denmark the Institute has for a number of years deemed it important to carry out demand analyses showing the correlations between business firms' use of the individual parameters of action and actual developments in consumption. Such analyses have also been employed in attempts to make prognoses of the future turnover on a number of important industrial sectors. Among these comprehensive demand analyses we mention "Cigaretforbruget" (Demand for Cigarettes), 1952, "Forbruget af pelsværk" (Demand for Furs), 1953, "Annoncemarkedets reaktioner" (Demand for Advertising Space), 1954, "Efterspørgselen efter radioer" (Demand for Radios), 1954, "Forbruget af øl og sodavand" (Demand for Beer and Soft Drinks), 1955 and "Dagbladssalget i København" (Sales of Daily Newspapers in Copenhagen), 1955.

In connection with the efforts made to determine some important features of marketing in Denmark by means of analysis in the field, or based on demand analyses, the Institute staff have planned and published a number of structural analyses. The analyses are above all concerned with the organization of business and the use of promotional activities and their importance in specific industrial sectors.

3. Contribution to the Development of a Theory of Marketing

The reason why we started our description of Danish research into marketing by going through practical analyses is not only that the results of these latter activities are dominant in quantitative terms. The activities were also the first to be launched, and later they formed the basis of the performance of the Istitute's second main function: to contribute to the international theoretical research into marketing problems. In the 1920's and the first half of the 1930's research activities were primitively concentrated on estimating the advertising effort of trade and industry and on conducting rational market analyses.

At the international level the break-through towards the development of scientifically valid theories of marketing took place at the beginning of the 1930's. It was macroeconomists, not microeconomists, who made the effort. Three works were of decisive importance: "Problems of Monopoly and Economic Warfare", by Fr. Zeuthen, London, 1930, "The Economics of Imperfect Competition", by Joan Robinson, London, 1933, and "The Theory of Monopolistic Competition", by Edward H. Chamberlin, Cambridge, Mass., 1933. In all three works the general economic tools available were used in expanding the insight into competition in the markets of our time. These works formed the basis of a rearrangement of the theoretical research activities in marketing, shifting the weight from pure description and primitive market analyses to economic analyses and evaluation on a scientific background. Towards 1940 it became clear to many marketing economists throughout the world that an extremely important, largely uncultivated field of activity lay before them. The task to be performed was to approach and deal with marketing problems on the basis of general economic viewpoints, and improve the scientific tools available for the purpose.

This approach determined the fate of the market researchers at the Copenhagen School of Economics and Business Administration. The fact that one of the pioneers, Fr. Zeuthen, was professor of economics at the University of Copenhagen made the new viewpoints of immediate interest to us. We now started planning our research activities on a general economic basis. Against this background the Institute tackled its international task. First of all we concentrated on expanding the knowledge of conditions relating to demand and competition. The writer has personally contributed to the formulation of certain of the modern problems and, to the best of his ability, participated in solving these problems. Above all we endeavoured to determine the parameters of action which are important in the present-day market under monopolistic competition and to create tools for measuring the influence of these parameters on demand.

In the field of parameters, which was of central importance to us, some notable results, several of them known also outside Denmark, were reached by *Børge Barfod, Hans Brems* and *Arne Rasmussen* while associated with the Marketing Institute. Børge Barfod is now professor of marketing at the Swedish University in Finland, Hans Brems is professor of economics at the University of Illinois, and Arne Rasmussen is professor of marketing at the Copenhagen School of Economics and Business Administration.

The research aiming at the development of a general theory of parameters is usually regarded as a characteristic of the theorists at the Copenhagen School of Economics and Business Administration, occasionally referred to as the "Copenhagen school" with a view to the theoretical marketing work performed. As is natural for research in a small country, activities could not be based exclusively on the knowledge obtained in Denmark. It was necessary to deal also with the different attempts at theory formulation made in the United States as well as in various European countries.

There is no doubt that the most important contributions to the creation of a general theory of marketing, quantitatively as well as qualitatively, were made by American researchers. However, in studying the American marketing literature in books and periodicals one gets the impression that research conducted in a large country is apt to be self-sufficient. Many European countries have made important, comprehensive contributions to the development of objectives and methodology in order to elucidate the problems confronting a modern business firm, but these contributions seem largely to have been disregarded by American theorists. Additionally, it has occasionally proved doubtful whether conclusions drawn under certain specifically American assumptions enjoy general validity.

The Danish activities in this field have generally been based on the often very different results attained in a number of larger countries. Thus, the Danish contribution has largely consisted in a comparative, critical evaluation of the knowledge obtained in various countries at the time in question.

Overall presentations of the Danish contribution in this field were published by Arne Rasmussen in "Pristeori eller Parameterteori" (Theory of Price or Theory of Parameters), 1955, and by Max Kjær-Hansen in "Salgets driftsøkonomi" (Economics of Selling), 1960. The latter work was translated into German and published as "Absatz, Markt und Nachfrage", 1965.

As mentioned above, the "Copenhagen school" has largely put its forces into action in creating a central economic theory of marketing based on evaluation and measurement of the application of the parameters of action. In addition, however, there are various specific areas in the heavily differentiated discipline of marketing in which a fairly intensive effort has been made. Among these areas we mention four: (1) consumer economics, (2) the interplay of legislation, which lays down the rules for the structure of competition, and practical promotional activities, (3) conducting research into the conditions of the press from a commercial standpoint and (4) cost, budgeting and control problems in modern marketing.

As the central theory of parameters rests on the reactions in demand, the problems relating to the motives and behaviour of consumers must be an important element in the basis for developing a valid and realistic theory. Consequently, *consumer surveys* have during the past twenty years become an integral part of the theoretical background of general marketing economics. In this field some scientific pioneer work had to be done, because this sphere is a boundary area which calls for both economic, sociological and psychological methods. The basic work was made by American researchers, but their effort was followed up and supplemented in several European countries, particularly in Germany. Also Denmark has contributed towards enhancing the insight into this field. *Karen Gredal,*

Lecturer at the Copenhagen School of Economics and Business Administration, has been working on these problems, teaching consumer economics as well as conducting reasearch activities. Through comments on international results as well as attempts at formulating new problems this reasearch has aimed to make the basic concepts of the discipline realistic, operational and verifiable. Karen Gredal's main work is "Moderne forbrugeres motiver og adfærd" (Motives and Behaviour of Modern Consumers), 1959. In this connection it should also be mentioned that one of the associates of the Institute, *Børge O. Madsen*, has endeavoured to evaluate the family's consumption behaviour in the light of family life cycle models, cf. "Familiens økonomiske livsløb" (The Economic Family Life Cycle), 1964.

Just as the international work in consumer economics has been concerned with the combination of economic, sociological and psychological methods, the Danish contribution towards elucidating *the relations between legislating and modern marketing activities* is a synthesis of legal and economic marketing viewpoints. Over the years Professor *Jan Kobbernagel* has been engaged on these problems. Besides writing a number of articles and treatises Kobbernagel is collecting his review and evaluation of legislation and competition in the Danish market in a large 3-volume work, "Konkurrencens retlige regulering" (The Law on Trade Marks and Unfair Competition). The first two volumes appeared in 1957 and 1961 respectively. As far as we are aware, this work is the first of its kind to be published in Europe.

In 1954 the *Institute of Press Research*, a sub-division of the Marketing Institute, was founded, with the object of exploring the economic problems relating to modern press, particularly the importance of the press as an advertising medium. In 1958 the Institute of Press Research became an independent institute, where all commercial research and publishing activities were placed in the hands of Professor *Ejler Alkjær*. Alkjær was associated to the Marketing Institute as early as in 1937. Thus, almost from the time the Institute was founded he has participated in planning and conducting the research work that was performed. Alkjær has contributed very considerably to the analyses mentioned above, whose object was to clarify various practical quantifiable problems. Alkjær's efforts to create new methods of analysis and improve existing methods are recognized also outside the Danish borders.

Besides developing commercial press research activities directed at an increasing proportion of overall mass media and constructing in particular the quantitative basis for carrying out analyses, Professor Alkjær has made various contributions to enhancing Danish insight into a number of specialized areas. Among these mention should above all be made of the new regional science theories and investigations of various marketing problems relating to the activities of the tourist industry.

Within the total marketing sector the problems relating to *the costs involved in marketing activities* have been a main object of the research conducted by the Institute.

Whereas cost considerations form the basis of all other microeconomic analyses, they have so far played a subordinate part in analyses of marketing problems. The explosive development in demand during the industrialization of the marketing process has resulted in a regular selling boom, which, in turn, has made the use of rational parameters of action profitable to an almost unlimited extent. Therefore, considerations of effectiveness have become of essential importance in the case of promotional activities. Accordingly, profitability has receded into the background: practically any effective marketing policy has been profitable.

However, the Institute staff have begun to doubt whether the present conditions of marketing will remain unchanged in the future. After a period of fifty years, during which demand has expanded at a steadily increasing rate, and the methods of influencing the market have been under constant development, the boom must be drawing to a close. Such reflections give rise to the question whether future marketing activities will not have to be approached on the basis of rational cost estimates to a far greater extent than previously.

During the last few years these viewpoints have caused us to explore the marketing cost problems with increasing energy.

Against this background we have brought into focus the basic nature of marketing costs, their variations, their control, and their budgeting. The starting-point was analyses of general economic importance of stepped (semi-fixed) costs and determination of their influence on the profitability of modern marketing methods. Whereas this field has attracted little interest at the international level, we place the subject in the centre of our research programme. In order to contribute to the international economic discussion with our viewpoints and provisional results we published our "Cost Problems in Modern Marketing", 1965, in the English language. This book contains a basic approach to various of the principal problems and also provides a broad outline of future research into this subject. Professors *Arne Rasmussen* and *Erik Johnsen* will be responsible for planning and conducting future research work in this important area.

4. Contribution to the Development of Methodological Studies

Whenever scientific investigations are made the results obtainable will depend both on the relevance of the problems formulated and on the expediency of the tools employed. Both the first and the second give rise to difficulties in the case of a new tradition-less discipline like marketing economics. In both respects researchers throughout the world have largely had to concentrate on surmounting the inevitable initial difficulties. These difficulties have also characterized our work. One of the consequences was that a considerable effort

2*

had to be devoted to the improvement of the tools avaiable and creating of more rational tools.

The fact is that methodological research and developments in this research have been mainly responsible for the results that could be achieved during the pioneer stage of our research in marketing. Accordingly, the Institute staff have eagerly followed the methodological discussion and the presentation of new procedures which have taken place not least in post-war years.

The work in developing more appropriate tools for research in marketing has been performed on two fronts: (1) technical innovations and (2) evaluating the applications of modern scientific methods in marketing and investigating the special adaptation of these methods to practice. The Danish efforts have largely been concentrated on the second front, i. e. Danish researchers have endeavoured to evaluate and discuss the new methods and to adapt these methods to solving existing marketing problems. As to technical innovations, some Danish attempt in this direction were made by Professors *A. Hald* and *Ernst Lykke Jensen* in pure statistics.

Throughout the years, evaluation and adaption activities have been conducted. At the initial stage, attention was concentrated in particular on rationalizing marketing research tools, i. e. efforts were above all concerned with the procedure involved in making sample surveys and constructing demand analyses on the basis of multiple correlation. As the work in developing some relevant parameter theories was brought into focus, the methodological studies were centred on various kinds of elasticity measurements and on other procedures by which the influence of the different parameters on demand could be determined.

In post-war years, as is well known, an enormous development has taken place in general scientific techniques. In many cases the starting-point was the solution of quantitative problems which had become of first importance during the war. The methods developed have later proved applicable in certain disciplines, where it is essential to be able to operate with concrete figures. As far as methodology is concerned these methods are above all based on modern computational procedures, usually referred to collectively as *operations research*. However, these procedures are essentially different, and many of them are related to modern statistical principles.

There seems to be no doubt that a great number of these techniques can be used profitably in clarifying various important problems in the marketing sector. In concrete terms we are thinking primarily of probability budgeting, linear programming, queuing theory, game theory, Markov matrices and simulation. As far as each of these techniques is concerned it has been necessary to determine which marketing problems could be solved by means of which tools. So far it has generally been agreed that probability budgeting can be used profitably in determining optimal inventory sizes, linear programming in determining the number of travelling salesman to be used in the case of a given number of calls and a given visiting frequency, queuing theory where a retail shop has to serve a volume of costumers that varies in point of time, game theory in determining the results of two or more rival firms' promotional efforts, and Markov matrices for the computation of penetration rates. This enumeration merely serves to exemplify applications. Several other uses have already been discovered, and continued research will bring more to light.

The Danish Marketing Institute staff have worked on these problems with great zeal. Additionally, they have participated in adapting and reformulating the original scientific models in the different fields in order that the models might be applied in solving existing marketing problems. Among the researchers mentioned above Arne Rasmussen, Børge Barfod and Erik Johnsen have achieved results which have added considerably to the current state of knowledge and have improved the possibility of using these computational procedures and models in marketing.

In connection with the operations research techniques it seems natural to mention the possibility of facilitating and intensifying scientific analyses in marketing that arises out of the use of electronic digital computers. Certain members of the Marketing Institute staff have been assigned the task of watching these technical developments closely, familiarizing themselves with the principles involved in order that programmes might be made for use in practical marketing. So far we have succeeded in constructing and carrying out a number of economic marketing simulation games, one of which was formulated in English and used abroad. The work on the application of simulation based on modern computer techniques performed under the auspices of the Marketing Institute has chiefly been carried out by Asst. Professor *Erik Trolle-Schultz.*

In concluding our review of Danish contributions to the methodological studies essential to the development of the theory of marketing, mention should be made of the Institute's attitude to the various principal lines of approach. In our research activities deductive and empirical methods have always been employed side by side. Both methods must be used if valid information about business conditions and the results of the activities performed in a market is to be obtained. Which method should form the primary basis depends on the nature of the problem in hand. However, in all problem-solving processes we have attempted to combine the two principles. Only the sequence of their use has varied. In certain cases we believe it is natural to start with deductive reasoning. Before the arguments are employed they are tested on a sufficient amount of appropriate data. Conversely, in other cases the procedure has been to draw conclusions on the basis of data which were available, or which had been collected for the purpose.

Both deductive and empirical research results will, as mentioned above, depend on the effectiveness of the methods used. For this reason we have devoted a good deal of time and attention to

21

methodological studies. However, the most refined technical tools will not avail if the problems on which research is based are not well-defined and relevant. The starting-point for the research conducted by the Marketing Institute has always consisted in economic arguments, from which hypotheses have been derived. The hypotheses which we have attempted to set up have been in the form of models, simplified but relevant.

5. Compilation of Readings in Danish Theory of Marketing

As mentioned above, the results of the research conducted by the Marketing Institute have primarily been published through two channels, i. e. the Institute's series of writings and its quarterly periodical "Det Danske Marked". Major works have appeared as books, but the majority of the attempts made at developing theories and contributing to the international methodological discussion have appeared in the periodical.

The first issue of "Det Danske Marked" was prepared in the autumn of 1941. The periodical has thus appeared for twenty-five years, and during this time it has served as organ for the theoretical marketing work performed in Denmark. The jubilee has caused us to reflect on past achievements and the present position of our research at the international level. It is next to impossible for us to evaluate our research objectively ourselves, and, consequently, we decided to have a selection of the articles published in "Det Danske Marked" translated into English and distributed abroad in order that our attempts and results might be evaluated by our foreign colleagues. This is our purpose in issuing these readings.

Also on account of the jubilee our book consists exclusively of articles which were published in Danish in our periodical. However, the articles selected are not representative of all the subjects that have been treated in "Det Danske Marked". Normally, a quarterly issue has contained 64 pages of text. Over the twenty-five years some 7.000 pages have thus been printed.

The main objective of the periodical has been for the authors to contribute to the scientific discussion of the marketing problems and point to a solution of practical problems by means of theoretical tools. In addition, however, "Det Danske Marked" has treated of sociological, psychological, organizational and economic descriptive subjects. In these fields the periodical has a permanent staff. The periodical furthermore carries a fairly large number of reviews, in which new international marketing literature is introduced, and attempts are made to evaluate its merits.

Each issue further publishes computations of Danish press advertising volume indices with comments, and once a year a detailed analysis is made of developments and shifts in the Danish daily newspaper market. This permanent press research material, which is intended in particular as a guide for business firms, is prepared and planned by Asst. Professor *Ulf Kjær-Hansen*.

In celebrating the jubilee of our periodical it would be natural for us to outline the different subjects dealt with by "Det Danske Marked" in the course of time. However, our intention is not only to mark the jubilee, but through a selection of articles published over the years to present the efforts we have made in the theory of marketing in narrow sense. This viewpoint has determined the selection of the readings. This is also the reason why the selection is not evenly distributed over the years. Developments in the theory of marketing during the pioneer years took place at such a speed that lines of thought which were most relevant a few years ago are hopelessly obsolete to-day. Consequently, the bulk of articles were published during the last few years. In order to outline the historical perspective, a few articles dating back to the early 1950's have been included. Although they may have lost part of the immediate interest which characterized them when they were first published, these articles should still be worth reading.

Even though all the articles making up our readings are related to problems in the theory of marketing, the individual contributions approach these problems from different standpoints. We have therefore divided the readings into four groups, in each of which we have collected articles with the same basic approach. The four groups are: (1) Danish research in marketing, (2) discussion of principal marketing problems, (3) contribution to the development of some theories of marketing and (4) practical marketing problems solved on a theoretical basis.

The choice of authors is no more than the selection of articles reprensentative of the theorists whose works were published in "Det Danske Marked". Although "Det Danske Marked" is a Danish publication, in which usually Danish articles appear, articles by leading marketing theorists in the United States as well as in a number of European countries have been printed every year.

As "Det Danske Marked" is the only theoretical marketing publication issued in the Scandinavian countries, it has in the course of time largely served also as organ for our Finnish, Norwegian and Swedish colleagues. Since more of these colleagues have performed part of their work on the basis typical of the "Copenhagen school", there was a strong argument for including examples of their contributions among our readings in order to provide a broader Scandinavian foundation for the publication. If this has not been realized, the reason is that the specific background is the development and treatment of the theories of marketing in Denmark. Thus, the list of authors includes only the names of Danish researchers who have been members of the staff of the Marketing Institute in Copenhagen, or have otherwise been associated with our Institute. There is but one exception to this: an article by the Finnish Professor *Gösta Mickwitz* has been included. Mickwitz's aticle which was published in our periodical, contains an evaluation of the influence exerted by the "Copenhagen School" on the theory of marketing in the Scandinavian countries.

[8]

COMPARATIVE MARKETING: THE FIRST TWENTY-FIVE YEARS[1]

JEAN J. BODDEWYN*
Baruch College

Abstract: This article reviews the field of Comparative Marketing in terms of scope, types, and depth of studies; methodological issues, conceptual and managerial payoffs, and teaching approaches. After its first quarter of a century as an international business topic, Comparative Marketing is still relatively green.

■ It has been fifteen years since Cox [1965] and Shapiro [1965] provided the first reviews of the then emerging field of comparative marketing.[2] This research and teaching area really started developing in the early 1950s; and most of its now out-of-print texts and books of readings by Bartels [1963], Carson [1967], Sommers and Kernan [1968], and Boddewyn [1969] were written in the 1960s. It is time to have another look at this field which now celebrates its silver anniversary and which remains most relevant for marketing theory and practice.

The 1965 Cox and Shapiro reviews were extensive, perceptive, and almost prophetic. Since they remain largely valid and well worth re-reading, several of their leading questions are used here.[3]

THE FIELD

Comparative marketing (CM) is about the systematic detection, identification, classification, measurement, and interpretation of similarities and differences among entire national systems or parts thereof [Boddewyn, 1969, p. 2; Jaffe, 1976 and 1980].[4] Cox and Shapiro saw in comparative marketing the potential for enriching our understanding of what marketing is all about (the marketing theory question par excellence) and of what forms it assumes in different national environments. It would also help refine marketing concepts, models, hypotheses, and theories [Wind and Douglas, 1980]. Such knowledge would have obvious international-marketing-management implications for the growing number of U.S. firms going abroad — a point also stressed by a contemporary Marketing Science Institute study urging the grouping of countries in terms of similarities [Liander et al., 1967].

Thus, conceptual frameworks, models, and theories developed in one setting assume a general character if found applicable in a variety of environments. Alternatively, they may be invalidated for being "culture-specific" and have to be modified to distinguish between what Cox [1965] has called universals discovered everywhere, limited generalizations found among particular countries only, and specific differences unique to some nations. [See also Boddewyn, 1966 and 1969]. For international marketing managers, comparative studies help identify common market segments which invite similar strategies or warn against such an approach because of significant differences.

The following sections analyze key issues, problems, and achievements in CM research and present major findings and conclusions. It was not possible to go into details in view of the vastness of the literature; nor are all relevant studies considered here since some of them were already analyzed in previous reviews.

---

*Jean J. Boddewyn is Professor of Marketing/International Business at Baruch College, City University of New York. His Ph.D. is from the University of Washington. Recent research interests have centered on international business-government relations, external affairs, MNC divestment, and advertising regulation.

TYPES OF COMPARATIVE STUDIES Macro comparisons of entire marketing systems or major parts thereof (for example, "Retailing in Mexico and the United States") are mostly institutional and descriptive without any explicit conceptual framework or underlying hypotheses so that the findings are hard to interpret. [See, however, Boddewyn and Hollander, 1972]. The obvious is usually compared (number of households and stores, education, per capita income), but the lack of comparable data often prevents or impairs generalizations. By and large, *differences* are uncovered and emphasized, with the contrasts being larger when the countries chosen differ considerably (for example, a developed vs. an underdeveloped one). This suggests that various variables— level of economic development for instance—be controlled in order to improve such studies which are relatively rare nowadays.

Micro CM studies, on the other hand, have dealt mainly with consumer behavior and segments: shopping [Green and Langeard, 1975; Douglas, 1976], innovator characteristics [Green and Langeard, 1975], female role perception [Douglas, 1976; and Douglas and Urban, 1977], media usage [Douglas, 1976], family buying decisions [Hempel, 1974; Green and Cunningham, 1980], life styles [Douglas and Urban, 1976; Plummer, 1977], information seekers [Thorelli et al., 1975; Becker, 1976], attitudes toward advertising [Anderson et al., 1978], reactions to product attributes [Green et al., 1976], media preferences [Urban, 1977], perceptions of foreign products [for example, Nagashima, 1970; Reader's Digest, 1970], risk aversion [Hoover, 1978], fashion involvement [Tigert et al., 1980], repeat-buying behavior [Ehrenberg and Goodhardt, 1968], and product evaluation by industrial buyers [Lehmann and O'Shoughnessy, 1974]—among others.

The emphasis in micro studies is more on uncovering *similarities* since the researchers are frequently testing abroad relational hypotheses developed in the United States (for example, between education and information-seeking behavior) for the purpose of uncovering comparable market segments in terms of lifestyle and other grouping factors. The facts that (1) most of these replicated studies deal with developed countries (that is, the United States and Western Europe); and (2) they focus on particular market segments, (such as innovators, working wives) also lead to uncovering similarities among countries in lieu of the national differences otherwise observed among undifferentiated average consumers.

THE SCOPE OF CM STUDIES From early general comparisons of the "Marketing in Country X" type, CM studies have come to encompass more specialized segments (for example, wholesaling, supermarkets, public policy) as well as many aspects of consumer behavior (lifestyle, satisfaction).[5] On the other hand, comparative-marketing scholars suffer from limited access to "foreign" sources of information; they read for the most part English-language publications, and they usually miss relevant publications outside of their ken. This has led to CM studies being limited to a dozen countries.

For one thing, the field of marketing itself is vast and segmented into sub-areas of specialization (for example retailing, consumer behavior, strategy making); this impedes a comprehensive view of marketing. Furthermore, perusing the multiple FAO/UN *Bibliography of Food and Agricultural Marketing* (in LDCs) makes one realize how many non-marketing sources there are, how few of them are readily available to and read by marketing scholars, and how we tend to ignore the marketing of commodities and of products not found in developed countries. For example, how many of us are even aware of the 1979 Australian study, "Corned Beef and Tapioca: A Report on the Food Distribution Systems in Tonga?"

The ignorance of foreign and non-marketing sources tends to create an ethnocentric bias manifested by a focus on middle-class consumers and on marketing-manager problems as found in high-consumption societies [Arndt, 1978; Dholakia and Firat, 1980]. Clearly, the search must be expanded for concepts, facts, and theories that transcend such country, class, and product limitations.[6]

There is general agreement that comparison is about similarities and differences since this is true by definition. The disagreement is more about how far the analysis should go. On the one hand, many authors readily accept that comparisons properly include purely descriptive elements — for example, comparing the relative proportion of small vs. large retailers, the functions of the wholesaler, and the purchasing habits of consumers in various countries. Bartels [1968], on the other hand, has stressed that the proper focus of the comparative approach is on the relationships between such marketing elements and various environmental factors that may explain them. Figure 1 adapted from Bartels illustrates the difference.

I have argued and still maintain that comparative marketing can deal with (A) and (B) alone as well as with (E), while Bartels insists that (E) is the proper domain of this discipline:

> The comparison of marketing in two countries . . . is simply a descriptive statement, not an analytical one. . . The relationships [between marketing and its environment], on the other hand, are statements of *environmentalism* . . . Comparative study is not simply a description of either marketing or environmental differences but rather a *comparison of relationships between marketing and its environment in two or more countries* [Bartels, 1968, p. 59].

Bartels' emphasis on these relationships is understandable in view of his long and deep interest in marketing theory which focuses on patterns, correlations and causes-and-effects. Shapiro [1965] also argued in favor of explanations because the similarities uncovered in a number of countries — such as, the combination of high-margin and low-volume policies in retailing — may not be due to a homogeneous set of underlying conditions. In the same vein, Douglas [1976] points out that the attitudinal and behavioral similarities and differences found among U.S. and French housewives may be due to differing product and channel availabilities rather than to cultural factors. More generally, Przeworski and Teune [1970] have commented that in comparative studies: "Systems differ not when the frequency of particular characteristics differ, but when the patterns of the relationships among variables differs (p. 45)."

Still, I believe that *the common deprecation of "descriptive" or "positive" studies ignores the usefulness of reliable facts as a basis for further investigation and as*

THE DEPTH OF COMPARATIVE STUDIES

FIGURE 1

What to Compare in Comparative-Marketing Studies

Source: Adapted from Bartels [1968].

a guide to action — at least in a field as young as comparative marketing where some critical mass of data must be obtained before conceptualization and theorizing can take place. After all, nobody rejected the comparative data provided by Kinsey on the sexual behavior of U.S. males and females because he did not explain why men had more premarital sex than women at a time when this kind of information was sorely missing. Similarly, knowing that French housewives spend more time shopping, examining items on shelves, and listening to the opinions of retailers than their U.S. counterparts who make greater use of television commercials and magazine ads to obtain similar information [Green and Langeard, 1975] constitutes valuable information even if we do not understand why they act that way. Such findings have practical implications as when these two researchers concluded that: "It is easier therefore to presell the U.S. housewife, whereas discounts to distributors and point-of-purchase displays are more important in France."[7]

This being said in favor of descriptive comparisons, it remains that *CM studies are frequently disappointing in terms of theorizing.* To start with, very few studies were designed to test relationships between some marketing phenomenon and particular properties of the societal system [Arndt et al., 1980]. Besides, as Van Raaij [1978] points out, alternative hypotheses are seldom considered [see however, Silverman and Hill, 1967]. Furthermore, uncovered similarities and differences often beg for deeper cultural and structural explanations than sucn elementary classificatory data as income and education [Arndt, 1978] — but more about this later.

Still, according to Wind and Douglas [1980], comparative consumer research has been helpful in clarifying the role of various *mediating variables* which both reflect and are part of the environmental context: (1) composition of the buying unit; (2) dominant value sets (such as modernity and ecological concern); (3) the retail structure (for example, number and size of stores, and interaction with store personnel); and (4) communication networks (mass-media availability).

METHOD-OLOGICAL ISSUES
The Use of Conceptual Frameworks

Various conceptual frameworks were presented in the 1960s for the comparison of entire marketing systems or at least as guidelines for research: Bartel's "marketing and its environment" scheme [1963]; Boddewyn's "actor-process-structure-function-environment" construct [1966 and 1969]; Cox' "flow approach" [1965]; and Fisk's "system" view [1967]. There is also the Sheth and Sethi [1973] "theory of cross-cultural buyer behavior" which is really an elaboration of the Rogers and Shoemaker [1971] adoption model with some indication of how to measure the relevant variables.

While some of these comprehensive shopping lists have received their due acknowledgements in footnotes and bibliographies and have probably influenced the teaching and learning of many scholars and students, their explicit use in research has been almost nil except perhaps in Bartels' volume on wholesaling [1967] and in the Boddewyn-Hollander compendium of analyses of national public policies toward retailing [1972] where some of the contributors used an "actor-process-structure-function-environment" framework.

Shapiro had already warned in 1965 against the practical impossibility of analyzing and comparing "total" marketing systems — not to mention an explanation à la Bartels of all the uncovered similarities and differences — and his prediction proved correct. In fact, the most common conceptual framework has been the traditional "4-Ps" when comparing the marketing policies of foreign subsidiaries vs. those of domestic firms [Kacker, 1972; Chong, 1973]. As far as consumer behavior is concerned, researchers have usually replicated U.S. studies abroad, typically using whatever research design, hypotheses, and instruments had been developed for the original study. On the other hand, the compendia of international statistics about the number and evolution of retailing and wholesaling institutions compiled by various national and supranational bodies have not utilized any conceptual framework at all.[8]

If scholars have not used these conceptual frameworks, neither have practitioners: "Prominent by its absence in appraising transferability (of marketing/advertising practices) is cross-cultural theory. The decision-makers came through mainly as pragmatists." [Dunn, 1976].

I do not think that the immediate need is for new conceptual frameworks but rather for greater discipline on the part of researchers to make explicit the one they are using; and dissertation advisers as well as book and article reviewers should be more demanding in that respect. In any case, the breadth of individual comparative studies is likely to remain narrow because of the complexity of comparing even a small part of whole systems. In commenting upon the first draft of this paper, Johan Arndt remarked that: "We cannot afford to wait for a comprehensive (comparative) scheme. Such a scheme, if it is ever developed, cannot be much less than a complex theory of marketing (or macro-marketing). For the time being, we have to work closer to the ground at the level of low- or middle-range conceptualizations." His suggestion seems to make sense.

Meanwhile, one can deplore the fact that there has been too much opportunism resulting in piecemeal research that does not "add up" but simply replicates abroad what is familiar and/or fashionable at home.

Cox [1965] deplored the lackadaisical attitude of many comparative researchers who simply assumed that such statistical categories as wholesalers, retailers, and supermarkets were identical and, therefore, comparable when, for example, the role of wholesalers differs considerably between the United States and Japan where their financial role is much more predominant and explains their captaincy of many channels. This is, of course, the classical problem of conceptual and functional[9] equivalence in cross-national research [Davis et al., 1980; Green and White, 1976; Van Raaij, 1978; Green and Langeard, 1979; Wind and Douglas, 1980] even if there are no simple ways of avoiding shortcuts and mistakes in this area:

Institutional Comparisons

> From a theoretical viewpoint, mere comparison of consumer responses to questionnaire items in different cultures does not guarantee meaningful and useful information for theoretical purposes and for managerial action. Functional (or conceptual) equivalence of constructs and instruments has to be established in order to guarantee "real" cross-cultural comparison. Plausible rival hypotheses that also explain the obtained differences/similarities have to be ruled out by using equivalent samples and functionally equivalent measures and quantification modes [Van Raaij, 1978, p. 700].

One cannot say that much progress has been made in this area since nations continue to collect their statistics in varying ways. At best, the major international comparisons [OECD, 1973; and U.K. National Economic Development Office, 1973] have carefully noted in footnotes and appendixes the differences in reporting systems and warned their readers against superficial comparisons and hasty conclusions.

Besides, institutional comparisons seldom explore in any depth what, for example, a French wholesaler in frozen foods specifically does in terms of bridging the space, time, perception, evaluation and ownership "separations" that form the substance of the marketing task. Detailed analysis of the sort is available only in relatively unknown articles, monographs, and dissertations such as Jaffe's [1969] analysis of four commodity-distribution systems in Israel, using a "flow" (of possession, title, risk, information, money) approach à la Cox.

Still, some recent analyses of foreign marketing systems offer richer analyses, comparisons, and interpretations in contrast to the more superficial treatments that prevailed in the 1950s and 1960s. Thus, Shimaguchi and Lazer's study [1979] of Japanese distribution channels provides a sound understanding of some of the crucial differences between Japan and the United States (for example, why there are relatively more Japanese wholesalers, and how wholesaling tasks differ in both countries). The cooperation of scholars from these two countries helps explain the quality of this analysis (some bi-cultural scholars such as Michael Yoshino have been equally successful) and reminds us of the futility of many impressionistic reports from monocultural traveling scholars. Here, the lack of research funds, the increased cost of foreign travel, and the stricter requirements of academic journals have certainly contributed to the decline of the "quickie" surveys which Foreign Trade or Commerce Departments around the world can perform just as well if not better in their "Marketing Conditions in Country X" reports.

Consumer-Behavior Comparisons

Recent cross-cultural studies based on cognitive consistency theory have concluded that:

> People do utilize a number of judgment continua that are related to each other in roughly comparable ways across the cultures studied so far. People from different cultures combine simple stimuli to make complex judgments in roughly similar ways. On the other hand, they do utilize different weights for various characteristics [H. C. Triandis as quoted in Klippel and Boewadt, 1974, p. 40].

Since these weights reflect the impact of culture,[10] the cross-cultural research agenda is to devise ways of: (1) ascertaining the cultural values that are relevant in a particular marketing situation; and (2) measuring the association of these cultural values with attitudes toward particular products, promotional appeals, etc. For example, in the case of an instant cake mix, one would compare: (1) the satisfaction derived from leisure time in different countries; and (2) the extent to which target groups in these countries associate instant cake mixes with the attainment of leisure time [Klippel and Boewadt, 1974, p. 42].

This proposed research strategy sounds simple but even industrialized countries exhibit significant cultural differences [Katona et al., 1971]. Besides, target groups are not always obvious, nor is their behavior necessarily identical. Thus, Thorelli and Becker [1975 and 1980] have identified similar groups of information seekers in the United States and Germany, but they do not share identical attitudes on all counts. In the same vein, Douglas and Urban [1977] point out that demographic segments, such as teenagers and working wives, may not exhibit similar behavior patterns across countries. Even similar life-style and attitudinal segments (for example, liberated working wives) do not necessarily behave similarly because much depends on their position relative to dominant cultural norms: what is considered avant-garde behavior in one country may be common somewhere else so that liberated working women in two countries may end up buying or using very different products (for example, prepared vs. unprepared foods). This illustrates the importance of considering *mediating variables* in comparative research [Wind and Douglas, 1980].

Besides, several factors may be needed to explain consumer behavior differences among countries. For example, hand-to-mouth shopping by housewives may be due to such structural (stage of economic development) elements as the absence of refrigeration facilities although preference for personal relations with neighborhood stores — a cultural factor — may also be an important factor [Holton, 1960; Kuznets, 1968; Goldman, 1974; Arndt et al., 1979]. In another case, Maddox et al. [1978] found similar patterns of relationships between information gathering and evoked set size for new-automobile purchasers in Norway and the United States. Norwegian respondents, however, generally reported higher levels or intensity of information search, which seems consistent with known structural differences between the two countries (for example, Norwegians had to commit a much higher proportion of their income to buying a car). *One-variable research must thus be considered suspect in CM research.*

Better qualified people than I can comment on the appropriateness of various statistical methods in comparative research because my own work has been mainly conceptual and institutional. Still, I am appalled by the cross-cultural mileage given to small convenience samples from one city in two or more countries (50 to 200 respondents per country are common; 1,000 to 2,000 are rare), carefully massaged by sophisticated statistical manipulations. **Statistical Analyses**

For instance, what are we to make of a comparison of a convenience sample of, say, 100 U.S. housewives in Peoria with 100 French ones in Nice to test the relationship between anxiety traits and the use of information sources — not to mention that such an article may be titled "What Makes French and U.S. Consumers Different?" Since no attempt is made to prove that these two cities are really representative of the United States and France, are we really getting closer to understanding the differences between these two countries — or are we simply going through a futile exercise possibly even less enlightening and more misleading than the old "Marketing in Country X" studies? It appears that analytical techniques designed for large random samples are too often used with a make-believeness that does not seem to faze journal reviewers and editors although some researchers are more careful and candid than others.

This small nonrandom sample problem is not unique to cross-national comparative studies for sure. However, the danger to be mistaken is greater here because the comparer usually has less knowledge and feel for the representativeness of his/her foreign convenience samples as well as for the validity of his/her interpretation of the findings, notwithstanding the disclaimer that it is only an "exploratory" study to be interpreted with care. Indeed, most comparative studies should be modestly entitled "A Comparison of a Small Convenience Sample of Manhattan and Parisian Middle-Class Women" rather than "What Makes U.S. and French Consumers Different!"

At the other end of the spectrum are the larger-scale media and market surveys sponsored by such publications as *Newsweek*, the *Reader's Digest* and *Time* or conducted in an omnibus fashion for a number of manufacturers or advertisers by international market-research firms. These studies can cover a dozen countries and thousands of respondents in a somewhat more sophisticated manner, including better sampling [for good examples, see Linton and Broadbent, 1975; and Plummer, 1977].

The only practical ways out of the small-sample quandary is: (1) to use multinational research teams to improve research design and interpretation; (2) to tack a few supplementary questions of academic interest to large-scale international surveys of a more commercial type, and/or (3) to recycle the findings of these large surveys to test various relationships among the data already available [Douglas and Urban, 1977; Arndt et al., 1979]. On the other hand, the usual appeal for large-scale, multicountry, multidisciplinary and multinational cross-cultural research keeps butting against the frustrating question of: "Where will the money come from in these recessionary and budget-cutting times?"

Two other methodological problems deserve more attention. One concerns *the level of statistical significance required to establish similarity* [Klippel and Boewadt, 1974, p. 44] since complete identicalness is never found. The other is that *causality is not always obvious*: do different consumer attitudes and behavior reflect different retail structures in two countries (for example, there are more small stores in France than in the United States) — or is it vice versa [Douglas, 1976; Van Raaij, 1978]? Macro-marketing studies (discussed next) are more ready to investigate both directionalities, and CM scholars should emulate them.

THE PAYOFF OF CM STUDIES
Conceptual Development

Comparative studies should help refine our understanding of marketing. Here, CM scholars tend to agree that the "marketing" compared among nations should be broadly conceived as a "social" process and as an institution that has numerous dimensions and ramifications as well as multiple connections with the broader environment (physical, economic, political, social, cultural, technological) with which it interacts.

This perspective blends in well with the more recent macro-marketing studies which focus on interpreting "exchange activities and exchange systems from a societal perspective" in lieu of the common marketing-research focus on individual choice processes [Shawver and Nickels, 1978, p. 41]. These studies—sometimes comparative and now available through proceedings [Slater, 1976; White and Slater, 1977; Fisk and Nason, 1978; and Fisk, Nason and White, 1979] and through the *Journal of Macro-Marketing*—will not be analyzed here, but they should be used to refocus the discussion of what constitutes "marketing" in different societies. Their emphasis on the two-way interaction between marketing and society should also prove helpful.[11]

This brings us back to an issue raised by Cox [1965]:

> To what extent are we justified in supposing that there is anything to compare?...Can we assume that marketing as a social process is itself a universal about which we can make generalizations applicable to all the societies...or even to any considerable number of societies? [p. 146 in Boddewyn, 1969].

In other words, does "marketing" really exist in such centrally planned economies as the U.S.S.R. or in the "peasant" societies of Bhutan and Niger? Cox was right to criticize other scholars for glossing over this conceptual issue:

> They do not tell us what systems can be considered equivalent to marketing although they are not marketing; what systems are substitutes for marketing; and the circumstances, if any, under which neither marketing, nor its equivalent, nor substitutes for it can be said to exist [ibid., p. 147].

This is a crucial issue, but I am puzzled by the fact that in addressing it neither Cox nor most other comparative-marketing scholars make reference to the excellent conceptual work of historians, anthropologists, and sociologists such as Polanyi [1957] and Smelser [1963, 1976].[12] The latter have classified exchange systems whose existence is universal because of the existence of scarcity and of division of labor in all societies, large or small, old or new. However, societies variously emphasize reciprocity (tradition), redistribution (command) and self-regulation (bargaining à la market system) as the prime ways of bridging the separations between suppliers and demanders. In this perspective, U.S. marketing is a representative of the self-regulatory type of exchange system even though some facets of U.S. exchange also partake of the reciprocative (for example, the discharge of obligations among relatives and friends) and redistributive (for example, transfer payments of the social–security type) modes of exchange.

Here, I can only recommend that comparative-marketing scholars go back to such sources—just as management academics quote their Max Weber about the nature of bureaucracy. This suggests, of course, that the very appellation "Comparative *Marketing* Systems" is erroneous and should be replaced by "Comparative *Exchange* Systems"—a trend that will be nurtured by macro-marketing studies [see also Baggozi, 1975; Hunt, 1976].

In any case, few CM scholars have devoted themselves to this issue although it is worth observing the emergence of comparative studies focusing on marketing forms intermediate between state-controlled and market-dominated ones. Thus, Arndt [1979] uses the concept of domesticated marketing to refer to such cooperative ventures as franchising, voluntary chains, and marketing boards [Izraeli and Zif, 1977] where many transactions are negotiated and controlled within a long-lasting "internal market" rather than left to the vagaries of competition or to government mandate.

Still, CM research has not yet contributed enough to our understanding of what "marketing" is all about, and much remains to be done here (for a thoughtful discussion of this topic, see Dholakia, 1980; and Dholakia and Firat, 1980).

Besides their theoretical payoff, comparative-marketing studies should lead to the uncovering of actionable similarities and differences. Here, Douglas [1976] makes the interesting point that marketing practitioners are more interested in similarities because they look for new foreign markets easy to penetrate since they are alike, while scholars are equally concerned about differences.

Managerial Applications

Practitioners, however, will not find easy answers in scholarly CM studies since some of them conclude that similarities predominate [Hempel, 1974; Thorelli et al., 1975; Becker, 1976] while others deduce the opposite [Douglas, 1976; Urban, 1975]. This disparity partly reflects different research focuses in terms of market segment, product, attitude, and behavior. The use of universal ("etic") concepts also increases the risk of overemphasizing similarities [Wind and Douglas, 1980]. Besides, as Douglas [1976, p. 12] points out, superficial comparisons tend not only to emphasize differences (rather than similarities) between countries but also to minimize the importance of differences in behavior patterns within a country.

For example, what are managers to make of a study showing that U.S., Brazilian, French and Indian consumers (small convenience student samples at that) differ in terms of the attributes (for example, taste and low price) they use to evaluate soft drinks and toothpaste [Green and Cunningham, 1975]? Superficially, such differences suggest different promotional approaches, but do they really? After all, some perceived product differences do not necessarily suggest different advertising strategies since some superarching theme could possibly be devised that transcends such differences. Moreover, the uncovered differences in preferences are not integrated into some broader cultural or life-style analysis which may cast a different light on their meaning. Nor are the respondents sufficiently broken down into segments which may reveal similar target groups in these countries. (For additional relevant comments, see the critique by S. F. J. Unwin, following the Green and Cunningham article).

Still, comparative studies do have implications for international marketers. If, for example, UK and U.S. female consumers differ significantly in their attitudes toward the home, then home-related U.S. products and promotions must be carefully reviewed before extension is attempted in the British market [Urban, 1975]. Besides, there is growing evidence that reaching average consumers requires more marketing adaptations than in the case of the more sophisticated information seekers who represent a fairly homogeneous market across developed countries [Thorelli and Becker, 1980].

Meanwhile, international firms have not left it entirely to scholars to come up with actionable comparative findings. A good illustration of how business firms use cross-cultural research is provided by Linton and Broadbent [1975] and Plummer [1977].[13] They use relatively large national samples to study: (1) life styles; (2) media usage and preferences; (3) product utilization, attitudes, and preferences; and (4) attitudes and behavior regarding such promotional devices as coupons. Three basic analytical models are developed for national analysis and cross-national comparisons: (1) shared cultural norms (for example, traditionalism); (2) market segments with homogeneous life styles as related to such variables as urbanization; and (3) correlates of usage (such as, heavy beer drinking with risk taking and pleasure seeking).

OTHER CM
RESEARCH
Consumption
Studies

Besides the micro studies previously reviewed, there are a few studies that analyze the overall evolution of consumption (rather than consumers) in various countries, often using the U.S. pattern as a reference point. For example, Ragone [1978] presents an interesting sociological classification of types of Italian consumer expenditures (standard package, physical and cultural continuity, status, and integrative purchases); while Kuznets [1966], Katona et al. [1971] and Musgrove [1978] have studied national differences in consumption expenditures. In a recent paper, Dholakia and Firat [1980] deplore the overemphasis on individual choice processes among brand objects, which ignores social choices and consumption modes (not just expenditure patterns) which are more socially significant than brand buying. Hence, they recommend greater study of consumption-formation patterns at the social level in various countries.

Market Groupings

Goodnow [1972], Ramond [1974] and Sethi [1971] have elaborated on the original Marketing Science Institute study [Liander, Terpstra, Yoshino and Sherbini, 1967] designed to determine what countries do cluster and therefore provide fairly homogenous targets for international marketers.

This kind of macro research is useful for market-entry and performance-control purposes, but is not per se aimed at providing an understanding of foreign marketing systems. Besides, this clustering is often meaningless for international managers when one realizes how the Scandinavian countries, which usually group well on the basis of the commonly used socio-economico-political indicators, differ significantly when the marketing of a particular product, such as suntan lotion, is considered [Johnsson, 1974]. Clearly, more micro variables should be used in lieu of the rather gross elements (population, income, education) typically used. Still, such groupings can be used for research purpose in selecting comparable countries since meaningful comparisons can be made only between societies at similar levels of development [Van Raaij, 1978].

Distribution
Structure and
Economic
Development

The issue of the relationship between the state or evolution of distribution structures and various environmental factors, particularly economic development, has been alive at least since Clark [1940] and Rostow [1960] published their original hypotheses. Cundiff [1965] and Wadinambiaratchi [1965] largely corroborated this relationship together with the lag or stage hypothesis that underdeveloped distribution systems resemble that of the United States at earlier periods of U.S. development.

Douglas [1971], however, has challenged this view, concluding among other things that the development of marketing structure does not closely parallel that of the environment:

... channel structure and relationships depend primarily on the relative size of firms at different stages of the channel rather than on the country's level of development... The variations of firms within a country suggests that individual firms may respond in different ways and in varying degrees to environmental conditions (pp. 45 and 48).

She also pointed out that a study of the evolution of marketing structures over time in various countries may be more appropriate than a simultaneous comparative survey of countries at different levels of development.

Arndt [1972], however, provided renewed support for some correspondence between channel structure and GNP per capita as far as supermarkets in fairly socio-politically homogeneous countries are concerned. With such an important qualification, his conclusion may be accepted although Arndt recognizes that it is still a loose relation, and that factors other than GNP per capita also account for similarities and differences (for example, government policy toward retailing). The research of Goldman [1974] on the low outreach (spatial, informational, attitudinal) of certain types of consumers certainly supports such a major caveat about accepting simplistic comparative associations between marketing and its economic environment – a point already made by U.S. marketing historians.

Aside from product-ownership surveys conducted by such organizations as the Economist Intelligence Unit and the *Reader's Digest,* there are unfortunately too few studies of why countries lead or lag in the adoption of new products and services. Among those who tried, Shipchandler [1972] found that per capita income, standard of living, percentage of working population in nonagricultural work, and level of literacy generally correlate with unit sales of television sets, refrigerators and washing machines in a score of countries; and that the speed of adoption of certain durables can be forecast.   **Diffusion Studies**

Such studies are still very macro in nature as they tend to focus on broad economic indicators which cannot explain why washing machines preceded refrigerators in some comparable countires, and vice versa. This is a comparative area well worth developing.

The 1979 curriculum survey conducted by the Academy of International Business uncovered only six comparative-marketing courses in the United States (J. J. Boddewyn/Baruch; R. S. Wilkinson/Ferris State; J. Knutsen/Puget Sound; C. Reierson/Baylor; J. H. Walters/Temple; and Douglas/NYU), but there are a few overseas too, such as, A. J. Brown at Strathclyde, UK. Even allowing for nonresponse and nonreaching, this is a small number although it is supplemented by the numerous teachers who touch upon the topic in the context of other general, theoretical, and international-marketing and consumer-behavior courses.   **THE TEACHING OF COMPARATIVE MARKETING**

It is of course difficult to teach such a subject because there are no textbooks left, and because we have few good multicountry studies to use. There are some cases providing descriptive data on alternative markets, but they are not geared to providing a systematic analysis of foreign marketing systems – limiting themselves instead to comparing how razor blades, for example, are marketed and used in several countries (for instance, the Gillette International cases).

At the system level, the comparative-marketing teacher must usually work with single country studies and use them to draw comparisons with the U.S. situation (or any other reference point), and to focus on explaining how features of the foreign marketing systems are linked to their environment. Actually, all of the approaches in Figure 1 can be used in comparative teaching. The same can be done with cases by pointing out how succeeding in a particular foreign market depends on determining the right adaptations that need to be made – but this is really more an international-marketing-management topic.

Comparative courses also typically include a review of the relevant conceptual frameworks. After that, most teachers choose from a variety of related topics, such as the role of marketing in economic development, the transferability of U.S. techniques, the desirability of introducing Western wants in LDCs, market grouping, and international marketing research – very much the topics already reviewed by Shapiro in 1965.

In view of these limitations, of the lack of trained teachers, and of the out-of-print state of textbooks and books of readings in this area, it is unlikely that the number of comparative courses will multiply. It seems more probable that comparative marketing will grow mostly through greater inclusion in international-marketing and, to a lesser extent, in marketing-theory courses.

Here, it would appear desirable to have a new or revised international-marketing text include a comparative-marketing scholar as co-author in order to replace the fairly conventional introductory chapters on the economic, political, social, cultural and legal environments of marketing with a more integrated comparison-cum-management approach.[14] Better still would be a basic marketing text written from an international and comparative perspective instead of a purely U.S. one—as is the common practice. In other words, U.S. marketing would be treated only as a subspecies of the genus "exchange."

SUGGESTIONS FOR FURTHER CM RESEARCH

Previous sections have already pointed out fruitful avenues for research as well as better ways of conducting comparative studies. Additional suggestions are in order, however.

The search for national consumer-behavior patterns should probably be held in abeyance for a while. Because there is so much heterogeneity within each nation, comparative studies will have to focus on the identification of comparable *segments*, such as, status-conscious consumers or information seekers, among countries rather than on what makes—say—*all* French and U.S. consumers different. As one anonymous reviewer pointed out:

> Comparisons of well-matched samples from two or more countries can provide interesting insights and, more importantly, provide some basis for future hypotheses as the field continues to develop. At the current level of development, researchers need some base on which to expand the knowledge and theory in this area.

In this context, Douglas and Urban [1977] have made useful suggestions to refine concepts such as life-style, to extend comparative studies to countries at comparable levels of economic and cultural development (market-grouping research should prove useful here), and to analyze how particular products are embedded in the life-style of similar target markets. There is also need to study more precisely the link between values, attitudes, and behavior instead of assuming that similarity at one level leads to similarity at the others.

Beyond consumer studies, another chance should be given to the comparison of major segments of marketing systems. Cox [1965] did not say so directly, but his plea for the study of flows of physical goods, authority over them, communications, payments, and risks amounted to a return to the commodity approach with which the study of U.S. marketing started around the turn of the century. It is from such analyses of the marketing of grain and other commodities that our concepts of function, institution, and policies emerged.

Therefore, I venture to say that a major mistake was made at the outset of comparative studies when we failed to make more comparisons of how grain, steel, automobiles, canned soups, life-insurance policies, etc. were marketed in various countries. The original Marketing Science Institute started work in that direction, but the output was limited [Douglas, 1971], and it found few if any emulators. There have also been too few functional and institutional comparisons although this is less true in the case of retailing [Cundiff, 1965; Boddewyn and Hollander, 1972].

The commodity, functional, and institutional approaches have long ceased to be glamorous; but by largely ignoring them we may have tried to run before we learned to walk. For that matter, these approaches remain of interest to practitioners who need to understand how their goods are distributed in other countries compared to the situation at home. Hence, a call for their academic resurrection in comparative-marketing studies may well be in order. While the question "Will marketing journals and publishers accept such studies?" can reasonably be raised, we can try to publish them in FAO-type journals if necessary.

A fruitful starting point for such studies would be the different prices charged for identical branded products in several countries (see the Gillette International cases, for example). This would require analyzing all sorts of societal and institutional variables in the search for explanations [see Elimelech, 1980].

One sadly neglected area of CM studies has been the *output* of marketing/exchange systems. There is need to update the productivity studies made earlier [for example, Bucklin, 1976] and to strike out in new directions beyond economic measurements of marketing outputs — for example, the socio-cultural impact of marketing systems and innovations in terms of quality of life for consumers and of social mobility for petty traders. Comparative studies of consumer satisfaction are already underway, for that matter [Arndt, Barksdale and Perreault, 1980]; while the whole issue of the role (positive and negative) of marketing in economic development deserves re-examination [see Dholakia, 1980].

Another area worthy of more comparative research is that of *marketing actors* [Boddewyn, 1966 and 1969] in terms of number, sex, age, background, attitudes, prestige and the like — as is frequently done in comparative-management studies. We know far too little about "who" engages in wholesaling, retailing, personal selling, advertising and so on.

CONCLUSIONS

Cox and Shapiro were both wary and hopeful when they analyzed the state of comparative studies in the early 1960s. On the one hand, they were aware of the real theoretical and practical difficulties connected with valid comparisons. Yet, they hoped that we would learn from our mistakes and do better.

Fifteen years later, their hopes remain largely unfulfilled. A perusal of marketing and consumer-behavior texts reveals little integration of cross-cultural comparative findings in terms of defining marketing and of analyzing its multiple forms. Even the now usual chapter on the impact of culture on consumer behavior and marketing policies does not go much beyond: (1) recognizing the importance of this important market-segmentation variable; and (2) recounting various marketing blunders abroad.[15]

What went wrong with comparative-marketing research? The simplest answer is probably the correct one — namely, that the methodological and financing difficulties have remained huge and that no genius has appeared who could cut through them to come up with major theoretical breakthroughs — but what business discipline has? Lack of consensus about purpose and methodology has also hampered progress.

Additionally, comparative marketing has not gained enough attention nor received much support in academic circles; and the American Marketing Association has repeatedly wavered in its recognition of international marketing. So, why study or research comparative topics if the rewards lie elsewhere?[16]

This is not to say that no advances have been made at all. The fact that "culture" (whatever the author means by it) is now recognized as a major marketing variable represents progress. Besides, the standardization vs. adaptation issue discussed in all international-marketing textbooks [for example, Terpstra, 1978] embodies in a concrete manner the contingency approach ("It all depends") based on the recognition of national and subnational similarities and differences — the very stuff of comparative marketing. Moreover, there have been interesting debates and research pieces which, if nothing else, have probed the limits and limitations of comparative marketing and have provided bases for further progress.

Therefore, we are not in trouble nor should we feel useless or impotent even though the agenda remains about as heavy as it was fifteen years ago. Some good trees and even patches stand up already but we are still a long way from seeing the forest![17]

FOOTNOTES

1. The following scholars provided helpful comments and suggestions for the revision of the original draft: J. C. Abbott (FAO, Rome); John Arndt (Bergen, Norway); Helmut Becker (Portland); Susan Douglas (NYU); S. Watson Dunn (Missouri-Columbia), A. A. El-Sherbini (In-

ternational Fund for Agricultural Development, Rome); George Fisk (Syracuse); Stanley C. Hollander (Michigan State); Dov izraeli (Tel-Aviv, Israel); Eugene D. Jaffə (Bar-Ilan, Israel); H. J. Mittendorf (FAO, Rome); Leon Schiffman (Baruch College); Stanley J. Shapiro (McGill); Helmut Soldner (Augsburg); and J. Hart Walters (Temple). Four anonymous reviewers were also most helpful.

2. For other reviews, see Demetrescu [1976]; Jaffe [1976]; and Douglas and Dubois [1977]. It is worth noting that Mulvihill's bibliography on foreign marketing systems has not been updated since 1966 but some relevant references can be found in Hanssens [1980] and Lorimor [1979]. Another review paper with very useful recommendations for research methodology has just been issued in draft form by Wind and Douglas [1980].

3. Left out are Shapiro's very relevant discussions of the relationships between marketing and economic development, the exportability of U.S. marketing techniques, and the stimulation of consumer wants in less-developed countries.

4. Comparative marketing also encompasses temporal (historical) and sub-national contrasts within the same country, but this dimension is usually subsumed under "domestic" marketing studies, and not discussed here. One interesting international aspect of the historical approach is the discussion of "lags" in the development of marketing systems as when people say: "Luxemburger advertising stands now where the United States was ten years ago." Another comparative focus is that of contrasting "headquarters" and "field" attitudes and practices as far as the development of multinational marketing policies is concerned, but this is more a "management" than a "marketing" topic since it deals essentially with the coordination problems of large enterprises rather than with a comparison of marketing systems.

5. There are very few comparisons of marketing management and personnel, as is common in comparative-management studies.

6. Fortunately, more Europeans (for example, Van Raaij and Arndt) are now writing on comparative-marketing topics and exposing us to other conceptual frameworks, methodologies and data; and Japanese studies are becoming more available too. Still, the impetus keeps coming from developed nations, and we know very little of what is done by scholars in less-developed countries.

7. For further discussion of the purpose, scope and methodology of comparative studies, see Wind and Douglas [1971], Jaffe [1976 and 1980] and Van Raaij [1978].

8. Kuznets [1968] and Preston [1968] have also made interesting comparative interpretations of the place of trade in the economy in terms of value added and employment. For productivity studies, see Bucklin [1976] as well as the older studies by Margaret Hall et al. [1961] and J. B. Jefferys et al. [1954] already reviewed by Cox [1965].

9. *Functional* equivalence of instruments for measuring a certain construct is a *validity* problem, while *formal* equivalence refers to identical questionnaire items. It appears that linguistic and conceptual equivalence in cross-national surveys is more difficult than for demographic and other background variables [Davis et al., 1980].

10. Culture is an elusive concept. For our purpose, it is probably best defined in terms of: (1) fundamental beliefs/values, (2) more superficial attitudes/opinions, and (3) habits/customs — all learned and shared by a significant proportion of a population. Other scholars, however, subsume the entire environment under that concept so that "cultural" becomes synonymous with "national." In any case, there is a co-relationship between culture and other environmental factors (physical, economic, political, social, etc.). For an excellent analysis of the relationship between consumption, culture and other environmental factors, see Smelser (1976).

11. As was mentioned before, most comparative studies look for explanation in the environment but seldom explore the impact of marketing and consumer behavior on it [see Douglas, 1976; Van Raaij, 1978].

12. There are many more anthropologists deserving mention such as Alice Dewey, Paul Bohannan and George Dalton.

13. The Linton-Broadbent and Plummer studies emanated from the Leo Burnett advertising agency.

14. An interesting development here is the ongoing indigenization of U.S. textbooks in Canada, France, South Africa and Australia — among others. A study of how this was done may provide interesting comparative insights into what was left untouched and what concepts and data had to be substituted.

15. A common and objectionable limitation of such chapters or sections is to label any *national* difference as "cultural" when it could equally be the effect of economic, social, physical or political factors. The Douglas-Dubois [1977] monograph on culture and consumer behavior is more careful in this respect; and they point out the need to sort out cultural influences from the impact of specific product and market situations as opposed to thinking in terms of describing entire cultural groups (for example, "the Mexican consumer"). Still,

Douglas and Dubois do not go much beyond recounting the anecdotal differences and market-segmentation implications already found in Carson's textbook [1967] as well as in numerous subsequent journal and magazine articles of the "Why Campbell Soup Bombed Out in England" type [see also Ricks et al., 1975].

16. The limited recognition granted comparative marketing is itself linked to the still restricted room accorded to international subjects in the business curriculum of many schools. In that context, comparative marketing assumes an even lower priority if not invisibility.

17. It is encouraging that a special 1981 issue of the *European Journal of Marketing* is scheduled to focus on comparative-marketing studies. For a recent example of the largely defunct type of "country" study, see: K. Kurtulus, "Marketing Channels in Turkey," *Management International Review*, X, 4/1980, pp. 38–46.

REFERENCES

Anderson, R. D.; Engledow, J. L.; and Becker, Helmut. "Advertising Attitudes in West Germany and the U.S.: An Analysis Over Age and Time." *Journal of International Business Studies*, Winter 1978, pp. 27–38.

Arndt, Johan. "Temporal Lags in Comparative Retailing." *Journal of Marketing*, October 1972, pp. 40–45.

_____. "Comments on Cross-Cultural Consumer Research." In H. K. Hunt, ed., *Advances in Consumer Research*, Vol. 5. Ann Arbor, MI: Association for Consumer Research, 1978, p. 705.

_____; Gronmo, Sigmund; and Hawes, D. K. "The Use of Time as an Expression of Life-Style: A Cross-National Study." Mimeographed. Bergen, Norway: Norwegian School of Economics and Business Administration, 1979. Forthcoming in *Research in Marketing*, Vol. 4, edited by J. N. Sheth.

_____. "Toward a Concept of Domesticated Markets." *Journal of Marketing*, Fall 1979, pp. 69–75.

_____; Barksdale, H. C.; and Perreault, W. D. "Comparative Study of Attitudes Toward Marketing, Consumerism, and Government Regulation: The United States vs. Norway and Venezuela." Mimeographed. Bergen, Norway: Norwegian School of Economics and Business Administration, 1980. Submitted to the *Journal of Marketing*.

Bagozzi, R. P. "Marketing as Exchange." *Journal of Marketing*, October 1975, pp. 32–39.

Bartels, Robert, ed. *Comparative Marketing: Wholesaling in Fifteen Countries*. Homewood, IL: Irwin, 1963.

_____. "Are Domestic and International Marketing Dissimilar?" *Journal of Marketing*, July 1968, pp. 56–61.

Becker, Helmut. "Is There a Cosmopolitan Information Seeker?" *Journal of International Business Studies*, Spring 1976, pp. 79–89.

Boddewyn, J. J. "A Construct for Comparative Marketing Research." *Journal of Marketing Research*, May 1966, pp. 149–153.

_____. *Comparative Management and Marketing*. Glenview, IL: Scott, Foresman & Co., 1969.

_____., Hollander, S.C., eds. *Public Policy Toward Retailing: An International Symposium*. Lexington, MA: Lexington Books, 1972.

Bucklin, L. P. "Trade Productivity: Comparison Between Japan and the USA." In Dov Izraeli et al., eds. *Marketing Systems for Developing Countries*. New York: Wiley, 1976, pp. 101–10.

Carson, David. "Comparative Marketing: A New-Old Aid." *Harvard Business Review*, May–June 1967, pp. 22 ff.

_____. *International Marketing: A Comparative Systems Approach*. New York: Wiley, 1967.

Chong, S-J. "Comparative Marketing Practices of Foreign and Domestic Firms in Developing Countries: A Case Study of Malaysia." *Management International Review*, 1973/6, pp. 91–98.

Clark, Colin. *The Conditions of Economic Progress*. London: Macmillan, 1940.

Cox, Reavis. "The Search for Universals in Comparative Studies of Domestic Marketing Systems." In P. D. Bennett, ed. *Marketing and Economic Development; Proceedings of the 1965 Fall Conference*, American Marketing Association, Chicago, IL, 1965, pp. 143–162. Reprinted in J. J. Boddewyn, *Comparative Management and Marketing*, pp. 142–160.

Cundiff, E. W. "Concepts in Comparative Retailing." *Journal of Marketing*, January 1965, pp. 59–63.

Davis, H. L.: Douglas, S. P.; and Silk, A. J. "A Cross-national Comparison of the Reliability of Selected Measurements from Consumer Surveys." Working Paper 80–20. Brussels, Belgium: European Institute for Advanced Studies in Management, June 1980.

Demetrescu, M. C. "Comparative Marketing Systems — Conceptual Outline." In Dov Izraeli, et al., eds. *Marketing Systems for Developing Countries.* New York: Wiley, 1976, pp. 111–17.

Dholakhia, Nikhilesh. "The Future of Marketing in the Third World." Working Paper 80–28. Manhattan, KS: College of Business Administration, Kansas State University, October 1980.

_____, and Dholakia, R. R. "A Framework for Analyzing International Influences on Third-World Marketing Systems." Working Paper 80–8. Manhattan, KS: College of Business Administration, Kansas State University, May 1980.

_____, and Firat, A. F. "Consumption Patterns as Core Analytical Categories for Macro-marketing." Working Paper 80–9. Manhattan, KS: College of Business Administration, Kansas State University, May 1980.

Douglas, S. P. "Patterns and Parallels of Marketing Structures in Several Countries." *MSU Business Topics,* Spring 1971, pp. 38–48.

_____. "Cross-National Comparisons and Consumer Stereotypes: A Case Study of Working and Non-Working Wives in the U.S. and France." *Journal of Consumer Research,* June 1976, pp. 12–20.

_____, and Dubois, B. *Culture and Consumer Behavior: Time for a Fresh Look?* Cambridge, MA: Marketing Science Institute, July 1977.

_____, and Urban, C. D. "Life-Style Analysis to Profile Women in International Markets." *Journal of Marketing,* July 1977, pp. 46–54.

_____, "A Cross-National Exploration of Husband-Wife Involvement in Selected Household Activities." In W. L. Wilkie, ed. *Advances in Consumer Research,* Vol. 6. Ann Arbor, MI: Association for Consumer Research, 1979, pp. 364–71.

Dunn, S. W. "Effect of National Identity on Multinational Promotional Strategy in Europe." *Journal of Marketing,* October 1976, pp. 50–57.

Ehrenberg, A. S. C., and Goodhart, G. J. "A Comparison of American and British Repeat-Buying Habits." *Journal of Marketing Research,* February 1968, pp. 29–33.

Elimelech, Raphael. "Pricing for the Japanese Market." *McKinsey Quarterly,* Autumn 1980, pp. 62–75.

Fisk, George. *Marketing Systems.* New York: Harper & Row, 1967, p. 16.

_____, and Nason, R. W., eds. *Macro-Marketing: New Steps on the Learning Curve.* Boulder, CO: University of Colorado, Business Research Division, Graduate School of Business Administration, 1978.

_____; Nason, R. W.; and White, P. D., eds. *Macro-Marketing: Evolution of Thought.* Boulder, CO: University of Colorado, Business Research Division, Graduate School of Business Administration, 1979.

Food and Agriculture Organization of the United Nations. *Bibliography of Food and Agricultural Marketing,* Second Series, Nos. 3 and 4. Rome: 1977 and 1979.

Goldman, Arieh. "Outreach of Consumers and the Modernization of Urban Food Retailing in Developing Countries." *Journal of Marketing,* October 1974, pp. 8–16.

Goodnow, J. D., and Hansz, J. E. "Environmental Determinants of Overseas Market Entry Strategies." *Journal of International Business Studies,* Spring 1972, pp. 33–50. (Their analysis is based on the Litvak-Banting model.)

Green, R. T.; Cunningham, W. H.; and Cunningham, I. C. M. "The Effectiveness of Standardized Global Advertising." *Journal of Advertising* 4, 3/1975, pp. 25–30.

_____, and Langeard, E. "A Cross-National Comparison of Consumer Habits and Innovator Characteristics." *Journal of Marketing,* July 1975, pp. 34–41.

_____, and White, P. D. "Methodological Considerations in Cross-National Consumer Research." *Journal of International Business Studies,* Fall/Winter 1976, pp. 81–87.

_____, and Langeard, E. "Comments and Recommendations on the Practice of Cross-Cultural Marketing Research." Mimeographed. Brussels: European Institute for Advanced Studies in Management, 1979.

_____, and Cunningham, I. C. M. "Family Purchasing Roles in Two Countries (United States and Venezuela)." *Journal of International Business Studies,* Spring/Summer 1980, pp. 92–97.

Hanssens, D. M. *A Bibliography of International Marketing.* Working Paper Series No. 12. Los Angeles, CA: Pacific Basin Economic Study Center, Graduate School of Management, UCLA, 1980.

Hempel, D. J. "Family Buying Decisions: A Cross-Cultural Perspective." *Journal of Marketing Research,* August 1974, pp. 295–302.

Hirsch, L. V. *Marketing in an Underdeveloped Economy: The North Indian Sugar Industry.* Englewood Cliffs, NJ: Prentice-Hall, 1961.

Holton, R. H. "Changing Demand and Consumption." In W. E. Moore and A. S. Feldman, eds. *Labor Commitment and Social Change in Developing Areas.* New York: Social Science Research Council, 1960, pp. 201–16.

Hoover, R. J., et al. "A Cross-National Study of Perceived Risk." *Journal of Marketing,* July 1978, pp. 102–108.

Hunt, S. D. "The Nature and Scope of Marketing." *Journal of Marketing,* July 1976, pp. 17–28.

Izraeli, Dov; Izraeli, D. N.; and Meissner, Frank, eds. *Marketing Systems for Developing Countries.* New York: Wiley, 1976.

Izraeli, Dov, and Zif, J. J. *Societal Marketing Boards.* New York: Wiley, 1977.

_____, et al. "Integrative Processes in Agricultural Marketing Channels." *Journal of the Academy of Marketing Science,* Summer 1977, pp. 203–20.

Jaffe, E. D. "A Flow Approach to the Comparative Study of Marketing Systems." In J. J. Boddewyn, *Comparative Management and Marketing,* pp. 160–170.

_____. *Grouping: A Strategy for International Marketing.* New York: American Management Association, 1974.

_____. "Comparative Marketing Revisited." *Marquette Business Review,* Winter 1976, pp. 143–153.

_____. "Are Domestic and International Marketing Dissimilar?" *Management International Review,* 3/1980, pp. 83–86.

Johnsson, L. G. "International Coordination of Marketing: The Scandinavian Experience." In S. P. Sethi and R. H. Holton, eds. *Management of the Multinationals.* New York: Free Press, 1974, pp. 238–56.

Kacker, M. P. "Patterns of Marketing Adaptation in International Business: A Study of American Business Firms Operating in India." *Management International Review,* 1972/4–5, pp. 111–118.

Katona, George, et al. *Aspirations and Affluence: Comparative Studies in the United States and Europe.* New York: McGraw-Hill, 1971.

Klippel, R. E., and Boewadt, R. J. "Attitude Measurement as a Strategy Determinant for Standardization of Multinational Advertising Formats." *Journal of International Business Studies,* Spring 1974, pp. 39–50.

Kuznets, Simon. *Modern Economic Growth.* New Haven, CT: Yale University Press, 1968.

Lehmann, D. R., and O'Shoughnessy, John. "Difference in Attribute Importance for Different Industrial Products (U.S. and U.K.)." *Journal of Marketing,* April 1974, pp. 36–42.

Liander, Bertil, et al. *Comparative Analysis for International Marketing.* Boston, MA: Allyn and Bacon, 1967.

Linton, Anna, and Broadbent, Simon. "Internation Life Style Comparisons." *European Research,* March 1975, pp. 6 ff.

Lorimor, E. S. "A Look at Some Current Articles on International Advertising and Marketing." In S. W. Dunn and E. S. Lorimor, eds. *International Advertising and Marketing.* Columbus, OH: Grid, 1979, pp. 55–66.

Maddox, R. N., et al. "Correlates of Information Gathering and Evoked Set Size for New Automobile Purchasers in Norway and the U.S." In H. K. Hunt, ed. *Advances in Consumer Research,* Vol. 5. Ann Arbor, MI: Association for Consumer Research, 1978, pp. 167–70.

Mulvihill, D. F. *Domestic Marketing Systems Abroad: An Annotated Bibliography.* Kent, OH: Kent State University Press, 1966. (Earlier edition in 1962.)

Munson, J. M., and McIntyre, S. H. "Developing Practical Procedures for the Measurement of Personal Values in Cross-Cultural Marketing." *Journal of Marketing Research,* February 1979, pp. 48–52.

Musgrove, Philip. *Consumer Behavior in Latin America: Income and Spending of Families in Ten Andean Cities.* Washington, DC: Brookings, 1978.

Nagashima, Akira. "A Comparison of Japanese and U.S. Attitudes Toward Foreign Products." *Journal of Marketing,* January 1970, pp. 68–74.

National Economic Development Office (UK). *The Distributive Trades in the Common Market.* London: HMSO, 1973.

Organization for Economic Cooperation and Development. *The Distribution Sector: Evolution and Government Policies.* Paris, 1973.

Plummer, J. T. "Consumer Focus in Cross-National Research." *Journal of Advertising,* Spring 1977, pp. 5–15.

Polanyi, Karl, et al. *Trade and Market in the Early Empires.* Glencoe, IL: Free Press, 1957.

Preston, L. E. "The Commercial Sector and Economic Development." In Reed Moyer and S. C. Hollander, eds. *Markets and Marketing in Developing Economies.* Homewood, IL: Irwin, 1968, pp. 9–23.

Przeworski, Adam, and Teune, Henry. *The Logic of Comparative Social Inquiry,* New York: Wiley, 1970.

Ragone, Gerardo, "Sociological Aspects of the Evolution of Consumption in Italy." *Review of the Economic Conditions in Italy,* March–May 1978, pp. 105–119.

Ramond, Charles. *The Art of Using Science in Marketing.* New York: Harper & Row, 1974.

Reader's Digest Association. *Survey of Europe Today.* New York and Paris, 1970. The French edition is called *Radioscopie de l'Europe.*

Ricks, David; Fu, M. Y. C.; and Arpan, J. S. *International Business Blunders.* Columbus, OH: Grid, 1974.

Rogers, E. M., and Shoemaker, F. F. *Communication of Innovations: A Cross-Cultural Approach.* New York: Free Press, 1971.

Rostow, W. W. *The Stages of Economic Growth.* Cambridge, England: The University Press, 1960.

Sethi, S. P. "Comparative Cluster Analysis for World Markets." *Journal of Marketing Research,* August 1971, pp. 348–354.

Shapiro, S. J. "Comparative Marketing and Economic Development." In George Schwartz, ed. *Science in Marketing.* New York: Wiley, 1965, pp. 398–429.

Sheth, J. N., and Sethi, S. P. "Theory of Cross-Cultural Buyer Behavior." Faculty Working Paper. Urbana-Champaign, IL: University of Illinois, College of Commerce and Business Administration, 31 May 1973.

Shimaguchi, M., and Lazer, M. "Japanese Distribution Channels: Invisible Barriers to Market Entry." *MSU Business Topics,* Winter 1979, pp. 49–62.

Shipchandler, Z. E. "A Cross-Country Study of Annual Unit Sales and Ownership Patterns of Three Consumer Durables (TV Sets, Washing Machines, Refrigerators)." Unpublished DBA dissertation, Indiana University, 1972.

_____. "Diffusion Patterns of Consumer Durables in International Markets: Implications for Management." Fort Wayne: Indiana University. Paper presented at the Annual Meeting of the Midwest Business Administration Association, April 1973.

Shawver, D. L., and Nickels, W. G. "A Rationalization for Macro-Marketing Concepts and Definitions." In George Fisk and R. W. Nason, eds. *Macro-Marketing: New Steps on the Learning Curve.* Boulder, CO: University of Colorado, Business Research Division, Graduate School of Business Administration, 1978, pp. 29–45.

Silverman, William, and Hill, Reuben. "Task Allocation in Marriage in the United States and Belgium." *Journal of Marriage and the Family,* May 1967, pp. 353–9.

Slater, C. C., ed. *Macro-Marketing: Distribution Processes from a Societal Perspective.* Boulder, CO: University of Colorado, Business Research Division, Graduate School of Business Administration, 1976.

Smelser, N. J. *The Sociology of Economic Life.* Englewood Cliffs, NJ: Prentice-Hall, 1976.

Sommers, M. S., and Kernan, J. B., eds. *Comparative Marketing Systems: A Cultural Approach.* New York: Appleton-Century-Crofts, 1968.

Terpstra, Vern. *International Marketing.* Hinsdale, IL: Dryden Press, 1973.

Thorelli, H. B.; Becker, Helmut; and Engledow, J. E. *The Information Seekers: An International Study of Consumer Information and Advertising Image.* Cambridge, MA: Ballinger, 1975.

_____, and Becker, Helmut. "The Information Seekers: Multinational Strategy Target." *California Management Review,* Fall 1980, pp. 46–52.

Tigert, D. J.; King C. W.; and Ring, L. J. "Fashion Involvement: A Cross-Cultural Comparative Analysis." In J. C. Olson, ed. *Advances in Consumer Research,* Vol. 7. Ann Arbor, MI: Association for Consumer Research, 1980, pp. 17–21.

Urban, C. D. "Life-Style Patterns of Women: United States and United Kingdom." Paper presented at the American Academy of Advertising, Knoxville, TE, 20 April 1975.

_____. "A Cross-National Comparison of Consumer Media Use Patterns." *Columbia Journal of World Business,* Winter 1977, pp. 53–64.

Van Raaij, W. F. "Cross-Cultural Research Methodology as a Case of Construct Validity." In H. K. Hunt, ed. *Advances in Consumer Research,* Vol. 5. Ann Arbor, MI: Association for Consumer Research, 1978, pp. 693–701.

Wadinambiaratchi, George. "Channels of Distribution in Developing Economies." *Business Quarterly* (Western Ontario), Winter 1965, pp. 74–82.

White, P. D., and Slater, C. C., eds. *Macro-Marketing: Distributive Processes from a Societal Perspective—An Elaboration of Issues.* Boulder, CO: University of Colorado, Business Research Division, Graduate School of Business Administration, 1977.

Wind, Yoram, and Douglas, Susan. "On the Meaning of Comparison: A Methodology for Cross-Cultural Studies." *Quarterly Journal of Management Development,* June 1971, pp. 105–21.

————, and Douglas, Susan. "Comparative Consumer Research: The Next Frontier?" Working paper, June 1980, 20 pp. Forthcoming in *European Journal of Marketing,* 1981.

[9]

Marketing and Economic Development: Review, Synthesis and Evaluation

Van R. Wood and Scott J. Vitell

The authors present a review, synthesis and evaluation of the published works on marketing and economic development over the last 30 years. Future research directions are also provided.

Twenty-five years ago Drucker's (1958) article entitled "Marketing and Economic Development" sparked widespread interest and concern for the role of marketing and economic development. Drucker argued that marketing activities make possible economic integration and full utilization of the productive capacity of nations by lifting the entrepreneurial spirit of the people. He concluded that it was marketing, more than the more overt economic activities of manufacturing or construction, that offered the greatest challenge and greatest potential payback to developing societies. Since this classic work many scholars have researched the role of marketing and economic development. However, progress has been slow and limited, with the subject remaining outside the mainstream of scholarly research in marketing.

Recently, two calls for additional research on this important topic have appeared. At the AMA 1982 Marketing Educators' Conference in Chicago, Kotler (1982), in a keynote speech, identified the role of marketing in developing economies as one of the five neglected areas demanding the attention of marketing scholars. Likewise, in a recent editorial of the *Journal of Marketing*, Cunningham and Hunt (1982) called for substantive research on the consequences of marketing systems on society.

To guide subsequent research in this area, thorough synthesis, classification and evaluation of the literature are needed. Such a review of the literature would be valuable to scholars,

Van R. Wood is Assistant Professor of Marketing, Texas Tech University, Lubbock, Texas. Scott J. Vitell is Assistant Professor of Marketing, University of Mississippi, Oxford, Mississippi.

practitioners and public policymakers. Unfortunately, such a comprehensive literature review has not been attempted since Shapiro (1965). Therefore, it is the objective of this article to (1) propose a model to review and synthesize the research on marketing and economic development, (2) evaluate that research, and (3) suggest directions for future research.

MODEL DEVELOPMENT

Economic development is generally defined to include improvements in material welfare, eradication of mass poverty, and shifts in the underlying structure of production away from agricultural toward industrial activities. Economic development also entails organizing the economy so that productive employment is widespread among the working-age population, who in turn have a high degree of participation in decisions concerning improvements in their economic welfare (Kindleberger and Herrick 1977). For the purposes of this article, marketing is defined as the creation and delivery of a standard of living (McNair 1968).

To organize and classify past research on marketing and economic development, a modification of the Hunt (1976) model is used in this article. Briefly, Hunt's model uses three dichotomies to classify the scope of marketing: (1) profit/nonprofit marketing, (2) micro/macro marketing and (3) positive/normative marketing. The model consists of eight (2x2x2) cells and can be used to categorize and analyze all marketing phenomena, problems, issues, theories, and perspectives. Arndt (1982) states the model has been successfully defended against numerous critics and has passed the initial tests for acceptance.

A review of past studies suggests that along with Hunt's three dichotomies, the topic areas shown in Exhibit 1 best capture the breadth and depth of the individual works on marketing and economic development.[1] Research may concentrate on conceptual and theoretical issues, or provide empirical tests of hypotheses. A specific geographic region(s) may be the focus of a study and a specific sector(s) of the economy in which marketing activities are found may be examined (e.g., agriculture, manufacturing, wholesaling and retailing). Finally, studies may have involved one or more marketing variables and activities (e.g., product, price, promotion, channels or market research). While some works have concentrated only on a specific country and the interaction between the environment (e.g., politics, economics, or culture), marketing, and subsequent development, other studies have looked at a number of countries, regions, or international environments for insights into marketing's role in economic development. Exhibit 1 displays examples of research in marketing and economic development from the 1950s through the 1980s and indicates the focal points of each study. The remainder of this article will explore each contribution cited within the context of Hunt's three dichotomies. Where researchers have made significant contributions to more than one perspective, they will be so noted.

PROFIT/MICRO/POSITIVE PERSPECTIVE

This perspective contains research on developing nations with respect to the marketing environment at a profit, micro level. The studies pertaining to this perspective are divided into three subcategories: (1) studies which examine the effects of consumer behavior on firms in less developed countries (LDCs), (2) studies which examine the marketing activities and strategies of firms in LDCs, and (3) studies which examine and describe the marketing environment faced by firms in LDCs.

Synthesis

Consumer behavior and consumer characteristics in LDCs are the target of a small but

---

[1]Exhibit 1 displays only 16 works on marketing and economic development. A complete table classifying all research reviewed in this article is available upon request from the authors.

insightful collection of studies. In a pioneering study, Hamilton (1965) focused on the U.S. market from the 1860s forward. The author noted that in primitive societies, production and consumption are not separated either temporally or spatially and, therefore, marketing is of limited importance. However, using the U.S. as a model he traced the importance of marketing in saving consumers time and money as a society advances economically.

On a more specific level, Goldman (1974) examined barriers to the success of modern food retailing outlets in LDCs. He found that barriers to consumer outreach, including spatial, informational, and sociocultural factors, make it difficult for modern supermarkets to reach the majority of consumers in developing countries. Specifically, consumers' consumption efficiency is hindered by high transportation costs, lack of awareness of shopping alternatives, and loyalty to more traditional, and sometimes more costly, food stores. This generally collaborated earlier works by Halper (1966) and Henley and Farace (1967) in Peru and Bolivia, respectively, which found "considerable time and energy" being spent in food shopping each day. In particular the Bolivian study found that families earning below a mean annual income of $1500 spent 54 percent of their income on food products.

Consumer shopping patterns for a variety of non-food products in Sao Paulo, Brazil were examined by Cunningham, Moore and Cunningham (1974). Their findings indicated that the market could be segmented by social class and that the primary source of information for all social classes was word-of-mouth. However, the upper classes also depended upon mass media for product information, whereas the lower classes did not. The lower social classes considered installment plans as the most important store service while the upper classes were concerned with delivery service. These differences imply that retail businesses in LDCs need to tailor their marketing strategies to specific social classes, to enhance their competitiveness and overall economic development.

A number of studies have focused on the strategies and behaviors of individual firms in LDCs. Most of these involve food distribution. An early work by Abbott (1963) concerned marketing food products in Western Europe. His study implied that firms in LDCs could improve their distribution efficiencies by

EXHIBIT 1
MARKETING AND ECONOMIC DEVELOPMENT LITERATURE

	Holton (1953)	Galbraith & Holton (1955)	Drucker (1958)	Cook (1959)	Boyd (1961)	Abbott (1963)	Slater (1965)	Ruttan (1969)	Preston (1970)	Holdman (1973)	Kirpalani (1975)	Jessop (1979)	Bartels (1981)	Nason & White (1981)	Dholakia & Dholakia (1982)	Etgar (1983)
Major Emphasis of Study																
Conceptual theoretical	X	X	X	X		X	X		X	X	X		X	X	X	X
Empirical		X						X								
Descriptive					X							X				
Geographical Emphasis																
Canada														X		
Latin America and the Caribbean	X	X				X	X							X	X	
Western Europe						X				X		X			X	
USSR and Eastern Europe															X	
Middle East and Egypt					X	X									X	
Africa (except Egypt)						X								X	X	X
Asia and the Far East				X				X					X		X	
Australia and New Zealand															X	
USA			X						X		X					
General																
Sectors of the Economy Examined																
Agricultural production		X		X	X	X	X						X	X		X
Food wholesaling	X	X		X	X	X		X	X				X	X		X
Food retailing	X	X		X	X	X	X	X	X				X	X		X
Non-agricultural production								X					X	X		
Non-food wholesaling								X	X				X	X		
Non-food retailing								X	X				X	X		
Marketing Variables and Activities Examined																
Product									X			X	X	X	X	
Price	X	X				X	X	X	X	X		X	X	X	X	
Promotion												X	X	X	X	
Channels of distribution						X	X	X	X						X	
Market research						X					X				X	
Market communications		X				X		X	X				X	X	X	X
Physical distribution activities		X						X	X	X	X			X	X	X
Training programs	X	X				X								X	X	X
Standardization and grading										X			X	X	X	X
Buying and selling													X	X	X	
Risk-taking								X					X			
Financing					X			X					X			
Environmental Factors Examined																
Political/legal		X		X	X				X				X	X		X
Economic		X		X	X				X				X	X		
Competitive	X		X	X		X			X				X	X		
Cultural		X							X					X		
Technological				X							X	X				
Geographics									X					X		
Consumer	X	X			X				X					X	X	
International/multinational														X	X	
Three Dichotomies																
Micro			X									X				
Macro	X	X	X	X	X	X	X	X	X		X		X	X	X	X
Positive	X	X	X	X	X	X	X	X	X		X		X	X	X	X
Normative	X	X	X			X	X	X		X	X			X	X	X
Profit	X	X	X	X	X	X	X	X		X	X	X	X		X	X
Non-profit										X				X	X	

observing more developed markets. In this vein, Kriesberg (1968) studied the marketing of food products in LDCs in general. He found inefficiencies in storage, transportation, and processing of food to be widespread.

Bucklin (1976), the Food and Agriculture Organization of the U.N. (FAO) (1975), and Dannehaeuser (1980) pointed out the barriers to the success of small scale food retailers in Asian LDCs. Government policy, lack of capital, poorly designed public food markets and inefficiencies in assorting and sorting products were noted. In a related study, Bucklin (1975a) found that supermarkets were catering primarily to the upper classes while the lower classes tended to frequent more traditional central food markets. The individual stall operators in these central markets over-utilized labor, leading to increases in the cost of food for their customers.

Various other studies examined the marketing activities of firms dealing with non-food products. Sherbini (1965) discussed product, price, channels of distribution and promotional decisions for the firm in LDCs. He found many firms operated with no specific plans concerning trade margins or markups. Yoshino (1971) traced the development of the Japanese system through the period of postwar economic growth and social change. His work discusses the behaviors of small Japanese retailers, wholesalers, and trading companies and the marketing efficiencies that led to one of the world's highest standards of living. Similarly, Garlick (1971) found that firms in Ghana were faced with numerous marketing barriers which prevented the individual firm from expanding.

A final subcategory of studies examined the marketing environment for the individual firm in specific LDCs. These "comparative" studies point out the differences between countries at different levels of development. These include works mentioned earlier by Yoshino (1971) and Garlick (1971) as well as studies by Lugmani, Ouraeshi and Delene (1980) on Islamic countries; Rae (1980) on Communist China; Thomson (1980) on Egypt; Goertz (1979) on Kenya; Worth (1978) on Ireland; Scherb (1980) on Brazil; Wheatly and Oshikawa (1979) on Japan; and Jessop (1979) on Greece. While these studies covered a number of different countries and markets, they are similar in that they examined relationships between a firm's success and the stage of development of the marketing

systems they deal in. Barksdale and Anderson (1982 a,b) provide an extensive overview of these works in a 25-year review of comparative marketing studies. They divide them into six categories including three which have special relevance for the profit/micro/positive perspective, namely (1) marketing institutions and activities, (2) buyer behavior, and (3) environmental conditions.

Evaluation

Studies examining consumer behavior and individual firm behavior in LDCs have revealed barriers and inefficiencies which act as inhibitors to economic development. The description and analysis of these barriers provide insight into the establishment of more efficient marketing systems. However, these studies have tended to concentrate on the food-product sector to the partial exclusion of non-food sectors of the economy. Likewise many of the studies looking at consumers and the marketing environment for individual firms focused solely on Latin American markets. However, as it is unlikely that the consumers and the environment of LDCs in other parts of the world are directly comparable to Latin American markets, studies are needed to examine other world areas as well. Of particular interest would be studies that examine the marketing variables that save consumers time and money, across a variety of world areas.

PROFIT/MICRO/NORMATIVE PERSPECTIVE

This perspective contains research on what the marketing environment "should be" at the micro, profit level in order for an economy to develop. The literature relating to this perspective is divided into the following subcategories: (1) studies suggesting how to improve the efficiency of individual firms in LDCs and (2) studies suggesting how to "improve" consumer spending, consumption, and the "quality of life" in LDCs.

Synthesis

A classic work in the area of improving the efficiency of profit oriented firms in LDCs is Drucker (1958). While taking a primarily macro viewpoint in supporting the role of marketing in economic development, Drucker illustrated the value of marketing at the micro level as well as through the development of managers and entrepreneurs. Such managers are willing to take the necessary risks needed for development and are familiar with the decision areas specific to marketing. Later Sherbini (1965) revealed the tendency of manufacturing firms in developing countries to overlook marketing for production considerations in the pursuit of profits. He indicated how profits could be improved by specifically examining the product, price, channels of distribution, and promotion decision areas. In support of this, Goldman (1974), studying urban food retailers, made a series of strategic recommendations to reach low-income consumers. These included differential pricing, improved delivery systems and the increased efficiency of market information systems.

Several studies have focused on coordinating and improving specific marketing operations of firms in LDCs. Bucklin (1975a) recommended improving the level of cooperation among small-scale urban food wholesalers and retailers in areas such as storage and transportation. Likewise, Bucklin (1975b, 1976) suggested a variety of training programs that would improve the profitability of food wholesalers and retailers in LDCs. Training should focus on site location, facility size, store layout, transportation, storage and product handling. A study by the FAO (1975) reached similar conclusions and made recommendations to improve wholesale and retail food operations in various Asian cities. In a more recent study, Taimni (1981) also concluded that marketing assistance and training programs could improve profits for traditional craft industries in India.

Cundiff and Hilger (1979) emphasized marketing innovations by individual entrepreneurs as a means to increase the level of economic development. In a followup work Cundiff (1982) reemphasized this position, stating that micro level improvements are the most effective means of encouraging economic development. He proposed the development of management training programs that increase the competency of local managers in using marketing techniques and stressed the need to develop and improve the marketing curricula in institutions of higher education.

A few authors have been concerned with recommendations for improving consumer spending, consumption, and the consumer's quality of life. Findings by Freedman (1970) indicated consumption of modern objects as being a positive contributor to economic development. Families who consume modern objects were found to be better educated, to work in more modern occupations, and more likely to use family planning. Nielsen (1974) looked at the impact of marketing communications on consumption in LDCs. First, he reviewed economic theory that suggests commercial communications cause money to shift from savings to consumption, making it more difficult for a developing society to invest in production facilities. He then countered this theory, stating that the relationship between commercial communications and consumption is modified by four factors: (1) the wealth of the audiences receiving the communications, (2) the degree of product differentiation involved, (3) the extent to which those doing the communicating are innovative in their operations, and (4) the degree to which the products involved are essential goods rather than luxury goods. He concluded that both efficient consumption along with a degree of savings are essential to economic development. Similarly, Bretherton (1977) made suggestions for improving the quality of life in LDCs. These included developing product, price, communications, and physical distribution strategies that improve living conditions, and regulating the consumption of non-essential "luxury" products. Cundiff and Hilger (1979) took an even broader perspective. Stating that developing societies need to maximize consumption potential to meet production output, they recommended increasing investments in promotion, consumer credit, market research and channel infrastructure.

Evaluation

Studies dealing with improving operations at the individual firm level have made substantial conceptual contributions. However, this area lacks empirical research. Therefore, a primary research need under this perspective is the empirical investigation of many of the propositions posed, but not yet tested, with respect to individual firms and marketing in LDCs.

Studies examining the individual consumer in LDCs and dealing with improving consumer consumption and the "quality of life" are sparse. There is a need for additional studies on improving the individual consumer's position in the marketplace. More specifically, while various works emphasize the training of individual small-scale traders in LDCs, few studies concentrate on the training of individual consumers. For example, while the home economics area of study has information programs designed to help the undernourished improve their food consumption by increasing the nutritional value of their food intake, little research has investigated the relationship between nutritional intake and overall economic development. Likewise, studies dealing with communications, emphasizing value for money spent, could improve consumer expenditure patterns.

PROFIT/MACRO/POSITIVE PERSPECTIVE

This perspective contains research on macromarketing issues in developing societies with specific emphasis on the profit sectors of such societies. Studies pertaining to this perspective focus on what the macro role of marketing is or will be in developing economies. Three areas of inquiry are reviewed here: (1) comparative studies, or the search for functional universal principles; (2) the role of government in the profit sector; and (3) channel structures, profit and economic development in LDCs.

Synthesis

The first area of this perspective reviews comparative studies that as a whole constitute an ongoing search for functional, universal principles of macromarketing in developing nations. Early researchers included Holton (1953) and Hirsch (1961), both of whom noted that the macro-profit sector of economic development devoted almost exclusive attention to the problems of increasing industry's production levels, correcting unfavorable balances of trade, and reducing capital shortages. They investigated the universally applicable marketing principles of profit growth through expansion of buying, selling, risk-taking, credit extension, and sorting and assorting of goods in the distribution channels. The need to change social attitudes to reflect an entrepreneurial spirit was emphasized as a major area of opportunity.

The research of the previous two authors was followed by works from Abbott (1963), McCarthy (1963), and Bartels (1963). These authors attempted to integrate the functions of production and marketing. Abbott (1963) and McCarthy (1963) investigated the loss of profits to the production sectors of developing economies owing to inefficiencies in the marketing institutions that bridge the gap between producers and consumers. They concluded that not just more wholesalers and retailers are needed, but more effective and efficient wholesalers and retailers. Bartels (1963) presented a collection of papers that described and compared the structures and operations of wholesalers in all major regions of the world. Taken together, these papers revealed that the structures and operations of wholesalers are directly related to producers' profits.

The year 1965 produced a series of works in this area by a variety of authors. Cox (1965) posed a number of questions on marketing and profit universals and suggested a "flow analysis" from producer to consumer to seek out such universals. Moyer (1965) outlined marketing functions and examined market entry and trade restrictions and their effect on profits. Lamont (1965) provided results that showed marketing functions to be just as important as production functions in profit realization. Wadinambiaratchi (1965) and Cundiff (1965) studied distribution and retail systems in eight regions and 19 countries, respectively. Their work indicated economic development depends on marketing innovation and aggressive actions to reach consumers.

The late 1960s and early 1970s also produced a variety of research on the relationship between economic development and macromarketing. Preston (1968) demonstrated that developing countries with higher percentages of their population working in commercial marketing activities also have higher gross domestic products. However, no causal direction was implied by this finding. Preston (1970) further elaborated on this finding, demonstrating that economic development required transformation of marketing activities with respect to market structures, product variety and volume, and marketing management behavior and goals.

In testing a number of "working hypotheses," Glade et al. (1970) found profits in developing nations to be related to whether the marketing facilities were foreign- or home-owned, whether professionals or owners managed the marketing activities, whether the firms were small or large, whether consumer or industrial goods were marketed, and whether the products marketed had high or low purchase values. A similar study with respect to agricultural products was undertaken by Ruttan (1969). Likewise, Arndt (1972) showed that retail performance depends on a number of environmental characteristics that affect market potential. Such characteristics included personal consumption expenditures per capita, passenger car ownership, geographic concentration of population, and inhabitants per retail establishment. Hansz and Goodnow (1973) found market performance to be related to such variables as the number of per capita television sets, the number of newpapers per capita, local assembly and content requirements and road density.

One study, Douglas (1971), in contrast to previous findings, concluded that the development level of marketing structures was independent of the level of economic development. This conclusion was based largely on the finding that channel structures depend more on the relative size of the firms in the channel rather than on levels of economic development.

The late 1970s and early 1980s also produced studies seeking functional, universal principles. Weinstein (1976) and Holton (1980) examined the nature of advertising in developing countries. Weinstein (1976) showed that the investment behavior of advertising firms entering developing markets results in economic gains for all parties involved when such investments are in the form of shared ownership through joint ventures. Holton (1980) reviewed advertising's influence on personal consumption and profits. He found the evidence inconclusive as to whether advertising has a positive effect on personal consumption and gross national product. However, he noted that advertising reduced consumer product search costs and resulted in market power and higher profits for advertisers.

Finally, in the subcategory of comparative studies, Dawson (1980) delineated a number of principles relevant to the multinational corporation's role in developing countries. Specifically, profitable relationships can be realized if multinational corporate marketing strategies (1) are compatible with national development plans, (2) reflect social responsiveness, (3) provide for local enterprise participation, (4) reflect understanding of inter-regional differences, (5) preserve national identity and culture, and (6) adapt to rapid changes.

The second area of this perspective addresses the issue of the role of government in the profit sector of developing nations. Early works included those of Cook (1959), Boyd et al. (1958) and Boyd (1961). These writings focused on the role governments can play to increase market demand and decrease production and marketing costs through incentives that help firms achieve economies to scale. They emphasized the need to reduce foreign controls that repatriate profits to home nations and to reduce the number of small-scale inefficient traders that give rise to marketing inefficiencies.

Abegglen (1967) and Preston (1967), using examples of Japan and the Arab nations respectively, pointed out how close cooperation between government and business leads to economic development and profit gains. Such gains are related to business decisions on pricing, new product development and market penetration, being made in conjunction with the advice and support of government. However, direct governmental intervention (i.e., ownership) in marketing activities was not recommended. On the other hand, Hilger (1977) points out how direct governmental intervention through operation of food stores has worked in Mexico to achieve development and profits.

Boddewyn and Hollander (1972) edited a symposium examining government's role in retailing for 20 different countries. They observed that many government policies work at cross-purposes and remain in effect long past their period of relevance. Such policies often run counter to goals of improving retailing efficiency while protecting established retailers and traders. The authors concluded that the role of public policy in retailing should not be overemphasized as most retail changes succeed or fail irrespective of any public policy toward them.

A final subcategory of studies under this perspective examines the channel structures and their relationship to profits. A pioneering study by Galbraith and Holton (1953) researched the efficiency of the marketing system in Puerto Rico. That study, examining food product channels, found little communication or coordination among channel members. The result was a relatively long and inefficient distribution system. Likewise, Martin (1959) observed that in Pakistan and India the major marketing problem was the lack of effective and efficient channels of distribution, including a coordinated transportation and communication system. In contrast, Bauer (1954), in a study of West African distribution systems, found that channels which appeared to be long and inefficient were actually quite sound, given the circumstances in the market involved. He noted that the special distance between markets and the relatively small number of consumers in such markets made longer channels more efficient.

The European distribution systems for foodstuffs were the subject of works by Collins (1963) and Guerin (1965). Collins (1963) concentrated on the different rates of adoption of self-service food retailing in various European countries. He theorized that such differences were related to differences in per capita income. He found low per capita income limited the sale of processed goods which best lend themselves to self-service. Guerin's (1965) study of supermarkets in Spain supported Collins' work. He found that conditions in Spain were not conducive to this type of self-service outlet. Consumers did not have the income nor the willingness to change their traditional buying habits, which were oriented more toward personal services.

An entire group of studies on channels, profits and development was pioneered by Charles S. Slater. These studies examined the marketing channels for food products in a number of LDCs. They began with Slater's (1965) article describing the role of food marketing systems in Latin American development, and included studies in Brazil (Slater et al. 1969b), Bolivia (Slater and Henley 1969a), Puerto Rico (Riley et al. 1970b), Colombia (Riley et al. 1970a), Costa Rica (Harrison et al. 1972) and Lesotho (Dahringer 1983). The results of these works were summarized in a later publication (Harrison et al. 1974) which reviewed the problems common to the LDCs studied. In general these problems included the following:

1. a lack of geographic and firm specialization in the production of many farm commodities,

2. a tendency toward spatial monopsonies or oligopsonies in local assembly markets,

3. high physical handling and transaction costs owing to operational inefficiencies and the lack of a grading system,

4. overly specialized food wholesalers and retailers,

5. a shortage of credit available to middlemen at reasonable interest rates,

6. assemblers failing to perform the communication function linking producers to potential markets,

7. a physical facilities bias on the part of many development projects,

8. a lack of a dynamic and effectively competitive market structure, and

9. severe fluctuations in prices.

In more recent studies, Slater (1976, 1977) developed a theory of market processes and profit generation. His theory focused on market demand and utilized the marketing concept, the marketing mix concept, consumer behavior theories, and the notion that operators of for-profit firms attempt to minimize risks and uncertainty while expanding revenues. This series of studies has been reviewed by Nason and White (1981).

The U.S. Department of Agriculture (1972) also identified food marketing and channel problems in LDCs. This study examined problems common to three different types of economies: (1) *traditional subsistence economies*, where most people earn their livelihood from the land, (2) *transitional agricultural economies*, which are only just becoming urbanized and market-oriented and (3) *market-oriented agricultural economies*, where the interdependence between rural and urban economies is more evident. In the traditional economy, the major problem is the lack of assured prices and subsequent lack of incentives to increase crop production. In the transitional economy, major problems in storage, transportation, and communication are common. In the market-oriented economy, capital and credit availability are the major problem in profit realization.

Anderson (1970) and Lele (1971) both noted the importance of investments in storage, transportation and food processing facilities to achieve more efficient channels of distribution. Anderson did his work in Thailand; Lele examined grain marketing in India. Langley and Foggin (1980) also emphasized the development of physical distribution facilities and infrastructure as a key to economic and market development.

Bucklin (1975c) examined the factors inhibiting change and innovation for food marketers in Asian LDCs. These included consumer patterns of daily purchases, a scarcity of capital, the subsidization of inefficient, traditional markets and high levels of unemployment. Oritt and Hagan (1977) looked at non-permanent markets common to many LDCs. They noted that producers and traders continually enter and leave these markets and that the price of any good is attributable solely to the markups of the intermediaries involved. They concluded that this condition was a significant deterrent to market expansion.

Examining the appliance trade in the Philippines, Dannehaeuser (1981) tested the hypothesis that as the wealth of an area rises

1. the number of channel levels are reduced and vertical integration occurs,

2. the relations between traders becomes more standardized, and

3. the international organization of channel members becomes more formalized.

His results, however, tended to disprove these relationships. This demonstrated the importance of carefully examining each individual LDC for its peculiar market characteristics, and their relationship to development.

A recent study, Kaynak and Cavusgil (1982) contrasted the food retailing systems in developed versus developing economies. In developing economies, they noted a trend on the part of large-scale food retailers to increase their channel power at the expense of suppliers. This compelled small-scale food retailers to form voluntary groups to compete. They concluded that traditional small-scale food retailers may need government protection as large-scale supermarkets are not the "total solution to the problem of increasing efficiency in food retailing." On the other hand, Etgar (1983), in studying rice distribution systems in the Ivory Coast, concluded that farmers and marketing intermediaries should be encouraged to adopt vertical integration, but without direct government involvement. The basis for this conclusion was that government-initiated vertical integration failed to achieve predicted profit improvements for the food distribution system.

Dahringer (1983) advocated reverse channel mapping (RCM) to evaluate the profitability of channel systems. This method (1) identifies subsystems in the channels and their relationship to each other, (2) determines their effects on the overall marketing system, and (3) identifies points of intervention where public policy may improve the effectiveness of the system. The major benefit of this approach is identification of areas where public policy can best aid channel structure profitability.

Evaluation

The profit, macro, positive perspective includes substantial and useful works in the areas of functional universal principles, the role of government and channel improvements for profit realization and economic development. In particular marketers' activities, the coordination of those activities, and the size, ownership, and dispersion of facilitators of those activities were found to play a major role in LDC development. Government activities to reduce foreign control of marketing activities and to provide incentives to achieve economies of scale were shown to affect profits and subsequent development. Finally, analysis of problems common to channels of distribution showed how profit gains and development can be realized.

These past works also lend insight into areas in this perspective that need to be addressed further. For example, aggregate consumption patterns and profit flows in LDCs need investigating. The behavioral aspects of power and the conflict in the distribution channels of LDCs and their relationship to profits and development need work. Finally, in light of the work on retailing and public policy by Boddewyn and Hollander (1972), the economic aspects of laws and regulations affecting marketing efficiencies in LDCs is ripe for research.

PROFIT/MACRO/NORMATIVE PERSPECTIVE

The issues addressed under this perspective revolve around what the role of marketing in economic development should be at the macro, profit level. As Bartels (1976) noted, marketing should be a "stimulator" of economic development and not just a passive functionary of economic development. Four sub-categories of inquiry are included here: (1) the importance of developing an effective and efficient infrastructure, (2) the kinds of marketing know-how that could best be transferred from developed to developing countries, (3) the social responsibility of marketing in developing countries and (4) the relative effectiveness of macro vs. micro inputs in aiding economic development.

Synthesis

The first area of inquiry raises the issue of the normative importance to developing nations of an infrastructure, particularly a distribution system. Two of the early theorists in this area, Holton (1953) and Hirsch (1961), theorized that the link between improved distribution techniques and economic development lay in the effect efficient distribution had on market expansion. Enhancing a nation's distribution system should lead to a savings in cost per item, owing to the efficiency and size of the transportation operation, particularly savings in inventory bulk carrying costs and spoilage costs. This in turn should decrease the ultimate cost of goods to consumers, allowing them more discretion in the quantity and variety of goods they purchase. This overall enhanced consumption translates into increased demand and leads to greater economies of scale in production runs. A synergistic process is thus placed in motion by improving the efficiency of a nation's distribution systems. Hirsch (1961) carried the theory one step further, stating that benefits from improved distribution should disseminate new ideas, new patterns of consumption, new techniques, and possibly new social relations. All are considered to be favorable to economic growth.

Abbott (1962, 1963) and Rostow (1965) expanded this topic by looking at the link between improved distribution systems and agricultural development. In particular they examined improvements in farm products moving to

urban markets and consumer products moving to rural markets. Likewise, Collins and Holton (1963) stressed that primary and secondary industries could be expanded if correlative changes in the distribution system were realized. Heldmann (1973) stated the normative link between transportation quality and market expansion even more succinctly. Transportation, like money, fulfills an elementary function in economic systems, namely conserving time and distances in the transfer of products, passengers and communications from one location to another. Heldmann also noted the effect that traffic junctions could have on attracting new commercial enterprises and extending existing enterprises. With more traffic going to more remote markets, industries should be able to extend their markets and improve their market positions. Oritt and Hagan (1977), reviewing the theoretical and empirical works on infrastructure and economic development, noted that "there is a clear and immensely important connection between the two." However, they also noted that fieldwork to date was mostly an afterthought and lacked systematic investigation.

Boddewyn and Hollander (1972) suggested that the distribution system for a country could be greatly improved if public policymakers would (1) provide resources for improving the efficiency of less productive retail forms, (2) set flexible policies to accommodate innovations in distribution and changing consumer needs, (3) restrict harmful and fraudulent practices in distribution, (4) leave the main regulatory role to self-regulation, (5) set policies to encourage those firms in distribution that are most likely to make positive contributions to the economy, and (6) provide social measures designed to lessen the human costs of economic development.

Langley and Foggin (1980), looking at historical trends in the U.S., noted a high correlation between population and manufacturing shifts (i.e., from the New England and Middle Atlantic states to the Southern and Western states) and the rapid growth in transportation and distribution. However, the relationship was primarily due to a sincere partnership between government, business and labor that resulted in the growth of infrastructure and industry. Mentzer and Samli (1981) elaborated further, stating that the key to economic development is the "construction of a production/marketing infrastructure" which combines the productive, distributive and cooperative aspects of a society.

Finally, in this area of infrastructure and economic development, Layton (1981a, 1981b) noted that to be truly successful development must match changes in the local distribution system with changes in social values and attitudes. Infrastructure development, driven only by political consideration, often results in a project that is disappointing to the local community and ineffective for a region as a whole. The process of industrialization must be matched closely with the rising expectations of the local populace, or the benefits realized may be minimal at the macro level. Infrastructure has a role to play, not only in the distribution of an economy's productive output but also in influencing living standards. That is, where expectations are changing positively, and the distribution sector is responding appropriately in terms of outlets and product assortments, attitudes towards industrialization are likely to be favorable. The result is a work force that accepts "newness" in jobs and economic structure in order to earn the income rewards that have meaning to them.

The second area of inquiry under this perspective addresses the issue of transfer of marketing know-how and technology from developed to developing nations. A dichotomy of views has developed in this area, with some authors favoring "transferring" contemporary marketing practices to foreign environments and others questioning the wisdom of such an approach.

Emlen (1958) was one of the earliest scholars to call for direct exportation of modern marketing know-how to developing nations. Citing the "obvious" logic for developing nations to follow a proven pattern of development (e.g., that of the United States), he also argued that developed countries were neglecting one of their most exportable commodities, marketing know-how. Elton (1967) took a very similar stand, stating that lack of a marketing management talent in the developing countries remains a major obstacle to economic development. He called for modern advertising and marketing procedures to become an integral part of business in LDCs.

Cranch (1974), probably the staunchest supporter of transferring modern marketing techniques to developing areas, stated that modern procedures in marketing research, distribution, promotion, packaging and media selection (with minor modifications for purposes of local adoption) can be applied directly in LDCs to reach the mass market.

A number of writers have taken the opposite view, expounding on the non-applicability of transferring modern marketing know-how to developing countries. One of the most articulate supporters of this view was Myers (1963). He argued that the U.S., because of its unique history and characteristics, had developed a marketing system that was only transferable to societies with similar traits. In particular, Myers noted the richness in U.S. resources and the quality of economic drive of its predominantly Calvinist population. This, along with its ready access to the technological and managerial know-how of Great Britain and the absence of rigid commercial traditions, made the U.S. unique to history, and helped foster new forms of business. Myers warned that extreme care should be exercised in attempting to transfer U.S. marketing institutions, concepts and practices to other societies. In particular, he noted that the transfer of U.S. marketing know-how has been most successful in Canada followed by the Northern European countries, but it has been of little relevance to the tradition-bound, agrarian, and nomadic masses that make up nearly half the world's population.

Preston (1967) held similar views but believed that economies in the "take-off" or early "post-take-off" stages of development could utilize government policy to overcome the unique environmental factors that favored development in the U.S. In particular, government control of consumption and production patterns could be combined with U.S. marketing techniques to improve overall standards of living.

Kirpalani (1975) and Mentzer and Samli (1981) lie between those who expounded the virtues of transferring U.S. marketing know-how and those who took exception to it. They acknowledged a growing demand among LDCs for such know-how and recognized the high rewards for the successful transfer of marketing know-how. However, they felt that until specific inefficiencies are overcome, the transfer of marketing technologies would be of minimal value. These inefficiencies included: (1) lack of primary data on developing markets, (2) conflicting attitudes between developing and developed nations as to who should control technology, and (3) incompatible perceptions between developed and developing nations as to the value of marketing know-how.

The third area of inquiry under the profit-macro-normative perspective addresses marketing's social responsibility in developing countries. Robinson (1961) stated that western marketers should place more emphasis on products that offer the greatest long-run benefit to developing nations. He noted that management sensitivity to social responsibility is needed and should be reflected in (1) awareness of the need to modify or redesign products to more appropriately match markets into which they are moving, (2) awareness of the need to measure products against the long run interests of developing markets, and (3) awareness of the extent to which products are politically vulnerable.

L. J. Hunt (1974) stressed adopting a marketing philosophy compatible with the societies in LDCs. Profit-making alone cannot be the only goal. Developed nations have a responsibility to aid in eradicating disease, overcoming malnutrition, and introducing family planning. The same zeal and techniques that modern marketers bring to researching, planning and promoting new products should be brought to solve the social problems facing developing economies.

Harper (1975) noted that developing countries are justified in questioning situations where families are poorly nourished and inadequately dressed, yet spend money on cigarettes, soft drinks, or confectionaries. Modern marketers should be aware of the role they play in forming a developing nation's way of life.

Three articles were found that address the fourth and final issue of this perspective, namely whether macromarketing or micromarketing inputs are more effective in aiding economic development. Kriesberg (1974) advocated that both macro and micromarketing inputs are of value to economic development. Measures of an individual firm's yearly performance and influence on economic development are meaningful at the micro level. For example, a transportation firm might measure performance as the cost per ton-mile of moving a particular commodity from the rural farmer to the urban city. Such a measure taken over a number of years and compared with other competing

firms could give an indication of a firm's efficiency and relative micro contribution to economic improvement in an area or region. On the other hand, a government economist concerned with a nation's overall development would evaluate marketing using "macro" measures. He might compare competing modes of transportation (rail, air freight, and trucking) at the macro level for purposes of evaluating performance. Kriesberg's essential argument was that societal and firm objectives often differ and hence different measures of marketing performance are needed.

Dixon (1981) argued that modern efforts to improve economic development should overcome the limitations of micromarketing with its overemphasis on analytical tools and its narrow behavioral orientation. He noted that the major strides in development made between 1500 and the mid-1800s were macromarketing dominated. Thus a lesson from history would dictate a return to a macro orientation if further strides are to be made.

Cundiff (1982) stated that macromarketing inputs have been the focus of economic development teams who were anxious to show quick results. While agreeing that macro programs have their place, Cundiff argued that macro solutions are, in many instances, not the most efficient. Micromarketing activities by individual businessmen frequently make more important contributions to economic development, particularly in the transfer of technology, and improvement of marketing support systems. A heavy reliance on central planners for macro solutions may stifle entrepreneurship, innovation, and risk-taking in developing nations.

Evaluation

The profit, macro, normative perspective has received considerable attention. Works investigating infrastructure, transfer of marketing know-how, social responsibility and macro-micro inputs to development have made substantial contributions. Areas where more research is needed, however, include the social desirability of advertising, the nature and effect of consumer sovereignty on economic development, advantages and disadvantages of vertical and horizontal integration of marketing systems, and the "optimal" laws to have for regulating marketing activities under various environments. With increased understanding in these areas, the contribution of this marketing perspective to economic development would be greatly improved.

NONPROFIT/MICRO/POSITIVE PERSPECTIVE

This perspective contains research concerning the not-for-profit marketing sectors of an economy at the micro level that influence development. Only one study was found which relates to this perspective. As such the synthesis and evaluation of this perspective are presented concurrently.

Berg (1970) examined the relationship between nutrition and income and noted that for many low-income consumers in LDCs there was actually an inverse relationship between income and the nutritional value of one's diet. This was attributed to the fact that as income increased many consumers shifted to more prestigious but less nutritious foods.

While this study does give some insight into the attitudes of individuals in LDCs, clearly more work is needed. Studies investigating the effect of consumer purchases of public goods on economic development as well as studies dealing with the promotion, pricing and product development for nonprofit organizations should be undertaken. In addition, more research such as Berg's which deals with the general attitudes and opinions of consumers in LDCs would be useful.

NONPROFIT/MICRO/NORMATIVE PERSPECTIVE

This perspective contains research on what the marketing impact should be at the micro, not-for-profit level in order that an economy might develop. Research in this area has also been minimal; only two studies were found that correspond. Again, the synthesis and evaluation of this perspective are undertaken concurrently.

Kriesberg (1968) observed that the production of food products in LDCs was adequate "to meet minimum needs of the population." However, he felt that the problem relating to world food supplies concerned both production and distribution. He pointed out specific public policy actions necessary to facilitate the modernization of food marketing in developing nations. For example, he advocated policies which would encourage farmers to produce

more products for commercial marketing. In addition, he recommended processes for preserving foods which would reduce spoilage. Finally, he recommended increasing the nutritional value of foods through various food supplements.

A second article in this area by Weinstein (1976) developed a strategic plan to market family planning programs in developing countries. The author illustrated how marketing skills can help social action efforts become more effective in achieving their goals.

Given the paucity of work in this area, more research is needed regarding how nonprofit organizations should market their ideas and services and marketing's relationship to economic development. For example, improving the marketing of family planning and energy management programs would assist economic development by reducing demands on resources. In addition, consumer education programs in nutrition, diet and general hygiene could improve standards of living.

NONPROFIT/MACRO/POSITIVE PERSPECTIVE

This perspective contains research on the not-for-profit, macro issues as they actually exist in developing societies. While only a few published studies can be classified under this perspective, various topics have been covered. Three subcategories are reviewed here: (1) studies examining the role of government in economic development especially as regulators of market activities, (2) studies classifying countries based on their level of economic development, and (3) studies concerning the macro nutritional level of LDC populations and its relationship to development.

Synthesis

Studies examining the role of government as regulator of market activities include Samli's (1978) study of Eastern European countries. He noted that economic development is linked to decentralization of government authority over marketing activities. By decentralization he meant a movement from a command economy to a "pseudo-market economy," with the end result being a "socialist regulated market economy." While Samli examined only Eastern Bloc countries, his observation that decentralization aids development may be applicable to other LDCs as well.

Dholakia and Dholakia (1982), examining the changes which are taking place in the world economic order, noted that the nation-state will increasingly become "the market," especially in the Third World and Socialist nations. This trend toward the direct involvement of government in market processes will affect marketing and its role in economic development. The authors observed that such situations will influence the nature of buyer-seller interactions to the extent that negotiations will resemble diplomatic and intergovernmental exchanges.

Bartels (1981) set forth a number of general "marketing principles." He stated that the relationship between government and marketing may be either *constructive* or *constrictive*, depending on the ability of the marketing system to provide society's consumption needs and protect its welfare. Thus, a diversity of market situations in LDCs leads to a diversity in relationships with government and may affect development either positively or negatively.

The previously cited work by Boddewyn and Hollander (1972) also addresses the role of government as a regulator of market activities. While primarily examining the retail sector, it does provide macro insights into government regulations and economic development.

Classification systems for countries based on their level of economic development have been widely recognized. Most notable among these are Rostow's (1960) framework based upon the level of economic growth and Dichter's (1962) framework based upon the development of the middle class. However, Dichter (1962) was primarily concerned with identifying markets for U.S. products rather than fostering economic development. Sethi (1971) examined 91 countries and classified them using a multidimensional approach with 29 different variables. His results indicate that any classification system needs to be multidimensional in nature. However, even using a multidimensional approach, no well defined continuum for economic development was apparent.

The final subcategory under this perspective involves issues concerning the improvement of nutrition at a macro level in LDCs. Only one article fell under this heading. Berg (1970) examined growth in per capita income and its relationship to nutrition in LDCs. He noted that most public policymakers assume that (1) an increase in per capita income among the poor leads to an increase in the amount spent on food products and that (2) an increase in the amount spent on food leads to an improvement in nutrition. Doing his research primarily in India, Berg observed, however, that there was often an *inverse* relationship between income and nutrition. As income increases, consumers in India often purchase non-food rather than food products, and if they do spend more on food, it is often to purchase less nutritional but more "prestigious" food products.

Evaluation

More research is needed concerning the growing trend toward government involvement in market processes and in buyer-seller interactions between nations. In what ways are governments participating in this process? How has such participation affected development? Similarly, additional research in other LDCs along the lines of that conducted by Berg (1970) in India would be useful in determining whether his findings are generalizable to other societies.

NONPROFIT/MACRO/NORMATIVE PERSPECTIVE

This perspective contains research on what marketing's influence should be in development at the nonprofit, macro level. The articles under this perspective can be divided into two categories: (1) those which have looked at the importance of improving the general state of consumer health and nutrition as a facilitator of development, and (2) those which have focused upon government policy as a fomenter of economic and market development and of consumer projection.

Synthesis

Along with various recommendations concerning the importance of increasing the efficiency of individual traders and the distribution system as a whole, Muller-Heumann and Bohringer (1973) recommended improving the general state of health of the labor sector with the objective of improving the efficiency of the work force. Unfortunately, the authors offered no specific recommendations as to *how* this is to be accomplished. Similarly, April et al.

(1974) recommended the use of consumerism to help solve nutritional problems in LDCs. They felt that consumerism as a mechanism for efficient resource allocation can aid developing societies in identifying needs relative to nutritional problems.

The second subcategory of articles under this perspective deals with various government policies and their use in facilitating market development. Myers and Smalley (1963) counseled governmental and private assistance programs to "export" the marketing system as developed in the United States rather than concentrating solely on exporting machinery and production-related ideas. They suggested that such "exporting" not be done without paying careful attention to the cultural pattern and stage of development of the LDC involved.

The role of government as a stimulus for agricultural development was the focus of Breimyer's (1963) article. He also used the U.S. example and noted that the development of U.S. agriculture was accomplished through the use of chemical fertilizers, diesel fuels and other agricultural inputs having an industrial origin. He recommended that governments provide the industrial materials necessary for improving agricultural output at minimum price levels. The downstream marketing of goods that facilitate output was also seen as an important impetus to economic development.

Bennett (1967) depicted the public sector as a facilitator of marketing, as a regulator of business, and as a promoter of entrepreneurship in the economic development process. To facilitate marketing he suggested that government assume some of the responsibility for new product research, for market research and for the building of a skilled labor force. To regulate business he recommended that government be responsible for licensing the foreign technology needed for development, for enforcing anti-trust regulations that enhance competition and for restricting the "unnecessary" consumption of luxury goods. Finally, to promote entrepreneurship, he held that governments should invest in industries such as transportation and communications which complement rather than compete with the private sector.

Gerlach (1963) and Heldman (1973) concentrated on the government's role as a promoter of entrepreneurship. Studying small-scale traders of Africa, Gerlach noted that they acted as

important catalysts of both economic growth and cultural change. He concluded that these traders needed to be recognized and encouraged by government and government policies.

Heldman was concerned with the public sector's development and extension of the transportation system as a necessary prerequisite to the growth of private entrepreneurship. He theorized that the development of a transportation system would attract new commercial firms as well as encourage the expansion of existing ones.

Likewise, Mentzer and Samli (1981) emphasized the importance of government involvement in developing a nation's infrastructure. They stressed first determining the infrastructure needs and then redirecting the work force into activities designed to develop the infrastructure. Finally, they recommended following this up with more advanced infrastructure systems using imported technology.

Like Bennett (1967), Katona (1982) proposed that the public sector conduct market research (i.e., act as a facilitator of business). Such research would be designed to determine public attitudes toward various government policies aimed at expanding the business and marketing systems. A second objective of such research would be to determine how these policies could best be explained to the public and to assess the impact of policies on consumers and businesses once the policies have been instituted. Dholakia et al. (1979) stated that normative policy models can be useful for purposes of policy formation to influence the availability, quality and price of mass consumptions in LDCs. However, such models require empirical and expository backup.

Recently the United Nations (1985) has adopted a series of guidelines concerning consumer protection policies. These guidelines involve policies that deal with (1) the protection of consumers from health and safety hazards, (2) the protection of the economic interests of consumers, (3) consumer education and information programs and (4) the ability of consumers to obtain redress.

Evaluation

The articles under this perspective have examined the public sector's role as a facilitator of public health, as a stimulator of the marketing system, and as a promoter of entrepreneurship. However, the marketing of public goods and social ideas to enhance economic development has not been addressed in sufficient detail. For example, Breimyer (1963) recommended that the public sector provide the agricultural inputs needed to improve agricultural production, but he made few suggestions as to how such inputs are to be marketed by the government. Similarly, while the general state of consumer and worker health and nutrition are seen as being critical to development, more research is needed on the role of health marketing in developing societies. How do we "market" the idea and value of improved nutrition to consumers in LDC's? Both theory development and empirical research are woefully inadequate in this area.

In addition, while Bennett (1967) does concern himself with the government's role as a regulator of business, he suggests *more* regulation in terms of antitrust and restrictions on consumption, but the impact of fewer regulations on marketing systems also needs to be addressed. For example, the reduction of restrictions which limit the activities of middlemen in developing areas has not been examined adequately as a possible catalyst for development.

CONCLUSION

Marketing's impact on economic development has been an area of concern and study for the past 25 to 30 years. Although marketing as a catalyst for development is a concept long accepted, the often intangible benefits of marketing have been overshadowed by the more visible results coming from manufacturing, construction, and agriculture. This article, through the review, synthesis, and evaluation of past works, has attempted to clarify marketing's role in economic development. Also, directions for future research have been suggested.

Table 2 utilizes Hunt's (1976) model to summarize the subcategories of research reviewed in this article. In this form, a parsimonious overview of the issues addressed to date on this topic can be grasped. Table 3 summarizes the topics and issues suggested for future research. Here again, categorization is based on Hunt's model.

Research to date clearly indicates the value of marketing to economic development.

Marketing, for example, provides utility to consumers in LDCs through savings in time and money spent in the buying process. However, many barriers still remain including high transportation, processing, assorting and sorting costs, lack of awareness of shopping alternatives and loyalty to tradition, labor intensive and more expensive retail outlets.

Marketing also develops managers, entrepreneurs and risk-takers in LDCs. However, lack of training and education has offset some of the gains realized by the innovativeness of such risk-takers. Improvements in marketing management skills with respect to marketing research and information systems, coordination of transportation, product handling and storage systems, and channel member communications are needed to fully realize the potential of the newly developing entrepreneur class in LDCs.

Profit levels of LDC firms have been shown to be directly related to the efficiency of their marketing activities, particularly in buying, selling, credit extension, communication and distribution functions. Systems flow analysis has been recommended as a means to identify where efficiencies exist and where they are lacking with respect to these activities. Market entry barriers and trade restrictions imposed by LDCs' public policies have been suggested as possible areas for future research on this topic.

Profits at the macro level have also been correlated with the nature and degree of marketing endeavors in a developing area. High gross national products tend to be related to the percentage of the population working in marketing activities, their level of professionalism and ability to adapt to rapid changes in the environment. The size of markets, the concentration of markets, and personal consumption patterns of consumers are all affected by marketing activities, which in turn affects profit realization.

The majority of findings in regard to public policy in LDCs emphasize government cooperation with, rather than government ownership of, marketing institutions. Government policy and marketing activities must, however, be coordinated with the stage of development of the particular LDC. Depending on the level of development, different problems arise that dictate different policies. Subsistance economies often require assured market prices as incentive to produce, while transitional economies

EXHIBIT 2

A SYNTHESIS OF MARKETING AND ECONOMIC DEVELOPMENT

Sector and Level	Positive	Normative
Profit Micro	- Effects of consumer behavior on firms in LDCs	- Improving the efficiency of firms in LDCs
	- Marketing activities and strategies of firms in LDCs	- Improving consumerism and the quality of life in LDCs
	- The marketing environment faced by firms in LDCs	
Macro	- Comparative studies that search for universal marketing principles applicable to most economic development situations	- The importance of developing an effective and efficient infrastructure
	- The role of government in stimulating marketing activities for profit realization	- The kinds of marketing know-how that could be best transferred from developed to developing countries
	- The relationship between channel structure, profit and economic development in LDCs	- The social responsibility of marketing in developing countries
		- The relative effectiveness of macro vs. micro inputs in aiding economic development
Nonprofit Micro	- Nutritional marketing	- Nutritional marketing
		- Family planning
Macro	- Government as marketing regulator	- Consumer health and development
	- Country classification schemas according to economic development	- The role of government policy towards marketing as a catalyst for economic development
	- Nutrition levels, marketing and development	

need improved storage, transportation and communication facilities. Market-oriented economies need credit availability support and policies to enhance vertical integration of all marketing activities. In other words, careful examination of individual LDCs' market characteristics is needed to guide government policy.

Normative theory on economic development and marketing has focused on the benefits to be derived from improving LDCs' distribution activities. Basically, improvements in distribution systems are seen as a catalyst for decreasing transportation and spoilage cost, which leads to decreases in costs of goods to consumers. This in turn increases consumer discretionary income and demand for goods. Increases in demand allows for increases in economies of scale in production runs and a further decrease in consumer costs. A synergistic process is thus set in motion, which eventually leads to new social behaviors, new patterns of consumption and increased standards of living (i.e., economic development). Government tax benefits, resulting from this process, allow for increased expenditures for disease and malnutrition erradications, family planning and similar social areas of concern.

Much research remains to be done in regard to marketing and economic development. A clear example of this lies in the realization that very little research has been conducted on the relationship between nonprofit marketing and development. Exhibits 1, 2 and 3 form the backdrop of the review, synthesis and evaluation presented in this article. These exhibits together with the text of this article, may provide future researchers firm ground by which to advance the study of marketing and economic development.

EXHIBIT 3

SUGGESTED TOPICS FOR FUTURE RESEARCH

Sector and Level	Positive	Normative
Profit		
Micro	- Individual firm and consumer buyer behavior in non-food industries	- Marketing roles in improving consumer consumption
	- Case studies on how firms determine factors as prices, products promotion and channels of distribution in markets other than Latin America	- Improving marketing training in small firms
		- Improving marketing communication between consumer and producer
Macro	- Aggregate consumption patterns and profit flows due to marketing activities	- The social desirability of advertising
	- Power and conflict in LDCs' channels of distribution	- Consumer sovereignty and economic development
	- Effect of LDCs' laws and regulations affecting marketing efficiencies	- Advantages of vertical and horizontal marketing systems in LDCs
		- Optimum regulations for marketing efficiency in LDCs
Nonprofit		
Micro	- Effect of consumer purchases of public goods on economic development	- How to market nonprofit services, ideas and and products, i.e., marketing family planning and energy use
	- Nonprofit marketing decisions including pricing, promotion, channels and service-product mix	- Consumer education on nutritional hygiene
Macro	- Government participation and effect on buyer-seller interactions	- Government marketing of public goods and ideas
	- Public policy effects on consumer consumption patterns and resulting effects on overall economic development	- The role of health marketing in LDCs' development
		- The impact of fewer regulations on marketing systems

REFERENCES

Abbott, J. C. (1962), "The Role of Marketing in the Development of Backward Agricultural Economies," *Journal of Farm Economics* (May), 349-362.

———(1963), "Marketing and Area Development Studies," in *Towards Scientific Marketing*, Stephen A. Greyser, ed., Chicago: American Marketing Association, pp. 424-438.

———(1967), "Agricultural Marketing Boards in Developing Countries," *American Journal of Agricultural Economics*, 49, 705-722.

Abegglen, James C. (1967), "Japan, Incorporated: Government and Business as Partners," in *Changing Marketing Systems: Consumer, Corporate and Government Interfaces*, Reed Moyer, ed., Washington, DC: American Marketing Association, pp. 228-232.

Anderson, Dole A. (1970), *Marketing and Development, the Thailand Experience*, East Lansing: Michigan State University.

April, Jay E., David J. Rogers, Gilbert N. Hersh, and Charles C. Slater (1974), "Consumerism—A Neglected Decision Tool

for Solving Nutrition Problems in Developing Countries," in *Marketing Systems for Developing Countries*, Dov Israeli, Dafna Israeli, and Frank Meissner, eds., New York: John Wiley and Sons, pp. 70-80.

Arndt, J. (1972), "Temporal Lags in Comparative Retailing," *Journal of Marketing*, 36 (October), 40-45.

———(1982), "The Conceptual Domain of Marketing: Evaluation of Shelby Hunt's Three Dichotomies Model," *European Journal of Marketing*, 16, 27-35.

Barksdale, H. C. and L. M. Anderson (1982a), "Comparative Marketing: A Review of the Literature," *Journal of Macromarketing*, 2 (Spring), 57-62.

———(1982b), "Comparative Marketing: A Program for the Future," *Journal of Macromarketing*, 2 (Fall), 52-58.

Bartels, R. (1963), *Comparative Marketing: Wholesaling in 15 Countries*, Homewood, IL: Richard D. Irwin.

———(1976), "Marketing and Economic Development," in *Macromarketing: Distributive Processes from a Societal Perspective*, C. Slater, ed., Boulder: University of Colorado, pp. 211-217.

_____ (1981), *Global Development and Marketing*, Columbus, OH: Grid Publishing.

Bauer, P. T. (1954), *West African Trade*, Cambridge: Cambridge University Press.

Bennett, P. D. (1967), "Marketing and Public Policy in Latin America," in *Changing Marketing Systems: Consumer, Corporate and Government Interfaces*, Reed Moyer, ed., Washington, DC: American Marketing Association, pp. 233-238.

Berg, Alan (1970), "Increased Income and Improved Nutrition: A Shibboleth Examined," in *Marketing Challenge: Distributing Production in Developing Nations*, Martin Kriesberg, ed., Washington, DC: U.S. Department of Agriculture, pp. 41-45.

Boddewyn, J. J. and Stanley C. Hollander (1972), *Public Policy Towards Retailing*, Lexington, MA: D. C. Heath.

Boyd, Harper W. (1961), "Marketing in Egypt," in *The Social Responsibility of Marketing*, W. D. Stevens, ed., Chicago: American Marketing Association, pp. 419-424.

Boyd, Harper W., Richard M. Clewett, and Ralph L. Westfield (1958), "The Marketing Structure of Venezuela," *Journal of Marketing*, 22 (April), 391-397.

Breimyer, H. F. (1963), "Functioning of Factor Markets and Economic Development," in *Towards Scientific Marketing*, Stephen Greyser, ed., Chicago: American Marketing Association, pp. 409-423.

Bretherton, I. S. (1977), "Does Marketing Activity in Mexico Help the Country's Development?" in *Macromarketing: Distributive Processes from a Societal Perspective, An Elaboration of Issues*, Phillip D. White and Charles C. Slater, eds., Boulder: University of Colorado, pp. 351-364.

Bucklin, L. P. (1975a), "Efficiency in the Retailing and Wholesaling of Food Products," *FAO Expert Consultation on the Development of Food Marketing Systems for Large Urban Areas in Asia*, Kuala Lumpur, Malaysia: FAO.

_____ (1975b), "Training for Improving Food Market Management," *FAO Expert Consultation in the Development of Food Marketing Systems for Large Urban Areas in Asia*, Kuala Lumpur, Malaysia: FAO.

_____ (1975c), "Change Agents in Marketing Development," *FAO Expert Consultation on the Development of Food Marketing Systems for Large Urban Areas in Asia*, Kuala Lumpur, Malaysia: FAO.

_____ (1976), "Intermediate Technologies for Improving Food Retailing Efficiency in Developing Asian Countries," in *Macromarketing: Distributive Processes from a Societal Perspective*, Charles Slater, ed., Boulder: University of Colorado, pp. 218-237.

Collins, Norman R. (1963), "The Development of a Coordinated Food Production and Distribution System in Western Europe," *Journal of Farm Economics*, 45 (May), 263-272.

Collins, Norman R. and R. H. Holton (1963), "Programming Changes in Marketing," *Kyklos*, 16, 123-137.

Cook, Hugh L. (1959), "Market Structures and Economic Development in the Philippines," *Journal of Farm Economics* (December), 1316-1322.

Cox, R. (1965), "The Search for Universals in Comparative Studies of Domestic Marketing Systems," in *Marketing and Economic Development*, P. D. Bennett, ed., Chicago: American Marketing Association, pp. 143-162.

Cranch, Graeme (1974), "Modern Marketing Techniques Applied to Developing Countries," in *The Environment for Marketing Management*, 3d edition, R. J. Holloway and R. S. Hancock, eds., New York: John Wiley & Sons, pp. 412-416.

Cundiff, E. (1965), "Concepts in Comparative Retailing," *Journal of Marketing*, 29 (January), 59-63.

_____ (1982), "A Macromarketing Approach to Economic Development," *Journal of Macromarketing*, 2 (Spring), 14-19.

Cundiff, E. and M. Hilger (1979), "Marketing and the Product Consumption Thesis in Economic Development," in

Macromarketing: Evolution of Thought, George Fisk, Robert Nason, and Phillip D. White, eds., Boulder: University of Colorado, pp. 177-186.

Cunningham, William H., Russell M. Moore, and Isabella Cunningham (1974), "Urban Markets in Industrializing Countries: The Sao Paulo Experience," *Journal of Marketing*, 38 (April), 2-12.

Cunningham, William H. and Shelby D. Hunt (1982), "From the Editor," *Journal of Marketing* (Summer), 7-8.

Dahringer, Lee D. (1983), "Public Policy Implications of Reverse Channel Mapping For Lesotho," *Journal of Macromarketing* (Spring), 69-75.

Dannehaeuser, N. (1980), "The Role of the Neighborhood Store in Developing Economies: The Case of Dagupan City, Philippines," *Journal of Developing Areas* (January), 157-174.

_____ (1981), "Evolution and Devolution of Downward Channel Integration in the Philippines," *Economic Development and Cultural Change* (April), 584-595.

Dawson, Leslie M. (1980), "Setting Multinational Industrial Marketing Strategies," *Industrial Marketing Management*, 9 (July), 179-186.

Dholakia, N. and R. R. Dholakia (1982), "Marketing in the Emerging World Order," *Journal of Macromarketing*, 2 (Spring), 47-56.

Dholakia, N., R. Khurana, L. Bhandari, and M. N. Vora (1979), "On Normative Policy Models in Developing Countries," *Omega International Journal*, 7, 359-360.

Dichter, Ernest (1962), "The World Customer," *Harvard Business Review*, 40 (July-August), 113-122.

Dixon, D. F. (1981), "Role of Marketing in Early Theories of Economic Development," *Journal of Macromarketing*, 1 (Fall), 19-27.

Douglas, S. (1971), "Patterns and Parallels of Marketing Structure in Several Countries," *MSU Business Topics*, 19 (Spring), 38-48.

Drucker, Peter (1958), "Marketing and Economic Development," *Journal of Marketing*, 22 (January), 251-259.

Elton, W. W. (1967), "The Developing World," in *Changing Marketing Systems: Consumer, Corporate and Government Interfaces*, Reed Moyer, ed., Washington, DC: American Marketing Association, pp. 242-243.

Emlen, Woodruff (1958), "Let's Export Marketing Know-How," *Harvard Business Review*, 36 (November-December), 70-76.

Etgar, Michael (1983), "A Failure in Marketing Technology Transfer: The Case of Rice Distribution in the Ivory Coast," *Journal of Macromarketing* (Spring), 59-68.

Food and Agriculture Organization of the United Nations (1975), *Development of Food Marketing Systems for Large Urban Areas*, Kuala Lumpur, Malaysia: FAO.

Freedman, Deborah S. (1970), "The Role of the Consumption of Modern Durables in Economic Development," *Economic Development and Cultural Changes* (October), 25-48.

Galbraith, J. K. and Richard H. Holton (1955), *Marketing Efficiency in Puerto Rico*, Cambridge: Harvard University Press.

Garlick, Peter C. (1971), *African Traders and Economic Development in Ghana*, Oxford: Clarendon Press.

Gerlach, Luther P. (1963), "Traders on Bicycles: A Study of Entrepreneurship and Cultural Change Among the Digo and Duruma of Kenya," *Sociologus*, 13.

Glade, W. P., W. A. Strang, J. G. Udell, and J. E. Littlefield (1970), *Marketing in a Developing Nation*, Lexington, MA: Heath Lexington Books.

Goertz, Janice (1979), "KETA: A Force Behind Exports," *International Trade Forum*, 15 (July/September), 16-20, 27-35.

Goldman, A. (1974), "Outreach of Consumers and Modernization of Urban Food Retailing in Developing Countries," *Journal of Marketing*, 38 (October), 8-16.

Guerin, Joseph R. (1965), "The Introduction of a New Food-Marketing Institution in an Underdeveloped Economy: Supermarkets in Spain," *Food Research Institute*, 5, 217-227.

Halper, D. G. (1966), "The Environment for Marketing in Peru," *Journal of Marketing*, 30 (July), 42-46.

Hamilton, David (1965), "Marketing Science: Usefulness to the Consumer," in *Science in Marketing*, George Schwartz, ed., New York: John H. Wiley & Sons, pp. 33-46.

Hansz, James E. and James D. Goodnow (1973), "A Multivariate Classification of Country Market Environments," in *Marketing Education and the Real World and Dynamic Marketing in a Changing World*, Boris W. Becker and Helmut Becker, eds., Chicago: American Marketing Association, pp. 191-198.

Harper, M. (1975), "Advertising in a Developing Economy: Opportunity and Responsibility," *European Journal of Marketing*, 9, 215-223.

Harrison, Kelly, Donald Henley, Harold Riley, and James Shaffer (1974), *Improving Food Marketing Systems in Developing Countries: Experiences From Latin America*, East Lansing: Latin American Studies Center, Michigan State University.

Harrison, Kelly, Donald Henley, and Michael Weber (1972), *Fomenting Improvements in Food Marketing in Costa Rica*, East Lansing: Latin American Studies Center, Michigan State University.

Heldman, Horst (1973), "The Role of Transportation Traffic in the National Economy," *Intereconomies*, 11, 343-350.

Henley, Donald S. and R. Vincent Farace (1967), "Consumer Buying and Communication Patterns in Bolivian Urban Food Retailing: A Preliminary Report," in *Changing Marketing Systems: Consumer, Corporate and Government Interfaces*, Reed Moyer, ed., Washington, DC: American Marketing Association, pp. 191-194.

Hilger, M. (1977), "Theories of the Relationship Between Marketing and Economic Development: Public Policy Implications," in *Macromarketing: Distributive Processes From a Societal Perspective, An Elaboration of Issues*, Phillip D. White and Charles C. Slater, eds., Boulder: University of Colorado, pp. 333-350.

Hirsch, I. V. (1961), "The Contribution of Marketing to Economic Development—A Generally Neglected Area," in *The Social Responsibility of Marketing*, W. D. Stevens, ed., Chicago: American Marketing Association, pp. 413-418.

Holton, Richard H. (1953), "Marketing Structure and Economic Development," *Quarterly Journal of Economics*, 67 (August), 344-361.

——— (1980), "How Advertising Achieved Responsibility Among Economists," *Advertising Age*, 51 (April 30), 56-64.

Hunt, Lawrence J. (1974), "Marketing Education in Developing Environments," in *AMA Combined Proceedings*, Ronald C. Curham, ed., Chicago: American Marketing Association, pp. 642-646.

Hunt, Shelby D. (1976), *Marketing Theory: Conceptual Foundations of Research in Marketing*, Columbus, OH: Grid, Inc.

Jessop, Guy (1979), "Greece: A Nation at the Crossroads," *Marketing* (December), 73-77.

Katona, George (1982), "Selling Government Programs," *Journal of Macromarketing*, 2 (Fall), 38-42.

Kaynak, E. and S. T. Cavusgil (1982), "The Evolution of Food Retailing Systems: Contrasting the Experience of Developed and Developing Countries," *Journal of the Academy of Marketing Science*, 10, 249-267.

Kindleberger, Charles and Bruce Herrick (1977), *Economic Development*, 3d ed., New York: McGraw-Hill Book Company.

Kirpalani, V. H. (1975), "Opportunities/Problems in the International Transfer of Marketing/Technology to the Third World," in *AMA Combined Proceedings*, Edward M. Mazze, ed., Chicago: American Marketing Association, pp. 285-288.

Kotler, Philip (1982), "Neglected Areas Demand Attention of Scholars if Marketing Discipline is to Reach Maturation," *Marketing News*, 41 (September), 3.

Kriesberg, Martin (1968), "Marketing Food in Developing Nations—Second Phase of the War on Hunger," *Journal of Marketing*, 30 (October), 55-60.

——— (1974), "Marketing Efficiency in Developing Countries," in *Marketing Systems for Developing Countries*, Dov Izraeli, Dafna Izraeli, and Frank Meissner, eds., New York: John Wiley and Sons, pp. 18-30.

Lamont, D. (1965), "A Theory of Marketing Development: Mexico," in *Marketing and Economic Development*, Peter D. Bennett, ed., Chicago: American Marketing Association, pp. 44-45.

Langley, J. and J. Foggin (1980), "Selected Aspects of Economic Development As Related to Distribution," *Survey of Business*, 15 (Spring), 30-35.

Layton, R. (1981a), "Trade Flows in Macromarketing Systems, Part I," *Journal of Macromarketing*, 1 (Spring), 35-48.

——— (1981b), "Trade Flows in Macromarketing Systems, Part II," *Journal of Macromarketing*, 1 (Fall), 48-55.

Lele, Uma J. (1971), *Food Grain Marketing in India*, Ithaca: Cornell University Press.

Lugmani, Mushtaq, Zahir A. Quraeshi, and Linda Delene (1980), "Marketing in Islamic Countries: A Viewpoint," *MSU Business Topics* (Summer), 17-25.

Martin, Lee R. (1959), "Some Marketing Problems in Pakistan and India," *Journal of Farm Economics* (December), 1323-1326.

McCarthy, E. J. (1963), "Effective Marketing Institutions for Economic Development," in *Towards Scientific Marketing*, Stephen A. Greyser, ed., Chicago: American Marketing Association, pp. 393-404.

McNair, Malcom P. (1968), "Marketing and the Social Challenge of Our Times," *A New Measure of Responsibility for Marketing*, Keith Cox and Ben M. Enis, eds., Chicago: American Marketing Association.

Mentzer, J. T. and A. C. Samli (1981), "A Model for Marketing in Economic Development," *Columbia Journal of World Business*, 16 (Fall), 91-101.

Moyer, R. (1965), *Marketing in Economic Development: International Occasional Paper No. 1*, East Lansing: Bureau of Business and Economic Research, Michigan State University.

Moyer, R. and S. Hollander (1968), *Markets and Marketing in Developing Economies*, Homewood, IL: Richard D. Irwin.

Muller-Heumann G. and R. Bohringer (1973), "Stimulating Consumption in the LDCs," *Intereconomics*, 11, 344-347.

Myers, K. H. (1963), "Marketing's Role in the Economy," in *Towards Scientific Marketing*, Stephen A. Greyser, ed., Chicago: American Marketing Association, pp. 355-365.

Myers, K. H. and Orange A. Smalley (1963), "Marketing History and Economic Development," *Business History Review*, 33 (Autumn), 387-401.

Nason, R. and P. White (1981), "The Visions of Charles C. Slater: Social Consequences of Marketing," *Journal of Macromarketing*, 1 (Fall), 4-18.

Nielsen, Richard P. (1974), "Marketing and Development in LDCs," *Columbia Journal of World Business*, 9 (Winter), 46-49.

Oritt, P. and A. Hagan (1977), "Channels of Distribution and Economic Development," *Atlanta Economic Review*, 27, 40-44.

Preston, Lee E. (1967), "Market Development and Market Control," in *Changing Marketing Systems: Consumer, Corporate and Government Interfaces*, Reed Moyer, ed., Washington, DC: American Marketing Association, pp. 223-227.

——— (1968), "The Commercial Sector and Economic Development," in *Markets and Marketing in Developing Economics*, Reed Moyer and Stanley Hollander, eds., Homewood, IL: Richard D. Irwin, pp. 9-23.

_____ (1970), "Marketing Organization and Economic Development: Structure, Products, and Management," in *Vertical Marketing Systems*, L. P. Bucklin, ed., Glenview, IL: Scott, Foresman and Co., pp. 116-133.

Rae, Ian (1980), "Solving the Chinese Puzzle," *Marketing*, 2 (August 27), 24-25.

Riley, Harold (1972), *Improving Internal Marketing Systems as Part of National Development Programs*, East Lansing: Latin American Studies Center, Michigan State University.

Riley, Harold, Kelly Harrison, Nelson Suarez, James Shaffer, Donald Henley, Donald Larson, Colin Guthrie, and David Lloyd-Clare (1970a), *Market Coordination in the Development of The Cauca Valley Region-Colombia*, East Lansing: Latin American Area Studies, Michigan State University.

Riley, Harold, Charles Slater, Kelly Harrison, John Wish, John Griggs, Vincent Farace, Jose Santiago, and Idalia Rodriguez (1970b), *Food Marketing in the Economic Development of Puerto Rico*, East Lansing: Latin American Studies Center, Michigan State University.

Robinson, R. D. (1961), "The Challenge of the Underdeveloped National Market," *Journal of Marketing*, 25 (October), 19-25.

Rostow, W. W. (1960), *The Stages of Economic Growth*, Cambridge: Cambridge University Press.

_____ (1965), "The Concept of a National Market and its Economic Implications," in *Marketing and Economic Development*, Peter D. Bennett, ed., Chicago: American Marketing Association, pp. 11-20.

Ruttan, Vernon (1969), "Agricultural Product and Factor Markets in Southeast Asia," *Economic Development and Cultural Change*, 7 (July).

Samli, A. Coskun (1978), *Marketing and Distribution Systems in Eastern Europe*, New York: Praeger Publishers.

Scherb, Otto (1980), "Brazil Pursues Industrial Eminence," *Advertising Age*, 51 (May 12), 5-8.

Sethi, S. Prakash (1971), "Comparative Cluster Analysis for World Markets," *Journal of Marketing Research* (August), 348-354.

Shapiro, S. J. (1965), "Comparative Marketing and Economic Development," in *Science in Marketing*, George Schwartz, ed., New York: John Wiley and Sons, Inc., pp. 398-429.

Sherbini. A. A. (1965), "Marketing in the Industrialization of Underdeveloped Countries," *Journal of Marketing*, 29 (January), 28-32.

Slater, C. (1965), "The Role of Food Marketing in Latin American Food Development," in *Marketing and Economic Development*, Peter D. Bennett, ed., Chicago: American Marketing Association, pp. 30-37.

_____ (1968), "Marketing Process in Developing Latin American Societies," *Journal of Marketing*, 32 (July), 50-55.

_____ (1975), "Comparative Marketing and Economic Development," in *Science in Marketing*, George Schwartz, ed., New York: John Wiley and Sons, Inc., pp. 398-429.

_____ (1976), "A Theory of Market Processes," in *Macromarketing: Distributive Processes from a Societal Perspective*, Charles Slater, ed., Boulder: University of Colorado, pp. 117-140.

_____ (1977), "Towards an Operational Theory of Market Processes," in *Macromarketing: Distributive Processes from a Societal Perspective, An Elaboration of Issues*, Phillip D. White and Charles C. Slater, eds., Boulder: University of Colorado, pp. 115-129.

Slater, C. and Donald Henley (1969a), *Market Processes in La Paz, Bolivia*, East Lansing: Latin American Studies Center, Michigan State University.

Slater, C., Harold Riley, Vincent Farace, Kelly Harrison, Ferdinando Neves, Alan Bogatay, Mark Doctoroff, Donald Larson, Robert Nason, and Thomas Webb (1969b), *Market Processes in the Recife Area of Northeast Brazil*, East Lansing: Latin American Studies Center, Michigan State University.

Taimni, K. K. (1981), "Employment Generation Through Handicraft Co-Operatives: The Indian Experience," *International Labour Review*, 120 (July-August), 505-517.

Thomson, John R. (1980), "Foreign Marketers Rush into Sadat's 'Open' Arms," *Advertising Age*, 51 (August 18), S-2.

United Nations (1985), "Resolution Adopted by the General Assembly 39/248, Consumer Protection" (April 9).

U.S. Department of Agriculture (1972), *Improving Marketing Systems in Developing Countries*, Washington, DC: U.S. Department of Agriculture.

Wadinambiaratchi, G. (1965), "Channels of Distribution on Developing Economies," *Business Quarterly*, 30 (Winter), 74-82.

Weinstein, D. (1976), "Marketing and Communication in Family Planning Programs in Developing Countries," in *Marketing Systems for Developing Countries*, Dov Izraeli, Dafna Israeli, and Frank Meissner, eds., New York: John Wiley & Sons, pp. 81-93.

Wheatly, John J. and Sadaomi Oshikawa (1979), "Marketing in Japan: Problems and Possibilities for American Business," *Journal of Contemporary Business*, 8, 63-79.

Worth, Don (1978), "The Wherein of the Green," *New Englander*, 25 (September), 51-52, 54.

Yoshino, M. Y. (1971), *The Japanese Marketing System*, Cambridge: The MIT Press.

Part II
Historical Method

[10]

RONALD SAVITT

Why history in marketing? Historical research in marketing offers opportunities for charting our past and better understanding our present. The author formulates a suitable method for undertaking historical research in marketing. It relates the principles of history to the study of marketing.

HISTORICAL RESEARCH IN MARKETING

WILL historical research in marketing continue to be undertaken mainly by nonmarketing scholars?

The question arises because marketing scholars have given little attention to this part of the discipline. More than 10 years have passed since the publication of the last major work in marketing history (Shapiro and Doody 1968), and business historians are wondering why the history of marketing has not interested marketing scholars (Hidy 1977, p. 19). Part of the void has been filled by *business* and *economic* historians who are making contributions to the marketing literature, but they are not writing marketing history. Such scholars have produced important works, such as the economic history of American wholesale middlemen in the nineteenth century (Porter and Livesay 1971). However, they do not do justice to marketing history in the way marketing scholars would.

Among the reasons advanced for the absence of historical research in marketing are the lack of appreciation of its importance and the lack of a method. The purpose of this article is to offer a rationale for such historical research and a method which can be applied in marketing. A brief sketch of the state of marketing history is presented as background.

Why Study Marketing History?

Historical study adds a robust quality to a discipline. It enables scholars within the discipline, as well as society at large, to gain an understanding of its origins and its patterns of change. Such study relates a discipline to its own past and to other disciplines. Historical study helps to establish an identity for a discipline by providing some idea of where it is and what it is.

Historical research can also be used in the verification and synthesis of hypotheses, "the cumulative result being the promotion of theory" (Doody 1965, p. 557). It can be done at the micro level as in the case of market segmentation. The study of Josiah Wedgwood, the English porcelain manufacturer, provides new bases for understanding the origins of segmentation (McKendrick 1960). Historical research can also add to the development of macro theories such as proposed by Alderson (1965) and more recently by Bagozzi (1978). Cassady, in his studies of food retailing, argued this point. Historical studies of market behavior would provide a better understanding of how markets and competitors do behave than the current theories based on how they are supposed to behave (Cassady 1963).

Some Basic Issues

Marketing history is defined by the content of marketing. Assume that marketing is the discipline which describes and explains the operation of markets in terms of all

Ronald Savitt is Professor, Department of Marketing and Economic Analysis, The University of Alberta.

Journal of Marketing
Vol. 44 (Fall 1980), 52-58.

prepurchase and postpurchase activities related to transactions of ownership or use rights to any factor, good,
or service (Narver and Savitt 1971, p. 4). Historical
research in marketing is a narration of events through
time in which their sequence is described. The writing
of history requires the analysis and explanation of the
causes and consequences of events with particular concern for change.

A historical study in marketing would focus on the
elements of want satisfaction, rather than on resource
allocation as in economics, or on spatial behavior as in
human geography. An illustrative hypothesis for a specific study might be:

> In spite of increasing marketing abilities, merchant
> wholesalers in foodstuffs in Great Britain declined in
> importance in the nineteenth and twentieth centuries
> because of improvements in the transportation system
> which provided a closer relation between food produc-
> ers and retailers.

Though the hypothesis includes concepts and ideas
from other disciplines, its central thrust is within
marketing. This is as it should be; however, research
from other disciplines is not to be ignored. It is to be
treated as complementary to the marketing issues. Good
historical analysis seeks to explore and analyze the
infinitely subtle relations between marketing events and
economic and geographic factors. Vance, a prominent
geographer who has studied wholesaling, makes this
point. He says that the geographer examines the economic landscape in terms of the components and the
activities that they serve, and the relations between and
among the physical and social elements that are present
(Vance 1970, p. 34). The marketing scholar, in contrast, must concentrate on the development of the
marketing system, the factors that affect it, and most
important, its management.

The Historical Perspective

An introduction to the concept of historical perspective
is required. It is defined in terms of *description* and
comparison.

Historical research and writing are basically descriptive; they begin with the narration of events in a time
sequence. Such an exercise might encompass a recognized historical period, for example, the industrial revolution. Specific events are identified and described as to
particular characteristics. Analysis addresses the questions of explanation, relationship, and consequences of
the events.

Historical studies are generally not predictive although
the historian does become involved in a type of prediction, sometimes called "retrodiction," in attempting to
work out what might have happened in the past. The
conclusions of historical study can form the basis of

prediction, to the extent that extrapolation to future
cases is desirable *and* realistic.

Historical studies are not deterministic in the sense
of an equilibrium model. *Probable cause*, rather than
deterministic cause, describes historical relationships.
Moreover, unlike quantitative analysis, historical analysis does not contain the axiomatic development of mathematical theory in which inferences are certain, the
theorems are absolutely determined, the axioms are given,
and hence the results are deterministic (Harvey 1969, p.
232).

Comparison is also part of the historical perspective
although it is important to note that comparison is only
a method and not historical research itself. Events in a
single place can be compared through time, and events
at different places in space can be compared in the
context of chronological time—at the same time, for
example. The former approach is an instance of traditional, chronological historical research. The latter is no
less an example of historical study. A project which
examines department stores in a series of economies in
1980 would be part and parcel of historical research in
marketing if emphasis were given to the time-related
differences among them. What is required of the historian is recognition of the complexities in the meaning of
time. This important topic is beyond the scope of the
article; however, anyone undertaking historical studies
should become acquainted with the problems (Whitrow
1975).

Types of Marketing History and the State of Historical Research

The historical dimension of the discipline consists of
two distinct but inextricably intertwined components.
One is the historical development of the doctrines or the
history of thought, the discipline's "intellectual history." The second is the history of the discipline's content. The two feed upon one another. "It may be
oversimplification to contrast the body of theory in
economics—whatever its deficiencies—with the absence
of a corpus of marketing theory and the respective
significant correlations with the presence and absence of
a strong historically oriented literature, but there remains
a reasonable suspicion that these factors are not unrelated"
(Smalley 1964, p. 366).

There is a historical tradition in marketing, although
it is not as well developed as in economics. Work has
been undertaken in both components, although marketing
thought has been given more attention than marketing
content. The writings of Bartels (1976) and Schwartz
(1963) capture the core of the history of marketing
thought. Bartels concentrated on the development of
marketing thought by documenting major academic contributions. His work is historical only to the extent that

it is chronological. He traced the development of concepts in a number of areas. The work is not analytical because he does not attempt to explain the circumstances that affected the topics. It is not comparative because he does not evaluate the relationships between various approaches to marketing, such as functionalism or the institutional approach. The readers gain few insights into the environmental conditions and intellectual forces that produced such marketing scholars as Wroe Alderson, Reavis Cox, E. T. Grether, David Revzan, and others. Marketers, unlike economists, know little about the forces that gave direction to their intellectual development (Gray 1931).

Only a few attempts have been made to produce marketing history. The major comprehensive work is the classic *Milestones of Marketing*, published in 1938, which documents progress in marketing to that date (Hotchkiss 1938). *Readings in the History of American Marketing* falls short of an actual history although it has served as an important stimulus for encouraging historical work (Shapiro and Doody 1968). Interestingly, marketing history has not been accorded a place in the study of the history of marketing thought. Bartels includes no entry for either "history" or "historical." In spite of his citing individuals who have contributed to marketing *thought*, he does not include their contributions to marketing *history*. For example, Frank M. Jones is acknowledged for his work in theory but not for marketing history (Jones 1937).

I do not mean to suggest that no work has been done in marketing history. The topics that have been addressed are advertising and distribution. In the former area the amount of study has led to the development of the *Journal of Advertising History* (Pollay 1977). In the latter, some work has been undertaken in retailing, most notably "the wheel of retailing" (Hollander 1963). More recent work by Goldman (1978) on the concept of "trading up" provides more hypotheses for historical study in retailing. Bucklin's comprehensive study of evolution in the distributive trades offers a broad framework for understanding growth and competition in retail and wholesale trade. Because of his reliance on economic analysis, the study is not historical in the sense developed in this article; however, it is rich in hypotheses for marketing history (Bucklin 1972).

Without condemning marketing scholars as neglectful, one can easily understand why, in general, marketing history has received little attention. As an applied discipline, marketing must cater to its client market of decision makers. Their concerns are directed toward, understandably, making better decisions in today's market. Looking backward to them is a luxury. Moreover, the discipline itself has had to absorb an ever-increasing set of new concepts and methods and then establish appropriate ways to apply them to the problems at hand.

Finally, the absence of historical methodology has also limited the opportunity to reflect upon the past.

To a great degree, marketing history is a victim of the endless flood of contemporary developments and the increasing specialization of academics (Shapiro 1964, p. 569).

Method for History in Marketing

The question: "What is the correct method for historical research?" is important and cannot be easily dismissed. All research should be based on the principles of the scientific method, although experimentation cannot be applied in history as it is applied in the biological and physical sciences or even in the social sciences. The fact that "historical experimentation" is impossible does not mean that historical research must be any less valid than research in those circumstances in which experimentation is used. Historical research must retain the objectivity of the scientific method, following its structure as closely as possible. The major principle is that historical research in marketing must conform in every way possible to experimental control as applied in the experimental method. It is beyond the scope of this article to argue how historical analysis might approach the structure of a well defined experiment (Marwick 1970, p. 105).

The Formulation of Historical Research

Figure 1 is a methodological diagram for historical research in marketing which includes the essence of the scientific method. The seven elements describe the sequential pattern of activities required to do historical research. They can be examined in the context of a specific project. Assume that a marketing scholar is interested in understanding the conditions which led to the development of *fixed store retailing*, namely, the transition from journeyman merchants to continuous selling at specific locations. The results of such a study could be used to understand the problems that must be faced in a developing economy, although they would have to be considered within the limitations of the predictive nature of history as previously discussed.

Activity 1. The beginning point for the researcher is to define his or her own perceptual experiences of the problem. These include, among other things, the researcher's beliefs about what has happened, perceptions about the conditions which lead to the changes, and assumptions about how the former relate to the problem at hand. This activity aims at understanding the nature and the amount of subjectivity held by the researcher which will have to be accounted for in the evaluation of the findings. Subjectivity is present in all historical research simply because of differences between the past and the present. This gap, much as the "gap"

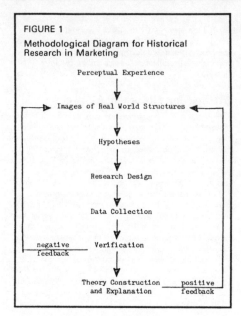

FIGURE 1

Methodological Diagram for Historical Research in Marketing

distance that buyers will travel to purchase that good (Hay and Beavon 1979, p. 27).

Within the formulation of the hypothesis, definitions of standards must be developed for the testing procedures, such as the meaning of "viable" and "profitable;" however, these do not differ from those employed in traditional research.

Activity 4. The research design to test the hypothesis will incorporate observation of examples of periodic markets as they operate in different environments, and surveys of the literature and individuals familiar with such markets as well as persons who possibly have seen the transition take place. The surveys will also examine materials that include descriptions of this type of transition over a variety of time periods. This activity is no different from the techniques used in traditional marketing research except in the types and sources of data found in historical research.

Activity 5. The sources of historical evidence differ from the traditional ones used in marketing research. Greater reliance is placed on archival materials, corporate records, and public and legal documents as well as business, economic, social, and urban histories. Artifact evidence including buildings and relics also is used.

Attention must be given to the distinction between primary and secondary sources as a means of minimizing the gap between the actor and the observer. Drawing a precise line between primary and secondary sources is difficult in historical research. Simply because a document is old does not mean that it is primary. On a spectrum from "purely primary data" to "purely secondary data" there is a greater overlap for historical data than for contemporary data. The marketing scholar can in part minimize this problem by attempting to view historical data as if he or she were a contemporary with them. This is no mean task and it requires that the researcher have some knowledge about the period of the study.

A researcher not only must understand his or her own subjectivity as previously described, but also must be prepared to understand the ways in which subjectivity can creep into primary data. Anyone who has examined legislative hearings will appreciate this problem. The verbal testimony of a witness as recorded in the hearings and the written testimony from which the oral statement is made often differ even though they are presented by the same person.

Being aware of the problems of such differences creates a degree of sensitivity which is necessary if correct statements about the validity of data are to be made. The historical researcher must closely question "official records" and "first-hand reports" in the same way that caution is exercised in accepting the information on completed mail questionnaires. In historical re-

of experimental error, must be acknowledged and accounted for.

Activity 2. The perceptual experiences are compared with the images of the real world as reported in the literature. This activity includes the preliminary investigation stage in which a literature search is undertaken to determine what is known about retail change of this type. In the case of marketing, the primitives, the basic functions, must be defined in a manner that allows comparison over time. For example, the contrast between fixed store retailing and journeyman merchants or periodic markets implies something about how storage and transportation functions are performed in the economy. Hence, the characteristics of the functions as well as the factors that influence them must be understood in terms of their effects on buyers and sellers, and the effects of buyers and sellers on them.

Activity 3. From that exercise will develop hypotheses which are to be verified. One hypothesis for historical investigation that has evolved from the images of the real world is:

A fixed location retailer will be established and will remain viable if the maximum range of a good exceeds the minimum range of a good, where the minimum range is defined as the distance from the fixed location incorporating sufficient demand to provide a profit and where the maximum range represents the maximum search, the failure to do so may be more damaging to the extent that the conclusions will often be drawn from a smaller number of observations.

First-person accounts of periodic markets will have to be evaluated in terms of the background of the writer so as to minimize the biases. A sociologist will see periodic markets in a different way than will a marketer. Because many marketing events have been reported by people who are not marketers, extra care must be exercised in the evaluation of such reports even when they are primary sources. Primary data include personal account books and ledgers, such as those used in the study of Andrew Melrose, an Edinburgh grocer. In such documents are recorded the accounts with suppliers, customers, and agents as well as banking activities (Hoh-Cheung and Muir 1973, p. 37). For the case of periodic markets, diaries, day books, public records, and the remembrances of traders will form the nucleus of primary data.

Another source of primary data is corporate records. When these are made available to the marketing historian, they can provide minute details about the development of marketing programs and activities including perceptions about the marketing activities of other firms. Access to these materials is often restricted because many corporations have had poor relationships with historians in the past. Unfortunately, some business historians have used their studies of corporations to ridicule business practices or to support self-serving views (Williamson 1966, p. 26).

Public records and litigative proceedings also offer primary and secondary data, although they are often difficult to categorize clearly. The legal approach to the study of marketing, even though it is not well developed, provides insights into what practices are acceptable and insights into the evolving legal structure which surrounds marketing decision making. The failure of a contract to meet the test of legality through litigation provides much understanding about the ways in which marketing practices evolve, though it would be incorrect to accept the test of legality as a measure of the success or failure of a specific practice. A fairly extensive literature in industrial organization and in the law offers important secondary materials (McCurdy 1978).

The question of the validity of a piece of evidence is related to the distance between the event and the user who subsequently interprets the information. Validity, or acceptability, becomes an issue when the data are drawn from studies in closely related fields. This is a precaution to the researcher in marketing so that he or she will be keenly aware of the differences in purpose of various types of historical research. Drawing upon the *business* historians, who are often interested in individual business leaders, may lead the marketing scholar to bypass marketing concepts. The problem is not that a study of a business leader contains inaccurate information, but that the information may not lead to marketing insights. Business history studies such as "The Development of the Retail Grocery Trade in the Nineteenth Century" (Blackman 1967) and "Marketing Organization and Policy in the Cotton Trade" (Lee 1968) provide interesting insights into entrepreneurial activities but they do not analyze historical developments in marketing as would be done by the marketing historian. These studies are valuable, however, because they direct the researcher to primary and secondary data.

In general, traditional statistical sources will not be available for all of the periods of historical study. What data are available may be limited in scope and may stem from sources not known to the marketing historian. For example, church records often include a listing of the names of merchants in a parish and medical records may report occupation-linked injuries. To the extent that data series in the traditional reporting form for marketing are not available and to the extent that unusual forms are not known, the work of the marketing historian will be made more difficult. The situation will be like that of the economic historian, who because of the shortage of great volumes of statistics must either muddle along with other evidence or specialize in those areas where statistics are sufficient to employ sophisticated statistical techniques (Johnston 1941, p. 46). The statistical data that are found, such as census reports, taxation reports, and transport movement documents, must be carefully scrutinized to determine their relevance to marketing activities. They also must be tested for validity (Marburgh 1960).

Hypothesis Verification and Theory Development

Activity 6. The verification procedures are the equivalent of hypothesis testing. Verification is accomplished by comparison of qualitative factors which may or may not be associated by numerical values. The choice of the term "verification" is deliberate, to draw attention to the differences between hypothesis testing in historical research and hypothesis testing in marketing research. Most historical research involves the qualitative comparison of events over time or between different places without regard to either a known or a theoretical standard as is used in statistical inference. Unlike the test of the null hypothesis as in the case of a sample and a population, no precise process is available which allows for error estimation. Comparison itself is based on the ability of the researcher to describe a certain phenomenon in two time periods or in two areas. The process is often thwarted because of differences in the description of events. For example, in the description of periodic markets it would be important to know clearly whether they operated randomly in an area, that is, were periodic in space, or whether they were periodic in time, that is, operated at the same place but at different times. Though these differences seem obvious, great care must be taken to ensure that the proper conditions are included. As a method, comparison is characterized by the isolation of similarities and differences and by the assessment of the factors which lead to change (Boddewyn 1966).

A second verification method, which has received great attention by economic historians, is the regressive method (Marwick 1970, p. 73). This method follows the general principles of statistical analysis; obviously, its use depends on the availability of significant quantities of data.

The regressive method involves the use of evidence drawn from one period which is extrapolated either backward or forward in time in order to understand the earlier or later period. "Cliometrics," the name given the method in economic history, is an application of econometric methods to historical data. It incorporates prediction as discussed heretofore. Cliometrics has been criticized along two lines. The lack of data limits the validity of some studies, and techniques have dominated some data to give to conclusions more weight than they might have under different conditions (McCloskey 1978, p. 28). Whether this approach will be useful in historical research in marketing is unknown, although it is reasonable to suspect that the dearth of data will limit its use.

For the hypothesis describing the conditions for fixed store retailing, verification would be undertaken by the comparison of the assembled data with the constructs of the hypothesis. The researcher must subjectively apply weights to the various pieces of evidence and then reach conclusions. Because of the absence of fixed standards, close attention must be paid to the specific factors that affect the acceptance or the rejection of the hypothesis. The end product of the verification process, regardless of the outcome, will be a set of conclusions which recognize, but do not necessarily strongly endorse, alternative explanations. The precision of statistical relations which clearly link events will not be present in most cases.

Activity 7. Theory development arises from the testing of the hypothesis in several environments. The development of explanatory theory is a process in which the results of positive and negative findings are merged, as shown in Figure 1. Those hypotheses which are not verified and not accepted become the negative feedback loop and are reexamined in further investigations. Those which are accepted form the basis for theory. There is no magic number of tests which signals the point when theory development can begin. Clearly, more than one case would be required.

Historical research by itself is not likely to lead to the development of predictive theory. The evidence collected and the inferences drawn can serve as the platform on which theory is built. Theory emerges when an attempt is made to predict the outcome of events. "A purely descriptive or historical treatment of marketing would not be marketing theory" (Alderson 1965, p. 23).

CONCLUSIONS

Marketing history can show meaningful interconnections and parallels among different events. Its role will be to isolate and illustrate the changes that marketing and its respective institutions have made, the factors which have been influential in effecting change, and the consequences of change. Though some scholars might choose to study the history of a firm or a single practice, greater value will come from studying marketing's role in the broader economic and social context. The history of specific events has value in itself but even more value when placed within the larger framework. Thus, if the limitations of such studies are fully recognized, marketing history might provide one avenue for preparing for the future (Carson 1978).

Because of the lack of methodological precision in historical studies, some marketing scholars may ignore them. What is lacking, however, is a full understanding of the aims of historical research. Although the development of general theory is a desired consequence of such research, more limited goals must be accepted. This fact should not detract from the search for a better knowledge of marketing's past.

REFERENCES

Alderson, Wroe (1965), *Dynamic Marketing Behavior*, Homewood, Illinois: Richard D. Irwin, Inc.
Bagozzi, R. P. (1978), "Marketing as Exchange: A Theory of Transactions in the Marketplace," *American Behavioral Scientist*, 21, 535–56.

Bartels, R. (1976), *The History of Marketing Thought*, Columbus, Ohio: Grid, Inc.
Blackman, J. (1967), "The Development of the Retail Grocery Trade in the Nineteenth Century," *Business History*, 9, 110–117.

Boddewyn, J. (1966), "A Construct for Comparative Marketing Research," *Journal of Marketing Research*, 3 (May), 149–53.

Bucklin, L. P. (1972), *Competition and Evolution in the Distributive Trades*, Englewood Cliffs, New Jersey: Prentice-Hall, Inc.

Carson D. (1978), "Götterdammering for Marketing?", *Journal of Marketing*, 42 (July), 11–19.

Cassady, R. Jr. (1963). "The Role of Economic Models in Microeconomic Market Studies," in *Models of Markets*, Alfred R. Oxenfeldt, ed. New York: Columbia University Press, 20–52.

Doody, A. F. (1965). "Historical Emphasis: Its Contribution to Marketing Education," in *Reflections on Progress in Marketing*, L. George Smith, ed., Chicago: American Marketing Association, 555–65.

Goldman, A. (1978), "An Updated 'Wheel of Retailing' Theory," in *Foundations of Marketing Channels*, Arch G. Woodside, J. Taylor Sims, Dale M. Lewison, and Ian F. Wilkinson, eds., Austin, Texas: Lone Star Publishers, 189–211.

Gray, S. A. (1931), *The Development of Economic Doctrine, An Introductory Survey*, New York: John Wiley & Sons, Inc.

Harvey, D. (1969), *Explanation in Geography*, London: Edward Arnold.

Hay, A. M. and K. S. O. Beavon (1979), "Periodic Marketing: A Preliminary Geographical Analysis in Part Time and Mobile Marketing," *Tijdschrift Voor Economisne en Social Geografie*, 70, 27–34.

Hidy, R. W. (1977), "Business History: A Bibliographic Essay," in *Research in Economic History Supplement 1*, Robert E. Gallman, ed., Greenwich, Connecticut: JAI Press, 1–27.

Hoh-Cheung and L. H. Muir (1973), "Andrew Melrose, Tea Dealer and Grocer of Edinburgh 1812–1833," *Business History*, 9, 30–48.

Hollander, S. (1963). "The Wheel of Retailing," in *Marketing and the Behavioral Sciences*, Perry Bliss, ed., Boston: Allyn and Bacon, 311–21.

Hotchkiss, G. B. (1938), *Milestones of Marketing*, New York: The Macmillan Company.

Johnston, E. A. J. (1941). "New Tools for the Economic Historian," *The Journal of Economic History, Supplement*, 1 30–38.

Jones, F. M. (1937), *Middlemen in the Domestic Trade of the United States 1800–1860*, Urbana: The University of Illinois.

Lee, C. H. (1968), "Marketing Organization and Policy in the Cotton Trade: M. Connel and Kennedy of Manchester," *Business History*, 10, 89–100.

Marburgh, T. F. (1960), "Income Originating in Trade, 1799–1869," in *Trends in the American Economy in the Nineteenth Century, Studies in Income and Wealth*, National Bureau of Economic Research, Princeton, New Jersey: Princeton University Press, 317–26.

Marwick, A. (1970), *The Nature of History*, London: The Macmillan Press.

McCloskey, D. N. (1978), "The Achievements of the Cliometric School," *Journal of Economic History*, 38, 13–28.

McCurdy, C. W. (1978), "American Law and the Marketing Structure of the Large Corporation 1875–1890," *Journal of Economic History*, 38, 631–49.

McKendrick, N. (1960). "Josiah Wedgwood, An Eighteenth Century Entrepreneur in Salesmanship and Marketing Techniques," *Economic History Review*, 12, 408–31.

Narver, J. C. and R. Savitt (1971), *The Marketing Economy: An Analytical Approach*, New York: Holt, Rinehart and Winston.

Pollay, R. W. (1977), "The Importance, and the Problems of Writing the History of Advertising," *Journal of Advertising History*, 1, 3–5.

Porter, G. and H. C. Livesay (1971), *Merchants and Manufacturers, Studies in the Changing Structure of Nineteenth Century Marketing*, Baltimore, Maryland: The Johns Hopkins Press.

Schwartz, G. (1963), *Development of Marketing Theory*, Cincinnati, Ohio: South-Western Publishing Co.

Shapiro, S. J. (1964), "Marketing in America: Settlement to Civil War," in *Reflections on Progress in Marketing*, L. George Smith, ed., Chicago: American Marketing Association, 566–9.

————— and A. F. Doody (1968), *Readings in the History of American Marketing*, Homewood, Illinois: Richard D. Irwin, Inc.

Smalley, O. A. (1964), "The Empty Boxes of Marketing Organization," *Toward Scientific Marketing*, Stephen A. Greyser, ed., Chicago: American Marketing Association, 366–71.

Vance, J. E., Jr. (1970), *The Merchant's World: The Geography of Wholesaling*, Englewood Cliffs, New Jersey: Prentice-Hall, Inc.

Whitrow, G. J. (1975), *The Nature of Time*, Middlesex, England: Penguin Books Ltd.

Williamson, H. C. (1966), "The Professors Discover American Business," in *Readings in United States Economic and Business History*, Ross M. Robertson and James L. Pate, eds., Boston: Houghton Mifflin Company, 25–34.

[11]

HISTORIOGRAPHIC PARADIGMS IN MARKETING

D.G. Brian Jones
University of Prince Edward Island

ABSTRACT

History is art and science, poetry and journalism,
explanation, narration, and criticism; it is epochal
and parochial, holistic and individualistic,
materialistic and spiritualistic, objective and
subjective, factual and normative, practical and
theoretical (Abelson 1963, p.167).... This paper
describes different approaches to doing historical
research - "scientific" and "traditional" paradigms -
and illustrates each with examples from historical
research in marketing.

INTRODUCTION

Historiography deals with the theory and methods of historical
scholarship. Certainly, historians are not known to be
methodological zealots. Indeed, one observer has complained that,
"historians show an almost pathological disinclination to commit
themselves to general statements about their work, its aims,
subject matter, and methods" (Gallie 1964, p.53). However, when
they do reflect on the nature of their work the issues of
interest include sources and types of primary data, research
method, and methodology.

Historical method refers to the techniques of data collection and
analysis as well as the writing of history, whereas methodology
refers to the philosophy of the research process - for example,
assumptions about epistemology, ontology, and voluntarism /
determinism. The distinction between primary and secondary
historical data is not always clear, but is nonetheless an
important one.

Occasionally important historical research is conducted
exclusively from secondary sources. In general, however,
significant historical work is rooted in primary sources. As one
historian has observed, "study of [primary] sources alone does
not make history, but without the study of sources there is no
history" (Marwick 1971, p.171). Primary, original, source
materials are derived directly from the persons or events one is
studying. It is not, however, necessary that a source be
unpublished in order to be considered primary. For example,
contemporary (to the persons or events being studied) pamphlets
and periodicals as well as other published materials can be
primary sources depending on the nature of the subject being
studied and the purpose for which the materials in question were
created.

3

Until recently most discussions by marketing historians of historiography focused on the relatively simple issue of justification (Jones and Monieson 1990, p.271), that is, why historical research was needed and legitimate. In the last decade, however, the discussion of historiographic issues has grown, both in the number of works as well as the range of issues examined. Savitt (1980) presented a thorough discussion of scientific historical method and followed this with a presentation (1983) of some sources and types of primary historical data. Firat (1987) described methodological perspectives (termed "traditions") of historical research ranging from Annales (positivistic) to Hermeneutics (phenomenological). Fullerton (1987a) contributed a discussion of the philosophy of German Historicism, a specific methodological perspective on historical research. Fullerton (1987b) was also one of the first marketing historians to distinguish historical method from methodology and to write about the essential connection between the two. And finally, there have been archival essays including Pollay's (1988) which describes source collections such as the Smithsonian Collection on Advertising, the Museum of Modern Mythology, and the History of Advertising Archives.

One point which, to date, has not been made clear, is that there are different methodological perspectives, corresponding methods of historical research, and sources and types of primary data - paradigms[1], if you will - of historical research in marketing. These paradigms are summarized in Table 1 together with citations of examples from the marketing literature, some of which are discussed in this paper.

The purpose of this paper is to describe those different paradigms of historical research in marketing and to illustrate them with examples from the literature. In this way I hope to organize, clarify, and expand somewhat, the discussion to date of historiography by marketing historians. It is not my intent to oversimplify any individual scholar's work by rigidly casting it into a category of one approach or another. Also, I will attempt not to advocate one specific approach since I believe that a range of approaches is useful and necessary. Often the nature of the research question being asked will demand one specific approach to historical research. In any case, as the examples cited here will demonstrate, no one approach to historical research has a monopoly on interesting and important contributions to our understanding of marketing history and the history of marketing thought.

---

[1] For the purposes of this paper the term "paradigm" refers to a general research tradition or approach to doing research shared by a significant number of scholars.

Table 1

Historiographic Paradigms in Marketing

Paradigm	Methodology	Method	Sources */Types of Primary Data	Examples *
			Demographics	
Scientific	Positivist epistemology	Quantification	Records of government, organizations, and firms	Savitt (1984)
	Realist ontology	Classification		Pollay (1985)
		Sampling	Census reports	Gross and Sheth (1989)
	Determinism	Hypothesis testing	Occupation listings	Zinn and Johnson (1990)
		Statistical analysis	Daybooks, ledgers	
		Theory & prediction	Advertisements	Hollander (1986)
Traditional	Idealist epistemology	Imaginitive reconstruction, creative interpretation	Personal & family records	Fullerton (1988)
			Artifacts & photography	Nevett (1988)
	Nominalist ontology	Synthesis	Correspondence	Jones and Monieson (1990)
	Voluntarism	Descriptive, narrative, story-telling	Diaries	Witkowski (1989)
			Unpublished manuscripts	

* These are representative only.

5

METHODOLOGY - THE PHILOSOPHY OF HISTORY

All historical research proceeds implicitly or explicitly from certain assumptions about the nature of history and historical phenomena. Such assumptions are related to ontology, epistemology, and human nature (Burrell and Morgan 1979, p.1).

Ontology is concerned with the essence of reality, the nature of "being". It is concerned with whether reality is something objective and external to individuals or is the product of individual consciousness. The Realist position assumes that the world is made up of tangible, empirical entities which exist independent of an individual's appreciation of them. On the other hand, the Nominalist position assumes that reality is created through the process of interpretation. The difference between the two views is perhaps best captured by Collingwood's distinction between the "inside" and "outside" of an event (1956), where the outside is the result or achievement itself, the "external of acts", the ready-made statements by individuals from the past (p. 213). The inside of an event (the essence of reality for a Nominalist) is "that which can only be described in terms of thoughts" (p.251), not accessible to observation. Individuals make sense of the world and give it meaning by using names, concepts and labels (Winch 1974). In short, Nominalists believe that reality is socially constructed.

Epistemology deals with the nature and grounds of knowledge - how we come to understand and communicate knowledge to others. Positivist epistemology has as its objective the search for causal relations, regularities and even laws. Using a rhetoric which is formal, quantitative, and sometimes mathematical, these laws are used to explain and predict what happens in the world. This epistemology is most typically characterized by the natural sciences, although it has often in the past been held as a model for social science as well. In history the Positivist epistemological position is most closely associated with Carl Hempel's covering-law model which builds on the premise that to explain a historical event is to show that a statement asserting it is deducible from certain empirically testable universal laws, or can be inferred from probabilistic-statistical laws (Hempel 1974). On the other hand, an Idealist epistemology asserts that we can only understand human action by occupying the frame of reference of the participant in the action, and therefore, that knowledge is relativistic. Again, drawing from Collingwood, to explain history is to understand it from the inside through a process of re-enactment of past experience; knowledge is an interpolation or imaginitive construction in the Kantian sense (1956, p.240).

Finally, in historical methodology there are assumptions about human nature - the relationship between actors and their environment. The deterministic view is that we are a product of our environment, that human behavior is conditioned by external circumstances (Nagel 1974). Alternatively, there is the view that voluntarism or human free will plays a more creative role in explaining human behavior (Dray 1974, Berlin 1974).

The alternate positions described with respect to the philosophical issues above create two different methodological perspectives from which one can approach historical research in marketing. From each of these methodological perspectives follows a consistent set of research methods as well as types and sources of primary data. These alternate paradigms or approaches to historical research are referred to here as "scientific" and "traditional" (see Table 1).

SCIENTIFIC HISTORICAL RESEARCH

The methodological perspective which is consistent with Realism, Positivism, and a deterministic view of human nature characterizes a <u>scientific</u> paradigm in historical research. The purpose of scientific historical research is to develop generalizations, descriptions of cause and effect and predictions involving observable events. Therefore, scientific history attempts to classify and quantify historical data and to develop formal hypotheses which are tested using statistical analysis (Savitt 1980). In practice, simple, descriptive statistics are most often relied on. However, some of this research makes use of sampling and statistical inference (Aydelotte 1971, p.27). Indeed, some types of historical data (especially in economic history) are analyzed using regression analysis or cliometrics. Not surprisingly the most common types of primary sources used in scientific historical research are aggregate, numerical data such as demographic and economic statistics (Aydelotte 1971, chap. 4) which are most often found in government collections. However, nonquantitative, verbal or pictorial data such as advertisements can analyzed when transformed into quantitative form using techniques such as content analysis.

There are several recent, classic examples of scientific historical research in marketing. Savitt's (1984) historical study of the wheel of retailing opens by pointing out that the wheel is not a "law", but rather an "untested hypothesis" (p.43). He goes on to deduce three specific hypotheses from McNair's original "postulate" and tests these under the assumption that the findings could be generalized to other firms and even (albeit with less certainty) to other economies (p.44). The sources of data for this study included regional and local newspaper advertisements as well as company annual reports. Sampling data for 20 points in time over a ten year period, the number of products, brands, and suppliers (categories representing inventory assortment) were counted. The totals for each of those categories were then observed in order to determine their correlation with the hypotheses and conclusions were drawn from that comparison. In its methodological assumptions, methods of data collection and analysis, and type of data used, Savitt's study conforms closely to the scientific paradigm described

7

above.

Another representative example is Pollay's (1985) descriptive history of print advertising. The purpose in that study was to identify (inductively) trends and styles in advertising since "no generally accepted theory [existed] to provide any detailed hypotheses regarding when and how advertising could be expected to display maturation phases" (p.25). A random sample of 2,000 print ads covering eight decades was subjected to content analysis in order to transform the ads into quantitative data for categorization. The results of the analysis were reported in the form of frequency counts and percentages of print ads which identified fads and trends in tactics and styles. An interesting methodological comparison can also be made of Pollay's study with that of Gross and Sheth (1989) which also used content analysis. However, the latter study made use of more formal hypotheses and conducted simple regression analysis of the proportion of print ads containing time-oriented appeals against chronological distance from the year 1890. In that way the Gross and Sheth study is archtypical of scientific history.

A final example from the scientific historical paradigm is the study by Zinn and Johnson (1990) which uses content analysis of selected marketing publications covering half a century to identify the frequency of publications dealing with the commodity approach. Their objective was to determine if the commodity approach was obsolete. This hypothesis was rejected in favor of one which suggested a cyclical pattern of adoption which the authors demonstrated using a graphical presentation of their findings.

Summary

In each of the examples cited above there is an attempt to develop theory, or at least "generalizations of a middle level" (Aydelotte 1971, p.26). In most of these cases formal hypotheses are tested using statistical analysis. The process of quantification and classification used in these studies is an efficient and convenient method of analysis given the type of historical data studied here (large volumes of readily observable, easily categorized characteristics) and it would appear that such data are becoming increasingly available, especially for advertising history. Clearly however, there are some historical questions and issues which do not lend themselves to this scientific approach.

TRADITIONAL HISTORICAL RESEARCH

Opposite the scientific paradigm is a perspective which follows Nominalism, Idealism and a belief in voluntarism or free will. This perspective characterizes the traditional paradigm of historical research. The objective of traditional historical research is to discover and imaginitively reconstruct the lives

of people in other times and places (Dray 1974), to offer
insights into possibilities and to inventory achievements (Tosh
1984). This type of research uses a descriptive or narrative form
of expression. In practice there is no formal technique for data
collection or analysis. The exact procedures vary with the type
of evidence used. Its reasoning is best described as common sense
and its form of expression is common language (Hexter 1971,
p.275), or story-telling. Typically, the most common primary
sources include collections of personal papers including
materials such as correspondence, diaries, and unpublished
manuscripts, anything containing verbal descriptions of events in
the past.

An example of traditional historical research is Fullerton's
(1988) study of the "Myth of the Production Era". Fullerton draws
explicitly upon Collingwood's philosophy of historical Idealism
(p.109) to recreate a contemporary conceptualization of marketing
which existed much earlier (although in a less developed form)
than commonly believed. Even in his development of a 'model' of
marketing's evolution, Fullerton maintains an essentially
antipositivist position since he rejects determinism and
predictability in favor of a "complicated and fluid process
involving simultaneous dramatic change, incremental change, and
continuity" (p.121). Consistent with the types of primary data
characteristic of the traditional paradigm, Fullerton uses a
combination of unpublished manuals which describe the marketing
practices of firms from the period being studied, descriptive
scholarly publications from the same period, and secondary data
in the form of histories which, in turn, draw from firm archives
and trade papers (p.110). This evidence is critically evaluated
by Fullerton in a "web of constructive imagination" (p.109).

A second example of traditional historical research is Nevett's
(1988) biographical study of Thomas Barratt and the advertising
for Pears Soap during the late nineteenth and early twentieth
centuries. Nevett focuses on Barratt as a distinct and profound
contributor to the development of British advertising and
examines the nature of those contributions which included unusual
budgetary practices and progressive creative strategies. Nevett's
study is a very good example of classic, descriptive, historical
story-telling. It draws on autobiographical materials of
Barratt's, newspaper stories from the period, secondary data from
published histories, and, of course, Pears advertisements. In the
interpretation of the latter Nevett's study stands in marked
contrast to those of, say, Pollay, or Gross and Sheth (cited
above).

Summary

The examples of traditional historical research described above
each focus on developing a detailed historical account of unique
events in order to interpret (or sometimes to reinterpret)
situations from the past. The knowledge objectives, means of
addressing them... the rhetoric and style as well as the types of

9

primary sources employed, differ considerably from those of the examples from the scientific paradigm discussed previously. However, a caveat given in the introduction to this paper bears repeating. There is a risk of oversimplifying the works cited here by categorizing them as being "scientific" or "traditional". Although some tend to represent one approach or the other, many historical studies fall somewhere in between these paradigms by integrating both approaches.

A good example is Hollander's (1986) critical assessment of the "standard chronology" involving the emergence of the marketing concept. Hollander sets up that standard chronology (where the marketing concept emerged during the 1950s or later) as a hypothesis (p.8) to test its fit with the reality of business practices from the mid-nineteenth to mid-twentieth century. To do so, he examines frequencies of publications (p.11), reports and citations of companies, economic statistics, interpretations of publications from the period in question, and secondary historical sources, to reconstruct the character of marketing activities from the era. Quantitative and qualitative data are combined; the hypothesis is rejected - "the standard chronology does not fit" (p. 22), but the written presentation by the author is a narrative one in the style of traditional historical research. For these reasons this study is shown between the two paradigms listed in Table 1.

CONCLUSIONS

The philosophic assumptions which we bring to our research efforts inevitably influence our choice of methods, data sources, and consequently, even the topics we study. In order to fully understand alternative points of view it is important to understand the assumptions upon which these points of view are based. By reflecting in this way on the nature of historical research done, marketing historians can become better aware of the range of perspectives and approaches to historical research in marketing.

This final observation is admittedly made from my own traditional (as opposed to scientific) perspective. Unlike the broader field of marketing which has been dominated by a scientific paradigm for most of this century, historical research in marketing has no such orthodoxy. Perhaps that is because of this field's relatively recent development of a critical mass of work. In any case, it is a healthy condition, one which will help in developing a rich variety of interesting questions and answers.

REFERENCES

Abelson, Raziel 1963. "Cause and Reason in History." in Sydney Hook, (ed.), Philosophy and History. 167 - 173.

Aydelotte, William O. 1971. <u>Quantification in History</u>. Reading, MA: Addison-Wesley Publishing.

Belk, Russell W. and Richard W. Pollay 1985. "Images of Ourselves: The Good Life in Twentieth Century Advertising." <u>Journal of Consumer Research</u> 11 (March) 887 - 897.

Berlin, Isaiah 1974. "Historical Inevitability." in Patrick Gardiner, (ed.), <u>The Philosophy of History</u>. London: Oxford University Press. 161 - 186.

Burrell, Gibson and Gareth Morgan 1979. <u>Sociological Paradigms and Organizational Analysis</u>. London: Heinemann Publishing.

Collingwood, R.G. 1956. <u>The Idea of History</u>, New York: Oxford University Press.

Dray, William 1974. "The Historical Explanation of Actions Reconsidered." in Patrick Gardiner, (ed.), <u>The Philosophy of History</u>. 66 - 89.

Firat, A. Fuat 1987. "Historiography, Scientific Method, and Exceptional Historical Events." in <u>Advances in Consumer Research</u>. Melanie Wallendorf and Paul Anderson, (eds.), Provo, Utah: ACR. 435-438.

Fullerton, Ronald A. 1987a. "Historicism: What It Is, And What It Means For Consumer Research." in <u>Advances in Consumer Research</u>. Melanie Wallendorf and Paul Anderson, (eds.), Provo, Utah: ACR. 431-434.

_____ 1987b. "The Poverty of Ahistorical Analysis: Present Weakness and Future Cure in U.S. Marketing Thought." in <u>Philosophical and Radical Thought in Marketing</u>. A. Fuat Firat, Nikhilesh Dholakia and Richard P. Bagozzi, (eds.), Lexington: Lexington Books. 97-116.

_____ 1988. How Modern is Modern Marketing? Marketing's Evolution and the Myth of the 'Production Era'." <u>Journal of Marketing</u>. 52 (January) 108 - 125.

Gross, Barbara L. and Jagdish N. Sheth 1989. "Time-Oriented Advertising: A Content Analysis of United States Magazine Advertising, 1890 - 1988." <u>Journal of Marketing</u>. 53, 4, 76 - 83.

Hempel, Carl G. 1974. "Reasons and Covering Laws in Historical Explanation." in Patrick Gardiner, (ed.), <u>The Philosophy of History</u>. London: Oxford University Press. 90 - 105.

Hollander, Stanley C. 1986. "The Marketing Concept: A Deja-Vu." in <u>Marketing Management Technology as Social Process</u>. George Fisk, (ed.), New York: Praeger. 3 - 26.

11

Hexter, J. H. 1971. The History Primer, New York: Basic Books.

Jones, D.G. Brian and David D. Monieson 1990. "Historical Research in Marketing: Retrospect and Prospect." Journal of the Academy of Marketing Science. 18, 4, 269 - 278.

_____ and _____ 1990. "Early Development of the Philosophy of Marketing Thought." Journal of Marketing. 54, (January) 102 - 113.

Mandelbaum, Maurice 1974. "The Problem of 'Covering Laws'." in Patrick Gardiner, (ed.), The Philosophy of History 51 - 65.

Marwick, A. 1971. The Nature of History. New York: Alfred Knopf.

Nevett, Terry 1988. "Thomas Barratt and the Development of British Advertising." International Journal of Advertising. 7, 267 - 276.

Pollay, Richard W. 1985. "The Subsidizing Sizzle: A Descriptive History of Print Advertising, 1900 - 1980." Journal of Marketing. 49, (Summer) 24 - 37.

_____ 1988. "Current Events that Are Making Advertising History." in Terence Nevett and Ronald A. Fullerton, (eds.), Historical Perspectives in Marketing, Essays in Honor of Stanley C. Hollander. Lexington: Lexington Books. 195-222.

Savitt, Ronald 1980. "Historical Research in Marketing." Journal of Marketing. (Fall) 4, 52 - 58.

_____ 1983. "A Note on the Varieties and Vagaries of Historical Data." in Proceedings of the First North American Workshop on Historical Research in Marketing, Stanley C. Hollander and Ronald Savitt, (eds.), Lansing: MSU. 30 - 34.

_____ 1984. "The Wheel of Retailing and Retail Product Management." European Journal of Marketing. 18, 6, 43 - 54.

Tosh, 1984. The Pursuit of History. London: Longman Books.

Winch, Peter 1974. "Concepts and Actions." in Patrick Gardiner, (ed.), The Philosophy of History 41 - 50.

Witkowski, Terrence 1989. "Colonial Consumers in Revolt: Buyer Values and Behavior During the Nonimportation Movement, 1764 - 1776." Journal of Consumer Research 16, 2: 216-226.

Zinn, Walter and Scott D. Johnson 1990. "The Commodity Approach in Marketing Research: Is It Really Obsolete?" Journal of the Academy of Marketing Science. 18, 4, (Fall), 345 - 354.

12

[12]

A WRITER'S GUIDE TO HISTORICAL RESEARCH IN MARKETING

Terrence H. Witkowski
California State University, Long Beach

ABSTRACT

Drawing from historical research in marketing journals, the literature on historiography, and the author's experiences with the review process, this paper identifies five important issues in writing marketing history: the mix of data sources, the narrative structure, the incorporation of relevant literature, the formal methods section, and the implications of historical findings.

INTRODUCTION

Since the publication of Ronald Savitt's (1980) seminal article, marketing academics have given much greater emphasis to historical research in marketing and its subdisciplines of advertising, retailing, and consumer behavior (Jones and Monieson 1990b). These investigations have covered substantive history as well as the evolution of marketing thought, primarily, but not exclusively, from the nineteenth century to the present. In addition to the many papers appearing in the five proceedings volumes from this conference, a number of articles have been published in other venues including some in major journals such as the Journal of Marketing, Journal of Consumer Research, Journal of Advertising, Journal of Retailing, Journal of Macromarketing, and the Journal of the Academy of Marketing Science.

Historians who seek to publish in marketing journals, need to consider how to best present the findings of their research. This goes well beyond paying close attention to editors' pages, manuscript guidelines, acceptance criteria, and statements of review philosophy. Marketing historians should seriously question how closely their writing should adhere to existing models of historiography. There are good reasons to believe that the specialty would be well-served if it developed its own prototypes. How marketing history is written determines not only the likelihood of acceptance by top journals in the field, but ultimately its contribution to the advancement of marketing thought.

This paper discusses five issues in the writing of marketing history: the appropriate mix of data sources, the narrative structure, the incorporation of relevant literature, the need for a formal methods section, and the implications of historical findings. The emphasis will be on writing histories of substantive marketing practice and consumption behavior somewhat more than on histories of marketing ideas. The purpose is twofold: first, to share a few ideas and experiences that may help marketing historians improve the written presentation of their research and, second, to inform journal editors and reviewers about these issues as well as the diversity of acceptable historiographic formats. This paper does not presume to offer the final word in marketing historiography, but rather to submit a few ideas suitable for further debate.

THE MIX OF DATA SOURCES

The collection, analysis, and synthesis of data sources is a very important topic in historiography and sometimes a matter of great controversy. This section considers the appropriate blend of primary and secondary data sources in the writing of marketing history. Some writers (Jones and Monieson 1990a; Savitt 1983) apparently favor heavy reliance on primary data; others (Fullerton 1988; Hollander 1986b) have made good use of both types; and still others (Witkowski 1989) have based their histories upon a reinterpretation of existing literatures. Because relatively few marketing academics are professionally trained historians, some current writing in the field might be overemphasizing the use of secondary sources.

Clearly, there is a danger when historical research in marketing relies too heavily on secondary data sources. They are sometimes based on haphazard or poorly conceived research that may not have subjected the evidence to internal criticism. The written presentation may be incomplete and rely too heavily on other secondary sources or the writer's imagination. Secondary sources do not always present both sides of a story with equal weight. The biases of a given generation, historical school, or individual writer with a specific purpose in mind inexorably enter into a discussion.

Outside of material culture studies (Schlereth 1982), historians use written evidence far more than any other primary data source. Written sources can range from a wide variety of business, legal, and governmental records, to popular writing and literature, to personal letters and diaries. Even the heavily descriptive works of early (pre-1930) academic marketers can now be considered a primary source (Fullerton 1988). Marketing historians have not often consulted physical evidence, such as art, artifacts, and architecture, although these alternative sources appear to have some potential for documenting the products actually sold, what they looked like, and how they may have been used (Witkowski 1989b). Advertising, typically a combination of both written and pictorial evidence, has been one of the most frequently consulted primary sources (see, for example, Belk and Pollay 1985; Gross and Sheth 1989; Pollay 1985). A fair number of primary sources have been published and are widely available. Many university libraries have good microfilm or microprint collections of newspapers and magazines dating back to the American colonial era.

Sources in manuscript form, on the other hand, are geographically restricted. For example, business records from the first part of the nineteenth century and before typically reside in east coast institutions such as the Hagley Museum and Library in Wilmington, Delaware. Although many historians must face the problem of access, marketing historians might find it comparatively difficult to obtain travel grants from business school deans who place a higher priority on funding new laboratory equipment or providing seed money for surveys and experiments. Further, reading and interpreting qualitative evidence can be extremely time consuming. Aside from advertising content analyses using predetermined coding categories, much historical research cannot be done well by using teams of student assistants. Thus, too great an emphasis on primary sources may effectively prohibit research on some topics in marketing history.

One factor that might determine the mix of data sources is the historical era
being investigated. There is an enormous amount of period material for late
nineteenth and twentieth-century marketing studies. In contrast, primary evidence documenting such things as managerial thinking or buyer attitudes is
far less abundant for the eighteenth century and earlier and, being scattered
over a great number of documents, quite difficult to locate. It seems repetitive and wasteful for marketing historians researching the earlier eras to re-
analyze the same primary sources that other historians have gone over repeatedly. A great deal of historical research from fields as diverse as women's
studies to material culture (Witkowski 1990) begs to be read, analyzed, and
incorporated into the body of marketing history. For many years, scholars in
marketing, advertising, and consumer research have borrowed theoretical ideas
and empirical findings from economics, psychology, sociology, anthropology,
and other fields. There is no reason to believe that the large body of historiography cannot contribute in a similar fashion.

THE NARRATIVE STRUCTURE

The present writer once received the following criticisms from two different
reviewers of the same paper. While one reviewer said "too much of the paper
concentrates on a simple narrative," the other noted that "Historical writing
has a pattern and rhythm. An important part of historical writing is narration. That is missing here." Contradictory comments such as these dismay
hopeful authors, but in this case underscore narration as an important issue.

Narrative history describes "What was the case?" Four basic elements --
character, setting, action, and happening -- interact to produce narrative
(Megill 1989). Character and setting are called <u>existents</u>, whereas actions
(taken by characters) and happenings (how settings impinge upon characters)
are <u>events</u>. The majority of historians write within a narrative structure
(Hexter 1971; Lavin and Archdeacon 1989). Although tradition identifies narration with the recounting of events, many historians emphasize existents.
For example, Fernand Braudel's <u>Capitalism and Material Life, 1400-1800</u> (1967)
focuses on food and drink, housing and clothing, and technology and towns.

Narrative history that concentrates on character or setting does not necessarily require a chronological arrangement. John Demos (1970) organizes his
highly regarded history of family life in the Plymouth Plantation (1620-1691)
topically rather than diachronically. He begins with a discussion of physical
setting, moves to household structure, and then examines themes of individual
development. Demos chose this approach not only because it seemed a better
way to highlight analytical issues, but also because changes in family structure generally come very slowly and, hence, elements of stability and continuity loom unusually large. If spread over too long a period, however, a topical arrangement may "seriously distort the objective reality of the past" and
"forfeit the fundamental historical essence of change through time" (Marwick
1970, p. 145).

Some historians prefer a more dramatic and literary style than others who fav-
or heavy documentation and elaborate presentation of empirical findings. Good
narrative depends upon a correct determination of historical tempo, the art of
expanding and contracting the scale of time to establish the significance of
events (Hexter 1971). Much narrative in historical writing can be termed "im-

15

pressionistic" (Demos 1970). General statements are followed (or preceded) by a small number of illustrative examples. Dissatisfaction with this approach has increased the emphasis on cliometrics or "scientific" history (Fogel and Elton 1983), the use of quantitative models and measures and statistical analyses. Sometimes, however, a paucity of evidence leaves no alternative to the impressionistic approach.

Marketing historians can face serious difficulties when editors and/or reviewers are biased against narration. Many scholars in the social and behavioral sciences, not to mention quite a few professional historians, view description as a less serious task than explanation. Explanation is deemed to be more scientific and generalizable than description of particulars. This position is being challenged, however, as evidenced by the current debates between positivistic and interpretive consumer researchers (Hudson and Ozanne 1988). Moreover, as Megill (1989) points out, even nominally descriptive writing will have a large component of explanation. That is, the ordering of events chronologically implies (but does not prove) causality.

Problems may also arise in the review process when referees are unfamiliar with the different ways in which history can be presented. As mentioned, narrative can be arranged topically as well as chronologically. There also can be a geographic organization, usually by the territories of political units (Shafer 1974). In argumentative or justificatory pieces the writer might limit the topic to an analysis of sources or, in the case of Fullerton (1988) and Morris (1990), assemble and criticize evidence in order to evaluate alternative representations of the past. In historiographic essays or surveys of prior studies, narration of events is likely to be relatively less important than thematic issues.

Finally, reviewers can sometimes introduce unexpected criteria, as indicated by the following criticism of a thirty-page manuscript: "There is absolutely no way that a piece as short and informal as this one can produce a 'history.'" This writer is unaware of any length requirements for historical writing or, for that matter, any other kinds of marketing research. If this criterion were taken seriously, few historical pieces could ever appear in marketing journals unless editors made special provision for articles far longer than the average submission.

INCORPORATING RELEVANT LITERATURE

Unlike the typical social science article in marketing and consumer research, papers written by professional historians often proceed without first integrating previous work on the subject or problem of interest into the text. This is not to say that historians ignore prior findings and interpretive essays, but just that their narrative structures do not always lend themselves to or require the kind of presentation that first "plugs into" existing literatures, theoretical perspectives, or research traditions. When included, such material is usually placed in footnotes, a hallmark of the rhetoric of history.

This lack of explicit "positioning" can be frustrating to reviewers and other readers accustomed to the social science tradition. It makes historical research seem atheoretical, which it frequently is, and consequently irrelevant to the accumulation of knowledge, which it is not. More important, a lack of grounding in the literature may detract from the drawing of implications and the building of theory, topics discussed later in this paper. Thus, whether and how to incorporate relevant material becomes another important issue for marketing historians.

Papers taking a positivistic stance, such as theoretically driven content analyses (Belk and Pollay 1985; Gross and Sheth 1989), will invariably review the literature to find loose theoretical ends and to develop hypotheses. Essays and argumentative pieces also discuss relevant literature, sometimes in great detail. Incorporation of prior research will probably be most difficult in narrative works, especially case studies that emphasize events.

THE METHODS SECTION

An anonymous reviewer once criticized a paper submitted by this author as "a piece of storytelling rather than formal research . . . There is no research method set forth that explains a systematic means of search for themes, and therefore there is not assurance that the finding of themes is conclusive in a scholar's sort of way." According to this position, historical writing in marketing should make explicit its data sources and methods. This seems to be a quite reasonable guideline, although one that is not always followed by professional historians.

Some historical writing proceeds with scant discussion of research methods. For example, the following sentence from Roland Marchand's (1987) "The Fitful Career of Advocacy Advertising" is as close as the article comes to a methods statement: "A historical survey of some early advocacy campaigns will reveal both the variety of experiments within this advertising mode and the ways in which earlier practitioners tried to deal with the problems that still beset the genre" (p. 129). Marchand, a professional historian, never explains what he means by the term "a historical survey." His text does not describe his sample of ads nor say how they were interpreted, although his references do suggest he consulted several archival collections. Other historians are more explicit about their methods than Marchand, but still relegate their methodological statements to footnotes or bibliographic essays.

Methods sections should contain a description of the data sources and, if applicable, how they were selected from a larger universe of sources. In addition, this section might discuss how the data was analyzed. A good example of one such methods section can be found in Fullerton (1988) who first discusses the philosophical support for his historical approach, including the rationale for a cross-national investigation, and then describes his sample of primary and secondary sources. Note that Fullerton was not just writing a narrative history, but was scrutinizing a marketing theory, the so-called "production era" concept inspired by Keith (1960).

THE IMPLICATIONS OF MARKETING HISTORY

Professional historians write history more as an end in itself, an independent contribution to knowledge, than as a vehicle for building theories or making policy. They are committed to the study of individual facts, the events, in-

17

stitutions, and personalities that have historical significance, rather than to the discovery of broad conceptual constructs. Historians believe that each period contains its own reasons why events occured and that these causes are usually not generalizable (Firat 1987). Although historians sometimes use theory as a means to their own particular ends, such as the application of psychology or psychoanalysis to explain the behavior of famous people, relatively few are willing to go very far in drawing implications. Historical research is a cumulative process and every generation builds upon and revises previous work.

This position characterizes much traditional, Anglo-American historiography. However, continental European "historicism" takes a rather different approach in stressing "historical laws, determining factors, and the meaning of the past as the source of the present" (Daniels 1981, p. 96). Further, cliometricians, who focus more on collectivities of people and recurring events than on particulars (Fogel and Elton 1983), are committed to the positivistic philosophy of building, testing, and refining historical models. Given these different schools and paradigms, marketing historians need to consider what are and how to present the implications of their research and writing.

Whatever pretensions marketing scholars may have, many people consider the field to be "applied research" that should have some utilitarian purpose such as refining marketing practice or, perhaps, contributing to public policy making. Similarly, it could be argued that historical research in marketing should also go beyond the accumulation of historical facts. Arguably, historical study is something of an intellectual luxury that should try to pay its way by somehow adding to the inventory of theoretical ideas. Although such opinions may have dubious validity, they appear to be held by some practitioners and professors.

Historical analysis can contribute to the field of marketing through the formulation and testing of hypotheses (Shapiro and Doody 1968) or, putting it more broadly, through the development, appraisal, and testing of theories. For example, the process of assembling and analyzing the historical record can generate emergent themes just as readily as can ethnographic and other qualitative methods (Belk, Sherry, and Wallendorf 1988). Writers can usually find room for this material in the final sections of their papers. In Does it Pay to Advertise?, John Philip Jones (1989) draws several specific lessons for advertising management at the end of each case history. Hollander's (1986b) article on the marketing concept concludes with separate "explanation" and "implications" sections.

Editors sometimes ask for the implications of historical research and may suggest additional areas that should be consulted. On the other hand, too much emphasis on hypothesis formulation might elicit a reviewer comment like the following: "It is not clear that the Journal of Marketing should be an appropriate forum for attempting to generate new research projects." Not all marketing academics consider theory development and/or interpretive methodologies acceptable for journal articles.

When used for theory testing, historical research can be thought of as diachronic analogy to cross-cultural investigations. By comparing a theory with the record of earlier periods, the researcher "may be able to show which of its parts are most unyielding, and which are most variable, in relation to particular cultural settings" (Demos 1970, pp. 129-130). The problem with using history for theory testing, however, is that so much evidence is biased, incomplete, and too often nonexistent. For many issues, particularly those pertaining to the internal states of long dead consumers, there is very little data whatsoever. Longitudinal analyses of advertising content appear most applicable to this purpose.

CONCLUSION

There is no best model for writing marketing history and it would be overly dogmatic to insist upon one. As the debate over cliometrics has shown (Fogel and Elton 1983), professional historians themselves often disagree, sometimes bitterly. Nevertheless, marketing historians, journal editors, and reviewers might benefit from the following guidelines which seem to have broad, although not universal, application.

1. Marketing historians should stress primary data sources quite heavily when researching and reporting twentieth-century topics. Research on marketing during the first part of the nineteenth century and earlier need not be as dependent upon primary data. So many historical studies are already available that it seems rather inefficient for marketing scholars to replow this turf too vigorously. Much can be gained from recasting findings into a marketing context -- a kind of historical "meta-analysis." Still, researchers should familiarize themselves with the primary source material from the earlier eras so that they can critically evaluate secondary sources.

2. The narration of marketing history can stress events or existents. It can be arranged chronologically, geographically, topically, or in some combination of the three. Whatever the organization, it should be synthesized through appropriate linkages, such as the comparative method, and it should be adequately balanced in its coverage (Daniels 1981). Marketing history needs to cover a topic adequately, but should also strive for economy in its written presentation.

3. Positivistic research, as well as critical essays, should be clearly positioned within the stream of prior research. Narrative historians do not have to present a formal literature review, but they should be prepared to answer editor and reviewer queries on this point. The better the literature review, the easier it will be to build theory.

4. Given the social science grounding of our field, as well as the realities of the review process, most historical writing in marketing should present a reasonably formal methods section incorporated into the body of the paper. This section should include both a description of data sources and how they were chosen, and also some indication about how they were analyzed.

5. Finally, to pay its way in the marketing discipline, historical research should try to draw some implications for theory building and, if possible, for management. Articles written from a positivistic perspective will test hypotheses as a matter of course, whereas more interpretive and qualitative narrative studies might consider a brief listing of emergent themes.

Assuming that marketing historians can reach some consensus about how to evaluate the written presentation of their work, the problems they confront in the review process will eventually diminish as the body of research expands and journal editors assemble a pool of published authors from which they can choose reviewers. In the meantime, however, marketing historians need to continue their educational campaigns, not only to stress the usefulness of their specialty (see, for example, Hollander 1986a), but also to inform their colleagues about what kinds of historiographic methods are most appropriate.

REFERENCES

Belk, Russell W. and Richard W. Pollay. 1985. "Images of Ourselves: The Good Life in Twentieth Century Advertising." Journal of Consumer Research 11 (March) 887-897.

_____, John F. Sherry, Jr., and Melanie Wallendorf. 1988. "A Naturalistic Inquiry into Buyer and Seller Behavior at a Swap Meet." Journal of Consumer Research 14 (March) 449-470.

Braudel, Fernand. 1967. Capitalism and Marterial Life, 1400-1800. New York: Harper and Row.

Daniels, Robert V. 1981. Studying History: How and Why. Englewood Cliffs, NJ: Prentice-Hall.

Demos, John. 1970. A Little Commonwealth: Family Life in Plymouth Colony. New York: Oxford University Press.

Firat, A. Fuat. 1987. "Historiography, Scientific Method, and Exceptional Historical Events." In: Advances in Consumer Research, Vol. 14. Melanie Wallendorf and Paul Anderson, eds. Provo, UT: Association for Consumer Research, 435-438.

Fogel, Robert William and G. R. Elton. 1983. Which Road to the Past?: Two Views of History. New Haven, CT: Yale University Press.

Fullerton, Ronald A. 1988. "How Modern is Modern Marketing? Marketing's Evolution and the Myth of the 'Production Era.'" Journal of Marketing 52 (January) 108-125.

Gross, Barbara L. and Jagdish N. Sheth. 1989. "Time-Oriented Advertising: A Content Analysis of United States Magazine Advertising, 1890-1988." Journal of Marketing 53 (October) 76- 83.

Hexter, Jack H. 1971. Doing History. Bloomington: Indiana University Press.

Hollander, Stanley C. 1986a. "A Rearview Mirror Might Help Us Drive Forward--A Call for More Historical Studies in Retailing." Journal of Retailing 62 (Spring) 7-10.

_____. 1986b. "The Marketing Concept--A Deja Vu," In: Marketing: Management Technology as Social Process. George Fisk, ed. New York: Praeger Publishers.

Hudson, Laurel Anderson and Julie L. Ozanne. 1988. "Alternative Ways of Seeking Knowledge in Consumer Research." Journal of Consumer Research 14 (March) 508-521.

Jones, D.G. Brian and David D. Monieson. 1990a. "Early Development of the Philosophy of Marketing Thought," Journal of Marketing 54 (January) 102-112.

_____ and David D. Monieson. 1990b. "Historical Research in Marketing: Retrospect and Prospect." Journal of the Academy of Marketing Science 18 (Fall) 269-278.

Jones, John Philip. 1989. Does It Pay to Advertise?: Cases Illustrating Successful Brand Advertising. Lexington, MA: Lexington Books.

Keith, Robert J. 1960. "The Marketing Revolution." Journal of Marketing 24 (January) 35-38.

Lavin, Marilyn and Thomas J. Archdeacon. 1989. "The Relevance of Historical Method for Marketing Research." In: Interpretive Consumer Research. Elizabeth C. Hirschman, ed. Provo, UT: Association for Consumer Research, 60-68.

Marchand, Roland. 1987. "The Fitful Career of Advocacy Advertising: Political Protection, Client Cultivation, and Corporate Morale." California Management Review 29 (Winter) 128-156.

Marwick, Arthur. 1970. The Nature of History. London: Macmillan and Company.

Megill, Allan. 1989. "Recounting the Past: 'Description,' Explanation, and Narration in Historiography." American Historical Review 94 (June) 627-653.

Morris, David J. 1990. "The Railroad and Movie Industries: Were They Myopic?" Journal of the Academy of Marketing Science 18 (Fall) 279-283.

Pollay, Richard W. 1985. "The Subsiding Sizzle: A Descriptive History of Print Advertising, 1900-1980." Journal of Marketing 50 (April) 18-36.

Savitt, Ronald. 1980. "Historical Research in Marketing," Journal of Marketing 44 (Fall) 52-58.

_____. 1983. "A Note on the Varieties and Vagaries of Historical Data." In: First North American Workshop on Historical Research in Marketing, Stanley Hollander and Ronald Savitt, eds. East Lansing, Michigan State University, 30-34.

Schlereth, Thomas J. 1982. "Material Culture Studies in America, 1876-1976." In: Material Culture Studies in America, Thomas J. Schlereth, ed. Nashville: The American Association for State and Local History, 1-75.

Shafer, Robert Jones, ed. 1974. A Guide to Historical Method. Homewood, IL: The Dorsey Press.

Shapiro, Stanley J. and Alton F. Doody, eds. 1968. Readings in the History of American Marketing: Settlement to Civil War. Homewood, IL: Richard D. Irwin.

Witkowski, Terrence H. 1989a. "Colonial Consumers in Revolt: Buyer Values and Behavior During the Nonimportation Movement, 1764-1776." <u>Journal of Consumer Research</u> 16 (September) 216-226.

_____. 1989b. "Probate and Property: Written and Material Data Sources for Consumption History." In: <u>Marketing History:The Emerging Discipline</u>. Terence Nevett, Kathleen R. Whitney, and Stanley C. Hollander, eds. East Lansing: Michigan State University, 120-131.

_____. 1990. "Marketing Thought in American Decorative Arts." <u>Journal of the Academy of Marketing Science</u> 18 (Fall) 365-368.

[13]

CLIO IN THE MARKETPLACE:
THEORETICAL AND METHODOLOGICAL ISSUES
IN THE HISTORY OF CONSUMPTION

Grant McCracken, University of Guelph[1]

Abstract

Modern consumer behavior is the work of several
centuries of social, economic and cultural
change in the west. The origins of this new
species of social action can be found in 16th
century Europe, and its vigorous development observed in the 17th, 18th and 19th centuries.
Happily, the investigation of this topic is a
matter of growing concern in the historical community. In the last 5 years three major studies
and a host of minor ones have appeared. The purpose of the present paper is to examine this
work, to identify the theoretical and methodological issues that have emerged from it, and
discuss the accomplishments and prospects of this
new and vital field of study.

Introduction

The "great transformation" saw the west move
from a relatively traditional, slow changing,
status-bound, sacred society to one that was
relatively innovative, quick paced, contract-
bound and profane. The literature under review
here represents a radical new approach to the
study of this transformation. It contends that
an essential and unexamined aspect of the great
transformation are the changes that took place
in consumption from the 16th century onwards.
It is this "consumer revolution", just as much as
the "industrial revolution" that has traditionally preoccupied historians, that is responsible
for the astonishing metamorphosis of the post-
medieval western world. This paper seeks to do
two things. It will review in highly schematic
terms some of the historical developments that
make up the consumer revolution. It will then
review recent historical scholarship that has
taken up the study of this previously neglected
aspect of the great transformation. The purpose
of this second section is to identify the theoretical and methodological issues that surround
this literature and to identify some of the prom-
ises and difficulties that now await this growing
field.

A Thumb Nail Sketch

The "consumer revolution" that took place as part
of the great transformation of the western world
is too recent a topic of historical study for
comprehensive understanding. Enough work has
been done that we are no longer quite so obviously blind men examining an elephant, but certain
topics and certain periods have been almost
completely neglected. Our present appreciation
of the development of consumption is therefore
still very limited. The following thumb nail
sketch must be treated as an exceedingly hasty
review of a very partial record. (A fuller

[1]Department of Consumer Studies, University of
Guelph, Guelph, Ontario N1G 2W1

treatment of this material may be found in
McCracken 1985e).

The history of consumption has no single beginning, no single line of development, no single
cause, no single set of consequences. It is
necessarily a vastly complicated social and historical process that can only be examined imperfectly and incompletely. For purposes of
exposition, however, arbitrary selections must be
made. Proceedingly arbitrarily, we can say that
an important origin of modern consumer behavior
can be found in the latter half of the 16th
century in England. Here a certain sector of
Elizabethan society, specifically the nobility,
engaged in a riot of consumption. Their expenditures on housing, clothing, furnishings, food,
servants and ceremony assumed the proportions of
the Northwest coast pot-latch. It appeared almost as if this class was bent on consuming its
wealth in a self-destructive gesture of extravagance (Stone 1965).

There are several apparent causes for this consumer boom. One of these was the effort of
Elizabeth I to make the members of her court
active participants in (and therefore underwriters of) the ceremony with which she ruled
(McCracken 1982b; Montrose 1980; Strong 1973).
Another was the fierce competition caused by
Elizabeth's new system of patronage and the new
proximity of noblemen living in London. The consumer boom also had several apparent consequences.
The new scale of Elizabethan consumption had the
effect of drawing the nobleman away from his
reciprocal bargain with his family and his locality (McCracken 1983a). Consuming with new competitive extravagance, the nobleman was unable to
engage in the consumption patterns with which he
traditionally met his obligations to the family
corporation (Stone 1977) and his local subordin-
ates (Heal 1984). He now engaged in consumption
behavior controlled by new concerns for fashion
and devoted to the aggrandizement of the self
rather than the material and symbolic needs of
the family and the locality. The nobleman's consumption behavior represents a dramatic transformation of the consumer decision-making, the unit
of consumption, the social context of consumption,
and symbolic properties of consumer goods. All
of these changes may be seen to draw consumption
away from its medieval constraints and give it
new potentially modern characteristics.

The 18th century saw another explosion of consumption (McKendrick et al., 1982). This explosion has the same startling quality of its 16th
century counter part. Contemporaries compared it
to an epidemic and to a collective act of mad-
ness. What particularly distinguished this consumer riot from its 16th century counter part was
its greatly enlarged scale of participation. The
nobility were now joined by the upper and lower
middle-classes as voracious consumers. The

causes of this consumer boom again appear to be those of social competition. New wealth and new mobility fuelled the competition between social classes and created a fury of spending and display. And again the consequences were dramatic. Consumer behavior was now more than ever governed by the dictates of fashion and the symbolic needs of the individual. It took place in a market place that was increasingly aware of the forces of the market place (such as diffusion driven by social competition) and prepared to exploit them with new advances in marketing and advertising. Once confined to "high days" and "local markets", consumption was spreading out in time and space to occupy more of the week and more of the town. Consumption was growing from a small corner of domestic life into a major preoccupation for both the individual and the collectivity.

The 19th century saw the steady unfolding of the consumer revolution (Williams 1982). A vital development in this period was the Department store which changed the context and nature of consumption. Individuals were now exposed to astonishing displays of merchandise in controlled environments where every medium was used to persuasive effect and every sense commandeered by the marketing process. The Department store served also to further discourage the barter process and encourage the use of the fixed price, a development which changed profoundly the nature of the interaction between buyer and seller. The Department store also succeeded in encouraging the use of credit, or more accurately, the possession of an object before its purchase. This had important implications for the new wish-fulfilling promise of consumption. A second vital development in this period was the tremendously expanded range of cultural meaning that consumer goods could express (Miller 1981). Both marketers and consumers began to explore the expressive potential of these goods. This exploration meant the eclipse of the "courtly model of consumption" that had prevailed from the Renaissance onwards and the development of new "consumer lifestyles", through which social groups who communicated their values and relationship to the larger society through the increasingly sophisticated deployment of the symbolic properties of consumer goods. The multiple realities of modern society were now under construction as consumer goods were used by all classes and sectors as means of self- and group-definition.

In sum the development of consumer behavior from the 16th century onwards sees it move from a small corner of domestic life to become a major preoccupation for the individual and society. In this period, the very definition of time and space was being changed to accommodate its expanded presence. The number of players allowed to participate expanded continually. Consumption was now an instrument of government and an instrument of competition, and in both these roles represented a newly sophisticated deployment of the symbolic properties of consumer goods. The consumption process was also increasingly understood by and subject to the control of manufacturers and retailers. Consumption was now governed by fashion and subject to obsolescence, and as a result less and less devoted to utilitarian considerations. Consumption was undertaken increasingly for the sake of the individual and less and less for the family, class or local cor-

poration and to this extent contributed to the growing disarray of culture and society in the west. But as goods became increasingly a means of communication and an opportunity for experimentation in cultural meaning, it also became a way of re-establishing new terms for social organization and self presentation. Consumption and consumer goods became an idiom for the expression and invention of new social and cultural orders.

The Methodological Issue

A single methodological issue dominates the present state and future of this nascent field. It is the skill and success with which it selects, imports and applies theories from the social sciences. This is an issue that students of consumer behavior will recognize. It is one with which they themselves have had to wrestle. They will appreciate as well as anyone the urgency and the difficulty of this undertaking. The remainder of the paper reviews the several theories that have been borrowed from the social sciences in order to examine the making of modern consumer behavior.

The State of a Nascent Art

McKendrick et al., (1982) have examined the explosion of consumer activity that took place in 18th century England in terms of two concepts from the social sciences, specifically Veblen's (1912) notion of "conspicuous expenditure" and Simmel's (1904) "trickle-down" theory. The fury of consumption of this period is seen as the result of fiercely competitive status display behavior within each social rank, and the downward diffusion of status markers between them.

There is no doubt that this dual theory serves as a useful way of explaining the consumption behavior of this period. But it is also clear that it offers no exhaustive account of this phenomenon. The astonishing intensity, novelty, and impact of 18th century consumption requires more, and more penetrating, theoretical perspectives. We must know the changes in "mentalitie" were necessary for this riot of consumption to take place. It is wrong and presentist to suppose that the English of the 18th century were merely waiting for the ways and means of consumption; that they took to it as "ducks to water". The ideas of Simmel and Veblen despite their values in this context are sometimes as much the substitute of insight as its opportunity. In defense of McKendrick et al., it must be acknowledged that in relying too heavily on this account of consumption behavior, they have merely reproduced a bias that already existed in consumer behavior research and the social sciences. These fields have for many years sought to explain the meaning contained in consumer goods as "status markers" and to understand the social uses of this meaning as "status competition". Rich and productive as this approach has been, it has helped create the notion that status information is the only or the chief kind of meaning contained in goods. It should not surprise us then that a visitor to the social sciences from the field of history should have been mislead on this score and moved to treat the ideas of Veblen and Simmel as if they were sufficient rather than merely necessary terms for the study of consumption behavior.

The second major contributor to the history of consumption, Rosalind Williams, is the author of "Dream Worlds: Mass Consumption in Late Nineteenth Century France". This work uses a much richer selection of social scientific theory than McKendrick et al. Williams gives due attention to the role of status competition but she moves on to consider several additional explanations. She follows Braudel's suggestion (1973) that consumption was used by European rulers of the Renaissance as an instrument of politics. This is a vital idea that will contribute to current attempts to establish the symbolic aspects of hegemonic control of society enjoyed by ruling families and their courts (cf. Thompson 1974). Williams also follow Elias' study (1978) of the "civilizing process" and suggests that consumer goods served as both a cause and consequence of the growing body of rules that constrained the individual in social situations by heightening the possibility of social embarrassment and shame. And finally, Williams takes up the notion of "lifestyle" and attempts to show how styles of life in 19th century France were indeed created as styles of consumption. The importation of this social scientific idea allows her to consider how goods in the 19th century were becoming the site of diverse social meanings and indeed instruments by which these meanings could be given coherence and expression.

Williams' work has several difficulties. The first is the continual tone of moral disapproval that attends her description of an emerging consumer society. She begins her treatment with the assumption that rising consumption must always have a corrupting influence (even while she presents evidence that it does not). Some pieces of analysis become mere recitations of articles of modern, liberal faith. The history of consumption will certainly become the opportunity for a variety of scholars to sound a variety of ideological horns, but this tendency must be discouraged. Williams' book also tends to confuse the exposition of an argument with its demonstration and leaves us wondering just what evidence justifies Williams' use of ideas from Braudel and Elias. If McKendrick et al. use too few of the social scientific resources at their disposal, Williams uses too many   rather too well. The ideas that are imported from the social sciences will surely be transformed by their application in this historical context. They must be used with sufficient care that this transformation can be observed. Finally, it is not clear that Williams controls the idea "lifestyle" with the precision it must have to make a real contribution to our understanding of experiments in the culturally constitutive powers of consumption. As with McKendrick, Williams' difficulty can be said merely to reflect the confusion and imprecision that surrounds this concept in the field of consumer research and sociology. Still, historical study will be no mere client of the social sciences when it uses social scientific concepts. It will almost certainly return with interest the ideas it borrows. This can not happen when care is not taken.

The third contributor is Chandra Mukerji, author of "From Graven Images: Patterns of Modern Materialism". Mukerji examines the "consumerist culture" of 15th and 16th century Europe and the rise of early modern printing and 18th century cotton. This is the most ambitious attempt to apply theories from the social sciences to the making of modern consumer behavior. It draws on theoretical innovations by Douglas and Isherwood (1978) and Sahlins (1976) and constructs a model of inquiry that ought to take this work far beyond the sociological transparencies of Veblen and Simmel. Mukerji seeks to consider the "symbolic properties" of consumer goods and to show how their meaning contributed to a "cultural system" that encouraged new demand, new production, and the birth of capitalism (1983:8-16). From Graven Images does not succeed in this attempt. Consistently, Mukerji studies the "cultural" aspects of consumption and consumer goods from a functional sociological point of view rather than a semiotic anthropological one (McCracken 1984).

Theoretical Imperatives in the Study
of the History of Consumption

The work of these three scholars has helped us see that the consumer revolution was as important to the transformation of the western world as the industrial revolution. They have also made it clear that this topic is a vital one to those who would understand the consumption of the present day. What they have failed to do is to establish an enquiry that takes us to the heart of this emergent species of social action. There is no question that consumption has made itself a kind of preoccupation of modern society. It has emerged as one of the major ways in which individuals and groups contend with the dislocation and constant innovation the west has made its permanent condition. It has become a source of cultural meaning and an instrument for the manipulation of this meaning (McCracken, 1985b, 1985c, 1985d). In short, the industrial and consumer revolutions have left culture and consumption inextricably linked. The historians who would demonstrate how this interpenetration of culture and consumption took place must resort to more, and more sophisticated, theoretical tools than those they have used to date. They must then apply these theories in a manner that is exacting enough to bring real insight and sensitive enough to see where the data demand theoretical reform. The theoretical and methodological challenges before this scholarly enterprise, then, are daunting. Interestingly, they are precisely those that now face scholars within the field of consumer research itself. The students of past and present consumer behavior have much to offer each other. Whether they will be mutually useful depends upon the success with which they meet this common problem.

References

Braudel, Fernand (1973), Capitalism and Material Life 1400-1800, Miriam Kochan (trans.) London: Weidenfeld and Nicolson.

Douglas, Mary and Baron Isherwood (1978), The World of Goods: Towards an Anthropology of Consumption. New York: W. W. Norton and Co.

Elias, Norbert (1978), The History of Manners, The Civilizing Process: Vol. 1. Edmund Jephcott (trans.) New York: Pantheon Books.

Heal, Felicity (1984), <u>The Idea of Hospitality in Early Modern England, Past and Present</u>, 102, 68-93.

McCracken, Grant (1982a), "Rank and Two Aspects of Dress in Elizabethan England," <u>Culture</u>, II(2), 53-62.

_____ (1982b), "Politics and Ritual Sotto Voce: The Use of Demeanor as an Instrument of Politics in Elizabethan England," <u>Canadian Journal of Anthropology</u>, 3 (1), 85-100.

_____ (1983a), "The Exchange of Tudor Children," <u>Journal of Family History</u>, 8(4), 303-313.

_____ (1983b), "History and Symbolic Anthropology: A Review and Critique of Four New Contributions to Their Rapprochement," <u>Culture</u>, 3(2), 3-14.

_____ (1984), "Review of From Graven Images: Patterns of Modern Materialism by Chandra Mukerji," <u>International Journal of Comparative Sociology</u>, XXV(3-4), 283-284.

_____ (1985a), "Colour in the Court of Elizabeth I: Historical Agent and Cultural Operator," <u>Canadian Review of Sociology and Anthropology</u>, Forthcoming, November 1985.

_____ (1985b), "Culture and Consumption I: A Theoretical Account of the Structure and Content of the Cultural Meaning of Consumer Goods." Working Paper No. 85-102, University of Guelph, Department of Consumer Studies Working Paper Series, pp. 1-38.

_____ (1985c), "Culture and Consumption II: A Theoretical Account of the Movement of the Cultural Meaning of Consumer Goods." Working Paper #85-103, University of Guelph, Department of Consumer Studies Working Paper Series, pp. 1-39.

_____ (1985d), "Culture and Consumption III: A Theoretical Account of Change in the Cultural Meaning of Consumer Goods." Working Paper #85-104, University of Guelph, Department of Consumer Studies Working Paper Series, pp. 1-32.

_____ (1985e), "The Making of Modern Consumption Behavior: The Historical Origins and Development of the Context and Activity of Modern Consumption," Working Paper #85-101 in the University of Guelph Department of Consumer Studies Working Paper Series, pp. 1-77.

McKendrick, Neil, John Brewer and J. H. Plumb (1982), <u>The Birth of a Consumer Society: The Commercialization of Eighteenth-Century England</u>, Bloomington, Indiana: Indiana University Press.

Miller, Michael (1981), <u>The Bon Marche: Bourgeois Culture and the Department Store, 1869-1920</u>, Princeton, New Jersey: Princeton University Press.

Montrose, Louis (1980), "Eliza, Queene of Shepheardes," and the Pastoral of Power, <u>English Literary Renaissance</u>, 10, 153-182.

Mukerji, Chandra (1983), <u>From Graven Images: Patterns of Modern Materialism</u>, New York: Columbia University Press.

Sahlins, Marshall (1976), <u>Culture and Practical Reason</u>, Chicago: University of Chicago Press.

Simmel, Georg (1904), "Fashion," <u>International Quarterly</u>, 10, 130-155.

Stone, Lawrence (1965), <u>The Crisis of Aristocracy 1558-1641</u>, London: Oxford University Press.

_____ (1977), <u>Family, Sex, and Marriage 1500-1800</u>, New York: Harper and Row.

Strong, Roy (1973), <u>Splendor at Court: The Renaissance and the Theatre of Power</u>, London: Weidenfeld and Nicolson.

_____ (1977), <u>The Cult of Elizabeth: Elizabethan Portraiture and Pagentry</u>, London: Thames and Hudson.

Thompson, E. P. (1974), "Patrician Society, Plebeian Culture," <u>Journal of Social History</u>, 7(4), 382-405.

Veblen, Thorstein (1912), <u>The Theory of the Leisure Class</u>, New York: Macmillan.

Warner, W. Lloyd and Paul S. Lunt (1941), <u>The Social Life of the Community</u>, New Haven: Yale University Press.

Williams, Rosalind (1982), <u>Dream Worlds: Mass Consumption in Late Nineteenth Century France</u>, Berkeley: University of California Press.

[14]

PERIODIZATION OF THE HISTORY OF MARKETING THOUGHT

Noel J. Stowe, Arizona State University

ABSTRACT

History is a valuable tool for marketers. Historical techniques aid in identifying and comprehending interconnections among events, in sifting conflicting viewpoints, and in understanding situations over time. Such tasks are encountered in studying the intellectual development of the discipline. Periodizing eighty years of market- ing thought is a difficult challenge. Problems of periodization are examined and questions posed to better grasp the development of marketing thought.

THE USEFULNESS AND COMPLEXITY OF PERIODIZATION

Establishing periods in the history of a discipline helps to reveal the flow of intel- lectual activity. It is a way of finding some order and coherence in the flux of ideas, trends, and events. Single periods can be studied to identify internal influ- ences and external stimuli; or several periods can be grouped to discover long-term issues.

Although the usefulness of periodization is apparent to anyone who must grapple with a variety of personalities and economic, social, political, and cultural factors, the task is not so simple or straightforward as it might seem. In particular, vary- ing strategies will produce different "periods." For example, suppose a historian wanted to use periods of Mexican history as a framework for tracing the roots of present thought. Which date marks the origin of "modern" Mexico--1917, 1890, the 1880s, 1876, 1848, 1821, 1810, 1750? All these dates have, in fact, been suggested. Which date marks the transition to modern development and thinking depends upon wheth- er the questions being posed are diplomatic, legal, political, institutional, econom- ic, social, cultural, or intellectual.

This diversity may seem to make the researcher's task hopelessly complex. How can order and coherence be derived from periodization if the periods themselves fluctuate? In particular, how can the periodization of marketing thought be informative?

These questions raise an even more fundamental issue that we should look at briefly: how history is being tapped and how it is being defined. Researchers who use history-- and, as we shall see, all researchers do--should have a clear understanding of what the discipline is being asked to do. They must consider what they think history is.

Using History as a Tool

What is history? Is it, for example, a set of facts conveniently arranged in a book or a series of events recorded in some chronicle? No, because a listing of facts or events does not have meaning in itself--and giving meaning to the past is what histo- rians are paid to do. Little in the past is fixed enough for us to use without apply- ing historical analysis. The past--which ended a second ago--is inert. A mere re- cording of events is no more informative than the markings on a gravestone. Giving life and voice to the past by moving beyond mere chronicling is what the discipline of history does.

Thinking historically means fashioning and refashioning the historical record to give it substance, meaning, and dimension. History makes the past active, allowing us to reach back for authority and guidance, and to disaggregate the web of events in order to comprehend more fully particular elements. This is history as process, a way of carving out information as it is needed, so that complicated mixtures of ideas, events, groups, and people can be analyzed. Like marketing, history must reach out to other disciplines to understand its material; this is history's horizontal dimension. Being historically minded means using the skills and techniques of the historian to control and manipulate the past. (Hughes 1964, Barzun and Graff 1977, Fischer 1970; see also Savitt 1980).

How can this concept of history as process be applied to marketing thought? Beginning in 1970, the dimension of marketing thought widened considerably as marketing scholars discussed such new topics as demarketing, macromarketing, and social marketing (e.g., Kotler and Levy 1971, Kotler and Zaltman 1971, Kelley 1971, Bartels and Jenkins 1977). A chronicler would list the publication of these articles and note the emerging discussion of these ideas. By contrast, a historian raises questions: Is the field changing? How do these new ideas reflect contemporary social, cultural, or political trends? How does this thinking change the discipline's conceptual base? Is there a tie-in to the rising concern over scarce resources, to the notion that "less is more," or to the idea that social values take precedence over other concerns? In other words, how does this literature relate to its social context? Is this just a natural broadening of the marketing concept (Kotler and Levy 1969), a normal growth of thought within the discipline? Or are the ideas and values of society compelling the discipline to give attention to these topics? Such a line of inquiry enables us to make more enlightened, critical assessments of conceptual development, and therefore to make better use of concepts because we understand how they were developed and the situations to which they correctly apply.

Much of marketing thought and theory development necessarily relies on the study and evaluation of the past. The historical character of marketing thought affects not only the work of scholars and theorists but also the decisions of practitioners who review experience in order to understand their contemporary setting, outline their expectations and alternative courses, and develop appropriate strategies. In fact, all report writing is history, because all report writing interprets the past.

Furthermore, several marketing conceptualizations naturally incorporate history into a marketer's thinking. Product life cycle analysis periodizes the past of a product and helps determine future action. Market penetration and market segmentation studies assess the recent past in an effort to develop effective strategies for the future. Marketing models can be thought of as descriptions of past action frozen for comparison to present or future situations. Conceptual approaches such as macromarketing involve applying past thought to current situations. Hunt's three dichotomies model of marketing, which was developed to set forth the scope of the discipline, is historical. It captures past trends and previous thinking, and it categorizes present and future activity to particular norms (defined according to past activity). Here is an example of current thinking being held captive to past development, the present tied conceptually to the past (Hunt 1983, pp. 9-14).

The value of the historical discipline lies in the techniques it has developed for recognizing the interconnected nature of events, sifting conflicting viewpoints and problems of evidence, and achieving depth of meaning and understanding between situations over time. Historical thinking allows us to use the past to develop new lines of thought instead of being controlled by past actions and influences.

The Problem

Given this understanding of the historical enterprise, how can marketing thought be periodized so that we can understand more clearly its emerging stages and the deeper meaning behind current thinking? Organizing the eighty years of intellectual devel-

2

opment in the discipline creates special tasks. To achieve a better grasp of the issues, this paper will (1) trace existing periodization schemes; (2) offer a generational comparison between a principles text of the 1920s and a principles text of the 1980s; and (3) discuss raising questions that periodization can answer.

EXISTING PERIODIZATION SCHEMES

Bartels' (1976) oft-cited and valuable monograph on the history of marketing thought approaches periodization from one primary perspective: decades. Virtually all of us fall into this habit: we talk about the thinking of the 1970s or the coming trends in the 1980s. But clearly this is arbitrary, for trends and thinking do not conveniently begin or end with years ending in zero.

Two special problems arise from applying this approach to marketing. First, the subareas are not considered on the basis of their own development and periodization. The inherent difficulty is obvious from Bartels' discussion of advertising thought, in which he sidesteps a decade-by-decade approach until 1950, casting the preceding era in topical divisions that permit study of influences extending beyond decade boundaries. Clearly, one cannot construct a general time structure into which every component subarea fits and at the same time preserve the historical integrity of each subarea.

The second problem, which derives from Bartels' attempt to place all marketing thought in the same linear time continuum, is that plural intellectual foundations are ignored. Such a discussion would jeopardize the decade categories and labels, for intellectual underpinnings cut across decade divisions and affect each thought area differently. Only late in his discussion (chapters 12-14) does Bartels grapple with this problem and examine field developments in a general manner, avoiding the period confines.

Jackson (1979) modifies Bartels' approach by incorporating the major environmental factors that have spurred marketing thought. His stages cross decades, with each segment carrying its own descriptive title. Particularly important to Jackson's structure is the development of an environmental approach that captures the evolution of marketing thought as it responds to influences from within and without the discipline. In contrast to Bartels', this time scheme carefully incorporates the changes in thought sweeping the discipline. Like Bartels, Jackson uses several subcategories to grasp the meaning of thought development: commodity, institutional, functional/systems, macromarketing, and functional. Thus, both writers move beyond a unified periodization strategy as the complex nature of the discipline and its inner structure demands.

Another method of periodization relies on carving out longer time spans for review. Converse (1951), for instance, examines the first fifty years of marketing thought. Converse's goal is to demonstrate the emergence of a scientific discipline with an organized literature supporting an organized body of knowledge. Therefore he considers some of the hypotheses, theories, laws, and techniques that originated during the first fifty years. Transcending narrow time structures, his topical discussion of costs, pricing, trade movements, and retail rents examines the ideas surrounding these subjects. Although he treats these topics only briefly, his work strikes at the meaning and substance of these matters and breaks out of the time sequence approach.

In 1976, on its fortieth anniversary, the Journal of Marketing published a group of articles evluating the Journal's contribution to the field. Classifying articles into twelve subject areas, Grether (1976) stressed the linking of external economic, political, scientific, and technological changes to the issues covered in Journal

writing. Stretching over forty years, as Grether saw it, was an evolving discipline
participating in and contributing to changes in the behavioral sciences and the quantitative, statistical, and econometric methodologies. In a manner reminiscent of
Converse, Grether treated this forty-year period as a unit of thought development,
avoided segmenting it, and characterized it according to the subjects addressed in
the writing of marketing scholars.

Similarly, Myers, Massy, and Greyser (1980) examine twenty-five years (1952-1977) of
discipline activity. In using this time span, the authors are studying a generation
of marketing research and knowledge development. According to their review, a marked
shift occurred during the early 1950s in the philosophy of teaching and research in
business education: "Economics as the core of business training . . . . evolved into
a social science core of economics, behavioral science, and quantitative methods."
The business schools adopting this approach became "the most productive generators of
new knowledge in all business fields, including marketing" (p. ix-x). At this time
model building (a new key research technique) and consumer research (based on the behavioral sciences) became important. New conceptual ideas appeared, such as the marketing concept, market penetration, market segmentation, and refined views on the product life cycle. Important external developments influenced these changes: in technology, the computer and television; in the sociopolitical setting, consumerism, increased government restrictions, and heightened ecological concerns; in the economic
area, an enlarging population, expanding corporations, and a rising gross national
product. By making the setting for marketing more complex, these external factors
stimulated new developments in marketing thought, resulting in the theoretical development of major new approaches and techniques. Indicative of the new economic and behavioral trends influencing the discipline were two new journals focusing on marketing
research and consumer research.

An examination of what Myers, Massy, and Greyser do in their study is useful in a discussion about periodization for several reasons. Their approach enables us to see
how a generation of scholars responded to a wide variety of new developments coming
from within and without the discipline. Furthermore, from their discussion we can
see the difficulty of establishing appropriate time divisions, either across the
whole discipline within a limited time setting, or in a rapidly changing era such as
the one following World War II. Although their analysis is more instructive than the
forty-or fifty-year studies because they confine their work to a single generation,
they ignore broader intellectual trends and pre-1952 influences. The narrowness of
their periodization outlook, stemming from the survey technique underlying the book,
hinders an adequate treatment of thought development.

A GENERATIONAL COMPARISON

We can isolate more precisely the problems involved in periodization and focus on possible solutions by comparing two titles written in distinctly different periods and
examining them as reflections of their intellectual contexts.

Copeland: 1924

Copeland's 1924 <u>Principles of Merchandising</u> presented the conclusions of his twelve
years as a professor of marketing and director of the Bureau of Business Research at
Harvard. The book centers on marketing costs and ways of reducing them. Philosophi-
cally, Copeland was concerned that merchandising take place "under competitive conditions which afford liberal opportunities for the manifestation of individual initiative" (p. iii). He was troubled by the inhibiting influences of federal legislation
(the Sherman Act) and by competition from cooperative marketing associations that expressed "the philosophy of socialism" and made up "a non-competitive society" (p. 18).
Throughout his discussion he dealt with the unsettling effects of World War I--partic-

4

ularly the war support drive to limit or restrict nonmilitary production and the
postwar collapse in prices that extended into the early 1920s.

In setting out his objectives, Copeland focuses on "the exchange of goods and services . . . effected for practical purposes with money as the medium of exchange"
(p. 2). The producer or merchant initiates the exchange process by soliciting patronage and plans for the efficient distribution of the product to consumers. Merchandising comprises these tasks. Effective merchandising increases demand and
thereby sales. Producers compete for consumer dollars not only with producers of
very similar goods but also with producers of goods that can satisfy the same range
of wants. Thus, a phonograph manufacturer competes with other phonograph manufacturers and with suppliers of musical instruments, rugs, radios, and garments.

Copeland carefully categorizes merchandising activities and related factors. His
now classic division of goods includes two broad categories: (1) consumer goods sold
for retail distribution and (2) industrial goods. The retailing discussion centers
on three classes of items: (1) convenience goods, (2) shopping goods, and (3) specialty goods. Other major topics he discusses include marketing industrial goods,
consumer buying motives, sales forces, advertising, stock-turn, and price policies.

The pricing discussion demonstrates the effect of the World War I era. The unsettled
conditions following the war were reflected in a recession, a decline in prices, and
the decisions (which Copeland laments) of the Supreme Court under the Sherman and
Clayton Antitrust acts. Clearly, the writing and thought of this title are couched
in the terms of the early 1920s. Copeland wrote out of his own experience and strongly held beliefs. Nevertheless, though he might be suspicious of a socialist trend
reflected in cooperative ventures such as the California Fruit Growers Exchange (Sun-
kist), and though he might angle off into a review of how to stock a store properly
a broader conceptual framework is in evidence.

Udell and Laczniak: A Recent Principles Text

Udell and Laczniak published a new principles text in 1981. Their use of definitions
and concepts as well as their topics and citations place this title in the mainstream
of the marketing literature of the 1970s. This text sets marketing within a dynamic
environment, assuming the reader must be in tune with "marketing in an age of change."
Consumers are the most important part of marketing, the purposes of which are to
serve the consumer well (the social function of business) and to earn a profit (the
private goal). Marketing activities lead "to the facilitation and consummation of
satisfying exchanges." Essential for both profit and nonprofit organizations, marketing is "the product planning, pricing, promotion, distribution, and servicing of
goods and services needed and desired by customers" (p. 5). The management of marketing is an art, but the discipline of marketing is a science involving explanation,
prediction, and understanding, and resulting in a body of systematized marketing knowledge.

Their discussion covers diverse subjects: consumer behavior; competitive strategy;
marketing research and forecasting; product, promotion, pricing, distribution, and
service management; societal issues; wholesaling and retailing; and international
trade. Udell and Laczniak explore the broad impact of marketing on society as well
as the external forces impinging on marketing activities and thought. Consumerism,
antitrust legislation, ecological issues, and resource shortages are challenges leading to new marketing opportunities. Their discussions of social values, technological
development, and resource problems couch their writing in the context of the 1970s.
Marketers must be aware not only of the nature of consumer and industrial markets but
also of the sociological and psychological determinants of buyer behavior. The marketing strategy of the future will become more ethical, constrained, value-oriented,
conserving, flexible, anticipatory, and broadened in order to cope with a society

caught up in change.

The Texts as Reflections of Periods of Thought

These two texts clearly reflect the periods in which they were written. Copeland directs his discussion to the tasks of the early 1920s, whereas Udell and Laczniak target the dynamism of the later 1970s and stress an ever-changing marketing strategy.

Copeland's views remain closed and finite, aimed at meeting the demands of the early 1920s. No foundation is laid for what lies in the future. His concern over socialism and stress on competition reveal a strong philosophical orientation and almost certainly reflect the Red Scare of the period. Udell and Laczniak assume a broader, more eclectic posture, viewing legal restraints and regulations as part of an evolving social setting. Their discussion emphasizes the free enterprise or free market setting. Their optimistic and open-ended orientation leaves the reader with the belief that marketing thought is dynamic, fully capable of meeting future societal change.

To a great extent the two books deal with similar material. In Copeland's definitions and ideas we can see the rudiments of the definition of marketing as exchange, a market segmentation approach, a consideration of the product life cycle, a nascent behavioral emphasis on buyer behavior, and the marketing mix concept. The contrast between the works lies in their emphasis and intellectual underpinnings, and reflects the changes stemming from the evolution and maturation of the discipline in the sixty years separating the two titles. Because one is grandfather to the other, it is easy to perceive a common base. For example, Udell and Laczniak reflect the discipline's continuing reliance on Copeland's categorization of retail goods into three categories. But Copeland's 113-page discussion contrasts with their 5. More pointedly their discussion of goods categories is embedded in a larger consideration of consumer markets that extends into an examination of population dynamics, changing life-styles, and income dynamics. Their view of buying motives, embodying the notion of an ever-changing social setting, is more sophisticated and complex than Copeland's, which remains static. The much emphasized discussions of advertising and the sales force in Copeland are reduced by Udell and Laczniak to smaller segments of a broad discussion on promotions management. His review of pricing policies is narrower, and begrudgingly admits of change. In contrast Udell and Laczniak discuss the several conceptual foundations upon which management may base pricing decisions, stressing the limits of applicability of each view and the need for flexibility.

Thus, despite their conceptual similarities, Udell and Laczniak's analysis is a springboard to the future, whereas Copeland's view is frozen, embracing the past, only tentatively viewing the present, and never reaching out to the future.

The Texts as Illustrations of the Problem of Periodization

This comparison is useful for several reasons. Obviously, whatever "periods" there may be in marketing thought, the two titles stem from two different thought periods. The importance of the sixty-year differential is intellectual, not chronological. As a piece of literature, each book conveniently freezes the thought of its period for us to examine.

When evaluating a piece of writing it is important to consider it on its own merits. It is always dangerous to assume that we are the sophisticates and the past authors the untutored. Instead, viewing each title within its own context reveals much about the intellectual process internal to the discipline, as well as the external forces that were influencing thought patterns at the time. Then the similarities and differences between the writings can be analyzed. When differences outweigh similarities, chances are the thinking of two periods is being expressed.

6

Earlier we saw that maintaining the unity of a discipline by using single, linked linear time periods for categorizing all thought development has the unfortunate effect of submerging the complexity of thought. But this complication of the work of periodizing also presents a significant opportunity. What richness might emerge if the individual integrity of the subfields within the discipline were maintained and examined separately, charting influences and internal thought development. Although the obvious disadvantage is the momentary casting aside of unified linear periodization, this technique allows us to pose a variety of interesting questions. Do all the subareas of thought have their own integrity? What are the interrelationships among them? Does each subfield have its own periods? Does a series of layers of marketing thought exist? How independent are these layers? When external forces confront the discipline--for example, demographic change, consumerism, the computer, model building, behaviorism--do they affect all areas equally? How does thought in each area respond to such factors?

A kind of stratification of development is suggested by Bartels' History of Marketing Thought (1976). As mentioned earlier, his discussion of early advertising development avoided periodization by decades. Instead, Bartels charts lines of personal influence. Yet his chart usually maintains the coherence of the formative years by showing strong linkages through 1927 (1976, p. 28). It might well be argued that the beginnings of thought in the discipline are best treated in such a holistic fashion. And it may be that reviewing even the first half-century of marketing thought as a unit has its merits. Once the more complex forces spanning the 1950s, 1960s, and 1970s have to be considered, though, that procedure becomes difficult to defend. To cope with the diversity of those years, Myers, Massy, and Greyser set narrower time boundaries, carefully delimited their discussions, and focused on particular topics.

It is probably impossible to organize large chronological chunks of writing in the postwar years because the intellectual dimensions of marketing thought expanded so significantly during this time. Two factors suggest that a more complex approach is needed. First, the discipline's well-acknowledged eclectic nature, manifested in its reaching out to the theories, concepts, ideas, and techniques of the other social sciences, resulted in a vast expansion of the thought horizon. Second, the broadening of marketing discussion may be the best evidence of the discipline's own self-adjustment to the recognition of diversity (Kotler and Levy 1969). Increased discussion or controversy over the generic concept, macromarketing, marketing as exchange, and social marketing may represent not only the charting of new directions but also the recognition and careful definition of the conceptual growth of the discipline. The retrospective comments of Levitt on the significance of his "myopia" article (1960) might be taken at face value as indicating such a situation: "'Marketing Myopia' was not . . . a new idea--Peter F. Drucker, J.B. McKitterick, Wroe Alderson, John Howard, and Neil Borden had each done more original and balanced work on 'the marketing concept' . . . . My contribution, therefore, appears merely to have been a simple, brief, and useful way of communicating an existing way of thinking" (Levitt 1975, p. 180).

In like fashion it might be well to consider whether the broadening of the marketing concept was a written recognition of a trend already in place (Kotler and Levy 1969). Without belittling any scholar's contribution, interrelationships with earlier literature as well as the development of the discipline need to be examined in order to place a discussion, trend, or piece of writing in its contextual niche. Does the writing in fact reflect the field's ripeness for a new direction? Is the field already moving that way? Do certain articles capture for us that important moment?

The case can be made that new, diverse directions manifested themselves in the 1950s, 1960s, and 1970s in the subfields of marketing thought. The point to consider is whether the individual subfields must be examined for their own separate periodization in order to test the breadth and depth of thought within them.

RAISING QUESTIONS TO GAIN A HISTORICAL PERSPECTIVE

Questioning the Disappearance of an Issue

As the issues of periodization are addressed and as time boundaries are drawn, certain questions should be raised to support the task. For instance, when an intellectual discussion seemingly lapses or disappears, it is vital to understand what has happened. A good example is the issue of whether marketing is a science or an art. Nowadays this subject seems dead. How and when did it die? What meaning can be attached to the submergence of this discussion? Has it disappeared or is it concealed in another subject?

Answers to these questions center on at least three points. First, the definition of marketing has broadened considerably over the past thirty years (see Hunt 1976 and Hunt 1983, 5-26). At the same time the exchange idea was extended to embrace a more intangible, idea-oriented concept (e.g., Bagozzi 1975, Bagozzi 1979, Ferrell and Perrachione 1979). The old science-and-art controversy, cast as a simple dichotomy became surrounded with ideas less tangibly focused in either/or terms. Second, a greater adaptation and use of economics and behavioral science concepts incorporated more scientifically based notions and techniques into marketing thought processes. These changes are particulary reflected in the direction marketing research has taken in recent years. Third, there is evidence that the entire issue has moved to a different plane. In 1982, a marketing theory conference was held under the subtitle "Philosophy of Science Perspectives" (Bush and Hunt 1982). Clearly, no one at that conference was debating an either/or subject. Instead it now appears more important to reflect whether marketing practice is grounded in the scientifically based thought of the discipline (that is, through the application of scientific theory or the scientific method) or in an artful practice learned through experience. Bringing experience and theory together appears to be the agenda for the immediate future. In addition, by 1980 marketing was being described as a process, a technical art—a description that is quite separate from the old art-or-science discussion (Carman 1980).

Analyzing what happened to a once significant issue can help us begin to shape periodization ideas. In this case the point at which the older art/science debate advanced to a different intellectual level may mark the existence of a new period of marketing thought.

Establishing a Generational Perspective

Generations of Thought. Another way to address periodization is to use a generational approach. Generational discussions may be delineated and charted in two ways. First, writings may be grouped according to the generations of which they are a part. Does a piece of writing mirror particular values or concerns? Can it be placed alongside a group of materials expressing a similar ethic? The earlier discussion of the Copeland and Udell-Laczniak examples illustrates this procedure. By examining a body of writings together, we can establish how a group of thinkers treated their subject, shaped it, and shared ideas, althought each writer set a separate course for his or her individual contribution. Well-selected questions can focus attention on what one group of thinkers believed important. What was the intellectual stimulation—new techniques or an infusion of ideas from an adjunct discipline? How important was the contextual stimulation? What internal and external forces encouraged thought to take on new dimensions? Were new thought patterns formed? What is the relationship of the thought under scrutiny to what had gone before and to what followed?

Generations of Thinkers. A second generational approach is to ask what generation dominates the discipline's ideas at any given moment. Here questions of age, academic preparation, and individual thought patterns and interests become important. Such questions focus attention on who is controlling a field and influencing its development and how long they will dominate.

For example a study might focus on the thirty marketing scholars identified as the most cited in books and articles for 1972-1975 (Myers, Massy, and Greyser 1980, p. 187). How long will this group of thirty be influencing thought? An examination of their birthdates might suggest much about those influencing the discipline. How important are these thirty in training graduate students? What legacy is being passed on? Even though Myers et al. suggest some aspects of influence, much more analysis should be done. What is the impact of a single scholar's work? What are the linkages of one scholar to another? In the distribution/channels area, the impact of Louis Stern might serve as an example. His influence is felt not only through his own writing (e.g., 1969) but through the writings of scholars he has trained (e.g., El-Ansary 1970), and the scholars they have trained (e.g., Robicheaux 1974).

Examining the Emergence and Influence of Trends

In conceptualizing periods, it is important to identify trends. Tracing the roots of current trends permits us to judge the impact of particular developments. For example, technology has affected marketing through the computer, which supports the much expanded use of statistics. In areas such as marketing research this influence is remarkable. Yet it is equally important to identify the thought areas in which such innovation had less impact and what that suggests. Behaviorism and systems ideas have strongly influenced some areas of thought but not others. Identification of trends can help us to understand narrower subfield aspects of thought development and gain a sense of how the discipline is responding to various influences.

Periodization as a Function of the Subject Being Studied

For some subjects, periodization emerges from the subject itself. A discussion of the shift from market research to marketing research instantly categorizes the discipline into two large divisions. A shift from being product-oriented to being consumer-oriented produces a like division for thought purposes. Conceptual schemes such as marketing mix, market segmentation, and product life cycle each have their own developmental histories. In reading a piece of marketing literature, it is possible to place it in its own time continuum. How does it fit into past thought, or what is new in the use of technique or conceptualization? Treating each writing as a historical document gives it more substance, dimension, and meaning.

Periodizing by Strata

Finally, if periodization is to move away from decade labels and begin to express the rich diversity of marketing thought, researchers must treat each thought area as having its own integrity and identifiable history. Historical techniques can be used to disaggregate marketing thought as a means of studying its structure. As a result, deeper patterns of thought may be identified and the impact of trends, ideas, and techniques on the substance of marketing thought better perceived. Once subfield periodization has been done, more effective periodization work can be achieved for the discipline as a whole.

Analyzing Schools of Thought. Sheth and Gardner (1982) recently demonstrated the value of studying schools of thought as a way to examine the layers of recent marketing theory. They probe the development of six schools: macromarketing, consumerism, systems approach, buyer behavior theory, behavioral organization, and strategic planning. Analyzing schools is an extraordinarily useful way of grouping thought patterns, identifying interrelationships, and uncovering influences cutting across several sub-

9

field thought areas. Such scrutiny permits both periodization within a specific school and comparisons of development between schools within the same time period. It also makes it possible to determine the ideas pertinent to each school and the persons responsible for the dissemination of those ideas. Also, linkages over time between individual scholars or between patterns of ideas are more easily established with such a framework.

CONCLUSION: HISTORY AS A TOOL

Historical measures can help us to understand changes in marketing thought over time and thus gain control over the past. Better questioning to create more sophisticated periodization is one step toward gaining that control. Such history has contemporary meaning, for it supports heightened self-awareness. Understanding the past can help practitioners and theorists evaluate lines of thought, build better theories, and make more effective decisions. As comparisons are made between the present and past and analogies are drawn, the experience of previous generations can be more skillfully selected and used. The past can be a useful tool if we are not controlled by it because we misapprehend what occurred.

Within the study of marketing, the history of marketing thought should be carefully delineated as an important field component. Study of the intellectual development of the discipline is too important to be left out. Periodization is but one aspect of this powerful historical tool. Specifically, periodization can lead to more awareness of the direction thought has taken and is taking, it can suggest the origins of the thinking in control of the field at any given time, and it can reveal the presence of schools of thought or the existence of a generation of thinkers strongly influencing the discipline.

REFERENCES

El-Ansary, Adel (1970), "Power Measurement in the Distribution Channel: An Empirical Investigation," Columbus, OH: Unpublished Ph.D. Dissertation, The Ohio State University.

Bagozzi, Richard P. (1975), "Marketing as Exchange," Journal of Marketing, 39 (October), 32-39.

_____ (1979), "Toward a Formal Theory of Marketing Exchanges," in Conceptual and Theoretical Developments in Marketing, O. C. Ferrell, Stephen W. Brown, and Charles W. Lamb, Jr., eds., Chicago: American Marketing Association, 431-447.

Bartels, Robert (1976), The History of Marketing Thought, Homewood, IL: Richard D. Irwin, Inc.

_____ (1951), "Influences on the Development of Marketing Thought, 1900-1923," Journal of Marketing, 16 (July), 1-17.

_____, and Roger L. Jenkins (1977), "Macromarketing," Journal of Marketing, 41 (October), 17-20.

Barzun, Jacques, and Henry Graff (1977), The Modern Researcher, 3rd edition, New York: Harcourt Brace Jovanovich, Inc.

Bush, Ronald F., and Shelby D. Hunt, eds. (1982), Marketing Theory: Philosophy of Science Perspectives, Chicago: American Marketing Association.

Carman, James M. (1980), "Paradigms for Marketing Theory," in <u>Research in Marketing</u>, 3, 1-36.

Converse, Paul D. (1951), "Development of Marketing Theory: Fifty Years of Progress," in <u>Changing Perspectives in Marketing</u>, Hugh Wales, ed., Urbana, IL: University of Illinois Press, 1-31.

Copeland, Melvin Thomas (1924), <u>Principles of Merchandising</u>, Chicago: A. W. Shaw Company.

Ferrell, O. C., and J. R. Perrachione (1979), "An Inquiry into Bagozzi's Formal Theory of Marketing Exchanges," in <u>Conceptual and Theoretical Developments in Marketing</u>, O. C. Ferrell, Stephen W. Brown, and Charles W. Lamb, Jr., eds., Chicago: American Marketing Association, 158-161.

Fischer, David Hackett (1970), <u>Historians' Fallacies: Toward a Logic of Historical Thought</u>, New York: Harper and Row.

Grether, E. T. (1976), "The First Forty Years," <u>Journal of Marketing</u>, 40 (July), 63-69.

Hughes, H. Stuart (1964), <u>History as Art and as Science: Twin Vistas on the Past</u>, New York: Harper and Row.

Hunt, Shelby D. (1983), <u>Marketing Theory: The Philosophy of Marketing Science</u>, Homewood, IL: Richard D. Irwin, Inc.

_____(1976), "The Nature and Scope of Marketing," <u>Journal of Marketing</u>, 40 (July), 17-28.

Jackson, Donald W., Jr. (1979), "The Development of a Marketing Thought Course: An Approach," in <u>Conceptual and Theoretical Developments in Marketing</u>, O. C. Ferrell, Stephen W. Brown, and Charles W. Lamb, Jr., eds., Chicago: American Marketing Association, 408-419.

Kelley, Eugene J. (1971), "Marketing's Changing Social/Environmental Role," <u>Journal of Marketing</u>, 35 (July), 1-2.

Kotler, Philip, and Gerald Zaltman (1971), "Social Marketing: An Approach to Planned Social Change" <u>Journal of Marketing</u>, 35 (July), 3-12.

_____, and Sidney J. Levy (1969), "Broadening the Concept of Marketing," <u>Journal of Marketing</u>, 33 (January), 10-15.

_____(1971), "Demarketing, Yes, Demarketing," <u>Harvard Business Review</u>, 49 (November-December), 74-80.

Levitt, Theodore (1960), "Marketing Myopia," <u>Harvard Business Review</u>, 38 (July-August), 45-56.

_____(1975), "Marketing Myopia," <u>Harvard Business Review</u>, 53 (September-October), 26-44.

Myers, John G., William F. Massy, and Stephen A. Greyser (1980), <u>Marketing Research and Knowledge Development: As Assessment for Marketing Management</u>, Englewood Cliffs: Prentice-Hall, Inc.

Robicheaux, Robert A. (1974), "Control in a Distribution Channel: A Field Study," Baton Rouge, LA: Unpublished Ph.D. Dissertation, Louisiana State University.

Savitt, Ronald (1980), "Historical Research in Marketing," Journal of Marketing, 44 (Fall), 52-58.

Sheth, Jagdish N., and David M. Gardner (1982), "History of Marketing Thought: An Update," in Marketing Theory: Philosophy of Science Perspectives, Ronald F. Bush and Shelby D. Hunt, eds., Chicago: American Marketing Association, 52-58.

Stern, Louis W., ed. (1969), Distribution Channels: Behavioral Dimensions, Boston: Houghton Mifflin Company.

Udell, Jon G., and Gene R. Laczniak (1981), Marketing in an Age of Change: An Introduction, New York: John Wiley and Sons, Inc.

Part III
Marketing Education

[15]

Excerpt from Lucy Black Creighton, *Pretenders to the Throne*, 69–82.

6

Advocacy and Education

If the current "consumerism" is to be a more effective force, people are going to have to give more importance to their roles as consumers.

Carol Foreman (October 1974)

Even though in recent years the most conspicuous efforts for the consumer have been identified with Ralph Nader and governmental consumer advocates, the consumer movement has found support from other quarters as well. Several national consumer organizations have been formed. *Consumers Union* and *Consumers' Research* have been joined by other publications and columnists seeking to help consumers in their search for the kinds of information that will give them their "money's worth." The labor movement has identified itself with the consumer's cause and has used its resources and influence in programs for consumer organization, legislation, and information. And finally, there has come to be a renewed interest in the possibilities for additional protection for consumers through formal programs of consumer education.

Consumer Organizations

A continuing goal of the consumer movement has been to establish a large, central organization at the national level. Such an organization would give a needed cohesiveness and coordination for the diverse elements supporting the consumer's cause and provide a national forum to lend weight and prestige to the various groups speaking in the name of the consumer.

The first such organization, begun in 1933 as the Emergency Conference of Consumer Organizations, got as far as setting up headquarters in Washington and starting a biweekly newspaper. It lacked any sort of financial backing, however, and lasted less than a year. Some four years later a second organization was started for the same purpose. The Consumers' National Federation, as it was called, contemplated individual consumer memberships as well as the affiliation of interested groups. The Federation continued for several years without any spectacular results, and it passed out of existence sometime during World War II. (Unlike people, organizations are more heralded at birth than at death.)

69

70

With the impetus given the movement by the renewed interest in consumers in the early 1960s, another national organization, the Consumer Federation of America (CFA), was begun in 1967. There are some 200 organizations—labor unions, state and local consumer organizations, credit unions, and rural electric cooperatives—which currently identify themselves with the CFA. The CFA sees its role as an action-oriented one, serving as a clearinghouse on consumer legislation and as a consumer representative appearing at public hearings and bringing pressure for consumer legislation. It is also active in encouraging and supporting grass roots consumer organizations. The CFA has a staff of about ten people and a budget of some 200 thousand dollars.

Currently the CFA is the most prominent consumer-organization voice being heard at Congressional hearings.[1] Its executive director, Carol Foreman, is an energetic and effective lobbyist who describes herself as an "agrarian radical." Under her direction, the CFA garnered the support of many in the 1974 Congress and has spoken out on many issues affecting the consumer interest, including controls on natural gas and petroleum, food price supports, and the proposed agency for consumer protection. Even though the political activism of CFA has done much to publicize the consumer in Washington, the long-run success of CFA will depend on the degree of support from the affiliated organizations and their members. It has, however, had a longer life than any such previous organization.

In addition to CFA at the national level, there are dozens of state and local consumer organizations active across the country.[2] Many of these are the PIRGs and Citizen Action Groups begun by Nader and his associates. Some are an outgrowth of neighborhood-development programs; others are associated with colleges and universities. Many are small, locally organized groups with constantly changing leadership and membership. The effectiveness of these organizations varies over time and from place to place; they are largely dependent on voluntary staffing and their viability is directly related to the prominence of consumer issues. In times of inflation or rising food prices, local organizations attract the interest and support of new members, but this is apt to be temporary and cannot be the basis for sustained development.

Consumer Publications

In contrast to the numerous consumer organizations that have come and gone and in contrast to the ebb and flow of consumer activity over the nearly fifty years since the consumer movement began in 1927, two consumer-information services, Consumers' Research and Consumers Union, have continued without interruption. These two services were organized to provide consumers with impartial information on goods and services on the premise, as Consumers Union states it, that "any economic system based on free choice succeeds only

71

insofar as its citizens are given useful information to choose rationally among competing products and competing services."[3] Though serving the same purpose, the two organizations have played essentially different roles in the consumer movement.

Consumers' Research, since its foundation in 1927, has been run by F.J. Schlink. Schlink has staunchly defended the concept of the independent consumer who, armed with sufficient information and energy, can make the kinds of decisions necessary to assure that he gets "his money's worth." Schlink stood outside the mainstream of the consumer movement in the thirties because he did not believe that government representation of the consumer would achieve any lasting benefits. In his view, government had "sold out to business," and consumers could expect little genuine help there. Schlink still holds this view. Editorializing in 1974 on the increasing activism for government support for the consumer, he wrote, "the alert and informed consumer is his own best friend."[4]

Consumers Union, like Consumers' Research, is engaged in testing consumer goods and services and funds this information service through subscriptions to its monthly publication, *Consumer Reports*. Though in its early days it concentrated on low-cost household items—like food, soap, clothing, and bedding—it now provides information on a wide variety of consumer products—automobiles, sports and hobby equipment, tools, TVs, and phonograph equipment—as well as the more usual items in household use. And, increasingly in recent years, CU has extended its concern to consumer "products" like safe drinking water, health insurance, mass transportation, and banking services. Its readers are primarily college-educated, upper-middle-income families. CU estimates a readership of about two million.

By contrast with Consumers' Research, CU has always seen itself as a part of the consumer movement. Its long-time president, Colston E. Warne, has been a central figure in the consumer movement since the end of the 1930s. CU has been critical of what it considers excessive and misleading advertising on the part of business. It has called for grade labeling and standards for consumer products, for the release of product information gathered by government agencies, and for a "department of consumers." It publicizes rulings made by the FDA and FTC on products and advertising and has consistently criticized government regulatory agencies for neglecting to uphold the consumer's interest. CU currently has a Washington office to foster and promote its consumer advocacy in government.

CU's joint policies of political advocacy and consumer information have caused some conflict within the organization. On the one hand, there are those who maintain that CU should restrict itself to product information based on testing and leave controversial issues alone. They disapprove of CU's interest in public issues such as national health insurance.[5] In this camp are also a number of CU employees whose union, in May 1975, accused CU's management

72

of "squandering money on social activism."[6] On the other hand, there are those who support CU's interest in political activities and are critical of what they see as CU's reluctance to participate in an even wider range of consumer activities. Criticism from this camp reached a peak in the summer of 1975 when Ralph Nader resigned from the Board of Directors of CU, charging that CU should devote more of its "energy and resources . . . toward changing major consumer injustices through consumer action" and should "realize more of its potential in the area of consumer investigation, advocacy and organization."[7]

In responding to these criticisms, CU has generally leaned toward those who favor testing and information over advocacy. In an editorial in early 1975, CU acknowledged the value judgments implicit in any stand on a public issue and stated that in the future it would "label clearly those reports that, on balance, present a viewpoint on a controversial issue rather than buying data on goods and services."[8] In responding to Nader later in the year, Rhoda H. Karpatkin, executive director of CU, recognized the need for greater advocacy but reaffirmed the "impartial product-testing and reporting program" as "CU's unique contribution to the consumer interest."[9] Whatever may be the predilection of CU's Board, it is surely the case that the activities CU elects to pursue are funded by the subscriptions to a magazine based on testing information.

Less closely associated with the consumer movement are a number of other magazines and syndicated columns carrying information and advice about spending and money. *Changing Times* is a monthly magazine published by Kiplinger as a "service for families," much as the Kiplinger newsletter is for businessmen. It covers a broad range of family expenditures including health, education, investment, and leisure. It does not recommend specific brands nor is it oriented toward consumer advocacy. Time Inc. publishes a similar monthly, *Money*. Both of these magazines are geared to the expenditures and life styles of upper-middle-income families. The most widely read newspaper column is that of Sylvia Porter whose daily column *Your Dollar* appears in hundreds of newspapers across the country. Porter's lively discussions combine consumer counsel with lucid explanations of the current economic situation.

Labor's Part in the Consumer Movement

The labor movement was late in coming to espouse the consumer's cause. During the thirties when the consumer movement had its initial growth, labor was preoccupied with securing its own position and could not afford to advocate any other special interests.[a] Nor was it always evident to labor that workers' goals were in harmony with consumers' goals. Increasingly, however, after World

---

[a]That CU grew out of a split with Consumers' Research on the issue of union membership did serve to tie labor to one element of the consumer movement. At the same time, F.J. Schlink's hostility to labor did not enhance the relationship between labor and consumer.

73

War II as labor became more secure in its economic position, it came to see the consumer movement's goal of more efficient consumer spending as consistent with labor's own goal of greater worker income. Labor now identifies workers as consumers, and organized labor as part of the consumer movement. In 1973, for example, the AFL-CIO Convention called for a "consumer protection agency, improved product warranties and no fault insurance." It asserted that "millions of consumers are defrauded in the market place every year when they are sold shoddy products and unsafe food."[10]

In labor's view, organization is a key to power. To this end, labor not only urges its local labor organizations to participate in consumer activities but also has promoted consumer organization at the national level. The AFL-CIO sponsored the 1966 Washington Consumer Assembly which was the impetus for the Consumer Federation of America. A number of unions were charter members of this organization and have been a significant source of support.

In its program for strengthening the position of consumers, labor also has relied heavily on legislation. It sees legislation and government regulation as "the major screen" for consumer protection against unsafe and poor-quality products. Labor has consistently backed consumer legislation—the truth in lending and truth in packaging bills, auto safety, meat inspection, and the establishment of a consumer-protection agency. One spokeman has asserted that "unions have been the single most influential force on both national and state levels in securing most of what legislative gains [have been] made on behalf of consumers."[11]

In addition to organization and legislation, the labor movement has made some efforts to promote consumer education, particularly at the local level. This program has been based on the proposition that without effective consumer education for workers, "the gains made at the bargaining tables are lost across the counters." Consumer education has tended to concentrate on specific problems such as credit, health insurance, and legal assistance and protection. There is also emphasis on avoiding fraud in door-to-door sales and useless and quack drugs. The monthly AFL-CIO publication, *The American Federationist*, carries a consumer column by Sidney Margolis which discusses the specific ways consumers can make dollars go farther. In recent years, however, there appears to be less organized-union support for consumer education.

Several explanations can be given for labor's efforts to promote the consumer interest. Labor's own explanation, of course, is that consumer protection becomes another, and necessary, service of unions to their members. A second explanation for labor's interest in consumers is that labor can in this way identify not just with workers but with all Americans who are consumers. Thus labor projects itself not as a special-interest group seeking the worker's advantages at the expense of others but as an ally of all consumers. Labor, like Congress, comes to support the consumer who is the "unrepresented man in our society."

74

Labor can profitably espouse the consumer's cause when consumers' interests complement rather than compete with labor's own interests. The consumer's interest in low prices and high quality, in more product information and in consumer representation does not threaten labor's interest in higher incomes and greater job security. Much consumer legislation affects producers rather than workers—truth in packaging and lending, meat inspection, and the various health and safety measures. Labor can urge this kind of consumer legislation without fear of hurting workers as producers of income. And there are cases where the consumer's interest coincides with labor's. In the discussion of grain sales to Russia, for example, labor could oppose increased deliveries (in Russian ships) on the basis of higher consumer prices rather than on the basis of lost worker income. Finally, if there is any advantage to unions to emphasize the old conflicts between labor and management, a consumer program works for the former as a consumer and against the latter as a producer.

When, however, there is a conflict between the interests of workers and consumers, labor has to look to its own defenses and to assert its own interests over and beyond those of the consumer. In the bargaining to get a passable consumer-representation bill, labor managed to get labor matters exempt from any review by the new consumer-protection agency. Such review could, of course, be damaging to labor as the consumer's interest in wage settlements, restrictive labor policies, strikes, and import duties and quotas would be different from that of labor. The militancy of public employees for higher wages is a good case in point here. In a similar conflict of interests, the Sheetworkers Union, which was a charter member of the Consumer Federation of America, opposed CFA's position in favor of the prohibition of throw-away cans.[12]

The prolonged economic downturn of the 1970s, the prospect of increased competition from foreign production, and the drive to protect the environment seem to have undermined the ties between labor's interest and the consumer's interest. Increasingly, labor's interest in jobs runs counter to the consumer's interest in lower prices. At the same time the growing political appeal of the consumer movement makes identification with it a source of strength for labor.[13] The basic issues between labor and the consumer movement, however, remain "unformulated," and it is too soon to predict what will be the long-term relationship between the two.[14] Likewise, in its search for support, the consumer movement necessarily counts on organized labor and cites "the new visibility of the consumer movement" as the carrot for labor's "forthcoming" support.[15]

Consumer Education in the Thirties

Consumer advocates have consistently viewed consumer education as an integral part of the work of the consumer movement. They have urged the adoption of consumer education as lifetime training—in school and college, as well as in adult and continuing education. In particular, consumer education has been held out as a way of ameliorating poverty among minority groups and the elderly. Within the movement, education has had the dual role of providing to consumers the information they need to be efficient in the marketplace and of creating among consumers the kind of awareness that would lead to support for political action on behalf of consumers. The consumer movement envisioned education as the primary vehicle by which it would seek to promote efficient consumers and effective consumer political pressure. Education came to outweigh other efforts that could have concentrated on establishing consumer organizations, on consumer action through strikes or boycotts, or pushing for government legislation or representation. The consumer movement has seen education in the community as well as in formal schooling as an efficient and noncontroversial way to achieve consumer efficiency and awareness.

This concentration on education came about partly because other efforts of the consumer movement were less successful. After the mid-thirties, as chances faded for accomplishing very much for the consumer through legislation and representation, the hopes for educating consumers grew brighter. It is hard to find any other similar movement—not even the cooperative movement—that has put so much emphasis on the process of education as a means to gain strength.

The early consumer movement conceived of consumer education in a very broad sense. Consumer education was not to be limited to providing consumers with information about buying but was to give people the background necessary to see and understand the whole role of the consumer in society. The concept of consumer education originally included a wide range of activities, as much *outside* formal education as within, by which people "of all ages" could be made to realize and act on their rights and responsibilities as consumers. But in particular, the movement wanted definite programs to provide various groups with specifically designed material in consumer education. These programs were to include the teaching of specially prepared material with specially trained instructors in elementary schools, high schools, and colleges, either in specific courses in consumer training or along with other courses in the curriculum. The movement sought also to extend the programs as far as possible to other groups in the community which would, or were felt should, be reached with information about how to become better consumers.

As general interest in consumer education grew during the 1930s, organizations developed committed to promote consumer education as a whole. The most significant of these was the Stephens College Institute for Consumer Education, established in 1937 at Stephens College (Columbia, Missouri) by a 250 thousand dollar grant from the Sloan Foundation. One of the major contributions of the Institute was a yearly National Conference on Consumer Education. Groups of as many as 400 or 500 gathered to attend lectures and participate in workshops devoted to increasing the quantity, and to improving the

76

quality, of consumer education.[16] The concern of the Institute was to provide consumer education not only within the framework of school and college but in the larger community as well. The life of the Institute coincided with the early years of success for the consumer movement, and in no small way contributed to its strength.

Other groups also took up the cause of consumer education. In the spring of 1939, the Consumer Education Association was formed for teachers with this special interest. Within a few years, the Association had a membership of more than 700 and was able to hold two annual meetings. The American Home Economics Association established a Consumer Education Service that distributed a newsletter with information of particular interest to home economists working in consumer education. The American Association of University Women considered the consumer's interest a part of its basic program and published consumer-education materials for use by its local groups.

Most important, however, for consumer education was the support of the public schools. By 1941, it was estimated that some 5 to 10 percent of American high schools were offering special courses in consumer economics and that many more schools were providing consumer-education material in business, social studies, and home economics courses. The Educational Policies Commission of the National Education Association in its *Purposes of Education in American Democracy* pointed out the importance of consumer education. Several years later the National Association of Secondary School Principals (a department of the NEA) set up curriculum guides for teaching consumer education. The consumer movement asserted that "the educational expansion of the past decade has witnessed no movement that has gained greater momentum than has Consumer Education."[17]

But the consumer movement's hopes for education were not fulfilled. The women's groups lost interest. More significantly, following World War II consumer education in the schools became entangled in the conflict between the consumer's interest and the viewpoint of business. The same kind of distrust and animosity that flared up in other parts of the consumer movement found its way into consumer education. Public education could not be insensitive to the fears of business, with the result that consumer education was considerably watered down from what the consumer movement expected it to be. The schools suggested that learning such things as "shrewdness in bargaining" and "the protection of one's own interests against exploiters, etc." might lead to "cynicism and a calculating 'me first' attitude."[18] The public schools could not handle the conflict between consumers and producers that is implicit in economic theory. Even though consumer education did not disappear from school curricula during the fifties, what was left did little to promote the consumer's cause.

Consumer Education in the Seventies

The consumer-education programs that have come with the revived consumer interest of the past decade are considerably more narrow than the consumer-education programs of the thirties. The earlier efforts for widespread consumer education were essentially an extension of the consumer movement, a means by which the consumer movement sought not only to help the consumer assume his "rightful" place in the economy but also to expand its influence and create effective consumer political pressure. By contrast, consumer education today is not so much a vehicle for the expansion of the consumer movement as it is the means to arm buyers for the confrontation with sellers. At the same time consumer education today, like forty years ago, is seen as a combination of providing straight information about price and quality and the knowledge and understanding necessary to be an effective consumer in the modern complex economy.

If the focus of consumer education is more narrow than before, it has achieved a wider group of advocates who have great faith in the ability of consumer education to help the consumer protect his position in the market. In addition to the traditional support shown by consumer groups and the public schools, there is support from Presidential consumer appointments, the labor movement, and, in recent years, from Congress in the form of funds for consumer education to the Office of Education in the Department of Health, Education, and Welfare. Business has also joined the ranks of supporters to espouse consumer education as a "vehicle for preventing future consumer unrest."[19]

The Presidential consumer assistants have advocated greater efforts for consumer education in the schools and among target groups of the population. Under Mrs. Peterson's leadership, several national conferences were held focusing on ways of implementing consumer education in the public school curriculum. In his 1971 message on consumers to Congress, President Nixon asserted that "consumer education is an integral part of consumer protection. It is vital if the consumer is to make wise judgments in the marketplace." Under Mrs. Knauer the Office of Consumer Affairs has developed several sets of materials to be used in consumer-education programs for adults and children, as well as for minority groups like the Indian, the elderly, or other low-income people. The Office of Consumer Affairs has also sought to make available to consumers some of the immense amounts of government information that may be of interest and help to consumers. Twice a month it publishes a *Consumer News* sheet that gives information about consumer-related actions and activities of the various agencies of the federal government. It also makes available a guide to Federal Consumer Services. Through the Consumer Information Center of the General Services Administration, Mrs. Knauer, as the President's Special Assistant for Consumer Affairs, issues a quarterly pamphlet, "Consumer Information," which is a compilation of federal publications that may be useful to consumers.

Congress has also expressed its interest in and support for consumer education. In 1968, it first authorized federal funds to states for "consumer and homemaking" education through the Office of Education in HEW. Four years

78

later Congress authorized the appointment of a "Director of Consumer Education" in the Office of Education and the preparation of curriculum materials that would "prepare consumers for participation in the marketplace." In 1974 it went one step further to direct HEW to set up an "Office of Consumer Education" to be responsible for preparing curriculum and curriculum materials and to award grants directed toward community education, workshops, and training. The Office of Consumer Education issued preliminary guidelines for these activities in the fall of 1975.

It is on the premise that consumer education for young people can be most readily and easily provided through the public school system that Presidential consumer advisors, and consumer groups in general, have continued to urge public schools to offer more in the way of consumer education. The educational system on the whole, however, has been slow to respond. Consumer education comes largely through home economics and business courses. Because there is no "standard" consumer education course, the materials are usually produced by local school districts and are heavily dependent on material from business sources. Even though the National Education Association has never repudiated consumer education, the Consumer Education Study material, for example, which was prepared between 1945 and 1955 has not been revised, and nothing has been substituted for it.

The rising interest in consumer affairs does seem to have moved some leaders in public education to revive programs in consumer education. The State Education Department of New York has developed a series of materials to be used in consumer education. The CU Consumer Educational Materials Project, set up under a grant from the Office of Education, offers a wide variety of techniques for dealing with consumer education for different age groups.[20] The Joint Council of Economic Education, in line with its goal of increased economic literacy, lists a wide number of district-wide and individual classroom units currently underway in various sections of the country. And the legislatures of several states, including Illinois, Oregon, and Wisconsin, have mandated consumer education in all public schools.

It is interesting to note that the fortunes of consumer education in the public schools have depended less on pressures arising through the consumer movement than on currents within the educational system itself. In the 1930s, consumer education coincided with the emphasis in education on "education for life" and "education for living." This was the idea that schools had the primary responsibility for training young people to find useful and satisfying roles in society. The suitability of a subject in the schools was measured by its "social utility or actual use in the 'real business of living.' "[21] Then, with the Sputnik events of the 1950s, education was criticized for its overemphasis on "practical" subjects and with the return to greater stress on traditional academic subjects consumer education lost much of its appeal to educators. Twenty years later, however, in response to the educational cry of "relevance," consumer

79

education has again found a place in the public schools. Cheering that it is in the limelight again, CU asserts that consumer education offers "great potential as a vehicle for reforming education in the U.S."[22]

Conflicts in Consumer Education

In general, the focus of consumer education has been in two areas. In one direction, it has emphasized the necessity for consumer information—about goods and services, about budgeting and credit, about fraud and deception—as a tool for bringing about increased consumer satisfaction. In another direction, consumer education has been built around the economic role of the consumer. Here the emphasis is on competitive theory, decision-making in the market, and the role of the consumer and consumption from the perspective of the economy as a whole.

In the first area, programs are necessarily limited to a "how-to" approach and are heavily weighted with descriptive material about how consumers do and should behave. Categories of expenditures are listed with sources of information about each. The assumption is that consumers should, and can, gain expertise in all areas of expenditures. The result is that the materials emphasize the work in shopping rather than the reward in the goods bought. Effort is made to avoid the appearance of "siding" with consumers against legitimate (as opposed to "unscrupulous") business. The materials are almost all uniformly dull and uninteresting.

In the second direction, consumer education tends to become *economics* rather than *consumer economics*. ("Consumer economics" has never gained much authority among academic economists.) Only by analyzing the competitive model—and the divergence from it of monopoly and corporate power—can this type of program focus on the consumer. And even here the consumer is not one of "flesh and blood" but one who is rational and utility-maximizing. Because economics takes wants as *given*, economists have not dealt with the question of basic consumer needs and how these might relate to the total economic system. Most importantly, these courses are taught by economists, and economists, given the whole range of economic problems that need to be dealt with, are not particularly interested in dealing with consumer problems as such. If consumer economics has been a stepchild of economics, it is also important to note that it has not been able to achieve an independent status outside of academic economics.

A continuing problem for consumer education in schools and other publicly funded agencies has been: What position should it take between the producer interest of business and the consumer interest in lower price and greater quantity? In urging consumer efficiency in the market, consumer education has to support the buyer's interest against that of the seller. Such a stance is

80

often interpreted as a direct and unwarranted attack on business. As a consequence, business often sees public efforts at consumer education as unfair to business. In matters of advertising, packaging, and consumer action as opposed to producer action, publicly supported consumer education has seldom taken a firm stand.

In particular, this question of point of view has been a problem in the development of consumer education for low-income groups. These groups are usually less educated, less informed, and less mobile than higher-income groups. They also seem more susceptible to the pressures of advertising and salesmanship in what David Caplovitz calls "compensatory consumption." Here, says Caplovitz, "appliances, automobiles and the dream of a home of their own can become compensations for the blocked social mobility."[23] Such consumers are more open than others to abuses from unscrupulous salesmen and lenders. Yet efforts to help these consumers to learn more rational patterns of spending is necessarily contrary to the interests of the businesses with which they deal. As a consequence, business often questions the legitimacy of government efforts at consumer education. For example, in 1966 *Nation's Business* called information from cooperatives and the consumer testing services "questionable weapons" in the "escalating consumer education phase of government's war on poverty."

In spite of the basic issues that divide business and consumers, business has consistently been in the position of supporting the idea of consumer education. The main reason for this is that business has found education to be a useful alternative to increased government protection of consumers. When consumer advocates call for further consumer legislation or consumer representation in government, business can advance consumer education as a means to an "informed and effective consumer directing the free enterprise economy." In the make-believe context of rational and informed individuals buying in competitive markets, consumer education is neither controversial nor a threat to the status quo.

The continuing frustration for consumer educators has not been so much a lack of support as it has been a lack of well-defined goals and methods. This inability to focus clearly on what *is* consumer education can best be understood in terms of the disparity between a very broadly defined set of purposes and the rather narrow set of concepts out of which consumer education must be taught. As a consequence of this divergence between task and tools, consumer education has been handicapped by an absence of sense of purpose and an ambivalence of viewpoint.

Two current definitions of consumer education suggest the almost limitless task assigned consumer education.

Consumer education seeks to provide consumers with the information and skills they need to deal effectively with the institutions, agencies, corporations, social conditions, and economic and ecological problems that affect them daily.
Education Division of Consumers Union, 1973

81

Consumer education should help each person understand his own value system; develop a sound decision-making procedure in the marketplace based upon his values; evaluate alternatives in the marketplace, and get the best buy for his money; understand his rights and responsibilities as a consumer and as a member of society; and fulfill his role in directing a free-enterprise system."

United States Office of Consumer Affairs, 1973

In both these statements consumer education is so broadly defined that it encompasses nearly every aspect of a person's life in a highly industrialized and monetized society. Consumer education is to provide people—young and old— with the knowledge of how to cope with "institutions, agencies, corporations, social conditions, and economic and ecological problems that affect them daily." To accomplish this, consumer education has to teach values clarification, decision-making, and economic theory, and provide an almost infinite amount of information—both private and government—about the wide variety of increasingly complex goods and services available to consumers and about the administrative procedures for intervention if consumer rights are abused. Then consumer education holds out the promise that if a person thus is informed and knowledgeable, he will be a sovereign consumer who can "fulfill his role in directing a free-enterprise system."

In contrast to education for life which consumer education sets as its goal, the theoretical concepts that consumer education can draw on are narrowly prescribed by the economic analysis of the consumer/buyer operating in competitive (or what should be competitive) markets. However broadly consumer goals may be defined, the theoretical model from which any analysis of consumers must proceed is that of conventional economic theory. In this model, wants and choices are a *given*, decision-making is defined in terms of the rational human being weighing prices of alternate goods, and consumer goals are a sterile concept of getting the most goods and services for the least expenditure. Most importantly, economic theory has no way at all, beyond the still unsatisfactory analysis of monopolistic competition and oligopoly, to deal with the social complexities of "institutions, agencies, corporations, social conditions, and economic and ecological problems" that make up the daily lives of most American consumers.

Advocates of consumer education hold out the promise that understanding is the solution to consumer problems. But when that understanding is bound within the narrow framework of conventional economic theory, it is little wonder that there has been a wide difference between promise and reward. Given this situation, there has been little consensus on what programs in consumer education should include. As a result, practitioners of consumer education have difficulty in setting their objectives and in evaluating the usefulness of any programs that are carried out.

As it is currently conceived, consumer education should be worthwhile because it contributes in some way to consumer satisfaction or well-being—either through an increase in the quantity of goods and services consumed or through

82

an increase in disposable income by way of lower prices and better goods. That consumers in general do not appear to be interested in consumer education and are not anxious to "study" in order to realize these benefits has led some economists to question the purposes and goals of consumer economics. D.I. Padberg argues that with increasing real incomes most people are no longer forced to watch every dollar of expenditure.[24] What he calls "survival shopping" is to most people less important than it used to be. He maintains that people are caught between their increasingly humanitarian interests and the "frugality" that has been "lauded and honored" as the traditional "survival and subsistence" consumer value. In a similar vein, Gerhard Scherf points out that current consumer education concentrates on enabling consumers to get more goods and services as a means of alleviating dissatisfaction.[25] He asserts, however, that higher incomes do not appear to bring greater consumer satisfaction and argues the need for education that will bring consumers an "increase in their level of life satisfaction." Scherf notes the work done to increase job satisfaction through involvement in decision-making and understanding. He calls for similar work in consumer education to emphasize interpersonal goal-orientation rather than the individual means-orientation of conventional consumer education.

These may be harbingers of coming changes. But to date consumer education has not made any significant impact on the lives of most consumers and has never made the hoped for contribution to the consumer movement. It has not created informed consumers who, through wise buying decisions, can direct the development of the economy. Nor has it created large groups of politically conscious consumers who see the necessity of bringing consumer pressure to bear on governments. Perhaps no program of consumer education can achieve these ends, but without real changes in its goals and methods, the increased interests in consumer education are likely to come to naught.

Chapter 6

1. *Wall Street Journal* (April 9, 1975), p. 1.

2. Cf. Consumer Federation of America, *Directory of State and Local Consumer Groups,* (Washington, D.C., January, 1975).

3. *Consumer Reports* (November 1966), p. 572.

4. *Consumers' Research Magazine* (August 1974), p. 3.

5. *Consumer Reports* (February 1975), p. 72.

6. *Wall Street Journal* (May 9, 1975), p. 1.

7. *Consumer Reports* (September 1975), p. 525.

8. *Consumer Reports* (February 1975), p. 72.

9. *Consumer Reports* (September 1975), p. 524.

10. *American Federationist* (November 1973), p. 27.

11. Sidney Margolis in *The American Federationist* (March 1974), p. 21.

12. *Wall Street Journal* (April 9, 1975), p. 1.

13. Solomon Barkin, "Trade Unions and Consumerism," *Journal of Economic Issues* (June 1973), pp. 317–321.

14. Ibid., p. 321.

15. Clinton L. Warne, "The Consumer Movement and the Labor Movement," *Journal of Economic Issues* (June 1973), pp. 307–316.

16. The proceedings of these annual conferences were published by the Institute for Consumer Education, Columbia, Missouri, as *Next Steps in Consumer Education* (1939), *Making Consumer Education Effective* (1940), and *Consumer Education for Life Problems* (1941).

17. Herbert A. Tonne, *Consumer Education in the Schools* (New York: Prentice-Hall, 1941), p. xiii.

18. National Association of Secondary School Principals, *Consumer Education in Your School: A Handbook for Teachers and Administrators* (Washington, D.C.: National Association of Secondary School Principals, 1947), p. 19.

19. Elisha Gray II, "Educating the Consumer," in The Conference Board, *The Challenge of Consumerism* (New York: The Conference Board, Inc., 1971), p. 79.

20. Consumers Union of U.S., Inc., Consumer Education Materials Project (Mt. Vernon, New York: 1973).

21. V.T. Thayer, *Formative Ideas in American Education* (New York: Dodd, Mead, 1965), p. 281.

22. *Consumer Reports* (March 1971), p. 133.

23. David Caplovitz, *The Poor Pay More* (New York: The Free Press of Glencoe, 1963), p. 13.

24. D.I. Padberg, "Today's Consumer," in *The Economics of Consumer Protection* ed. Loys L. Mather (Danville, Ohio: The Interstate, 1971), pp. 11–21.

25. Gerhard Scherf, "Consumer Education as a Means of Alleviating Dissatisfaction," *Journal of Consumer Affairs* (Summer 1974), pp. 61–75.

[16]

By Quentin J. Schultze
ASSOCIATE PROFESSOR OF JOURNALISM
DRAKE UNIVERSITY

"An Honorable Place": The Quest for Professional Advertising Education, 1900–1917

¶ The opening decades of the twentieth century saw various advertisers embark on a concerted effort to create professional instruction at American universities. They had two objectives. They thought that such instruction might help individual firms determine precisely how advertising worked in the marketplace—and thereby create a science of advertising—and they hoped that university education would transform their business into a full-fledged profession. Yet these efforts brought mixed results. As such instruction came into being, advertisers found that they had little influence over the education they had sought to promote, and they found that such training had chosen to follow one of two divergent paths, neither of which the industry thought wholly acceptable. Even more to their dismay, advertisers found that this education did not in fact convert their business into a profession.

It should be no surprise to anyone associated with advertising instruction in American universities that businessmen have often criticized academicians for the way they approach the subject in the classroom. The major trade journal, *Advertising Age*, has frequently printed letters and editorials from disgruntled agency personnel complaining that colleges generally do a poor job of preparing students for advertising careers, and many practitioners today would no doubt agree with Claude Hopkins, who wrote in 1927 that he was "exasperated" because the courses offered were "so misleading, so impractical."[1]

Such criticism has stemmed from the inability of educators to resolve a number of fundamental problems. Integrating vocational instruction into traditional liberal arts programs, teaching managerial concepts or decisionmaking or even entry-level skills, determining the proper relationship between business and the academy, and defining "advertising education," are unresolved issues that must share the blame. It was especially the latter problem—defining the nature and purpose of advertising education—that the business and the academy failed to address in

Business History Review, Vol. LVI, No. 1 (Spring, 1982). Copyright © The President and Fellows of Harvard College.

[1] Claude C. Hopkins, *My Life in Advertising* (New York, 1927), 7.

any adequate fashion during the formative years of advertising instruction. Educators and businessmen together established the nation's first advertising courses and programs, but they did so without elucidating the scope and purpose of advertising education. Although businessmen were the prime movers in the development of such instruction, they were motivated primarily by a symbolic ideal of professionalism, and ironically, that preoccupation with professionalization hindered their ability to grasp the complexities of creating professional education for business in the early twentieth century.

The movement to establish respected advertising instruction was but one of the many crusades launched by a myriad of self-conscious occupational groups seeking to transform their business or craft into a profession. Like engineers and administrators, businessmen created special-interest organizations that became preoccupied with the issue of professionalism. As Robert Wiebe has cogently shown in his book, *The Search for Order*, this new middle class of business and technical experts burst upon the American landscape during the Progressive Era.[2]

Such groups almost invariably looked to higher education as a training ground for their occupation and to the university as a source of professional credentials. Progressivism for them became an ethos of professionalism; they estimated their self-worth according to the degree to which their occupation displayed the typical characteristics of professionalism, notably ethical codes, licensing or certification requirements, and standardized instruction. The latter trait occupied the hopeful minds of many aspiring businessmen, including advertisers who began in 1901 to look to the academy for help. Like many progressives, advertisers believed that extending the fruits of university instruction to the advertising business would benefit society. Although they lacked any unified view of the form that advertising education should take, advertisers convinced themselves that university-level instruction would elevate the status of their business as well as contribute to the democratization of the American university.[3]

WALTER DILL SCOTT

Formal cooperation between advertisers and academicians began in 1901, when Walter Dill Scott, a psychology professor

[2] Robert Wiebe, *The Search for Order 1877–1920* (New York, 1967).

[3] For two good discussions of professionalization within the university, see Burton J. Bledstein, *The Culture of Professionalism* (New York, 1976) and Mary O. Furner, *Advocacy and Objectivity* (Lexington, 1975). Some of the consequences of the merging of science and business are cogently analyzed in David F. Noble, *America By Design* (New York, 1979).

at Northwestern University, accepted an invitation to address the Agate Club of Chicago. Scott's subject was the psychology of advertising. Although Harlow Gale of the University of Minnesota had already investigated the application of psychological principles to the study of advertising, Scott was one of the first psychologists to challenge publicly the traditional academic view that it was inappropriate to apply the principles of social science to business.[4] Most social scientists differed from Scott in their view of the academy. Some years later in 1912, Jacob Gould, president of Cornell University, told the trade journal *Printers' Ink* that if he did not see his way clear to a university course of instruction in advertising, it was because he did not believe that the "calling," however important or practiced, rested on exact science that could be taught in a university.[5]

Not surprisingly, Scott's early pre-occupation with the utility of psychological experimentation had elicited harsh criticism from his university colleagues, who repeatedly asked him to disassociate himself from applied research, particularly its applications in business. Several years earlier Wilhelm Wundt, his instructor at Leipzig, had cautioned him against the pernicious effects such research might have on the reputation of the scientific community. Then in 1900, Scott was relieved of his teaching duties at Cornell University because of a similar disagreement. Scott's vision of the academy, though unpopular among colleagues in 1901, eventually led him to the presidency of Northwestern University. Rebuke turned to praise, and during his later career, he was heralded by many as a champion of democratic education.

Yet that was all in the future. Scott's appearance before the Agate Club in 1901 signaled that at least some members of the business community accepted the scientific method. Yet many practitioners continued to believe that good advertising depended upon factors such as "good judgment, good taste, good ideas, and a whole lot of other good things that [could not] be dissected or classified by the college professor." [6] As another anti-science proponent wrote, any "attempt to reduce [advertising's] influence to a science is futile. Advertising must be studied from the relation of debit and credit so long as an advertiser is a business man and not a dreamer." [7]

[4] Gale was, like Scott, a rebel personality in the psychological community. For his own reflections on the state of psychology during the turn-of-the-century period, see Russell Roth, "One Man's Story," *Ski-U-Mah* (University of Minnesota student magazine), October 1940, 10. The information in the next few paragraphs about Scott's life is taken from J. Z. Jacobson, *Scott of Northwestern* (Chicago, 1951).

[5] "Advertising As a University Subject," *Printers' Ink* (cited hereafter as *PI*), 79 (June 20, 1912), 19.

[6] "For and Against Psychology in Advertising," *PI*, 97 (December 28, 1916), 25.

[7] *PI* (August 26, 1903), 35.

A growing number of advertising men were not so skeptical, however. Many began to call for collaboration with universities in the belief that, for the first time, scientific research might reduce risk in the marketplace by elucidating the laws of human behavior that presumably undergirded the actions of all consumers. "It would be as foolish for the advertiser to refuse the help of the faithful psychologists," wrote the trade press, "as it would be for the invalid to refuse the aid of the faithful physician, or the manufacturer to disregard the knowledge accumulated by the students in the realm of theoretical chemistry, physics, and mathematics." [8] The natural vicissitudes of the economy, along with the difficulty of analyzing increasingly vast and impersonal markets, turned the business away from self-reliance and toward a dependence on social scientists. "Although human choice is reputed to be indeterminable and the unknown factor in the world," wrote Scott, "the results of human choice can be foreknown by the statistician." [9] He promised advertisers that psychologists could now predict the "action of large groups of people." [10]

Scott's presentation on "The Psychology of Involuntary Attention as Applied to Advertising," along with his subsequent lectures at the Agate Club, were publicized far beyond the Chicago advertising community. His remarks were printed in *Mahin's Magazine*, a trade journal established by agency owner John Mahin to spread the concept of scientific advertising across the country. Then in 1903 Thomas Balmer, a magazine advertising salesman, subsidized the printing of Scott's lectures as a book entitled *The Theory of Advertising*, which became the first text on that subject written by an academician. [11] Although Scott's theory became a topic of heated debate among members of the advertising business, none could refute the apparent success of advertisers who relied on his simple laws of association and suggestion. [12] Scott became a symbol of progress for supporters of

[8] "Empiricism or Psychology?," *Mahin's Magazine*, 2 (October 1903), 521.

[9] "The Psychology of Selling," *The Business World*, 25 (November 1905), 609.

[10] Ibid. For additional insight into the merging of business and social science, see Daniel Andrew Pope, "The Development of National Advertising, 1865-1920" (Ph.D. Thesis, Columbia University, 1973); Loren Baritz, *The Servants of Power* (New York, 1960); Merle Curti, "The Changing Concept of 'Human Nature' in the Literature of American Advertising," *Business History Review*, 41 (Winter 1967), 335–357; Stuart Ewen, *Captains of Consciousness* (New York, 1976); Michal A. McMahon, "An American Courtship: Psychologists and Advertising Theory in the Progressive Era," *American Studies*, 13 (Fall 1972), 5–18; Quentin J. Schultze, "Advertising, Science and Professionalism 1885–1917" (Ph.D. Thesis, University of Illinois, 1978); and David P. Kuna, "The Concept of Suggestion in the Early History of Advertising Psychology," *Journal of the History of the Behavioral Sciences*, 12 (1976), 347–353, "Early Advertising Applications of the Gale-Cattell Order-of-Merit Method," *Journal of the History of the Behavioral Sciences*, 15 (1979), 38–46, and "The Psychology of Advertising, 1896–1916 (Ph.D. Thesis, University of New Hampshire, 1976).

[11] Jacobson, *Scott of Northwestern*, 69–73. The influence of the earliest books on the development of advertising and marketing is discussed in Frank G. Coolsen, "Pioneers in the Development of Advertising," *Journal of Marketing*, 12 (July 1947), 80–86.

[12] H. Addington Bruce, "Psychology and Business," *The Outlook*, September 1911, 32.

scientific approaches to the study of advertising, and by 1904 he was offering the nation's first course in the psychology of advertising, although Gale may have conducted a course in the experimental psychology of advertising in 1900.[13]

For many advertisers Scott's ideas revealed the potential benefits of cooperation with the academic world. Scientific experimentation, they thought, would eventually yield theoretical principles applicable to all marketing situations. The university might help the practitioners create more effective campaigns and more efficient media schedules. Most importantly, academia might help advertising agents and media salesmen persuade manufacturers of the advantages of advertising as a promotional technique. As one advertising manager suggested in a controversial article, "it would pay the business interests of this country to get together and take steps to overcome the tremendous waste that is now going on. The first step to be taken in the direction of intensive cultivation is the establishment of schools—great schools, thoroughly equipped, and endowed with ample funds, to carry out extensive research and wide investigation, to collect statistics, to make experiments and to bring to their aid the experience and knowledge of all allied sciences."[14] After psychologists perfected models of consumer behavior, manufacturers were told, advertising would be virtually risk free, and advertisers would become specialists essential in the inchoate industrial nation. After all, wrote Scott, "every advertiser is searching for the easiest method of securing the desired action on the part of the public." [15]

ADVERTISING JOURNALS

Between 1902 and 1906 advertising journals printed a plethora of articles assessing the new cooperation between the university and business. The benefits of scientific advertising were invariably expressed in social and economic terms: science would increase the profitability of advertising and would help make advertising an indispensable and respected profession. In cultural terms, the business had linked its own professionalization to its ability to develop a formal relationship with the academicians who dispensed scientifically validated knowledge. Like other occupations during the same period, advertisers sought

[13] "Teachers of Advertising Organize," *Judicious Advertising*, 13 (July 1915), 89. Also see Frank Gordon Coolsen, "The Development of Systematic Instruction in the Principles of Advertising" (M.A. Thesis, University of Illinois, 1942), 38–42.

[14] J. H. Craig, "A Plea for Advertising Endowment," *Advertising and Selling*, 19 (February 1910), 1222. Also see "Can Advertising Be Scientized?," *Agricultural Advertising*, 23 (June 1911), 46–48.

[15] Walter Dill Scott, *The Theory of Advertising* (Boston, 1903), 33.

ways of instituting professional advertising instruction at the university level. "With Harvard installing a 'chair of advertising,' and with the special study and training which the subject requires, we may reasonably expect more and more to see advertising take an honorable place among the recognized professions," predicted an employee of an eastern agency.[16]

Of particular concern to many advertisers was the fact that other forms of education, especially correspondence courses and business schools, would probably subject the business to public criticism for its lack of professionalism. "When teaching law in college was first talked of, old lawyers shook their heads," wrote George H. Whitney in *Printer's Ink* in 1910, "College presidents couldn't see it, and so special schools and unreliable business colleges took it up. Then the old lawyers saw that their profession would soon be cheapened and they begged colleges to introduce such courses. This is exactly what has happened to the advertising profession today. Outside of the correspondence courses, there are probably 150 business colleges and Y.M.C.A.'s throughout the country that will graduate advertising men in from ten to thirty lessons. This is not right." [17]

The most cogent argument for professional advertising education during this period appeared as a two-part article published in *Profitable Advertising*, a journal primarily for national advertisers. Written by Earnest Elmo Calkins, the piece began with a declaration: "I believe that advertising can be taught . . . I fully believe that the time will come when there will be a fully-equipped advertising school and this school will teach advertising as other professional schools now teach other professions." [18] In his "advertising college," Calkins would have the introductory course include an analysis of product distribution, media usage, and sales management. He proposed that the college then offer a dozen courses "devoted to a special study of some one of the departments of advertising," including business conduct, managership, commerce, mail order advertising and retail advertising. Students would then take "technical courses" in topics such as printing and typography. Finally, in the third year the student would complete his study of advertising with an investigation of the "higher branches" of advertising, including psychology, statistics, and copywriting styles. "Such a school will make its appeal to the public in the same dignified, con-

[16] William P. Tuttle, Jr., "Advertising as a Profession," *Profitable Advertising*, 15 (December 1905), 863.
[17] George H. Whitney, "Advertising Courses in Universities and Colleges," *PI*, 73 (December 8, 1910), 5.
[18] "Advertising As It's Taught," Part I, *Profitable Advertising*, 14 (March 1905), 1101.

servative way that a good law or medicine school makes its appeal," he wrote.[19]

THE ASSOCIATED ADVERTISING CLUBS

A year after the appearance of Calkins' articles, the desire for professionalism took on collective dimensions. In 1906, advertising clubs from around the nation formed the Associated Advertising Clubs of America to "advance the advertising profession" through such activities as teaching professional skills, correcting abuses, exposing fraudulent advertising, and maintaining a bureau for the registration of advertising men.[20] The Associated Clubs addressed some of the typical characteristics of professionalism: ethical codes, certification and licensing restrictions, and educational requirements. For the first time the business formally stated that standardized advertising instruction was necessary for it to become a profession. Emulating law and medicine especially, members discussed ways of instituting educational programs associated with the most respected professions, and they came to believe that professional instruction would benefit the business in two ways, each of which would elevate its social status and enhance its profitability.

First, formal advertising instruction would provide a forum for establishing a corpus of "scientific" principles that would, as Scott told them, eliminate the advertiser's dependence upon intuition and subjectivity. One proponent wrote that "throughout the history of the world, mystery has been used to take the place of substance," but "advertising could be proven today to be more nearly exact, more nearly a science than medicine." [21] By science, practitioners typically meant the "systematized, assimilated and digested collection of all the available facts bearing on a subject." [22] Similarly, they viewed psychologists such as Scott as specialists trained in the experimental collation of empirical "facts" into general principles. Advertising clubs were initially formed to help aid in the establishment of such a "science" of advertising. The serious clubs were "energetically endeavoring to put the *science of advertising* where it belongs—in the forefront of efficient methods of modern merchandising," wrote one

19 "Advertising As It's Taught," Part II, *Profitable Advertising*, 14 (April 1905), 1249.
20 "The National Federation of Advertising Clubs," *Agricultural Advertising*, 15 (October 1906), 366.
21 L. W. Reiner, "Mystery—Advertising's False God,"*Judicious Advertising and Advertising Experience*, 9 (August 1911), 45.
22 "Can Advertising Be Scientized?," *Agricultural Advertising*, 23 (June 1911), 46.

EARNEST ELMO CALKINS as a young man. An early advocate of professional education for advertisers, Calkins outlined a complete curriculum that would be offered in what he called an "advertising college."

trade journal.[23] "Advertising must be standardized and formed into a tangible business factor," and the clubs would "exert a tremendous and wide-spread influence towards the betterment, the uplift and the standardization of advertising." [24]

Second, the Associated Clubs hoped that formal advertising instruction might be used in conjunction with certification or licensing to regulate entry into the profession. It created a Committee on Standard of Qualifications of an Advertising Man, which concluded that all practitioners should be required to "study and understand psychology as it controls advertising. . . . While there were many able advertisers who would combat this position," wrote chairman George French, "if a man has an open mind and

[23] "Why Is An Advertising Club?," *Judicious Advertising and Advertising Experience*, 11 (January 1913), 43–44.
[24] George L. Louis, "Standardizing Advertising," *Judicious Advertising and Advertising Experience*, 8 (September 1910), 101–103. Also see Homer McKee, "Advertising Efficiency and Standardization of Sales," *Agricultural Advertising*, 25 (October 1913), 48–55.

ADVERTISING EDUCATION, 1900-1917   23

is willing to go to the bottom of the question, it will always appear that there has never been an advertising success that was not due to the operation of the laws of psychology." [25] Another practitioner asked his colleagues, "why shouldn't the advertising man be required to show a license, just as a doctor must?" He recommended that for purposes of improving ethical standards, local examining committees should be empowered to grant certificates." [26]

As the Associated Clubs discussed alternate methods of instituting professional education, it also raised the question of standardized instruction. Advertisers assumed that education could not be used to regulate entry into the profession unless there existed some teachable corpus of "scientific" principles, and advertisers increasingly looked to the university to provide them. Although the Associated Clubs never devised a workable plan for licensing, as late as 1912 the organization considered working with chambers of commerce and school officials to "encourage, standardize and recognize by examination and certificates those who attain the first elements of the standard after study in proper courses." [27]

The concept of formal education germinated among advertisers as a professional ideal, but members of the Associated Clubs were never able to agree on an institutional structure. Some members believed that the business ought to provide course materials and choose the teachers. Since many universities in 1910 were unwilling to offer advertising courses, let alone permit businessmen to design a curriculum, the Associated Clubs began offering its own courses. The Committee on Lectures wrote a "Standard Course" for use by local clubs wishing to provide instruction at the community level. Lesson plans resembled church catechisms; subjects included "Why This Club Exists," "Who Pays for Advertising," "The Practical Use of Science in Advertising," and "The Moral Essentials of Good Advertising." [28] Novices learned in these club-sponsored courses that advertising should be practiced "fairly and honestly" because it played an essential role in stimulating the American economy and promoting a high standard of living. Yet the Standard Course effectively integrated professional ideology and vocational instruction, the basis of all introductory textbooks.[29] Clearly, advocates of

[25] *Proceedings of the Eighth Annual Convention of the Associated Advertising Clubs of America* (n.p., 1912), 336–37.

[26] "A Plan to License Advertising Men," *PI*, 77 (October 5, 1911), 64.

[27] *Proceedings of the Eighth Annual Convention of the Associated Advertising Clubs of America*, 129.

[28] "The Ad Clubs' Educational Program Outline," *PI*, 73 (November 10, 1910), 54.

[29] For a provocative review of recent advertising textbooks, see Vincent P. Norris, "Advertising History— According to the Textbooks," *Journal of Advertising*, 9 (1980), 3–11.

business-controlled education were motivated partly by a desire to ensure a favorable assessment of the fledgling profession's role in society, which could not be guaranteed if the university were to oversee instruction.

BUSINESS-SPONSORED RESEARCH

The most detailed and provocative plan for business-sponsored advertising research was presented in 1910 by Chicago copywriter John E. Kennedy. Although his proposal did not deal directly with the need for educating new practitioners, it represented a novel approach to the problem of creating a science of advertising. Like many other practitioners, Kennedy argued at club meetings and in the trade press that advertisers urgently needed to establish a unified, tested set of theorems or axioms that would hold true irrespective of time or place. Caught in the scientific spell cast by Walter Dill Scott, he insisted that academicians and businessmen must cooperate.

The "Kennedy Plan," as it became known, resembled the case-study approach adopted by a number of business schools only a few years after he first advocated such a method of instruction. Kennedy proposed the creation of an "Institute for Advertising Research," which would "officially investigate and record actual experiences of advertisers, in a wide range of test cases, as a basis for conclusions in study and practice." According to Kennedy, the personnel of the Institute would compare the results obtained by the use of various media, advertisement sizes, copy appeals, layouts, and colors. Empirical data supplied by advertisers and agencies would eventually lead to the inductive development of a science of advertising. "The profession of medicine was once where we are today," Kennedy told his colleagues, "composed of a lot of individuals each acting on his own initiative and guided by his own limited insight." [30] He believed that the success of the proposed Institute would be dependent upon finding a man to supervise its research projects, and he suggested an initial budget of $50,000 to cover the salary of a prestigious director, preferably a "college president" who would be "unfettered" by advertisers and "free to carry out neutral work." Additional funds would come from subscriptions to the Institute's quarterly journal of research.[31]

Although Kennedy's plan became by far the most popular plan

[30] "A Further Brief for Advertising Institute," *PI*, 73 (October 20, 1910), 61.
[31] "An Institute for Advertising Research," *Advertising and Selling*, 20 (June 1910), 67–72.

ADVERTISING EDUCATION, 1900-1917 25

Judicious Advertising (July 1904)

JOHN E. KENNEDY, as he appeared in 1904. In various speeches and articles, Kennedy advocated business-sponsored advertising research and formulated what became known as the "Kennedy Plan" to collect and analyze data gathered in the field.

for business-sponsored research, it was only one of many proposed in the decade that preceded World War I. Another proposal suggested that the Associated Clubs sponsor four or five fellowships for graduates of "respected colleges" who wished to further the study of advertising. One half of the fellows would conduct theoretical research independently; the other half would carry out applied research by working directly with particular advertisers.[32] All such plans, however, were bitterly attacked by many advertisers and agencies who refused to release data on the effectiveness of their advertising. Kennedy and others failed to distinguish between professional ideals and the highly competitive structure of the business. Individual firms sought a science of advertising, but not if it meant the possible loss of competitive advantage. There were limits to professional cooperation.[33]

[32] C. H. Weller, "Advertising, a Science or an Art?," *Judicious Advertising and Advertising Experience*, 12 (July 1914), 107–109.
[33] See "Opinions on Kennedy's Institute Plan," *PI*, 71 (June 9, 1910), 51–52 and "Difficulties Facing Proposed Advertising Institute," *PI*, 73 (October 20, 1910), 65.

BUSINESS SCHOOLS VS. JOURNALISM PROGRAMS

Meanwhile, the stigma against psychologists who ventured into applied science was rapidly disappearing, and the Associated Clubs formed a Committee on Colleges and Universities to encourage joint university-business projects and persuade university administrators to initiate advertising instruction at major schools in the nation.[34] At Columbia University, Edward L. Thorndike, Harry L. Hollingworth, and Edward Kellogg Strong collaborated with the Advertising Men's League of New York to refine the scientific advertising principles first developed by Gale and Scott. At Harvard University the Committee on Publications enlisted psychologist Paul T. Cherington to write the first advertising textbook specifically designed for business programs, *Advertising as a Business Force,* which appeared in 1914. The publisher sold more than 8,000 copies in the next year. Cherington also promoted the introduction of advertising courses at other universities and encouraged advertisers to write educational materials for use in university classes, a reversal of Scott's pledge to write for the business. The mutual dependence of university and business was becoming a reality.[35]

Cherington became so strongly committed to helping advertisers that his research and writing were always attuned to practical concerns. Unlike Scott, who spoke in the jargon of the experimental psychologist, Cherington framed his questions and answers in the language of the new field of marketing, and his text, *Advertising as a Business Force*, was more a treatise on effective marketing than it was a handbook on the psychology of advertising. Cherington's activities, moreover, showed that by 1914 it was possible for applied business studies to be undertaken with dignity in an American university. Cherington eventually transferred from the psychology department at Harvard to the new Graduate School of Business Management, where he helped establish a case study approach similar to that envisioned by Kennedy.[36]

Although New York University had initiated advertising instruction in 1905, with guest lectures by managers and agency owners, not until 1912 did Harvard, Dartmouth, and Cornell take

---

[34] Lewellyn E. Pratt, "Educational Work of the A.A.C.W. Grows," *PI*, 91 (June 24, 1915), 101.

[35] Ibid. Also see "Associated Ad Clubs Publish Two More Books," *PI*, 90 (February 4, 1915), 58, Paul T. Cherington, "How the Colleges are Teaching Advertising and Selling," *PI*, 80 (July 18, 1912), 54–64, and "Get That Cherington Book Out," *PI*, 85 (November 20, 1913), 102.

[36] The seeds for the case-studies approach were evident in Cherington's book, which was "mainly a compilation of the experiences and ideas of others." See the review in the *Journal of Political Economy*, 21 (December 1913), 966–967.

it up.[37] By then it was clear that psychology would no longer be the host of advertising instruction or of applied research; many of the early psychologists had already left their departments to take up residence in business programs.[38]

The future of advertising education in American universities might have been firmly established in business programs had it not been for the success of the state schools. While business programs in private universities focused on managerial and marketing approaches to advertising education, land-grant schools admitted advertising through the new discipline of journalism. Advertising instruction thus became a Janus-headed affair with no clearly defined purpose or direction. In journalism departments, advertising was viewed as a natural aspect of newspaper publishing, with instruction centering on the skills of retail copywriting, advertisement layout, and especially newspaper space sales. Business programs, meanwhile, emphasized the relationship between advertising promotion and the management of large business in a marketing environment.[39]

At the University of Missouri, John B. Powell, a vocal advocate of practical instruction, started the first journalism course in "Advertising and Publishing" in 1908. Two years later his school offered the nation's first advertising degree and Powell became the first full-time instructor of advertising in the United States. The courses in his curriculum were Principles of Advertising, The Writing of Advertising, Current Problems in Advertising, The Soliciting of Advertising, and Rural Newspaper Management.[40]

The wide divergence between advertising instruction at business schools and that at the newer land-grant universities was obvious in Powell's writings for *Printers' Ink*. He and other authors hammered away at the need for practical instruction in advertising design, layout, and sales. They viewed social science as merely a "systematizing of common sense" and believed that the formal study of psychology would not make a significant impact on the business. [41] Consequently, Powell designed the Missouri curriculum to meet the needs of agencies and news-

[37] Coolsen, "The Development of Systematic Instruction in the Principles of Advertising," 59–60. Also see Billy I. Ross, *Advertising Education: Programs in Four-Year American Colleges and Universities* (n.p., 1965), 16 and Cherington, "How the Colleges are Teaching Advertising and Selling," 56–64.

[38] Such psychologists included Albert Poffenberger at Columbia, Edward K. Strong at Stanford, Harry Hollingworth at New York University, and Daniel Starch at Harvard.

[39] For statistics on the early years, when business and journalism courses developed simultaneously, see Ross, *Advertising Education*.

[40] John B. Powell, "A University Course in Advertising," *Judicious Advertising*, 12 (May 1914), 76.

[41] John B. Powell, "Principles of Advertising as Taught at the University of Missouri," *Judicious Advertising*, 14 (February 1916), 67–69.

papers for advertising talent, which he determined through a survey of operators and owners.[42] Obviously, he thought that the university should serve business directly and not waste time with the theoretical study of advertising.

In 1913 Powell became a self-appointed spokesman for vocational advertising education, searching for ways to graft courses in the skills into traditional college curricula. "The average university offers sufficient courses in Economics, English, Psychology, Sociology, History, Political Science, and Public Law to qualify an advertising man on the theoretical side," wrote Powell, but "the problem is to combine these courses with the practical courses in advertising and selling in a professional school." [43] A stream of anti-intellectualism seemed to flow through Powell's writings. Although he never stated that only practical courses should be taught in the university, he apparently placed little inherent value on the liberal arts, viewing them primarily as a source of credentials for the professional man.[44]

Although Powell recognized early the lack of uniformity in advertising instruction, he apparently failed to see how his narrowly defined approach to advertising education, based loosely on a professional school model, exacerbated the problem.[45] As an advertising manager for a cement company put it, "I find, in the little inquiry that I have had time to make, that the demands of employers on schools and teachers of advertising are very varied, because in the first place the interests of employers vary greatly and their ideas and standards also vary. The publisher, the manufacturer, the retailer, all need the advertising man, but their fields call for different qualities." [46] When Cherington analyzed the current state of advertising instruction in 1912, he completely ignored the work at Missouri, apparently believing that journalism programs did not represent an important contribution to what Harvard University called "business administration." [47] Powell, on the other hand, concluded that "schools of journalism . . . have perhaps offered the best places for the development of courses in advertising." [48] Obviously Powell and Cherington had

[42] John B. Powell, "What a Young Man Should Know Who Goes into Advertising," *PI*, 94 (January 13, 1916), 45–52.

[43] John B. Powell, "How Advertising is Being Taught," *PI*, 85 (November 6, 1913), 57.

[44] For an idea of the extent to which Powell sought to integrate liberal arts and advertising, see his "Principles of Advertising as Taught at the University of Missouri."

[45] Powell, "How Advertising is Being Taught," 73.

[46] S. Roland Hall, "What Advertisers Expect From Teachers of Advertising," *PI*, 95 (June 29, 1916), 94.

[47] Cherington, "How the Colleges are Teaching Advertising and Selling." Cherington undoubtedly knew about the work at Missouri, since Powell's articles were published in the same trade journals that published Cherington's articles.

[48] John B. Powell, "Advertising as It Is Being Taught in Schools and Colleges," *PI*, 90 (January 28, 1915), 38.

very different notions of the practice of advertising, not just of advertising education.

These two routes to advertising instruction—business schools and journalism programs—set the course of future development in the United States. Between 1910, when New York University, Missouri, Northwestern, Kansas, Indiana, and Iowa offered courses in advertising, and 1914, by which time the list included California, Columbia, Cornell, Dartmouth, Harvard, Illinois, Marquette, Michigan, Minnesota, Ohio State, Pennsylvania, and Pittsburgh, the two contrasting approaches to instruction continued to plague the Associated Clubs. Lacking any unified vision of the nature and scope of instruction, advertisers found themselves largely powerless over those programs that they had originally hoped to control. While the business continued to rhapsodize publicly about professionalism, it increasingly looked as though professional education would be a long way off.

A professional ideal was simply insufficient for the creation of specific curricula compatible with the institutional idiosyncracies of the nation's private and state universities. One observer remarked in 1912 that each educational unit worked along its own lines. Instead of "universality and organization" there was "individuality and irregularity." [49] Hoping to standardize curricula, educators began an annual "conference of teachers of advertising" in 1915, but the first meeting showed how irreconcilable the differences were.[50] George B. Hotchkiss of New York University, for example, argued that "to regard advertising permanently as a function of journalism would seem to me unwise . . . The college may well give some instruction in advertising as applied economics, psychology and English composition. But college traditions make it likely that such instruction will be in the hands of those whose interest in the subject is purely academic and theoretical. The best place for teaching the practice of advertising is the school of commerce or business administration." [51] The trade journal *Advertising and Selling* editorialized in 1912 that it hoped "to see in the coming year better coordination between advertising clubs on educational matters; a clear understanding of what advertising education really means; [and] the adoption of systematic methods of study." [52] Five years later Bruce Bliven of the University of Southern California surveyed advertising

[49] Gerald B. Wadsworth, "The Education of the Advertising Man," *Advertising and Selling*, 21 (March 1912), 128.
[50] "Teachers of Advertising Organize," *Judicious Advertising*, 13 (July 1915), 89–90.
[51] George B. Hotchkiss, "The Place of Advertising in a University Curriculum," *Advertising and Selling*, 25 (July 1925), 58.
[52] "Club Work for the Coming Year," *Advertising and Selling*, 21 (May 1912), 36.

teachers and concluded that instruction was still unstandardized, "unqualified" persons were not prohibited from entering advertising programs, educators were unable to provide instruction that approximated the conditions of the market, and advertising academicians still disagreed on which department advertising instruction belonged in—business or journalism.[53]

CONCLUSION

As the United States entered World War I in 1917, more schools began offering courses in advertising, but to the business itself the nature and purpose of advertising education appeared ever more ambiguous and contradictory. Businessmen were not solely to blame, however, because they had never held any significant control over the planning and operation of advertising programs. For these people, the idea of professional education was a dream that grew out of their desire to elevate the occupation's social status and to solidify its economic position in the emerging industrial nation. That dream obscured the complexity of creating professional education for a business that was itself not a profession. The dream also ignored the difficulty of working with educational institutions that had their own priorities and status interests.

It is interesting to see how ineffective was the new class of advertising academicians in convincing businessmen that professional instruction would directly benefit manufacturers and advertising agencies by supplying them with trained employees. Businessmen voiced support for the concept of professional advertising education, but they were never firmly committed to hiring graduates. The historical record clearly suggests that advertisers have typically believed that advertising majors are insufficiently trained in the skills necessary to secure an entry-level position, and that an advertising degree in itself is worth very little. Instead, employers have looked favorably upon job applicants who have the personalities and skills associated with the needs of the business. Advertising agencies have frequently hired the friends and relatives of employees rather than unknown applicants. Furthermore, large agencies have usually developed their own training program to teach new employees basic advertising skills as well as to inculcate them with the agency's own philosophy. As a result, advertising majors have always been little more then members of a large labor pool for the business.

[53] "Working to Make the Teaching of Advertising More Practical," *PI*, 98 (January 18, 1917), 57–60.

The motivation behind the establishment of advertising instruction at American colleges and universities was complex and self-serving. Complex because the quest for advertising instruction was only part of the general movement in society to expand the role of higher education by opening the university to the middle class and by establishing a plethora of so-called "practical" courses that would presumably lead to employment for students. The life and pedagogy of Walter Dill Scott best symbolizes those developments. In 1900 he was castigated by his university peers for supporting applied research in advertising, but after World War I, as the new president of Northwestern University, he established the school's first programs in business and journalism. Motivations were self-serving in the sense that the advertisers supported professional instruction because they thought it would elevate the standing of the business in American society, and because they hoped it would increase the profitability of their trade by providing trained personnel. Advertisers, however, were not concerned with examining the purpose of professional education, nor with articulating their responsibility for helping to provide society with truly educated practitioners. Although advertisers wished to create a profession, that was a dream that would not become real even with university instruction.

Part IV
Macromarketing Policy Issues

Part 2

Manufacturing Policy Issues

A
Marketing Under Varied Economic Systems

[17]

Excerpt from *Essays in Canadian Business History*, 13–23 and notes.

1

An Introduction to the Nineteenth-Century Business World

Douglas McCalla

It was once the task of the student of business history, like his counterparts in political and military history, to study great men, to identify the heroes who, it was assumed, were the makers of history and of the modern world. Peter Newman, for example, has often depicted in such terms the businessmen who "transformed Canada from a community of traders and land tillers into one of the world's economically most advanced nations. They changed history and the face of their country."[1] At the other extreme, but in fact with a similar orientation to great men, were those who searched for villains. Unfortunately this has seemed to some, who would suspect the approach in any other field of history, still to be a legitimate avenue to understand the history of business in Canada; there is even a school of thought that depicts Donald Smith, Lord Strathcona, as a kind of arch-villain, almost single-handedly dominating and manipulating more than half a century of Canadian history.[2] Such approaches as these, however, by their emphases on businessmen's individual qualities, have tended to over-simplify the past and have insufficiently explored the context in which their individual stories should most appropriately be set. Even without Newman's particular collections of businessmen, after all, other western economies have undergone the same transition, which suggests structural rather than individual explanations.

Reprinted from *The History and Social Science Teacher*, 18, 2 (1982), with the permission of the author and editor.

14   CANADIAN BUSINESS HISTORY

Recognizing this difficulty of the great-man approach, Canadian historians have increasingly sought to focus on political, economic, and social structures and their ordinary and typical institutions and behaviour, rather than on the heroic exceptions. Although much of the research of business historians has continued to focus on individual firms and businessmen, the questions posed have very much reflected this concern with structures. Because of the importance of business institutions in Canadian economic life, their roles have become of considerable interest to a much wider historical community, including regional, urban, labour, economic, social, and political historians.[3] From all this work has come a growing sense of the shape and significance of Canadian business history.

I

One fundamental role of recent research has been to combat anachronism by sharpening our knowledge of the chronology of the transformation of business organization in Canada. Until at least 1850, the scale and structure of Canadian business might, but for a variety of institutional factors, be said to have been eighteenth-century in nature. The largest businesses were mercantile and did general rather than specialized trades. The widespread industry of the society was small of scale by the standards of the leading industrial societies of the day, very much oriented to local markets, and, in a variety of ways, quite traditional in the organization of work.[4] More modern financial institutions had been organized, including incorporated banks, insurance companies, and even mortgage loan companies; but even the largest such institutions did business on a scale and in a way familiar to the eighteenth century.

Although Canadian railroads have thus far been studied more in terms of promotion and construction than of subsequent operations, it would not be unreasonable to hypothesize that in Canada as in the United States, it was railroads which from the 1860's or 1870's first began to epitomize the structure of more modern business. Not only did they develop a growing appetite for fixed capital, but they needed to confront the physical and accounting problems of depreciating such capital. They needed larger and more bureaucratic organizations and specialized skills in fields such as engineering. Their labour problems took on new levels of complexity, and management became generally divorced from ownership.[5]

The railroad also, with the steamship, the telegraph, and the Atlantic cable, began to change the significance of distance, as the risks hitherto associated with slower movement of information diminished. This permitted major expansion in the trade volumes of some firms, especially in bulk trades, and a bypassing of some links in the chains of middlemen that earlier characterized the structure of business. Increasingly, such changes in communications would also permit effective management and supervision from a distance, an important prerequisite for the development of larger and more complex organizations.

Such changes were not immediate; rather, throughout the second half of the nineteenth century, in a gradual and cumulative process marked by the end of extensive agricultural growth in eastern Canada, the rise of urban centres, and the workings of comparative advantages in the industrial sector, Canada developed an economy characterized by a larger and more urbanized industry, a very much enhanced and commercialized service sector, and an increasing predominance of incorporated and larger firms, as measured in terms of capitalization, number of employees, and volume of output. Because the scale, swiftness, and simultaneity of these interrelated transitions can readily be exaggerated, there is great need for research on the history of individual business sectors to permit generalizations more precise than these.[6]

It was not until about 1900, however, that market forces, the capital and other business requirements of new technologies such as electrical power, and the cumulative example and experience of successful incorporations in various economic sectors began to produce in Canada something like the "big business" that we tend to associate with late nineteenth-century capitalism. Only after 1900 did the Toronto Stock Exchange, for example, take on the characteristics of an important component of the workings of the Canadian business system.[7] Even by 1914 the predominance of bigger business was anything but complete or comprehensive.

Throughout the nineteenth century, in short, the Canadian business world was one of relatively small-scale firms, usually owner-operated, functioning in competitive markets. It was a world of growing specialization and complexity of business institutions and, increasingly, an urban business world in which fewer and larger centres dominated in most areas of economic activity. But not until virtually the end of the period, in 1914, could the modern bureaucratic, multi-branch, multi-product company be said in any sense to have typified Canadian business.[8]

II

Traditionally, one central concern of the business historian has been

16   CANADIAN BUSINESS HISTORY

to identify and consider the significance of entrepreneurship as a factor in economic development and change. Entrepreneurship, something in a culture or at least in some individuals within the culture, was the quality that led the independent, risk-taking, profit-seeking economic agent, the entrepreneur, to innovate by combining economic resources in new ways. This, it was argued, was an essential part of the process of economic progress, and to many it was the key variable that explained varying growth patterns in different regions or countries. Such behaviour needed to be differentiated from what was thought of as merely managerial behaviour, in which the businessman simply responded to economic stimuli in predictable ways. Failing this distinction, "entrepreneur" became merely a synonym for businessman.

Thus, for example, Atlantic Canada's relative economic stagnation after about 1870 has been attributed in part to the failure of the region's entrepreneurs to make appropriate investment decisions, especially in the previous two decades. When they persistently invested in traditional trades such as timber and wooden shipping, they ignored the chance to encourage or invest in secondary industry, and thereby "they contributed to the retardation of a viable industrial base" in the region.[9] On the other hand, the large-scale quantitative investigation of entrepreneurial behaviour that is being carried out by the Atlantic Canada Shipping Project is enabling us to see more clearly the rationality of Maritime businessmen in the shipping industry. Wooden shipping continued to be a most reasonable investment, in a number of ports, until the 1870's. Moreover, "when new markets and new opportunities appeared in the domestic economy, shipowners and their sons responded, not in undue haste, but with the same prudent calculation which earlier had guided them into the ocean trades of the North Atlantic."[10]

More generally, it seems implausible that one region of a society in which there is much mobility of population should lack such a cultural quality as entrepreneurship unless other, prior factors caused the migration away from the region of some of those possessing it.[11] There is in fact great danger that the often met concept of entrepreneurial failure will be little more than a label employed to explain why a particular economy did not take a road that it was never destined to take. As H.C. Pentland once tartly and succinctly put this point, "it seems to me that in societies of a northwest European type (at least), development is dependent upon supplies of resources, capital and labour, but not upon promoters, who are always in excess of supply."[12]

NINETEENTH-CENTURY BUSINESS WORLD 17

Even if this is true and the use of business history to study entrepreneurship is something of a dead-end street, the approach has reflected and helped to highlight the importance of cultural and organizational factors in the economic world. The significance of such factors is suggested also by the failure in the last twenty-five years of so many efforts at economic development, both within some of Canada's less developed areas and elsewhere in the world and by the relative success of some economies not notably better endowed with measurable and quantifiable resources than others.

It is an important virtue of business history that it considers economic change and development at a less abstract level than economics; in so doing it can reveal much about the mechanisms of economic change in a society. The same point can be made in socio-logical terms: if one wishes to understand, investigate, indeed, see at all the role and influence of a dominant class in society, rather than simply to assume and assert, then examination of the institutions and the inner workings of that class can be very much to the point. With this perspective in mind, let us review briefly a few contributions of relatively recent work in nineteenth-century Canadian business history.

III

An appropriate starting point lies in the structure of commercial enterprise, the dominant business form of the period. That structure has often been misunderstood, and it has tended to be seen largely through the eyes of its critics. One of the first of these was John Graves Simcoe, who was convinced that a merchant monopoly was obstructing his plans for Upper Canadian prosperity by holding up prices of wheat and flour to the government, yet paying the farmers only a small proportion of such high prices, keeping the rest for themselves.[13] Doubtless the merchants wished for such power to control prices and margins, but in fact Simcoe, and those who have echoed his opinion of the merchant class in the almost two centuries since, blamed the individuals who visibly represented the business system, entirely ignoring the underlying structure of trade and the inescapable realities of the market forces that actually determined prices.

The mercantile firm depended on credit, from suppliers, banks, and other mercantile intermediaries, in order to acquire and ship its goods to the colonies, where it sold them, also on credit. The usual retail term was twelve months, reflecting the economy's harvest and timber marketing cycles. The entire world of credit focused on the

18   CANADIAN BUSINESS HISTORY

metropolitan centres of Britain – London and, especially important
in the Canadian context, Glasgow and Liverpool. There, in expansionary times, competition meant that credit was liberally available,
at least to appropriate borrowers, and this prevented the formation
of monopolies such as Simcoe feared.

When the business cycle turned downward, credits were tightened
or withdrawn. Because trust was central to the granting of credit,
easiest and earliest access to it in expansionary times and preferential
treatment in contractions went to those on whom the creditor considered he could rely most fully, that is, to people whose characters
he knew and to those personally recommended or guaranteed by
those he knew and trusted. Thus the commercial world was struc-
tured not only in the competitive yet mutually supporting business
communities of individual cities, with which research has made us
increasingly familiar in recent years, but also, in some respects more
importantly, along international chains of personal connections.[14]

As work progresses in Canadian business history, the reality of
risk for businessmen is repeatedly emphasized. In a commercial
world that required the merchant to decide what to buy as early as
the autumn of one year to obtain goods to be sold in the summer of
the next and on which payment would not follow until the ensuing
summer, much could happen to undermine a business. Too little or
too much expansion, a wrong estimate of future wheat and timber
supplies and prices, extension of credit to the wrong people, or a
sudden commercial collapse in Britain could all bring serious loss.
Bankruptcy, especially in the recurrent cycles of credit stringency,
was a frequent and normal feature of the business world.[15]

These risks, plus the personal nature of business, in which death
or retirement could bring a change of business partnership and
name, meant that relatively few enterprises spanned multiple generations, although we are likely to hear most about the exceptions that
did survive. If the departure of firms left opportunities to be grasped,
it was likely that the business world would produce successors, either
through the formation of new firms or the expansion or adaptation
of existing ones. Where opportunity had shifted, would-be successors
either did not appear or did not succeed; such was the case, for
example, as independent wholesaling declined at Hamilton after the
1850's.[16] These general points on the nature of the Canadian business
world in the merchants' age help to explain the shifting fortunes of
competing nineteenth-century urban centres, and they have much to
say about larger social changes in the period.

IV

One of the crucial issues in the interpretation of the Conquest and the development of Quebec and its élite thereafter has been the takeover of the St. Lawrence economy by English-speaking, notably Scottish, merchants in the generation after 1763.[17] How and precisely when did this happen, what did it have to say about British policy and practice and about French-Canadian business abilities, and, of course, what did it mean for French-Canadian society to have at the head of its business system a Scottish-dominated mercantile élite? While a variety of answers have been offered to these questions, it is our interest to view them in the perspective of business history. From this angle, it comes as no surprise that the economy of a colony that became dependent on British supplies, markets, and credit was increasingly dominated by those with superior access to the metropolis.

Such a transition did not occur all at once, because the French-Canadian merchants had knowledge of their local markets and of the indigenous credit mechanism, which was of real advantage in a competitive world. But as the normal turnover of firms took place, the successful among the aspiring replacements were very likely to be those with more immediate connections in Glasgow, Liverpool, or London than any Lower Canadian could have. After 1800 this probability was still further increased by the fact that the Upper Canadian frontier region, now almost entirely English-speaking, was the most dynamic commercial sector in the St. Lawrence valley.

It has not usually been recognized that the Lower Canadian situation was in many respects paralleled in Upper Canada, where commercial leadership soon fell largely into the hands not of men of Loyalist, military, or American background, as the composition of the population might have suggested, but into those of newly arrived merchants, especially Scots, with solid connections to the Montreal, Quebec, and Glasgow commercial worlds. As Bruce Wilson has argued this point in his excellent account of the enterprises of Robert Hamilton, the Niagara area's leading merchant at the beginning of the nineteenth century, economic power in the first generation in Upper Canada stemmed directly from the ability to be part of that commercial and communications system.[18] Even in the 1830's and 1840's, it is clear that suitably connected Scots had better opportunities for commercial leadership in Upper Canada than the native born.[19] Thus it was that the economic leadership of the St. Lawrence economy acquired and long retained its markedly Scottish character,

20   CANADIAN BUSINESS HISTORY

and this in turn had real consequences in determining the personnel of its business élite.

Related to, yet distinct from, the question of domination of the Lower Canadian economy by English-speaking merchants was the question of the entrepreneurial spirit and values of French Canadians. It was once usual to contend that, either through decapitation of the society, that is the removal of its commercial élite by the Conquest, or because it was a Catholic-peasant-seigneurial-professional culture that was inimical to entrepreneurship, French Canadians lacked the business values and commercial drive that produced great entrepreneurs. Recent research has made that view difficult to sustain. Certainly in those areas of trade and business where connections in the French-speaking community gave an advantage, French Canadians were much involved in business enterprise. They were, for example, active in a venturesome and risk-taking way in the domain of urban land development and associated real estate speculation, where international ties mattered less than local ones.[20]

At the same time, economic historians are increasingly noting contrasts in the basic resource endowments for agriculture between Upper and Lower Canada, thereby revealing the basis for the lower per capita output and income of French-Canadian farmers. Of course, this in turn left a smaller and less dynamic market, one that experienced real economic crisis and decline in at least the second quarter of the nineteenth century, as the basis for French-Canadian commerce.[21] Here, in short, is a classic case where observed differences in economic behaviour have in the past been attributed to that elusive quality, entrepreneurship, when they should probably have been attributed to quite other factors.

Given the merchants' concern with the problems of credit, aspects of their business and political behaviour also become more explicable. It was one of the merchants' earliest priorities to improve the banking and insurance systems in order to obtain assistance in carrying credit burdens, controlling risks, and effecting interprovincial and international transfers of funds. Needing and knowing these financial services, which could, moreover, be built up incrementally, they were very ready to establish the appropriate institutions themselves, though the state had a role to play in chartering such companies. By contrast, they consistently avoided personal investment, except in certain promotional stages or when given ample government aid, in such desirable but capital-consuming and altogether unsafe investments as the shares of most canals and railroads. For these ventures, they predicted large returns to society and urged and

NINETEENTH-CENTURY BUSINESS WORLD 21

often obtained state support in such forms as subsidies, share purchases, loan guarantees, and land grants.

At the same time, merchants were markedly involved in politics and legal efforts to develop and improve other aspects of a credit-based society, such as laws relating to promissory notes and currency, bankruptcy, the role of the courts in enforcing contracts, land tenure (important in terms of securing debts), etc.[22] In all of these, merchants were at once debtors and creditors and hence as a class they had a particular interest in the certainty and efficacy of procedures. Given their awareness of the importance of maintaining and increasing the stream of British-based credit, they were naturally attentive to the worries of overseas lenders. Indeed, the Canadian businessman's often met litany of fear of giving offense to foreign creditors and investors had a genuine basis in his actual economic activity, particularly in this early period.[23]

We have in the twentieth century come to view with suspicion the intertwining of politics and business engendered by these and other merchant concerns. We have also, perhaps paradoxically, both pursued a wide variety of state interventions in business and economic life and enacted laws (e.g., on conflict of interest, public tendering, political party funding, etc.) to separate the two domains in an effort to reduce what we see as undesirable links between business and politics. We are, however, liable to misunderstand the politics of the nineteenth century if we apply our current standards on these matters anachronistically, or, alternatively, if we assume that the interrelationship of business and politics is largely a modern phenomenon.

The nineteenth-century spheres of government, politics, and business were not discrete or separate from each other; they overlapped in wide areas and it was altogether natural that businessmen and politicians should have many connections. If, as politics developed, this common ground led to situations in which political capital could be made by opponents of one or another element in the process, the consequence was the gradual buildup of a set of political and institutional barriers attempting, seldom successfully, to separate the spheres. As often as not, however, the issue in political debate in such cases was not the appropriateness of links between politics and business, but inappropriateness of particular links, especially ones that appeared to favour one set of development ambitions over another. This most often happened when the interests of one generation of businessmen collided with another, or of one city with another, or of one element in the business community with another,

22   CANADIAN BUSINESS HISTORY

or of established business institutions with newer ones.[24] Only gradually did debates of this kind create a more general sense of the need
for limits beyond those supplied by the common law. But it is not
helpful to apply those standards moralistically to the business-political world of most of the nineteenth century.

As Keith Johnson has shown so well, especially in his perceptive
studies of John A. Macdonald's earlier years, the aspirant local
politician and the aspirant local businessman had much in common,
and it is artificial and harmful to our understanding of the behaviour
of either to separate one sphere too much from the other. The leaders
of the age, as Johnson notes, spoke a "common legal-entrepreneurial
language," which also had clear equivalents in French, as the careers
of Cartier and others indicated.[25] Certainly an understanding of how
the world looked to a typical Kingston businessman has much to say
about Macdonald's guiding tenets in politics as a whole. That the
state existed to promote economic development and the interests of
businessmen (a distinction easier to make now than then, and easier
to make even now by the observer than by the businessman) was not
really in question; politics was, in significant part, about how that
would be done.

These then are among the conclusions and perspectives raised by a
focus on the commercial world of business in nineteenth-century
Canada. As they indicate, that earlier world deserves understanding
in its own terms, and not merely as a distant prelude to the real world
of big business today. Indeed, while bigger business, with its far more
complex structure and its greater wealth, power, and institutional
permanence, has overlaid that earlier structure, it has not completely
overwhelmed it. Traces of that earlier period can, after all, be found
almost everywhere in Canada.

Thus, some sense of its outlook can be gained from the boosterism
that even now characterizes the business outlook of most local
business communities in Canada. The intricate connections and
barriers among our government and business institutions can be
given historical roots once an idealized, usually *laissez-faire*, model
of the past is abandoned and the actual history of nineteenth-century
business behaviour is considered. Entrepreneurial failure and inadequacy, on which so much historical research has focused, continue
to be cited frequently as explanations for why something in the
Canadian economy or business world has not happened as the
observer would have preferred, just as entrepreneurial skill and
success are often assumed to be explanations for the growth of new
areas of the economy.

NINETEENTH-CENTURY BUSINESS WORLD   23

Finally, as is vividly exemplified still in the financial districts of Canada, where one finds the headquarters of, for example, most of the country's resource-extracting companies, the history of nineteenth-century Canadian business illustrates clearly the centrality of credit and the institutions by which it is managed in the overall structure and functioning of an economy.

Notes

Chapter 1 McCalla,
Nineteenth-Century Business World

1. Peter C. Newman, *Flame of Power* (Toronto, 1959), p. 12.
2. Gustavus Myers, *A History of Canadian Wealth*, vol. 1, 2nd ed. (Toronto, 1972), *passim*; T. Naylor, *The History of Canadian Business, 1867-1914* (Toronto, 1975), I, p. xx.

178

NOTES   179

3. This paper necessarily draws on a very selective range of potentially relevant sources; for a good review of recent literature in Canadian business history, see Christopher Armstrong, "Recent Books in Canadian Business History," *History and Social Science Teacher*, XIV (1978-79), pp. 171-7.
4. But see G. Kealey, *Toronto Workers Respond to Industrial Capitalism, 1867-1892* (Toronto, 1980), for an excellent account of the complex transition to a larger and more modern industrial structure in Toronto after about 1860.
5. A.D. Chandler, Jr., *The Visible Hand: The Managerial Revolution in American Business* (Cambridge, Mass., 1977), pp. 81-187. For a Canadian account paying some attention to issues of railroad management, see Peter Baskerville, "The Boardroom and Beyond: Aspects of the Upper Canadian Railroad Community" (Ph.D. thesis, Queen's University, 1973), pp. 207-93.
6. On this transition, see Michael Bliss's outstanding work, *A Canadian Millionaire* (Toronto, 1978), pp. 110-37 and *passim*; also Paul Craven, *"An Impartial Umpire": Industrial Relations and the Canadian State, 1900-1911* (Toronto, 1980), pp. 90-110, 375-80.
7. John F. Whiteside, "The Toronto Stock Exchange to 1900: Its Membership and the Development of the Share Market" (M.A. thesis, Trent University, 1979).
8. See also, on this transition, David Coombs, "The Emergence of a White Collar Workforce in Toronto, 1895-1911" (Ph.D. thesis, York University, 1978).
9. T.W. Acheson, "The Great Merchant and Economic Development in Saint John, 1820-1850," *Acadiensis*, VIII, 2 (Spring, 1979), p. 27. See also D. Sutherland, "Halifax Merchants and the Pursuit of Development, 1783-1850," *CHR*, LIX (1978), p. 11.
10. Eric Sager and Lewis Fischer, "Patterns of Investment in the Shipping Industries of Atlantic Canada, 1820-1900," *Acadiensis*, IX, 1 (Fall, 1979), p. 43. See also D. Alexander and G. Panting, "The Mercantile Fleet and its Owners, Yarmouth, Nova Scotia, 1840-1889," *Acadiensis*, VII, 2 (Spring, 1978), pp. 19-28.
11. David Alexander, "Some Introductory Thoughts on Entrepreneurship," in Lewis Fischer and Eric Sager, eds., *The Enterprising Canadians: Entrepreneurs and Economic Development in Eastern Canada, 1820-1914* (St. John's, 1979), pp. 3-4. See also Barry Supple, "A Framework for British Business History," in Supple, ed., *Essays in British Business History* (Oxford, 1977), pp. 12-15. Of course, under more modern business conditions it is possible for the entrepreneur to remain in an area but for his capital to leave.
12. H.C. Pentland, "Further Observations on Canadian Development," *Canadian Journal of Economics and Political Science*, XIX (1953), p. 410. The context of this note makes clear that "promoters" is used very much analogously with "entrepreneur."
13. For example, J.G. Simcoe to George Ross, Navy Hall, 21 October 1794, in E.A. Cruikshank, ed., *The Correspondence of Lieut. Governor John Graves Simcoe, III, 1794-5* (Toronto, 1925), pp. 38-9. See also Lillian Gates, *Land Policies of Upper Canada* (Toronto, 1968), pp. 35-6.

180   CANADIAN BUSINESS HISTORY

14.   D. McCalla, *The Upper Canada Trade, 1834-1872* (Toronto, 1979), pp. 151-5. Regarding the structure of the timber trade, see Graeme Wynn, *Timber Colony: A Historical Geography of Early Nineteenth Century New Brunswick* (Toronto, 1981), pp. 113-37; A.R.M. Lower, *Great Britain's Woodyard: British America and the Timber Trade, 1763-1867* (Montreal, 1973), pp. 139-57.

15.   For a few examples of the importance of the theme of failure and insecurity, see Dale Miquelon, *Dugard of Rouen: French Trade to Canada and the West Indies, 1729-1770* (Montreal, 1978), pp. 147-50; Michael Katz, *The People of Hamilton, Canada West: Family and Class in a Mid-Nineteenth Century City* (Cambridge, Mass., 1975), pp. 176-208; Michael Bliss, *A Living Profit: Studies in the Social History of Canadian Business, 1883-1911* (Toronto, 1974), pp. 139-40.

16.   D. McCalla, "The Decline of Hamilton as a Wholesale Centre," *OH*, LXV (1973), pp. 247-54.

17.   Dale Miquelon, ed., *Society and Conquest: The Debate on the Bourgeoisie and Social Change in French Canada, 1700-1850* (Toronto, 1977); Fernand Ouellet, *Lower Canada, 1791-1840: Social Change and Nationalism* (Toronto, 1980), pp. 2-20; also F. Ouellet, "Dualité économique et changement technologique au Québec (1760-1790)," *HS*, IX (1976), pp. 258-9, 296.

18.   Bruce Wilson, "The Enterprises of Robert Hamilton: A Study of Wealth and Influence in Early Upper Canada: 1776-1812" (Ph.D. thesis, University of Toronto, 1978), p. 96.

19.   McCalla, *The Upper Canada Trade*, pp. 38-9.

20.   Paul-André Linteau and Jean-Claude Robert, "Land Ownership and Society in Montreal: An Hypothesis," in G. Stelter and A. Artibise, eds., *The Canadian City: Essays in Urban History* (Toronto, 1979), pp. 17-36. See also G. Tulchinsky, *The River Barons: Montreal Businessmen and the Growth of Industry and Transportation, 1837-53* (Toronto, 1977), p. 17.

21.   John McCallum, *Unequal Beginnings: Agriculture and Economic Development in Quebec and Ontario until 1870* (Toronto, 1980).

22.   R.C.B. Risk, "The Golden Age: The Law about the Market in Nineteenth-Century Ontario," *University of Toronto Law Journal*, XXVI (1976), pp. 307-58; Risk, "The Nineteenth-Century Foundations of the Business Corporation in Ontario," *University of Toronto Law Journal*, XXIII (1973), pp. 270-306.

23.   For example, C. Armstrong and H.V. Nelles, "Private Property in Peril: Ontario Businessmen and the Federal System, 1898-1911," in G. Porter and R. Cuff, eds., *Enterprise and National Development* (Toronto, 1973), p. 20.

24.   For such internecine business-political conflicts, see, for example, Peter Baskerville, "Entrepreneurship and the Family Compact: York-Toronto, 1822-1855," *Urban History Review*, IX, 3 (February, 1981), pp. 15-34.

25.   J.K. Johnson, "John A. Macdonald," in J.M.S. Careless, ed., *The Pre-Confederation Premiers* (Toronto, 1980), pp. 197-245, with quotation from p. 212; see also Johnson's "John A. Macdonald, The Young Non-Politician," *CHAR* (1971), pp. 138-53. For Quebec, see, for example, Brian Young,

NOTES   181

Promoters and Politicians: The North Shore Railways in the History of Quebec 1854-85 (Toronto, 1978), pp. 138-44; Young, *George-Etienne Cartier: Montreal Bourgeois* (Montreal, 1981). For a Maritime example, see Carman Miller, "Family, Business and Politics in Kings County, N.S.: the Case of F.W. Borden, 1874-1896," *Acadiensis*, VIII, 2 (Spring, 1978), pp. 60-75.

[18]

Excerpts from Marshall I. Goldman, *Soviet Marketing: Distribution in a Controlled Economy*, 1–6, 12, 203–7.

[1] *INTRODUCTION*

THE NATURE OF MARKETING

THE TRANSFER of goods from one person to another constituted one of man's earliest social acts. Whether the action was negotiated by means of force and violence or barter, man's inability to satisfy all his desires by producing everything himself has forced at least a partial reliance upon others for both necessities and luxuries. Initially this inability may have been due to weakness, but gradually with increased socialization, physical coercion became less important and increasingly the transfer of goods was marked by mutual exchange and trade.

The basic motive for trading is that somebody possesses something you desire more than something you have in your possession. By bringing such people into contact with one another, it is frequently possible to arrange a mutually satisfactory transaction. For the most part, therefore, trade is the exchange of surplus items for deficit items. Geographical and resource variations are one reason for surpluses. Among other factors are division of labor, variation

1

2 SOVIET MARKETING

of skills, and differences in taste. One is led to create a surplus of some product in the hope that he may then bargain and exchange it for some other product for which he has a stronger desire.

As society and production grow in complexity and mass production and improved communications make it possible to expand the limits of the market, both the range of goods and the distance between negotiators increases. It becomes more and more difficult for the producers to locate one another and arrange mutually satisfactory exchanges between themselves without the aid of some sort of intermediary or middleman. The middleman, in this role of bringing together interested parties, has come to perform a variety of functions, which include buying, selling (which may involve advertising), transporting, storing, grading, financing, assembling, informing, bearing risk, packaging, refining, and altering the form of goods.

The nature of the contribution made by the middleman has long been a subject of controversy. While some functions (refining, packaging) are conceded to be completely productive in nature and others relatively productive (transporting and assembling), others are sometimes held to be parasitic (advertising, bearing risk, and, in some contexts, storing) to the basic processes of producing and consuming. Oddly enough, two of the most pronounced critics of these "parasitic" marketing practices have been the Catholic Church and the Marxists. Under the influence of Aristotle, the Church was opposed to anything or anybody who interposed himself between production and consumption and made a profit thereby. Undue transfers of title not affecting the nature of the goods themselves were felt to lead invariably to increases in price at the expense of both producers and consumers:

The essence of the argument was that payment may properly be demanded by the craftsmen who made the goods, for both labor in their vocation and serve the common need. The unpardonable sin is that of the speculator or the middle man who snatches private gain by the exploitation of private necessity (Tawney, 1926, p. 36).

Marx was similarly opposed to such "unproductive exploitation." Distribution activities were divided by him into two categories: "supplemental," those that were a continuation of the production process, and "pure," those that arose only because of the process of buying and selling (Marx, 1925, pp. 147–72). "Supplemental" production expenses were given the Marxian seal of approval. The cost of such activities, as determined by the labor expended, added to the value of the product. He included here such activities as packaging, storage, and transportation. It was assumed, of course, that no one was engaged in any of these practices in a socially unproductive manner, that is, by storing a good for an undue period of time merely to raise the price or by storing outmoded goods. In Marx's ideal society, such supplementary activities were really a continuation of the productive process. As a result, it was only natural that the value of labor expended in such work should normally be included in the final valuation of the commodity. If these same practices were undertaken in a capitalistic environment, however, the danger existed that the capitalist would use them to bring about an artificial price increase. Hence, even this potentially creative type of expense might not add to value as defined by Marx.

"Pure" costs of distribution were regarded by Marx as expenses arising solely because of a conversion of form (that is, the needless transfer of title among speculators, commission merchants, and others). Thus, as distinct from supplementary expenses, he felt that such costs could not add to the value of a good no matter how or when they were incurred. He considered all such merchandising activities to be uncreative. Essentially, anything more than simple retailing—that is advertising, operating commodity markets, speculating, carrying out commission activities, accounting, and so forth—was felt to be parasitic and of no value to society as a whole. "The general law is that *all expenses of circulation which arise only from changes of form do not add any value to the commodity*. They are merely expenses required for the realization of value or for its conversion from one form to another" (Marx, 1925, p. 169; italics in original).

Consequently, both the scholastics and the Marxists believed that elimination of pure costs of distribution and reduction of supplemental cost excesses would be in the best interests of society.

On the other hand, while modern Western authorities acknowledge that marketing has its excesses, it is generally asserted that a function is undertaken only if it performs a service and fulfills a need. This follows, they assert, because the act will not be carried out if it is unprofitable, and it will only be profitable if someone feels it provides a service worth the money. It is argued that almost all marketing activities do therefore contribute to the real value of a good, although there may be a difference between private and social value.

While it is difficult to assess the real contribution of certain marketing functions in any definitive manner, it may nevertheless be interesting to study an economic system in which there is the political power, as well as the ideological desire, to dispense with various "nonessential" functions. This may allow us to further our understanding of the nature and value of trade and to ascertain whether or not certain aspects of it can actually be eliminated. A study of the marketing operations in a country like the Soviet Union, where the marketing structure has such a different orientation, should prove valuable in illuminating the essence of the phenomenon.

THE AIMS OF THIS STUDY

The following examination of trade and distribution in the Soviet Union is thus undertaken for several reasons. On the one hand, this study may aid our understanding of the phenomenon of marketing. Even though there seems to be general agreement that trade is the one field of competition in which the West is safely ahead of the Russians and, therefore, about which we should know enough, there is still much we have to learn about the essence of marketing. If nothing else, we will be able to see ourselves and our activities better after subjecting someone else to examination.

On the other hand, any survey of the marketing process in the Soviet Union is highly desirable in itself. In the course of the last decade, Western economists have devoted considerable attention to many aspects of the economy of the Soviet Union. Economic investigations have ranged from the particular problem of transportation to the general problems of national income and growth. However, the area of domestic trade and distribution has been relatively neglected. Some earlier studies have been made, but the opportunity (one might say need) for research since 1953 has widened considerably.

The publication of detailed statistical handbooks and extensive descriptions of marketing operations enables the researcher to devote more time to analysis and less to detective work, thereby broadening his scope. At the same time, the extensive Soviet organizational changes and the increased concern with improvements in marketing following Stalin's death have all but necessitated a revision of the now outdated surveys of earlier years. Consequently, even if there were no implications in such a study for the basic marketing phenomenon, there nonetheless seems to be a need for an up-to-date survey of marketing in the Soviet Union.

Before outlining the structure of the monograph, something should be said regarding the limits of the proposed study. First, distribution is considered here only as it relates to the domestic sale of consumer goods, not to producers' goods or exports. Second, with minor exceptions, the basic production-goal decisions are assumed to be given. In the Soviet Union such goals are centrally determined by the policy makers, who steadfastly have emphasized heavy industry. Consequently, it is only within such circumscribed boundaries that the roles of consumer sovereignty, demand estimation, and product assortment are studied. The main concern here, then, is with the problems of allocating and delivering within the Soviet Union such goods as are produced. The establishment of basic production goals themselves is beyond the competence of this book.

Table 1—Retail Sales Volume by Trade Network
(in Million Rubles, Prices of Respective Year)

Year	Government Trade	Cooperative Trade	Commission Trade	Total (1), (2), & (3)	Private Trade	Total (4) & (5)
	(1)	(2)	(3)	(4)	(5)	(6)
1924	99	186		285	319	605
1925	160	352		512	386	898
1926	215	546		761	521	1,282
1927	233	706		939	496	1,435
1928	250	927		1,177	364	1,541
1929	334	1,186		1,520	243	1,763
1930	448	1,445		1,893	112	2,006
1931	726	2,068		2,794		
					Kolkhoz market	
1932	1,445	2,581		4,036	750	4,786
1933	2,512	2,467		4,979	1,150	6,129
1934	3,682	2,499		6,181	1,400	7,581
1935	6,315	1,856		8,171	1,450	9,621
1936	7,981	2,695		10,676	1,560	12,236
1937	9,285	3,309		12,594	1,780	14,374
1938	9,988	4,014		14,002	2,440	16,442
1939	11,606	4,977		16,583	2,990	19,573
1940	12,808	4,700		17,508	2,910	20,418
1941				15,280		
1942				7,780		
1943				8,400		
1944				11,930		
1945	12,460	3,554		16,014	13,640	29,654
1946	19,853	4,870		24,723		
1947	25,174	7,906		33,080		
1948	23,248	7,775		31,023		
1949	24,286	9,225		33,511	4,570	38,081
1950	26,104	9,854		35,958	4,920	40,878
1951	27,401	10,584		37,985	5,080	43,065
1952	28,489	10,870		39,359	5,370	44,729
1953	30,868	12,196	7	43,071	4,880	47,951
1954	33,565	14,399	224	48,188	4,900	53,088
1955	34,736	14,968	490	50,194	4,782	54,976
1956	38,062	16,016	665–704	54,743	4,210	58,953
1957	43,296	18,432	773–823	62,501	3,960	66,461
1958	46,794	20,055	871–939	67,720	4,050	71,770
1959	49,807	21,244	872–950	71,923	3,831	75,754
1960	54,904	22,906	745–795	78,555	3,604	82,159
1961	56,800	23,400	847	81,000		

SOURCE: TsSU 3, pp. 740-41, 787; TsSU 5, pp. 673, 681, 696, 736; TsSU 6, pp. 14, 16, 19, 20; TsSU 8, p. 425. Lifits 1950, pp. 11, 236, 317; 1955, p. 85. Dadugin and Fedorov, 1957, pp. 9, 12. TsSU 13, p. 356; Pravda, Jan. 23, 1962.

Appendix

HISTORICAL

BACKGROUND

FORTUNATELY there have been at least three competent historical descriptions of Soviet trade covering the period up to 1950 (Hubbard, 1938; Chossudousky, June, 1941, Nov., 1941; Ware, July, 1950, Oct., 1950). Since detailed discussion is available to the reader in English, it will only be necessary here to describe the more significant trends.

At an early date after the revolution, a new type of cooperative society was formed to supply the needs of the population. Despite the fact that membership was compulsory, the organization failed for the simple reason that the chaos that followed in the wake of the revolution left little semblance of order or organization in domestic distribution. In the following NEP period, conditions improved

203

and sales by cooperative organizations increased significantly. (See Table 1.) Private trade was permitted, if not encouraged, until the early 1930's when the state felt itself strong enough to eliminate it. Actually, private trade did continue, but under the pseudonym of *kolkhoz* market trade.

The inauguration of the five-year plans and the collectivization of agriculture once again disrupted the normal distribution channels that had been reconstructed during the NEP period. The solution in this instance was rationing. However, the full impact of rationing was often averted by recourse to the use of special stores selling to privileged customers or other stores selling to all customers, but at prices far above the official rates.

By the time rationing was abolished in 1936, the basic pattern of retail trade had been established. Cooperative stores, at one time the largest retail network, were confined to rural areas, and government stores were permitted an operating monopoly in urban areas. This pattern persisted until the outbreak of war in 1941, when rationing and the privileged-store system of shopping was reintroduced. It was as if conditions existing during the last crisis period of the early 1930's had been duplicated in exact detail. It was even decided to allow cooperative stores in the cities again.

The war years were extremely difficult. Despite all the attempts to provide new trading methods, the *kolkhoz* market often became the only source of food. In 1945, 51 per cent of total food sales volume was transacted in *kolkhoz* markets. Because of heavily inflated prices, the absolute volume of goods sold was much smaller, but other outlets often had no supplies at all.

The currency reform of 1947 brought an end to rationing and a return to normalcy, albeit an austere form of it. The basic structure of the retail network was converted to its prewar pattern when the consumer cooperatives were again returned to the countryside. More important for the people, however, was a series of yearly price reductions and an increasing sales volume that combined to bring about a gradual improvement in the standard of living. The fluctuations of trade and the shifts in prominence between various retail outlets can be traced in the sales statistics given in Table 1.

The history of changes at the wholesale and administrative levels follows closely the changes at the retail level. As Figure 7 indicates, there were many changes at the upper echelons. The evolution of the present wholesaling system took place in the twenties and thirties as the state gradually asserted itself and attained more and more control over the distribution sections. The state replaced the private enterprises, but not the essential functions. It was discovered that the basic operations could be assigned to different organizations, but they had to be performed none the less.

One interesting instance of this is cited by Hubbard. An attempt was made to abolish certain wholesaling functions of the consumer societies. Intermediary cooperative wholesale depots were abolished, and it was reasoned that the *sbyt* organizations of industry could deliver the goods directly to the retail outlet, thereby eliminating an unnecessary and expensive distribution operation. Unfortunately, it was not so simple:

> the managers of the rural cooperative societies were generally ignorant of which manufacturing enterprises were in a position to supply their requirements, and in any case it was a greater tax on their intelligence to write out

Figure 7—Evolution of Central Organization for Domestic Trade

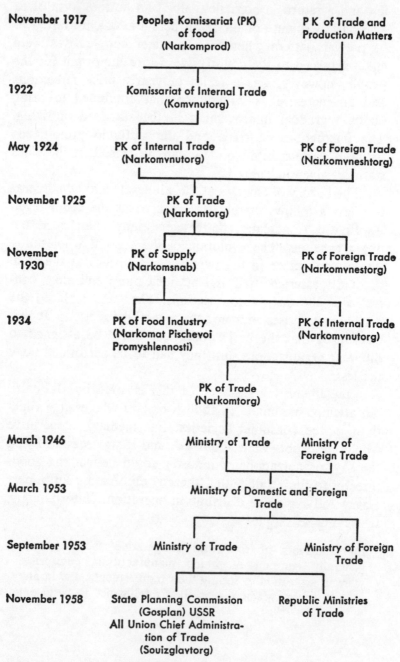

November 1917	Peoples Komissariat (PK) of food (Narkomprod)	P K of Trade and Production Matters
1922	Komissariat of Internal Trade (Komvnutorg)	
May 1924	PK of Internal Trade (Narkomvnutorg)	PK of Foreign Trade (Narkomvneshtorg)
November 1925	PK of Trade (Narkomtorg)	
November 1930	PK of Supply (Narkomsnab)	PK of Foreign Trade (Narkomvnestorg)
1934	PK of Food Industry (Narkomat Pischevoi Promyshlennosti)	PK of Internal Trade (Narkomvnutorg)
	PK of Trade (Narkomtorg)	
March 1946	Ministry of Trade	Ministry of Foreign Trade
March 1953	Ministry of Domestic and Foreign Trade	
September 1953	Ministry of Trade	Ministry of Foreign Trade
November 1958	State Planning Commission (Gosplan) USSR All Union Chief Administration of Trade (Souizglavtorg)	Republic Ministries of Trade

NOTE: See Figure 2a for November, 1962, reorganization.

orders for goods on distant enterprises than to go to their
nearest wholesale depot and pick out what they wanted
on the spot. This naturally led to delay in the receipt of
goods and the accumulation of stocks in the manufacturers'
warehouses (Hubbard, 1938, p. 41).

It was quickly discovered that because of the significantly higher transportation costs of sending small, special,
broken-lot shipments of goods and the delays in shipments
resulting from an already overcrowded transportation system, it was actually cheaper and certainly more efficient
to reintroduce intermediary and seemingly parasitic wholesale operations. All the state could hope to do was to transfer the responsibility for the performance of the wholesaling
functions from one agency to another. The increased bookkeeping resulting from the broken-lot ordering not only
led to immeasurably poorer services but it in no way
reduced costs.

Amid countless reorganizations and redesignations, the
basic administrative and wholesale organizations described
in Chapter 2 came into being. The organizational pendulum
seems to have shifted continuously between increased centralization and decentralization. The apogee of centralization seems to have been reached in the early 1950's before,
and shortly after, Stalin's death; but even in that confusing
era, a movement toward decentralization seemed to be
forming. The resulting trend ultimately reached the stage
described in Chapter 2 when the abolition of the Ministry
of Trade of the USSR was announced. While at this writing
the move toward decentralization seems to be continuing,
it certainly would be an unwise prophet who predicts that
there will never be any movement in the opposite direction.

REFERENCES

Chossudousky, E. M. 'Derationing in the USSR', *Review of Economic Studies*, November, 1941 [a].

———. 'Rationing in the USSR', ibid., June, 1941 [b].

Dadugin, A. P. and Fedorov, P. N. *Organizatsiia Kolkhoznoi Rynochnoi Torgovli*. Moscow, Gostorgizdat, 1957.

Hubbard, Leonard E. *Soviet Trade and Distribution*. London: Macmillan & Co. Ltd, 1938.

Lifits, M. M. (ed.). *Ekonomika Sovetskoi Torgovli*. Moscow: Gostorgizdat, 1950.

———. Ibid., 1955.

Marx, Karl. *Capital*, Vol. II. Chicago: Charles Kerr, 1925.

Tawney, R. H. *Religion and the Rise of Capitalism*. New York: Harcourt, Brace and World, 1926.

Tsentral'noe Statisticheskoe Upravlenie. *Narodnoe Khoziaistvo SSSR v 1958 Godu*. Moscow: Gosstatizdat, 1959 (TsSU 3).

———. *v 1960* Godu. *Ibid.*, 1961 (TsSU 5).

———. *Sovetskaia Torgovlia*. Moscow: Gosstatizdat, 1956 (TsSU 6).

———. *SSSR v Tsifrakh*. Moscow: Gosstatizdat, 1958 (TsSU 8).

———. *SSSR v Tsifrakh v 1961 Godu*. Moscow: Gosstatizdat, 1962 (TsSU 13).

Ware, Henry. 'Costs of Distribution in Soviet Domestic Trade', *Journal of Marketing*, July, 1950 [a].

———. 'The Procurement Problem in Soviet Retail Trade', *ibid.*, October, 1950 [b].

[19]

Excerpt from Ruth Prince Mack, *Controlling Retailers: A Study of Cooperation and Control in the Retail Trade with Special Reference to the NRA*, 135–49.

CHAPTER I

THE NATIONAL INDUSTRIAL RECOVERY ACT

AT this point in the stream of events which spun the story of retail collective activity, the river flows through a lake. The history of retailer cooperation is merged with that of group relations in all industry by the National Industrial Recovery Act. We will pause for a moment to study the genesis of this act before resuming the story of the retailer by inquiring into the gestation and birth of the Code of Fair Competition for the Retail Trade.

Two full years of depression had swept the Democratic Party into national office. The country was in the process of a physical and psychic deflation. The red hue of balance sheets is easy to recall, as is the downward plunge of indices of production and payrolls. The psychic deflation is more difficult to recreate in memory than the deflation of monetary and physical values; yet a recollection of its quality is necessary background to an understanding of the NIRA.

By the spring of 1933, the popular mood was unsure to the point of panic. Solid things seemed to have lost their weight and dissolved into a time-sequence; there was no knowing whether they would be there tomorrow. Individuals were losing their poise, their necessary feeling of adequacy; as a group, they were losing confidence in their collective power. When Roosevelt took the oath of office on March 4, 1933, he slaked a popular thirst. He focussed and fed the need for faith that grew out of the enveloping unsureness of the time. He was bewilderingly confident in the adequacy of man. He was a tonic to national morale.

136   *CONTROLLING RETAILERS*

The first days of the new administration were dramatic. Staccato commands from the White House were bringing order out of chaos.   There must be an end of submission, there must be action, action and faith.   " We do not distrust the future of essential democracy.   The people of the United States have not failed.   In their need they have registered a mandate that they want direct, vigorous action " . . .[1] " I assume unhesitatingly the leadership of this great army of our people, dedicated to a disciplined attack upon our common problem," [2] to the " larger purposes, to the pursuit of social values, to the forgotten man."   " The relation between government and business will necessarily be in process of redefinition during the coming years."   " Our new national administration . . . is going to bring about governmental action to mesh more with the rights and essential needs of the individual man and woman."   " *These are not merely hopes.   They are the battle orders imposed upon myself and my party.*" [3]

There could not be the slightest doubt that there would be rules of the game laid down in Washington.   The only question was what the rules would be.

SECTION I.   DRAFTING THE NIRA

Obviously, in a democratic government, lobby-infested and shackled with vested interests, pressure groups would have much to say concerning legislation which affected them.   The organized groups most vitally interested in the NIRA were industry and labor.

Both organized labor and business were wary of letting the camel's head into the tent.   Neither was anxious for gov-

[1] Franklin D. Roosevelt, *Looking Forward*, John Day Co., New York, 1933, p. 269.

[2] *Ibid.*, p. 267.

[3] *Ibid.*, p. 246.   Italics mine.

THE NATIONAL INDUSTRIAL RECOVERY ACT 137

ernment regulation, although the thought was certainly far from new. Comprehensive industrial planning had been seriously considered since the Economic Council Hearings in the fall of 1931 and had reached the preliminary stages of legislative drafting prior to the spring of 1933.[4] Moreover, even the Chamber of Commerce was not opposed to industry-controlled regulation.[5] But the issue was precipitated by the relatively clear road in both Houses that greeted the Black-Connery 30-hour bill. Clearly, regulation of some kind was inevitable. Accordingly the obvious job for the guardians of business interests to perform was to get into the control bill the measures and principles which they advocated and to keep out of the bill clauses adverse to business interests.[6]

[4] At the hearing before the Ways and Means Committee of the House of Representatives, May 18-20, 1933, Mr. Richberg, in speaking of his role in the writing of the NRA says: "Before the final draft of this measure there has been prepared a very large number of measures under the auspices of many groups, including a measure approved by the U. S. Chamber of Commerce and measures brought in by the various trade associations. There had been various kinds of committees of a semi-official nature working on these measures. The final basis for the production of this particular bill was the suggestion that all that work should, if possible, be conducted in a small group to *endeavor to bring out one bill of this multitude of counsel,* in which there might have been wisdom but in which also there was much confusion." (Hearings before 73 Congress on H. R., 5664, House Committee on Ways and Means, p. 84.)

At the Senate Committee hearing of the same bill on May 22, Mr. Richberg speaks of the "multitude of counselors in the preliminary stages" of this particular bill "having within the last two or three years been as the sands of the sea": also within the last two years "a large part of the members of both Houses" were brought into these conferences. (Hearings before the 73rd Congress on S. 1712, p. 30 before Senate Committee on Finance.)

[5] Chamber of Commerce of the U. S. Referendum, No. 59. Quoted by Mr. Harriman at House Hearing on H. R. 5665, p. 137.

[6] At the 22nd annual meeting of the Chamber of Commerce of the United States, the Board of Directors, in their annual report, quote a resolution adopted by the membership of the Chamber in annual meeting held May 3, 4, 5, 1933, which advocates that " Federal legislation affording

138   *CONTROLLING RETAILERS*

Likewise the trustees of labor welfare would, if true to their
trust, attempt to counteract paternalistic influence of government regulation of hours and wages through guarantee
of collective bargaining.[7]   It is important to note that executives and directors of business and labor organizations alike
would have been disloyal to their constituencies and to their
own standards had they failed to attempt to influence control
legislation.

Control of the framing of an act could presumably be
achieved in two ways: through having individuals engaged
in the actual drafting who were sympathetic to the point of
view to be advanced; and by having the act framed in constant consultation with the proponents of the interest in question.   The personality of the inner core of drafters changed

opportunity for this [Trade Association] form of self-regulation under
government supervision would produce conditions which assure fair competitive opportunity to each enterprise and permit immediate increase in
employment, raise earnings, and free the public from the results of
destructive competition on the part of the least responsible industrial
elements. All enterprise could be held to standards of fair competition
properly determined."   Concerning this resolution, the directors state:
"When that resolution was passed, there was pending in Congress a
bill that had been passed by the Senate to impose compulsory 30-hour
law limitations on the work week. We urged as a *constructive substitute* that trade organizations be permitted to formulate their standards,
in line with conditions in the industries, subject to approval by the
Federal government."   (Chamber of Commerce of the U. S. Board of
Directors Annual Report, Twenty-Second Annual Meeting, 1933-34,
pp. 5-6.)

[7] Organized labor throughout the major portion of its history had
worked on the hands-off-government theory. The union was the phalanx
of the traditional labor attack. Even during the hearings of the Black
Bill, the major groups of organized labor demanded only a drastic
reduction of hours; they were opposed to the public fixing of wages, even
of minimum wages. Traditionally, they wanted higher wages and shorter
hours together with certain specified rights, achieved through unionization. The change, then, from the traditional A. F. of L. position in regard to the relations of labor and government was significant in determining what type of clauses the NIRA would contain.

THE NATIONAL INDUSTRIAL RECOVERY ACT 139

as April and May wore on. These changes seem to have, in general, decreased the liberal and increased the business-minded influence urging self-rule in industry.[8] At the same time, the lines of communication seem to have been kept open between the framers of the Act and certain of the business groups that were interested[9] in it. Section 7A of the labor provisions, on the other hand, seems to have been interpolated into an early draft of the Act by the Department of Labor. In spite of the importance among the Code drafters of Mr. Richberg, who was considered to be sympathetic to the labor cause, modifications in the 7A clause were made

[8] General Hugh Johnson and Mr. Donald Richberg sifted to the top in the final stages of code drafting. The first page draft of a bill submitted by Johnson "was an outright grant of power to the President to organize industry, to give to trade associations authority to regulate prices, production, trade practices, wages and hours. It provided for suspending the Sherman Anti-Trust Law. It contained the authority to the President to license industry." It made no mention of collective bargaining for labor. (*Harpers' Magazine*, September, 1934, p. 392, article by John Flynn, "Whose Child is the NRA?".)

[9] At the House Hearing on H. R. 5664: Mr. Treadway: "I assume, from your statement, that you, like the rest of us did not see this bill until it was made public yesterday,"

Mr. Harriman: "Not as a whole. I had seen paragraphs of the bill..."

Mr. Treadway: "Then you were possibly consulted by the proponents of the bill?"

Mr. Harriman: "To a certain extent. Not as to language, but as to the principles involved in it" (p. 137).

At the same Hearing:

Mr. Richberg: "In the process of drafting this measure those conferences and consultations continued, and I had nothing to do with that phase of it. *But I do know, as a matter of fact that there was constant touch kept with those who have been working on this matter for a long time.*" (73rd Congress, Hearings; H. R. 5664, p. 84.)

At the Senate Hearing on S. 1712: Mr. J. A. Emery, representing local, state, and national industrial trade associations, with a membership of manufacturers employing in the aggregate about one-half of the employees in manufacturing, said that "a standing committee of 50 industrialists had engaged in continual study of the measure" (p. 273).

140   CONTROLLING RETAILERS

which were thought to outlaw the closed shop.[10]   Moreover,
the indirect control of organized labor over the proceedings
of the inner chamber was deficient in certain respects:[11] the
amendments to Section 7A proposed at the Congressional
Hearing were submitted at that time because there had been
no other opportunity to do so.[12]

Congressional committees introduced two important
changes in the proposed bill.   In the first place, the immunity
from the anti-trust acts which was presumably afforded by
the original draft[13] was modified to apply only to practices

[10] The section as recommended by the committee read: " No employee
or no one seeking employment shall be required as a condition of employment to refrain from joining a labor union of his own choosing."   In
the final draft presumably recast by Richberg, it read: " No employee or
no one seeking employment shall be required as a condition of employment to join any organization or refrain from joining a labor organization of his own choosing."   (*Harpers' Magazine*, Flynn, *loc. cit.*, p. 393.)

[11] John L. Lewis, writing of "Labor and NRA", said: "Moreover,
representatives of organized labor took an active part in the Conferences
leading to the drafting of the law.   What was being done was known in
detail by the United Mine Workers, and we had Senator Wagner's
assurance, as chairman of the legislation drafting committee, that no law
would be drawn which did not meet with the approval of organized labor."
(*Annals of American Academy of Political and Social Science*, March,
1934, p. 58, John L. Lewis, "Labor Under the NRA.")

[12] When William Green proposed his amendments to Section 7A at the
House Hearing, he was asked by Mr. Treadway: "Were those amend-
ments submitted to the gentlemen who prepared this bill?"   He answered,
"No sir, we had no opportunity to present these amendments."   (73rd
Congress Hearings, H. R. 5664, p. 122.)

[13] A comparison of the NIRA and the draft of the act submitted at the
Hearing before the Committee on Ways and Means of the House, dis-
closes the following differences in clauses relating to the trust acts.

Both drafts contained substantially the same clauses granting immunity
from the anti-trust laws to practices approved in the codes (Section 5).

The last two sentences of Section 3B in the early draft were: "Any
violation of such standards in any transaction in or effecting interstate
commerce shall be deemed an unfair method of competition in commerce
within the meaning of the Federal Trade Commission Act, as amended.
A violation of any provision of any such code shall be a misdemeanor and

THE NATIONAL INDUSTRIAL RECOVERY ACT 141

performed in compliance with the provisions of approved codes:[14] moreover a code could be approved only if in the opinion of the President, it would not operate to promote monopolies or eliminate or oppress small enterprises or permit monopolies or monopolistic practices.[15] In the second place, Section 7A was substantially changed after the Congressional Hearings in conformity with two modifications presented by William Green as the price of the " full, complete and hearty endorsement " of the bill by labor.[16] A

upon conviction thereof, an offender shall be fined not more than $500 for each offense." (73rd Congress Hearings, Committee on Ways and Means, May 18-20, 1933, H. R. 5664, p. 2.)

The NIRA in its final form contained in Section 3B the first sentence quoted above and transferred the second sentence to a different section. To the first sentence was added the phrase, " But nothing in this title shall be construed to impair the powers of the Federal Trade Commission under such Act as amended." It was thought that this phrase would destroy the immunity from the Anti-Trust Acts which it had been hoped would be granted to practices not specifically included in codes. (Public No. 67, H. R. 5755, 73rd Congress, NIRA.)

[14] Section 5, NIRA. This change seems to have been bitterly resented by some business men on the basis that the attack by Senator Borah which introduced the modification was made subsequent to the notification of business men concerning the provisions of the Act and the messages of endorsement sent to congressmen and senators by business men from all parts of the country who approved the Act on the basis of the long-sought-for relief from the anti-trust acts.

[15] NIRA, Section 3A, paragraph 2.

[16] Mr. Green suggested that to paragraph one, which read, " That employees shall have the right to organize and bargain collectively through representatives of their own choosing" should be added: " and shall be free from interference, restraint, or coercion of employers of labor, or their agents, in the designation of such representatives or in self-organization or in other concerted activities for the purpose of collective bargaining or other mutual aid or protection". He explained that the amendment which he proposed was a verbatim quotation taken from one of the laws of the country—the Norris-La Guardia Anti-Injunction Law. The second change which was suggested by Mr. Green and incorporated in the bill was the substitution of " company union" for " labor organization" in the paragraph referring to employment con-

142   CONTROLLING RETAILERS

third change of less general importance but of particular concern to retailers was the stipulation that persons in other steps in the economic process whose interest was affected by provisions in a code should have the right to be heard prior to the approval of the code by the President.[17]

The Act " to encourage national industrial recovery, to foster fair competition, and to provide for the construction of certain useful public works and for other purposes," emerged in early spring with the approval of the House and the Senate. On June 16, it was signed by the President. Section 7A had been vociferously fought by business; congressmen and senators had shied at the licensing clause; labor representatives had blessed the final draft. The consumer was silent except for the voice of Benjamin Marsh of the People's Lobby, who liked it not at all. " Government cannot repeal economic laws, nor make profiteering trusts good by going into partnership with industry." [18]

Political events can only be evaluated in terms of politically possible alternatives. In the face of the social and economic philosophy of the President, the political temper of both houses of Congress, and the virtual *fait accompli* of the Black-Connery Bill, the NRA must be adjudged a feather in the cap of industry's spokesmen.

Labor had achieved, in addition to the still to be defined reduction of hours of work and established minimum wages,

ditional to the employee undertaking to "refrain from joining a labor organization ['company union' as amended] of his own choosing." (73rd Congress Hearing on H. R. 5664, pp. 3, 117 and 118.)

[17] Section 3A, paragraph 2, *NIRA*. This clause was added in Senate Committee (73rd Congress Senate Hearings S. 1712, May 26, 1933) and had been suggested and advocated by the NRDGA (*Bulletin*, June, 1933, Editorial, p. 7) and endorsed by the Retailer National Council on June 1st (June 1st session at Palmer House, Chicago, of Retailer National Council. Reported in NRDGA *Bulletin*, June, 1933, p. 13.)

[18] *Cf.* Senate Hearings, *op. cit.*, p. 316.

THE NATIONAL INDUSTRIAL RECOVERY ACT 143

a clause which some thought would result in the unionization of industry.[19]

Industry, on the other hand, gained three outstanding advantages. Minimum wages and maximum hours of work were not, under the codes, stipulated rigidly for the country as a whole, but would be determined separately for each industry. The members of the industry would have an important part in determining the rates which would be established. Their knowledge of the implication of what might be thought by an outsider to be unimportant detail frequently afforded a bargaining advantage of great importance. The point will be illustrated from experience with the Retail Code. The right to determine wage rates separately for each industry carried with it the further advantage of a subtle, though very significant, weighting of the balance of power between industry and government. It implied a tacit admission that a knowledge of intimate conditions in an industry was necessary to intelligent social legislation. In the second place, the NIRA was to be administered by NRA rather than by established government bureaus. Later events proved this a chieftain's scalp. NRA, being young, was educable. Finally the NIRA underwrote industrial agreements on codes of fair competition. Fair business practice was to be defined and enforced. Destructive price competition and overproduction might be forbidden; survival value was to be based on efficiency rather than on the willingness to mulct labor, mislead the public and lay waste to competitors. The era of the " just price " was ushered in as [20]

[19] It would seem that certain outstanding leaders of labor felt that time was the essence of the advantage, and that, with speed and decisive action, the position of labor could be substantially improved before the rest of the country awakened to the innocuousness of the clause.

[20] For an interesting discussion of the " just price " and the NRA see *A Short History of the New Deal* by Louis M. Hacker, F. S. Croft and Co., New York, 1935.

144   *CONTROLLING RETAILERS*

the Sherman Anti-Trust Act was ushered out.[21]   Fair price
to labor, fair profit to business, fair cost to purchaser was
to be achieved through the certain magic of the Code of Fair
Competition.

A judgment rendered in the light of the political and economic situation of May, 1933 must pronounce NIRA a clear
tactical victory for representatives of business. Nevertheless
in the minds of many business men it was at best a Pyrrhic
victory.   Clear it was that business had joined hands with
Government.   Even the good trade association cooperator
grows strangely jumpy at the thought of " government in
business ".   To those business men who disapproved not
only of government regulation but also of trade association
regulation, the jumpiness approached St. Vitus' dance.   As
has been suggested at other points in this discussion, the ideology of *laissez-faire* is root and soil to American business
enterprise.   Such things do not change as the result of a
quixotic national mood.   In so far as business men *thought*
they were giving up, under the NIRA, independence of judgment and action, they were making a genuine and significant
sacrifice.   It is immaterial whether they actually were making
any substantial sacrifice or whether the sacrifices which they
would have made under the Black-Connery Bill or substitute
legislation would have been worse.   The fact that under the
NRA they thought they were giving up significant elements of control, is of the utmost importance in determining the actions of business men and their attitude towards
the NRA.

   [21] The extent to which the Anti-Trust Acts would be suspended would,
of course, depend upon the clauses contained in the Codes.   Nevertheless,
a clear change in pricing theory was involved.   No longer was the mere
preservation of competition through prevention of acts in restraint of
trade, acts tending to promote monopolies, etc., considered an adequate
assurance of a proper price structure.

THE NATIONAL INDUSTRIAL RECOVERY ACT 145

SECTION II.   THE NATIONAL INDUSTRIAL RECOVERY ACT

It will be recalled that the purpose of the NIRA, as stated in the preamble, was to " remove obstructions in the free flow of interstate and foreign commerce which tend to diminish the amount thereof." This was to be achieved by the elimination of unfair competition, by the promotion of the fullest possible utilization of the present productive capacity of industry and by increasing consumption through a large public works appropriation, the relief of unemployment, and an improvement in the standards of labor. The means whereby these desiderata were to be obtained and maintained was through the benevolent effect of " the organization of industry for the purpose of cooperative action among trade groups," and the " united action of labor and management under adequate governmental sanctions and supervisions ".

What was envisioned, then, was recovery and reform through an initial stimulation and the medium of the " just price ". Business was encouraged to organize; labor was encouraged to organize; labor and business were encouraged to cooperate. And in this broad-gauge get-together, the government was assigned the triple role of umpire, catalyst and shepherd. The first two functions were assigned to the administrator and his core of assistants, deputies and assistant deputies and respective staffs. The sheep over which it was the function of government to watch were the black, white and mottled little lambs of public interest. In connection with each code, the general interest of all employers, all labor and the consumer interest were guarded by three boards: the industrial, labor, and consumer advisory boards respectively. Collateral divisions of research and planning and a legal division were constituted to advise on appropriate questions.

146 *CONTROLLING RETAILERS*

The newly fostered cooperation of labor was cast in old forms: industrial, or craft, or company union. Industry also typically utilized as the unit of cooperative activity the time-tested device of the trade association or institute. The final draft of the NIRA seems to have provided no set form in which the cooperation of labor with industry was expected to materialize. This was left essentially to separate determination for each code, although NRA plans clarified in the spring of 1934.

The NIRA was, except for the public works section, essentially an enabling act. Government participation in and cooperation with industry could take one of four forms: (1) voluntary agreements between the President and an industry; (2) voluntary agreements, between employers and employees in an industry, approved by the President. (3) voluntary codes of fair competition; (4) imposed codes. The last mentioned method of effecting Title I of the Act was thought of more as a method of ensuring voluntary agreements than as a desirable method of organizing industry. As further emergency implementation, the President was empowered to require the licensing of firms. The third method, that of the voluntary code of fair competition, was the focus of most of the discussion between trade groups and the Government.

A code of fair competition would, it was intended, be applied for by " one or more trade or industrial associations or groups ".[22] Such codes could be approved by the President if he found that various stipulations were fulfilled: (1) That the associations or groups " impose no inequitable restrictions on admission to membership " and are truly representative of the trade or industry or subdivision for which the code is requested; (2) That the codes " are not designed to promote monopolies or to eliminate or oppress small enterprises and will not operate to discriminate against them,

[22] 73rd Congress Hearings S. 1712, May 22, p. 2.

THE NATIONAL INDUSTRIAL RECOVERY ACT 147

and will tend to effectuate the policy of this title." " Provided: that such code or codes shall not permit monopolies or monopolistic practices. Provided further that where such codes affect the services and welfare of persons engaged in other steps of the economic process, nothing in this section shall deprive such persons of the right to be heard prior to the approval by the President of such code or codes." [23] The codes were required to contain Section 7A, to regulate minimum wages and maximum hours of labor, and to define fair business practice.[24]

The original Administration plans contemplated a two-staged process of code-making. The labor provisions were to be the primary and immediate concern of Administration spokesmen. Trade practice provisions were to be the subject of more leisurely analysis. Code clauses would be formulated by reconciling conflicting interests.

But the expected and actual job of code-making diverged in several significant respects. In the first place it was found that conflicting interests could not typically be reconciled but had to be bargained off. The corresponding change in the function of the Deputy from a chairman of a forum to the umpire of an arena complicated as well as altered the task with which Government representatives were confronted.

[23] National Industrial Recovery Act, Section 3A.

[24] In the words of Senator Wagner: "A code of fair competition will set forth the best judgment of those engaged in the particular trade or industry as to the competitive conditions within the industry, specifically: (1) the standards of fair competition; (2) the trade practices which should be banned as unfair, oppressive and designed to give advantage to the employer with the lowest standards; (3) the methods which should be employed to rehabilitate the industry, increase its capacity to give employment, and raise the living standards of those who labor in it." " In this manner we lift the plane of competition to the level of the highest ideals prevailing in the particular industry, and at the same time we avoid the regimentation of all industry under a single inflexible set of rules." (73rd Congress Hearings, S. 1712, May 22, p. 2.)

148 *CONTROLLING RETAILERS*

In the second place, the early planning for code-making had envisaged negotiations starting with ten and ending with perhaps fifty large associations.[25] The 400 codes filed in the first month surprised the Administration and greatly magnified the task which had been undertaken, at the same time that it was welcomed as an opportunity to extend the benefits of the program.[26] In the third place the task undertaken by the Administration was further complicated by the fact that industry soon indicated that it was not interested in negotiating codes governing wages and hours and a few of the more flagrant and destructive trade abuses, but was primarily concerned with the regulation of trade practices,[27]

[25] Brookings Institution, *National Recovery Administration*, George Banta Publishing Co., Menacha, Wis., 1935, p. 87.

[26] *Ibid.*, p. 88. The unexpected character of the rush for codes is indicated further by the fact that on July 26, 1933, there were less than 400 persons having fixed employment in NRA. (*NRA Release* No. 93 quoted *ibid.*, p. 88, footnote 5.)

[27] The National Industrial Conference Board drafted a model code which appeared four days after the President signed the NIRA. The code developed the elements in the act which permitted direct and indirect (through statistics) price and production control. It restated Section 7A, contained a section devoted to minimum wages and maximum hours, and significantly contained no provisions concerning prohibition " of reductions of wages " above the minimum. It contained a list of unfair competitive methods, it forbade selling below cost of production, except for valid reasons, cost of production being defined as the average cost of firms submitting figures to the Association. It contained clauses which linked the code to the Trade Association in a variety of ways which ranged from encouraging membership in the Association to requiring, on pain of violation of the code, the submittal of statistics to the Association or " any agency acting on behalf of the association to determine whether there has been compliance with the provisions of the NIRA and this code ".

The bond between the Trade Association and the code was finally cemented by the clause on arbitration which read: "Any complaint, difference, controversy or question of fair competition arising under or out of this code or relating to standards as to maximum hours of labor and minimum rates of pay or other working conditions provided for

THE NATIONAL INDUSTRIAL RECOVERY ACT   149

particularly with controlling and improving prices through collective action.[28]

The Field Day was on. The invitation to write a code had been extended and accepted. Obviously there would be a rush to write into the fair practice provisions of the codes the wish fulfillment of decades of business experience, together with the pet foibles of many business men. The dance began: various industrial agencies of cooperation already existing, together with individual industrialists interested in individual practices, together with contingently interested organized groups, together with government officials, began the intricate masque, with its varied movements ranging from minuet to tarantella, which culminated in the grand finale—the President's signature on another Code of Fair Competition for the ————— Industry.

therein or concerning the interpretation of application of any provision thereof, shall be submitted to arbitration . . ." (Conference Board Information Service, Domestic Affairs, Memo. No. 7, NIRA, *Formulation of Codes of Fair Competition*, June 21, 1933.)

The position taken by the NICB was further bulwarked by the subsequent pamphlet which they issued entitled, "Organization of Industry for the Administration of the Act in the Light of German Cartel Experience". (NICB Conference Bd. Information Service, Domestic Affairs, Memo No. 8, July 7, 1933.)

General Johnson seemed to concur in the thought of trade-association governed industry. "In our eventual pattern, these associations will, in the first instance, and in truly representative fashion govern their trades and industries. The Government will sit in with a veto power, but without vote, to prevent the abuses of monopoly and the oppression of small enterprises and the exploitation of consumers." (Address by General Johnson, quoted in NRDGA *Bulletin*, October, 1933, p. 14.)

[28] Brookings Institution, *op. cit.*, pp. 92-94.

[20]

Excerpt from Ruth Prince Mack, *Controlling Retailers: A Study of Cooperation and Control in the Retail Trade with Special Reference to the NRA*, 304–16.

CHAPTER IV

ADMINISTRATIVE MACHINERY AND THE PUBLIC INTEREST

WE have reviewed some of the major problems involved in the administration of the Retail Code. Some of the difficulties encountered under NRA could doubtless be circumvented by analogous legislation that viewed objectives more clearly and was more realistic in calculating and facing the cost of desired achievements. But basic to specific difficulties was a fundamental problem of control which it will be useful to outline at this point.

Operation under a code of fair competition meant that the trade or industry had purchased power in enforcing aspects of trade ethics by acceding to specified labor standards and to government supervision. The NRA lent the dignity of the law to trade ethics, it encouraged self-government of industry, but it insisted on government supervision. The NRA was watch-dog for the public interest. This exchange of power for control was embodied in a pervading dualism of code administration: the work of code authorities was checked at every turn by NRA divisions.

A system of this kind could serve the public under one of two circumstances: either the code authorities spontaneously acted in accord with the public interest and therefore required no watching; or the officials of NRA were effective guardians of the public interest wherever and whenever it required protection.

The elasticity of each code achieved through interpretation and amendment, the newness of compliance problems, and the changeableness of NRA organization meant that the

304

ADMINISTRATIVE MACHINERY 305

entire process was in constant flux. Subtle changes could occur all along the line of intricate control machinery; major changes occurred through the formal channels of code modification which were duplicated for each of the several hundred codes and were of necessity only indirectly connected with any central person or board. *The public interest could only be guarded at these many points at which change occurred.* Accordingly, it was imperative that the NRA officials to whom authority was delegated have the ability to judge where the interest of labor and consumer lay and to urge their opinions with effectiveness in the event of a disagreement with the code authority. But two sets of difficulties tended to aid the trade and hamper the government in the inevitable jockeying for control: In the first place, important centrifugal forces were exerted by the nature of code problems; in the second place, NRA faced a terrific personnel problem.

SECTION I. NRA AS GUARDIAN OF THE PUBLIC INTEREST

In the first place, the magnitude of the task of enforcing the codes seems to have been largely unanticipated: the self-policing machinery as a *preventative* of code violation did not work as well as expected; there seems to have been more non-compliance than was foreseen; complaints did not disclose all of the violations; the ambiguity of fact made non-compliance, when discovered, difficult to correct. The resultant disorder and the terrific press of work made it highly desirable to delegate work to any group ready and willing to assume the burden. The Retail Code Authority was organized speedily. Retailers wanted to handle their own compliance problems. Willing cooperation of members of the trade was essential to code enforcement; especially was this true in the retail field since Federal regulation of retail trade had a highly questionable legal status. When we reflect that

306   *CONTROLLING RETAILERS*

the situation in retailing was multiplied by similar situations
in many other industries, we can readily understand why the
government seemed more willing than it might otherwise
have been to permit code authorities to assist in handling
labor complaints on a temporary basis prior to the code
authorities having arranged for bipartisan labor boards.
But typically responsibility breeds further responsibility and
in the Retail Code the typical sequence seems to have been
followed.

Significant centrifugal influences made it difficult to keep
control centralized in Washington. It would, under any
circumstances, have been difficult to devise a system which
would have been at once elastic and adequately coordinated
to answer the needs of a country as large as the United
States, but several factors tended to magnify the problem.
We have noted that retailers, not unlike most men and
women, are jealous of their personal and civic rights and
therefore in most cases favor home rule.[1] But the con-
scientous administration of the Code actually required a
certain amount of usurpation of power and accordingly re-
enforced an individual's inner necessity to be important. We
have noted that a substantial amount of bluffing was necessary both in determining whether firms were complying and
in correcting non-compliance. The bluff of official peroga-
tive ranged from the impressive noise of a complaint ad-
juster trying to prevent a respondent from committing future
violations, through official emblems on letterheads [2] to the

---

[1] It should be noted that the store which used methods which many of
its competitors thought improper was often opposed to home rule, or the
" lynch law of competitors ", and in favor of central control.

[2] On December 22, in Bulletin A 3 signed by Lew Hahn, the temporary
chairman, the Code Authority gave instruction concerning insignia: names
of officers and name of local Code Authority could be stated on letterheads. It also said, " No attempt shall be made on such printed matter to

ADMINISTRATIVE MACHINERY

use of the government franking privilege by the New York Code Authority.[3] We have also noted the unavoidable necessity when applying Code clauses to specific cases, for local offices to make judgments concerning which reasonable men might well differ. Thus both the nature of compliance work and the nature of people encouraged separatism.

The personnel problem of NRA lay in collecting a large group of men who had the necessary knowledge, ability and independence effectively to champion the public interest in all the codes.

The nature of the subject matter of the Retail Code, and in fact of most codes, meant that it was necessary to have

indicate that a LRCA is a branch or agency of the NRA of any other department of the Government."

The change in name from "Council" to "Authority" was related to the need for official sound. Whatever the actual cause of the shift, it would seem that most of the trade groups would have shared Grover Whalen's objection to the word "council". It was thought at the New York office that in order to enforce the Code a certain show of officialdom was essential. The necessary quality seemed entirely lacking in "council" and present in "authority". The office, in applying for a certificate of authority requested to be permitted to call itself Retail Code Authority —City of New York. Bulletin A-1 (Order No. 8) issued December 6th by General Johnson changed the name of the National Retail Trade Council to National Retail Code Authority. A similar change was authorized for local bodies and embodied in the Code as an amendment.

[3] Franked envelopes had been used by the Chairman of the Code Authority in his capacity of Compliance Director. The desire to continue to use them was motivated in part by the economy that would result in collecting assessments from the many thousands of retailers, many of whom would require three or four communications. Moreover, the penalty privilege is used for government business; therefore if the Code Authority could be empowered to use the frank they would, by definition, be engaged in official business. There ensued elaborate discussions, in which Mr. Whalen insisted that the sanction of a Code Authority came directly from the Government, and without official backing no compliance could be achieved, whereas NRA, with the exception of General Johnson, and Post Office officials held that no such privilege could be granted. The N. Y. office discontinued using the frank on January 8, 1934.

308   *CONTROLLING RETAILERS*

an intimate and sure knowledge of the practices of the trade
in order to be aware of the implication of actual or suggested
phrasing and to be proof against being told that " it can't
be done ".   In any argument over a phrase, which took place
between two individuals, one of whom had, the other of
whom did not have such knowledge, the former had a distinct
and most important advantage.   But winning a point at a
code authority meeting or in the informal conference preceding the meetings involved not only knowledge but technique.   This is a fact which can not be over emphasized.
Skill in negotiation is a fine art that takes time and experience to master : the human animal is not born with the ability to play off factions against each other, to inject the proper
remarks at the proper time, to know when to press a point
and when to let it ride.   Moreover, only certain men and
women have the natural attributes necessary to the acquisition of the technique : mental ability, judgment, tact, insight.

The nature of the administrative jobs meant that their
proper execution required, in addition to a rather rare combination of abilities, an unusual independence.   Many of the
officials of the Government were men who had come from
trade or industry.   But if officials of the NRA came from
business life, there was considerable probability of their
returning to it.   Governmental positions paid relatively low
salaries, they paid lower salaries than many code authority
jobs,[4] or many business jobs of equal responsibility.[5]   Work

[4] Interesting in this connection is an order issued by General Johnson
(NRA Release No. 3226, Feb. 9, 1934) " No person who has served with
the National Recovery Administration will be permitted to appear before
the Administration in the interest of any trade or industry with which his
former official duties brought him into relationship or to serve on the
Code Authority of such industry ... except as a government member in
an industry in which he has no interest."

[5] The salaries of men occupying important positions were : Divisional
Administrator between $6800 and $8000, a Deputy not over $6800, As-
sistant Deputy not over about $4500.   It is interesting to note that a secre-
tary of a deputy or divisional administrator might receive $2600.

ADMINISTRATIVE MACHINERY   309

for the government, in spite of its lower monetary remuneration might well have been preferred by many individuals for various reasons including a genuine idealism and joy in doing something that seemed worth doing; this idealism seemed to fire a very significant group of NRA employees, particularly in the early days of NRA.[6] But even had men preferred to dedicate the rest of their lives to government service, the uncertain future of NRA made the possibility of having to return to business as a means of livelihood, failing a university position, a probability that needed to be faced. Accordingly, the direct alienation of business interests in defense of the public interest required courage, inward honesty and independence. We have noted in the previous paragraph that it also required knowledge, a specialized skill and high mental ability of a particular kind. A set of attributes of this sort meant that the number of really effective government officials would necessarily have to be counted well at the upper end of a Bell curve. At the same time, as in the case of the specially appointed Retail Trade Authority, people who possessed the necessary attributes were often too busy to attend even the formal meetings of the Code Authority, whereas, in order actually to exert important influence, it would doubtless have been necessary to have been present at many of the informal conferences as well.

But the " Government " in terms of any individual code was Mr. Jones of the Labor Board, Mr. Smith of the Consumers' Board, Assistant Deputy Black, etc. If these men were less free, less knowing, or less skilled in the art of negotiation than their brothers in trade, then to these brothers belonged control. If their job was, either because of

[6] The hours which were kept and the amount of work which was accomplished by some NRA officials during the summer of 1933 and winter of 1934 were astounding. Professor Dameron, in the ten months during which he was working in NRA, put in ninety days, or over three months of overtime.

its subjective or objective characteristics, a nearly impossible
job to perform, then the public interest, their ward, must
suffer. In the Retail Code, in spite of conscientious effort,
the active representatives of advisory boards and government were, it would seem, unable adequately to protect the
labor interest. Much of benefit was accomplished, but the
much was not enough to warrant confidence in the machinery. Interpretation, formal and informal, broke down Code
restrictions on the reduction of wages above the minimum;
moreover, long negotiation failed to develop adequate labor
control over national and local Code administration. Such
representation would have become increasingly important for
adequate Code enforcement as well as for proper Code interpretation had the life of NRA been prolonged and a change
in popular sentiment made members of the Code Authority
less interested in enforcing the letter of the law.

SECTION II.   THE CODE AUTHORITY AS GUARDIAN OF THE
PUBLIC INTEREST

But the control over the Code administration which was
gained by the Code Authority could well have been entirely
consistent with the public interest: The members of the
Authority were able men; they gave a great deal of time and
conscientious effort to their jobs; the office staff was able
and hard working.

The difficulty lay in the nature of the job, given the nature
of man. Adequate performance of all the aspects of the
administration of the Retail Code by members of the Code
Authority would have meant a disregard for self-interest
which ran counter to all the training that American society
imposes on an individual. Each member of the Authority
was caught in a paradox that only a magician's wand could
dissolve. In the first place, the members were either individual retailers occupying high offices in their companies or

ADMINISTRATIVE MACHINERY   311

officials of retail trade associations. In the second place, they were representatives appointed by trade associations to a representative assembly. In the third place, they were representatives of the trade as a whole as opposed to labor or customer or resource. In the fourth place, they were members of a governing body charged with the administration of a law designed to achieve the well being of labor, consumer and retailer. Moreover, this bewildering fourheaded monster had three functions—he was executive, legislator, and judge. There was little wonder that members of the Authority had considerable difficulty in deciding which head was speaking at any given time.[7]

The multiheadedness of the Code Authority members became important when the animal disagreed within itself. The incidence of this conflict of interest between I, the President of Blank Company; I, the Trade Association member; I, the Retailer; and I, the citizen, depended on the particular subject or circumstances under consideration. The adequacy of the Code Authority as a piece of Government mechanics depended, therefore, on the subject before the meeting.

When the subject under debate was one in which the interests of individual retailers conflicted, the round table afforded a very adequate method of reaching a reconciliation or at least, a decision.

Also when the issue under discussion involved a conflict between trade associations, the representative assembly was perfectly adequate. It meted out justice in the manner of

[7] The struggle would assume the most amusing and confused form in the New York Code Authority. A decision would be reached. Then someone would say, " But speaking as a Code Authority, I don't think we ought to say that." The voice of the Code Authority might then boom for awhile. Or else it might be decided to let the opinion issue from store offices rather than from the Authority. The variations of this theme were infinite.

312   CONTROLLING RETAILERS

a representative assembly—on the thoroughly unrealistic
assumption that the just and right cause, rather than the
most skillfully argued cause, would win. The trading, bargaining, badgering, and maneuvering brought forth an
answer which, if not a good answer, was a democratic answer
and would pass.[8]

But difficulty might arise when the subject before the
assembly was one on which the Authority spoke for the
trade. Here the question of adequacy of representation entered. It was clear that small retailers whose interests in
many matters were substantially different from those of the
chain, mail order houses and large stores, were noticeably
absent from the council.[9] The absence of any association
of wide enough membership to constitute a genuine voice
of the trade, together with the increased need for retailers

[8] Obviously the jockeying for power by different trade associations
representing somewhat divergent groups and interests was marked. The
appointment of Mr. Peterson of the Hardware Association, and Mr.
Young of the NRDGA as joint directors of the Code Authority represented an initial attempt to trade off conflicting interests of different
groups. The process was almost bound to continue in the National and
most of the local code Authorities, although it often took a subtler form.
When a group of men meet, questions of skill in negotiation are often
more important than a forthright trial of strength. In the National Code
Authority certain of the members became the most important individuals
in the group because of their superior penetration into the significance of
what was transpiring and their ability to shape and lead discussion. In
the New York Code Authority this ability was exercised by certain of
the members with a smooth and conservative precision that was a joy
to watch.

[9] The officials of the Retail Hardware Dealers Association on the Code
Authority might, in representing trade association interest, be said to
urge the cause of small retailers. The National Shoe Retailers Association was also composed of independents rather than chain stores. But
all associations had some small members. It was only when the controlling body of merchants in the association were small and the individual representative on the authority was not himself a large retailer that
the small merchant in that branch of trade could, for the purpose of the
present discussion, be said to be adequately represented.

to present a unified front on several subjects, created pressure
for representatives of the Code Authority to appear on behalf of retailers. The matter was put to a vote in an Authority meeting and favorably reported in connection with the
question of sending a representative of NRCA to express the
opinion of retailers at the NRA price fixing hearing. The
problem is perhaps best illustrated in a proposed amendment
to Article X, Section 2, of the Retail Code which was passed
by the Authority and ordered submitted to the signatory
trade associations: (The words added to the original section
are in italics) " That the NRCA, Incorporated, may from
time to time present to the Administrator *objections* or
recommendations (including interpretations) based on conditions in the trade, which *will promote the interests of the
Retail Trade* or tend to effectuate the operation of the provisions of this Code and the policy of the National Recovery
Act." [10]

When the problem before the meeting involved the interests of labor and to a lesser extent the consumer, the absurd-
ity of the Code Authority as a governmental form grew
blatant. Here were nine Code Authority members—for the
most part employers of labor—sitting as an impartial judicial
body on interpretations of labor clauses under which they
operated their own businesses. As watch-dog at their meetings was a young man whose function was to defend the
interests of labor; he formed judgments according to his
humanly fallible opinion; he defended them as best he could,
having for his chief bargaining instrument a nuisance value.
The Administration members and representatives of the
Advisory Boards could also debate for the public interest.
They had no vote. As a matter of workaday and reliable
motives, it would seem that to *count* on altruism from
members of the Code Authority was a rank injustice

[10] NRCA meeting, December 12, 1934, Minutes.

314   CONTROLLING RETAILERS

to the intelligence of the group. Their adequacy as a governing body would accordingly depend upon the extent of the conflict between the public interest and that of the members of the Authority, and on the nature and strength of the motives that influenced their behavior.

Code Authority members had to conform to the *clear* tenets of the Code. They ran retail businesses which are curiously vulnerable to public opinion. To be a member of the Code Authority and to pay employees less than the minimum wage or work them longer than maximum hours would "look bad". It might, if found out, actually alienate customers. Thus, in enforcing the Code, the members of an Authority were, in a sense, seeing that their competitors did what they themselves were obliged to do. Besides, if they did not do what seemed to be a fairly good enforcement job, the Compliance Division might cease to refer complaints to the Authorities, which would weaken their position with NRA.

From the point of view of self-interest then, the code authorities could be expected to perform the executive aspect of their work with reasonable efficiency. In other words— if a definite and adequate plan of procedure had been laid out, it seems likely that it would have been followed by the code authorities, although this might have ceased to be true had NRA continued and codes become increasingly less popular. Moreover this does not mean that code authorities would generally have taken the initiative in planning aggressive enforcement. A certain essential lack of sympathy of the employer for the point of view of the employee, as well as a group solidarity among employers—the feeling that attached the word "snitch" to reporting a labor violation of a competitor—would in many cases, particularly in the smaller communities, have prevented over-playing the role of compliance officer. But it would seem that had expectancies been clearly defined they would have been met. The inadequacies in enforcement were due primarily to the essential difficulty of the problems, to lack of any adequate plan for enforcement work, and to the innate fear of employees of bringing their troubles to a tribunal of employers. This last was probably particularly marked in small towns.

It was when expectancy and meaning were not clear that social sanctions no longer required action identical with group interest. The inadequacy of the code administrative form increased in inverse relation to the clarity of the law —it increased as functions grew interpretive and judicial as opposed to executive. It was when retailers were, within margins, writing their own laws, after the fervor of the early days of Code writing had cooled, that the inadequacy of the Code Authority as a social tribunal sharpens. Moreover if the National Code Authority bent the law to its advantage, meeting as it did in Washington under the hard gaze of ardent young eyes, how much more obviously unable to function as administrators of social law would the local code authorities have been.

This inability is illustrated by the answers to a questionnaire that was sent out by the National Code Authority to the local authorities asking for suggestions for Code modification. The covering letter stated: " What is sought is your earnest judgment on the provision of the Retail Code as a reflection of your experience in its administration ". " This questionnaire is submitted not to your merchant members as individual retailers, but as official representatives of their trades on your LRCA." [11] The questionnaire mentioned a specific section of the Code and asked: " What difficulties have you experienced in the administration of this provision? " [12] There were 353 comments in response to

[11] Letter, November 7, 1934, " To All Local Code Authorities ".

[12] The following groupings are made on the basis of summaries of the

316   CONTROLLING RETAILERS

the questions on labor clauses. Fifty-four of these comments appeared to deal with difficulties in administration
from the point of view of a code authority trying to enforce them; twelve of the comments urged difficulties which
pleaded inconvenience or hardship for labor. (Ten of these
claimed that minimum wages were too low.) The other
287 referred to management problems in stores.

The questionnaire also asked: " As a result of your experience, what modification and changes do you suggest "?
There were 566 answers to this question. Seventeen of
these answers suggested changes for the purpose of facilitating administration; eleven proposed changes that might be
said to advocate modification in favor of labor. (Ten of
the eleven claimed that minimum wages should be raised,
in five cases to correspond to state laws.) The other 538
suggestions aimed to make the Code less burdensome for
store management.[18]

The incidence of the many cross pressures that have been
outlined may perhaps best be tested by the final result—the
effect of the Code on retailers, employees, consumers and
resources. In the next part of this study we will accordingly attempt to picture the changes in established practice
which occurred contemporaneously with the Code and to
evaluate the causal relationships that seem to have existed.

answers made at the office of the National Retail Code Authority. It is
possible that the grouping would have been slightly different had the
original questionnaires rather than the summaries been used; it seems
most unlikely, however, that the changes would have been very extensive.

[18] Twenty-eight answers to the first question suggested that limitation
of hours of work caused hardship for trainees; forty-three answers to the
second question suggested that trainees be permitted to work longer hours.
The reader may feel that these answers should be classifid as advocating
a change advantageous to labor.

[21]

Excerpt from Paul N. Bloom and Stephen A. Greyser, *Exploring the Future of Consumerism*, 25–8.

The Co-ops

These organizations (whether legally organized as a co-op or not) serve the interests of consumers by providing mechanisms through which people can pool their resources to obtain better information and/or better buys than they could obtain on their own. Some of these organizations are national, such as Consumers Union, the publishers of Consumer Reports. A national buying service (albeit a for-profit one) is also growing rapidly in the form of Compucard. However, co-op retail organizations are mostly local, such as Chicago's Hyde Park Cooperative, the Harvard Coop in Cambridge, and the Greenbelt Cooperative in Maryland. They manifest themselves as department stores, grocery stores, auto-repair clubs, credit unions, and neighborhood day-care centers and babysitting networks. The growth of local co-ops (especially food co-ops where some members volunteer working time) has been spurred by inflation, as more people have become willing to trade their own time for lower prices and better services.

These organizations range from the conservative to the radical: some promote cooperative activity as a way to inject increased competition into a market while others promote it as a vehicle for circumventing or challenging the power of big business. In general, the "Co-ops" seem to be doing reasonably well in selling their services. One recent report estimates that one in three Americans belong to a cooperative of some type (Cooperative League of the USA, 1979). Table 11 contains data on how the growth of cooperatives has progressed over the last decade. In addition, the 1980 opening of the National Consumer Cooperative Bank -- a quasi-government institution that can receive up to $300 million in Federal monies over the next five years -- gives the "Co-ops" a resource base they can draw upon to expand their "market share."

The Corporates

The large number of corporate consumer affairs offices established during the last decade were set up to have people working within corporations on behalf of consumers. Many were established to provide a form of internal self-regulation that might eliminate the need for proposed regulatory changes. The offices were theoretically supposed to resolve consumer complaints, conduct consumer education efforts, and serve as advisors to top management in making decisions about product safety features, advertising claims, and so forth.

Although consumer affairs offices in companies such as Giant Foods and J.C. Penney have apparently had considerable influence on the policies and actions of

Table 11

Number and Size of Cooperative Organizations
(1973 and 1979)

	1973	1979
Consumer Goods*		
Number	150	920
Membership	544,800 families	1,000,000 families
Dollar Volume	$457,520,000	$750,000,000
Credit Unions		
Number	23,469	22,272
Membership	28,500,000	39,600,000
Dollar Volume (savings)	$24.6 billion	$53 billion
Dollar Volume (loans outstanding)	$12 Billion	$51.8 billion

---

* Includes grocery stores, furniture stores, pharmacies, service stations, and hardware stores.

Source: Cooperative League of the USA (1973, 1979).

their companies, several recent research studies suggest that most of these offices are working on behalf of their companies first and on behalf of consumers second (Fornell, 1976; Hise, Gillett, and Kelly, 1978). This is, of course, the central issue surrounding the purpose and positioning of the consumer affairs function in business: To what extent is the aim to represent the company's interests to the consumer? . . . Or to represent the consumer's interests to the company? The possibility of conflict between these two aims is high.

Whatever their formal mission, many consumer affairs personnel tend to see themselves as not having much influence over corporate policies, but instead see themselves as responsible for keeping their companies out of trouble through their complaint-handling and education activities. As the results displayed in Table 12 suggest, only a minority see themselves as having much influence over product design, advertising, or distribution decisions (Hise, Gillett, and Kelly, 1978). In a sense, business consumer affairs offices have been having problems selling consumer representation to corporate executives, particularly during an era of few new regulatory initiatives. They have, however, been reasonably successful at selling redress assistance and consumer education to the general public. For instance, a recent Conference Board study found that the use of corporate complaint-handling services has increased markedly in the last few years (McGuire, 1980). Although this could also be a sign that consumers have become more dissatisfied with products and services, we think it is more likely that improved complaint-handling processes both have made it easier for complaints to be voiced and have, to some extent, elevated consumers' expectations about the likely success of their own complaining efforts.

Table 12

Level of Influence Indicated by Chief Consumer Affairs Officers for 18 Decision Areas

Decision area	Individuals Indicating Decision Area Is Applicable to Consumer Affairs Department		Individuals from Total Sample Indicating Decision Area Is Not Applicable to Consumer Affairs Department	
	Number and percentage indicating much influence	Number and percentage indicating little or no influence	Number	Percentage
Handling consumer inquiries	140 (93.3)	10 (6.7)	3	2.0
Processing consumer complaints	125 (86.8)	19 (13.2)	6	4.0
Consumer education programs	108 (79.4)	28 (20.6)	13	8.7
Researching consumer satisfaction	107 (74.3)	37 (25.7)	4	2.7
Developing consumer orientation among executives	103 (72.5)	39 (27.5)	7	4.7
Improving employee attitudes toward consumers	104 (72.2)	40 (27.8)	4	2.7
Public relations programs	90 (65.7)	47 (34.3)	10	6.8
Product safety	46 (51.1)	44 (48.9)	56	38.3
Developing consumer orientation among dealers and distributors	39 (46.4)	45 (53.6)	60	41.6
Developing warranties and guarantees	34 (44.2)	43 (55.8)	70	47.7
Advertisement	60 (43.5)	78 (56.5)	11	7.4
Packaging and labeling	39 (40.2)	58 (59.8)	54	35.8
Quality control	39 (38.2)	63 (61.8)	42	29.1
Training service personnel	33 (31.4)	72 (68.6)	44	29.5
Establishing industry standards	27 (23.8)	86 (76.2)	35	23.6
Product design	22 (22.9)	74 (77.1)	50	33.8
Training sales personnel	22 (22.0)	78 (78.0)	47	31.8
Selecting suppliers	16 (17.8)	74 (82.2)	60	39.9

Source: Hise, Gillett, and Kelly (1978).

References

Cooperative League of the USA, *Co-op USA: Facts and Figures* (Washington, D. C.: Cooperative League of the USA, 1973, 1979).

Fornell, Claes, *Consumer Input for Marketing Decisions: A Study of Corporate Departments for Consumer Affairs* (New York: Praeger Publishers, 1976).

Hise, Richard T., Peter L. Gillett and J. Patrick Kelly, 'The Corporate Consumer Affairs Effort', *MSU Business Topics*, 26 (Summer 1978) pp. 17–26.

McGuire, E. Patrick, 'Consumerism Lives! ... and Grows', *Across the Board*, 17 (January 1980), pp. 57–62.

[22]

Excerpt from *Encyclopaedia of the Social Sciences*, 4, 285–91.

CONSUMERS' COOPERATION. Consumers' cooperatives are to be distinguished from consumers' leagues or other public or semi-public organizations which seek to protect consumers' rights in the course of their dealings with producers or purveyors of consumption goods. Consumers' cooperatives are actual economic enterprises in the form of stores or shops, set up by associations of consumers to distribute fundamental consumption goods, usually staple food items, but also at times clothing, furniture and the like. In the process of expansion a group of stores may set up a wholesale distributive and may even establish its own factories and farms for the production of these goods. Or consumers' cooperatives may furnish other consumption needs, such as housing, insurance against risk, provision of gas, light, transportation. In order to set up these enterprises it is necessary to acquire capital and to found a joint stock society.

These economic enterprises differ, however, from ordinary joint stock companies not only in their aims but in their actual economic and legal characteristics. In the first place, they are not restricted as to the number of members and the number of shares but are open to anyone who wishes to join, and the last comers, moreover, are on an equal footing with the first. From this initial rule necessarily follows the corollary that the value of the shares at no time can be higher than their price at issuance and that speculation on rising values is therefore impossible. This constitution, practically impossible in an association for production purposes because of limitations both of capital and of demand, is advantageous in an association of consumers in which each new arrival brings with him his consumption capacity.

In the second place, capital as such does not play the same role or have the same rights in government or profits as in ordinary joint stock enterprises. In the consumers' cooperatives every member has an equal vote in the assemblies regardless of the number of shares he may possess. The profits of the enterprise are divided pro rata for purchases and not for shares, so that it might be said that profits are returned to those who originally paid them. In fact, in describing the return French cooperative enterprises prefer the term *ristourne*, or *trop-perçu*, to the English cooperative term dividend with its profit making connotations. Thus it might well be asserted that these returns to purchasers are not a form of profit but rather the negation of profit. Cooperatives have protested against a tax on alleged profits which they claim are non-existent because the surplus redistributed to members was based on overpayment arising from the practise of marking goods at current competitive prices.

As a result of these rules capital, whether obtained in the form of loans or of shares, is restricted to a mere return based on the cost of obtaining it or as limited remuneration for its share in the services rendered and is no longer the dominant factor in the government of the enterprise or in the distribution of profits. Within this voluntary association therefore capital and profit in their ordinary forms are virtually abolished by pacific legitimate means, without any imposition of exterior restraint or any change in the basis of the social and economic order as to property, inheritance, interest, salary or even competition. There is nothing in the nature of the association to prevent its spread by the formation of similar voluntary associations and by federation throughout the nation or even on an international scale.

These economic and legal limitations on the role of capital and profits are supplemented by certain further ethical limitations self-imposed by the majority of consumers' societies. These include the provision that not all profits are to be returned to the individual members but that a portion is to be devoted to enterprises for collective welfare, such as the propagation of cooperative ideals and the provision of educational and recreational facilities for workers.

The special characteristics of consumers' cooperative enterprises require special legislation, for they do not easily conform to common law concepts. Thus there are special laws on consumers' cooperatives in most countries today, including countries such as Mexico and Argentina where the movement is still in its infancy.

Consumers' cooperatives, which now include over 40,000,000 members in about 60,000 societies in thirty or more countries, began in 1844 with the association of twenty-eight English weavers in Rochdale near Manchester. As early as 1827, however, consumers' societies had existed and had even developed sufficient strength to establish a wholesale; one or two societies still in existence antedate the experiment of the "Equitable Pioneers of Rochdale." Nor did the theory of cooperation arise with the Rochdale weavers. They were in fact somewhat under the influence of Robert Owen, whose use of the term cooperation made it synonymous with communism but who is often credited with the paternity of the movement because he coined the term and said: "You must become your own merchants and your own manufacturers . . . to be able to supply yourselves with goods of the best quality and at the lowest price." Both in Owen's plans and experiments for communistic settlements and in those of the French socialist Fourier in his *Traité de l'association domestique agricole* (2 vols., Paris 1822) social transformation into these forms of society was to come about through outside intervention of philanthropists. But the Rochdale Pioneers began to express this social transformation through the voluntary and independent association of groups from the very midst of the masses and thereby gave it its voluntaristic and democratic form. It was one of their members, Charles Howarth, who devised the method of disposing of surpluses which is described above, and which proved to be the indispensable practical as well as ideological tool for the accumulation of membership, capital and patronage. Prior to that time profits had been distributed to shareholders (a practise which encouraged the limitation of membership), equally divided among all members without regard to their patronage of the enterprise or else buried in

an inalienable reserve fund. The essential characteristics of all consumers' cooperatives, including the sale of goods at current prices and for cash and the device of voting by membership instead of by shares, were also inaugurated by the Rochdale weavers. Although in several countries individual consumers' enterprises mainly under the influence of Fourierist disciples had been experimented with before the Rochdale enterprise, the history of consumers' cooperation throughout Europe is mainly one of the founding of societies patterned on the Rochdale practises. It is true that the Rochdale Pioneers in their original statement of aims included the emancipation of the workers from their employers through self-employment and even the founding of cooperative communities. But they themselves never carried these principles into practise, and in England it remained for a group under the moral leadership of the early Christian Socialists to attempt the fulfilment of this aim.

The development of consumers' cooperation has proceeded instead along the assumption, not clearly articulated at the outset, that production was not an end in itself but must be a response to consumption needs of society. This is illustrated in the development of consumers' societies within a country or community. Small consumers' societies commonly begin with, and often limit themselves to, the provision of simple uniform daily needs which requires neither large capital nor special technical equipment. Groceries and bakeries are usually the first types of store to be established. Somewhat later, as in the case of large English cooperatives, they extend their scope to include haberdashery, clothing, furniture and the like. Usually housing or insurance societies take the form of separate organizations. When the societies have reached the second state of development, that of a regional union among themselves, they set up a wholesale society. In the course of time these wholesales have themselves entered upon the field of production, both because the consumers' cooperatives wish to procure the articles as close to the source of production as possible in order to reduce costs and because they have found themselves at times in conflict with capitalistic production—as when a large soap concern in England objected to the dividend as a price cutting scheme and when, on the other hand, the cooperative movement joined with other socially minded organizations in a protest against the treatment of labor on native planta-

Consumers' Cooperation

tions. Thus the wholesale societies of Manchester, Glasgow, Hamburg and Stockholm and the Centrosoyus of Moscow have established large industrial plants which at times have been able to defeat capitalist trusts.

With the entry of the consumers' cooperative into the fields of production and distribution there arose the question of its relations to the labor employed by society. In England and Germany, for instance, while a large proportion of the membership of the consumers' societies is drawn from the laboring classes, the workers employed by the cooperatives regard them as employers. These workers have of course the opportunity, of which they usually avail themselves, of joining constituent societies and thereby benefiting as consumers from the operations of the cooperatives. In fact, such students of the cooperative movement as Beatrice Webb see in the consumers' cooperative movement a new social organization which would supplement the trade union movement by organizing the workers as consumers. This has generally been the attitude of the trade union leaders and the basis of their support in most countries of the cooperative movement. On the other hand, the cooperative societies have in most cases been willing to recognize and deal with their workers as an organized group and in some cases have been of great aid to the trade union movement. In Germany standard agreements with the unions have been worked out with reciprocal obligations on both sides. This has checked the tendency of the specific trade unions involved to ask for standards above those which they set in their agreements with ordinary commercial and industrial enterprises. A highly praised expedient for dealing with this problem is that employed by the Scottish wholesale of making workers eligible to membership not only in the constituent societies but in the national federation itself, in which they are granted voting power in proportion to the total membership. A suggestion has been made of permitting representation of the employees either upon the board of management or upon the advisory board of the wholesale society.

Moreover, the English societies in particular found themselves in competition not only with capitalistic trusts but with workers' producing cooperatives, which in many cases they finally absorbed. When the field of production is agriculture, new conflicts arise with agricultural cooperators, who are a far more powerful group than the workers' producing cooperatives ever

were. In Scandinavian countries and elsewhere, where on the whole agriculture and industry are equally important, central clearing houses functioning between the various types of organizations have been set up with varying degrees of success. The wholesale cooperative of so industrialized a country as England has entered into cooperative agreements with the central clearing houses of other countries, but it has come into conflict with the agricultural cooperative movement within the empire, especially in Ireland. The problem is by no means resolved and is a matter of great concern for the cooperative movement.

Conflict with other types of cooperatives either in practise or in ideology arises also in the second state of development of the cooperatives, when individual scattered local societies form into a national organization. The tendency at first is to unite all types of cooperatives in one federation, but inevitably conflict has arisen which has led to the establishment of separate types of nationals. Similar conflict arose in the third stage of development, when national federations formed in 1895 the International Cooperative Alliance. Although it is nominally an alliance of all types of cooperation, conflicts have resulted in the withdrawal of many agricultural and credit societies and in the refusal to admit that type of profit sharing enterprise known as copartnerships, until now more than three fifths of its membership are affiliated with consumers' cooperatives.

These three stages of development—the formation of local consumers' societies (which in most countries of Europe began about 1865), then the formation of national associations about a decade later and finally the affiliation with an international organization—have not been undergone by the cooperative movement in all countries, for development has not been equal in all countries. In France and to some extent in Switzerland large numbers of individual societies are not affiliated with the national federation, and the consumers' society membership of the International Cooperative Alliance includes only 33,000,000 out of 40,000,000 in all countries. Cooperation is far more active in the north than in the south. Thus in the north are the three great countries of cooperation—Russia, Great Britain, Germany— and the two smaller countries which are from the point of view of intensity and quality of the movement of great significance—Denmark and Finland. In Belgium, Switzerland, Czecho-

288   Encyclopaedia of the Social Sciences

slovakia, Austria, Hungary and Poland the movement also flourishes. But in Italy, Spain, Rumania, Portugal and even in the southern half of France itself consumers' cooperation is poorly developed. In some of these countries, however, agricultural and credit cooperative movements are more flourishing.

More specifically, the development of cooperative movements and of their particular types is bound up with the stage of development of general economic and social forces. In countries but poorly developed except in agriculture and there suffering from certain defects of primitive organization it is only natural to find credit and agricultural and not consumers' societies. Moreover, consumer's cooperatives flourish best in societies of large membership— in London they reach numbers of 100,000 or even 300,000—whereas other cooperative forms can be founded among small groups. Since the interest of the consumer is far less apparent than that of the producer and since he is usually passive in his role, the consumer's cooperative is more difficult to develop.

The success of the consumers' cooperatives within a country can be judged by membership figures, by the proportion of the total population which this membership includes, by the total extent of its sales, by the average sales per member and by the proportion of the member's income which is spent in his cooperative store.

Russia with a membership of over 15,000,000 in consumers' cooperatives accounts for almost half of the total consumers' membership of the International Cooperative Alliance; Great Britain follows with a membership of 5,600,000, almost a sixth of the total membership; Germany and France follow with about 4,000,000 and 2,500,000 respectively. But the movement in some of the smaller countries, such as Switzerland and Hungary, represents as high a proportion of the total population as in Great Britain and a great deal higher than in France. There is a similar variation in the proportionate purchases per member. In Great Britain, Hungary, Russia and Switzerland, for instance, the membership of consumers' cooperatives represents one tenth of the total population, and since this usually includes only one member of a household of four or five persons it is apt actually to represent almost half of the population. In the community of Basel practically the entire population belongs to cooperatives.

Another test of the strength of the movement is in the degree to which it has pervaded the lives of its membership. This is shown not only in the extent of membership or of sales but in the development of education along cooperative lines, in the development of the cooperative press and of educational courses within the movement itself and in the introduction of courses on cooperation in the schools and universities of the country; in the establishment of "people's houses" as in Belgium, in the extent to which the women and children have been drawn into the movement and in the democratic participation of its entire membership. It is true of course that, as the movement gains in numbers and geographic extent, the last named activity becomes a problem. This is closely linked, however, with the development of an able leadership both for the technical administration of the business of the cooperatives and for its educational work.

Broadly speaking, the consumers' cooperative movement has certain fundamental rules, evolved by the weavers of Rochdale, which are everywhere observed. They are: absolute equality in elections—one man, one vote; the return of profits to the buyer pro rata for purchases after the deduction of a specified levy for collective works of education, recreation and solidarity; and sale at current price for cash.

In addition to these basic principles there have appeared attempts to give the movement a broad theoretical and ideological basis. Theorists have not been in complete agreement—a natural situation when the origins of the separate movements and the variations in nationality, social background, political affiliation and even economic grouping of the membership are considered. Internationally the movement is politically neutral. In certain countries and communities, however, it is socialistic or socialistically inclined. Thus the Belgian cooperative movement was begun by socialists and although not restricted to them in membership still maintains its socialist character; in Russia the movement is of course communistic. In certain countries separate socialist federations have been formed, and almost everywhere there exist socialist minorities.

Diversity of opinion within the movement itself in the determination as to what attitude it should take toward other forms of cooperative endeavor, toward socialism, trade unionism, profit, the capitalistic order and the state has accelerated the formulation of a theory. In England the work of Beatrice Potter (Mrs. Sidney Webb) in her *The Cooperative Movement*

Consumers' Cooperation

(London 1891) was epoch making. In Germany, under fire from the socialists on the one hand and the marketing and credit cooperatives on the other, the leaders of the consumers' societies were slow in evolving an ideology. Earlier than any of these attempts, however, was that begun in 1886 by the group which came to be known as L'École de Nîmes and which has most emphatically stated the doctrine of cooperation.

This group sees economic government passing from the hands of the producers and capitalists to the hands of the consumers, whose ranks include all classes. This placing of the consumer in the first rank was a new idea, for previously he had been accorded the most negligible of roles in theory and practise. The English cooperatives, for instance, even today carry not the name of consumers' societies but rather that of distributive societies. This point of view means to consumers' cooperatives the loss of a specific working class character. It does not, however, imply any desire to ignore the essential working class origins of the movement in most countries or even its general socialistic and radical leanings, especially as exemplified by the Belgian socialist cooperatives and political and economic alliances between the English cooperatives, the trade unions and the Labour party. It refuses to accept the Marxist statement that labor is the sole creator of wealth and declares that it is consumption, or need, which creates value. With equal force cooperation refuses to capital the right to control production and to draw profit, and it has thus encountered the opposition of the middlemen and manufacturing capitalists. Where the state is markedly capitalistic it too has reflected the opposition to consumers' cooperation.

The socialists on their side have had a rather varied and complicated attitude toward cooperation. At the beginning of the cooperative movement in the middle of the last century they were very sympathetic to the idea, especially to producers' cooperation, since it was a specific proposal of such socialists as Owen, Fourier, Louis Blanc, Lassalle, Mazzini. The failure of this type of cooperation and the formulation of Marxism caused a rejection of all cooperation on the grounds that it was a purely reformist and bourgeois program. Nevertheless, in actual practise such examples as the reciprocal role of cooperation and socialism in Belgium, the actual assistance rendered by consumers' cooperatives in many countries during periods of industrial struggle and a recognition of their general importance have led to a revision of the socialists' attitude. They recognize cooperation, however, only as an annex of socialism for the purpose of furnishing them with resources at times of strikes and political elections. Thus the cooperative, the trade union and the party are all three yoked to the socialist chariot and must be proletarian in character. If the cooperative remains neutral it is more of a hindrance than a help, for then it will be more serviceable to the petty bourgeoisie than to the workers or might even transform the proletarians into small capitalists greedy for bonuses and completely uninterested in all revolutionary action. Nor do the socialists accept the thesis of L'École de Nîmes that the control of the economic world should belong to the consumers; they naturally claim it for labor.

The claim of the French school has also been criticized by economists, especially those of the "liberal" school. Part of their criticism of cooperation centers about the relation of the movement to the state. The "liberal" economists of course profess a strong antipathy to the intervention of the state in the economic order, and thus they object to the existence in some countries of favorable legislation, subventions, exemptions from taxes and other privileges which are accorded to cooperative societies. It is necessary to point out that on the whole these privileges have been more frequently accorded to agricultural societies, credit or marketing or producing societies, than to consumers' organizations. In some countries the consumers' movement has been initiated with state aid, although in others municipalities and other public bodies have expressed hostility by forbidding their employees to be members of consumers' cooperatives. The cooperative movement has carried on an effort, sometimes against great odds, for legislation recognizing its peculiar status; and its sponsors cannot be classed with those advocates of voluntary mutual aid who will not recognize any right of legislation on the part of the state. In certain countries, as in Russia, and in such communities as the city of Basel where practically the entire population belongs to the cooperatives, the state can with justice be considered merely as the political expression of the economic unity. On the part of the state itself there has been a tendency to enter the field of consumers' cooperation, which is best illustrated perhaps by the cooperative public boards developed in Belgium and to some extent in Italy and Austria. These consist of cooperative

Encyclopaedia of the Social Sciences

organizations set up by national, provincial or municipal government bodies for the purpose of providing gas, light, water, transportation, credit and housing for these communities. The dividends of these operations are divided according to consumption use. They are an example not of "stateizing" the cooperatives but of placing certain functions of public administration on a cooperative basis. In this identification, however, there is no retreat from the cooperative ideal of opposition to constraint. It was the element of constraint which led the International Cooperative Alliance between 1917 and 1921 to refuse to admit the Russian cooperatives because of their obligatory character, and it is for the same reason that the alliance still refuses to accept the Fascist cooperatives. The relation of the cooperative movement to the state during the period of the World War was of a similar character. In every country the cooperative movement rendered so great a service in the supply of food and other necessities to the population as to merit governmental approval. The International Cooperative Alliance, however, at all times held fast to its ideal of peace between the nations as embodied in its endorsement of such pacifist measures as disarmament, arbitration, commercial union and the removal of tariff barriers; and during the war it was one of the few international bodies which maintained relations between warring countries.

Within the field of economic endeavor itself the criticism of the "liberal" economists has centered on the claim that consumers' cooperation introduces a new element into economic theory and practise. A few of their number have chosen to see in the attempt of the cooperatives to formulate standards as to a "just price" and a "just measure" interference with the salutary effects of competition as it operates in supply and demand under a regime of self-interest. Others, however, look upon the fact that consumers' cooperatives base their prices on current "fair" prices, as established by ordinary competition, as proof that they too are governed by supply and demand and that the dividends, so called, are in reality a form of profit.

On the whole, however, the economists have not condemned cooperation, since in the last analysis it is a form of free association. They are willing to admit that it is of considerable service: to the consumer in serving as a check on the extortion of merchants and in reestablishing the desired effect of competition, which so far as the consumer is concerned is threatened today by the coalition of producers; and to the worker in permitting him to utilize most advantageously the purchasing power of his wages and even by the redistribution of bonuses to realize savings which may permit him to acquire property.

This limited concept of cooperation, particularly as formulated in the second half of the last century by Paul Leroy-Beaulieu, Léon Say and M. Pantaleoni and reaffirmed more recently by Robert Liefmann in his article "Monopolies and the Interests of the Consumers" (in *Review of International Cooperation*, vol. xxii, 1929, p. 201–10), has been accepted by some groups of cooperators and is held in high repute by the leaders of Fascist cooperation. The French school realizes that this program in itself allows a vast field of action, but it reaffirms its belief in the capacity of the consumers' cooperative to go beyond these limits. In the economists' criticism is implied a denial of the assumption that an economic order based on a recognition of the needs of the consumer can replace one in which production operates through the motive of individual self-interest expressed in the form of profits. L'École de Nîmes does not postulate its assumption on the abolition of personal interest or the hedonistic principle, but it insists that mutual help is more efficient than self-help and points to the existence of the widespread consumers' movement as proof of the fact that enterprises can live and prosper without the profit motive as it exists in commercial enterprises. This is all the more remarkable because even by definition consumers' cooperation, in contrast to producers' organizations, is an association of non-professionals. Nevertheless, they have developed technical and administrative ability of a high order, and the questions of sharing profits or even of paying high salaries to management, although they have occasionally come up for discussion, have never had to receive serious consideration. As Alfred Marshall pointed out in a presidential address to the Cooperative Congress in 1889, this is probably because cooperation is "at once a strong and calm and wise business, and a strong and fervent and proselytizing faith." It is, in other words, an economic enterprise not wholly in the service of Mammon.

CHARLES GIDE

See: COOPERATION; COOPERATIVE PUBLIC BOARDS; CONSUMER PROTECTION; HOUSING; FOOD INDUSTRIES; RETAIL TRADE; MIDDLEMAN; COST OF LIVING; PRICE REGULATION.

Consult: Webb, Sidney and Beatrice, *The Consumers'*

Consumers' Cooperation — Consumers' Leagues   291

Cooperative Movement (London 1921); Totomianz, V. F., *Theorie, Geschichte und Praxis der Konsumentenorganisation* (2nd ed. Berlin 1923); Gide, Charles, *Les sociétés coopératives de consommation* (2nd ed. Paris 1910), English translation (London 1921); Staudinger, Franz, *Die Konsumgenossenschaft* (2nd ed. Leipsic 1919); Wilbrandt, Robert, *Konsum-Genossenschaften* (Stuttgart 1922); Poisson, Ernest, *La république coopérative* (Paris 1921), tr. by W. P. Watkins (London 1925); Warbasse, J. P., *Cooperative Democracy through Voluntary Association of the People as Consumers* (2nd ed. New York 1927); Göhring, Friedrich, *Zur Theorie der Konsumgenossenschaften* (Ulm 1921); Sonnichsen, Albert, *Consumers' Cooperation* (New York 1919); Harris, Emerson P., *Cooperation, the Hope of the Consumer* (New York 1918). See also bibliography for COOPERATION.

B
Government Support and Control

[23]

Mandell, Lewis, *The Credit Card Industry: A History,* Boston: Twayne Publishers, 1990, 176 pp., $26.95 (cloth), $12.95 (paper).

The Credit Card Industry: A History is a concise, comprehensive, and chronological overview of the birth and development of the credit card. The selected bibliography is appended but source citations have been abandoned in order to provide a flow that makes this book a quick read for the business person, teacher, student, or consumer interested in obtaining a general understanding of the credit card industry from its inception to the technological advances that may soon make the over 1.25 billion cards in circulation obsolete.

The introduction of Express Travelers Checks in 1890, retailer-issued credit cards in 1914, charge-plates in 1928 and 1948, Wanamakers' revolving credit in the late 1930s and Standard Oil cards in 1939, led to the birth and development of the Diners Club Card in 1949. The growth of this powerful marketing tool is discussed as the competition among banks, oil companies, retailers, and third party organizations evolved over 50 years.

The earliest historical mention of credit is found in "The Code of Hammurabi" written about 1750 B.C. in Babylonia (chapter 2) followed by the Old Testament, writings of Plato and Aristotle, the roles of Jews and Catholics, and the Protestant Reformation. Both installment and a form of revolving credit started with the founding of our nation and remain the same today except for technological innovations. Credit cards were used in small numbers prior to WWI by some hotels, oil companies, and department stores and grew until the depression of the 1930s.

The transformation of the credit card into an industry was accomplished in 1949 with introduction of the Diners Club Card. The process and ensuing trials are described in chapter 1. As Americans began to obtain more discretionary income, they began purchasing more and the door opened for consumer credit which grew from $5.7 billion in 1945 to $375 billion in 1980.

Initially the credit card was a marketing tool to bind customers to specific retailers (i.e., Sears) not as a profit making operation; however, others saw this as being too restrictive and the universal credit card was conceived. Mandell sees this as "without a doubt, the most important development in the history of credit cards."

Early years (chapter 3) saw the development of monthly installments, revolving credit, rotating charge accounts, and interest free periods. However, the mathematical variations and traps for the consumer of the many methods used to extract cost of overhead and profit by the industry are not discussed in depth.

The growth years (chapter 4) followed with the availability of numerous bank cards but the economies of scale led to the prevailing cards being Master Charge and Bank Americard later to become

MasterCard and Visa, respectively. The development of a large client base was crucial and the marketing techniques employed resulted in problems of unsolicited cards, theft, fraud, duality, antitrust, international markets, and the invasion of department store credit.

With growth came pain (chapter 5) and the legal issues of equal access, privacy, lost or stolen cards, and billing errors. Consequently government intervention and regulation entered the industry with the passage in 1974 of the Federal Privacy Act, in 1975 of the Equal Credit Opportunity Act, and in 1978 of the Financial Institutions Regulatory and Interest Rate Control Act.

With the large well-established client base came the age of "pursuit of profitability" (chapter 6). The initial focus of marketing began to take a back seat to profits and the grantors of cards were challenged to find new means of turning a profit. With usury laws limiting the amount of interest charged profits needed to be extracted in other ways. This led to initiating an annual fee to customers, raising merchant percentage costs, "cross selling programs," selling card holder lists, selling of advertising space, and the "biggie," adjusting the method of calculating finance charges.

Saturation of the credit card market created a new angle which resulted in the affinity, secured, prestige, Discover, Optima, and telephone charge cards.

With the history and growth of the credit card fully discussed, Mandell takes a closer look at retail and oil company cards (chapter 7) and travel and entertainment cards (chapter 8). Though many of these cards still exist, none exists at the level of American Express, which now finds itself in stiff competition with MasterCard and Visa.

In chapter 9, Mandell discusses the impact of ever increasing and more sophisticated technology. The advent of the Automated Teller Machine (ATM) launched the United States into the era of electronic funds transfer (EFT), Point of Sale System (POS), telephone applications with at-home banking, and the unmanned supermarket: all part of the move toward totally paperless banking.

The final chapter (10) is devoted to the development of the card itself in order to secure it against fraudulent use and yet maintain simplicity for both customer and business operations, both being crucial to its continued success.

Mandell has produced an understandable, easy to read overview of the history and development of credit cards. Though redundant at times it is enjoyable reading and puts the evolution of that marvelous but dangerous plastic card into historical perspective.

Marilyn A. Chase
Center for Human Resources

State University of New York
Plattsburgh, NY

[24]

Excerpt from Charles E. Magoon, *Photos at the Archives: A Descriptive Listing of 800 Historical Photographs on Food Marketing at the National Archives*, 12–19.

Food Markets Throughout Recorded History—a brief review

On markets in general.—As stated earlier, this book includes photos of various types of food markets. Urban public markets, for instance, are one of the world's oldest social and cultural institutions. "In many cities and cultures the marketplace grew out of the development of a village into a town and the town into a city. In the medieval city...it was often found at the most important intersection in town."* Unquestionably, food markets have been a fixture in human society for thousands of years.

---

* Padraic Burke, "To Market, To Market," *Historic Preservation,* Vol. 29, No. 1, January-March 1977, p. 33.

Clay tokens in ancient times.—The existence of markets is sometimes traced back to the development of urban centers in Iraq and Iran. This would have been early in the Bronze Age, between 3500 and 3100 B.C. The author's view, however, is that markets existed long before that. Indeed, an intricate system of record keeping can be traced back 11,000 years. One of the most interesting glimpses of ancient times is provided by Denise Schmandt-Besserat in an article in the *Scientific American.** In her analysis of the use of clay tablets she recounts the following:

In 1969, I visited museums in the United States, Europe and the Middle East that had collections of clay artifacts dating back to the seventh, eighth and ninth milleniums B.C. This interval of time, beginning around 11,000 years ago and ending a little more than 8,000 years ago, saw the firm establishment of the first farming settlements in western Asia.

I encountered what was to me an unforeseen category of objects: small clay artifacts of various forms. . . . Could these artifacts, some of them 5,000 years older than the tokens from Susa [in Iran], also have served as tokens?

After compiling a catalog of hundreds of tokens, she concluded that these far earlier artifacts were indeed tokens.

As I extended my investigations to include later clay artifacts, dating from the seventh millenium B.C. to the fourth millenium, and later, I found to my surprise that similar clay tokens had been found in substantial numbers at sites representative of the entire time span. Evidently a system of accounting that made use of tokens was widely used, not only at Nuzi [in Iran] and Susa but throughout western Asia from as long ago as the ninth millenium B.C. and as recently as the second millenium.

Ms. Schmandt-Besserat notes that the system had some 15 major classes of tokens, further divided into some 200 subclasses on the basis of size, marking or fractional variations. Why so many? It is more than coincidence that the first tokens appear in the early Neolithic period—when human society was changing profoundly. Subsistence based on hunting and gathering was transformed by plant and animal domestication and the evolvement of a farming way of life. It is easy to visualize that this new agricultural economy would have been accompanied by new problems.

Perhaps the most crucial would have been food storage. Some portion of each annual yield had to be allocated for the farm family's own subsistence and some portion had to be set aside as seed for the next year's crop. Still another portion could have been reserved for barter with those who were ready to provide exotic products and raw materials in exchange for foodstuffs. It seems possible that the need to keep track of such allocations and transactions was enough to stimulate development of a recording system. . . . The Neolithic period and the succeeding Chalcolithic period, or Copper Age, in western Asia lasted about 5,000 years. Over this substantial span one finds surprisingly few changes in the tokens, a fact that may indicate how well suited to the needs of an early agricultural economy this recording system was.

* Denise Schmandt-Besserat, "The Earliest Precurser of Writing," *Scientific American*, June 1978.

14 / Photos at the Archives

As stated at the beginning of this discussion, it was at this point then—between 3500 and 3100 B.C.—that a significant change occurred. This was the rapid increase in the population of Iraq and Iran, and the appearance there of urban centers located close to earlier village settlements. Ms. Schmandt-Besserat adds this observation:

> The development of an urban economy, rooted in trade, must have multiplied the demands on the traditional recording system. Not only production but also inventories, shipments and wage payments had to be noted, and merchants needed to preserve records of their transactions. By the last century of the fourth millenium B.C., the pressure of complex business accountancy on the token system becomes apparent both in the symbols and in how the tokens were used.

Ms. Schmandt-Besserat goes on to trace further events: the proliferation of subtypes of tokens, the appearance of clay bullae (a type of envelope), the substitution of two-dimensional portrayals of the tokens for the tokens themselves, and consequently the earliest examples of writing—the representative signs inscribed on clay tablets. However interesting those connections may be, they are beyond the scope of this review/book.

Early mention.—Although these included infrequent fairs as well as daily markets, markets are mentioned in both the Old and New Testaments, and markets are known to have existed in China, Burma and India before the time of Christ. Among other facts, it is known also that control over markets in ancient Greek cities was exerted by special boards. Later, in Italy, the Roman senate claimed the right to establish markets.

In medieval times.—In medieval towns and cities it was after the collapse of trade which accompanied the fall of the Roman Empire that markets achieved their greatest growth. The market often was found at the most important intersection in town, and it might be adjacent to or attached to the church, the same as markets in Islamic countries were linked to mosques and shrines. Expansion of the market street might be into a central market square, or into lesser squares, or it might be just affixed to neighboring houses.

"Although historians differ as to the exact date and cause, by the late 16th or early 17th century the public character of the medieval market in England and Europe had significantly eroded. But well into the 20th century markets survived in various stages of decline in the poorer sections of European cities." *

The market's public character.—It may be appropriate to pause a moment in this brief historical narrative to note the social significance of shopping for food.

In any age, in any society, the act of going into the marketplace—whatever type market facilities and surroundings there may be—is one of

* Burke, *Ibid.,* p. 36.

the most basic social functions. An important element of the medieval market—and of the early American market, too—was its public character. That is, it was administered by a public agency (church, king, state or municipality) and it was intended to serve a variety of public needs, including court and meeting place as well as a source of food.

"The economic foundation (and to some extent the ethical and social as well) on which the public market rested was an egalitarian one that guaranteed access to all producers. Free access to and from the market was guaranteed by the *king's peace* and, later, *the market peace*. The enforcement of market regulations was handled either by a special office (such as Britain's Royal Clerk of the Market), special market courts or a market master, as in the United States. Every market possessed a pillory, including the markets in Boston and Philadelphia, and offenders often were tried and pilloried on the day the offense took place. The most serious offense was *forestalling the market*, or interfering with the pricing of goods entering the market. This was usually done by monopolizing sale of a particular commodity and artificially inflating its price." *

The colonial era.—Although the public character of markets was declining in Europe, this was not the case in the growing villages and towns of North America. Here, the public market shared a leading position in the community, along with the meeting house or church and town hall. Mr. Burke notes, "By 1690 the major colonial towns (Boston, Philadelphia, New York, Charles Town, S.C. and Newport, R.I.) held weekly markets at a given time and place and under regulated conditions. . . . By the beginning of the 18th century there were seven public markets in the city and New York City surpassed all other places in the number of people that used its markets."

In some localities a section of one of the streets was laid off into stalls where growers could park their wagonloads of farm products for display and sale to city consumers. In other cities buildings were constructed where growers could obtain display space. During this period of slow transportation and poor roads, most cities did not hold markets more than one or two days each week. Most of the products offered for sale were produced within 5 to 10 miles of the city. Out of a total population of only 3,929,214 in 1790 in the U.S., over 90 percent lived on farms.

In the 1800s.—As roads improved and urban population increased, farm produce from somewhat greater distances might be brought in for sale on the market. Markets were a feature of all towns, and most cities had several. Prior to the Civil War, over half the people lived on farms and there was no need for an intricate food marketing system—and this condition extended for many more years. (A more complex system did not evolve

* *Ibid.*

until after the turn of the century, when larger, year-around wholesale businesses and related middlemen developed.) Even as late as 1900, an estimated 38 percent of the [75,994,575] population still lived on farms.

In this era it is interesting to note that 1880-1890 was the decade of greatest railroad construction, with 71,000 miles of new track built. Perishables were a negligible part of the traffic for many years, however. Indeed, from Colonial days clear into the 1900s the horse and wagon supplied most cities with produce from local farms.

The wholesaling of perishables.—In addition to produce from local farms, there was considerable local movement by boat from nearby producing areas into Washington, Baltimore, Philadelphia, New York, Boston and other coastal and river cities. This was seasonal movement, of course. There also was considerable coastwise movement of perishables by boats with ventilating hatches—from Virginia, North and South Carolina, Georgia and Florida to Baltimore and other port cities. This traffic continued until railroad mergers and the establishment of through routes drove these boats out of operation because of ruinous competitive rates by the railroads.

Since commodities other than produce also were subject to transportation limitations, cities had first developed around ports. And since it was as difficult to deliver produce after arrival as it was to get it to market in the first place, wholesale markets developed as near the center of the city as facilities for boat arrivals would allow. Inland cities, also having only horse-drawn vehicles for delivery, located wholesale markets as near the center of the city as they could. Those were the days of the commission merchant, since few dealers would assume transit risk; they preferred not to buy anything until they saw its condition on arrival.

Prior to the late 1800s, wholesale fruit and vegetable markets were local and usually seasonal, operating part or all of the year in conjunction with other commodities. Transportation, when by rail, was without protective (refrigeration or heater) service, was limited to the life of each commodity under prevailing weather and temperature conditions, and was physically limited to short and one-line hauls. Any so-called **expedited service** was provided by the old express companies, some of whom covered in their charter the right to handle merchandise on commission.

Following the development of the refrigerated rail car, another major development in the late 1800s was the wide availability of manufactured ice in the southern and western states. Also, it was around the turn of the century when railroads were forced to furnish refrigerated cars and some degree of protective services as a necessary public service.

The perishable terminal market dates from about 1900, then, and was a natural marketing development based mainly on: through rail transportation, the availability of ice, and refrigerated railroad cars.

A notable feature of the 1920s was the construction of quite a number of railroad market terminals for perishables. This was done by the larger railroad companies and was designed to enhance the respective company's competitive position in the particular city. (See pages 28 to 32 for Dr. Crow's observations about such construction.) Also, there was a need to get refrigerated rail cars unloaded promptly and moving again. (It was common practice for small [perhaps inadequately financed] dealers in particular to sell direct from the rail car, often detaining it unduly.)

On occasion the trade also would build a large terminal, e.g., Chicago's South Water Market, which still serves as the city's major produce terminal in 1980, 55 years after it was opened.

It is interesting to note the carryover into the 1930s and 1940s—and even beyond—of the thinking of salesmen and dealers based on the earlier days of little/inadequate refrigeration of perishables. This involved the quick unloading of rail cars and the immediate sale of their contents. The trade thought in terms of a daily clean-up, with leftovers being a sign of poor marketing and being subject to quick-sale or even distress pricing. The exception to this rule was potatoes, apples, etc. stored perhaps for months in multiple-floor commercial cold storage facilities, of which there were many throughout the United States. Construction of these on a large scale had begun around 1915.

It was in that period of time around World War I, and before trucks took over the traffic, that considerable produce was shipped via interurban trolley. Often this involved a two-day delivery schedule to connections with grocery stores in surrounding towns and to company stores. Understandably, there was a great deal of spoilage in transit.

Although more efficient than in most other countries, the food marketing system of the U.S. in the 1930s showed considerable variation in efficiency from city to city. Some of the newer wholesale produce markets were very efficient, at the same time as many other cities struggled along with obsolete, inefficient markets. See pages 20-36 for Dr. Crow's portrayal of that latter category of wholesale markets.

A change in marketing channels.—The relative decline of farmers' markets throughout much of the 20th century was accompanied by the expansion of wholesaling. Contributing factors included: the loss of farmland on the edge of towns and cities because of the growth of suburbs; farms tending to become larger and to produce a less diversified array of crops; and improving transportation and refrigeration, which expanded the radius from which a city could draw its food supplies.

By the 1930s, too, an increasing number of supermarkets were making heavy inroads into the public market. This trend was accentuated as cities

18 / Photos at the Archives

expanded and it became progressively more difficult for the homemaker to reach a public market on the converging web of streetcar lines. At the same time, the automobile enabled her to reach suburban stores. Also, improved preservation techniques (i.e., refrigeration) in the home permitted buying in quantities sufficient to eliminate the daily shopping trip.

Last three decades not covered here.—Since very few photos listed in this book are more recent than 1950, it is not within the scope of this book to review the marketing scene in the U.S. for the last three decades A final remark on the 1930s: the reader is encouraged to read Dr. Crow's fascinating glimpse of wholesale produce markets in the 1920s-1930s, the next major section of this book.

Federal government interest in marketing.—Caroline B. Sherman* briefly traces back to 1869 an organized interest in "the processes of marketing farmer products and their improvement." She notes that "The first scientific study of marketing problems appeared in 1900 when the United States Industrial Commission...deemed the question of marketing to be of such fundamental importance that it submitted an advance report on the distribution of farm products..."

Ms. Sherman notes further that "Approximately ten years after the publication of the report by the Industrial Commission, the interest of the people in marketing problems began to crystallize into rather insistent demands for governmental assistance. There were many and diverse opinions on the proper way to meet these demands." One response was exercised by Congress in 1910. Since no funds were made available, however, no real results were achieved at that time.

In succeeding years work was being conducted on harvesting, transporting, storing and marketing many kinds of fruit and truck crops; on grading, transporting and handling cereals; and on grading and marketing cotton. In addition, studies were being made of market methods and the conditions surrounding the transportation and marketing of eggs, milk, butter and other animal products.

Authority for the marketing work conducted by USDA was conveyed by a regular agricultural appropriation act—the one for 1914. On May 16, 1913, the Office of Markets was created by the Secretary of Agriculture.

In 1914, rural organizations work and the Office of Markets were combined and designated the Office of Markets and Rural Organization. In turn, this office finally became the Bureau of Markets through the agricultural appropriation act for the fiscal year ending June 30, 1918, approved March 4, 1917. Work continued on such projects as the standardization, collection and dissemination of market information nationwide;

---

* Caroline B. Sherman, "The Legal Basis of the Marketing Work of the United States Department of Agriculture," *Agricultural History* 11 (July 1937): 289-301.

on improvement in preparation of farm products for market; and on improvement in transportation conditions including methods of loading and refrigerator car service.

Formation of BAE.—By 1922 the Bureau of Markets, the Bureau of Crop Estimates and the Office of Farm Management and Farm Economics had been consolidated to form the **Bureau of Agricultural Economics.** It was this bureau which supervised the acquisition of most of the photographs now stored at the National Archives and listed in this book. The Bureau was organized around three functional headings: production, marketing, and general. The marketing divisions were Cotton; Fruits and Vegetables; Warehousing; Livestock, Meats and Wool; Hay, Feed and Seed; City Markets—Washington Center Market; Grain; Dairy and Poultry Products; and Cost of Marketing.

In 1939 the Divisions of Marketing and of Transportation Research were combined to form the Division of Marketing and Transportation Research. Various other reorganizations too numerous to cover here are enumerated in the *Century of Service.* *

Users of this book will notice some photo numbers which include the prefix PMA. This refers to the Production and Marketing Administration, established in 1945 as the successor to the War Food Administration, a relatively short-lived agency. (World War II had just ended.) On July 1, 1947, the Marketing Research Branch of PMA was established. This was related to the transfer from BAE to PMA of responsibility for research programs for marketing and marketing research activities with reference to technical improvement of market facilities, transportation methods, packing and packaging, and wholesale and retail marketing practices.

A major reorganization occurred in 1953 when the Agricultural Marketing Service was established—centralizing the marketing and distributive functions of USDA. "Marketing research and service work, the administration of marketing and regulatory legislation, work on food distribution, and food trade activities were transferred from the Production and Marketing Admin. (Secretary's Memo. 1320, Supp. 4, Nov. 2, 1953.)."*

The functions of BAE not transferred to the Agricultural Marketing Service were assigned to the Agricultural Research Service. At the same time (November 2, 1953), PMA ceased to function and was succeeded by the Commodity Stabilization Service. There, PMA's remaining responsibilities (i.e., those not already transferred to AMS or to ARS) included adjustment activities, stabilization of sugar production, price supports, foreign supply programs, commodity disposal, and administration of the International Wheat Agreement.

_____
* *Century of Service—the first 100 years of the United States Department of Agriculture.* Centennial Committee, USDA, Washington, D.C., 1963, 560 pp.

[25]

Marketing Legislation

By Ewald T. Grether

MARKETING legislation is an organic part of the great body of law relating to all economic activity. Further, legislation per se is merely a section of the larger field of regulation. Hence, marketing legislation should be interpreted in the perspective of the larger regulative field of which it is a part.

The forms of regulation for purposes of general appraisal may be classified as voluntary and involuntary. Voluntary regulation is essentially self-regulation, either through the independent decisions of enterprises, or by formal or informal group effort through associations composed of firms in the same fields, or through more inclusive groupings such as Better Business Bureaus and Chambers of Commerce. Involuntary regulation may take place through the pressures of (1) custom and tradition, (2) competition, or (3) governmental controls. But these categories, as is always true of classifications of social phenomena, are not entirely exclusive, and have their validity merely as convenient and broad divisions for general analysis. For instance, it is extremely difficult in practice, in fact often impossible, to distinguish between the relatively voluntary adaptations of individual enterprises to market situations in which they have considerable latitude of choice, and those adjustments which are predetermined by competitive forces so rigorous and impersonal as to leave scant room for individuality in expression. Legislation, also, cuts across boundaries, for it may take the form of mandatory rules and hence become a third general type of involuntary regulation, or it may be merely ancillary to the other general regulative procedures

intended to expedite or mold their functioning. Further, it is highly unrealistic to examine legislation separate from common law, judicial law built out of the review of statutes by the courts, and administrative law. In the United States, particularly, the *Law* is an organic whole.

Finally, since lawmaking and law interpretation involve Federal, state, and local governmental bodies, the field is a bewildering maze, much of which has never been systematized sufficiently for orderly appraisal.[1] The comments to this point are intended not merely to clear the path in an introductory manner, but to indicate that the writer is fully aware that the brief interpretation to follow must inevitably be selective and oversimplified.

Types of Legislation

Federal, state, and local laws affecting marketing may be classified as follows: (1) those governing the conditions of entry into and exit from business; (2) those facilitating the pursuit of legitimate business interests; (3) those intended to preserve competition in markets; and (4) those intended to establish the plane of competition in markets.[2] Even though much legislation overlaps and hence does not fall clearly in these divisions, these categories, like the initial ones, are useful bases for general interpretation. In this

[1] It is to be hoped that the *Marketing Laws Survey* of the W.P.A. will eventually furnish some guidance as far as state legislation is concerned.

[2] See L. S. Lyon, M. W. Watkins, and V. Abramson, *Government and Economic Life*, Washington, 1939. These writers distinguish between the implementing and regulating activities of government. The terminology "plane of competition" is also used by them.

paper, attention will be centered upon groups (3) and (4) above, since there is some discussion of the first two categories elsewhere in this volume. Further, only the more important legislative developments since the World War will be discussed, except for brief general characterizations and references to historical antecedents.

LEGISLATION GOVERNING ENTRY AND EXIT

The rights and obligations of the various forms of enterprise have a long common-law and statutory history. Further, in many professions and in the service trades, restrictions upon free entry and regulations governing entry are well-established procedures rooted in precedents running deep into the past. The most important recent developments affecting entry have been (1) the expansion of licensing regulations by state and local governments in the professions and the service trades, and (2) an endeavor to use licensing or a combination of licensing and regulatory taxation to restrain certain types of enterprise, such as itinerant vendors and chain stores. These devices are discussed elsewhere in this volume, hence need not be reviewed here.

Until the depression period, the bankruptcy law of 1898 governed the conditions of exit or of reorganization for insolvent enterprises. In 1933 and in 1934 important revisions were made; these culminated in the Chandler Act of 1938.[3]

FACILITATING LEGISLATION

State, Federal, and local laws designed to facilitate marketing activities take so many forms that adequate listing would in itself require many pages.

[3] For an excellent brief historical review and analysis of the provisions of the existing law and suggestions for further modifications, see Lyon *et al.*, *op. cit.*, Chap. V.

Hence it is possible here merely to characterize. It is useful to classify these enactments into two groups: (1) passive—i.e., intended merely to provide the conditions essential for the ordinary marketing pursuits; and (2) active—i.e., intended in a positive manner to make such endeavors more effective. The "active" types of facilitating legislation are distinguished from laws intended to establish the plane of competition in that they are not directly concerned with problems of trade ethics or with general conflicts of interests. Obviously, this category has very elastic boundaries.

The "passive" category should be considered to comprise at least legislation concerned with: (1) basic contractual rights and obligations (the common law is assumed); (2) facilitating the meeting of minds in markets (trade-marks, trade names, copyrights, standardizing, grading, and inspecting); (3) financing (money, banking, and credit in their diverse manifestations); (4) risk bearing (insurance, speculation, trading in futures, and so forth); (5) transportation (railway, waterway, motor, or other forms); and (6) storing and warehousing. "Active" facilitating legislation provides for: (1) collection and dissemination of statistical data in order to improve general knowledge; (2) educational work; (3) favored conditions in order to encourage certain types of enterprises, as farmers' co-operative associations and consumers' credit unions; and (4) special rights, privileges, and subventions for certain classes, as agricultural producers.

Facilitating legislation, both active and passive, has expanded greatly in recent years. It is in this field that legislators have made their finest contributions because of the general service nature of such statutes and the common absence of sharp conflicts of interest. This type of legislation will not be reviewed in this paper because other contributors to the volume make reference to leading statutes.[4]

LEGISLATION TO PRESERVE COMPETITION

The traditional American belief concerning the economic system is that it would achieve its maximum efficiency only if free competition were preserved. This doctrine showed itself in the common law of restraint of trade and in Federal and state antitrust legislation. The Sherman Act of 1890, with its sweeping prohibitions of monopolies and of attempts to monopolize, and of combinations in restraint of trade, still is the theoretical base of Federal legislation. The Clayton Act of 1914 put labels upon a small group of specific practices that Congress deemed in violation of the Sherman Act. The Federal Trade Commission Act enacted during the same year set up an administrative agency with broad, flexible powers, to work out rules and procedures to grapple with the infinite variety of methods intended to depart from or subvert the theoretical competitive pattern. But the Commission's role was not merely to guard against monopoly, but also to regulate competition in a positive manner, as will be noted below.

The faith in free competition was also expressed in state laws. All the states except Delaware, Nevada, New Jersey, Pennsylvania, Rhode Island, and West Virginia have general statutes intended to prohibit the development of monopolies.[5] In addition to the general codes, or incorporated within them,

there often appeared prohibitions of certain practices that were considered monopoly tactics. For instance, twenty-three states by 1916 had statutes dealing with local price cutting with monopolistic intent.[6]

The Clayton Act carried a similar provision, but with more general reference than the state laws, since it was not restricted to local price cutting although it was so considered at first.

The most significant new Federal legislation relating to marketing in the direct line of descent from the Sherman Act was the Robinson-Patman Act of 1936, which amended the price-discrimination prohibition of the Clayton Act. It is difficult to characterize the act in a few words; and its full meaning will not be known for years, since it has raised a host of problems of interpretation which are being litigated only gradually. In the main, though, it prohibits price variations on goods of like grade and quality, when the effect of such discrimination "may be substantially to lessen competition or tend to create a monopoly . . . or to injure, destroy or prevent competition with any person who either grants or knowingly receives the benefit of such discrimination." But a seller may make due allowance for cost differentials, and there are exceptions to meet changing market conditions, deterioration, obsolescence, and the like. Subsidiary sections of the act govern payments for brokerage services, the provision of services to customers, and the payment for services rendered by purchasers. The act culminates in a criminal section (the Borah-Van Nys Bill), which will not be discussed here.

The prohibitions of *personal* price discrimination, as under the Robinson-Patman Act, have largely supplanted

[4] For a summary of laws relating to standards, research, and the dissemination of knowledge, see Lyon *et al.*, Chap. IX; see also F. E. Clark, *Principles of Marketing* (New York, 1932), Chap. 23.

[5] "A Collection and Survey of State Anti-Trust Laws," *Columbia Law Review*, Vol. 32 (1932), pp. 347–66.

[6] For details see E. T. Grether, *Price Control Under Fair Trade Legislation* (New York, 1939), pp. 33–36.

the older issue of locality price discrimination. As yet, the Robinson-Patman Act has not exercised the influence that its more ardent supporters hoped for and some frightened business interests feared. If the complaints, orders, and court cases under it to date are indicative of the ultimate outcome, then its prime influence will be to remove some of the monopoly bargaining power of large firms, such as chain stores and mail-order houses. Many sellers appear to be pleased to have this legal bludgeon to assist them in working out their higgling relations with large buyers. A secondary contribution of the act is that it forces cost calculations in connection with price variations. Unfortunately, though, cost accounting is a weak instrument for assuming this burden. In this connection, one paradoxical result does stand out, however. In so far as costs can be known, it appears that large buyers often were not receiving discounts as large as the cost differentials; that is, the discrimination often was against them instead of the smallest buyers.

It is impossible at present to know or to predict the full effects of this statute. On the whole, it appears that the adjustments of American business to the act will be so relatively mild and gradual as to make radical changes in trade relations unnecessary. Further, the more hopeful opponents of chain stores and other large distributive enterprises are learning that the bases of success and survival of these enterprises are much broader than mere buying advantage. There are many sound bases for price variations between buyers, and no doubt most of these will ultimately be tolerated under the act.

ESTABLISHING THE PLANE OF COMPETITION

The Robinson-Patman Act also typifies a pronounced drift which is pulling American trade regulation away from its 1890 moorings, because monopolistic intent is no longer the sole basis of action. Slowly and often imperceptibly, but surely, regulation has veered from the clear-cut and simple anti-monopoly objective to the more positive attempt to make qualitative distinctions concerning the functioning of competition. This tendency without doubt reflects the growing awareness (1) that the simple, forthright prohibitions of the Sherman Act were too unsophisticated (witness the "rule of reason"), and (2) that actually monopoly and competition are inextricably interwoven into an infinite variety of patterns; i.e., that competition inherently is somewhat "imperfect." Hence, regulation to preserve competition is merging more and more with that intended to establish its plane. More specifically, the great bodies of law governing the restraint of trade and unfair competition are tending to become fused instead of flowing down separate channels, and are becoming interlarded by attempts to mold the nature of competition in a positive manner.

The National Industrial Recovery Act gave open, public recognition of the extent to which the American public had given up its traditional point of view or was unwilling to fight for it under emergency conditions. For good or for ill, the experience under the N.R.A. codes left a deposit which will linger long in the American trades and may be expected to continue to affect legislation. But it should be noted that important breaches had been made in the "free trade" position prior to the recent depression legislation. American tariff policy, of course, for years had shown the trend in external relations. Even before the Great Depression and prior to the New Deal, strong endeavors were made to soften the play of full and free competition in the agricultural field. The Agricultural Marketing Act of

MARKETING LEGISLATION

1929, for instance, which set up the Federal Farm Board with its broad powers (1) of assisting farmers in co-operative marketing activities, (2) of financing the withholding of crops from the market, and (3) of entering the market directly in order to control surpluses, was the immediate Republican precursor of the crop of Democratic legislation along similar lines. The point is that this particular lapse of faith in the beneficence of unrestricted competition is no surface phenomenon with mere short-run party significance.

FAIR TRADE AND UNFAIR PRACTICES ACTS

The Fair Trade and Unfair Practices Acts show the same trend in an unmistakable manner. Forty-four states now have so-called Fair Trade Laws in effect which allow producers of trade-marked goods to control resale prices in the distributive channels. The Federal Government in 1937 cleared the way in interstate commerce with the Miller-Tydings Amendment to the Sherman and Federal Trade Commission Acts. Not only is a long line of precedents broken negatively, but manufacturers are given powerful, positive assistance through the famous non-signer's clause which makes given contractual prices binding upon noncontractors. It is alleged that these new rights do not abridge the antitrust laws because horizontal combination is still specifically prohibited in practice. But they of course inevitably reduce or remove the play of *price* competition between distributors on the products under contract, and involve a large amount of group activity in enforcement. Although the fruition of this movement was a depression phenomenon, it would be a serious error to interpret it merely as a reaction to short-run conditions, for it has roots that go deep into the last decades of the nineteenth century.

Further, it has arisen in about the same manner in all capitalistic countries.

At the time of writing, the so-called Unfair Practices Acts [7] appear to be moving towards a culmination in the various states, similar to that of their companionate Fair Trade Laws. The nature of the shift in American regulative conceptions is also indicated by these statutes, for they are rooted in the antitrust laws but have greatly broadened these initial prohibitions. In the first two decades of this century a small number of states, in addition to local price-cutting prohibitions, added general bans upon price cutting with monopolistic intent.[8] At present, twenty-seven states have built general price-cutting prohibitions upon this base, but now the avowed purpose is to curb "loss leader" or other predatory price cutting in the distributive trades. These laws may well be characterized as "market-floor" acts, for their effect is to fix floor prices in markets either at the level of the most efficient enterprise or at an arbitrary level. In the majority of these statutes it is no longer necessary to prove monopolistic intent, as in their earlier antitrust form; hence, broad bases for restricting the depth of price variations have been provided. Further, in some states [9] trade associations are specifically empowered to bring action. Thus in these instances horizontal combination is specifically allowed as under the N.R.A., but without governmental supervision and without the labor provision. It should be noted, too, that the coverage of the acts is general (with numerous exceptions and al-

[7] Other titles are also employed for acts in this category, such as "Fair Sales Act," "Unfair Sales Act," "Unfair Trade Act," "Fair Trade Practices Act." In the trade press these acts are also sometimes dubbed "loss leader laws."

[8] For detail, see Grether, *op. cit.*, p. 36.

[9] I.e., the states following the pattern of the 1935 California Unfair Practices Act.

lowances) instead of being limited to trade-marked goods as under the Fair Trade Acts.

At present in the United States, there is much discussion of the effects of resale price control and market-floor acts. A considerable amount of formal research has been made or is in process. It appears to this point that the alarmists have painted too dark a picture, for the mal-effects are not nearly so large as stated. The Fair Trade Laws apply to only a minority of goods, and within this field they have made for significantly higher prices to consumers primarily on some of the best-known products that entered heavily into price competition and in the popular price of cut-rate types of enterprise. That is, it is a mistake to assume that consumers in general and on all of their purchases have been forced to pay higher prices. But, unfortunately, the price increases that have appeared have been concentrated upon the lower income and/or thrifty members of the community. But there are some compensatory factors that offset some of this loss.

Market-floor acts

The market-floor laws, in so far as they have had wide coverage, have similarly achieved their benefits (if any) at the expense of the same consuming groups that, either through economic pressure or from choice, shop carefully and rationally for items featured at low prices. But neither consumers as a whole nor dealers have much at stake when floors are kept low, as, say, at merchandise cost or a small percentage above it. The most serious aspect of these laws, as is true also of the Fair Trade Acts, is their portent, for there is a strong hazard that they will be merely an entering wedge for more ambitious ventures to fix prices in general. At present in this country (as well as in Europe) it has become widely believed

that aggressive price cutting in the distributive trades is an unsocial practice and hence properly subject to governmental regulation. This attitude was supported and incited by the master code for the retail trades under N.R.A., which stated that the use of loss leaders "works back against the producer of raw materials on farms and in industry and against the labor so employed." [10]

In addition to the reversals of public policy which have shifted the purpose of much legislation from the mere preservation of competition per se to an attempt to mold it in a positive manner, there are those enactments which intend primarily to provide rules for the competitive game without altering it fundamentally. Thus, there is a great body of law which is either directed at unfair competition between rivals or at practices that run counter to the interests of consumers. It is this type of legislation that was originally considered separate from the antitrust laws. More and more, however, it is becoming clear that it was highly unrealistic, except for purposes of preliminary analysis as in this discussion, to keep these strands separate in public policy.

FOOD AND DRUG LEGISLATION

The Federal and state laws regulating the sale of foods, drugs, and cosmetics are the best examples of legislation in the consumer interest. The dominance of the earlier beliefs that free competition is largely beneficent is portrayed by the fact that it was not until 1906 that the Federal Government enacted comprehensive legislation in this field. The purpose of the 1906 Federal Pure Food and Drugs Law,[11] as amended in

[10] For a criticism of this point of view see Grether, *op. cit.*, pp. 214–22, 386–90.

[11] For a brief review of the act and its amendments, see W. C. Waite and R. Cassady, Jr., *The Consumer and the Economic Order* (New York, 1939), pp. 103 ff. Several excellent brief statements are available elsewhere.

MARKETING LEGISLATION   171

1912, 1913, 1930, and 1934, was to prohibit the adulteration and misbranding of foods and drugs in interstate commerce.

The 1906 law was passed only after a long battle, and was an important phase in the general movement away from *caveat emptor*. But the act had a number of pronounced weaknesses, chief of which were: (1) food compounds were not considered to be adulterated if they contained no poisonous or deleterious ingredients, irrespective of the proportions of the ingredients; (2) branded food mixtures, when the place of manufacture was indicated, were likewise considered adulterated or misbranded only if they contained poisonous or deleterious ingredients; (3) although the labeling requirements curbed much misrepresentation in a narrow sense, they did not enforce positive descriptions adequate for sound consumer judgment; (4) the government had to establish fraud with respect to claims made for drug products; this burden of proof seriously weakened the protection of consumers in a field in which consumer ignorance is particularly dangerous; (5) the prohibitions of the act did not carry through to advertising, but only to labeling; (6) the coverage of the act was too limited—e.g., cosmetics and therapeutic devices were not included; (7) there were no definitions of standards for foods in the act; hence, the burden of determining reasonable standards rested with the government.[12]

In 1938 Congress enacted a new Food, Drug, and Cosmetic Act which remedied most of the weaknesses listed above, although it still does not offer full protection to consumers. The provisions of the new act will not be reviewed in detail here; instead, the degree to which the weaknesses of the old act were not corrected and substantive changes ranging beyond this enumera-

12 Lyon, *et al.*, p. 345.

tion will be noted.[13] The chief defect of the 1938 bill is the absence of provisions governing advertising; but this weakness was overcome entirely or in part by the Wheeler-Lea Amendment to the Federal Trade Commission Act. Further, positive labeling requirements are still relatively weak for foods except in the case of those for special dietary purposes. It is not required to state the ingredients of cosmetics. But the provision declaring labeling misleading if it fails to reveal "facts material" (i.e., in the light of representations that have been made) ". . . with respect to the consequences which may result from the use of the article" may be the basis for overcoming some of this weakness with vigorous enforcement. One important new provision in the food field is the grant of power to the Secretary of Agriculture to license food manufacturers, if necessary, to protect against contamination. Some additional protection is given consumers in the purchase of drugs through a provision requiring the testing of new drugs before they are marketed. Enforcement is expedited and strengthened by increasing the penalties and providing broader powers in addition to the changes already noted. Some observers believe the provision for court review will weaken enforcement.

Many state and local political bodies had enacted legislation governing the sale of foods and drugs even prior to the 1906 Federal act. Now every state of the Union has laws in this field, which often include other malpractices affecting public health, safety, and welfare. Fortunately, state, local, and Federal agencies are increasingly finding means of co-operating in enforcement.

THE FEDERAL TRADE COMMISSION

The Federal Trade Commission Act

13 For a brief digest of the provisions, see Lyon, *et al.*, pp. 357–60.

of 1914 is the most important Federal law to date relating to the maintenance of the ethics of competition. Under this statute the Commission was given blanket authority to take action against "unfair methods of competition" in interstate commerce. The sponsors of the act purposely did not define "unfair methods of competition," apparently because they wished the Commission to work out standards of ethical conduct in a flexible, creative manner.

Early in its career the Commission discovered that it was impossible to set up a broad, well-rounded program of regulation in the trade and public interest, because of (1) the tendency of courts to interpret its powers narrowly, based upon the common-law conception of "unfair competition"; and (2) the necessity for establishing the existence of both a specific competitive interest, and a direct public interest in the practices deemed "unfair." Administrative and personnel difficulties and the limitations set up by courts combined to restrict the Commission's efforts to a point much below that envisaged by many of the sponsors of the act. Yet, as the years have passed, the Commission's vigilance over the channels of trade has become increasingly important. Its complaints and orders to cease and desist, the stipulations accepted, and the voluntary rules established in trade-practice conferences, have accumulated a great body of specific rules which greatly assist in giving form, direction, and content to the generally accepted principles of social ethics in relation to business conduct. Consequently, those engaged in marketing goods in interstate commerce now know, for instance, not merely that deceit and fraud are in general prohibited, as throughout the centuries, but that specific methods of branding and describing products are violations and subject to action. Further, the Com-

mission's endeavors to maintain a proper level of business conduct clearly demonstrate the organic interrelations of "monopolistic" and "unfair" practices. Hence, a large portion of the Commission's attention has been directed to monopolistic practices.

In 1938, in the Wheeler-Lea Amendment, the powers of the Federal Trade Commission were broadened so that it might take action against practices harmful to consumers even when no injury to members of the trades is demonstrated. Further, increased penalties and procedural changes should assist it in making its will much more effective than in the past.[14] The new power which has been exercised most since 1938 is specific control over false advertising of foods, drugs, devices, and cosmetics. Many of the supporters of the Food, Drug, and Cosmetic Act of 1938 had hoped to write a similar provision into that law. Because of heavy opposition this task was given to the Federal Trade Commission, partly because it already was exercising some supervision over advertising, but chiefly because the industries concerned seemed to prefer Commission supervision to that of the Department of Agriculture.

STATE TRADE COMMISSIONS

The various states to date have not followed the example of the Federal Government by establishing trade commissions with broad powers of regulation over trade practices. The Utah Trade Commission set up in 1937 is the only state agency with general powers at all similar to those of the Federal Trade Commission.[15] There are, how-

[14] The Commission may bring injunctive proceedings in district courts to prevent the dissemination of false advertising of foods, drugs, devices, and cosmetics, while an order is pending. Further, the violation of a final order is subject to a penalty of $5,000.

[15] For detail, see Grether, *op. cit.*, p. 400.

ever, special agencies, boards, and commissions in numerous states with limited grants of power in specific fields, as the service trades, alcoholic beverages, and agricultural products.

Space limitations make it impossible in this discussion to examine numerous other types of legislation that are intended to regulate the plane of competition. Fortunately, brief summaries are available to readers elsewhere.[16]

CONDITIONS INFLUENCING RECENT MARKETING LEGISLATION

Marketing legislation should be interpreted in the perspective of the social mores and ethical precepts distilled by centuries of human commercial intercourse and the specific crystallization developed in the common law. The interpretation of the historical setting, as well as of legislative developments, would be inadequate without an awareness of basic evolutionary forces that are more important than their specific expression in any one brief period of time. But evolutionary forces do not move at a uniform rate. In the modern period, particularly in the United States, industrial trends became so accelerated toward the end of the nineteenth century as to produce major conflicts of interests out of which appeared the Sherman Act intended to preserve competition. The ways in which this act has since been implemented have already been indicated.

Following the World War, acceleration of trends in the distributive channels also appeared as large-scale distributors, particularly chain-store systems, made rapid strides. The impact of this increase in the evolutionary tempo inevitably aroused the organized opposition of the established distributive types that were forced to give ground, even as

[16] Lyon, *et al.*, pp. 343 ff.; H. H. Maynard, W. C. Weidler, and T. N. Beckman, *Principles of Marketing* (New York, 1939), pp. 360 ff.

small-scale industrialists had reacted in the 1880's. The most significant *single* factor (there are others) that accounts for much of recent marketing legislation is the political pressure of distributive interests which have suffered from the expansion of large-scale distribution.

The effectiveness of this pressure was maximized by the conjuncture of a number of conditions. First, general intensive, *qualitative* regulation had gradually received at least passive acceptance in public opinion. Second, farmers and small shopkeepers both found themselves struggling against adverse economic trends; hence, often they joined forces politically to gain governmental aid. In many states, and for the most part in Congress, this active co-operation, or the tacit absence of opposition of either party, in itself insures the control of legislative channels. There are a number of important similarities of purpose and procedure in the agricultural and distributive control acts. Third, the 1920–21 depression and the Great Depression beginning in 1929 added the fuels of emergency and despair to the fires that were already well kindled. It is important to note, though, that the legislative demands were not merely depression phenomena, but had a broader evolutionary base; depression merely acted as a powerful stimulant. Fourth, the N.R.A. assisted in breaking down some portion of the traditional public opposition to formal co-operation among the members of given industries and trades to serve their own economic ends, and gave American industry a taste of long forbidden fruits. This experience left its direct deposit in the current market-floor and price-discrimination statutes as was noted above. In spite of the tremendous opposition that the N.R.A. program produced before its end, it would be a serious error to assume that all its aspects were distasteful to American business. On the contrary, it gave pattern and form to many sub rosa or latent activities and desires.

In this connection, too, it needs to be stressed that the pressure of the larger, powerful forces of impersonal competition in our period make local, independent, and co-operative adjustments to competition increasingly less effective. For instance, small dealers typically find themselves in a welter of competition with not only their own types, and direct sellers and large-scale distributors in their own fields, but also with firms in other fields. Consequently, distribution is a labyrinth of intertwining highways and bypaths, and the weight of competition is increased and impersonalized. Hence, even group activity within given fields often would no longer be able to protect the interests of the members of the trades.

Inevitably, most legislation, although couched in terms of the public interest, expresses most largely the desires of specific groups. "Public opinion" is more influential as a passive nonresisting factor than as an active influence. Only occasionally, as in the case of food and drug legislation, does the "public" become an active force. Much of the legislation described above would not have been enacted at all, or would have been greatly modified, if consumers, for instance, had expressed themselves as efficiently as producers and distributors. The passive, uncritical acceptance of laws that run counter to the interests of consumers reflects not only the characteristic apathy of most voters, but also their extraordinary difficulty, if not impossibility, of forming sound judgments concerning complex problems. It will be interesting to watch the development of the current "consumers' movement." Perhaps it will for a brief period focus an aroused public opinion upon a few issues in this field.

CONCLUDING OBSERVATIONS

Marketing legislation in recent years has reflected the state of flux in both the system of marketing and the philosophic rationalization of competition and its regulation. Ours appears to be a transitional period; hence, it is not surprising that trade relations and the sets of ideas about them should be confused. Fortunately for all of us, the marketing mechanism seems able to perform its proper function of supplying goods and services to consumers with considerable efficiency in spite of great legislative abuse. The prime public issue of our period as far as the regulation of marketing is concerned is to direct legislative zeal into sound channels—if this be possible. Industrial and regulative evolution has carried the American economy (as well as that of the capitalistic world in general) along to the point where regulation no longer can be intended merely to facilitate trade passively or to preserve competition quantitatively. It is a hopeful sign that the concept of "competition" is leaving the shibboleth stage.

In the meantime, though, regulation in the public interest has become greatly more difficult by contrast with the assumptions and beliefs of the past generation. Regulative procedures today, to be sound, must find ways and means of bringing expert analysis and judgment to bear upon public problems in a manner which allows the long-run general interest to be served, instead of a presumed short-run vested interest. Most marketing legislation is the product of the political pressures of special groups who wish to conserve their own short-run positions. Unfortunately for them, time and again they are unaware of the immediate compensatory forces and the long-run consequences which subvert their short-run objectives.

Much of the current legislation serves

MARKETING LEGISLATION 175

the public interest chiefly because its proponents misunderstood the full, ultimate effects of their laws; not because it was intended to enlarge the general welfare. Sponsoring members of trades and the public would gain if greater wisdom and criteria derived from the public welfare could be brought to bear. Basic clashes of interest in markets ideally should not and cannot be resolved by the political strength of the parties to the conflicts, but only in terms of relative contribution to social welfare. In an ideal system of regulation, Federal, state, and local legislation would be so oriented and integrated. There is, of course, some cause for optimism in a few directions, as, e.g., food and drug legislation. But the larger tasks are still ahead.

Ewald T. Grether, Ph.D., is professor of economics on the Flood Foundation at the University of California, Berkeley, and managing editor of the Journal of Marketing. He was visiting professor of marketing at the University of Pennsylvania, 1938–39, and has had summer session and other appointments at Columbia University, University of California at Los Angeles, Montana University, and the University of Nebraska. He is author or co-author of "Resale Price Maintenance in Great Britain" (1935), "Essays in Social Economics" (1935), "Price Control under Fair Trade Legislation" (1939), and "Restriction of Retail Price Cutting" (1936).

[26]

Excerpt from Morton Keller, *Regulating a New Economy: Public Policy and Economic Change in America, 1900–1933*, 102–14, 259–62.

Prices, Products, and Sales

The regulatory system most directly confronted the new consumer economy in the realms of prices, products, and sales. Here basic yet conflicting policy goals—to stimulate innovation and growth yet guard against overproduction and harmful price cutting—came to a head. But these intensely modern regulatory problems arose within a structure of law and government designed to deal more with the problems of production and competition than with the problems of consumption and distribution; to make war on scarcity rather than to come to terms with abundance.

A case in point is that innocuous appliance the electric refrigerator. By the 1930s about seventy manufacturers faced classic problems of overproduction and cutthroat competition. And their marketing techniques raised a host of legal issues. Devices such as conditional sales and time payments dated from the nineteenth century. But now they functioned in a larger and more complex economic and social setting, with commensurately more complex legal consequences.

Apartment house builders, and retailers such as meat markets and florists, were the first major customers for refrigerators. Often they failed before they paid for these appliances. As a result the manufacturers were enmeshed in sticky legal controversies involving foreclosures and creditors' claims, possession and repossession. Time payments and other personal finance plans were necessary to create a mass market for refrigerators. Manufacturers made arrangements with finance companies to buy installment paper from retail dealers, but this led to difficulties with state usury laws. Litigation stretching from conflicts over sales contracts with dealers to personal injury claims by consumers completed this Hobbesian scene. One observer understandably concluded: "the list of legal problems in national merchandizing might be multiplied without limit."[54]

Price regulation was rare in the market economy of the nineteenth century. But two new issues became important in the early 1900s: resale price maintenance by manufacturers, and the threat to independent retailers posed by department and especially chain stores.

At first few doubted that producers could make enforceable resale price maintenance contracts with their distributors and retailers. True, the Department of Justice challenged one such contract soon after the passage of the Sherman Antitrust Act. But a federal circuit court sustained the agreement in 1892, and the government did not challenge resale price maintenance again for twenty-three years.[55]

During the early twentieth century increasing numbers of consumer brands came to be marketed nationally, usually with contracts

104 · Regulating Business

tying wholesalers, distributors, and retailers to a price structure determined by the manufacturer. "Price maintenance," said an observer in 1918, "has developed in part as a concomitant of national advertising." It became a matter of substantial political and legal concern— distinct from trust control, yet, like the concentration of corporate ownership, raising old fears of unfair competition in a new form.[56]

A number of lawsuits challenged the right of firms holding patents on new products to make price maintenance a stipulation in their licensing contracts. The courts consistently upheld the validity of these contracts. A circuit court of appeals decision affirmed the right of the Cream of Wheat Company to refuse to let the price-cutting A&P stores sell its product: "We have not yet reached the stage where the selection of a trader's customers is made for him by the government."[57]

Similar policies prevailed abroad, where cartel practices were much more widely accepted. A leading British case in 1901 held that price maintenance agreements did not restrain trade, and thus could be enforced in the courts. Decisions in the 1920s involving Dunlop tires and Palmolive soap came to a similar conclusion. French law went further: it held that to cut prices in itself might be a form of unfair trade.[58]

But as large-scale consumer marketing spread, policy considerations similar to those that fueled antitrust began to take hold. The first Supreme Court caveat came in *Miles v. Park* (1911). This case had to do with patent medicines, one of the oldest (and shadiest) of mass consumer products. Justice Charles Evans Hughes's majority opinion concluded that in this instance resale price maintenance was contrary to public policy. These were commodities in the "channels of trade," and under the Sherman Act the manufacturer could not interfere with the "traffic." Holmes dissented. A fair price, he thought, would emerge from "the competition of conflicting desires" and "the equilibrium of social desires." In any event, "the most enlightened judicial policy is to let people manage their own business in their own way." Louis D. Brandeis, too, favored resale price maintenance, but for his own, familiar reasons: it would help small manufacturers compete against large integrated firms and protect them from the coercion of big mail order and chain distributors.[59]

The issue of resale price maintenance grew in intensity as manufacturers and retailers competed for profits and consumer goodwill. The American Fair Trade League appeared in 1913 to support price main-

tenance, the National Trade Association in 1915 to resist it. Department, chain, and cut-rate stores—growing powers in retailing—led
the opposition. Manufacturers and jobbers with a stake in the market
value of brand-name products, and lesser retailers and wholesalers
suffering from the competition of the large retail outlets sparked the
defense. By 1916, Massachusetts, North Carolina, and South Dakota
had laws outlawing resale price maintenance as an illegal restraint of
trade. And about thirty "fair trade" laws enforcing price maintenance
came before Congress from 1913 to 1932, though none passed.[60]

The Supreme Court responded cautiously to this complex new issue. Justice James McReynolds held in 1919 that a manufacturer
could set the price at which his product might be resold and might
refuse to sell to noncooperative dealers, as long as there was no monopolistic intent. But in 1922—Holmes and Brandeis dissenting—the
Court upheld the contention of the Federal Trade Commission that
the Beech-Nut Packing Company's resale price schedule violated the
antitrust laws. This encouraged the FTC to issue complaints against
a number of manufacturers and distributors. In the traditional pattern
of regulator's thrust and regulatee's parry, large producers began to develop their own sales networks, with retailers acting as the manufacturer's agents and the firm holding title to its product: a practice upheld in *U.S. v. General Electric* (1926).[61]

Closely related to resale price maintenance was the growing demand of independent storekeepers (weak singly, politically potent in
aggregate) for checks on large-scale retailing. Several states around the
turn of the century tried to impose punitive taxes and otherwise restrict department stores, but the courts blocked these efforts on due
process grounds.

Chain stores—"foreign-owned, community-wrecking"—posed a
greater threat. Local retailers could not match their purchasing and
competitive power. Pressure for regulation to preserve the independent storekeeper came to a head with the Depression: "The feeling
aroused by the sight of the rapid expropriation of the field of merchandising by the chain store is of the same type, psychologically, as the
fear of the growing power of the corporation and the consequent dis-
couragement of individual initiative, so common fifty or seventy-five
years ago."[62]

From 1929 to 1931 about 80 anti-chain-store laws were introduced
in state legislatures. Six passed: in Georgia, Indiana, Kentucky, Mississippi, North Carolina, and South Carolina. They either imposed a

106 · Regulating Business

license tax on each unit of a chain above a certain number or limited outright the quantity of retail units under central control. But like antitrust, the anti-chain-store movement faced substantial legal, political, and economic obstacles. Advocates of chain stores argued that these restrictions violated the due process and equal protection clauses of the Fourteenth Amendment; and there was an obvious consumer interest in the efficiencies and economies of large-scale retailing.[63]

Some state courts frowned on the anti-chain-store laws as violations of equal protection. The Supreme Court upheld Indiana's chain-store-license tax act in 1931. But in 1933 it struck down a Florida law outlawing chains with stores in more than one county: this, the Court said, was an unacceptable classification. Brandeis in dissent reviewed the history of the American corporation—"the Frankenstein monster which States have created by their corporation laws"—and warned that the decision unduly limited the power of the commonwealth to control that fearsome economic force.[64]

As the Depression went on, ever more deeply eroding the economic position of small retailers, pressure grew for state and national action against chain-store price-cutting. The Supreme Court accepted price-fixing by a trade association of coal producers in 1933, and a New York milk price-fixing law in 1934. But it did so on the ground that the Depression constituted a national emergency. The more ambitious attempts of the NRA and the first AAA to put a floor under industrial and agricultural prices ran into constitutional roadblocks. And in 1936 the Court upheld a government effort to dissolve the Sugar Institute for price-fixing.[65]

Meanwhile, state legislatures—about half of them by 1935—passed "fair trade" laws imposing controls on retail pricing. An extensive FTC report on the adverse impact of chain stores, together with political pressure from retailers, induced Congress to pass the Robinson-Patman Act of 1936. This law extended the constraints of the Clayton Act to chain and other multiple-outlet retailers and empowered the FTC to act against quantity discounting, advertising allowances, and other practices that made things difficult for independent retailers. A further attempt to buttress the position of small retailers came with the Miller-Tydings Act of 1937, which exempted state resale price maintenance laws from federal antitrust provisions.[66]

By the late 1930s an impressive regulatory dike had been erected to stem the erosive power of large-scale retailing. But in the long run it was not possible so to contain economic change. As the economy recovered, the courts looked less favorably on pricing regulation. The chains, labor unions, and consumer groups maintained a continuing pressure to secure the pricing and other advantages of mass marketing. And in the decades since World War II these restraints have all but disappeared.

The control of products, like the control of prices, attracted ever more regulatory attention during the early twentieth century. Patents and copyrights—traditional ways of signifying product ownership—had to respond to new issues and interests. So too did trademarks and advertising, the major modes of product identification.

Patent and copyright laws, based on the constitutional provision empowering Congress "to promote the Progress of Science and useful Arts, by securing for limited Times to Authors and Inventors the exclusive Right to their respective Writings and Discoveries," were among the earliest federal regulatory acts. The patent system was much admired for the protection accorded inventors (few countries matched its coverage of seventeen years) and for the efficiency of its examiners.

But by the beginning of the twentieth century, Anglo-American patent law seemed less than adequate to the conditions of modern economic life. The spur of German and American industrial competition led to a turn-of-the-century British movement "to restore the integrity of a corrupted theory and deteriorated practice of the law." Britain's new patent law of 1907 was supposed to increase the protection extended to its inventive citizens. But dissatisfaction persisted with a system that did not appear to be attuned to the needs of modern industry.[67]

The American patent system also came in for criticism. Well-founded complaints mounted that large corporations used patents to stifle competition and to assure their control of distribution and sales. But firms, too, complained that patenting was time-consuming, out of sync with the character and complexity of new technologies. Pressure rose for structural reform, along familiar Progressive lines of centralization and uniformity. Proposals were made for a separate patent court, and for a court of patent appeals in Washington. A 1906 congressional act (supported by the American Bar Association) sought to extend the period of patent protection, primarily to give inventors a

108 · Regulating Business

longer period in which to protect themselves from infringement suits.[68]

The most heated issue was the degree to which the use of patents by large corporations conflicted with antitrust. From one point of view a patent granted "a true monopoly," bringing corporate patentees in interstate commerce within the purview of the Sherman Act. But a patent was also a privilege granted by law. Thus it could be—and was—argued that it escaped the sanctions of antitrust, which aimed at restraints of trade emerging from the play of the market.[69]

The Supreme Court accepted that distinction: patent protection, after all, was enshrined in the Constitution. The Court held in 1902 that fixing the price of a patented article did not violate the Sherman Act. A decade later it passed on the right of a patentee (the A. B. Dick Company, maker of the mimeograph) to require purchasers to use its own ink, paper, and other accessories. Traditionally, the Court said, the law of sales "permits one who by purchase becomes owner of a machine to use it in any way not forbidden by that law. But such right of user is in conflict with the right of the patentee to exclude others from all use of the invention. Which right shall yield?" By a four-to-three vote the justices upheld the mimeograph company.[70]

A bill before Congress sought to bring patent holders under the Sherman Act by compelling them to grant licenses after three instead of seventeen years. Manufacturers, patent attorneys, inventors, and representatives of commercial and scientific organizations testified in opposition, arguing that this would stifle inventiveness. President Taft, typically, proposed to appoint a patent commission to study the situation, and the bill failed to become law.[71]

By 1914 General Electric held an estimated 10,000 to 15,000 patents and International Harvester 17,000, stirring fears that they posed serious threats to industrial progress. After America entered the war, the number of German-held patents in the chemical and other industries reinforced the view that limits should be placed on the degree to which possessors of patents could control their use. The Supreme Court reflected this attitude in a pair of 1917 decisions. One struck down the requirement that users of a patented film projector restrict themselves to specified (but unpatented) films. The other rejected an attempt by the owners of a phonograph to fix the price at which the machine reached the "ultimate user." A changing Court appeared to be more aware of the danger implicit in unified control over the manufacture and sale of goods.[72]

These conflicts over patent policy continued—indeed, intensified—during the 1920s. The major function of many trade associations was to establish and enforce patent pools for their members.
Providers of new products and services such as the telephone, radio
broadcasting, motion pictures, cameras, electric appliances, and automobiles relied heavily on these pools to exclude the entry of competitors and enjoy the profits of invention and innovation. But in so
doing they constantly ran the risk of prosecution under the Sherman
Act. In 1926 the Supreme Court allowed General Electric to fix the
price of patented products but struck down the company's attempts
to control their resale. Soon afterward the Court refused to review a
federal court finding that the Radio Corporation of America had substantially reduced competition by entering into licensing agreements
with other radio tube manufacturers. In 1931 the Court for the first
time passed on an extensive intercorporate system of patent pooling
and cross-licensing—in this instance, the gasoline cracking process.
But since the agreement affected only one-fourth of total gas output,
it found no violation of the Sherman Act.[73]

As in other areas of business practice, the advent of the Depression
toughened judicial attitudes. From 1901 to 1931 the Supreme Court
heard an average of two patent cases a year; from December 1930 to
December 1932 it decided eleven such cases, and all went against the
patent holder. Still, the overall record of early twentieth-century patent law was not of a clear and distinct policy, but of an increasingly
complex, continuously uncertain response.[74]

Copyright, like patents, protected property—but property with distinctive social and cultural overtones. The tendency in the law to
equate literary or artistic creation with product invention was strong.
Nevertheless, copyrighted works had their own special character.

Thus—in contrast to the policy for patents—nineteenth-century
American copyright policy placed greater value on access to the product than on protecting its creator. Americans could freely pirate British and other foreign writing. And for all its length—twenty-eight
years plus a fourteen-year renewal—the extent of American protection was less than that of other nations, whose copyright laws extended for the life of the author and beyond.[75]

But the exploding commercialization of words and pictures around
the turn of the century brought pressures for change in copyright law
similar to those at work in the realm of patents. A 1903 review of
"Our Archaic Copyright Laws" observed that "the reproduction of the

110 · Regulating Business

varying things which are the subject of copyright has enormously increased. The wealth and business of the country and the method and means of duplication have increased immeasurably. The law requires adaptation to these modern conditions. It is no longer possible to summarize it in a few sections covering everything copyrightable."[76]

The courts soon confronted a new world of words and images. A federal court in 1901 extended copyright protection to *The Black Crook*, widely regarded as a pornographic work; a Boston Sunday paper was sued for $150,000 for printing the text of a current Tin Pan Alley favorite, "Daddy Wouldn't Buy Me a Bow Wow"; a federal court in 1903 and statute law in 1912 brought moving pictures within the purview of copyright. Holmes in the Supreme Court set out a broad view of what might be copyrighted. Even circus scenes used for advertisements, he held, qualified as a "personal reaction . . . upon nature."[77]

The copyright law of 1909 reflected the play of new interests and ideas. The nation's leading publishers, seeking to control a chaotic market, created the American Booksellers' Association in 1901. The association set (higher) standard prices for books, blacklisted dealers who discounted, and lobbied for a new copyright law. A draft bill emerged from two Library of Congress conferences attended by representatives of authors and artists, lawyers, playwrights, librarians, book, newspaper, and music publishers, theater managers, and typographers—the community of word and picture makers.

The statute enacted by Congress codified existing copyright law. But it also served the interests of copyright holders (authors or publishers): it doubled the renewal period to twenty-eight years and extended copyright protection to lectures, sermons, speeches, sheet music, drama and art, compilations and abridgments, and works of a scientific or technical character. Though vague in its general principles, this was "a peculiarly busy piece of legislation, crammed with details," an open invitation to continuing judicial interpretation.[78]

One thing it did not do: give publishers permanent control over the prices charged for their books. Publishers, like other producers catering to a mass market, wanted to control the retail prices of their products. They argued that copyright like patenting implied the power of resale price maintenance. Librarians and Macy's department store, a leading book discounter, took issue. In the course of a decade of litigation, the Supreme Court held that copyright did not entitle holders to fix retail prices, nor did it exempt them from state and national antitrust law.[79]

But changing technology, not antitrust, shaped copyright law in the 1920s. The sudden rise of radio posed distinctive new problems. Early radio performers often were unpaid, and of course no direct charges were levied on listeners. Could broadcasters claim exclusive performance rights "publicly for profit" under the 1909 copyright act? A few judges initially thought not. But from the mid-1920s on the courts agreed that what went out on radio was unquestionably a public performance, and that profit was indeed the name of the broadcasting game. Another issue: did the unauthorized broadcasting of a musical production infringe its copyright? Brandeis, speaking for the Supreme Court, settled the matter in 1931: "Reproduction . . . amounts to a performance."[80]

In the same year the Vestal Copyright Act strengthened the claim of authors and composers to their work in radio and the movies. It also authorized the government to become a signatory to the Bern Copyright Convention. The increasing popularity overseas of American books, plays, and movies finally overrode the traditional view that Americans gained more than they lost by staying out of the International Copyright Union.

Only a few Democrats opposed the bill: advocates of the old belief that copyright infringed on the people's right to free access to ideas and information. But facts and thoughts increasingly were products disseminated in commercial contexts, and copyright was the only practical way to connect "the Progress of Science and useful Arts" to the world of the big media and massive consumer audiences.[81]

The appearance of a rich body of law and legislation dealing with trademarks was an even more vivid demonstration that the rise of a consumer economy gave new meaning to the concept of property. Common law doctrine held that the property right in a trademark derived from priority of use. An 1870 congressional act tried to add a federal registration requirement. But in 1879 the Supreme Court severely limited the impact of the law.[82]

As in patent and copyright law, constitutional limitations, jurisdictional infighting, the clash of interests, and economic change made it difficult to provide the protection that trademarks in theory afforded. Congress passed a law in 1905 (the same year as a new British trademarks act) that tried to clarify matters by declaring that an infringement existed if a similar trademark was used for merchandise with "substantially the same descriptive properties as those set forth in the registration." But this was a "slovenly piece of legislation." And courts added to the confusion by accepting any trademark "actively and ex-

112 · Regulating Business

clusively used." The result: "what Congress left uncertain the Courts have made incomprehensible."[83]

Meanwhile, the number of trademarked consumer products kept rising. By 1912, 62,500 trademark applications had been filed in the Patent Office under the 1905 law. One captain of industry declared, "I would rather have a celebrated trade-mark than a million dollar plant." The American Tobacco Company's trademarks were valued at $45 million, one-fifth of its total assets. Like patents, trademarks had become a major instrument in the creation and marketing of the consumer products that fueled the modern American economy. The commissioner of patents and the District of Columbia Court of Appeals (which acted as the appellate tribunal for the commissioner's decisions) heard an ever-larger number of trademark disputes.[84]

The states now got into the act. The California and New York legislatures passed laws providing for state trademark registration. But the United States Trade-Mark Association opposed this challenge to a national system of registration and got the California law repealed on the ground that Congress's interstate commerce power enabled it to exercise exclusive control over trademarks.[85]

As the commercial importance of trademarks grew, so did their entanglement in the law of antitrust. In 1916 the Supreme Court defined trademarks not as a form of property, but as a business practice: "The common law of trade marks is but a part of the broader law of unfair competition."[86] By the 1920s, courts generally assumed that the purpose of a trademark was not to define prior claim to a product, but to foster consumer brand loyalty. A mark of ownership had become an instrument of sales. The chief policy concern now was to protect trademarks from exploitation by competitors, while not allowing them to stultify competition and innovation.

This changing view did not produce greater legal or regulatory clarity. If anything, trademarks became more difficult to define. Some product names—Kodak, Victrola—became part of the language; others—Blue Ribbon, Gold Medal—had doubtful claims to originality or exclusiveness. Nor did their sheer number help. By 1934 some 300,000 trademarks were registered with the Patent Office, and this was thought to be only about one-fifth of the total in use.

The courts paid increasing attention to the degree to which a trademark stood for some unique aspect of the product that it represented. As such it had real commercial value and needed to be protected in a mass consumer economy. Judge Learned Hand wryly took note of a growing "consciousness of the need for breadth and liberality in coping with the progressive ingenuity of commercial depravity." The Supreme Court in 1936 upheld an Illinois ban on the sale of trademarked items at a cut-rate price. But this was far from the last word on the subject. The legal future of this instrument of product differentiation would be no less complex and uncertain than its past.[87]

As trademarks were to patents, so advertising was to copyright: an application of ideas and images to the marketing demands of a consumer economy. It was in the early twentieth century that advertising assumed a place in American economic life substantial and distinctive enough to evoke a regulatory response. And as elsewhere, that regulation had a dual character: it dealt with the way in which the advertising business was conducted and with its impact on the society at large.

Advertising grew in pace with the consumer economy that it did so much to foster. The major advertisers were the companies whose products dominated the mass consumer market: packaged food, automobiles, tobacco, drugs. By 1929 advertising costs amounted to almost 3 percent of the gross national product, twice the pre-1914 level. But influence had its price. A federal law in 1872 forbade the use of patent medicines. In 1916 the Supreme Court held that a Florida real estate company's fanciful claims did not gain legitimacy from the fact that the land turned out to be worth its price: the mails could not be used for false representation.[88]

As the advertising business grew, it turned to the preemptive self-regulation favored by other major industries. Leading admen backed a model act that held advertisers responsible for falsity even in the absence of foreknowledge or of direct harm to an individual. Fourteen states passed versions of the model law in 1913, another fourteen by 1919. The Maine and Georgia legislatures rejected it because rural newspapers feared its effect on patent medicine revenue.

Like most general prohibitory legislation, these statutes were too broad-gauged to be enforceable. During the 1920s an increasing number of state laws dealt with common, specific practices of deception. Most required that labels accurately describe the products to which they were attached. But the variety and extent of advertising, the industry's political influence, and a reluctance to clamp down too tightly on a form of expression put severe constraints on regulation.[89]

After 1914 the Federal Trade Commission made false and deceptive

114 · Regulating Business

advertising one of its concerns at the behest of, among others, the Associated Advertising Clubs, which like other spokesmen for large enterprises saw advantages in uniform, federal regulation. By 1920, 67 percent of the FTC's workload dealt with false and misleading advertising; by 1929, 85 percent; by 1932 (despite the Depression), 92 percent. Critics charged that the FTC went beyond its mandate to maintain competition, and entered the realm of censorship.[90]

The federal courts were divided between their distaste for commercial immorality and their disinclination to allow the FTC to encroach on what they saw as their jurisdiction. Thus the Supreme Court in 1920 weakened federal regulation of the advertising business by holding that, like insurance, it was not interstate commerce per se. When the FTC issued a cease-and-desist order against the Winsted Hosiery Company for advertising cotton goods as wool, a federal court set it aside, observing that the commission was "not a censor of commercial morals generally." But the Supreme Court reinstated the order on the ground that false advertising was a form of unfair competition.[91]

Judges, legislators, and regulators appear to have been uncertain whether the primary purpose in restricting fraudulent advertising was to protect competing producers or the consuming public—objectives that were by no means always compatible. Not surprisingly, their response was halting and ambiguous. Congress's authority rested primarily on its power over the mails—tempered by fear of censorship. The FTC intervened to check unfair or improper business practices—tempered by the courts' concern lest the commission overreach its mandate. The courts wavered between their commitment to an open market economy and their distaste for commercial fraud. Here as in so many other areas of business regulation, it was evident that the rise of a consumer economy did not clarify or concentrate but, instead, complicated and diffused the regulatory role of the state.

54. Richard Ford, "Legal Problems in National Merchandizing," *Mich LR*, 32 (1913–14), 433–450.
55. E. R. A. Seligman and Robert A. Love, *Price Cutting and Price Maintenance: A Study in Economics* (New York, 1932), pp. 44–45.
56. H. R. Tosdal, "Price Maintenance," *American Economic Review*, 8 (1918), 31. See also Waldemar Kaempffert, "Price Maintenance and Modern Merchandising," *Sci Am*, 108 (1913), 566; *Sci Am*, 109 (1913), 7, 20; Myron W. Watkins, "The Change in Trust Policy," *Harv LR*, 38 (1921–22), 830.
57. A&P v. Cream of Wheat Co., 224 Fed. 566 (2nd Cir., 1915); Sumner H. Slichter, "The Cream of Wheat Case," *Pol Sci Q*, 31 (1916), 392–412.
58. Elliman v. Carrington [1901] 2 Ch. 275; "Price Maintenance Agreements in England," *Am LR*, 49 (1915), 271–274; "Price-Maintenance Agreements," *Law Times*, 164 (1927), 263–264; on France, Charles L. Miller, *Legal Status of Maintenance of Uniform Resale Prices* (New York, 1916), p. 22.
59. Hughes and Holmes in Miles v. Park, 220 U.S. 373, 408–409, 411–412 (1911); A. D. Neale, *The Antitrust Laws of the United States of America*, 2d ed. (Cambridge, 1970), chap. 10. See also "Price Cutting as a Tort," *Harv LR*, 27 (1913–14), 374–375; "On Maintaining Makers' Prices," *Harper's Weekly*, 57 (June 14, 1913), 6.
60. Tosdal, "Price Maintenance," pp. 33–35; "Fair Trade Legislation: The Constitutionality of a State Experiment in Resale Price Maintenance," *Harv LR*, 49 (1936), 811–821. See also "Price Maintenance at Common Law and under Proposed Legislation," *Harv LR*, 30 (1916–17), 68–75.
61. U.S. v. Colgate, 250 U.S. 300 (1919); F.T.C. v. Beech-Nut Packing Co., 257 U.S. 441 (1922); U.S. v. General Electric Co., 272 U.S. 476 (1926); Gilbert H. Montague, "Price Fixing, Lawful and Unlawful," *Am LR*, 62 (1928), 505–528; Seligman and Love, *Price Cutting*, p. 87.
62. *Nation*, 72 (1901), 125; on department stores, Chicago v. Netcher, 55 N.E. 707 (Ill., 1899); State v. Ashbrook, 55 S.W. 627 (Mo., 1900); Samuel Becker and Robert A. Hess, "The Chain Store License Tax and the Fourteenth Amendment," *North Carolina Law Review*, 7 (1928–29), 127. See also F. J. Harper, "'A New Battle in Evolution': The Anti–Chain Store Trade-at-Home Agitation of 1929–1930," *Journal of American Studies*, 16 (1982),

260 · *Notes to Pages 106–108*

407–426; "Organizing Retail Trades," *New Republic,* 1 (1915), 19–20; John T. Flynn, "Chain Stores: Menace or Promise?" *New Republic,* 66 (1931), 270–273.

63. J. Ross Harrington, "The Chain Store Era and the Law," *Notre Dame Lawyer,* 4 (1929), 491–505; Edward Simms, "Chain Stores and the Courts," *Virginia Law Review,* 17 (1931), 313–324.

64. Brandeis in Liggett v. Lee, 288 U.S. 517, 567 (1933); Tax Commissioners v. Jackson, 283 U.S. 527 (1931). See also Juliet Blumenfeld, "Retail Trade Regulations and Their Constitutionality," *Cal LR,* 22 (1933–34), 86–105.

65. Appalachian Coals, Inc., v. U.S. 288 U.S. 344 (1933); Nebbia v. New York, 291 U.S. 502 (1934); Robert L. Hale, "The Constitution and the Price System: Some Reflections on Nebbia v. New York," *Col LR,* 34 (1934), 401–425; Sugar Institute, Inc., v. U.S., 297 U.S. 553 (1936); George J. Feldman, "Legal Aspects of Federal and State Price Control," *Boston University Law Review,* 16 (1936), 570–594.

66. Ewald T. Grether, "Experience in California with Fair Trade Legislation Restricting Price Cutting," *Cal LR,* 24 (1935–36), 640–700; Charles D. Evans, "The Anti–Price Discrimination Act of 1936," *Virginia Law Review,* 23 (1936–37), 140–177; Milo F. Hamilton and Lee Loevinger, "The Second Attack on Price Discrimination: The Robinson-Patman Act,"*Washington University Law Quarterly,* 22 (1937), 153–186. See also Karl G. Ryant, "The South and the Movement against Chain Stores," *Journal of Social History,* 39 (1973), 207–222; Ellis W. Hawley, *The New Deal and the Problem of Monopoly* (Princeton, 1966), pp. 249–254; Joseph C. Palamountain, Jr., *The Politics of Distribution* (Cambridge, Mass., 1955), chaps. 6, 7.

67. J. W. Gordon, "Reform of the Patent Law," *Law Magazine and Review,* 31 (1906), 31; R. W. Wallace, "The Working of the Patent Acts," ibid., pp. 257–272; "American vs. British Patent Protection," *Sci Am,* 119 (1918), 523, 526, 539; "Reform of the British Patent System," *Nature,* 122 (1928), 757–761. See also G. H. B. Kenrick, "The Development of Patent Law," *Law Magazine and Review,* 26 (1901), 5–19.

68. Frederick P. Fish, "The Patent System in Its Relation to Industrial Development," *Forum,* 42 (1909), 8–22; William Macomber, "Patents and Industrial Progress," *NAR,* 191 (1910), 805–813; "Proposed Bill for the Extension of Patents," *Sci Am,* 94 (1906), 267; H. Ward Leonard, "The Legal Monstrosity of Our Patent System," *Forum,* 41 (1909), 496–505; Isaac L. Rice, "Suggestions for Amendments to our Patent Laws," ibid., pp. 189–198. See also David F. Noble, *America by Design* (New York, 1977), chap. 6.

69. Edwin H. Abbot, Jr., "Patents and the Sherman Act," *Col LR,* 12 (1912), 709–723.

70. Henry v. A. B. Dick Co., 224 U.S. 12 (1912); Bement v. National Harrow Co., 186 U.S. 70 (1902); Thomas R. Powell, "The Nature of a Patent Right," *Col LR,* 17 (1917), 666. See also *Lit Dig,* 44 (1912), 573–574.

71. "The Sherman Anti-Trust Act and the Patentee," *Sci Am,* 107 (1912), 434; Gilbert H. Montague, "The Proposed Patent Law Revision," *Harv LR,* 26

(1912–13), 128–145; idem, "The Spirit of the American Patent System," *NAR*, 196 (1912), 682–693; *J Pol Ec*, 20 (1912), 633–635; Montague, "The Bogey of the 'Patent Monopoly,' *Annals*, 42 (1912), 251–262.

72. William Macomber, "The War and Our Patent Laws," *Yale LJ*, 25 (1915–16), 396–404; Straus v. Victor Talking Machine Co., 243 U.S. 490 (1917); Motion Picture Patents Co. v. Universal Film Mfg. Co., 243 U.S. 502 (1917).

73. Floyd L. Vaughan, "The Relation of Patents to Industrial Monopolies," *Annals*, 147 (1930), 40–50; U.S. v. General Electric Co., 272 U.S. 476 (1926); R.C.A. v. Lloyd, 278 U.S. 648 (1928); Carbice Corp. v. Amer. Patents Development Corp., 283 U.S. 27 (1931); Standard Oil Co. of Indiana v. U.S., 283 U.S. 163 (1931). See also "Patent Pools and the Sherman Act," *Yale LJ*, 40 (1931), 1297–1303; Horace R. Lamb, "The Relation of the Patent Law to the Federal Anti-Trust Laws," *Cornell LQ*, 12 (1927), 261–285; Alfred McCormack, "Restrictive Patent Licenses and Restraint of Trade," *Col LR*, 31 (1931), 743–777.

74. John Dickinson, "Some Recent Developments in Patent Law," *ABA Journal*, 20 (1934), 576.

75. George H. Putnam, "The Copyright Law of the United States and the Authors of the Continent," *Critic*, 44 (1904), 60–64; PRO, *Cab 37*, 103 (1910), no. 31.

76. Samuel J. Elder, "Our Archaic Copyright Laws," *Am LR*, 37 (1903), 225.

77. Holmes in Bleistein v. Donaldson Lithographing Co., 188 U.S. 239 (1903); Hegeman v. Springer, 110 Fed. 374 (1901); Edward S. Rogers, "Copyright and Morals," *Mich LR*, 18 (1919–20), 390–404; Edison v. Lubin, 122 Fed. 240 (1903); on song, Elder, "Archaic Copyright Laws," p. 223. See also George P. Brett, "The Need of a New Copyright Law," *Ind*, 56 (1904), 612–614; Benjamin Kaplan, *An Unhurried View of Copyright* (New York, 1967), p. 34–37.

78. Kaplan, *Unhurried View*, p. 38; W. P. Cutter, "The Book Trust and the Copyright Bill," *Ind*, 63 (1907), 1239–41; Thorvald Solberg, "Copyright Law Reform," *Yale LJ*, 35 (1925–26), 62–65; "The New Copyright Law," *Outlook*, 91 (1909), 755–756.

79. Bobbs-Merrill Co. v. Straus, 210 U.S. 339 (1908); R. H. Macy & Co. v. Amer. Publishers' Assn., 231 U.S. 222 (1913); H. R. Tosdal, "Price Maintenance in the Book Trade," *Q J Ec*, 30 (1915–16), 86–109.

80. Brandeis in Buck v. Jewell-LaSalle Realty Co., 283 U.S. 191 (1931); W. Jefferson Davis, "Copyrighted Radio," *Virginia Law Review*, 16 (1929–30), 49; Lawrence P. Simpson, "Broadcasting as Copyright Infringement," *Air Law Review*, 1 (1930), 134–139.

81. Thorvald Solberg, "The Present Copyright Situation," *Yale LJ*, 40 (1930–31), 184–214; on Vestal bill, *Publishers Weekly*, 119 (1931), 296–297, 826–827; Lawrence P. Simpson, "The Copyright Situation as Affecting Radio Broadcasting," *NYU Law Quarterly*, 9 (1931–32), 180–197. See also Charles B. Collins, "Some Obsolescent Doctrines of the Law of Copyright," *Southern California Law Review*, 1 (1927–28), 127–140.

82. Keller, *Affairs of State*, pp. 420–421; Baker v. Selden, 101 U.S. 99 (1879).

262 · Notes to Pages 112–116

83. Edward S. Rogers, "The Expensive Futility of the United States Trade-Mark Statute," *Mich LR,* 2 (1913–14), 668, 665, 667; Arthur P. Greeley, "The Proposed New Trade-Mark Law," *Sci Am,* 92 (1905), 19.
84. "Trade-Mark Development during the Last Seven Years," *Sci Am,* 106 (1912), 569; Arthur W. Barber, "The Constitution and Trade-Marks," *Lawyer & Banker,* 5 (1912), 210–217.
85. "Trademarks: Relation of Trademark Infringement to the Law of Unfair Competition," *Cal LR,* 7 (1919), 201–204; Frank I. Schechter, "The Rational Basis of Trademark Protection," *Harv LR,* 40 (1926–27), 814–818.
86. Hanover v. Metcalf, 240 U.S. 403, 413 (1916).
87. Hand in Ely-Norris Safe Co. v. Mosler Safe Co., 7 Fed. 2d 603, 604 (2d Cir., 1925); Schechter, "Rational Basis," pp. 822–831; idem, "Fog and Fiction in Trade-Mark Protection," *Col LR,* 36 (1936), 69; Old Dearborn Distributing Co. v. Seagram Distillers Corp., 299 U.S. 183 (1936).
88. Roland Marchand, *Advertising and the American Dream* (Berkeley, 1985); on percentage of GNP, Daniel Pope, *The Making of Modern Advertising* (New York, 1983), p. 26; Tom E. Shearer, "The National Government and False Advertising," *Iowa Law Review,* 19 (1933–34), U.S. v. New South Farm and Home Co., 241 U.S. 64 (1916), James H. Young, "Legalized Morality in Advertising," *Outlook,* 111 (1916), 300–301.
89. "Untrue Advertising," *Yale LJ,* 36 (1926–27), 1155–62; "The Imitation of Advertising," *Harv LR,* 45 (1931–32), 542–548.
90. On FTC statistics, "Comments," *Mich LR,* 32 (1933–34), 1145; Milton Handler, "False and Misleading Advertising," *Yale LJ,* 39 (1929–30), 22; "Scope of the Jurisdiction of the Federal Trade Commission over False and Misleading Advertising," *Yale LJ,* 40 (1930–31), 617–631.
91. Winsted Hosiery Co. v. F.T.C., 272 Fed. 957, 960 (2d Cir., 1921); Blumenstock Bros. Advertising Co. v. Curtis Publishing Co., 252 U.S. 436 (1920); F.T.C. v. Winsted Hosiery Co., 258 U.S. 483 (1922).

[27]

Were Freight Rates Used to Keep the South and West Down?

Carole E. Scott
West Georgia College

ABSTRACT

Some claim that the scale of the conspiracy required to confine the South and West to producing raw materials via discriminatory freight rates was unreasonably great, therefore, it couldn't have happened. Would they say blacks couldn't have been held back by discrimination because millions of whites would have had to conspire? Individual self interest accompanied by facilitating circumstances can lead to behavior identical to that produced by a conspiracy, and it is reasonable to assume this was true of freight rates in the past.

Truth or hyperbole? These were the comments of Arne Wiprud, a former railroad counsel, in 1945:

> Agriculture, mining, manufacturing, merchandising, and many other activities are vitally affected by the adequacy and the cost of transportation. Indeed, the character of available transportation determines the life of communities and of whole states, permitting one industry to flourish and condemning another to decay, stimulating the development of some resources and leaving others untouched. Public transportation is one of the basic determinants of the social and political life of a nation....The distance between the farmer, the manufacturer, and the merchant is not to be measured in miles but in rates....

> The 'colonial system' in our national economy--whereby the West and the South produce basic raw materials and do little manufacturing, and

51

the East emphasizes the production of high-unit-value manufac-
turers--condemns the country to an unbalanced economy and a lower level
of income than would result from the full use of all productive resources.

Whatever the historic origins of the 'colonial economy,' it is now
clear that its perpetuation is pre-eminently the result of
freight-rate handicaps...[1]

Complaints that the South and West were held in colonial bondage
via discriminatory freight rates have a long history. For example, the
railroad industry was convulsed in the 1870s with rate wars which
sometimes led to freight being sent by very circuitous and, thus, wasteful
routes. To deal with this situation, in 1878 representatives of southern
and northern railroads and steamship lines operating along the Atlantic
Coast met for the purpose of protecting eastern freight for easterners and
western freight for Westerners. Eastern roads insisted that they be the
ones to carry eastern manufactured products to southern markets, while
western lines were content so long as they carried western grains, meats,
and other food products to the South.
William Jourbert wrote in 1949:

...The Southern Railway and Steamship Association conceded that
it was in the best interests of the carriers for lines in the western
part of Southern Territory to leave manufactured goods to the
Eastern lines. This objective was to be accomplished by
requiring the Western lines to charge prohibitory rates on
manufactured goods from Western points to the South. As a
concession to the Western routes, rates of Eastern lines on
Western products bound for the South were thereafter to be
made uniformly 10 cents higher than the Western rates on such
products.[2]

As the importance of manufacturing in the West grew, shipping and
commercial interests in Cincinnati became dissatisfied with this
arrangement. Both Cincinnati and Chicago were unhappy because it was
virtually impossible for them to distribute western manufactured products
by rail directly into the South. The 1892 agreement of the Southern
Railway and Steamship Association, which contained the principles of the
agreement of 1878, caused the Cincinnati and Chicago shipping interests
to complain to the Interstate Commerce Commission (ICC).
An article in this agreement provided that, in order to obtain the
greatest amount of net revenue for the member companies, "the Western
lines of Southern Territory were to protect the revenue from shipments
to Eastern lines of Southern Territory by the exaction of high rates." The
eastern lines, in turn, were to protect western revenue.[3] This agreement
"virtually excluded the sale of goods manufactured in Cincinnati and
Chicago from the richest part of the Southern market."[4] Complaints to

52

the ICC about this discrimination against western manufacturers resulted in what were called the freight-bureau cases.

Defenders of the status quo argued that eastern rates had to compete with combined water-rail rates by steamship from Boston, New York, Philadelphia, and Baltimore to Norfolk, Charleston, and Savannah and via rail from these points. The Supreme Court reversed the ICC's decision in favor of the Westerners, claiming it was one thing to say rates were unreasonable, but it was another to prescribe rates to be charged in the future. This was a legislative function, not an ICC function; thus this discrimination continued until 1928. Before 1947 the nation's railroad freight rate structure rested on ICC orders issued between 1925 and 1931 that gave legal sanction to the five rate territories into which the railroad companies had divided the country for purposes of setting freight rates.

The ICC was only concerned with variations and disparities within territories. The South and the West, however, were very concerned about rates between territories. Therefore, the ICC had hardly equalized intraregional rates before it was faced with complaints from shippers in these regions about interterritorial rate differences which favored the Official (Eastern) Territory. Their concern arose out of two factors: (1) the fact that just over half--and the wealthiest half at that--of the nation's people lived in Official Territory and (2) an ever larger percent of rail traffic was interterritorial.

As Gavin Wright has observed, less than 30 years ago the "regional economic backwardness in the states of the traditional American South was considered an intractable problem of continuing national concern."[5] "The South," he observed, "was a quasination."[6] Its society--native born, sharply racially-divided, one party, agriculturally-based, producer of crops not grown elsewhere in the nation, etc.--as well as its factor endowment made it the nation's most distinct region. Few, however, have considered why "the perception and reality of the Southern economy has changed so drastically in such a short time."[7]

Because of the high degree of outside ownership of its industry and the fact that it was basically a producer of a narrow range of cheap, standardized, low-skill commodities, which added little value to the region's raw materials, many southerners believed they resided in colonial (exploited) economy. This attitude was well summarized by historian Sheldon Hackney: "profits that might have been re-invested in southern enterprise or helped to stimulate the local economy were drained off to the North. More important, decisions affecting the economic health of the region were made by men in northern boardrooms who had a vested interest in maintaining it in its colonial status."[8]

However, Gavin Wright has observed that, "economists who have looked into the subject have found almost no merit in the views of Hackney and Arnall" [a Georgia governor]. The intensive use of natural resources and unskilled labor was, after all, a logical reflection of the region's comparative advantage. The idea that an anti-southern conspiracy could have been maintained among business interests across the entire rest of the country is implausible on its face; and the idea that increased inflows of outside capital would damage southern growth seems utterly fallacious....A partial exception is the case of the Birmingham steel industry, where slow progress after 1900 has often been attributed to the dominance of U.S. Steel and its notorious "'Pittsburgh Plus' pricing formula."[9]   On the other hand, he observes, "the fear of low-wage Southern competition *united* Northern workers and Northern employers."[10]   (Emphasis added.)

New Deal legislation raised the minimum wage; thus high-wage industries were not directly affected, but the migration of low-wage industries, such as New England's textile mills, to the South accelerated. Clearly increasing this industry's minimum wage rate made moving to the South--where average wage rates were the lowest--more attractive. Some southern economists, such as John Van Sickle, believed that national wage standards imposed on the South in the Roosevelt years had a desired effect: southern industrial growth was stifled.[11]   However, Gavin Wright contends that subsequent industrial progress in the South can hardly be described as an example of stifled growth.[12]

The belief that the South was an oppressed colony of the North was widespread among both the general public in the South and its politicians. Georgia's governor in the early forties, Ellis G. Arnall, recounts that, when he grew up in Newman, Georgia, in the early twentieth century, "I realized that the South was merely a colonial appendage of the imperial domain called the North; that the South was the economic doormat of the United States as Ireland was of the United Kingdom. Eastern and Northern writers had field days in steady criticism of the South, its poverty and our problems."

He added:

> After the Civil War, instead of rehabilitation, the North inflicted upon our people a program of retribution, discrimination, and restrictions. I determined that if ever the opportunity came I would do something to bring about the readmission of the states of the South into our Union as equals with comparable economic and commercial opportunities....I found that the only way the few textile mills in the South could stay in business competitively with their Northern counterparts was by paying low wages, requiring the workers to live in mill villages owned by the companies and requiring high rentals from the workers, requiring the workers to trade with the mill commissaries on credit terms which were much higher than offered by non-company stores, to use child labor and other devices which the mill owners did not want to employ but which were required for them to stay in business.[13]

Arnall got the chance to do something about this when he became Georgia's Attorney General and, later, when he was elected Governor.

To what did the liberal Arnall attribute the South's relative poverty? He attributed it, at least in part, to discriminatory freight rates, which were applied both to the South and the nation's other colonial economy, the Mountain States. (See Table One.) The South, Arnall claimed, was handicapped almost irremediably by the exclusion of its manufacturers from the most lucrative markets and by the effective limitation of its industrial production to unfinished heavy goods.

Encouraged by President Franklin D. Roosevelt, who, because he treated his paralysis by spending part of the year in Warm Springs, Georgia, had developed an interest in what he called the nation's number one economic problem, the nine Southern governors belonging to the Southern Governors Conference in 1937 filed a complaint with the ICC about freight rate discrimination against the South. (Concern over discriminatory freight rates was what had led to the formation of this group.) In their complaint the governors asked the ICC to reduce railroad rates on freight moving from the southern to the Official Territory.

The Official Territory encompassed the area north of the Ohio River and east of the Mississippi River, a portion of West Virginia, and most of Virginia. The Southern Territory was south of the Official Territory and east of the Mississippi River. The Western Trunk Line Territory was between the Mississippi River and the Rocky Mountains north of a line following the northern boundaries of Arkansas and Oklahoma. During that same month the governors filed their complaint, J. Haden Alldredge, a TVA economist subsequently appointed to the ICC by President Roosevelt, issued a report which strengthened their case, because it claimed to provide incontrovertible proof that freight rates on manufactured goods shipped from either the West or the South into the Official Territory were higher than those within the Official Territory.

Large shippers, who could threaten to take their business elsewhere and/or afford to challenge rates in hearings before the ICC, could obtain what are called commodity rates rather than a higher class rate. Commodity rates apply to a specific commodity, whether it be a raw material or manufactured good, rather than to a class of commodities as is true of class rates. In some cases a class-rate type of structure of related commodity rates existed. Those shipping bulky, low value commodities, such as gravel, which would not move except at a low rate, were charged commodity rates.

Some freight moved on class rates, which were higher. By far the majority of goods moved on commodity rates, and the use of class rates was declining. (See Table Two.) Increasing competition from water and highway transport played a major role in increasing the proportion of traffic moving on commodity rates. Intraterritorial class rates differed significantly from interterritorial class rates. An ICC class rate study begun in 1939 revealed that first class rates within the Southern Territory averaged 37.7 percent higher than those in the Official Territory. A third type of rate was the exception rate, a modified class rate applicable to a specified commodity within specific shipping limits. In the South few

55

manufacturers of high value goods existed, and they were of a relatively small size; thus, they had to pay the higher class rates.

Shipments into Official Territory were much more important to the South and West than shipments to the South and West were to the North (Official Territory). (See Table Three.) Northerners argued that on a ton-by-ton basis, southerners were actually paying less to ship to the North than northerners were paying to ship to the South. This fell on deaf southern ears, because this was not the issue. The issue was that existing and potential southern manufacturers of high-value goods could not compete in given northern markets with northern firms located no closer to them because southerners had to pay higher transportation charges. On the other hand, northern producers located at the same distance from southern markets as southern firms could compete in these southern markets because of the lower transportation charges they enjoyed. Thus, existing high-value southern firms were kept small by denying them the chance to obtain lower commodity rates and the resulting economies of scale which northern firms were able to obtain because lower freight rates sufficiently enlarged their market. These economies of scale made northern firms more competitive and/or profitable and kept new, competing firms from being established in the South.

During the Great Depression, railroads' revenues fell precipitously, and they were desperate to maintain their revenues and cut costs. At the close of 1938--after the 1937 repression within a depression--the Association of American Railroads reported that the nation's railroads were earning only one-half of one percent on their investment, and nearly one-third of the nation's railroad mileage was in bankruptcy or receivership. In the first three months of 1938 the railroads piled up a deficit of more than $100,000,000.

The brief for the Southern governors condemned the argument of Northern industrialists that the South, being more generously endowed by nature, should have a handicap in the form of a higher rate level. The contention of Official Territory shippers that Northern industry was less prosperous than Southern industry was also placed under attack. Further, the Southern governors assailed the argument of Northern industrial interests that lower wages in the South justified charging shippers higher rates.[14]

Northern industrialists claimed higher southern rates were fair because the South was more generously endowed by nature than the North and had lower wage rates; thus the South should, like the race horse with the lighter jockey, be handicapped. They also claimed that southern industry was more prosperous than northern industry. The governor of Connecticut claimed that one of the functions of the ICC was to prevent great migrations of industry. The governor of Vermont feared that lower freight rates out of the South would enable Georgia's marble industry to destroy his state's. Northerners also argued that higher rates were justified by southern railroads' higher operating costs, however, in 1939 the ICC ruled that higher southern rates were not justified by higher costs. (For 20 years the ICC had been arriving at the opposite conclusion, that is, that the operating costs of southern railroads were higher.) In 1965, the ICC reversed its position, declaring that the northern roads had the higher costs.

Many of the northern roads' defenses were clearly fallacious. For example, they claimed that transportation charges were too insignificant a portion of a manufacturer's total costs to affect where he located his firm. However, it is obvious that the relatively small size of transportation costs only means that a comparatively small percentage increase in a much larger cost will cancel out any transportation advantage. Because the South had more natural resources and lower average labor costs than the North (Eastern or Official Territory), having lower transportation costs than the South was probably of more importance to the North than freight rate equality for the South. (The North's advantage over the South largely lay in its much larger local market and more skilled labor force.)

In their 1984 article in *Growth and Change*, Gerald S. Goldstein and Robert H. Pittman disagreed with the usual contention that transportation costs are not very important and that in regional development, transportation networks have mainly simply accommodated growth and trade rather than directly influencing their composition. Their regression results provided evidence that the transportation system can influence the commodity composition of trade.[15]

The fact that manufacturing firms had for many years, on balance, been relocating to the South did not, as the northern roads claimed, prove that higher transportation charges were not hurting the South. Industries not heavily dependent on the South's natural resources and cheap, unskilled labor were both relatively and absolutely few in number. For them transportation charges would be relatively more important in determining where they would locate than would be the case for firms serving a national market which were dependent on the South's resources. Thus, higher freight rates in the South might explain the scarcity of firms not dependent on southern resources in the South.

[Between 1929 and 1954]...the New England and Middle Atlantic states... experienced large declines in manufacturing employment relative to the rest of the country, thus continuing a trend which was evident in the first quarter of the century.

The 1919 period was a favorable one for all three southern divisions. Each of them had comparative gains in manufacturing employment...Abundant supplies of cheap labor provided the major attraction in the South Atlantic; natural resources were more important in the East South Central, and most important in the West South Central.

The comparative gains of the South Atlantic were predominantly in Textiles. The shift of this industry has been the major force in the growth of manufacturing in the division...In North and South Carolina, the [low skill, low wage, cotton using]. Textile industries accounted for more than 50 percent of the state's total manufacturing employment in 1954.[16]

In 1939 the ICC concluded that northern railroads as a group effectively controlled the rates both within the North and northbound interterritorial rates. Northern carriers were much larger, and the majority of southern carriers' stock was in northern hands. The National Resources Committee estimated that the investment banking firms of Morgan and Kuhn Loeb had financial interests in 98 percent of all American railroad assets.

In February 1939, Senators Hill and Bankhead of Alabama, Connally of Texas, and McKellar of Tennessee proposed that regional freight-rate discrimination be eliminated by statutory law. In July of that year the ICC responded to years of increasing pressure from southern governors and Congressmen and launched what was called the class rate investigation. In 1940 a resolution of Robert B. Ramspeck (Ga.) outlawing discrimination against a region, as well as against individual transportation users, was included in the Transportation Act.

Although southern Congressmen were not able to get passed any of the many bills they introduced to eliminate discriminatory freight rates, their efforts may have been responsible for a change in the attitude of the ICC, because it granted the South the freight-rate relief the region desired. (While only five of 41 men who had previously served on the ICC were southerners, after the southern campaign against discriminatory freight rates began in the early thirties, the South gained a majority on the ICC. The vote on the discriminatory freight rate issue was split, with southerners and westerners agreeing that discrimination had taken place, while northern commissioners said it had not.)

Galvanizing northern Congressmen into action was the Department of Justice. In 1942 it accused the railroads' rate bureaus of violating the Sherman Antitrust Act. That another factor was also involved is suggested by the fact that in 1935 the Transportation Association of America was formed. Its objective was to obtain a legislative exemption from the antitrust laws for the rate bureaus. (The Wheeler Committee in 1940 revealed that between 1930 and 1936 $182,000,000 was spent on lobbying by the railroad industry.)

In 1944, in tandem with a suit by the Department of Justice, Governor Arnall, a New Deal loyalist, decided to bypass the ICC by appealing to the Supreme Court. The State of Georgia filed suit against the principal eastern (northern) and southern railroads under the Sherman Antitrust Law, requesting that it strike down a purported, man-made set of discriminatory freight rates favoring the manufacturers of one part of the nation at the expense of the others by making it more costly to ship manufactured goods into this region than out of it. Rates on shipments of commodities used by northeastern manufacturers were, however, cheaper going into this region than out of it. (It cost the North relatively little to import southern raw materials and to export to the South its manufactured goods. It cost the South more to ship its manufactured goods to the North than it did for the North to ship manufactured goods to the South.)

Georgia's suit was based on the organization, in 1934, of a new nation-wide, private rate-making organization (the Association of American Railroads) whose objective was to prevent freight rates from declining. Arnall's suit attacked not the rates, but the method of setting them, that is the rate bureaus, claiming they violated the antitrust laws. The Justice Department's brief in its parallel suit noted that the steering committee which had drawn up the Association of American Railroads' covenant consisted entirely of men affiliated with Morgan and Kuhn Loeb financial interests.

The people of the South [Arnall said] had reason to know that he who controls the means of production has a vehicle for tyranny. Though the degree of corporate overlordship may have varied in different places, the rank and file of Southern people have long been subjected to a rule which, though far short of total occupation, was equally far from real freedom....

The end of the Civil War intensified the North's strangle-hold, since the exhausted South was left entirely without capital with which to develop its own manufacturing. The North concentrated on the exploitation of the Southern natural resources which were so plentiful. The Northern owners of Southern plants confined their efforts to crude processing of these raw materials, shipping them North for final fabrication into usable articles. Since the essence of this primitive type of industry is the payment of low wages, the South could not prosper.

The entire South was forced into the position where its income was dependent on the growing of cotton, tobacco and other crops, the mining of coal and iron, and the felling of trees....These operations required little skill or machinery....The real increase in value could only come when the tree had been worked into fine furniture, the cotton into fine textiles, and the iron ore into machinery or appliances....

The poverty of the South created racial hatred since there was only half a loaf of bread for both races. The black man was the economic competitor of the white man and there were not enough jobs for the Southerners who were trying to keep body and soul together....In 1945 the 13 southern states had 28% of the U.S. population and more than 40% of the country's natural resources. Yet the 13 southern states produced only 10% of all manufactured goods produced in our nation. Accordingly, the South had only 10% of the financial and money resources of the country.[17]

Arnall claimed that the freight rates precluded even the manufacture of finer cotton textiles in the South. So Georgia, despite all its cotton mills, had not a single fine-goods bleachery. At the same time, the commodity rates on raw materials moving from the South were set so low that they amounted to a subsidy to manufacturers in Official Territory, especially in parts of New England where obsolete plants might have to be refitted or junked if they did not enjoy an effective subsidy on their raw materials and a domestic tariff to protect their goods from the competition from more efficient industrial establishments.

On work clothing, Macon, Georgia, he said, had a rate 39 percent above that of Philadelphia to the Midwest. On shoes, the rate to Chicago from Atlanta (728 miles) was almost identical with that from Boston (977 miles). The first-class rate from Atlanta to Youngstown, Ohio, was $2.31 a hundred-weight while that from Manchester, Massachusetts, to Columbus, Ohio, was $1.52, although the distances were identical.[18]

Arnall received no support from his fellow governors, who thought relief should be sought from the ICC, not the courts. Apparently they thought the young governor's actions were motivated by a desire for national publicity.

Arnall's brief alleged that "...a combination was formed in 1934 in an effort to ward off indulgence in competitive business practices by the operating officials of the railroads. The depression of the early thirties genuinely alarmed the managers of industrial and railroad investments. They believed that the only way of preventing a wholesale decline in the value of securities of railroads and of other favored industries controlled by them was to maintain a structure of high freight rates. To achieve this objective it was necessary to curb the tendency of operating railroad officials to engage in competitive practices. The State of Georgia charges that a combination of investment bankers and holders of railroad securities amalgamated all railroad rate-making bodies into a new nation-wide private organization for the purpose of preventing downward reductions in freight rates.[19]

To shut off these Sherman Anti-Trust attacks on discriminatory freight rates, northern Congressmen began efforts to exempt the railroads from the Sherman Act, and this was accomplished in 1948 when, over President Truman's veto, the Reed-Bulwinkle Bill was passed.

To the charge that the Association of American Railroads maintained regional rate bureaus to eliminate intra-industry competition, the Association is clearly guilty. That this action violated the Sherman Act is practically indisputable. However, the rate bureaus had received tacit ICC approval and surely seemed consistent with the economic philosophy advanced by the National Recovery Act and the Emergency Transportation Act. The question was finally resolved in 1948, with the passage of the Reed-Bulwinkle Act which gave the railroads authority to operate rate agencies if they received advance ICC approval.[20]

Weak support by southern business interests for the attack on discriminatory freight rates, and how they were set, was blamed on northern control of southern businesses and by southern commodity shippers who feared lower class rates for the South would be offset by higher commodity rates. Arnall's failure to enlist the support of the governors of the Mountain States has been attributed to the fact that commodity shippers there were even more politically powerful than those in the South and manufacturers less politically powerful.

In their complaints the southern governors had received some support from southern carriers. But southern carriers threw their full support behind the northern carriers in opposing Arnall's attempt to have railroad rate-setting groups outlawed. Presumably this was because southern carriers did not want to see the industry stripped of this competition-reducing system.

Only a few weeks after the Supreme Court agreed to accept Arnall's case, the ICC finally handed down a decision based on the investigation begun in 1939. It announced that it had found that the higher class rates in the South and West and in interterritorial rates from these territories into Official Territory constituted undue and unreasonable prejudice and disadvantage and, thus, violated the Interstate Commerce Act. (A study done for the ICC revealed that average class rate charged on traffic between 12 typical Southern Territory cities and 14 typical Official Territory cities was 128 percent of the average class rate within the Official Territory.[21] The dispersion around this mean was wide.) The ICC's order providing for the gradual elimination of discrimination in class rates affecting the South and West was challenged by northern interests, who spent several times as much money on this issue as the South spent on it.

In 1947 the Supreme Court upheld the ICC's decision. Rates ending this discrimination did not go into effect, however, until 1952. Georgia's Public Service Commissioner, Walter R. McDonald, estimated that the ending of this discrimination would save southern shippers $28,000,000 a year.[22]

[According to Milton S. Heath the impact of the ICC's decision would depend on]...comparative prices and costs and elasticities of supply and demand in each case. Tariff rates [which a higher transportation charge equals in effect] that are apparently nominal because seldom paid may, nevertheless, be protecting monopolies of high-cost producers, or holding back the development of certain industries; and consequently their removal may have far reaching effects. On the other hand, if domestic costs and prices of the 'Protected' articles are already as low or lower than international [or inter-regional] costs and prices, the elimination of the tariff rates could have slight effect other than that of broadening somewhat the basis of competition.[23]

Subsequent to the 1939 ICC decision requiring that a uniform rate structure east of the Rocky Mountains be established (costs to the West being deemed to be higher than to the East), the ICC required that a uniform divisional scale be used by both northern and southern railroads in dividing revenues from North-South traffic. In 1956 the northern roads complained, and in 1965 the ICC, based on its finding that northern roads' costs were higher, increased the percent of the revenues from interterritorial freight traffic going to the northern roads; thus reducing southern roads' revenues by $8,838,000.

The southern roads appealed the ICC's decision in the New Orleans District Court (Aberdeen and Rockfish Railroad Company et al., Plantiffs versus the United States of America and the Interstate Commerce Commission, Defendants, no. 15454). The District Court, in a decision sustained by the Supreme Court, overturned the ICC's decree, declaring

61

that it had improperly included, in determining a fair division of freight revenues, the passenger deficits northern roads were experiencing. Thus, it was not until the late 1960s that both southern shippers and railroads gained equality with the North.

Clearly, the freight rate issue was not, at least in the short run, settled on a purely economic basis. Throughout the years FDR was in office, the issue is covered with the highly political fingerprints of the President in a typically contradictory fashion. Before, during, and after his administration, others, too, played politics as well as economics. (Due to the fact that railroading is a regulated industry, politics was bound to play a role.)

In 1946, Milton S. Heath forecast that the South might gain from the equalization of freight rates in the East. The most likely gain would be a decentralization of industry, that is, the South would have more industry and the North less than otherwise, but Heath believed this would be via branch operations, rather than independent manufacturing firms, setting up shop in the South.[24] This, of course, seems to have been pretty much what has happened.

Gavin Wright finds it impossible to believe, because so many people would have to be involved, that there was a conspiracy to keep the South down. Yet, is it not equally unlikely that the white people of the United States or even just the millions of them in the South could form a conspiracy to keep blacks down, but--most assuredly--blacks were kept down. Clearly, therefore, it is not necessary for a conspiracy to exist in order for a person or persons to be "kept down." All that is necessary is a common interest(s), the means, and facilitating circumstances. That the North had the motive to do the holding back seems clear. That it had the means and opportunity seems likely.

Various data suggest that the South was held back. However, railroad freight rate's role cannot be pinned down because the necessary data is not available. In addition, the impact of railroad rates is obscured by many factors, including railroads' loss of high-unit-value business to trucks. Like lower railroad rates, this has made the Official Territory more accessible to southern shippers.

In 1919 the combined value added by manufacturing in the South Atlantic, East South Central, and West South Central regions was 31 percent of the combined total for the New England and Middle Atlantic regions, even though the former regions had a larger population. By 1929 this ratio had risen to 36 percent. By 1972 it had risen to 97 percent, which meant that the pace at which the South was closing in on these northern regions speeded up appreciably. All this increase cannot be accounted for by the greater population growth in the South, because the ratio of value-added by manufacturing per capita in the South relative to that in the North had more than doubled. However, per capita value-added was still well below the North.

Because the South Atlantic region includes a good deal of territory which lies within the Official Territory, let's consider the West South

Central region by itself. In 1929 it accounted for just under four percent of the value-added by manufacturing in the whole nation. By 1972 it accounted for nearly seven percent. Georgia, a state in both the Southern Territory and the South Atlantic region, accounted for 1.5 percent in 1929; 2.1 percent in 1972; and 2.8 percent in 1986.

Relative to the national average, incomes outside the Official Territory have risen since freight rates were equalized. Within the South, the coastal states in the South Atlantic region have, led by Florida--now in possession of a large domestic market--fared the best. The Rocky Mountain region has not fared as well as the South Atlantic region. It is, of course, less favorably located in terms of accessibility to the nation's major markets. The Pacific region, which today has a very large domestic market--California if standing alone would be the world's third-wealthiest country--has, of course, done exceptionally well. Like Florida, a great deal of its growth has been due to people migrating to a better climate. Yet, if fewer jobs based on selling things to the residents of other states had been available there, would so many have done so? (Does people moving somewhere in and of itself provide them with adequate employment? It hardly seems likely.)

There is, of course, no reason to ever expect income equality throughout the nation, because various studies indicate that labor responds to nonprecuniary attractions like climate as well as to monetary rewards.[25] (In 1986 the Mountain states--those worse situated in terms of reaching the nation's markets--became the nation's lowest income region.)

A.G. Mezerik sums up recent events:

> What started [the] process? Originally, the populous East was the best market. There the enterprising men settled. Very naturally they built their factories where they lived. Any other course would have looked very silly to them. Bankers liked investments close to home, where they could watch over them, which also seems the natural way for a banker to behave. Banker and businessman were alike intent on one goal--profits. To safeguard these they organized associations, demanded legislation which sanctified their patents and tariffs, and, when necessary, they backed a war which would crush competition for a long time to come. (Like more recent wars, different people were fighting on the same side for different reasons.)

So the system was growing, more perhaps like Topsy than by plan. Competition was held down and as sources of profit were discovered in the South and the newly opened West, these were gobbled up for the sake of profit and interest at ten percent.[26]

63

NOTES

1. Wiprud, Arne C., *Justice in Transportation, An Expose of Monopoly Control,* Chicago: Ziff-Davis Publishing Company, 1945, pp. 3, 70, 71, 72. Wiprud, formerly a railroad's counsel, studied this subject at the behest of Thurman Arnold, who was then Assistant U.S. Attorney General. Attorney General Francis Biddle in July 1942 authorized an investigation of monopoly in transportation.

2. Jourbert, William H., *Southern Freight Rates in Transition,* Gainesville, Florida: University of Florida Press, 1949, p. 118.

3. *Ibid.,* p. 120.

4. *Ibid.,* p. 121.

5. Wright, Gavin, "The Economic Revolution in the American South," *Economic Perspectives,* Summer 1987, p. 161.

6. *Ibid.,* p. 164.

7. *Ibid.,* p. 161.

8. Hackney, Sheldon, "Origins of the New South in Retrospect," *Journal of Southern History,* 38, 1972, p. 195.

9. Wright, *Op. Cit.,* p. 166.

10. *Ibid.,* p. 171.

11. VanSickle, John V., *Planning for the South: An Inquiry into the Economics of Regionalism,* Nashville: Vanderbilt University Press, 1943.

12. Wright, *Op. Cit.,* p. 172.

13. Arnall, "The South's Readmission to the Union," Franklin Forum Lecture, Atlanta Historical Society, February 2, 1982.

14. Jourbert, *Op. Cit.,* p. 325.

15. Goldstein, Gerald S. and Pittman, Robert H., "Transportation and the Commodity Composition of Interstate Trade," *Growth and Change,* 15, 3, July 1984, p. 15-24.

16. Fuchs, Victor R., *Changes in the Location of Manufacturing in the United States Since 1929,* New Haven: Yale University Press, 1962, pp. 234-235.

17. Arnall, *Op. Cit.*

18. Arnall, Ellis G., "The Freight Rate Cartel," *The New Republic,* April 16, 1945, p. 497.

19. Shott, John G., *The Railroad Monopoly, An Instrument of Banker Control of the American Economy,* Washington: Public Affairs Institute, 1950, p. 30.

20. Carson, Robert B., *Main Line to Oblivion,* Port Washington, New York: KenniKat Press, 1971, p. 112.

21. Heath, Milton S., "The Uniform Class Rate Decision and Its Implications for Southern Economic Development, *The Southern Economic Journal,* XII, 3, January 1946, p. 222.

22. Flint, Sam Hall, "The Great Freight Rate Fight," *Atlanta Historical Journal,* 28, 2, 1984, p. 5.

23. Heath, *Op. Cit.,* p. 230.

24. *Ibid.,* p. 235.

25. See Goldstein and Pittman, *Op. Cit.,* for citations.

26. Mezerik, A.G., *The Revolt of the South and West*, New York: Duell, Sloan and Pearce, 1946, pp. 11-12.

TABLE ONE

NONAGRICULTURAL WEALTH OWNED BY STATE RESIDENTS
AS A PERCENTAGE OF TOTAL NONAGRICULTURAL WEALTH
1820 - 1920

	1880	1900	1920
Middle Atlantic	118	121	125
New England	105	114	122
Pacific	104	108	112
South* including Texas	90	84	82
South excluding Texas	91	80	73
Mountain	44	54	60

*Alabama, Arkansas, Georgia, Louisiana, Mississippi, North Carolina, South Carolina, Tennessee, Texas, Virginia.

Source: Lee, Everett S., et. al., *Population Redistribution and Economic Growth: United States, 1870-1950.* Volume 1, Philadelphia: American Philosophical Society, 1957, 729-33. (Regional aggregates are weighted averages of state figures.)

TABLE TWO

RATES APPLICABLE TO ALL CARLOAD* TRAFFIC
TRANSPORTED ON SEPTEMBER 23, 1942

	Percent of Carloads		
	Class Rates	Exception Rates	Commodity Rates
United States	4.1	10.7	85.2
Intraterritorial:			
Official	5.8	17.6	76.7
Southern	1.8	6.0	92.2
Western Trunk-line	0.6	0.2	99.2
Southwestern	2.4	4.4	93.2
Mountain-Pacific	1.7	.0**	99.7
Interterritorial:			
Official to Southern	12.6	36.3	51.1
Southern to Official	0.9	4.9	94.2
Western Trunk-line to Official	3.1	1.0	95.9
Southwestern to Official	1.5	3.4	95.9
Mountain-Pacific to Official	0.7	0.0	99.3

* Accounted for nearly 99% of traffic
** Less than 0.05%

Source: Heath, Milton S., "The Uniform Class Rate Decision and Its Implications for Southern Economic Development," *The Southern Economic Journal*, XII, 3, January 1946, p. 219.

TABLE THREE

DISTRIBUTION OF FREIGHT CARLOAD TRAFFIC
DECEMBER 13, 1933

Origin Territory	Destination Territory				
	Official	Southern	Western Trunk Line	South-Western	Mountain Pacific
Official	23,060	739	1,227	182	193
Southern	1,638	4,281	202	143	9
Western Trunk Line	2,103	241	4,941	308	183
Southwestern	489	428	712	2,804	65
Mountain Pacific	689	87	596	181	3,594

Source: President of the United States, "The Interritorial Freight Rate Problem of the United States" (the TVA report; referred to the Committee of the Whole House on the State of the Union), June 7, 1937, p. 47.

C
The Fight for Protection

[28]

THE JOURNAL OF ECONOMIC HISTORY

VOLUME XXXVIII   SEPTEMBER 1978   NUMBER 3

American Law and the Marketing Structure of the Large Corporation, 1875-1890

By CHARLES W. McCURDY

This paper employs the techniques of legal history to explore the relationship between the rise of big business and the size of the American market. It emphasizes law as a determinant of market size, and it analyzes judicial construction of the Constitution's commerce clause over time to delineate the role of integrated corporations in generating legal change. Specifically, the paper suggests that if the American market is defined as a free-trade unit, enlargement of the market was a result of, rather than a prerequisite for, the post-Civil War revolution in business organization.

T HE "secret" of American economic growth, English legal scholar Sir Henry Maine wrote in 1886, lay in "the [constitutional] prohibition against levying duties on commodities passing from State to State. . . . It secures to the producer the command of a free market over an enormous territory of vast natural wealth, and thus it secondarily reconciles the American people to a tariff on foreign importations as oppressive as ever a nation has submitted to."[1] The debate on

Journal of Economic History, Vol. XXXVIII, No. 3 (Sept. 1978). © The Economic History Association. All rights reserved.

The author is Assistant Professor of History, University of Virginia. An earlier version of this paper was read in March 1978, at the Twenty-Fourth Annual Meeting of the Business History Conference. A printed version of this paper will also appear in *Business and Economic History*, second series, Volume 6. The author is indebted to Fred V. Carstensen, William H. Harbaugh, Jonathan Lurie, and Harry N. Scheiber for comments that proved helpful in revising the essay for publication.

[1] Sir Henry Maine, *Popular Government* (New York, 1886), p. 247.

632   *McCurdy*

the tariff's contribution to industrial development has not been resolved any more satisfactorily by modern scholars than it was by
nineteenth-century politicans. But virtually everyone has long agreed
that a division of the United States "into a number of smaller market
areas separated from each other by tariff walls," as in Europe, would,
as Stuart Bruchey stated it, "have abridged the possibility . . . of
large-scale production." For Bruchey, as for Maine, "of the many
contributions to growth made possible by the adoption of the Constitution, perhaps the most fundamental was that it laid the foundations for a national market."[2]

Yet on close inspection the sweeping statements of Maine and
Bruchey claim too much. Neither the Philadelphia Convention nor
the Supreme Court under Chief Justices John Marshall and Roger
Taney had, in fact, deprived the states of all power to interpose
obstacles to the movement of products throughout the nation. Although the framers of the Constitution proscribed outright tariff
barriers, state governments retained ample authority to devise more
subtle forms of protection through occupational-licensing and inspection laws. Before the last quarter of the nineteenth century, moreover, appellate courts routinely sustained such statutes. On the eve of
the post-Civil War revolution in the structure of American marketing,
there remained a host of barriers to free intercourse among the states.

This paper attempts both to describe the late-nineteenth-century
emergence of the "free trade" doctrine in American commerce law
and to offer some generalizations about economic growth and the
dynamics of legal change. It further endeavors to shed some new light
on Alfred D. Chandler, Jr.'s contention that the growth of a national
market was the chief prerequisite for the rise of large-scale,
vertically-integrated corporations in the manufacturing sector.[3] Specifically, it suggests that if the national market is defined in terms of a
free-trade unit, rather than in terms of an integrated transport network, then the post-Civil War pioneers in business organization were
instrumental in the creation of the market. Instead of responding to
an existing free market of continental dimensions, producers of sewing machines and dressed beef actually ignored legal barriers devised
by state governments and instructed their local marketing agents to
invite arrest and conviction. At that point, the companies' headquar-

---

[2] Stuart Bruchey, *The Roots of American Economic Growth, 1607-1861* (New York, 1965),
pp. 96-97.
[3] Alfred D. Chandler, Jr., "The Beginnings of Big Business in American Industry," *Business
History Review*, 33 (1959), 1-31.

Marketing Structure 633

ters mobilized the substantial financial resources necessary to press the Supreme Court for relief, and hired counsel who succeeded in persuading the Court that existing canons of constitutional construction had to be modified to accord with the changing structure of business enterprise. Earlier efforts to evoke similar mandates from the judiciary had failed because prior plaintiffs had not been affiliated with big business firms. They had lacked the resources to engage in protracted litigation; equally important, their interest in a free-trade unit had not been sufficiently compelling to induce an innovative response from appellate judges. From the legal historian's perspective, in short, the rise of big business was a prerequisite for the emergence of a national market.

I

Among the chief motives for calling the Philadelphia Convention in 1787 was the "interfering and unneighborly [state] regulations" that had created "animosity and discord . . . between different parts of the confederacy" under the Articles of Confederation.[4] The power of the several states "to impose duties on imports and tonnage," Justice Levi Woodbury acknowledged in 1849, "had caused so much difficulty, both at home and abroad, that it was expressly and entirely taken away from the States."[5] On questions of internal commerce, however, the framers had been "characteristically Delphic."[6] They vested Congress with plenary power over "Commerce with foreign nations, and among the several States," and Alexander Hamilton, in particular, viewed that provision as an instrument to facilitate "an unrestrained intercourse between the states" that would "advance the trade of each by an interchange of their respective productions, not only for the supply of reciprocal wants at home, but for exportation to foreign markets."[7] But the permissible scope of state activity in the silence of Congress neither attracted attention nor fomented instructive debate at the Philadelphia Convention.[8]

Participants in the pamphlet war generated by the ratification

---

[4] Clinton Rossiter, ed., *The Federalist Papers* (New York, 1961), p. 144.

[5] *Passenger Cases*, 7 How. 283 (U.S. 1849) at 545.

[6] John P. Roche, "Entrepreneurial Liberty and the Commerce Power: Expansion, Contraction, and Casuistry in the Age of Enterprise," *University of Chicago Law Review*, 30 (1963), 682.

[7] Rossiter, ed., *Federalist Papers*, p. 89.

[8] Albert S. Abel, "The Commerce Clause in the Constitutional Convention and in Contemporary Comment," *Minnesota Law Review*, 25 (1941), 432-94; Charles Warren, *The Making of the Constitution* (Boston, 1928), pp. 567-89.

634   *McCurdy*

controversy also devoted scant space to the internal commerce question. When commentators did treat the commerce clause, moreover,
they gave no indication that the states' police and tax powers would be
affected unless Congress occupied the field with its own legislation.
Hamilton, for example, flatly promised state governments that "with
the sole exception of duties on imports and exports," they would
retain their power to tax "in the most absolute and unqualified
sense."[9] James Madison, too, accorded wide policy latitude to state
governments. "The regulation of commerce, it is true," he stated in
The Federalist, "is a new power [of Congress]; but that seems to be an
addition which few oppose, and from which no apprehensions are
entertained." Indeed, Madison explained, "the powers reserved to
the States will extend to all the objects which, in the ordinary course
of affairs, concern the lives, liberties, and prosperity of the
State[s]."[10]

The commercial-policy objectives of state governments were, in
fact, extraordinarily broad. Throughout the nineteenth century,
Americans looked primarily to state and local officials to promote
internal improvements and regulate commercial traffic, tended to
regard "each State as a community of interest . . . operating in a
hostile environment of rival State communities," and expected governmental agencies closest at hand to be responsive to their particularistic interests.[11] In an era when constitutional scruples and
regional power groupings forestalled vigorous congressional action
under the commerce clause, state and local interventions did play an
important role in overcoming the physical obstacles that for generations had circumscribed inter-regional trade within narrow limits.[12]
State governments facilitated the expansion of interstate transactions,
generally, and also protected shippers, passengers, and consumers
against negligence or fraud on the part of carriers and merchants.[13]

But the state legislatures also spun an effective web of barriers to
internal commerce. Measures designed to protect consumers or to
promote inter-regional transactions joggled incongruously with statutes frankly adopted to impede the introduction of out-of-state prod-

[9] Rossiter, ed., *Federalist Papers*, p. 198.
[10] Ibid., pp. 292-93.
[11] Harry N. Scheiber, *The Condition of American Federalism: An Historian's View* (Washington, D.C., 1965), p. 5.
[12] Carter Goodrich, *Government Promotion of American Canals and Railroads, 1800-1890*
(New York, 1960), pp. 3-165.
[13] Albert S. Abel, "Commerce Regulation Before Gibbons v. Ogden: Interstate Transportation Facilities," *North Carolina Law Review*, 25 (1946), 121-71.

ucts on a bargaining parity with local goods. State and local officials prescribed marketing practices, enacted discriminatory schemes of mercantile licensing and taxation, proscribed the entry of unfavored articles of commerce, and devised inspection laws to improve the competitive position of their citizens relative to producers in other states.[14] In short, state governments acted freely on all matters concerning commercial traffic—whatever their interstate ramifications—as if they were unaware, or at least unconcerned, that the commerce clause might have divested them of powers they had exercised under the Articles of Confederation.

Before 1875, the federal courts said nothing that disturbed the states' impulse to intervene on behalf of local interests. In the landmark cases of *Gibbons v. Ogden* (1824) and *Brown v. Maryland* (1827), the Marshall Court established two principles of profound importance: "Commerce is intercourse" and it includes transportation and traffic, which comprise "its essential ingredients."[15] In both instances, however, the Chief Justice deftly avoided a direct confrontation with the question, as he put it, "whether this [commerce] power . . . is surrendered by the mere grant to Congress, or is retained [by the states] until Congress shall exercise the power."[16] Although he handed down *dicta* which looked toward a "dormant" theory of the commerce clause, Marshall preferred to invoke unlikely federal statutes—a federal coasting-license act in the one case, and national tariff laws in the other. As a result, the Court virtually ignored the broad policy issues raised by counsel, and held that the "sole question [was], can a state regulate commerce . . . while Congress is regulating it."[17] Anchoring his opinions as much upon the supremacy and import-export clauses as upon the commerce clause, Marshall flatly stated that state laws must give way once Congress occupied the field with its own legislation.

The legitimacy of state and local commercial interventions in the silence of Congress was too vital an issue to be long suppressed by Marshall's penchant for "esoteric statutory construction," and between 1837 and 1851 the Taney Court split into a bewildering array of shifting factional alignments as the Justices attempted to devise a

[14] Albert S. Abel, "Commerce Regulation Before Gibbons v. Ogden: Trade and Traffic," *Brooklyn Law Review*, 14 (1947-48), 38-77, 215-43; Stanley C. Hollander, "Nineteenth Century Anti-Drummer Legislation in the United States," *Business History Review*, 38 (1964), 479-500.
[15] *Gibbons v. Ogden*, 9 Wheat. 1 (U.S. 1824) at 189; *Brown v. Maryland*, 12 Wheat. 419 (1827) at 466.
[16] *Gibbons v. Ogden*, 9 Wheat. 1 (U.S. 1824) at 200.
[17] Ibid.

636 *McCurdy*

workable canon of constitutional construction.[18] Not until *Cooley v. Board of Wardens* (1851) was the protracted intra-Court controversy over whether the regulation of internal commerce belonged exclusively to Congress or admitted of a concurrent power in the states ultimately stilled. Justice Benjamin Curtis there pointed out that commerce embraced a great variety of subjects, some of such a nature as "imperatively" to require a uniform, national rule whereas others admitted of local control until such time as Congress occupied the field.[19] The *Cooley* rule, the Court later noted, was "as satisfactory a solution as perhaps could be obtained . . . [on a] question which had so long divided the judges."[20] As an adjudicatory mechanism, however, it was virtually useless. As Kent Newmyer observed, "the *Cooley* decision was less a doctrinal clarification than it was an agreement to stop looking for one."[21]

For the purposes of the postwar Court, the most important aspect of *Cooley* was its unarticulated premise: when Congress remained silent, the Court might supply its voice. In exercising the enormous discretion inherent in the *Cooley* rule, moreover, the Court had ample room to resolve disputes on the basis of frankly instrumentalist, extra-constitutional criteria. Between 1851 and 1875 the question of how the Court might employ that self-created power, and for what purposes, remained uncertain. Then the revolution in the structure of American marketing generated a period of extraordinary ferment that culminated with the creation and systematic application of the "free-trade" doctrine.

II

Through the first five decades of the nineteenth century the independent, "sedentary" merchant integrated the American marketplace. Urban-based wholesalers supplied manufacturers with capital for building plants, purchasing equipment, and paying wages; they also managed the flow of finished goods to retailers. Direct contacts between manufacturers and consumers were rare. Indeed, as late as 1860 the word "drummer"—which later became the popular term for

[18] Felix Frankfurter, *The Commerce Clause Under Marshall, Taney and Waite* (Chapel Hill, 1937), p. 20. See also Carl Brent Swisher, *Oliver Wendell Holmes Devise History of the Supreme Court of the United States*, vol. V, *The Taney Period, 1836-1864* (New York, 1974), pp. 357-422.

[19] *Cooley v. Board of Wardens*, 12 How. 299 (U.S. 1851).

[20] *County of Mobile v. Kimball*, 102 U.S. 691 (1880) at 701.

[21] Kent Newmyer, "History Over Law: The Taney Court," *Stanford Law Review*, 27 (1975), 1378.

Marketing Structure   637

traveling salesmen—was used to refer to the men wholesalers placed in hotel lobbies to greet the hinterland buyers who made annual visits to eastern marketing centers.[22] But changes generated by a swiftly developing new technology, by the expansion and integration of the nation's transport network, and by Civil War financial innovations which created new ties between manufacturers and commercial bankers all contributed to a revolution in the structure of American marketing.[23]

The pioneers were the manufacturers of new, expensive, and technologically complex products such as sewing machines. By 1860, I. M. Singer & Company had learned that existing wholesalers were unable to provide consumer credit or handle demonstration and repair services; consequently it moved into the wholesalers' domain and began to create its own distribution network.[24] It was not an instantaneous process, however. Operation of company-owned retail outlets entailed high overhead costs, and fewer than 100 such stores were opened as late as 1872. Not until 1873, when Singer's enormous new Elizabethport, New Jersey factory neared completion, did the central office commit itself to expanding the firm's marketing organization to the entire domestic market. By 1879 the company had severed its relations with all independent merchants, and its distribution network consisted of 530 retail stores which also served as the base of operation for a still larger force of door-to-door salesmen.[25]

Legal barriers posed immediate problems for the architects of Singer's aggressive sales organization. State governments, prodded by the local merchants and manufacturers whose interests were threatened, not only stepped up enforcement of long-established licensing laws for peddlers but also enacted new revenue statutes to buttress the competitive position of local businessmen. The very size of Singer's marketing organization after 1873 meant that there were substantial profits to be made by breaking down these barriers. As a result, Singer coupled its final drive to integrate its manufacturing and distribution operations with a determined effort to challenge protectionist state legislation in the nation's courts.

In choosing to mount a legal assault on state trade barriers, Singer

[22] Hollander, "Nineteenth Century Anti-Drummer Legislation," p. 481.
[23] Glenn Porter and Harold C. Livesay, *Merchants and Manufacturers: Studies in the Changing Structure of Nineteenth-Century Marketing* (Baltimore, 1971).
[24] Andrew B. Jack, "The Channels of Distribution for an Innovation: The Sewing Machine Industry in America, 1860-1865," *Explorations in Entrepreneurial History*, 9 (1957), 113-41.
[25] The data on Singer's post-Civil War marketing strategy were generously supplied by Fred V. Carstensen.

638   *McCurdy*

faced a formidable task. Statutes that required non-resident salesmen
to pay higher licensing fees than local merchants violated the privileges and immunities clause of the Constitution; thus they had been
subjected to the judicial veto in a long line of cases culminating in
1870 with an authoritative ruling by the Supreme Court.[26] When
state and local governments discriminated against out-of-state products rather than the salesman's domicile, however, tax and licensing
laws had been sustained routinely by the courts.

Through the mid-1870s, the state judiciaries regularly treated the
1827 case of *Brown v. Maryland* as the Court's final word on state and
local taxation of commercial traffic. There the Marshall Court had
invalidated a state law that required wholesalers of foreign merchandise, and only dealers in foreign merchandise, to pay an annual
license tax. Speaking through the Chief Justice, the Court held that
Congress had already forced importers to pay tariff duties on their
wares, and had thereby conferred upon them the right to sell in an
unfettered market—a right which, if abridged by state law, would
have made the right to import of little value. As Felix Frankfurter
later observed, "the circumstances of the case furnished a ready
opportunity for curbing state taxation discriminating against interstate commerce."[27] Nevertheless, Marshall focused the bulk of his
discussion on the import-export clause, and he suggested that the
states might tax all commodities imported from abroad, or from any of
the several states, once the "original package" had been broken and
the goods had "become incorporated with the general mass of property."[28]

The state judiciaries readily discerned "an immeasurable difference" between the act nullified in *Brown* and discriminatory taxation
of goods offered for sale by peddlers.[29] Statutes of the latter variety,
the Indiana court ruled in 1835, did not impede the operation of the
federal revenue laws, for the commodities thus taxed had already
"become incorporated with the great mass of property in the state."
Moreover, the Indiana court asserted, the power to tax "is insepara-
ble from sovereignty, essential to its existence, and one which all the
expounders of the Constitution admit to have been reserved" by the

[26] *Ward v. Maryland*, 12 Wall. 418 (U.S. 1870). See also the long line of state court decisions
collected in Thomas M. Cooley, *A Treatise on the Constitutional Limitations Which Rest Upon
the Legislative Power of the States of the American Union* (Boston, 1868), p. 487.
[27] Frankfurter, *Commerce Clause*, p. 36.
[28] *Brown v. Maryland*, 12 Wheat. 419 (U.S. 1827) at 447.
[29] *Beall v. State*, 4 Blackf. 107 (Indiana 1835) at 109.

Marketing Structure 639

states.[30] It was an inexorable corollary, an Alabama judge added a generation later, that a state legislature might tax all merchandise sold within its jurisdiction, whatever its state of origin, while encourag-[ing] manufacturers in its [own] borders, by exempting the articles so manufactured from taxation for a time, or altogether."[31]

The line of reasoning pioneered in Indiana comported with the particularistic needs of local merchants and manufacturers everywhere, and other state courts quickly adopted a similar position.[32] In an often-cited opinion in the *License Cases* (1847), moreover, Justice Woodbury observed that "it is perfectly competent for [the states] to assess a higher tax or excise, by way of license or direct assessment, on articles of foreign rather than domestic growth belonging to her citizens; and it has ever been done, however it may discourage the use of the former."[33] When Thomas Cooley published the first edition of his *Constitutional Limitations* in 1868, then, the principle of unrestricted state taxation of commercial traffic, in the silence of Congress, had already attained the status of a settled rule. "The states may unquestionably tax the subjects of commerce," Cooley wrote in his influential treatise, "and no necessary conflict with that complete control which is vested in Congress appears until the power is so exercised as to defeat or embarrass the congressional legislation. Where Congress has not acted at all upon the subject, the state taxation cannot be invalid on this ground."[34]

Despite the weight of precedent, Singer persevered with remarkable success. In the fourth edition of his *Constitutional Limitations*, published in 1878, Cooley had already begun to note exceptions to the rule he had formulated so confidently a decade earlier; when the sixth edition appeared in 1890, the passage on state taxation of commercial traffic had been excised altogether. The leading case in this crucial doctrinal transformation came up from Missouri in 1875. Thirty years earlier the Missouri legislature had enacted a revenue measure that defined peddlers as persons selling commodities "not the growth, produce, or manufacture of th[is] State," and required them to pay a license fee for the privilege of engaging in local

---

[30] Ibid.

[31] *Seymour v. State*, 51 Ala. 52 (1874) at 54.

[32] *Raquet v. Wade*, 4 Ohio 107 (1829); *People v. Coleman*, 4 Cal. 46 (1854); *State v. Pinckney*, 10 Rich. L. 474 (South Carolina 1857); *Davis v. Dashiel*, 61 N.C. 114 (1867); *State v. Hogdon*, 41 Vt. 139 (1869).

[33] *License Cases*, 5 How. 504 (U.S. 1847) at 622.

[34] Cooley, *Constitutional Limitations*, p. 486.

640   *McCurdy*

business.[35] M. M. Welton, an agent of I. M. Singer & Company, had been convicted under the statute and the law had been sustained by the state's highest court.[36]

On appeal to the Supreme Court, counsel for Missouri simply stood on the precedents in a terse, five-page brief. Singer, on the other hand, hired two luminaries from the Missouri bar who compiled lengthy briefs that spoke directly to the policy issues involved in the dispute. Stated simply, they argued that existing doctrines were "not practical in this case."[37] Missouri's equation of peddlers with hawkers of out-of-state goods, they contended, was such "linguistic legerdemain" that the legislature might as well have "define[d] a peddler to be one who deals in boots and shoes manufactured in Lynn, or salt produced in Syracuse."[38] In short, counsel emphasized that the statute was simply a protective tariff disguised as a licensing law. Because peddlers of local products were exempt, the Missouri law was "not a tax on the occupation of selling, but a burden on the goods themselves."[39] It followed, counsel concluded, that "[i]f this is a valid exercise of the taxing power, the legislature may wholly exclude . . . products of sister states; for a lawful exercise of a power knows no limitation except such as are to be found in the discretion of the lawmakers."[40]

The Supreme Court concurred. Speaking through Justice Stephen Field, the Court readily conceded that under the *Brown* doctrine the Singer machines had lost their interstate character before their sale had become subject to the Missouri licensing law. Nevertheless, Field flatly asserted that Marshall's "guarded language" could not be expected to control disputes arising in an integrated national economy.[41] Paraphrasing counsel's brief, Field asserted that it was unnecessary to consult an economist to discern that "where the business or occupation consists in the sale of goods, the license tax required for its pursuit is in effect a tax upon the goods themselves."[42] It was equally clear, Field added, that unless the "original package" doctrine were

[35] Evans Casselberry, ed., *The Revised Statutes of the State of Missouri* (St. Louis, 1845), pp. 404-05.

[36] *State v. Welton*, 55 Mo. 288 (1874).

[37] James S. Botsford, *M. M. Welton, Plaintiff in Error vs. The State of Missouri: Brief for Plaintiff in Error* (Jefferson City, Mo., 1875), p. 9.

[38] S. M. Smith, *M. M. Welton, Plaintiff in Error vs. The State of Missouri: Brief for Plaintiff in Error* (St. Louis, 1875), p. 5.

[39] Botsford, *Brief*, p. 12.

[40] Ibid., p. 13.

[41] *Welton v. Missouri*, 91 U.S. 275 (1876) at 281.

[42] Ibid., p. 278.

modified, a barrage of interstate tariff wars, like those which had
"depressed [the] condition of commerce and [created] obstacles to its
growth previous to the adoption of the Constitution . . . might follow,
and the experience of the last fifteen years shows would follow, from
the action of some of the States."[43] Because of new developments in
the structure of American marketing, he concluded, it had become
necessary to extend Marshall's *Brown* doctrine, and "to hold now that
the commercial power [of Congress] continues until the commodity
has ceased to be the subject of discriminating legislation by reason of
its foreign character."[44]

The protectionist impulse in the states was not easily curbed, and
the Missouri case established only a beachhead for large-scale,
vertically-integrated firms. As Harry N. Scheiber has demonstrated
for the antebellum era, state governments were extraordinarily adept
at initiating successful "counterthrusts" to the Supreme Court's nationalistic doctrines.[45] After the postwar marketing revolution, however, the ingenuity of local lawmakers rarely went unchallenged.
Firms such as Singer whose interests were national in scope were
quick to muster test cases in response to each new statutory innovation. Thus, in 1880 Singer's counsel was back in Washington to
challenge a Virginia law enacted five years earlier.

The measure disputed in *Webber v. Virginia* (1880) apparently was
designed to compel Singer and all other out-of-state firms to disband
their sales forces and deal exclusively with local wholesalers. Under
the act, all salesmen who peddled "manufactured articles or machines
. . . of other states or territories" were required to pay the state a
license fee of $25 and an additional $10 fee in every county where
they did a local business. Only distributors who actually owned
products manufactured outside Virginia were exempt.[46] For the
Singer Company, whose Richmond agency supervised salesmen
working door-to-door in a dozen surrounding counties, the Virginia
law had a potentially disastrous effect. Nevertheless, the Virginia
Court of Appeals sustained the statute, distinguishing the Missouri
case on the ground that there was no discrimination against out-of-
state products as long as the manufacturer had the option of distributing his wares through local wholesalers.[47]

[43] Ibid., pp. 280-81.
[44] Ibid., p. 281.
[45] Harry N. Scheiber, "Federalism and the American Economic Order, 1789-1910," *Law
and Society Review*, 10 (1975), 84.
[46] Virginia, *Acts of Assembly*, 1875-1876, p. 184.
[47] *Webber v. Commonwealth*, 33 Gratt. 898 (Va. 1880).

642   *McCurdy*

The Supreme Court, after having been briefed about Singer's organizational structure, voted unanimously to reverse the decision rendered below. Speaking again through Field, the Court disposed in a single sentence of the issue emphasized by the Virginia bench. "Sales by manufacturers," Field proclaimed, "are chiefly effected through their own agents."[48] Once the postwar marketing revolution had been thus ratified, the result flowed inexorably from the principles announced in *Welton v. Missouri:*

> It matters not whether the tax be laid directly upon the articles sold or in the form of licenses for their sale. If by reason of their foreign character the State can impose a tax upon them or upon the person through whom the sales are effected . . . she may place the tax at so high a figure as to exclude the introduction of the foreign article, and prevent competition with the home product. It was against legislation of this discriminating kind that the framers of the Constitution intended to guard, when they vested in Congress the power to regulate commerce among the several States.[49]

The last sentence above merits special attention, for it reveals in disarming fashion the degree to which I. M. Singer & Company had succeeded in fomenting a doctrinal revolution. As Field conceded, the framers of the Constitution had vested Congress—not the Court—with the authority to regulate interstate commerce. Nevertheless, the Court believed that the idea of a unitary national market would be nullified if large-scale firms were required to press Congress for relief each time the states disguised protectionist legislation in the form of licensing laws. As Justice Robert Jackson later observed, "the balkaniz[ing]" policies of state governments were just "too petty, too diversified, and too local to get the attention of a Congress hard pressed with other matters."[50]

The Court's decisions in the license-tax cases also marked a decisive break with prior doctrinal formulations. In *Gibbons* and *Brown*, the Marshall Court had curbed the states in order to protect rights that Congress had conferred on persons engaged in interstate and foreign commerce. Then, during the Taney era, the majority's concerns had shifted from protecting the prerogatives of Congress to maintaining the territorial integrity of the states. Consequently, the Taney Court tended to classify powers—taxation, police, commercial regulation—and then assign control of public policy to the proper governmental agencies. The *Cooley* doctrine looked to the subject matter of state policies; since regulation of chattel slaves, prevention of disease or

[48] *Webber v. Virginia*, 103 U.S. 344 (1880) at 350.
[49] Ibid., pp. 350-51.
[50] *Duckworth v. Arkansas*, 314 U.S. 390 (1941) at 400.

Marketing Structure   643

pauperism, and licensing of liquor dealers and steamboat pilots were all "local" matters, the Taney Court had held that they were subject to state laws. Once faced with questions generated by the rise of big business, however, the Court began to conceptualize issues in terms of free trade and free markets. In *Welton* and *Webber,* the Court looked to the incidence of state laws; if barriers had been erected to impede the inter-regional flow of commodities, revenue measures were held to be invalid despite the fact that the states' power to tax had been "admit[ted] to have been reserved . . . [by] all the expounders of the Constitution."[51] In effect, then, Singer's counsel prompted the Court to deduce from the commerce clause a new, fundamentally important constitutional right: the right of American businessmen, even without congressional license, to engage in interstate transactions on terms of equality with local merchants and manufacturers.

As late as 1885, the "free trade" doctrine had been applied only to state tax laws. Eventually, however, the rule formulated in *Welton* spilled over and controlled the Court's position on inspection laws. Appropriately, the key agents of the latter development were the "Big Four" meatpackers.

The development of railroad refrigeration exerted a revolutionary impact on the American meat business.[52] For centuries prior to the 1880s, cattle and swine had been driven on the hoof, and later by rail, to highly localized processing plants. When fresh meat was available, consumers knew it had been slaughtered nearby. Beef and pork prepared for interstate and foreign commerce had to be salted and barrelled, or canned with preservatives, in order to prevent spoilage. The refrigerator car not only extended the potential market for dressed beef but, since unsaleable parts of the animal need not be shipped, it also permitted the processor to save up to 35 percent on freight costs. By combining refrigeration with mass-processing techniques and a strategic location amidst the Chicago stockyards, the "Big Four" packers were able to ship dressed beef thousands of miles and still undersell local butchers by a substantial margin.

The combination of factors that enabled Chicago packers to obtain a virtual monopoly on the dressed-beef trade is still a matter of some dispute among scholars.[53] In testimony taken at St. Louis in 1888,

[51] *Beall v. State,* 4 Blackf. 107 (Indiana 1835) at 109.

[52] Mary Yeager Kujovich, "The Refrigerator Car and the Growth of the American Dressed Beef Industry," *Business History Review,* 44 (1970), 460-82.

[53] See e.g., Rudolf A. Clemen, *The American Livestock and Meat Industry* (New York,

644   *McCurdy*

however, a Senate Select Committee discovered that old-style local
butchers believed almost unanimously that the "Big Four" packers
had conspired to "freeze out" all competitors.[54] Chicago packers, the
small-scale butchers testified, had extorted from carriers special rates
for handling refrigerator cars; they had ordered their wholesale agents
to employ predatory pricing tactics in local markets; and they had
conspired with the stockmen's commission merchants to ensure that
live cattle were sold only by the carload. Witness after witness nevertheless informed the senators that no federal intervention was necessary. A national organization, the Butcher's Protective Association,
had been created, they explained, and it intended to seek relief in the
several state legislatures. One witness, Detroit butcher John Duff,
testified as follows:

Q. What is your remedy for it [collusion among Chicago packers]? —A. Give us a
   livestock inspection, and when meats are not inspected do not allow them to be
   sold.
Q. Do you want State or national inspection? —A. Give us State inspection.
Q. Do you think that a State inspection would be all that would be necessary? —A. I
   think so. I think it would cover the case.
Q. You think that would cover all the evils. —A. Yes, sir.[55]

The small packers' faith in the efficacy of state action should not be
surprising: the Butcher's Protective Association's model statute prohibited the sale of dressed beef, mutton, or pork unless it had been
inspected by state officials twenty-four hours before slaughter. In
short, the B.P.A. proposed to banish the "Big Four" packers from all
but the Chicago market.

In 1889, the B.P.A. persuaded lawmakers in Minnesota, Indiana,
and Colorado to enact their panacea for monopoly in the dressed-beef
trade.[56] Bills providing for pre-slaughter inspection failed to pass in a
score of other states because, according to one proponent, "of the
presence of a powerful lobby representing the most colossal
monopoly, perhaps, that any government was ever confronted

1923); Richard J. Arnould, "Changing Patterns of Concentration in American Meat Packing,
1880-1963," *Business History Review*, 45 (1971), 18-34; Robert Aduddell and Louis Cain,
"Location and Collusion in the Meat Packing Industry," *Business Enterprise and Economic
Growth: Essays in Honor of Harold F. Williamson*, Louis P. Cain and Paul L. Uselding, eds.
(Kent, Ohio, 1973), pp. 85-117.
   [54] U.S. Senate, *Testimony Taken by the Select Committee on the Transportation and Sale of
Meat Products to Accompany Senate Report No. 829*, 51st Congress, 1st Session (Serial 2705).
   [55] Ibid., p. 156.
   [56] Minnesota, *Laws*, 1889, p. 51; Indiana, *Laws*, 1889, p. 150; Colorado, *Laws*, 1889, p. 244.

Marketing Structure   645

with."[57] Where lobbying had proved ineffective, however, the "Big Four" had no choice but to ignore the inspection laws; thus their local agents were promptly indicted by state authorities. Within a year the leading case of *Minnesota v. Barber* (1890) was on the docket of the Supreme Court. The lawsuit was so vital to the interests of Indiana butchers that the state's attorney general asked for, and received, the Court's permission to join his Minnesota counterpart in defending the statutes.

Counsel for Minnesota and Indiana presented compelling arguments. Inspection laws had long been used by the states to improve their producers' competitive position, and the framers of the Constitution had deemed inspection measures to be of such great importance to local economies that the states' power to enact them, and to charge fees for their operation, had been expressly recognized in the Constitution. In *Gibbons v. Ogden,* Chief Justice Marshall had accorded further legitimacy to existing practices by observing that the states' power to enact inspection laws had "not [been] surrendered to the general government" despite the fact that they "m[ight] have . . . a considerable influence on commerce."[58] Moreover, counsel argued, as late as 1878 the Court had quoted Marshall's language in an opinion that sustained a Kentucky law providing for pre-sale inspection of illuminating oil manufactured in St. Louis.[59] But in the event long-accepted constitutional construction and the weight of precedent were not enough, counsel for Minnesota and Indiana also implored the Court to take judicial notice of what they considered to be a well-established scientific fact. Studies of diseased meat, including one cited in the Senate Select Committee's own report to Congress, demonstrated that

it is impossible to tell, by an inspection of fresh beef, veal, mutton, lamb or pork . . . whether or not it came from animals that were diseased when slaughtered; that an inspection on the hoof, within a very short time before the animals are slaughtered is the only mode by which their condition can be ascertained with certainty.[60]

[57] Gordon E. Cole, *In the Matter of the Application of Henry E. Barber for a Writ of Habeas Corpus: Points and Authorities for Appellant* (St. Paul, 1889), p. 43.

[58] *Gibbons v. Ogden,* 9 Wheat. 1 (U.S. 1824) at 203.

[59] *Patterson v. Kentucky,* 97 U.S. 501 (1878).

[60] Louis T. Michener, *Brief in Behalf of Appellants in the Matter of Henry E. Barber for a Writ of Habeas Corpus, Filed by Leave of the Court and Consent of the Parties Herein, by Counsel for the State of Indiana* (Indianapolis, 1889), pp. 30-31. See also Dr. Henry Behrend, "Diseases from Butcher's Meat," *Nineteenth Century,* 26 (1889), 409; U.S. Senate, *Report of the Select Committee on the Transportation and Sale of Meat Products,* Senate Report No. 829, 51st Congress, 1st Session (Serial 2705), p. 26.

646   *McCurdy*

And science, it was argued, only confirmed what common sense suggested: "The examination of the hind quarter of an ox will not detect tubercles in his lungs or cancerous tumors upon his neck."[61]

Counsel for the defendant, an Armour agent, filed a remarkably candid brief. They agreed at the outset that all the inspection cases on the books supported their opponent's position. Having made that concession, however, they urged the Court to "bear in mind" its prior decisions in the license-tax cases and to recognize that unless the principles laid down in *Welton* were extended, the idea of a free-trade unit would necessarily be sacrificed at the altar of plenary state inspection power. "If the State [of Minnesota] can prohibit interstate commerce in beef, unless the livestock is first inspected [t]here," counsel for Armour contended,

it may in fish unless they are first inspected when caught. It may in butter and cheese and milk and leather, unless the cow from which they are drawn is first inspected [t]here. It may in wool and all clothing made from it, unless the sheep is first inspected [t]here. It may in cotton and clothing made from it, unless the cotton and the ground that produces it is inspected in Minnesota before the cotton is picked; and there is no product of the agriculture or manufacture of other States that this State may not thus exclude; none of this State that every other may not exclude.[62]

The parade of horribles likely to proceed from an affirmative ruling thus laid bare, counsel took up the problem of whether the Court ought to take judicial notice of the scientific studies adduced by the states' attorneys general. Counsel's tactics on this issue were extraordinary. Rather than attempting to rebut the contention that only pre-slaughter inspection was effective, counsel emphasized that "fresh meats consumed by Minnesotans were never inspected on the hoof by State or city inspectors before April, 1889, and yet population has increased and the death rate has been low."[63] It followed, counsel concluded, that the Minnesota statute must have been enacted to protect the competitive position of local butchers rather than to promote the public health.

The Supreme Court concurred with Armour's counsel. The propositions Justice Field had formulated in *Welton*, rather than previous cases involving inspection laws, controlled its decision. We cannot "shut our eyes," Justice John Marshall Harlan declared for a unanimous Court, "to the fact that the act, by its necessary operation . . .

----

[61] Cole, *Points and Authorities for Appellant*, p. 9.

[62] Walter H. Sanborn, *In the Matter of the Application of Henry E. Barber for a Writ of Habeas Corpus: Points and Authorities for Respondent* (St. Paul, 1889), p. 49.

[63] Ibid., p. 48.

Marketing Structure 647

directly tends to restrict the slaughtering of animals . . . to those engaged in such business in that State."[64] Moreover, Harlan observed, there was "no real analogy" between the pre-slaughter inspection laws and the Kentucky inspection statute the Court had sustained 12 years earlier. Pre-sale inspection of illuminating oil was "neither unusual or unreasonable," nor did implementation of that law ineluctably discriminate against commodities "because of the locality of production." As for the "alleged" necessity for pre-slaughter inspection, the Court concluded disingenuously, "we are not aware that such is the view universally, or even generally entertained."[65] If government had a duty to protect consumers against the dangers of unwholesome meat, as counsel for Minnesota and Indiana had indicated, another strategy would have to be pursued.[66]

The obvious remedy for otherwise legitimate concerns about public health was, of course, the creation of a federal inspection force. But in *Barber*, as in the license-tax cases, the Court correctly perceived that unless the federal judiciary supplied the voice of Congress, federal lawmakers would not move with dispatch, if at all, to displace discriminatory state regulations with a uniform rule. The report of the Senate Select Committee, which appeared two weeks before *Barber* was decided, looked to state action for protection of American consumers and recommended federal inspection only of meat products prepared for export.[67] Not until five weeks after the Court had spoken did Congress appropriate the meat inspection provisions of a comprehensive pure food bill destined to die and tack them on to the Select Committee's bill.[68] The Court therefore forced Congress to apply the same solution for state barriers against "Big Four" meat that the

[64] *Minnesota v. Barber*, 136 U.S. 313 (1890) at 322-23.

[65] Ibid., pp. 327-28, 321.

[66] The "Big Four" packers, like I. M. Singer & Co., had to contend with "counterthrusts" by the state legislatures; counsel for Armour & Co. was back in court a year later to challenge a Virginia statute that provided for post-mortem inspection of all dressed beef slaughtered more than 100 miles from the place of sale and also required the processor to pay the cost of inspection (Virginia, *Acts of Assembly*, 1889-1890, p. 63). The Court, again speaking through Harlan, held that "the heavy [inspection] charge of one cent per pound" was, "in reality, a tax" which divested out-of-state packers of the right to "compete upon equal terms in the markets of that Commonwealth" (*Brimmer v. Rebman*, 138 U.S. 78 [1891] at 81-82). The last B.P.A.-sponsored law to fall was the Colorado statute (cited at note 56), which was struck down in *Schmidt v. People*, 18 Colo. 78 (1892).

[67] U.S. Senate, *Report of the Select Committee*, p. 40; *Congressional Record*, 51st Congress, 1st Session (1890), pp. 3056-58, 5928-31. The international dimensions of the meat-inspection issue are thoroughly treated in John L. Gignilliat, "Pigs, Politics, and Protection: The European Boycott of American Pork, 1879-1891," *Agricultural History*, 35 (1961), 3-12; Richard Perren, "The North American Beef and Cattle Trade with Great Britain, 1870-1914," *Economic History Review*, 24 (1971), 430-44.

[68] Oscar E. Anderson, *The Health of a Nation: Harvey W. Wiley and the Fight for Pure Food*

648   *McCurdy*

Select Committee had prepared already for European barriers against all American meat. The Federal Meat Inspection Service, established in 1891, was authorized to conduct pre-slaughter and post-mortem inspections of meat products produced for interstate and foreign commerce alike.[69]

IV

The Supreme Court's commerce clause decisions of the 1875-1890 period were of immediate importance to large-scale manufacturers and had an enduring influence on American economic growth, for they firmly established the Supreme Court's role as the umpire of the nation's free-trade network. Even Justice Oliver Wendell Holmes, a persistent critic of many late-nineteenth-century decisions, ardently believed that review of state commercial regulations was an essential judicial function. "I do not think the United States would come to an end if we lost our power to declare an Act of Congress void," he announced in 1913.

[But] I do think the Union would be imperiled if we could not make that declaration as to the laws of the several States. For one in my place sees how often a local policy prevails with those who are not trained to national views and how often action is taken that embodies what the commerce clause was meant to end.[70]

Holmes's suggestion that the commerce clause was "meant to end" discriminatory state policies was, as we have seen, correct only insofar as the Constitution empowered Congress to intervene. Before the Court could establish fully its claim to monitor the free-trade unit in the silence of Congress, two prerequisites had to be fulfilled. First, the Court had to be apprised by skillful counsel of the growth-eroding potential of state laws and to be persuaded that new juridical principles must be forged to preserve free trade among the states. Second, the legitimacy of protectionist state legislation had to be challenged by litigants with sufficient resources to finance scores of lawsuits in order both to secure initial favorable decisions and to combat the tendency of state governments to mobilize "counterthrusts" against the Supreme Court's nationalistic doctrines. For students of the NAACP's operations in the twentieth century, neither of these

(Chicago, 1958), p. 78; *Congressional Record*, 51st Congress, 1st Session (1890), pp. 5674, 6514, 10191.

[69] *United States Statutes at Large*, XXVI, p. 1089. See also A.D. Melvin, "The Federal Meat-Inspection Service," *Twenty-Third Annual Report of the Bureau of Animal Industry* (Washington, D.C., 1908), pp. 65-99.

[70] Oliver Wendell Holmes, *Collected Legal Papers* (New York, 1920), pp. 295-96.

Marketing Structure   649

caveats is apt to be startling. But their implications for the development of a national market supervised by appellate courts were simply
enormous. What the NAACP Legal Defense fund accomplished for
black Americans under the Fourteenth Amendment in the twentieth
century, the legal-defense war chests of I. M. Singer & Company and
the "Big Four" meatpackers accomplished for vertically-integrated
corporations under the commerce clause between 1875 and 1890.

[29]

Excerpt from *A Living Profit: Studies in the Social History of Canadian Business, 1883–1911*, 33–54.

Chapter 2

The Flight from Competition

> Men go into business to earn a living. There are often circumstances which seriously interfere with their ability to do so. The greatest of these is competition.
>
> *– Canadian Grocer*, 1891

In the autumn of 1883 the wholesale grocers of Hamilton and Toronto met to discuss the possibility of doing something about ruinous price-cutting in the articles they sold. By early 1884 Montreal grocers had formed an association to deal with the same problem and in June the two groups came together to form the Dominion Wholesale Grocers' Guild, branches of which were soon established in other Ontario and Quebec wholesale centres. The Guild's first actions were to regulate terms of credit and discounts, but it soon began arranging price-fixing agreements with manufacturers of tobacco, starch, baking powder, pickles, and other products. In each case the Guild fixed the prices under which the manufacturer's goods were to be resold to retailers and the manufacturer enforced the terms by refusing to sell to any price-cutting wholesaler except at higher prices. The most significant of these agreements was reached with the sugar refineries in the summer of 1887; sales of white sugar would be made to Guild members on more favourable terms than to non-members, membership in the Guild being conditional on accepting its fixed prices and doing no retailing. The Guild promised the refiners that members' profit margin on sales of sugar to retailers would not exceed one-half cent per pound. Sugar accounted for about 40 per cent of the grocery trade in the late 1880s and had been the article in which price-cutting had been universal.[1]

Outrage at the price-fixing arrangements entered into by the wholesale grocers was a major cause of Canada's first investigation

A LIVING PROFIT

of combinations in restraint of trade, carried out by a Select Committee of the House of Commons in the spring of 1888. Neither the investigation nor the ensuing anti-combines legislation of 1889 had the slightest effect on the Wholesale Grocers' Guild's price-fixing arrangements. Old agreements stayed in effect; new agreements on woodenware, rice, starch, and molasses were reached in 1890 and 1891. Discipline of price-cutting wholesalers was tightened. The only change in the Guild's method was that the press was no longer supplied with the details of decisions, although the trade press still had inside information.[2]

Continual battles with renegade wholesalers and frustrated retailers led to the collapse of the sugar agreement in 1892. The combines in other articles soon dissolved and the Guild was largely moribund in the mid-1890s, the period that not coincidently saw a major weeding out of wholesale grocers. Beginning in 1898 there was a gradual reorganization and reconstruction of the agreements and the Guild began to function effectively once again. Its methods became standardized into an insistence that manufacturers practise resale price maintenance (legal in Canada) under the covert threat of a boycott (illegal after 1900) by the Guild members. A typical threat was delivered to a manufacturer by the Guild secretary in 1908:

> As you are aware conditions of trade are such that the only authority which can fix prices is the manufacturer and in his own interest and that of the trade it is clearly advisable that the manufacturer protect all wholesalers handling his goods, as otherwise, should a fair profit not be assured, the wholesale trade will cease to take an interest in the sale of his goods and will instead endeavour to push the sale of those goods on which he [sic] can with certainty count on a fair profit.[3]

In these situations the Guild's Price Committee informed the manufacturers what a fair resale price would be. Proceedings were now wholly secret. In 1906 a prosecution for conspiracy was brought against the Guild under the combines section of the Criminal Code. Four years later it was acquitted and went on into World War I stabilizing the trade in its usual way.[4]

The Dominion Wholesale Grocers' Guild was one of the most visible and persistent business organizations in the forefront of a massive flight from domestic competition in the 1880s and 1890s, hard on the heels of the barriers to foreign competition erected by the National Policy tariff. Businessmen formed guilds, associations, pools, trusts, and mergers with the aim of restricting the free market in every form of enterprise – transportation, manufactur-

34

ing, finance, and distribution. They used a wide variety of methods to attain this end, including written agreements, sworn oaths, bonds, fines, expulsions, boycotts, legally enforced contracts, dumping on foreign markets, "friendly" persuasion, mobilizing public opinion, and bringing in the power of the state. They denied the maxim that competition was the life of trade, and justified their combinations as being in the public interest and in the reasonable interest of honest businessmen who only desired to obtain a "living profit."

Agreements among Canada's great railway systems to fix rates and limit other competitive practices dated from at least 1855 when the Grand Trunk and Great Western agreed to avoid competition. For the next generation agreement after agreement broke down only to be renegotiated and break down again. The amalgamation of the two lines fixed rates permanently in 1883. By then the Grand Trunk was faced with much more serious competition from the Canadian Pacific. Despite their well-publicized antagonism, the management of the two roads turned instinctively to the idea of limiting their competition. The Stephen-Tyler agreement of 1883 "to avoid competition and work together in all respects for mutual benefit" was never implemented, but a working agreement on rates was reached between the general managers in 1884. Other expensive competitive practices, such as running dining cars between Montreal and Toronto, were also eliminated by mutual consent.[5] Formal pacts tended to break down quickly, negotiations were always characterized by mutual distrust and charges of bad faith, and quiet arrangements were sometimes hindered by such public indiscretions as Sir Henry Tyler's remark to the Grand Trunk shareholders just before the 1891 agreement came into effect: "We will now get all we can out of the people of Canada." Nevertheless, efforts to limit competition in transportation continued, for both companies could not help but realize that what Van Horne called "reform in traffic matters" could lead to a saving that "may soon be counted in millions."[6] The Canadian trunk lines were also regular participants in the pools and other associations established by the major American railway systems to regularize rates.

The manufacturers most concerned about competition in the 1880s were the cotton magnates who found their industry in a crisis of surplus capacity by 1883 because of the rush of new capital into the industry after the 1879 doubling of the tariff. A well-publicized "Cotton Congress" in 1883 arranged a scheme of combination that broke down immediately, as did several other attempts to formulate "a price which allows a living profit to the manufacturer." The Canadian Cotton Manufacturers' Association

A LIVING PROFIT

was formed in 1886 to control production, fix minimum prices, and organize dumping of surplus stocks in China. It operated successfully for two years before its collapse from rivalry among New Brunswick manufacturers. The two chief cotton barons of Montreal, David Morrice and A. F. Gault, then organized negotiations resulting in the mass amalgamation of the Canadian mills into the Dominion Cotton Mills Company Limited (1890) and Canadian Coloured Cottons Limited (1892). Controlling approximately 70 per cent of Canadian capacity, these two companies led a general stabilization of cotton production and prices until new mills constructed in the early 1900s necessitated a further merger in 1905, creating the Dominion Textile Company. That merger reduced competition in the industry so much that, with the added help of the tariff on cottons, the shareholders who invested $500,000 in Dominion Textile common stock in 1905 received for the next generation an average annual return of 98 per cent on their capital.[8]

Salt combines had existed off and on in Canada since at least 1871. On March 1, 1889, when anti-combines legislation was before the House of Commons, a new salt syndicate came into effect to purchase the products of all the salt wells in the Dominion, raising the price to consumers from 55 cents to $1.05 per barrel in one day.[9] The Canadian Packers' Association also reorganized in 1889 under the guiding hand of trade paper editor J. B. Maclean, and arranged a very satisfactory limitation of the fruit and vegetable "pack" for that year as well as steady sales at fixed prices.[10] The Canadian Iron Founders' Association had been in existence since 1865, fixing a uniform price for stove and other foundry wares and apparently maintaining regular prices through the whole period. Other manufacturers who had formed associations to fix prices or control entry in the 1880s included biscuit and confectionary makers, cordage and barbed-wire manufacturers, oatmeal millers, and manufacturers of undertakers' supplies.[11]

In 1891 the Canadian Bankers' Association was formed in response to desires that banks exert more political influence and pull together to limit competition. Though the C.B.A. claimed to emphasize bankers' education and professional improvement as its primary goal, it was rightly interpreted in the business press as part of the general movement to restrict competition. There was a successful nation-wide attempt in the early years to fix the maximum rate of interest on savings deposits, and local agreements were reached regarding the handling of certain forms, bills, and special deposits. Rate-fixing agreements seem to have broken down with the founding of new chartered

36

banks in the early years of the twentieth century, but at the time
of its incorporation in 1900 the C.B.A. was authorized to supervise the note issues of all chartered banks, manage the system of
clearing-houses, and supervise the affairs of any bank that suspended payment.[12]

The most frantic and varied attempts to limit competition
were in the areas of wholesaling and retailing, both characterized
by too many small businesses struggling for shares of a limited
trade. At the local level a simple custom like the giving of Christmas presents could pose a great problem for the ordinary merchant.
Grocers, for example, were expected to curry favour with substantial Christmas presents of wine and spirits to customers who played
one shop off against another. The only way to end the annual levy
was for local grocers to make agreements among themselves –
signed pledges not to give any Christmas presents. The anti-
Christmas present movement organized by the editors of *Le Prix
Courant* in 1889 was estimated to have saved Montreal grocers
$12,000. Other centres followed suit.[13] Similarly, early-closing
movements were a regular feature of municipal business life in the
1880s and 1890s as merchants struggled to end the competitive
scramble of each staying open until there was no more business to
do. The first early-closing movements consisted of draft agreements
circulated among local merchants for their signature, each pledging
to restrict his hours as long as everyone else did. The regular
break-down of voluntary agreements led businessmen to ask for
government intervention in the form of early-closing by-laws which
would restrict hours of business at the request of a certain percentage of merchants in a given trade. Several provinces passed enabling statutes to this effect in the late 1880s and mid-1890s. They
were put into effect only with difficulty, for dissenting merchants –
usually small retailers struggling to neutralize the advantages of
large stores – were able to make much of this legislative interference with the freedom of trade.[14]

Price-fixing agreements to stop the disastrous results of "cutting" were a commonplace of local merchants' associations. In
most areas there would be no need for a formal agreement; where
there was, a central organization would circulate a standard price
list. The Retail Jewellers' Association of Canada, for example, was
formed in 1886 and by 1890 had compiled a "living profit price
list" which was accepted all over the country and was still in effect
for watch repairs in 1900.[15] Local merchants' associations also
struggled to limit the number of bankrupt sales at which the stocks
of insolvents were sold at cut prices, tried to pressure wholesalers to
stop extending credit to incompetents or price-cutters setting up in

A LIVING PROFIT

business to compete with established customers, compiled lists of "deadbeats," and organized restrictions on credit.

The central theme of small business restrictionism was the attempt to maintain lines of demarcation between levels of trade and lines of trade. Wholesalers who sold directly to the public were warned to mind their own business and boycotted by retailers if they did not. At the other extreme, established merchants tried to close off their markets against the "guerilla trade" of salesmen with no stake in their communities – farmers, pedlars, and other transient traders. The pedlar problem, for example, was brought under control by the manipulation of local licensing, although in the city of Toronto not before the Hawkers' and Pedlars' Association had successfully fought a restrictive by-law all the way to the Privy Council.[16] Still more perplexing was the problem of preserving horizontal lines of demarcation between retailers in different lines of trade. "Single-line" merchants found it profitable to carry other lines of goods for the convenience of their customers, as loss-leaders, or as new sources of profitable trade. Druggists tried to carry everything in the way of toiletries, household products, and fancy goods; jewellers stocked hardware; everyone stocked jewellery; grocers sold dry goods and dry goods men sold groceries. The ultimate implications of this kaleidoscopic retailing were brought home to single-line retailers in the 1890s when the founders of Canada's first big department stores moved into one line of goods after another, proclaiming their intention of selling everything. The pioneer department store men, notably Timothy Eaton and Robert Simpson in Toronto, operated on low margins, heavy advertising, and the use of loss-leaders. They also broke with precedent by eliminating credit and by-passing wholesalers in their purchasing. In the early 1890s the department stores wrought havoc with small retailers in Toronto and Montreal; by the end of the decade their mail order business was affecting retailers throughout the Dominion.

Merchants threatened by the department stores fought back with price-fixing schemes, boycotts, and attempts to obtain restrictive legislation. After 1897 the attack on open competition in retailing was led by the Retail Merchants' Association of Canada, whose first action was to sponsor a successful suit against the T. Eaton Company for fraudulent advertising. The R.M.A.C. lobbied for discriminatory taxes on department stores (say, assessing a separate tax on each department in a store), tighter controls on transient traders, and the general institution of resale price maintenance. As its final solution to the problem of stabilizing trade and nullifying the effect of the department stores, the Association proposed "that

38

it would be greatly in the interests of all the laboring, manufacturing, commercial and purchasing classes of the Dominion to have all lines of goods belonging to each trade defined in groups by the mutual consent of the Merchants, and a record of them placed upon the Statute books of the Province, and that power be asked to regulate and control by license or otherwise all such groups or lines of trade in cities having a population of 30,000 or more."[17] The R.M.A.C.'s most successful campaign in the early 1900s was the achievement of both provincial and Dominion legislation to prohibit the use of trading stamps. These had been introduced in the late 1890s, had become very popular among small merchants, and were quickly seen to be profitable only for the trading stamp companies. It was a classic instance of state intervention being the only means of ending a competitive situation from which none of the competitors was benefitting.[18] By 1910 the R.M.A.C. was leading resistance to the incorporation of consumer co-operative societies, posing as the champion of "individualism" in business.

After about 1900 economic expansion and/or fear of the law* may have reduced the incidence of formal agreements in restraint of trade. At the least members of trade associations were now much more careful about the legal implications of their constitutions and by-laws, had little to say to the press, and had mastered techniques of evasion before investigating bodies. When Ontario lumbermen held a special meeting to discuss their situation in 1908, for example, it was evident that a recent prosecution of Western lumber dealers significantly moderated their desire to reach a formal agreement on prices. Telling the press that they were meeting to talk about how to have better times, they did pledge to reduce their cut by 25 per cent; as for prices, the best each man could do was follow one member's advice to "keep your pecker up."[19]

Other businessmen had turned to organic mergers rather than

---

*   The combines investigation of 1888 had led to the passing of an utterly useless anti-combines act in 1889, which had been incorporated into the Criminal Code in 1892. In 1900 the law was accidently given baby teeth when an amendment to the relevant section of the Criminal Code omitted the crucial invalidating word. This happened without anyone, including its initiator, realizing the significance of the change until 1903 when the first of several actions was launched against price-fixing trade associations. The handful of prosecutions in the next few years heightened public awareness of and opposition to combines, as did the continuing anti-trust agitation in the United States, and eventually forced the Federal Government to a further attempt to clarify the legislation in the Combines Investigation Act of 1910. This, too, was a largely ceremonial attack on combinations and did not represent a serious legislative attempt to restore open competition in business. For further detail see my article, "Another Anti-Trust Tradition: Canadian Anti-Combines Policy, 1889-1910," *Business History Review* 47, No. 2 (Summer, 1973), pp. 177-88.

39

A LIVING PROFIT

loosely knit trade associations as a way of ending open competition. Although the classic merger movement of 1909-1912, in which some 275 individual firms were reduced to 58, was largely defended in terms of the desirability of achieving economies of scale in production and distribution, the need to eliminate "wasteful" competition was obviously a factor in some of the outstanding mergers.[20] And whether legal or not, trade associations continued their restrictive practices. "Notwithstanding ... the Statute books," commented the *Retail Merchants' Journal* in 1907, "it is well known to most businessmen in Canada that agreements are now made and entered into in many lines of trade, with a view of preventing ruinous and unfair competition ... and to act as a pendulum to regulate and steady trade."[21]

This brief description of restrictive activities has concentrated on only the most successful, the most persistent, or the most publicized of the combines and associations formed in the period. An exhaustive list of the combinations mentioned in trade journals or claimed to exist by newspapers would extend into every nook and cranny of the Canadian business world. When hardware men convened in Toronto in 1894, for example, meetings were held of the Wire Nail Association, the Wire Association, the Screw Association, the Bolt and Nut Association, the Rivet Association, the Barb Wire Association, the Bar Iron Association, the Cut Nail Association, the Horseshoe Association, the Tack Association, and the Paint Grinders' Association. All discussed prices. As early as 1887 the *Journal of Commerce* remarked, "there are few branches of trade in this or any other country which are not represented by associations which seek to prevent unprofitable competition." In 1890 N. Clarke Wallace, who had been chairman of the 1888 Select Committee, complained about attempts to burden the people with combines "from the cradle to the grave ... – from Nestle's food in infancy to the coffin in which they were carried to the grave."[22]

A number of businessmen and business organizations actively resisted the tendency to limit free competition. The consolidation of the railroad systems in central Canada in the early 1880s, for example, produced an outburst of anti-monopoly sentiment among shippers frightened at the freedom the Grand Trunk and C.P.R. now had to raise rates without check. Writing in the *Trader* on behalf of small shippers, W. K. McNaught, a Toronto jeweller, rang the changes on railway monopoly as skillfully as any Granger:

From present appearances it seems doubtful whether in the near future the railways won't control this country, instead of the country controlling the railways. . . . Corporations are said to be soulless, and these are not exceptions to the rule, as any one may judge from the past record, either of the Grand Trunk or the Canadian Pacific. They have each bled the public. . . .

We have often pointed out the fact that these railroads are like huge vampires, slowly sucking the life-blood of this country's commerce. They charge the extreme limit the law allows, and in many cases go beyond it, and the sufferers from their legalized tyranny have no chance of redress.

The *Canadian Manufacturer* chimed in with mutterings about "the oppressive and depressing feeling, in the public breast, of utter helplessness, and of being in forced submission to the despotism of a railway monopoly." In the same years in Manitoba the Winnipeg *Commercial* made common cause with farmers in attacking the monopoly rights of the C.P.R., "a horse-leech, which sucks at the life of the country and in its voracity is ever shouting for more." Pressure from urban Boards of Trade led to the establishment of the Royal Commission on Railways in 1886 at which many Manitoba and Ontario shippers called for a railway commission to regulate the systems; when the Canadian Board of Railway Commissioners was finally established in 1902 the Canadian Manufacturers' Association proudly took credit for leading the movement on behalf of government intervention.[23]

All the time it had been trying to shackle railways with government regulation, the C.M.A.'s main aim had been to encourage limiting the competition of foreign manufacturers in the Canadian market. The *Commercial* was the Winnipeg Board of Trade's mouthpiece in the anti-monopoly agitation; but representing other sections of its constituency it also led the campaign for price-fixing in Manitoba retail circles. W. K. McNaught, advocate of railway competition, was an enthusiastic supporter and member of the wholesale jewellers' combine, which at one time offered a $300 reward to anyone bringing evidence of price-cutting by any member. He believed that "combination for protection was a perfectly praiseworthy and legitimate thing to do" and the "very foundation stone" of their association was "honor."[24] Like many other Ontario manufacturers of this period he would go on to play a prominent role in the fight against private power monopolies in the province. At exactly the same time he was lobbying for federal legislation to restrict competition in the jewellery trade.[25]

The same pattern of tarnished virtue was revealed in the struggles against the Wholesale Grocers' Guild. George Light-

41

A LIVING PROFIT

bound, a Montreal wholesale grocer, was the key witness against the Guild and its sugar combine at the investigation of 1888. He objected to anyone trying to tell him how to run his own business, claimed a perfect right to buy or sell at whatever price he chose, and suggested that businessmen who could not conduct their affairs without a combination should choose another line of business. Under close questioning, however, it was revealed that Lightbound had been one of the charter members of the organization, had taken the lead in originating the combines on tobacco, baking powder, and starch, and had been the first to suggest it was time to fix a combined price on sugar. The trouble with the sugar agreement had arisen only because Lightbound would not join it for the territory west of Montreal, though he was perfectly willing to combine on prices for the south and east. Lightbound was in fact back in the Guild at the time of testifying against it. He claimed he had been squeezed back in only to be able to purchase sugar; actually his firm continued to participate in the sugar combine until November 1893 when it withdrew from all price-fixing because of what it called the "foolish policy" adopted by some members in "demoralizing" the fruit business.[26]

Other witnesses at the 1888 inquiry were caught in similar contradictions. In certain competitive situations they had broken with combines. In other real or posited competitive situations they would go along with combines in the interests of "fair" profits or "legitimate" trade. Walter Paul, a Montreal retailer who testified against the Guild, was "strongly in favour of freedom of business, the survival of the fittest," and yet he had recently been a member of a deputation of retailers insisting that wholesalers not sell directly to the public.[27] In 1890 retail grocers across Ontario and Quebec turned against the Guild, damning it as "the most selfish and unjust organization on the face of the earth today," and calling on its members to "act like business men, not afraid of one another, no matter how low the cut." At exactly the same time these local retailers' associations were continuing their price-fixing – entering new arrangements regarding bread in Toronto and liquor in Montreal – and their attacks on the Guild ended immediately when it agreed to revise credit terms and give larger volume discounts.[28]

Only a small handful of businessmen adopted a consistent, principled resistance to combinations in restraint of trade. A crusty old Montreal wholesale grocer, J. A. Mathewson, had refused to join the Wholesale Grocers' Guild from the beginning, testified against its "malicious blackmail" and "slavery" at

42

every opportunity, and alone among the businessmen opposed to combines in 1888 continued to fight for strong laws against "these infamous, unlawful organizations." The T. Eaton Company was adept at identifying itself as the consumer's friend and made backhanded slaps in its catalogues at merchants who worked merely for profit and wanted to divide the trade so everyone could ride in carriages. Eaton's aimed to do the best it could by each customer, sold good products at the lowest possible prices, and, "we mind our own business." Joseph Flavelle of the Davies meat-packing company took great pride in never having participated in a price-fixing agreement and complained bitterly to Mackenzie King in 1910 that the Combines Investigation bill pending before Parliament would subject honourable firms like his to unfair harassment. The more common objection to that Act was uttered by Senator W. C. Edwards, president of the Canada Cement Company (a firm resulting from a merger that had been directly aimed at achieving monopoly) who thought the Act would deny people "the profit of their industry." He delivered this speech the same week he told the *Monetary Times* that Ben Franklin had written all a young man needed to know about success.[29]

Sporadic complaints by businessmen subjected to the prices charged by combinations and monopolies and the objections to combinations by a few principled free traders were almost totally submerged in a climate of business opinion that attacked open competition as being destructive of profits, security, and business morality. Although lip service was often paid to the notion of competition as the life of trade, the arguments of trade restrictionists subverted the maxim by noting that unfair or illegitimate competition was the death of trade and then defining these unacceptable forms of competition so widely that they stretched almost all the way around the concept.

The "unfair" competitor was thought to be someone who had a privilege not available to his rivals. But what did this mean? Most small-town merchants thought it was unfair for pedlars to be permitted to compete with them without having to pay local taxes. Wholesalers selling at retail or even large retailers who could obtain volume discounts seemed to be operating from a basis of special power if not special privilege. When they took advantage of their position to launch price wars by cutting prices below cost or using loss-leaders, they were treating their competitors particularly unfairly. Indeed, any kind of underselling based on a superior capital position seemed unfair. The merchant who laid aside certain portions of his capital as a kind of "war

43

A LIVING PROFIT

reserve," argued a writer, "and spends it in price cutting just as an honest man may spend it in advertising or wages, is guilty of an act which it is hard to distinguish from the course of the man who hires some one to burn down the factories and warehouses of troublesome competitors."[30]

It was a small step from the idea of unfair competition to the belief that any competition involving price-cutting was illegitimate. Doing business on "sound business principles" seemed obviously to mean selling goods at a profit. Therefore, according to the *Canadian Grocer*, "selling below cost . . . is commercial idiocy." It hurt oneself, one's creditors, and, as another journal claimed, meant "doing an injustice to the general mercantile community – whose honest aim it ought to be to make a profit." There was no way that merchants in a community could avoid adopting the methods of ignorant or unscrupulous competitors, for the cut prices of one businessman set the levels of the market. A single reckless trader operating on borrowed capital could destroy the profitability of the trade of a whole community while he pursued his stupid course to bankruptcy. A typical outbreak of this "promiscuous" price-cutting in an "out of the way place" like Edmonton in 1887 led the Winnipeg *Commercial* to sermonize on the general issue:

> Cutting prices is an offence the most senseless and at the same time the least excusable which any business man can engage in. It is an offence against legitimate trade of a most grave nature, and which should not be condoned in any quarter. No rules or principles in commercial economy can be deduced to prove that any permanent advantage can come from cutting prices below a fair or living profit. . . .
> The only legitimate way to do business is to obtain a fair, living profit upon all commodities . . . the opposite system of cutting prices is demoralizing and destructive to legitimate trade, under whatever circumstances indulged in.[31]

The "demoralization" of trade as a result of price-cutting was a favourite business term. It had the obvious implications of a collapse in the regular price structure, leading to furious price juggling. But it also connoted the literal de-*moral*-izing effect of extreme competition in forcing businessmen back into unethical practices they would rather avoid. A retail grocer wrote to the *Canadian Grocer* in 1889 complaining that the only way he could make a profit under prevailing conditions was to deceive his customers by selling six plugs as a "pound" of tobacco when it actually took seven to make that weight. How could a retail man "hold up the

44

THE FLIGHT FROM COMPETITION

dignity of his manhood," "do right," and still stay in business, he asked. "It seems almost impossible for a man behind the counter to be truthful, honourable, straightforward and honest, and succeed." In a similar vein the *Journal of Commerce* argued that when cotton was sold at "cut-throat" prices the only way manufacturers could show "a living profit" was by "the employment of all those tricks of adulteration which have gained some European mills such an unenviable notoriety." Regulation of competition, then, was necessary to preserve the ethical as well as the material bases of business success.[32]

A further connotation of "demoralizing" trade was the effect it had on competitors' morale. Ruthless competition forced the businessman to be on his guard at all times, never secure from day to day. One fierce battle could ruin a life's work. A retail grocer described a situation in his town where four different travellers had appeared in succession quoting four different prices on sugar. By luck he had made a profit in his sugar transaction, but it was pure luck. The local trade "felt sick" at this kind of situation, and all favoured the Guild's one-price system under which "there is not that feeling that every one is buying goods cheaper than you." Commenting on the Guild, Professor W. J. Ashley of the University of Toronto also worried that worship of the consumer led people to forget "the worry and laceration of the spirit" (as well as "the vulgarization of business") involved in perpetual competition. The longing among businessmen for security, financial and otherwise, prompted the *Monetary Times* to suggest that the guild system of early times, though it occasionally seemed "to bear hard upon individual liberty," alleviated many of the scandals of modern trade: "The pushing and 'cutting' and striving for business which characterizes modern methods were then almost unknown. . . . The life of a trader in those days was one of comparative comfort and ease. Yet the wants of the community were as well supplied as they are now. This is the essential matter, after all."[33]

Members of combines always asked what was unreasonable about joining together to ensure one another "a living profit." Many of them claimed that the alternative to combines was to go out of business and pointed out that "the consumer must not expect the trade of the Dominion to work for them [*sic*] for nothing." This implied that profits in business were nothing more than the wages of businessmen. The Retail Merchants' Association called for "fair wages – improperly called by some, profits"; and a Quebec pharmacist thought it was necessary to

45

A LIVING PROFIT

interfere with the "incontestablement bon ... *principe*" of free trade because "dans tout corps social bien organisé, ceux qui exercent les divers états ou métiers qui le composent ont droit à une protection efficace qui leur assure un part des revenus proportionée à leurs aptitudes, à leur application au genre et au montant d'affaires qu'ils transigent." This strain of thought was based on the idea of there being a reward "justly" due to the man who provided a service to the community.[34]

Some people could and did say that open competition was justified as leading to "the survival of the fittest." This was heatedly denied. "To say that a half-witted man, who has money enough to outstay a poorer but able rival, shows himself thereby to be a fitter man than his rival is nonsense," argued the *Canadian Grocer* in an article attacking this usage of "the cant of the evolution theory." Generally, when businessmen used the catch phrases of Social Darwinism, they used them to describe the competitive situation as it existed, not as they hoped it might be. "If this competition continues, it is simply a question of the survival of the fittest," complained a cotton man trying to organize a merger. Another writer agreed that modern society did encourage the survival of the fittest. He meant that only the strongest of the strong could survive. Self-preservation therefore required combination. "What better argument could we have for the existence of the Canadian Bankers' Association?"[35]

The enthusiasts of combination always argued that restraints on competition either actively benefitted or at least did not harm the public. Almost everyone admitted there were limits beyond which trade restraints should not be pressed. It was common to distinguish between good and evil combines, responsible and extortionate ones, just as the distinction was drawn between fair and unfair competition. Just as they could find very little competition that was fair, however, restrictionists seldom found any unfair or extortionate combines operating in Canada, except possibly the railways. The only really evil ones were almost always American: Standard Oil, the American Tobacco Company, the United Shoe Machinery Company.

No one seemed to want to combine to set high prices. "There was no desire to combine with a view to pushing up the prices," a member of the first cotton combine was reported as saying, "but merely to advance the price a little."[36] Some combiners argued that they were not raising prices at all, merely "stabilizing" or "regulating" them. Others maintained that prices to the consumer had even dropped under combination.[37] The Canadian Canners' Association was congratulated by a Member of Parliament for having formed a combination "not to force up prices,

46

but to get fair prices." And the *Canadian Grocer* once reported that the Wholesale Grocers' Guild had achieved "a restriction on the price of graded sugars to that determined by the open market."[38]

When questioned about safeguards for the consumer in combines arrangements, some restrictionists fell back on their personal sense of duty. The scheme of fixing retail prices on the basis of a 20 per cent mark-up, claimed a member of the executive of the Western Retail Lumbermen's Association (under investigation in 1907 and later prosecuted) had been introduced "with the object of keeping the prices from being excessive to the consumer." As manager of the Association he felt he had "a duty to perform to the public, which is to see that there is no undue advantage taken."[39] Years earlier George Drummond of the Canada Sugar Refinery had made a memorable statement of his sense of public responsibility in response to questioning regarding his superintendency of the Guild's attempts to get what Drummond called "a fair reasonable living advance" on sugar:

Q. It is an agreement as long as you are satisfied with the list?
A. As long as I am satisfied that the thing is being, as I believe it is, honestly and fairly conducted.
Q. Fairly and honestly as between you and the guild?
A. And the public.
Q. Well, the public, according to you, have no say in the matter whatever. Their interests are simply affected as to the advance which you and the guild agree upon, that the sugar must be sold at. The public have no control over the agreement in any way whatever. The agreement is not an agreement between the guild and you and the public, it is an agreement between you and the guild which affects the public. Is that not so?
A. Well, that is a very long question.
Q. Has the public any control over the agreement?
A. Well, you covered that.
Q. I understand the public has no control over the agreement?
A. Well –
Q. Do you say that they have?
A. I don't know; we will see.
Q. I want you to answer that question; I put the question; I would like an answer.
A. I don't think a gentleman should ask a question like that; it is wasting time.[40]

47

—Facing up to combines, 1888.

THE GOVERNMENT "INVESTIGATING" MONOPOLY

A more sophisticated defence of profit margins under combines stressed the residual forces of the marketplace. An "unreasonable" advance in prices would be sure to offer opportunities for competitors to step into a field or for the members themselves to violate agreements. Even in 1910 when mergers had given single companies up to 85 per cent of the Canadian market, Fred Field of the *Monetary Times* felt it was still "almost impossible" to prevent competition in a new and growing country. As soon as one company was seen to be operating without restraint, "capital and enterprise will quickly change the situation."[41]

No combine, of course, ever admitted to exorbitant profit-taking. The Wholesale Grocers' Guild maintained that its sugar profits ranged between 2.75 per cent and 4.25 per cent on costs, whereas the accepted average rate of return on wholesale groceries was 4.5 per cent. Well aware that these issues often hinged on the manipulation of statistics, a spokesman for the Guild offered to place a $1,000 cheque in the hands of the mayor of Toronto to be distributed to city charities if his figures were not found to be substantially correct. They were not disputed in the press or by the Select Committee on combines. Others made a less persuasive case. The 20 per cent mark-up allowed by the Western Retail Lumbermen's Association, it turned out, was calculated to provide a 10 per cent net profit on turnover which could produce a 100 per cent annual return on capital.[42]

Restrictionists also claimed that combines served the public by preserving and increasing efficiency. The distribution of sugar through wholesale grocers was the cheapest way of bringing this article to the public, Guild spokesmen claimed. Did the public really want to force the wholesalers to go out of the business and compel the refiners to set up their own expensive distribution system? Was it truly in the public interest to encourage bankers to lend money on unsound principles because of competition, leading nowhere but to impaired capital, disastrous failures, and scandals? After all, said George Hague of the Merchants' Bank, "To lend the community too much money is not beneficial." As trade associations gave way to holding companies and organic mergers in the twentieth century, claims of economies and efficiencies to be gained through consolidation were their most common justification. It was admitted that the formation of the Steel Company of Canada, for example, would end competition among its constituents. But the savings created by lower shipping costs, specialization and longer production runs, and consolidation of the sales force, it was predicted, would allow products to be sold at a lower price ("if necessary") than in the past, but at a larger profit to the company. Most other amalgamations made similar claims.[43]

49

A LIVING PROFIT

Alternatively, some members of combines justified their actions by maintaining they prevented the growth of giant enterprises tending to monopoly. Totally free competition, they argued, would lead to the survival of the fittest in the form of either trusts or monopolies. In a campaign to have the Criminal Code changed to legalize small businessmen's combines, the Retail Merchants' Association maintained that the existing anti-combines sections induced the creation of monopolistic corporations by permitting businessmen to combine and fix prices through joint stock companies while prohibiting them from doing the same thing on an individual basis in trade associations. Far better to permit and even encourage the regulation of competition than to foster an end to competition by making sane regulations illegal. After all, the department stores were obviously inaugurated with "the prime motive of destroying your opponents and then creating a monopoly for selfish purposes, and public inconvenience."[44] An eminently respectable academic economist had defended the Wholesale Grocers' Guild for the same reasons in 1890, charging that unrestrained competition would lead to "the destruction of the trading and manufacturing middle class and the growth on its ruins of a few colossal businesses." Accordingly, "the tendency of the combines will, in this respect, seem conservative in the best sense of the word."[45]

Effective regulation of competition hinged on the ability to force would-be mavericks to obey the regulations. This posed the question of commercial liberty in its starkest form (since the outsider was often the victim of boycotts and other discriminatory devices) and was the point at which many otherwise sympathetic observers of the combination movement balked. Responding to the *Monetary Times'* stated belief that the sugar combine's attempts to interfere with third parties could not be tolerated in a country where commerce was free, Hugh Blain, a leading Toronto wholesaler, offered a common defence of coercion in the interests of a majority of traders:

Man's liberty is met in every direction by man's safety. The two stand in juxtaposition to each other. You cannot abnormally increase the one without infringing on the other. Safety so increased gives opportunity for oppression, and liberty so increased becomes a dangerous license. Whichever one of these may be of most consequence to the community should be secured and protected, and if necessary even by an encroachment on the other. The liberty of these individual merchants is curtailed to the extent only, that he or they are

50

required to observe laws voluntarily adopted by nearly all the trade in the general interest, just as a citizen is obliged to obey laws passed by a majority of the voters in the general interests of the community.

To talk of a dangerous violation of man's liberty, and British freedom under such circumstances, seems to me a mere device for popular applause, thoughtless hereditary buncombe, . . . No person will advocate liberty for the ordinary lunatic, especially if dangerous to others. May I ask, why be so solicitous about the liberty of the commercial lunatic?[46]

Businessmen who stayed out of combines, or, worse still, broke free from arrangements they had been a party to, were condemned as commercial mavericks, selfish, unprincipled, and immoral. Price-cutters lacked the courage to "meet rivals on fair ground and succeed"; their business life was "conceived in selfishness and nurtured by methods the very antithesis of business-like."[47] Very probably they were able to cut prices only because they sold inferior goods, exploited their employees, or both. The Retail Merchants' Association never tired of pointing to the low wages and poor working conditions in the department stores and their allied factories. These institutions, it charged, were engaged in "the vicious process of pauperizing labor" (and were also, according to the *Canadian Pharmaceutical Journal*, "the supreme personification of egotism, selfishness, and greed"). Surely the merchant who refused to join an early-closing movement and give his clerks free time to enjoy life, thought *Le Moniteur du Commerce*, "a moins d'égards pour son employé qu'il en aurait pour son cheval ou pour son chien!" By contrast, the men who came together in the new association movement were dedicated to stopping dishonest and unfair competitive practices and were the guardians of business ethics, lifting whole trades onto a new, higher plane of commercial morality. "The old business principles," said T. J. Drummond of the Lake Superior Corporation, "were a distrust of one's competitors, the idea that to succeeed yourself you must thrust out your rivals, and the solid belief that your rivals are mean enough to feel the same way towards you . . . the law of distrust was our basic principle." The new principle, he said, quoting Judge Gary of U. S. Steel, was "I believe what is good for my competitors is good for me."[48]

A final, very significant defence of business collectivism hinged on relating it to other, more socially acceptable forms of combination. Surely the statutes governing the liberal professions were laws giving private groups the right to form combines restricting

51

A LIVING PROFIT

access and fixing prices in their trades. Why should there be a
public hue and cry against combines designed to make sure
staple articles were sold at a profit, asked the *Commercial,* but
no thought of interfering with the fixed fees of doctors, lawyers,
and other professionals, "many of which are a much more
flagrant fraud upon the public than has ever been heard of in the
field of commerce?" "We meet together the same as doctors
do," said a Western lumber dealer defending his combine, "for
mutual benefit." The actions taken by the Western Retail Lumbermen's Association to prevent manufacturers from selling to
consumers were simply a matter of business ethics, "the same as
you may charge some person with violating professional eti-
quette." Bankers openly preached the doctrine that professionalism in banking meant an end to unwise competition. "If banking
is worthy the name of a profession," ran an article in the
Journal of the Canadian Bankers' Association, "there should be
certain things universally considered unprofessional within our
ranks. Giving service without profit or at an actual loss should
be unprofessional. Solicitation of business by offering to work
more cheaply should be as unworthy a banker as we consider it
unworthy a doctor."[49]
   At the other end of the social scale, workingmen had their
own combinations, trade unions. Was there any real difference
between a trade combination and a trade union? Referring to the
cotton combine of 1886, the *Journal of Commerce* suggested
that manufacturing combines were "in aims, powers and results
achieved . . . almost identical with those enjoyed by trades
unions, though they are seldom endowed with the authority
wielded by officials of labor organizations; and as we seldom
hear of any evil results to the public at large resulting from the
latter associations, it seems idle to fear that the establishment of
a body so essentially businesslike as the one in question, can in
any way prove prejudicial to public interests." The Canadian
Manufacturers' Association was told at its annual meeting in
1889 that the main pressure for laws regulating combines seemed
to come from labour organizations, "which in themselves are
perhaps the most notable instance of combines on record"
because of their attempts to control the labour market. When the
anti-combines act of that year was understood to exclude trade
unions there were bitter objections in the Senate about class discrimination, and for the next twenty years businessmen argued that
the law of combinations should be applied equally: either trade
associations should be given the same exemptions as trade unions,
or trade unions should have their exemptions removed. It seemed

52

odd that workers should be permitted to combine to achieve a living wage and businessmen forbidden to combine to achieve a living
profit.[50]

One reason why the condemnations of competition in business
were so frequent was because of the general failure of most
attempts to limit it. The failure rate of trade association agreements, combines, and attempts at monopoly was very high. It was
inherently difficult to build barriers around a free market. The
peculiarity of associational activities among businessmen was that
"scabbing" was even more effective in their field than when it was
employed against trade unions. A single non-union worker could
have little effect breaking a normal strike. A single price-cutting
Timothy Eaton or Robert Simpson could demoralize thousands of
retailers across the country. A single renegade manufacturer could
delight in undoing the most complicated stabilizing arrangements:

> What is it that doth shake the trade
> And make each grocery man afraid
> To buy, lest he may pay too dear,
> The fall in prices being near?
>   'Tis Brantford Starch.

> What is it that doth make Rome howl
> And cause the Guild to fight and growl,
> And harbor naughty vengeful feelings
> Towards the firm who loves fair dealings?
>   'Tis Brantford Starch.[51]

Organic mergers leading to oligopoly could ease the competitive
problems of some businessmen. As with the early-closing movement and the trading-stamp "evil," governments did occasionally
meet the demands of businessmen to have their trade restrictions
sanctioned by law. On the whole, though, government attitudes
ranged from benign neutrality and the passing of merely ceremonial
anti-combines laws through alarming and zealous prosecution of
combines by some provincial attorneys-general.[52] Without the
force of law behind them, combinations in restraint of trade
remained purely voluntary agreements, apt to be shattered at the
whim of any enterprising merchant.

Although there were enough of these enterprising individual-
ists in most areas of business to frustrate much of the flight from
competition, the strength of resistance to competition by businessmen must not be underrated. In a purely competitive marketplace a businessman had no security, no certainty, no sense of

53

A LIVING PROFIT

control over his own fate. He could be hard-working, honest, and thrifty, but still find his business and his livelihood destroyed by competitors who were wealthier, more efficient, or less scrupulous. In the real world of business most participants in the market would have amended the formula for material success to read Industry, Integrity, Frugality, and Fixed Prices. The continued freedom of enterprise was a function of the impersonal forces of the marketplace, not of the desires of a majority of traders. In these years the free market survived because businessmen did not have the power to control decisions affecting their livelihood.

Notes

1. S.C., pp. 3-5, 505-7, 526-27.
2. Montreal Board of Trade Archives, Montreal Wholesale Grocers' Association, Minutes, 1888-1891, *passim*.
3. *Ibid.*, Letterbooks, J. S. Cook to Messrs. Walter Baker & Sons, Dec. 14, 1908.
4. *Ibid.*, Minutes, 1900-1915, *passim*.
5. G. R. Stevens, *Canadian National Railways*, Vol. 1 (Toronto: 1960), pp. 347-53; Public Archives of Canada, C.P.R. Papers, Van Horne Letterbooks, No. 5, Van Horne to James Stephenson, April 29, 1884; *ibid.*, No. 6, Van Horne to W. Wainwright, May 22, 1884; *ibid.*, No. 10, *passim*.
6. Walter Vaughan, *The Life and Work of Sir William Van Horne* (New York: 1920), p. 166; C.P.R. Papers, Van Horne Letterbooks, No. 14, Van Horne to G. M. Bosworth, Dec. 8, 1885.
7. *C.M.*, Oct. 19, 1883, p. 764.
8. *Report of the Royal Commission on the Textile Industry* (Ottawa: 1938), p. 119.
9. House of Commons, *Debates*, April 8, 1889, p. 1112.
10. *C.G.*, March 7, 1890.
11. S.C., *passim*.
12. *J.C.B.A.*, Oct., 1895, p. 20; *J.C.B.A.*, Jan., 1900, pp. 97, 98.
13. *P.C.*, 27 déc., 1889; *C.G.*, Oct. 22, 1890.
14. *C.J.F.*, March 1887, pp. 59, 83; *M.T.*, June 1, 1888, p. 1482; *Commercial*, June 18, 1888, p. 996.
15. *Trader*, Oct., 1890, p. 31; *Trader*, Nov., 1900, p. 1.
16. *C.G.*, Feb. 26, 1892; *C.G.*, Nov. 22, 1895.
17. *R.M.J.*, July 20, 1903, p. 12.

A LIVING PROFIT

18. *Ibid.*, Aug., 1905, p. 255.
19. Public Archives of Ontario, Lumberman's Association of Ontario Papers, transcript of "Special General Meeting of Lumber Manufacturers," May 6, 1908; also, House of Commons, *Journals*, 1906-1907, Appendix 6, "Proceedings of the Select Committee . . . Inquiring into the Prices Charged for Lumber in the Provinces of Manitoba, Alberta and Saskatchewan."
20. *M.T.*, Sept. 24, 1910, pp. 1325-28; *F.P.*, July 30, Sept. 17, Oct. 22, 1910.
21. *R.M.J.*, Aug., 1907, p. 257.
22. *J.C.*, Jan. 19, 1894, p. 135; *J.C.*, July 15, 1887, pp. 66-67; *C.G.*, Nov. 7, 1890.
23. *Trader*, April, 1883; *C.M.*, Aug. 18, 1882, p. 469; *Commercial*, June 23, 1885, p. 769; Public Archives of Canada, The Royal Commission on Railways, "Evidence," *passim; I.C.*, Oct. 1903, p. 117.
24. *Trader*, March, 1890, p. 23.
25. Public Archives of Canada, Laurier Papers, pp. 111449-53, W. K. McNaught to Laurier, June 22, 1906.
26. S.C., pp. 19-25, 88-89, 113; Montreal Wholesale Grocers' Association, Minutes, Nov. 17, 1893.
27. S.C., pp. 84-85.
28. *C.G.*, Dec. 12, 1890; *C.G.*, Oct. 17, 1890; *C.G.*, May 15, 1891.
29. S.C., pp. 29-32; Laurier Papers, p. 5770, J. A. Mathewson to Laurier, July 20, 1896; T. Eaton Co., *Spring and Summer Catalogue. 1894*, p. 3; Public Archives of Canada, R. L. Borden Papers, Joseph Flavelle to Borden, Feb. 21, 1910; Senate, *Debates*, May 2, 1910, pp. 886-88; *M.T.* May 7, 1910, p. 1915.
30. *C.J.F.*, April 1896, p. 100.
31. *C.G.*, May 17, 1889; *M.T.*, Dec. 10, 1886, p. 664; *Commercial*, March 15, 1887, p. 510.
32. *C.G.*, April 11, 1889, *J.C.*, Aug. 20, 1889, p. 529.
33. S.C., pp. 122-24; W. J. Ashley, "The Canadian Sugar Combine," *University Quarterly Review* 1 (Feb., 1890), 38; *M.T.*, Aug 23, 1889, p. 223.
34. S.C., p. 110; *R.M.J.*, Oct. 20, 1903, p. 73; *P.C.*, 8 mai, 1894, pp. 272-73.
35. *C.G.*, Oct. 2, 1891; *C.J.F.*, April, 1886, p. 186; D. M. Stewart, "What Constitutes Unwise Competition Between Banks," *J.C.B.A.*, Jan., 1898, p. 223.
36. *C.M.*, Sept. 28, 1883, p. 703.
37. S.C., pp. 88, 355; "Select Committee on Lumber, 1907," pp. 655-57.
38. *M.T.*, May 25, 1888, p. 1448.
39. "Select Committee on Lumber, 1907," pp. 601, 602.
40. S.C., pp. 45-46.
41. *M.T.*, Sept. 24, 1910, p. 1327.
42. Hugh Blain, *Combines: An Address Delivered Before the Board of Trade of the City of Toronto by Mr. Hugh Blain Against the Bill Introduced in the House of Commons by Mr. N. Clarke Wallace Intitled "An Act For the Prevention and Suppression of Combinations in Restraint Trade."* (Toronto: 1889), pp. 11-12; "Select Committee on Lumber, 1907," p. 657.
43. Blain, *op. cit.;* Stelco, *M.T.*, Sept. 24, 1910, pp. 1326-27; see also Herbert Gordon Stapells, "The Recent Consolidation Movement in Canadian Industry," (M.A. Thesis, University of Toronto, 1922).
44. *R.M.J.*, Dec., 1906, p. 389.
45. *Ibid.*, May, 1904, p. 91; Ashley, *op. cit.*, p. 38.
46. *M.T.*, April 5, 1889, p. 1185.
47. *C.G.*, July 10, 1891; *C.G.*, Dec. 4, 1896.
48. *R.M.J.*, Aug. 20, 1903, pp. 48-49; *Canadian Pharmaceutical Journal*,

March, 1897, p. 313; *M.C.*, 6 août, 1886, p. 548; T. J. Drummond, *I.C.*, Nov., 1909, p. 428.

49. *Commercial,* Sept. 16, 1889, p. 1269; "Select Committee on Lumber, 1907," pp. 238, 278; David R. Forgan, "Banking as a Profession," *J.C.B.A.,* Oct., 1898, p. 52.

50. *J.C.*, Aug. 20, 1886, p. 529; *C.M.*, March 15, 1889, p. 178; Senate, *Debates,* April 29, 1889, pp. 643, 650; *I.C.*, May, 1910, p. 978.

51. *C.G.*, Feb. 26, 1892, p. 26.

52. Bliss, *op. cit.*

[30]

By *Stanley C. Hollander*

PROFESSOR OF MARKETING
MICHIGAN STATE UNIVERSITY

Nineteenth Century Anti-Drummer Legislation in the United States*

❆ *The rise and fall of discriminatory legislation against traveling salesmen is fully documented in this study of a negative vein of American business history.*

Traveling salesmen did not begin to play a role of any real significance in American marketing until about 1840 or 1850. Both their number and their importance to the domestic distribution system then increased vigorously throughout the second half of the nineteenth century. But during the period from 1850 to 1890 they were harassed by restrictive and hostile licensing laws adopted in numerous cities and states. This note is concerned with the development and effects of those laws.

I

During the early part of the nineteenth century, comparisons of British and American business methods often contained a note of surprise at the fact that commercial travelers were not used in this country. English textile houses had long sent traveling representatives out to solicit business.[1] Consequently, a number of writers were astonished that a similar method of marketing was not used in this country.[2]

But problems of distance, poor transportation, and poor communications were barriers against traveling salesmanship in the United States. Of course, traveling to a central market was as difficult for the resident merchant as traveling to the merchant would have been for the salesman. Going to market, however, enabled the merchant

* Support from the Michigan State University All-University Research Fund is gratefully acknowledged. A preliminary, abridged report on this research was presented at the American Marketing Association December, 1963 meeting, and was published in its proceedings, *Towards Scientific Marketing* (Chicago, 1964), pp. 344–51.

[1] A. P. Allen, *Ambassadors of Commerce* (London, 1885), p. 102.
[2] Isaac Holmes, *An Account of the United States of America* (London, 1823), p. 355; A. L. Stimson, "Commercial Travellers," *Hunt's Merchants' Magazine*, vol. I (July, 1839), pp. 37–41.

to inspect the goods he bought instead of being forced to depend upon unreliable samples. This was important in a period of poor transportation and little standardization, since it would have been difficult to return any goods that did not live up to sample. Visiting a central market also provided increased opportunity to buy at auction, a bitterly criticized but significant marketing institution in the early nineteenth century. The merchandise that was bought in the course of the annual or semi-annual market visit could be pooled for easier and cheaper shipment to the hinterland. In many cases, the central market firms provided elaborate entertainment so that the visiting buyer often enjoyed his trip in spite of all the difficulties. And shopping trips to the eastern seaboard gave the merchant selling prestige within his own community.[3]

The very smallest dealers were dependent upon nearby wholesalers and semi-jobbers but the merchant of any stature traveled to the market center that seemed appropriate to his size and location. Moreover, at least one early attempt, that of the Scovills, to send out a traveling salesman ran into wholesaler resistance that reinforced the traditional way of doing business.[4]

Of course, there were some traveling businessmen prior to 1850. Peddlers, hawkers, and similar itinerant merchants, who carried their goods with themselves and who sold directly to consumers, had long been known in this country.[5] There were even a few traveling wholesalers who carried stocks of such portable merchandise as jewelry and pistols directly to the retailers.[6] A number of eastern textile firms and other businesses sent out traveling agents who were primarily bill collectors but who also had some responsibility for attempting to maintain and encourage dealer goodwill toward their principals. Selling, however, was not their basic duty. And if they attempted to sell, these men were likely to encounter a sort of "critical mass" problem. As Atherton points out, the "representatives were not common enough to be of any great help to storekeepers who wished to order by mail and therefore wanted the latest possible information concerning eastern stocks and prices." [7] Consequently, the storekeepers could not forego the market trips by simply relying on the representatives, and at the same time, the market trips left

<hr>

[3] See Lewis E. Atherton, "Predecessors of the Commercial Drummer in the Old South," *Bulletin of the Business Historical Society,* vol. XXI (February, 1947), pp. 17–18; William H. Baldwin, *Travelling Salesmen: Their Opportunities and Their Dangers* (Boston, 1874), pp. 4–5.

[4] Theodore F. Marburg, "Manufacturer's Drummer, 1832," *Bulletin of the Business Historical Society,* vol. XXII (April, 1948), pp. 52–53.

[5] See Richardson Wright, *Hawkers and Walkers in Early America* (Philadelphia, 1927).

[6] Atherton, "Predecessors of the Commercial Drummer," p. 21.

[7] *Ibid.,* p. 22.

the storekeepers disinclined to buy from any traveling representative.

So the traveling salesman, whose main job was to solicit orders from wholesalers and retailers on the basis of samples, was almost unknown in the United States during the first four decades of the nineteenth century. In fact, the word "drummer," which later became the popular, slightly derogatory term for the traveling man, was used during the early part of the century to refer to men the wholesalers placed in depots and hotel lobbies to greet the visiting buyers.[8] Even as late as 1870, a businessman could mix pride and nostalgia with apology in a statement that his firm did not use commercial travelers. Responding to a speech by a delegate from Charleston, South Carolina in favor of salesmen's licensing laws during the 1870 meeting of the National Board of Trade, a Mr. Chittenden of New York said:[9]

> I am so old fogyish, and old-fashioned, that I refuse to be a drummer, or to allow my commercial establishment to act as a commercial drummer, in the sense referred to by several speakers. Having been for twenty-five years in business in New York, we do not send out travellers to sell our goods; but there are dealers in Charleston who complain that we do not, and there are dealers in other places where these [licensing] restrictions exist, who complain to us, that they are prevented by them from getting their goods on the best terms. . . . I could instance scores and hundreds of cases within the last five years, where the old dealers with my firm have complained to us, that we do not give them our goods at their counters as other houses do.

Mr. Chittenden was, as he admitted, a good bit behind the times. Marketing methods began to change in the 1840's, '50's, and '60's. Improvements in transportation and communication, particularly with the development of the railroads, began to eliminate many of the obstacles to traveling salesmanship. Increases in manufacturing capacity created needs for new competitive tactics and new marketing outlets. The combination of pressure and opportunity led to first a trickle and then a tide of traveling salesmen. Some of the first steps were hesitant and secretive. William H. Baldwin, a pioneer commercial traveler for a Boston house reminisced in 1874: [10]

> Again, well do I remember what profound secrecy was enjoined by the Seniors when the idea of sending out "Travelling Salesmen" was first practically inaugurated in this city twenty-five to thirty years ago.

[8] See Lee M. Friedman, "The Drummer in Early American Merchandise Distribution," *Bulletin of the Business Historical Society,* vol. XXI (April, 1947), pp. 39–44.

[9] Apparently Simon B. Chittenden, a successful dry goods wholesaler, later Congressman, publisher, and philanthropist. *Proceedings of the Third Annual Meeting of the National Board of Trade (1870)* (Boston, 1871), pp. 97–98.

[10] Baldwin, *Travelling Salesmen,* p. 5.

19TH CENTURY ANTI-DRUMMER LEGISLATION   481

That mysterious trunk in one of the upper rooms, samples and pattern books privately collected together and privately packed, the trunk as privately sent to the depot, the young "Traveller" and those remaining at home, having the words "say nothing" firmly impressed upon them.

The Scovills, who had found the market unprepared for their first venture into traveling salesmanship in 1832, sent another man out in 1852. Their second commercial traveler faced a very different situation, and his letters home were filled with comments on the activities of rival drummers.[11]

All the estimates of the actual number of traveling salesmen circulating in the years after 1850 are likely to be clouded in the uncertainties of fuzzy definitions and inadequate census methods.[12] But even the least reliable and most self-serving of these statements are indicative of the growth of the trade, since they indicate what must have at least had the semblance of reasonableness. No one in 1840 could have offered an estimate of about 95,000 commercial travelers, as the New York *Times* did in 1882.[13] Some other estimates of interest were: 1861: 1,000 commercial travelers;[14] 1869: 50,000;[15] 1885: 100,000;[16] and 1903: 300,000.[17] These estimates, which undoubtedly were just plain guesswork, are certainly far above the Census reports of 7,300 commercial travelers in 1870, 28,000 in 1880, 59,000 in 1890, and 93,000 in 1900.[18]

The Census figures probably seriously understated the total number of commercial travelers, since many of these men must have been included in other classifications, such as "agents," "salesmen," and the various kinds-of-business groups. The President of the Commercial Travelers' National League, P. E. Dowe, was very critical of the Census enumerations in his testimony before the Industrial Commission in 1899. Dowe pointed out that one of the many commercial travelers' associations then operating, The Commercial Travelers Mutual Accident Association of Utica, New York, alone had approximately 20,000 members. He also noted that the 1870

    [11] Theodore F. Marburg, "Manufacturer's Drummer, 1852; With Comments on Western and Southern Markets," *Bulletin of the Business Historical Society*, vol. XXII (June, 1948), pp. 106–14.
    [12] For a discussion of some of the weaknesses and ambiguities of nineteenth century Census data concerning salesmen, see Harold Barger, *Distribution's Place in the American Economy since 1869* (Princeton, 1959), pp. 106–108.
    [13] "Taxing Commercial Travelers" (editorial), July 9, 1882.
    [14] E. P. Briggs, *Fifty Years on the Road* (Philadelphia, 1911), p. 52.
    [15] The Society of Commercial Travellers, *The System of Commercial Travelling in Europe and the United States* (New York, 1869), pp. 18–19.
    [16] Allen, *Ambassadors of Commerce*, p. 190.
    [17] "Commercial Traveler," *Encyclopedia Americana*, 1903, vol. 5.
    [18] U. S. Bureau of the Census, Ninth Census of the United States, *Statistics of Population* (Washington, 1872), vol. I, table XXVII A, p. 676; Tenth Census, *Statistics of Population* (Washington, 1883), vol. I, table XXXII A, p. 746; Eleventh Census, *Report on Population* (Washington, 1897), vol. I, part 2, table 78, p. 304; Twelfth Census, *Occupations* (Washington, 1904), table 1, p. 7.

Census showed a ratio of almost four hotel keepers for every single traveling salesman in the country, a figure that seemed unreasonable.

The relationship between the total number of manufacturing and wholesaling concerns reported in 1890 (approximately 385,000) and the number of commercial travelers reported (approximately only 60,000) also suggested an undercounting of the travelers.[19] Whatever the true figure, it is clear that traveling salesmanship was well on its way after the Civil War. Mr. Chittenden, the "old fogy" who would not send out salesmen, was right in saying: [20]

> I hold, Sir, that there is not a merchant . . . who understands his business to-day, not a merchant in any of those remoter cities, who naturally is brought to New York, or to the principal markets, twice a year, who is not interested to have the merchants of the great markets send their agents to his own counter, without restrictions, to sell him, on the best possible terms, such goods as they have to offer. . . . The time will come very soon, when there will be no division of public sentiment, or of sentiment in this Board on such a question as that.

II

Many merchants, particularly the wholesalers outside of Boston and New York, feared that these salesmen would undermine the traditional marketing channels. As one might expect, a plea for legislative intervention was part of the reaction to this change in selling methods. Apparently starting with Pennsylvania (1851), Maryland (1852), and Virginia (1853), states and cities throughout the country adopted licensing laws that made the traveling salesman pay a costly, and in some cases prohibitive, fee for a license to do business. Fees of $50, $100, and $200 per annum were not uncommon; and in some instances such as that of Georgia, a separate license was required in each county in which the salesman wanted to do business.

The exact number of states, territories, and cities that attempted to license traveling salesmen is somewhat uncertain for two reasons. First, many of the municipal and county ordinances did not appear in the compilations of state statutes and did not lead to trials that are included in the state reports. Second, in some, but not in all, jurisdictions the local peddler laws were stretched to hamper commercial travelers in the wholesale trades. The list of states and terri-

---

[19] U. S. Industrial Commission, *Preliminary Report on Trusts and Industrial Combinations*, House Doc. 476, part 1 (Washington, 1900), testimony section, p. 27. Dowe's testimony in general, however, seems somewhat vague and unsatisfactory. Consequently his own estimate of the sales population should not be given too much credence.
[20] *Third Annual Meeting of the National Board of Trade*, p. 99.

19TH CENTURY ANTI-DRUMMER LEGISLATION   483

tories that enacted drummer laws between 1850 and 1890 includes at least: Alabama,[21] Connecticut,[22] Delaware,[23] District of Columbia,[24] Florida,[25] Georgia,[26] Kentucky,[27] Louisiana,[28] Maine,[29] Maryland,[30] Michigan,[31] Montana,[32] Nevada,[33] North Carolina,[34] Pennsylvania,[35] Rhode Island,[36] Tennessee,[37] Texas,[38] Virginia,[39] West Virginia,[40] and Wisconsin.[41] It also seems probable that state laws were used against commercial travelers in Arizona,[42] Colorado,[43] Dakota,[44] and South Carolina.[45] In addition, there were isolated, although possibly less accurate, complaints about state legislation in California,[46] Illinois,[47] Iowa,[48] and New Hampshire.[49]

[21] *Ala. Code* (1886), par. 629 (35); Frederick B. Goddard, *The Art of Selling with How to Read Character, Laws Governing Sales, etc.* (New York, 1889), p. 87; U. S. House of Representatives, Committee on Commerce, *Sale of Goods and Merchandise by Sample: Views of the Minority*, 49 Cong., 1 Sess., *Report* 1762, Part 2, 1886.

[22] *Conn. Laws of 1867*, Chap. 119, p. 137.

[23] *Dela. Rev. Stat.* (1874), vol. 13, Chap. 117, pp. 131–33.

[24] Act of Aug. 23, 1871. *D. C. Rev. Stat.* (1872), Pt. I, Title IX, Chap. 1, Sec. 23.

[25] *Dig. Fla. Laws* (McClellan, 1881), Chap. 174, Sec. 24–26.

[26] Act of Dec. 15, 1859; *Ga. Rev. Code* (1873), Part I, Title XVII, Sec. 1631–38. *Ga. Code* (Clark, Cobb & Irwin, 1861), Part I, Title 16, Par. 1566, later repealed, prohibited non-residents from selling by sample.

[27] *Ky. Rev. Stat.* Appendix (Act of 1860), p. 805, cited in "Abstract of State Laws Relating to Non-Resident Traders and Peddlers," *Proceedings of the Second Annual Meeting of the National Board of Trade (1869)* (Boston, 1870), pp. 340–46.

[28] *La. Rev. Stat.* (1886), Art. 101, Sec. 12.

[29] *Maine Laws of 1866*, p. 29, cited in "Abstract of State Laws," *loc. cit.*

[30] *Laws of Maryland*, 1852, Chap. 339, cited by Fred M. Jones, *Middlemen in the Domestic Trade of the United States 1800–1860* (Urbana, 1937), p. 17; *Md. Acts of 1868*, Chap. 413.

[31] Act 272, 1865. *Mich. Gen. Stat. Ann.* (Howell, 1887), par. 1257–59.

[32] Act of July 22, 1879. *Mont. Comp. Stat.* (Webb, 1888), 5th Div., Chap. 81, Sec. 1359.

[33] *Nev. Rev. Act*, Sec. 67 as amended, Feb. 20, 1877. *Nev. Gen. Stat.* (Bailey & Hammond, 1885), Sec. 1269–75.

[34] *N. C. Pub. Stat.* (Battle, 1873), Chap. 102, Sec. 82; *N. C. Act* (1885), Chap. 175, Sec. 28.

[35] Public Law 489, April 12, 1851. *Penna. Digest* (Brightly, 1883), p. 1696.

[36] *R. I. Rev. Stat.* (1857), Chap. 119, 120.

[37] *Tenn. Act of 1881*, Chap. 96, par. 16.

[38] Act of May 4, 1882. *Tex. Civ. Stat.* (Sayles, 1888), art. 4665.

[39] *Acts of Virginia* (1853) cited by Jones, *loc. cit.* *Va. Code* (1873), Chap. XXXIV, Sec. 26, Chap. XXXV, Sec. 21. *Va. Acts of 1859–60*, Chap. 2, Sec. 1. (*Va. Code*, 1860, Chap. XXXVIII, Sec. 2, later modified, provided that sales could be made only at specific locations specified on the licenses required for all sales, thereby prohibiting any form of transient selling.)

[40] *W. Va. Code* (1870), Chap. 33, Sec. 4.

[41] *Wisc. Gen. Laws* (1868), Chap. 177, Sec. 3. *Wisc. Rev. Stat.* (Taylor, 1871), Title XI, Chap. 50.

[42] House of Representatives, *Sale of Goods by Sample, Minority Views; Ariz. Rev. Stat.* (1887), Sec. 2239, cited by William B. Lockhart, "The Sales Tax in Interstate Commerce," *Harvard Law Review*, vol. 52 (1939), p. 621.

[43] House of Representatives, *Sale of Goods by Sample, Minority Views; Colo. Gen. Stat.* (1883), Sec. 2096–98, cited by Lockhart, *loc. cit.*

[44] House of Representatives, *Sale of Goods by Sample, Minority Views.*

[45] See *S. C. Rev. Stat.* (1893), par. 1451–54, amending *S. C. Code* (1876), Chap. XVI, Sec. 64 so as to exempt wholesale commercial travelers from the state requirements for hawkers and peddlers' licenses.

[46] "Commercial Traveler License Laws," *The Commercial Travelers' Magazine*, vol. I (September, 1883), p. 79.

[47] *Illinois Compiled Stat.* (1869), p. 414, cited in "Abstract of State Laws."

[48] L. P. Brockett, *The Commercial Traveller's Guide Book* (New York, 1871), p. 35.

[49] House of Representatives, *Sale of Goods by Sample, Minority Views*, but note that *N. H. Gen. Laws* (1878), Chap. 119, Sec. 2, contain a specific exemption from licensing for agents "whose business is to carry samples or specimens for wholesale trade."

Some of these laws, such as the Maryland act of 1868 and the Tennessee law of 1881, imposed licensing obligations only upon salesmen selling in designated cities. State-wide licensing systems were more common, however. Many of the statutes, particularly until Maryland's 1868 law was held unconstitutionally discriminatory, placed the licensing obligations only on non-residents or on the representatives of out-of-state firms. Of course, even if no ostensible discrimination appeared on the face of the statute, this sort of law was likely to have an uneven impact since most of the commercial travelers operating in the protectionist states were likely to be outsiders. In some cases, such as in Virginia, the legislation provided moieties, or rewards, to informers who reported unlicensed salesmen.[50]

In addition to the states, numerous cities established their own licensing ordinances. A very partial roster of these cities would include Augusta, Ga., Charleston, S. C., Cincinnati, Chicago, Detroit, Lancaster, Memphis, Mobile, Nashville, Omaha, Pensacola, Philadelphia, Pittsburgh, Portland, Ore., Providence, Richmond, Savannah, St. Louis, St. Paul, and Vicksburg.[51] This list only covers a small fraction of the communities involved. One salesman said that by 1869, sixty-four towns and villages in the Northwest had not only adopted, but had repealed, their licensing ordinances.[52] A later writer noted that "At one time this license law was in effect . . . in hundreds of cities."[53] Similarly, an old-time drummer reminisced:[54]

> It was in 1867 that I made my maiden trip through the oil regions of Pennsylvania for a Cleveland house, and I made Meadville my base of operations. In those days it was quite a different thing to be a commercial traveler from what it is to-day, as you had to be continually dodging tax-collectors, owing to the fact that nearly every little town imposed a license tax on traveling men.

About half of the Canadian provinces also had drummer licensing laws.[55] And a Honolulu drug firm issued a circular announcing a

[50] See, for example, *Virginia License and Tax Act,* approved April 22, 1882, Sec. 32.
[51] "Commercial Travelers' Meeting on Licenses," New York *Times,* June 24, 1869; Briggs, *Fifty Years on the Road,* pp. 48–50; Brockett, *Commercial Travellers Guide Book,* p. 35; Society of Commercial Travellers, *The System of Commercial Travelling,* pp. 6–8, 19; "Commercial Travellers' License Laws;" Detroit Common Council Ordinance #42, March 7, 1865; Portland Ordinance #4817, March 4, 1886, cited in *ex parte Hanson,* 28 Fed. 127 (1886); *ex parte Taylor,* 58 Miss. 478; 38 Am. Rep. 336 (1880).
[52] "Commercial Travelers' Meeting on Licenses."
[53] Harry Z. Griffin, "A Convention of Traveling Men," *The Bostonian,* vol. IV (July, 1896), p. 276.
[54] "A Veteran Commercial Traveler," *Salesmanship,* vol. 1 (July–August, 1903), p. 28.
[55] "Taxing Commercial Travelers," New York *Times,* July 9, 1882.

19TH CENTURY ANTI-DRUMMER LEGISLATION   485

willingness to buy by correspondence, since heavy license fees prevented visits from overseas salesmen.[56]

The yearly license fees plus, in some cases, the nuisance of registering the license in each county in which the drummer wanted to do business, could easily become burdensome. One Baltimore merchant declared: [57]

> As a question of money, the firm of which I am a member pays out several thousand dollars a year for these taxes. If we send a man from Baltimore to go through the South we have to pay over a thousand dollars in annual licenses for him. We pay two hundred dollars in this District [the District of Columbia], seventy-five dollars in Virginia, one hundred dollars in North Carolina, fifty dollars in one city in South Carolina, and so on. . . . We pay from two dollars a day to ten dollars a day in various localities.

The New York *Times* reported that one traveler paid $3,000 a year for his licenses, while many paid $1,000 or so.[58] In comparison, in 1889 the average earnings of *good* wholesale jewelry and drug salesmen were reported at about $2,500 per year, and the *top* men in such lines as boots and shoes, dry goods, and wholesale groceries earned from $6,000 to $10,000.[59]

Several arguments were advanced for the laws. Southern legislators at times claimed that the northern drummers carried abolitionist sentiments along with their samples.[60] A xenophobic suspicion of travelers may have reinforced the desire for barriers against them. To quote a delegate from Charleston at the National Board of Trade: [61]

> How easy it would be for me to say that there is less confidence in strangers who are passing through the country than in well known mercantile houses, who are engaged in distributing their goods in the usual way. How is it possible to maintain trade if strangers can come and sell goods in this way?

The argument that commercial travelers would not otherwise contribute to the tax burden of the communities where they sold goods provided a somewhat more plausible justification for the license statutes. George F. Bagley, a prosperous Detroit wholesale grocer, urged before the National Board of Trade: "I think, if the

[56] Circular issued by Hobron Drug Co., cited by Charles Austin Bates, *The Art and Literature of Business* (New York, 1903), vol. 3, p. 158.
[57] Mr. Supplee, *Proceedings of the Annual Meeting of the National Board of Trade (1886)* (Boston, 1887), p. 82.
[58] Editorial, December 17, 1882.
[59] Goddard, *Art of Selling*, pp. 59–60.
[60] See Atherton, "Predecessors of the Commercial Drummer in the Old South," p. 24.
[61] Mr. Lathers, of Charleston, *Proceedings of the Third Annual Meeting of the National Board of Trade*, p. 92.

Board will reflect upon it, they will see the injustice done to people who live in a State, and hold their merchandise there, by these persons who come in and exhibit just the same kind of goods, and pay none of the State or local taxation." [62] Or to quote the highly articulate Charleston delegate again: [63]

> But it has been said that these drummers pay taxes at home; that is very much as if a man should come to my house and propose to eat my dinner, and comfort me by telling me that I might pay the butcher's bill, because his wife paid a butcher's bill at home.

The tax burden argument proved appealing to many of the state courts that were asked to rule on the license requirements, since it seemed to be a matter of equitable treatment. Thus the Maryland Court of Appeals noted in *Ward* v. *State* (1869): [64]

> A custom, however, has grown up in recent times, with merchants and manufacturers in the large manufacturing and commercial cities and States, of travelling or sending agents or runners through other States and cities, with samples, cards, catalogues, or trade lists of their goods, and thereby selling by retail or wholesale large quantities of merchandise, located beyond the limits of the States, where they thus sell, and not subject to the local State, county, or municipal taxation, as are like goods in the hands of resident merchants or traders, to the great detriment of the business and trade of the latter. Large sales are thus made, and an extensive and lucrative business is thus carried on, and it is the object of the law in question to search and subject to taxation, by means of a license, the trade and business thus transacted within the limits of the principal city of the State.

The salesmen, though, felt that the advocacy of these laws rested not so much on the question of equal taxation, as on the matter of detriment to local business firms. In speeches, pamphlets, and articles, the travelers complained of "an epidemic of local 'protection.'" [65] They said: "The instigators . . . are well known to be small jobbers who desire to monopolize the trade of their own town." [66] "There are certain States and cities, whose merchants are so very narrow minded and contracted in their business views, that they practically clog the wheels of commerce in their own cities by enacting laws compelling the drummer to take out a license or abandon his profession in these particular localities." [67] "These

[62] *Proceedings of the Second Annual Meeting of the National Board of Trade*, p. 37.
[63] Lathers, *loc. cit.*, p. 101.
[64] 31 Stockett (Md.) 285 affirming conviction in Balto. City Court; later reversed U. S. Supreme Court, 12 Wall (US) 418.
[65] George S. Forbush, "Familiar Legal Talks — Discriminatory License Laws," *The Commercial Travelers' Magazine*, vol. 1 (September, 1883), p. 49.
[66] Society of Commercial Travellers, *The System of Commercial Travelling*, p. 15.
[67] George M. Hayes, *Twenty Years on the Road or the Trials and Tribulations of a Commercial Traveler by One of Them* (Philadelphia, 1884), Chap. VII, no p.

cities had an idea that by pursuing this policy, they were benefitting the business of the resident houses." [68]

The complaints seem justified. The licensing laws, although onerous, were not likely to produce sufficient amounts to be considered as revenue measures or as substitutes for local property taxes. In many cases, although by no means invariably, the salesmen were calling upon merchants who otherwise would have traveled out of State to buy their wares. In such cases there were no changes in the flow of the actual goods upon which the property taxes were levied. The real issue was that the drummers were beginning to sell, or constituted an implicit threat of selling, to the merchants who would otherwise depend upon local jobbers.

Many of the proponents of licensing urged this point. [69] The Charleston delegate, who again warrants quotation, declared: "These laws were made because so many were coming in and taking away the trade from the local merchants who should have supplied the people with flour and other articles." [70] Or as another Board of Trade delegate, who himself opposed licensing, said: "I know that some of my neighbor merchants in Milwaukee feel that it is a matter of some importance to them that the Philadelphia merchant should be prohibited, to some extent, from coming into Wisconsin, and from selling his goods, through an agent, by their side." [71] In 1884, a Congressional committee concluded that: ". . . these laws are made to please the selfishness of local jobbers and unscrupulous informers . . . and are not for the purpose of raising revenue for the States." [72] Professor F. E. Melder, who looked at the drummer laws as part of a 1937 study of interstate trade barriers, has offered the interesting thought that some of the support may have come from the larger retailers who were able to go to market themselves and who were upset at the emergence of a new source of supply for smaller competitors. [73] In any event, the major pressure for the legislation certainly came from traditional businessmen who feared a major marketing innovation.

[68] Charles S. Plummer, *Leaves from a Drummer's Diary* (Chicago, 1889), p. 63.
[69] See Atherton, "Predecessors of the Commercial Drummer," p. 24 for the argument of a representative of a New Orleans wholesale house in the Louisiana legislature.
[70] Lathers, *Proceedings*, p. 91.
[71] Mr. Holton (of Milwaukee), *Proceedings of the Second Annual Meeting of the National Board of Trade*, p. 33.
[72] U. S. House of Representatives, Committee on Manufactures, *Report to Accompany Bill H. R. 986* (48 Cong., 1 Sess., *Report* No. 1321), April 15, 1884.
[73] *State and Local Barriers to Interstate Commerce in the United States* (*The Maine Bulletin*, vol. 40, No. 4; The University of Maine Studies, 2d Series, No. 43) (Orono, Maine, 1937), p. 55.

III

In some jurisdictions the licensing laws were dead letters practically from the moment of adoption. Apparently in those communities the legislature or the city council simply followed the old political maxim that one of the best ways to deal with a political problem is to pass a law and then forget it. The Detroit ordinance of 1865, which imposed a $25.00 annual fee upon commercial travelers, appears to have been such a law. No trials or arrests seem to have arisen under the Detroit law, the contemporary newspapers seem to have ignored it, and relatively few licenses were issued. Receipts in fiscal 1866 were only $297, or the equivalent of twelve licenses minus a mysterious $3.00 shrinkage somewhere along the way. In fiscal 1867, receipts rose to $400; but by 1869 they dropped to $12.50, or half a license.[74] The ordinance was repealed in 1870, as part of a general effort to clear up a mass of miscellaneous matters before the city council.[75]

A Michigan state law (Act #272, Session of 1865) that set a $50.00 fee for an annual drummer license was almost equally ineffective, although the Detroit *Free Press* did report one arrest in the law's early days.[76] The surviving records of the State Treasurer are neither very detailed nor very complete, but they do show, that in the years from 1869 to 1880, total receipts from all types of peddlers' licenses, including the drummer's license, fluctuated between $300 and a maximum of only $600.[77] The salesman's licensing law was cited by three out of eight contestants, including the winner, for a prize offered by Governor Pingree in 1897 to the University of Michigan law student who could find the largest number of inoperative or dead letter laws on the state's statute books.[78] In fact, the Michigan law was so thoroughly forgotten that in 1894 the Grand Treasurer of the Grand Council of Michigan, Order of United Commercial Travelers of America could erroneously boast: [79]

I am happy to say that in Michigan no such restriction to commerce [as the drummer's tax] has ever been placed upon our Fraternity. Here

[74] "Report of the Controller of the City of Detroit," *Journal of the Detroit Common Council, passim.*
[75] Ordinance of the Common Council, approved February 17, 1870.
[76] September 28, 1866, p. 367.
[77] *Annual Report of the State Treasurer of the State of Michigan* (Lansing, 1870–1881), *passim.*
[78] *Journal of the House of Representatives of the State of Michigan, 1897* (Lansing, 1897), vol. I, pp. 583 ff.
[79] "Response of Grand Treasurer George A. Reynolds to the Toast, 'Commercial Freedom,'" *The Sample Case* (Order of United Commercial Travelers of America), vol. IV (May, 1894), p. 309.

we have always enjoyed the utmost freedom of speech, action and intercourse, and as a result this State has developed her natural resources,
encouraged her education and stimulated her civilization far beyond a
natural growth.

The more venturesome salesmen devised ways to evade the laws
in other communities. By 1886, even a delegate from Baltimore
could declare to the National Board of Trade that licensing taught
young men evasions and led them to creat the state.[80] The practice
grew up in Washington, D. C., and perhaps elsewhere, of borrowing
or renting licenses that had been issued to other salesmen.[81] Thus
A. W. Gage, a veteran in the shoe business, in reminiscing about a
fellow traveler, W. Preston Moses, commented on how he used to
rent Moses' license for $5.00 a day to avoid being arrested in Wash-
ington.[82] In 1886 an agent for the Travelers and Traders Union of
New York reported that license rental bureaus existed in some
southern cities, and especially in Washington and Baltimore.[83]
Representative James of New York asked for a Congressional investigation of the license brokers that year. He declared that 7,000
commercial travelers visited the District in 1885, but that only 38
licenses were issued because of the work of the brokers.[84]

Another tactic was used in those states where there was discrimination against out-of-state travelers, either in the enforcement
of the law or in the basic law itself, although such discrimination had
supposedly been ruled unconstitutional in *Ward* v. *Maryland*
(1871). A traveler would sometimes persuade a friendly local merchant to list him as an employee or agent, so as to benefit from the
preferential treatment accorded resident salesmen.[85] The dislike
that some of the wholesalers and retailers had for the licensing laws
undoubtedly increased their willingness to participate in such sub-
terfuges.

One of the simplest ways to evade the laws was to fail to obtain a
license. E. P. Briggs said that while he paid $50 for his license in

[80] Mr. Supplee, *Proceedings of the Annual Meeting (1886)*, p. 82.
[81] Copies of the Washington license form do not seem to have survived. However, a
Cincinnati license, reproduced in the Society of Commercial Travellers' pamphlet, bears
nothing to identify the licensee except a statement of his name. A similar lack of descriptive
information and/or pictures on the Washington license, which seems quite likely, would,
of course, have facilitated this bootlegging practice.
[82] A. W. Gage, "Sketches of Traveling Shoe Salesmen of Twenty-Or-More Years'
Standing and Whose Portraits Are Here Shown," in Joel C. Page, *Recollections of Sixty
Years in the Shoe Trade* (Boston, 1916), p. 89.
[83] "Protest of the Drummers," New York *Times*, January 23, 1886.
[84] "Commercial Agents," *House Mis. Doc.* No. 330, 49 Cong., 1 Sess., June 14, 1886.
[85] "Protest of the Drummers." Also note, "Petition and Remonstrance of Merchants
and Traders of Baltimore, Md., Setting Forth Frauds Committed in the District of Columbia
by Renting Out of Drummers' Licenses and by Drummers Pretending to be Partners in Local
Firms," U. S. House of Representatives, 49 Cong., 1 Sess., April 16, 1886, cited in
Congressional Record, vol. 17, p. 3582.

Washington and $150 in St. Louis, he never took out a license in Charleston, Savannah, or Baltimore. Yet he always escaped arrest in those cities.[86] As we have already noted, R. N. Hull just dodged the tax collectors while traveling through the Pennsylvania oil country.[87] George Hayes was arrested in Richmond in 1877 when he tried this method of evasion, even though he had gone to the trouble of shipping his samples to his customer in advance of his visit, so that he would not look like a drummer.[88]

Generally, those salesmen who were not encumbered with conspicuous samples were the ones most likely to escape the vigilance of the enforcement officers.[89] In his fictionalized autobiography, Charles Plummer describes the efforts that a group of salesmen in a Baltimore hotel exerted to appear as members of different trades as comical in the extreme. He says that any stranger with a package under his arm was likely to be apprehended as a salesman in that city. Yet he goes on to describe a false arrest hoax that several of the drummers played upon an unpopular fellow who traveled with trunks but did not have a license.[90]

Bribery of the enforcement agents was a common method for dealing with a threatened arrest. The salesman involved in Plummer's hoax, which may or may not have actually occurred, immediately tried to bribe the pretending agent; but apparently this tactic was used frequently in real life. An editorial in *Iron Age* pointed out that the men charged with the execution of the laws were often open to compromise.[91]

If neither evasion nor attempted bribery availed, the final tactic was to attempt to avoid the penalties through argument, bluff, or cheating. When Hayes was arrested, he persuaded the officials to accept a draft on his firm, then quickly skipped town and wired the home office to dishonor the draft. The major disadvantage of this tactic was that he was thereafter unable to return to Richmond.[92] Edward P. Briggs was arrested in Memphis on a charge that would have gladdened any sales manager's heart, that of "suspicion of offering to sell." Tried the next day, he successfully challenged the prosecution to prove that he had made any sales in the establishment where he was arrested, and was released. Fortunately for him,

[86] Briggs, *Fifty Years on the Road*, pp. 49–50.
[87] "A Veteran Commercial Traveler," p. 28.
[88] Hayes, *Twenty Years on the Road*, chap. VII.
[89] "Protest of the Drummers."
[90] Plummer, *Leaves from a Drummer's Diary*, pp. 62–67.
[91] January 7, 1869, quoted by The Society of Commercial Travellers, *The System of Commercial Travelling*, p. 20.
[92] Hayes, *Twenty Years on the Road*, Chap. VII.

19TH CENTURY ANTI-DRUMMER LEGISLATION   491

both the prosecution and the judge were unaware that the bail money he had posted for his overnight freedom while awaiting trial came out of an advance that he received against a sale to another Memphis house earlier in the day.[93] L. R. Shyrock, sometime president of the Board of Trade of St. Louis, stood on his dignity with only partial success when arrested in Atlanta: [94]

> I find it necessary in the prosecution of my business to travel through the Southern States. . . . so heavy has the taxation become upon persons travelling from the Northern and Western States, into that part of the country, that it amounts to a prohibition. I myself once came very near getting into the Atlanta jail. I suggested to the Mayor, it would be a pretty spectacle to see the President of the Board of Trade of St. Louis in the jail of his city. I was tapped upon the shoulder by a gentleman in disguise, who took me aside and said: "Do you know you are violating the laws of this State?" "No, I do not," I said. Said he, "You are liable to a fine of five hundred dollars, for offering to sell the people flour." I was waited upon by the Mayor and told finally, that I could, for the sum of fifty dollars, exhibit my samples of flour in that city. From there, I went to another city, and so on, and beginning to calculate the cost, I found that my expenses, and the licenses I had to pay for to do business in the State of Georgia would amount to more than all the profits on the goods I would sell there, so I returned home.

But elsewhere, as many of the comments already noted suggest, the laws were definite nuisances to the trade. The Society of Commercial Travellers probably exaggerated when it said, in its pamphlet, that it could cite fifty cases of honorable citizens who had been thrown into a criminal's dungeon for pursuing the honorable calling of showing new textures and explaining new processes.[95] Some salesmen, though, did go to jail. In 1869 Henry Dreshler of Newark was held in the Baltimore jail, "and kept for forty-five days the forced companion of murderers, thieves, and vagabonds," before his release could be arranged.[96] Ray T. Thornton, in turn, was jailed in Norfolk in 1882, in a test case arranged by a group of Baltimore merchants.[97] Thornton lost the case. In this he had less luck than William B. Barrett who was jailed eleven years earlier, also in Virginia, until he obtained a local court ruling that the Virginia license law was unconstitutional.[98] William G. Asher, a salesman

---

[93] *Ibid.*

[94] *Proceedings of the Third Annual Meeting of the National Board of Trade*, p. 90.

[95] The Society of Commercial Travellers, *The System of Commercial Travelling*, p. 5.

[96] *Ibid.*, pp. 5, 19.

[97] "Traveling Agents in Virginia," New York *Times*, June 7, 1882; "Decision against Commercial Travelers," *ibid.*, June 23; *Ex parte Thornton*, 4 Hughes 220, 12 Fed. 538 (C. C., E. D. Va., 1882).

[98] "A Commercial Traveller Released from Arrest in Virginia," New York *Times*, January 3, 1872.

of rubber stamps and stencils for a Louisiana firm, was arrested in Texas in 1882, and apparently he too was imprisoned for a time.[99]

Many others were forced to pay fines. A New York hat manufacturer, William H. Seymour, made good will calls on some of his customers and incidentally booked a few orders while traveling through the western states in 1869. His only samples were one of his products on his own head and another that he carried in his hand. Nevertheless, he was arrested in Cincinnati, where an apologetic judge fined him $50 plus costs. Another drummer, who apparently presented less of a borderline case, was fined $100 and costs in the same court the same day.[100] Virgil P. Humason was fined $250 in the District of Columbia police court, and the penalty was upheld on appeal.[101] An unidentified drummer told the New York *Times* that he had been arrested in Memphis, where he was forced to take out a license, and that he had been approached for a bribe by a "cadaverous" enforcement agent in Augusta, Ga. A friend had been fined a small amount for selling without a license in Charleston.[102] Since, as a Congressional committee pointed out, appeals were costly, most drummers or their principals either bought the licenses or paid the fines imposed in the local courts.[103] The drummer's aversion to long costly legal battles enabled some states to enforce their license requirements in spite of adverse higher court rulings.[104]

IV

Three forces finally eliminated the licensing requirements. One was merchant opposition to the legislation. This came from the small storekeepers who wanted salesmen as a source of supply and, to an increasing degree, from wholesalers and others who wanted to send their own salesmen on the road. The second force was composed of salesmen's associations, while the third, and probably most effective, was the United States Supreme Court.

Many small town and rural merchants fought even the earliest attempts to establish licensing requirements. According to Atherton, an attempt on the part of New Orleans wholesaling interests to ob-

[99] *Asher v. Texas*, 128 U. S. 129, 9 Sup. Ct. 1, 32 L. Ed. 368, reversing 23 Tex. App. 662, 50 Am. Rep. 783, 5 S. W. 91.
[100] *Cincinnati Commercial*, February 17, 1869, quoted by Society of Commercial Travellers, p. 6.
[101] *District of Columbia v. Humason*, 2 MacArthur 158 (D. C. Sup. Ct., 1875).
[102] Letter to the editor, June 12, 1882.
[103] U. S. House of Representatives, 48 Cong., 1 Sess., *Report No. 1321*, April 15, 1884.
[104] *Ibid.*, also "The Drummer Tax in Texas," New York *Times*, November 18, 1887.

19TH CENTURY ANTI-DRUMMER LEGISLATION   493

tain a state licensing law in 1860 was defeated through the opposition of the rural legislators.[105] Moreover, as already noted, many of the country merchants were willing to help the drummers evade the law. The changing attitude of the wholesalers, who became increasingly interested in developing their own outside sales forces, is particularly intriguing.

One commentator felt that the wholesalers would not boggle at the inconsistency of demanding protection in their own community while fighting it elsewhere: [106]

> It is urged by those who favor the continuance in force of these laws *at home*, that their business is injured by the appearance among their customers, *at their places of residence*, of foreign traders; yet at the same time these very men do not hesitate to solicit customers *away from home* by means of travelling salesmen; and if one of these employees happens to be punished for the infraction of local license laws abroad, no one is louder in denouncing their existence than these very gentlemen.

Nevertheless, many of the contemporary sources reported that the communities that were sending out salesmen were the ones most likely to repeal their own legislation.[107] The Baltimore merchants, who had espoused protection in the 1860's, were the ones who organized to test the Virginia law in the 1880's.[108] During the 1880's, "Merchants of Atlanta," "A large number of merchants of Baltimore," the Philadelphia and Louisville boards of trade, "Merchants of St. Louis," fifty-five merchants of Yazoo City, Miss., the wholesale liquor dealers of Chicago, seventy-eight firms in Columbia, Miss., the Merchants' Exchange of Memphis, one hundred and twenty merchants of New Orleans, sixty-one business firms of Yankton, Dakota, and many other merchant groups throughout the country petitioned Congress to do something about the licensing laws.[109] The change in attitude that resulted from a change of economic interest was exemplified in the speech of a Minnesota delegate to the National Board of Trade in 1886:[110]

> I have been a merchant in Minnesota for twenty-five years, and I have seen some of the workings of the system of commercial travellers who come into our part of the country and sell goods as against men who are

[105] Atherton, "Predecessors of the Commercial Drummer in the Old South," *loc. cit.*
[106] Mr. Seemuller, *Proceedings of the Second Annual Meeting of the National Board of Trade*, p. 34.
[107] Briggs, *Fifty Years on the Road*, p. 49; Society of Commercial Travellers, *The System of Commercial Travelling*, pp. 19, 22.
[108] "Traveling Agents in Virginia."
[109] *Congressional Record*, vol. 13, p. 4098; vol. 14, p. 2889; vol. 15, pp. 4654, 4709; vol. 17, pp. 2474, 3955, 4117, 4343, 7428, and *passim*.
[110] Mr. Loring, *Proceedings of the Annual Meeting of the National Board of Trade* (1886), p. 85.

paying thousands of dollars a year for taxes, and who come with their samples and pay nothing. There are, certainly, two sides to this question. . . . I say to you, that we in Minneapolis, whose jobbing trade has got to be something like one hundred million dollars, are going to favor this proposition [i.e., repeal of the license laws]. At the same time, I do not want gentlemen to think that every city that has been mentioned as charging a tax upon commercial travellers is entirely wrong. The time was when we in Minneapolis and in St. Paul could not afford to have our country overrun by men who were not paying local taxes.

The salesmen too tried to make themselves heard in opposition to the laws. Some commercial travelers' organizations, such as the Society of Commercial Travellers (New York) and the Merchant & Commercial Travellers Association (Chicago) were formed as early as 1869. These seem to have been *ad hoc* anti-licensing groups with considerable support from the salesmen's employers. The Society of Commercial Travellers gave at least some assistance in the Ward case (1871) which served as the first major Supreme Court test of the licensing laws.[111] Other early groups included the New York State Commercial Travellers Association (1871),[112] The Michigan Commercial Travellers Association (1874),[113] The Western Commercial Travelers Association (1878),[114] and many others. Two national organizations established in the 1880's, The Traveler's Protective Association (organized 1882, reorganized 1890) and The Order of United Commercial Travelers of America (1887) as well as some of the local associations still operate today as fraternal insurance societies.

Most of the commercial travelers' organizations were concerned with other things besides the licensing laws. The major purpose, particularly in the case of the larger associations, seems to have been to provide some sort of accident indemnity and/or death benefit protection.[115] Fraternal insurance, in general, evolved according to Kip from the conditions of the post-Civil War America.[116] The

---

111 "Meeting of Commercial Travelers."
112 See "10th Annual Convention of New York State Commercial Travelers," *New York Times*, January 11, 1881.
113 Michigan Commercial Travelers Association, *Constitution and By-Laws* (Detroit, 1878).
114 "Insurance and Fraternal Association Notes," *The Commercial Travelers Magazine*, vol. 17 (March, 1911), p. 92.
115 See, for example, "Inception, Organization and Progress of the Commercial Travelers' Association of the State of New York," *Commercial Travelers' Magazine*, vol. I (September, 1883), p. 78; "A Historical Sketch of the Order of United Commercial Travelers of America," Souvenir Program, Natchez (1913) meeting, O. U. C. T. A. (Library of Congress).
116 Richard deR. Kip, *Fraternal Life Insurance in America* (Philadelphia, 1953), p. 31. See also, B. H. Meyer, "Fraternal Insurance in the United States," *Annals of the American Academy of Political and Social Science*, vol. XVII (1901), pp. 80–106; *ibid.*, "Fraternal Beneficiary Societies in the United States," *American Journal of Sociology*, vol. VI (1900), pp. 646–61.

19TH CENTURY ANTI-DRUMMER LEGISLATION   495

travelers had the same needs as the members of the fraternal societies. The hazards of riding the early railroads lent even extra
urgency to the drummers' desire for protection. So the commercial
travelers' organizations were among the first promoters of mutual
insurance in America.

The groups also sought more comfortable and more sanitary hotel
accommodations. Even as late as 1907, the Ohio chapter of the
U. C. T. of A. was waging war on the germ-transmitting hotel wash-
room common roller towel. It sought legislation that would require
an individual towel for each hotel guest.[117] This, along with a desire for full-length sheets on hotel beds, was one of the aims of the
Knights of the Grip, a short-lived group organized in Jackson, Michigan.[118] Improved railroad, baggage, and express service were among
the other objectives of the salesmen's associations, as was a desire
for preferential hotel and railroad rates. The Commercial Travelers'
National Association discreetly announced that in addition to
securing special railroad and steamboat fares for its members and
increased free baggage allowances, "There are many ways in which
we can effect a saving for our members which it is not politic for us
to spread before the public, but concerning which information may
be had from any of our agents or at our offices." [119] The Travelers
and Traders Union of New York sold its members hotel tickets at a
discount price of $1.00 each. These tickets were worth $1.25 each at
some 700 hotels throughout the country.[120]

Fraternal and social objectives were also important to the associations, particularly in view of the rather difficult and lonely life that
their members led. The Albany (N. Y.) Commercial Travelers'
Club (1888) offered its members a club room, where among other
things, "light games for amusement may be indulged in." [121] The
United Commercial Travelers was founded by some dissident members of the Travelers' Protective Association who desired a larger
measure of fraternalism and ritualism than that organization provided in addition to an insurance program.[122] Banquets, picnics,
and the like seem to have played an important role in the life of
many of the state and local associations.

---

[117] *Proceedings of the Eighteenth Annual Session of the Grand Council of Ohio,*
U. C. T. of A., 1907, p. 26.
[118] Frank W. Smith, *Beyond the Swivel Chair* (New York, 1940), p. 20.
[119] Commercial Travelers' National Association, *Descriptive Handbook and Abstract*
(New York, C. T. N. A., 1872), p. 6. See also Civil Aeronautics Authority, Bureau of
Economic Regulation, "History of Railroad Interchangeable Mileage Tickets," (typescript,
undated, *circa* 1939), Interstate Commerce Commission Library, Washington.
[120] Goddard, *Art of Selling*, p. 92.
[121] Albany Commercial Travelers Club, *1891 Directory*, p. 3 (Library of Congress).
[122] "A Historical Sketch of the Order of United Commercial Travelers of America," p. 5.

But in addition to all of these activities, the salesmen's groups were active in the fight against licensing regulation. The Society of Commercial Travellers subscribed to the defense of Elias Ward, a New Jersey resident who was charged in 1869 with having disturbed the peace and tranquillity of Maryland through the unlicensed sale of twelve bridle fronts and six horse blinders. When this case, which had been arranged as a test of the Maryland law, was carried to the U.S. Supreme Court, Ward was represented by William M. Evarts, one of the outstanding lawyers of the period. Evarts was then a former U. S. Attorney General, well known for his defense in the Johnson impeachment case, and also was generally considered as one of the leading tax specialists in the national bar.[123] A well-furnished defense fund was undoubtedly useful in this sort of legal battle.

The subsequent role of the salesmen's associations in the struggle is not entirely clear. An editorial in the New York *Times* in December, 1882 referred to attempts of a "National Commercial Travelers Association" to persuade businessmen throughout the country to seek repeal of their local licensing laws. The attempts were finally abandoned as inexpedient, although they had succeeded in Augusta, Ga.[124] In 1885 the Travelers and Traders Union of New York sent an agent south to study the impact of licensing there.[125] This may have involved only a request to an obliging member or organization official for a few letters on the local situation, or it may have been intended as the start of a fairly ambitious program, since the Union at that time claimed a capital of over $200,000.[126]

P. E. Dowe, who became president of the Commercial Travelers National League, which was formed in 1896 and which included a number of former officials of the Travelers Protective Association, also claimed some of the credit for the abolition of the licenses. While testifying before the Industrial Commission, Dowe asserted that he had been actively identified with a successful fight against the licenses between 1882 and 1884. However, Dowe's statement that congressional action ended the taxation of commercial travelers

[123] See Frederick C. Hicks, "William Maxwell Evarts," in *Dictionary of American Biography*, vol. VI, pp. 215–18.
[124] December 17, 1882, p. 8. Apparently this was not the same organization as the Commercial Travelers National Association founded in 1870, although that body also listed "the abrogation of certain oppressive license laws" among its objectives. (*Descriptive Handbook and Abstract*, p. 4). Goddard (1890) says that the 1870 C. T. N. A. died "from a lack of harmony among its members, after a few years of active life." The *Times*, which reported the formation of the C. T. N. A. in 1870, also reported the organization of a similarly named association in 1881. ("Commercial Travelers National Association Organized," January 13, 1881). Thus the editorial cited above seems to have referred to this second C. T. N. A.
[125] "Protest of the Drummers."
[126] "The Drummers' Convention," New York *Times*, July 10, 1884.

was erroneous, and other gaps in his testimony leave his assertions open to some doubt.[127]

The strongest and most successful association efforts seem to have come from the Travelers Protective Association. The Order of United Commercial Travelers of America, which had splintered from the T. P. A., strongly denied that its parent deserved any credit. In fact, the O. U. C. T. A. magazine was quite vitriolic on the subject:[128]

> The Supreme Court of the United States has again vindicated the right of the commercial traveler to go where he will and solicit orders from all who will listen to him, unmolested by the constables and tax gatherers of other states than that in which his principals conduct their business. . . .
> The abolition of the "Drummers Tax" has been considered by some, and even claimed to be the exclusive work of a certain traveling men's association [T. P. A.] From the above we infer that the honor and credit of the "wipe-out" is largely due to the Supreme Court of the U. S. . . .
> Now we say it without fear of contradiction that this association [T. P. A.] as a National Association, has never accomplished any work, either mental, moral, social or commercial that has ever given dignity and increased business character to "that class of men popularly known as drummers."

Nevertheless, the T. P. A. was active in the fight against the laws. Apparently working in cooperation with the Travelers and Traders Union, it attempted to muster grass roots support for relief bills pending in Congress.[129] The effort was not successful. Bills that would have prohibited local taxation of interstate drummers were favorably reported out of committee in the House in 1884, 1886, and 1888, but apparently never came to a vote there and were never reported out in the Senate.[130]

The T.P.A. was also active in the courts. The association's president later claimed that it had sponsored the legal actions that led to the Supreme Court's final verdict, that the license laws were unconstitutional.[131] There are no indications available now as to whether the association participated in the really crucial 1887 *Robbins* case discussed below. However, several additional actions were needed to convince the legislatures and the lower courts that the Supreme Court had meant what it said in *Robbins*. The T. P. A.

[127] *Preliminary Report on Trusts and Industrial Combinations* (testimony section), pp. 40–41. See also testimony of L. V. LaTaste (T. P. A. president), *U. S. Industrial Commission Report*, vol. XIII (U. S. House, 57 Cong., 1 Sess., Doc. No. 182), pp. 31–32.
[128] "Not Constitutional," *The Sample Case*, vol. 5 (July, 1894), pp. 40–41.
[129] *Congressional Record*, vol. 17, pp. 642, 1932, 2423, 2474, 3103, 4074, 5839, 6068; vol. 18, pp. 349, 350, 385, 2051; vol. 19, p. 2464; "Objecting to Being Taxed," *New York Times*, January 24, 1886.
[130] U. S. House of Representatives, 48 Cong., 1 Sess., *Report* No. 1321; 49 Cong., 1 Sess., *Report* No. 1762; 50 Cong., 1 Sess., *Report* No. 1310.
[131] Lucien V. LaTaste, "His Givings Out Were an Infinite Distance from His True Meant Design," *The TPA Magazine*, vol. III (July, 1907), p. 22.

joined in providing representation for the drummer in at least one of these cases, that of Robert C. Stockton, a Kansas City tea salesman arrested in Texas.[132]

The courts, particularly the U. S. Supreme Court, were the drummers' best friends. The Supreme Court had held in 1871, in *Ward v. Maryland,* that a state could not establish a special tax for drummers from out of state. The Court went considerably farther in 1887 in the case of *Robbins* v. *Taxing District of Shelby County.*[133] Sabine Robbins, a Cincinnati stationery wholesaler, was arrested for violating a Tennessee statute (Act of 1881, chap. 96, sec. 16) that required all drummers and other persons selling by sample in Shelby County (Memphis) to buy a license at $10 per week or $25 per month, unless they operated a licensed business within the county. Even though this law technically applied to both Tennesseans and non-Tennesseans, Supreme Court Justice Bradley held for the majority that it was *de facto* discriminatory, since the Memphis merchants would not be likely to use drummers. But the Court's major attack on the law came under the commerce clause:[134]

It is strongly urged, as if it were a material point in the case, that no discrimination is made between domestic and foreign drummers — those of Tennessee and those of other States: that all are taxed alike. But that does not meet the difficulty. Interstate commerce cannot be taxed at all [by the states], even though the same amount of tax should be laid on domestic commerce, or that which is carried on solely within the State. This was decided in the case of *The State Freight Tax Cases* (*supra*). The negotiation of sales of goods which are in another State, for the purpose of introducing them into the State in which the negotiation is made, is interstate commerce. A New Orleans merchant cannot be taxed there for ordering goods from London or New York, because in the one case it is an act of foreign, and, in the other, of interstate commerce, both of which are subject to regulation by Congress alone.

This dictum was reiterated in *Corson* v. *Maryland,* decided on the same day as *Robbins.*[135] A series of subsequent cases was needed to drive the point home.[136] Legal scholars have debated the exact impact of the *Robbins'* decision, but at least some writers feel that for

---

[132] "Drummers' Licenses," New York *Times,* November 7, 1887; "The Drummer Tax in Texas," New York *Times,* November 18, 1887; *Ex parte Stockton,* 33 Fed. 95 (E. D. Texas, 1887), affirmed *Asher* v. *Texas,* 128 U. S. 129, 9 S. Ct. 1, 32 L. Ed. 368 (1888).
[133] 120 U. S. 489, 7 S. Ct. 592, 30 L. Ed. 694.
[134] 120 U. S. 498, 7 S. Ct. 596, 30 L. Ed. 697.
[135] 120 U. S. 502, 7 S. Ct. 655, 30 L. Ed. 699.
[136] *Asher* v. *Texas,* 128 U. S. 129, 9 S. Ct. 1, 32 L. Ed. 368 (1888); *Stoutenburgh* v. *Hennick,* 129 U. S. 141, 9 S. Ct. 256, 32 L. Ed. 637 (1888, District of Columbia tax); *Ex parte Stockton,* 33 Fed. 95 (E. D. Texas, 1887); *Simmons Hardware Co.* v. *Sheriff,* 39 La. Ann. 850, 2 So. 593 (1887); *Ex parte Rosenblatt,* 19 Nev. 441, 3 Am. St. Rep. 901, 14 P. 299 (1887); *State* v. *Bracco,* 103 N. C. 350, 9 S. E. 404 (1889); *State* v. *Rankin,* 11 S. Dak. 144, 76 N. W. 299 (1898).

19TH CENTURY ANTI-DRUMMER LEGISLATION   499

a long period it was a powerful factor in curbing the taxing and regulatory powers of the States.[137] In more recent years the Court has receded from its *Robbins'* position.[138] But in any event, local taxation of wholesale drummers was over.

Thus the Court's decision ended another manifestation of the ever-recurring movement toward protectionism in American marketing. This episode in many ways was similar to the earlier attempt to curb the auctions and to the later attempts to restrain department stores, mail order houses, and chain stores.[139] The anti-drummer laws were another expression of an often overlooked vein of pessimism that runs counter to the supposed universal optimism of the American business community.[140] But, happily, it also once again illustrated the ultimate failure of an attempt to block change.

[137] See, for example, Frank J. Goodnow, "State Taxation of Interstate Commerce," *Papers and Proceedings of the Sixteenth Annual Meeting, American Economic Association* (Amer. Econ. Assoc. Pub., 3rd. Ser., vol. 5, no. 2, pp. 307–35) (New York, 1904), p. 65; John Hemphill, "The House-to-House Canvasser in Interstate Commerce," *American Law Review*, vol. 60 (1926), pp. 641–48.

[138] See, for example, Nathan Isaacs, "Barrier Activities and the Courts: A Study in Anti-Competitive Law," *Law and Contemporary Problems*, vol. 8 (1941), pp. 382–90. *Robbins* did not preclude local taxation when the goods came to rest in the taxing state prior to being sold, nor did it permanently prevent attempts to regulate retail canvassers and peddlers under the police powers of the local jurisdictions. See 39 *Corpus Juris Secundum*, "Hawkers and Peddlers," pp. 784–803.

[139] Joseph Cornwall Palamountain, Jr., *The Politics of Distribution* (Cambridge, 1955); Joseph S. Gould, "Legislative Intervention in the Conflict between Orthodox and Direct Selling Distribution Channels," *Law and Contemporary Problems*, vol. 8 (1941), pp. 318–33.

[140] The persistence of pessimism and provincialism in American business is discussed at some length in Melder, *State and Local Barriers*, pp. 167–69.

[31]

By Robert Griffith
PROFESSOR OF HISTORY
UNIVERSITY OF MASSACHUSETTS, AMHERST

The Selling of America: The Advertising Council and American Politics, 1942–1960*

¶ *From its inception in the 1940s the Advertising Council was part of a broad, loosely coordinated campaign by American business leaders to contain the anti-corporate liberalism of the 1930s and to refashion the character of the New Deal State. In this campaign the Council generally aligned itself with the more liberal wing of the business community, usually identified with the newly organized Committee for Economic Development (CED), rather than with the older and more conservative National Association of Manufacturers (NAM). Like the CED, the Advertising Council often espoused a "corporatist" ideology which emphasized cooperation between business and government; and like the Business Advisory Council, the National Petroleum Council, and other quasi-public corporatist bodies, it sought to establish close, reciprocal relationships with the executive branch. The Council enthusiastically supported the new foreign and national security policies of the Truman Administration, but strongly opposed its domestic programs. By contrast, the Council supported both the foreign and domestic policies of the Eisenhower Administration, and helped promote the administration's economic programs in a series of major advertising campaigns. Through its millions of "public service" advertisements, the Council sought to promote an image of advertising as a responsible and civic-spirited industry, of the U.S. economy as a uniquely productive system of free enterprise, and of America as a dynamic, classless, and benignly consensual society.*

The leaders of American business entered the post-World War II era shaken to a degree not generally appreciated by the economic and political upheavals of the 1930s and apprehensive that the continued popularity of the New Deal at home and the spread of socialism abroad foreshadowed drastic and undesirable changes in the American economic system. Though they differed widely among themselves on such important questions as international trade, labor relations and the role of the state, they nevertheless shared a common commitment to halting the more radical features of the New Deal, such as public power, progressive taxation and pro-consumer regulation, and preserving the

Business History Review, LVII (Autumn 1983) Copyright © The President and Fellows of Harvard College.
*I would like to thank the Harry S. Truman Library Institute, the American Philosophical Society, and the John Simon Guggenheim Memorial Foundation for making possible the research and writing of this article. I am grateful for the valuable comments of Charles C. Alexander, Paul S. Boyer, Robert D. Cuff, Frank W. Fox, Burton I. Kaufman, and Ronald Story. I owe a special debt to the dedicated archival staffs of the Harry S. Truman and Dwight D. Eisenhower libraries. A somewhat shorter version of this essay was presented as a paper at the Seventy-Fourth Annual Meeting of the Organization of American Historians, held in Detroit, April 1–4, 1981.

autonomy of corporate enterprise. Following World War II, they set out to achieve these goals in a fairly purposeful and self-conscious manner, spending enormous sums of money not only on lobbying and campaign financing, but also on a wide variety of public relations activities — institutional advertising, philanthropy, the sponsorship of research, and industrial and community relations.[1]

Some of these activities were directed toward fairly specific ends — for example, in 1947 the National Association of Manufacturers spent nearly five million dollars, mostly in support of the Taft-Hartley labor bill.[2] Still other efforts were designed more broadly to sell the system itself. The U.S. Chamber of Commerce, the National Association of Manufacturers, and the Committee for Economic Development all launched broad "economic education" programs. So did many trade associations, foundations, and individual corporations. Indeed, by 1952 *Fortune* editor William H. Whyte, Jr., estimated that corporations were spending more than 100 million dollars annually to sell "free enterprise" to the American people.[3] Founded in 1942, the Advertising Council was one of the most important and influential purveyors of such business propaganda.

ORIGINS OF THE ADVERTISING COUNCIL

The Advertising Council was originally organized in response to the shocks produced within the advertising industry by the Great Depression, the rise of the New Deal, and the advent of World War II.[4] The depression had sent advertising revenues crashing and had intensified popular suspicions of the industry, while the New Deal raised the specter of massive state intervention to limit the industry's profits and prerogatives. For those in advertising the Wheeler-Lea Amendment of 1938, which empowered the Federal Trade Commission to prohibit deceptive advertising of foods, drugs, and cosmetics, seemed to foreshadow far more radical consumer attacks on the industry. The approach of war seemed especially threatening. Conversion to wartime

[1] On lobbying, see Karl Schriftgiesser, *The Lobbyists* (New York, 1951); on campaign financing see Alexander Heard, *The Costs of Democracy* (Chapel Hill, 1960); on public relations see especially J.A.R. Pimlott, *Public Relations and American Democracy* (Princeton, 1951) and Edward L. Bernays, *Public Relations* (Norman, Oklahoma, 1952); on institutional advertising see George A. Flanagan, *Modern Institutional Advertising* (New York, 1967); on philanthropy see Morrell Heald, *The Social Responsibilities of Business* (Cleveland, 1970); on sponsorship of research, see David W. Eakins, "The Development of Corporate Liberal Policy Research in the United States, 1885–1965," (Ph.D. diss., University of Wisconsin, 1966); on industrial and community relations see Wayne Hodges, *Company and Community* (New York, 1959) and William H. Form and Delbert C. Miller, *Industry, Labor and Community* (New York, 1960).
[2] Heard, *Costs of Democracy*, p. 96n.
[3] William H. Whyte, Jr., *Is Anybody Listening?* (New York, 1952), 7. See also C. W. McKee and H. G. Moulton, *A Survey of Economic Education* (Washington, 1951).
[4] On advertising before the war see especially Stuart Ewen, *Captains of Consciousness: Advertising and the Social Roots of the Consumer Culture* (New York, 1976); Otis Pease, *The Responsibilities of American Advertising: Private Control and Public Influence, 1920–1940* (New Haven, 1958); and Ralph M. Hower, *The History of an Advertising Agency: N. W. Ayer and Son at Work, 1929–1949* (Cambridge, Mass., 1949).

production would eliminate many consumer durables and with them the need for large advertising budgets; while the government, through defense contracts and tax rulings, might disallow advertising as a business expense altogether.

It was against this background that 700 industry executives gathered in November 1941, at a special meeting sponsored by the Association of National Advertisers (A.N.A.) and the American Association of Advertising Agencies (A.A.A.A.) to consider the dangers posed by "those who would do away with the American system of free enterprise" or who sought to "modify the economic system of which advertising is an integral part." The attack on advertising, a Columbia Broadcasting System presentation charged, was part of "the vast, world-wide struggle between two philosophies, the totalitarian idea, with people as the vassals of the state against the American philosophy of free enterprise and free competition and free opportunity for the individual to realize his own destiny under free institutions." The response to such attacks, declared industry leader James W. Young of the J. Walter Thompson Company, in the meeting's most dramatic speech, was to enlist advertising itself in the campaign on behalf of American business. "We have within our hands the greatest aggregate means of mass education and persuasion the world has ever seen — namely, the channels of advertising communication," he declared. "We have the masters of the techniques of using these channels. We have power. Why do we not use it?" Stirred by Young's appeal, the conference concluded with the adoption of a resolution to answer attacks on the industry by publicizing the benefits of advertising, by "reteaching a belief in a dynamic economy," and by improving the industry's public relations through the use of advertising "in other than commercial ventures, and specifically in the public interest."[5]

Young's proposal to employ "public service" advertising as the cornerstone of a broad public relations campaign on behalf of the advertising industry and its corporate clients was quickly overtaken, however, by Pearl Harbor and American entry to war, by the Roosevelt Administration's desire to sell its home front programs through advertising, and by the industry's need to secure its own place in the new wartime order. The result was the organization in early 1942 of the War Advertising Council. Made up of leading representatives from the advertising agencies, from large corporate advertisers and from the advertising media, the Council was designed to "contribute" tax deductible advertising to

[5] *New York Times*, November 14, 1941, pp. 35, 42; November 15, 1941, p. 25; November 16, 1941, III, p. 1. C. B. Larrabee, "If You Looked for a Miracle—," *Printer's Ink* (November 21, 1941), 13–15, 79–80. "Business at War/The Advertising Front," *Fortune* 26 (November, 1942), 60, 64. On advertising during the war, see Frank W. Fox, *Madison Avenue Goes to War: The Strange Military Career of American Advertising, 1941–45* (Provo, Utah, 1975).

the war effort. Working closely with the newly created Office of War
Information (O.W.I.), the Council thus served as a private vehicle for
public information and persuasion, launching massive advertising campaigns on behalf of war bonds, victory gardens, conservation and salvage
and other home front programs.[6] By war's end, the Council had coordinated more than 100 "public service" campaigns at an estimated cost, in
time and space contributed, of more than a billion dollars. High wartime
excess profits taxes and a generous I.R.S. ruling which permitted corporations to deduct the costs for institutional and public service advertising, of course, made such a contribution inexpensive for business, if not
other taxpayers, and helped produce rising revenues for the advertising
industry, which by 1945 had at last regained its pre-depression levels.

The Council's wartime program also produced enormous public relations dividends for the advertising industry, taught those in government
"a new appreciation of the power and impact of advertising in a free
economy" and stilled what one industry executive called "the clamor of
the reformers." "Wartime public opinion polls confirmed the rising
popularity of business," the Council reported. "All polls showed that
good opinion universally held for the advertiser who enlisted in the
public service. And scattered surveys made among men in the service
— the men who will make our laws and run our nation — show that they
give a hand and a heart to the advertiser who backed them up."[7] Thus
during the war the advertising industry had not only entered into an
intimate and profitable relationship with the federal government, but
had also sought, apparently with some success, to shape public opinion
in the interests of business and advertising.

CHANGES IN THE POSTWAR ERA

As the fighting drew to a close and wartime unity gave way to increasingly sharp conflict, especially between business and labor, industry
leaders became more and more worried. According to the Council's
1945 report, the world beyond America's shores was threatened by the
growth of communism and "the spread of state socialism throughout
much of Europe and perhaps Asia," while at home "group clashes
promise to be renewed, old hatreds revived, new war-born discords . . .

[6]Fox, *Madison Avenue Goes to War*, 22, 49–55. *Business Week* (February 7, 1941), 58–59; (February 21, 1942), 48–49. On the early history of the Council, see especially Harold B. Thomas, "The Background and Beginning of the Advertising Council," in C. H. Sandage (ed.), *The Promise of Advertising* (Homewood, Ill., 1961), 15–58.
[7]War Advertising Council, "From War to Peace: The New Challenge to Business and Advertising" (New York, 1945), 3–7. James W. Young, "The Advertising Council at Work," September 18, 1946, and Theodore S. Repplier, "How the American Enterprise System is Being Re-sold to the American People," October 1, 1946, both speeches in box 1, Dallas C. Halverstadt Files, Harry S. Truman Papers, Harry S. Truman Library. Stuart Peabody, "Advertising and Total Diplomacy," April 1, 1950, speech in box 16, Charles W. Jackson Files, Harry S. Truman Papers, Harry S. Truman Library.

almost inevitable." Business, which had risen in prestige during the war, was "again being pictured as the 'villain' in the American drama," according to Theodore S. Repplier, the Council's Executive Director. "Everybody agrees," he concluded, "that the American enterprise system needs 'reselling' . . ."[8]

As a result, the War Advertising Council was not demobilized when the war ended but was instead reorganized and renamed, becoming simply the Advertising Council. As before, its constituent organizations included the A.A.A.A., representing the agencies, the A.N.A., representing corporate advertisers, and the National Publishers Association, the Bureau of Advertising of the American Newspaper Publishers Association, the National Association of Broadcasters, and the Outdoor Advertising Association of America, all representing various advertising media. Theodore Repplier continued to head the Council's professional staff, though his title was changed from Executive Director to President. James W. Young continued as Chairman of the Council's Board of Directors, succeeded in 1947 by Charles G. Mortimer, Jr., of General Foods. The Council maintained its intimate connections with the federal government. The clearing house functions previously performed by the O.W.I. were now transferred to the Office of War Mobilization and Reconversion and then later to the Office of Government Reports, both situated in the Executive Office of the President. From these offices White House aides, usually advertising men themselves, served as liaison between the information divisions of all government agencies and the Advertising Council, thus institutionalizing what industry leaders would describe as "a unique relationship." It was a relationship that not only gave Council and industry leaders access to the President, it also conferred considerable prestige on them as well. So did commendatory letters from the President and, beginning in 1945, the annual meetings of the Council in Washington at which advertising and business executives gathered to hear the President and his cabinet discuss national issues.[9]

In reorganizing, the Council also sought to broaden its activities and to avoid any restraints that the government might impose on it. To begin with, Council leaders would no longer, as during the war, automatically accept any government proposal, but would rather reserve the right to accept or reject messages as they saw fit. Neither the Council nor its

[8] War Advertising Council, "From War to Peace," 8; Repplier, "How the American Enterprise System is Being Re-sold."

[9] Advertising Council, "In the Wake of the War: The Fourth Year of the Advertising Council" (New York, 1946), 7–16; Advertising Council, *Manual for Council Executives* (1948), in box 13, Jackson Files. Memorandum by Charles W. Jackson, January 13, 1948, box 1, John T. Gibson Files, Harry S. Truman Papers, Harry S. Truman Library. The Council was not unwilling to exploit this relationship to lobby the President on behalf of the tax breaks which made the Council's programs possible. See Repplier to Charles W. Jackson, October 11, 1950, and Jackson to Repplier, November 29, 1950, both in box 20, Jackson Files.

corporate constituencies, for example, were anxious to run a campaign on price controls requested by the Office of Price Administration; and did so in an only perfunctory manner. Secondly, the Council would accept requests from private organizations as well as from the government. Such applications would be screened by the President and the Board of Directors and, if approved by them, would be referred to a "Public Policy Committee" comprised of prominent citizens from "all phases of American life." In 1948 the Council also created an Industries Advisory Committee under the chairmanship of General Electric President Charles E. Wilson. Made up of executives from large corporations, the Industries Advisory Committee was created primarily as a means of securing financial support and of providing business leaders with more direct access to the Council.[10]

As during the war, the Council's role was chiefly one of coordination. Having determined to support a particular campaign the Council would name a coordinator, usually an executive on loan from an advertising agency or the advertising department of a large corporation. The campaign coordinator would then work with the advertising agencies which had volunteered their services in preparing materials for the campaign, with the large advertisers who used some of their product or institutional advertising budgets to support Council programs, and with newspaper and magazine publishers, broadcasters and other media, who contributed free time or space to the Council.[11]

The Council's political philosophy reflected the emerging corporatist ideology often associated with liberal business organizations such as the Committee for Economic Development. "You might say that whereas CED is concerned with the *manufacture* of information in the public interest," Council President Repplier once observed, "the Advertising Council is concerned with the *mass distribution* of such information." Leaders of the Council generally placed less emphasis on competition

[10] Advertising Council, "In the Wake of War," 15; *Manual for Executives*, 13–15; Advertising Council, "What Helps People Helps Business: The Sixth Year of the Advertising Council" (New York, 1948), 9. "In the old days the advertisers agreed to take any message which we prepared for them," wrote Charles W. Jackson, White House liaison to the Council. "Under this new arrangement they reserve the right to accept or reject messages as they see fit." The Council allocated the O.P.R. two weeks of radio time. Jackson to Douglas Bennet, December 19, 1945, box 2, Jackson Files.

[11] The resources thus assembled were enormous. In 1946, for example, Council radio spots generated over 300 million "listener impressions" (one message heard by one person) each week; 900 magazines with a combined circulation of 120 million carried Council ads; the outdoor advertising industry contributed 2,000 highway billboard spaces and the car card industry 100,000 spaces on buses and streetcars; newspapers frequently ran as many as 7,000 individual advertisements on a single Council campaign. By 1951, as the Council's activities increased, national radio produced an estimated four billion "listener impressions," while television, still in its infancy, added over a billion more. One thousand one hundred magazines contributed an estimated 16 million dollars worth of space annually, and the outdoor advertising industry displayed more than 50,000 Council-prepared billboard ads. Newspapers contributed over 110 million lines while the car card industry increased its contribution to over one million spaces, the equivalent of one card in every public vehicle in the country every month. By 1956 it was estimated that industry contributed over 149 million dollars annually to Council campaigns, and in 1958 it was estimated that television spots alone produced more than 16 billion "home impressions." Young, "The Advertising Council at Work." Advertising Council, "10th Annual Report of the Advertising Council" (New York, 1952), 14–21. *New York Times*, February 23, 1959, 22.

and the marketplace than on cooperation and planning, opposed those New Deal policies which seemed to threaten private enterprise but nevertheless saw in the state a powerful positive instrument for sustaining economic growth, opposed the more radical demands of militant trade unions but were willing to endorse collective bargaining in return for restraint on the part of labor, and stressed the consensual character of modern American capitalism, the stake which everyone was presumed to hold in the economic order. "There must continue to be competition, even conflict, I suppose, between our institutions, such as labor, management, capital, government for their respective rights and what they believe in," wrote Council founder Chester J. LaRoche to President Truman. "This competition can be good. But there must also be cooperation. The areas of conflict must be defined, and, through collaboration, lessen. And the areas of cooperation must be increased." The Advertising Council, observed James Young, was an "and/or" organization. "It believes that there are some things in the public interest that business is best fitted to accomplish, some which government is best equipped to accomplish, and some which government *and* business, working together, can best get done."[12]

The role of advertising in such a system was to secure public action informally through mass persuasion rather than through force of law, "voluntarily," as the Council termed it, rather than through "compulsion." During the war Americans had been, for the most part, persuaded rather than compelled. As Council publications explained, "There were no compulsory savings. No national service act, no labor draft . . . Thus, our great wartime information mechanism [the Council] enabled this nation to fight through our first global war — with a minimum of compulsion. In a period when the trend toward centralized controls might well have become an irresistible force, this was a service of lasting significance to every business and every citizen." The need for such persuasion did not, however, end with the war. Indeed, had the Council demobilized itself, there would have been "no coordinated method for informing and inspiring the people, or securing public action — no matter how grave the problem might be or its effects upon the welfare of the people and business itself." More importantly, advertising would safeguard the economy against the possibility that an undisciplined special interest (e.g., labor) would insist on too much or that the American people, not understanding the economic system and possessed of

[12]Repplier to Sumner Slichter, July 10, 1956, box 31, James M. Lambie, Jr., Records, Dwight D. Eisenhower Papers, Dwight D. Eisenhower Library, Abilene, Kansas. Chester J. LaRoche to Harry S. Truman, July 11, 1947, in PPF 2151, Truman Papers. Young, "The Advertising Council at Work." For a discussion of corporatism, see Ellis W. Hawley, "The Discovery and Study of a 'Corporate Liberalism,'" *Business History Review*, 52 (1978), 309–20. On the Committee for Economic Development, see especially Robert M. Collins, *The Business Response to Keynes*, 1929–1964 (New York, 1981). On business ideology in the 1950s also see especially Frances K. Sutton et al., *The American Business Creed* (Cambridge, Mass., 1956).

"an emotional hostility toward business," would demand public policies which might impair the system itself. Mistrustful of the untutored responses of ordinary citizens, the Council feared that Americans did not truly understand the economic system, that they could be "misled by exaggeration of its faults" or "be made to forget its benefits" by propaganda attacks "from within and without." As Council Chairman Charles G. Mortimer, Jr., explained, "If the national information job is badly done, the national decision may be tragically wrong. Correctly done, it constitutes the soundest assurance of that kind of decision." "American business has a tremendous stake in the proper education of the public," warned Leonard W. Trester of the General Outdoor Advertising Company, "and if it does not accept its responsibility, the field will be left wide open to the rabble rousers."[13]

The Council saw its campaigns primarily as a form of public relations — for advertising in particular and for American business in general. As Council founder James Young declared in 1946, business had learned during the war "that public service advertising was, in fact, the best kind of public relations — that it was not mere altruism to continue it, but hard-headed business sense." Many Council campaigns, moreover, were aimed directly at groups which had in the past been highly critical of advertising, including educators, physicians, and clergy. Campaigns in support of Better Schools, Nursing Recruitment, and Religion in American Life were thus designed to enhance the prestige of advertising among specific and presumably influential sectors of American life. As Council Chairman Stuart Peabody later pointed out, "teachers and educators learn first hand through the Better Schools campaign that advertising will benefit both them and their schools. Ministers, through the Council's Religion in American Life project, see with their own eyes how advertising can boost church attendance. Doctors watch advertising fill up schools of nursing, see it create an awareness of disease, and so on. Thus converts are won to advertising," he concluded, "by the most surefire of all methods — tangible, personal benefit — and a result is obtained that no amount of impassioned argument could bring about."[14]

Many Council campaigns were also expected to produce collateral benefits for industry as well. Thus preventing forest fires, a cause popularized through the invention of "Smokey the Bear," would help industries such as lumber and those using lumber; preventing highway accidents would aid the automobile and insurance industries, and so on. "In fact," declared Peabody, "when you stop to figure it out, there is

[13]"From War to Peace," 4–10; Explanatory Notes on Public Service Campaigns, September 12–18, 1948, in box 13, Jackson Files. Mortimer is quoted in "What Helps People Helps Business," 10. Trester Speech, February 7, 1950, in box 16, Jackson Files.
[14]Young, "The Advertising Council at Work." Peabody, speech to the Association of National Advertisers, November 10, 1954, box 11, Lambie Records.

hardly any Council campaign which doesn't make some contribution to the health of American business."[15]

Many Council campaigns carried subtle political messages, if sometimes only by omission. Thus the Better Schools campaign carefully refrained from any discussion of federal aid to education. Indeed, Time, Inc. President Roy E. Larsen boasted that the campaign had helped combat "the trend toward socialism" by depicting education as a local problem to be solved by local citizens rather than by the federal government. Similarly, the Council's campaign on behalf of highway safety stressed only the need for individual caution and avoided any discussion of poor automotive or highway design as a cause of deaths. The peacetime sale of Savings Bonds was favored by the American Bankers Association, the Committee for Economic Development and other business associations as a means of restraining inflation and maintaining "a sound federal financing structure." It would also give "every American as big a financial stake as possible in his country and the American way of living" and make him "a poor prospect for crackpot economic theories."[16]

Some of the Council's campaigns were closely tied to American foreign policy and to the increasingly conservative new diplomacy of the Cold War — trade expansion, the Marshall Plan, Armed Forces prestige, C.A.R.E. (whose relief packages the Council described as "a valuable diplomatic and political weapon"), civil defense and Radio Free Europe. "As the unfolding of our new foreign policy points the way," declared Council Chairman Stuart Peabody in early 1950, "advertising must devote its skills and its resources to assuring the support and cooperation of the American people to the demands of that policy, just as it did in the late war."[17]

DOMESTIC CAMPAIGNS

At least two of the Council's major postwar campaigns, however, were more preoccupied with domestic than with foreign affairs, and were more overtly political and illiberal in character. The first of these, "Our

[15] Peabody, *ibid.*

[16] *Advertising Council News* (October, 1949). Advertising Council, "Business Steps up its Candle Power: The 5th Year of the Advertising Council" (New York, 1947), 6. Advertising Council, "How you can help check inflation, avoid depression, give free enterprise a boost, defeat the 'isms, and make more and better customers for your business all at once!" (Washington, 1946).

[17] "Advertising and Total Diplomacy," April 1, 1950, box 16, Jackson Files. "What Helps People Helps Business," 2–3, 7, 14–16. "Tenth Annual Report," 23–31. Advertising Council, "Advertising: A New Weapon in the World-Wide Fight for Freedom" (New York, 1948), copy in box 13, Jackson Files. In August 1947, Council President Repplier wrote Assistant to the President John R. Steelman to emphasize his concern over "the grave situation which confronts the country" and to promise the Council's support for the Marshall Plan. While there was "a general vague realization that we are involved in an ideological war," he warned, few people realized how serious things really were. "In my opinion, the concern will need to penetrate very deep if we are to have the radical measures that would seem to be called for." Repplier to Steelman, August 5, 1947, box 9, Jackson Files.

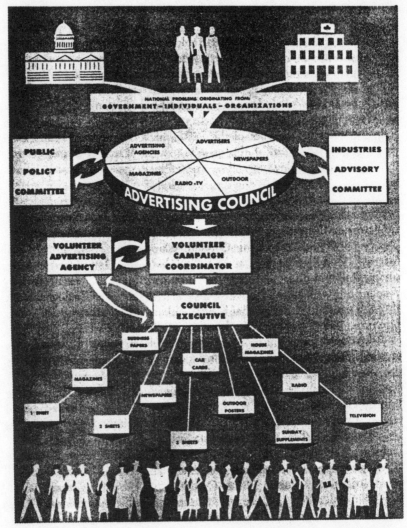

Courtesy of the Advertising Council

Advertising Council Organization Chart

The wide scope of the Advertising Council's activities is suggested by this 1951 organization chart.

American Heritage," was originally conceived by Council director Thomas D'Arcy Brophy, President of the advertising agency Kenyon and Eckhardt, Inc., who in late 1946 told his fellow board members that the causes of "our national unrest" were deep and complex and that there were "forces at work in the country that are attempting to destroy unity." He warned that these influences were "insidious and powerful," and that what was being done to combat them was "wholly inadequate." What was needed, he declared, was a patriotic campaign which "would help by attacking the root of the evil, which is a loss of faith in our traditions. And it would help by selling the rewards still open to us, individually and collectively, if we are willing to put American grit and sweat into our jobs."[18]

The following month Brophy and Council President Repplier attended a large meeting of business and professional leaders sponsored by Attorney General Tom C. Clark. The Attorney General's thinking clearly paralleled that of the Council. Clark warned that subversive forces, "aided by economic and political dissentions [sic], may seek to undermine and discredit our system of government." Since it was his responsibility to guard against "the impact of foreign ideologies . . . through constant scrutiny of subversive elements and through affirmative programs of education in democracy," he had concluded that "indoctrination in democracy" was badly needed in order to "blend our varying groups into one American family." In order to do this Clark proposed a traveling exhibition of original American documents such as the Constitution, the Declaration of Independence, and the Emancipation Proclamation.[19]

The proposals of Brophy and Clark were quickly merged. Brophy helped organize the American Heritage Foundation, under the chairmanship of prominent banker Winthrop W. Aldrich, to serve as official sponsor for the campaign; and the Advertising Council, with the approval of its new Public Policy Committee, agreed to promote the project in order "to strengthen the nation against the poisonous flood of Communist propaganda from within and without." The campaign was coordinated by W. B. Potter of Eastman Kodak and involved the combined efforts of ten advertising agencies. It featured the "Freedom Train," traveling about the country with its cargo of historic documents (now expanded to include the Truman Doctrine!), a program of local "Community Rededication Weeks" timed to coincide with the train's arrival, and a national campaign "to raise the level of active citizenship."[20] By 1949 over 3.5 million people had visited the Freedom Train

[18]"Our American Heritage Campaign," January 8, 1947, box 9, Jackson Files.
[19]*Ibid.* Memorandum, Annabelle Price to Charles W. Jackson, December 11, 1948, box 9, Jackson Files.
[20]Conference at the White House, May 22, 1947, box 1, Jackson Files. "What Helps People Helps Business," 3.

in 322 cities; newspapers had placed more than 26,000 orders for mats (molds from which advertisements are produced); over 3,000 billboards and over 300,000 car cards had carried the Council message; magazines had run over 2,000 articles and editorials; and radio had produced 6 billion "listener impressions." The Council distributed over 1.5 million copies of a booklet on the "duties and privileges" of citizenship prepared by the Leo Burnett agency, and even succeeded in having "Our American Heritage" adopted as the theme of the January 1, 1950, Rose Bowl Parade in Pasadena, California.[21]

The publicly stated goals of the campaign were broad and, according to the Council, nonpartisan: to encourage more active participation by citizens, to enhance awareness of individual rights and liberties, to increase pride in the American past and to encourage "a wider recognition of our obligations to the world to maintain our free institutions." The intent of the campaign, on the other hand, was quite conservative, subtly echoing attacks on the New Deal state from throughout the business community, and reinforcing the strident themes of the new, Cold War politics of anticommunism. In a democracy the people are the masters, warned the Council's Public Advisory Committee, but they must "either *exercise* that mastery or become, as others have become, the pawns of a master state." Corporations were urged to support the campaign as "an unparalleled opportunity to build public goodwill for themselves and enhance respect for American business at the same time that they make an important contribution to the country's welfare when, because of both world and internal conditions, that contribution is most needed."[22]

Closely related to "Our American Heritage" but far larger and more important was the Council's campaign on behalf of the "American Economic System." Unlike most of the Council's previous campaigns, it was almost exclusively the product of the advertising industry itself. It was first proposed to the Council in 1946 by the newly created Joint A.N.A.-A.A.A.A. Committee on Understanding Our Economic System, a group of industry leaders who were worried, according to Council Chairman Mortimer, by "the ominous pressures developing abroad and

[21]"What Helps People Helps Business," 3, 13. "What Helps People Helps Business: The Seventh Year of the Advertising Council" (New York, 1949), 15 (hereafter cited as "What Helps People Helps Business . . . Seventh Year"). "How Business Helps Solve Public Problems," 17. Progress Report, December, 1949, in box 13, Jackson Files.

[22]"Our American Heritage—Campaign Policy," May 28, 1947, box 9, Jackson Files. Charles C. Mortimer to Advertisers, Advertising Agencies and Media, July 1, 1947, box 1, Jackson Files. For analagous efforts by the more conservative U.S. Chamber of Commerce, see Peter H. Irons, "American Business and the Origins of McCarthyism: The Cold War Crusade of the United States Chamber of Commerce," in Robert Griffith and Athan Theoharis (eds.), *The Specter* (New York, 1974), 72–89. In subsequent years the American Heritage campaign was tied to the celebration of national holidays, including the 175th anniversary of the signing of the Declaration of Independence in 1951. By 1952 it had evolved into a campaign to encourage registration and voting, and as such would continue throughout the next decade. See Conference Report — Our American Heritage, March 18, 1949, box 14, and Allen Wilson to Staff, May 2, 1951, box 18, Jackson Files. "Tenth Annual Report," 22.

the disturbed situation at home." Americans, Mortimer and other Council leaders believed, were "staggeringly ignorant" of the benefits of the American economic system and hence susceptible to the danger of subversion by foreign ideologies. Economic "education" through advertising, they further believed, would help remedy this problem. Because of the politically sensitive and unprecedented nature of the proposal — it was a case of "angels rushing in," recalled one Council leader — it was first sent to the newly created Public Advisory Committee, which in turn referred it to a subcommittee composed of Studebaker President Paul G. Hoffman, A.F.L. economist Boris Shiskin, and Hunter College President George Schuster. These three men, together with representatives of the Joint Committee and members of the Council staff, worked out the broad outlines of the campaign. The support of labor was especially important. Although Shiskin succeeded in making several important alterations in the campaign plan, the result was a basically conservative document. Nevertheless his agreement, and the subsequent endorsement of the campaign by A.F.L. President William Green and C.I.O. President Philip Murray, were widely used by the Council to certify its nonpartisan character.[23]

The resulting campaign plan stressed freedom of enterprise and expanding productivity through mechanization and increased efficiency, recognized labor's right to organize and bargain collectively, acknowledged the need to protect the individual against those "basic hazards of existence over which he may have no control," and endorsed limited state intervention "when necessary to ensure national security or to undertake socially desirable projects when private interests prove inadequate to conduct them." It was not intended "to explain the complicated mechanisms of business, finance and trade that make up this 'American system,'" the Council declared, "but to make clear to everyone the most important features that distinguish it from that of all other countries — relating these features to past benefits but more especially to possible future gains, both material and cultural." Or as Evans Clark, director of the Twentieth Century Fund and chairman of the Public Policy Committee, put it, to show "why, in spite of its shortcomings, the American economic system has given us the highest standard of living and the greatest freedom in the world and to rally all groups in the nation for a common effort to improve our system through constantly increasing productivity and a wide distribution of its benefits." "If skillfully handled," the campaign's planners concluded, "this copy would create a national urge to work together, each in his own field,

[23]*New York Times*, October 17, 1948, III, 1. Robert M. Gray, Report to the Board of Directors on the Economic Education Campaign, November 8, 1950, box 20, Jackson Files. Draft of Possible Revised AAAA-ANA Presentation, January 20, 1947, in box 69, Paul G. Hoffman Papers, Harry S. Truman Library. *New York Times*, April 24, 1947, 37; *New York Herald Tribune*, April 24, 1947; *P.M.* (New York City), April 24, 1947.

toward greater things, toward a greater America and inevitably toward a finer world." More importantly, as Mortimer told a meeting of the A.N.A., "if people really understand what our private enterprise system had done for us and exactly how it had done it, they will not be very good prospects for swapping this system for government ownership and control."[24]

The Council raised unprecedented amounts of money for the new campaign through its recently created Industries Advisory Committee. Led by Charles E. Wilson of General Electric and Clarence Francis of General Foods, the Committee sponsored a meeting of more than 100 corporate presidents and advertising directors in September 1948, to introduce the campaign and solicit business contributions. "Many business leaders are of the opinion that the Republicans will take over the Administration in January, and they won't have anything more to worry about," Council director Donald David, Dean of the Harvard Business School, warned the meeting. "This is dangerous thinking, since the Communists will be on the march as strong as ever, and the American people will be in as much need of economic education as ever."[25]

During the next several months, many large corporations responded to the Committee's appeal. General Foods and General Electric each contributed $100,000, while smaller, though still substantial amounts were contributed by General Motors, International Business Machines, Eastman Kodak, Esso Standard Oil, Standard Oil of Indiana, Burlington Mills, Procter and Gamble, Remington Rand, the Ethyl Corporation, Republic Steel, Johnson and Johnson, and many, many others. Four large advertising agencies contributed their energies to the campaign — Batten Barton, Durstine & Osborne, Inc., McCann-Erickson, Inc., J. Walter Thompson, Co., and Young & Rubicam, Inc. — creating nearly 200 advertisements of which eleven were finally placed in production. The most popular one featured Uncle Sam rolling up his sleeves above the caption "The Better We Produce, the Better We Live." "SURE AMERICA'S GOING AHEAD IF WE ALL PULL TOGETHER," announced another. "American teamwork is management that pays reasonable wages and takes a fair profit [and] . . . labor that produces efficiently and as much as it can — that realizes its standard of living ultimately depends on how much America produces. . . ." By late 1949 advertisers, media and agencies had contributed more than $3,000,000 in time and space. As the Council's annual report boasted, "Perhaps no Council campaign since the war has had such enthusiastic cooperation of

[24] Draft of Possible Revised AAAA-ANA Presentation, January 20, 1947, in box 69, Hoffman Papers. *New York Herald Tribune*, April 24, 1947. *P.M.* (New York City), April 24, 1947. "What Helps People Helps Business," 11. *Advertising Council News* (October, 1949).
[25] Summary of the Advertising Council's Activities, September, 1948, box 13, Jackson Files.

members of the Council's constituent organizations, advisory committees and affiliated groups."[26]

The campaign began officially in mid-November, the week following Truman's surprising victory, and was one of the largest in Council history. By late 1950, campaign coordinator Robert M. Gray of Esso Standard could report that in two years publishers and national advertisers had sponsored more than 600 pages of Council-prepared magazine ads, that newspapers had ordered over 13 million lines of advertising, that the Council's message had appeared on 300,000 car cards and on two billboard postings of 4,000 each, while radio had carried the campaign into "almost every home in America." Most of the advertisements offered, free on request, a small pamphlet prepared by the Twentieth Century Fund and McCann-Erickson, entitled "The Miracle of America." In its pages Uncle Sam explained the American economic system to Junior and Dad, showing "Why Americans live better," "How machines make jobs," and "Why freedom and security go together." "In America we have won freedom and we are winning economic security," declared Uncle Sam. "Dictators promise security if the people will give up freedom. But experience shows that freedom and economic security *must* grow together." "If everybody who plays a part in making things will team up," he concluded, ". . . we can raise productivity so far and so fast that we can share the benefits and have real security for *all* our people." By 1950 more than 1.5 million copies of the "Miracle" had been distributed, and it had been reprinted or digested in *Look*, the *Scholastic* magazines, *Opportunity*, and nearly 50 company publications.[27]

The Council's campaign was, of course, only one among many similar drives launched by American business during the late 1940s and early 1950s. Indeed William Whyte's estimation, that by the early 1950s American businesses were devoting over $100,000,000 of their advertising, public relations, and employee relations budgets each year to economic "education," was probably a conservative one. A survey by the Opinion Research Corporation showed that economic education was the chief goal of most corporate public relations, while a study by the Brookings Institution noted "a great intensification of interest in mass communication" prompted by "fear over the future of free enterprise." By 1952 the detritus of these campaigns lay scattered about America's cultural landscape in books, articles and pamphlets, in motion pictures,

[26] Summary of the Advertising Council's Activities, September, 1948; Summary of the Advertising Council's Activities, October, 1948, box 13, Jackson Files. *Advertising Council News* (October, 1948). *New York Times*, October 17, 1948, III, 1. "What Helps People Helps Business—Seventh Year," 14. For sample advertisement, see *Saturday Evening Post* 221 (November 6, 1948), 115.
[27] Gray, Report on Economic Education Campaign. "The Miracle of America" (New York, 1948). Summary of Advertising Council Activities, November, 1949, box 13, Jackson Files. Ordinary citizens were, unfortunately from the Council's point of view, highly resistant to the blandishments of the campaign and initial requests for the "Miracle" proved "discouraging." In the end, more than half of all copies sent out were requested by corporations for distribution to their employees and stockholders.

Courtesy of the Advertising Council

Advertisement for "The Miracle of America"

In conjunction with the Twentieth Century Fund, the Advertising
Council ran thousands of billboards like this one in the late 1940s
extolling the virtues of corporate capitalism.

on billboards and posters, on radio and television, on car cards in buses,
trains, and trolleys, even in comic books and on matchbook covers.
Though the message varied, both in form and content, from the sophisticated studies of the Committee for Economic Development to the hard
sell comic books of the National Association of Manufacturers, the
purpose was invariably the same — to arrest the momentum of New
Deal liberalism and create a political culture conducive to the autono-
mous expansion of corporate enterprise.[28]

[28]Whyte, *Is Anybody Listening*, 7. *New York Times*, February 10, 1952, III, 1. *Fortune* (July, 1951), 84–86.
McKee and Moulton, *A Survey of Economic Education*, p. 24. While some campaigns were subtly understated,
many others bordered on the ridiculous. For example, the National Association of Manufacturers offered a
comic book entitled *The Fight for Freedom* which showed how in 1776 American patriots had rebelled against
"government planners" in London, as well as a series of films such as "The Price of Freedom," "Joe Turner,
American," and "The Quarterback," all of which stressed "concepts of freedom, security and the advantages
enjoyed by the worker under free enterprise." In a slide film produced by a Detroit firm, "Tom Smith"
discovered that mankind had for centuries faced problems "surprisingly similar" to our own, and that, for
example, while the ancient Spartans waited behind their Iron Curtain, the foolish Athenians indulged themselves with expensive public works and "soak the rich" taxes until at last they fell prey to their sinister
neighbors. RKO Pathé made a short film entitled "Letter to a Rebel" for the Motion Picture Association, in
which a small town newspaper editor defended capitalism and the American way from the attacks of his son, a
radical college student. MGM and Harding College collaborated on an educational cartoon entitled "Meet King
Joe," which closely followed the themes of the "Miracle of America" pamphlet, while Teamwork Publications,
Inc., put out a 32-page comic book containing "an economic adventure story built around a character called
Steve Merritt." Junior Achievement, a national organization founded in 1919, was extremely active in the
economic "education" of young people. Financed by corporate contributions it was "frankly intended to get
across the principle of free enterprise to youngsters in the 15–to–21 age bracket." Dorothy Barclay, "Teen Age
Business Lessons," *New York Times Magazine*, November 26, 1950, 44. On Junior Achievement, see especially
Edwin Gabler, "The Way That Good Folks Do: Junior Achievement and Corporate Culture," (M.A. thesis,
University of Massachusetts, Amherst, 1981).

THE EISENHOWER YEARS

Between 1945 and 1953, the relationship between the Advertising Council and the Democratic Administration of Harry Truman was at best characterized by ambivalence. Council leaders enthusiastically supported the new diplomacy of the Cold War, but remained generally opposed to Democratic domestic programs. As we have seen, the American Economic System campaign was but a thinly veiled attack on New Deal and Fair Deal liberalism.

No such ambivalence characterized the response of Council leaders to the election of Dwight D. Eisenhower, however. Indeed, they saw in him a chief executive whose philosophy and style were close to their own. A product of the organizational revolution that had transformed American society in the twentieth century, Eisenhower fully accepted the place of large and powerful interest groups in the national economy, though he also feared that the unbridled self-interest of these groups posed a grave danger. The system could only be preserved, in his view, through enlightened and disinterested public management by leaders such as himself, through self-discipline and voluntary cooperation by business, labor, and agriculture, and through the skillful use of advertising and public relations to dampen partisanship and secure public support for those policies dictated by enlightened management.[29] In 1948 Eisenhower had encouraged the Advertising Council "to sell . . . an understanding" of the free enterprise system. In 1953 he warned the Council that "the only way to avoid centralized domination" was "through an increased readiness to cooperate in the solution of group problems. As problems became more complex," he continued, "we must find new ways to achieve cooperation — new mechanisms for discovering our problems and getting them over to the American people." The Advertising Council, he declared, was precisely such a mechanism and thus was "one of our great agencies for the preservation of free government." The Council reciprocated the feeling, finding in the new President, as one industry leader expressed it, "a reassuring understanding of business, of advertising and of the true purpose of the Advertising Council which this writer has never heard before from anyone in the Treaty Room or any other government Chamber."[30]

During the Eisenhower years the Advertising Council continued, as before, its public service campaigns on behalf of fire prevention, highway safety, savings bonds, and other similar concerns. It also continued its campaigns associated with American foreign policy — C.A.R.E., civil

[29]Robert Griffith, "Dwight D. Eisenhower and the Corporate Commonwealth," *American Historical Review*, 87 (February, 1982), 87–122.

[30]*New York Times*, October 28, 1948, 45. Leo Burnett, "Cherry Blossom Time in Washington: An Informal Report on 'The Ninth White House Conference'," March 23–24, 1953, box 1, Lambie Records.

defense, and Radio Free Europe. The relationship between the Council and the government grew even closer. Council leaders were called to the White House for consultation on the promotion of "Operation Candor" — Eisenhower's United Nations speech on "Atoms for Peace"; and later urged to organize a *Get Out the Vote Drive* that White House advisors hoped would encourage more Republicans to vote. The Council also organized, in cooperation with the United States Information Agency, an exhibit on "People's Capitalism" designed to show the world how in America the rewards of capitalism were "shared with the workers," how "class lines [had begun] to disappear," and how "almost everybody became a capitalist." Council leaders were so pleased by the People's Capitalism exhibit that they also sought to popularize the concept at home — inspiring speeches and articles on the subject by prominent business leaders, sponsoring conferences of academics and businessmen to discuss it, and planting the phrase in publications such as the *New York Times* and *Saturday Review*.[31] The most important of the Council's activities during the decade, however, was a series of campaigns tied closely to the economic policies of the Eisenhower Administration and designed to promote the political interests of both the Administration and American business.

One of the most critical political issues facing the new Administration was that of managing the economy. Eisenhower had won election on the basis of his personal popularity and the hope that he would bring an end to the war in Korea. But could the Republicans maintain prosperity and high employment? Could they escape the popular image created by Hoover during the depression and sustained by two decades of Democratic campaign rhetoric? These questions were not academic, for by late 1953 economic indicators pointed to an approaching downturn in the business cycle, a downturn which would unhappily coincide with the 1954 offyear elections. Democrats were already attacking the Administration's economic policies, while Eisenhower, in a nationwide radio and television address, charged that his critics were "peddlers of gloom and doom."[32]

Against this background the Joint Committee of the A.N.A.-A.A.A.A. once again called on the Advertising Council to initiate a campaign, in

[31]On Operation Candor see C. D. Jackson log, April 2, 14, June 3, July 20, 1953, box 56, Jackson Papers, Eisenhower Library. On voting see Memorandum, Tom Hall Miller to Public Relations Advisory Council, National Citizens for Eisenhower Congressional Committee, April 3, 1954, box 5, William E. Robinson Papers, Eisenhower Library. On People's Capitalism see especially Memorandum of the Conversation between the President and T.S. Repplier, August 3, 1955, box 23; Advertising Council, "People's Capitalism: The Background—How and Why This Project Was Developed" (n.d., but c. 1956); "People's Capitalism in the USA" Test Preview, February 14–22, 1956; Notes on People's Capitalism Program, (July, 1956); Repplier to Evans Clark, June 12, 1956; Repplier to Andrew H. Berding, June 19, 1956; Lambie to Claude Robinson, July 25, 1956, all in box 31, Lambie Records.

[32]*New York Times*, January 5, 1954, 1. "I know," the President told his audience, "that you have unbounded confidence in the future of America." House Speaker Joseph Martin (R.-Mass.) was blunter, charging that left-wing "eggheads" were trying "to promote us into hard times for political reasons." *New York Times*, January 24, 1954, 61.

effect an extension of the earlier American Economic System campaign, to promote confidence in the American economy. The danger, as the Joint Committee saw it, was that "gloomy, often slanted forecasts" were undermining faith in the economy and raising the prospect that what was "a normal readjustment might become a real depression." "The number of whispering campaigns taking place and the gloom and doom being spilled in many quarters defy both faith and reason," declared William C. McKeehan, Jr., vice president of J. Walter Thompson and Chairman of the Joint Committee. To counteract this danger, the Joint Committee urged the Council to mount an aggressive campaign which would create confidence in the economic future both among businessmen and the general public. Quickly approved by the Public Policy Committee (at the time chaired by Eisenhower's close friend and political supporter Paul G. Hoffman) and by the Board of Directors, the campaign was launched in May 1954, under the title "The Future of America." "By acquainting more people with the actual facts and figures of the nation's astonishing postwar development, and the coming needs in terms of goods and services, we might help to prevent a normal business readjustment from being turned into a major depression by the contagion of fear," declared Council President Repplier. "We propose to tell this story in such a way that the businessman, the banker, the manager and the employee can each see in it his own individual opportunity and have a reasoned faith in a secure economic future," agreed campaign coordinator Robert Gray. "Success in creating informed public opinion about the dynamic nature of America and about the age of promise which can lie ahead, could produce effects of utmost importance to every businessman and every individual in the country."[33]

The Eisenhower Administration was involved in the preparation of the campaign from the very outset. Both the Administration and the Council, moreover, were keenly aware of the political implications of the project. As White House aide James R. Lambie, Jr., wrote Assistant to the President Sherman Adams, the campaign could have "a significant part in creating the kind of business conditions which would put the Administration in a favorable light." Robert R. Mullen, a Washington public relations executive with close ties to the Administration, warned the Council that it might need "protection" from the possibility of adverse publicity. Above all, we have to avoid "the taint of working with or for a special interest lobby," agreed a member of the Council staff. "It

[33] Press Release, Joint ANA-AAAA Committee (n.d., but early 1954); Robert M. Gray, "The Future of America Campaign," March 19, 1954, box 12, Lambie Records. Press Release, the Advertising Council, January 12, 1954, box 62, O.F. 127–A–1, Dwight D. Eisenhower Papers. Boris Shiskin, the A.F.L. representative on the Public Policy Committee, had some reservations about the campaign but agreed to go along with the majority. Shiskin to Paul G. Hoffman, February 16, 1954; Hoffman to Shiskin, February 25, 1954, box 69, Hoffman Papers.

could be a very controversial campaign if it were not handled properly."[34]

Like the AES campaign on which it was patterned, the "Future of America" was coordinated by Robert Gray of Esso Standard Oil and the copy was prepared by McCann-Erickson. It was initially presented to a meeting of 200 prominent business executives who in turn helped raise $100,000 dollars to cover production costs. The campaign included the usual bank of radio and television spots (257 million "impressions"), newspaper and magazine advertisements, car cards and billboards. Like the AES campaign it also featured a pamphlet extolling America's bright economic future. All in all, American business contributed an estimated $10,000,000 to the Council's campaign. The recession, which ended in August 1954, proved relatively mild and shortlived, for which the Advertising Council claimed some credit. The campaign was slowed down during the late summer, then resumed during the fall, climaxing on January 2, 1955, when each of the major television networks contributed a half hour for the showing of a film on "The Future of America" narrated by Paul Hoffman. During 1955 the campaign continued on a more modest scale, even though the threat of recession had disappeared, with television and radio advertising producing over 90 million home impressions.[35]

For Eisenhower, the results were hardly less satisfactory. Though the Republicans lost control of Congress in the November elections, their losses were quite modest, while the President's personal popularity remained extremely high. Thus both economic and political developments seemed to confirm the wisdom of the administration's new fiscal policies. As the President boasted in his January 20, 1955, economic report, "Instead of expanding federal enterprises or initiating new spending programs, the basic policy of the Government in dealing with the contraction was to take actions that created confidence in the future and stimulated business firms, consumers, and states and localities to increase their expenditures."[36]

In 1958, when recession once again threatened the precarious stability maintained by the Eisenhower Administration, the Council turned to yet another mass campaign to promote confidence in America's eco-

[34]Lambie to Sherman Adams, December 9, 1953, box 3; Max Fox to Theodore S. Repplier, April 5, 1954; Paul West to Sherman Adams, March 5, 1954, box 12, Lambie Records. The week before the campaign officially began, former President Truman accused the Administration of "creeping McKinleyism," possibly prompting campaign coordinator Robert Gray's declaration that "this is not a political campaign in any sense" but rather represents "the forces of advertising against the forces of depression." *New York Times*, May 14, 1954, 1; May 21, 1954, 30.
[35]Plan for the "Future of America" Campaign, box 12, Lambie Records. Advertising Council, "The Future of America" (New York, 1954). *Business Week* (March 13, 1954), 58.
[36]Press Release, Advertising Council, August 17, 1954; Theodore S. Repplier to Lambie, September 11, 1954; Repplier to Arthur Burns, July 30, 1943; Press Release, Advertising Council, December 27, 1954; Richard E. Deems, "Who Killed Cock Robin," speech, August 16, 1954, all in box 12, Lambie Records. Advertising Council, Annual Report (New York, 1955), 4–19. Advertising Council, Annual Report (New York, 1956), 19. *New York Times*, January 21, 1955, 8.

nomic future. As before, the Council's campaign was developed in close cooperation with the White House. Charles G. Mortimer, the president of General Foods and a former Chairman of the Council, was the principal organizer of the campaign, conferring frequently with the Secretary of Treasury, Federal Reserve Board members, and White House aides, and bringing together a group of major corporate executives to raise money for production costs. Once again the target was "the statements and gloomy predictions now being made on the present recession." And once again the campaign took place within a highly charged political setting. The Administration, more fearful of rising prices than of rising unemployment, was attempting to hold down the budget, while the Democrats, led by Senate Majority Leader Lyndon B. Johnson, were calling for accelerated public works spending, aid to depressed areas, and other measures to combat joblessness.[37]

Financed initially by $262,000 in corporate contributions, the 1958 campaign, "Confidence in a Growing America," quickly became one of the largest in Council history, surpassing even the earlier American Economic System campaign. During the first three months television alone accounted for more than one billion home impressions, radio 41 million more. Council advertisements ran in 76 national magazines, in 371 trade and business papers, and in over 1,000 newspapers, and appeared on 60,000 car cards and 5,000 outdoor billboards. Sinclair Oil tied its annual advertising campaign to the Council theme: "Your Future is Great in a Growing America — Remember to Drive with Care and Buy Sinclair." General Electric stressed the "confidence" theme in its own advertising of what it called "Operation Upturn," while American Can, U.S. Steel and Prudential Insurance all filmed television spots with a similar message.[38]

By the fall of 1958 Administration and Advertising Council leaders were congratulating one another on the success of the campaign. "You have helped let the economy prove again that it has great basic resilience, inasmuch as the better turn has come about without the heavy intervention by government which was urged by some in the early months of this year," wrote Treasury Secretary Robert B. Anderson to Repplier. "By helping the American people remain confident about the ability of our economy to right itself, the Advertising Council's campaign has been, and continues to be, most important." The Council, agreed Charles Mortimer, "focused national attention on the relationship between public attitudes and psychology and the economic swings which

[37] Mortimer to Lambie, April 2, 1958; List of Conferees at Advertising Council Anti-Recession Meeting, April 11, 1958, box 44, Lambie Records. *New York Times*, April 15, 1958, 1; April 20, 1958, 1; April 24, 1958, 1.
[38] Progress Report, Confidence in a Growing America, c. August, 1958, box 44, Lambie Records. The Council also established what it called a "Good News Bureau" to distribute "positive" information about the economy supplied by the Administration. *Advertising Council News* (May–June, 1958). Maxwell Fox to Lambie, March 27, 1958; Lambie to Fox, April 2, 1958, box 44, Lambie Records. *New York Times*, April 24, 1958, 1, 26; May 7, 1958, 21; May 27, 1958, 43; July 9, 1958, 43; September 18, 1958, 30.

ARE YOU
one of
STALIN'S PUPPETS?

Marionettes and puppets are fun for
kids but when grown people begin to
act like puppets it's dangerous.

Puppets don't think for themselves. They
do and say just as their master instructs.

Many of us today are being puppets for Mr.
Stalin and not even knowing it.

If you spread rumors about other people's religion,
race or culture—you're a puppet. If you refuse to accept
people on their individual value and insist on classifying
everybody into groups—you're a puppet.

Communism and Uncle Joe thrive on dissension — Management
against Labor—Christian against Jew and White against Negro. Don't
be one of Uncle Joe's puppets. Think your own thoughts, say what you
think and make sure to judge each person individually and not as a group!

Support BROTHERHOOD WEEK and live Brotherhood the year 'round!

BROTHERHOOD WEEK
FEBRUARY 17 THROUGH 24

Advertisement for
"Brotherhood Week"

As this 1952 poster demonstrates, the
spectre of Communism was sometimes explicitly incorporated into public service messages.

Courtesy of the Advertising Council

This shameful waste
WEAKENS AMERICA !

Remember — only **you** can
PREVENT FOREST FIRES !

Courtesy of the Advertising Council

Advertisement for
Fire Prevention

Smokey the Bear — one of the Advertising Council's best-known public
service campaigns.

must always be part of our economy, if that economy is to remain free and is to function with a minimum of government intervention." Though the evidence was, as in 1954, ambiguous, the Council nevertheless claimed a share of the credit for having arrested the recession, citing a study by the Survey Research Center at the University of Michigan which concluded that "many more people believe, today, that a year from now conditions will be better, than believe that they will be worse."[39] Unfortunately, the campaign was far less successful politically, and in the November off year elections the Republicans suffered their worst defeat since 1936. Confidence in a growing America did not, apparently, extend to the party in power.

The victory of the Democrats in 1958 in turn intensified the debate over economic policy between the Administration and its critics and set the stage for the last Council campaign undertaken during the Eisenhower years. The 1957–58 recession had produced the largest peacetime deficit in budget history and the Administration, fearing renewed inflation, was determined to impose fiscal and monetary restraints. Unemployment, on the other hand, remained fairly high, over five percent as late as December 1959, and Congressional Democrats were pressing for expansionist policies. Against this backdrop the Advertising Council, once more in step with the Administration, shifted its attention from recession to inflation and began recasting its economic campaign as a weapon in the battle to maintain wage and price stability. As former Secretary of Treasury George Humphrey warned a Council meeting in early 1959, "with too much inflation, the whole free enterprise system could go out of the window."[40]

The anti-inflation campaign, however, quickly ran into opposition from labor representatives on the Public Policy Committee who strongly objected to copy which proposed to stress "making certain that government income is sufficient to cover expenditures, . . . not demanding government services unless willing to pay for them through taxes, . . . [and] not asking for special advantage for any interest as a group at the expense of the country as a whole." We quickly discovered, Repplier wrote Humphrey, "that labor had an unreasoningly antagonistic attitude."[41] The Public Advisory Committee, deeply divided over the proposed campaign, rejected the initial copy prepared by McCann–Erikson and it was not until the fall of 1959 that the Council staff was able to produce copy acceptable to both the anti-labor Industries Advisory

[39] Anderson to Repplier, August 18, 1958; Mortimer speech, September 17, 1958; Progress Report, Confidence in a Growing America (c. August, 1958), box 44, Lambie Records; *New York Times*, September 18, 1958, 44.

[40] Maurice Stans to Lambie, November 28, 1958; Lambie to Stans, December 10, 1958, box 49; Minutes of Meeting, Board of Directors, Advertising Council, January 15, 1959, box 46, Lambie Records.

[41] Suggested Copy Policy, The Problem of Inflation, March, 1958; Lambie to Humphrey, May 4, 1959, box 46, Lambie Records.

Committee and the Public Policy Committee. Even then the union representatives on the Public Policy Committee remained opposed but were outvoted by a three-quarters majority.[42]

The President's economic advisors were not overly enthusiastic about the final result, but nevertheless endorsed it as a means of dampening pressure for wage increases. As Henry C. Wallich of the Council of Economic Advisors wrote, "to the extent that wage push can be considered a cause of inflation, a reduction in labor's demands and a more conciliatory attitude on their part would help curb inflation."[43] The anti-inflation campaign was shortlived, however, for by May 1960, another recession was underway and the Council was once again trying to devise an anti-recession campaign. The decade ended, much as it had begun, with a Council decision to support a "Promise of America" campaign to promote confidence in the economy.[44]

CONCLUSION

The impact of this enormous amount of cultural production neverthe-less remains extremely difficult to assess. It would be easy, of course, to take too literally the often inflated claims of the Council's leaders and to exaggerate its influence on postwar politics. It would also be easy, and equally misleading, to suggest a simple cause and effect relationship between the Council's efforts and the seemingly consensual character of American culture in the 1950s. The universe of advertising and public relations does not readily submit to such easy measurement, however, especially when the product to be measured is as diffuse as attitudes about the economic order. How, for example, would one measure the influence of the Council's "economic education" campaigns as over against similar campaigns by the U.S. Chamber of Commerce, the National Association of Manufacturers, and many other groups? Or, to take a somewhat different example, how would one compare the influ-ence of the more or less overtly political advertising of the Council's "public service" campaigns with the far larger volume of "commercial" advertising? Surely this, too, sold the system, if only in less direct and more subtle fashion. How, finally, would one separate the impact of the Advertising Council from the influence of, say, the Cold War, or high

[42]Report of Public Policy Committee Meeting, June 29, 1959, box 49; Report of Public Policy Committee Meeting, November 20, 1959, box 46, Lambie Records.
[43]Wallich to Lambie, August 24, 1959, box 46, Lambie Records. Also see Raymond J. Saulnier to Lambie, September 4, 1959; Maurice H. Stans to Lambie, August 28, 1959; and Allen Wallis to Lambie, August 22, 1959, box 22, Lambie records.
[44]Minutes of Meeting, Board of Directors, Advertising Council, October 20, 1960, box 53, Lambie Records. The Advertising Council continued its public service campaigns, including those emphasizing "economic education," throughout the 1960s and 1970s. See, for example, David L. Paletz et al., *Politics in Public Service Advertising* (New York, 1977); Glenn K. Hirsch, "Only You Can Prevent Ideological Hegemony: The Advertis-ing Council and Its Place in the American Power Structure," *The Insurgent Sociologist* (Spring, 1975); and Bruce Howard, "Selling Lies," *Ramparts* 13 (December, 1974), 25–32. On the controversy surrounding a recent economic education campaign, see *Newsweek* 88 (September 20, 1976), 74.

employment, or the rapid, if uneven, spread of consumer goods and homesteads in suburbia?

It would also be easy to underestimate popular resistance to the Council's campaigns, especially since ordinary Americans had little or no personal power over the channels of mass communication and since their attitudes and concerns were but imperfectly registered by the era's pollsters. Public opinion surveys do show that throughout the 1950s large and indeed growing majorities believed that the federal government should guarantee employment and help people get medical care at low cost. Large majorities remained critical of the influence of big business on American society, and advertising executives still met to worriedly discuss their public image. Despite the millions of dollars spent by the Council to sell consensus, there is considerable evidence that at the grass roots, at least, many Americans were not buying.[45]

Yet it would also be a serious mistake to *underestimate* the impact of the Council, if for no other reason than the frequency and ubiquity with which its advertisements appeared and the zeal with which its leaders sought to publicize their highly selective view of American society. If the Council was but one of many organizations promoting such a view, it was nevertheless unique in its access to what its founders had called "the greatest aggregate means of mass education and persuasion the world has ever seen." If the portrait of America it sought to popularize was the product of diverse and complex economic and social forces, it was also the deliberate product of the Council and its powerful corporate constituencies. If, as William Whyte claimed, much of the propaganda produced by American business was "naive . . . psychologically unsound . . . abstract . . . defensive, and . . . negative," it was nevertheless repetitious, pervasive and unchallenged, surrounding Americans in all walks of life with an omnipresent if distorted reflection of their society and thus helping shape, to a degree no less real for being difficult to measure, the political culture of postwar America.[46] If consensus did indeed characterize America's national culture in the 1950s, it was perhaps to a degree we have not fully appreciated, a consensus manufactured by America's corporate leaders, packaged by the advertising industry, and merchandised through the channels of mass communication.

[45] Richard F. Hamilton, *Class and Politics in the United States* (New York, 1972), 89–112. See, for example, Minutes of Meeting, Committee on the Prestige of Advertising, October 1, 1958, in box 46, Lambie Records. C. W. McKee and H. G. Moulton, who surveyed early economic education programs for the Brookings Institution, concluded that "While 'audience research' on some campaigns shows that economic advertising has been noticed and remembered, there is no evidence to indicate how it affected the people who read it." *Survey of Economic Education*, 57–58. William Whyte, whose breezily impressionistic essay on business propaganda asked "Is Anybody Listening?", concluded that no, nobody was. Whyte, *Is Anybody Listening*, 1–20.

[46] Whyte, *Is Anybody Listening*, 8. The most recent study of public service advertising concludes that while such communications may be limited in their ability to actually change behavior, they nevertheless serve to "canalize viewers' predispositions and reinforce existing behavior." Paletz et al., *Politics in Public Service Advertising*, 58–59, 73–76, *et passim*.

Part V
Marketing Research

[32]

THE ADOPTION OF STATISTICAL METHODS IN MARKET RESEARCH:
1915-1937

Richard Germain
Michigan State University

ABSTRACT

The goal of this research is to determine
whether or not known, readily available
statistical methods were discussed in market
research textbooks during the 1915-1937 time
period. A content analysis of market research
and statistics texts indicated that basic
statistical concepts were omitted from market
research books of the period. An adoption of
innovation framework was used to identify and
discuss possible causes of the delay. Three
potential factors which could have slowed the
adoption of statistics were identified: the
personality of Ronald Fisher, statistics as a
discipline, and market research practices of
the period.

INTRODUCTION

In a recent article Charnes et al. (1985, p. 96) state:

Survey design, statistical sampling, and related
methodologies developed at Rothemstead Experimental
Station in England [by Sir Ronald Fisher] and at the U.S.
Census Bureau in the 1920s and 1930s - and as extended
for marketing in the 1940s and 1950s - provided important
stimuli for market research.

The purpose of this paper is to examine this phenomenon in more
detail. The research questions that will be addressed are: (1) did
market research textbooks published between 1915 and 1937 include
readily available statistical techniques that are now routinely
included in today's market research texts? and (2) if so, then how
rapidly were they adopted, or if adopted after considerable delay,
what seems to have caused the delay?

A content analysis of fifteen statistics texts from various
disciplines and ten market research texts published between 1915
and 1937 was conducted. Comparisons were then made to two recently
published market research textbooks. The results indicate that a
considerable number of routine statistical methods were not
incorporated into market research books.

Given this finding, three potential causes of the delay were
identified: (1) the personality of Sir Ronald Fisher which impacted

317

the dissemination of his ideas; (2) the discipline of statistics;
and (3) market research practices of the day. This discussion of
potential causes is cast in an adoption of innovation framework.
The discussion of the last factor will partially focus on the
relevance of statistical methods to market research during this
period, an issue which has received little attention (Bartels
1976).

IDENTIFICATION OF UNUSED STATISTICAL METHODS

The Statistics Texts
        Exhibit A lists statistical topics in each of fifteen
statistics texts published between 1913 and 1937. These texts fall
into one of three categories. First, the texts of Forsyth (1924),
Kelly (1924), Bowley (1926) and Camp (1930) relied on calculus, and
are devoted to statistics as an abstract or generic subject. The
remainder of the texts are application oriented in specific
disciplines (e.g., Secrist 1925 on business; Thurstone 1925 on
psychology). They can be characterized as either: (1)
sophisticated insofar as statistical content (i.e., Fisher (1925)
and Snedecor (1937) both on biology); or (2) less sophisticated
(i.e., the remaining nine books).

        The Fisher (1925) and Snedecor (1937) texts were designated
statistically sophisticated because, as shown in Exhibit A, their
works were the only ones to discuss: (1) experimental design; (2)
the chi-square test of independence, as presented in most
contemporary texts, and the chi-square goodness of fit test; (3)
the "student" t and chi-square distributions; (4) tests of two
means, two variances and paired means; and (5) analysis of variance
including advanced methods of analyzing experiments. Among the
texts reviewed here, Fisher's was the first to discuss these
methods. Also, of the many innovations in his book was his focus
on significance (i.e., the use of a small alpha value) as opposed
to probable error (i.e., equivalent to an alpha level of 50%).
Snedecor, in addition to covering all these topics, also discussed
the F-distribution and analysis of covariance.

        As can be seen in Exhibit A, most books adequately covered:
(1) measures of central tendency and dispersion; and (2) graphs,
tables and time series. The use of secondary, survey and/or
internal time series data was treated in the majority of less
sophisticated texts. Only Bowley (1926), among the calculus based
textbook authors, covered some data collection methods. The most
complete treatments of probability and probability distributions
(i.e, the normal, binomial, Poisson, and "student" t distributions)
were found in the calculus based books and in the two sophisticated
application texts. Among the less sophisticated books Davis'
(1937) is the exception which deserves mention because of his
coverage of these topics.

        While the majority of textbook authors adequately discussed
simple linear correlation and regression, treatment of more
advanced correlation and regression methods (e.g., coefficient of

Exhibit A

CONTENT ANALYSIS OF THE STATISTICS TEXTS

x represents discussion of topic
i represents incomplete
  discussion of topic

	King (1913)	Forsyth (1924)	Kelly (1924)	Kent (1924)	Secrist (1925)	Crum & Patton (1925)	Thurstone (1925)	Fisher (1925)	Bowley (1926)	Dittmer (1926)	Elmer (1926)	Camp (1930)	Day (1930)	Davis (1937)	Snedecor (1937)
Measures of Central Tendency and Dispersion															
– mean	x	x	x	x	x	x	x	x	x	x	x	x	x	x	x
– mode	x	x	x	x	x	x	x	x	x	x	x	x	x	x	x
– median	x	x	x	x	x	x	x	x	x	x	x	x	x	x	x
– geometric mean	x	x	x	x	x			x		x	x	x	x	x	x
– weighted mean	x	x	x	x	x			x		x	x	x	x	x	x
– standard deviation	x	x	x	x	x	x	x	x	x	x	x	x	x	x	x
– skewness	x	x	x	x	x	x		x	x	x	x	x	x	x	x
– moments		x	x			x		x			x	x		x	
– grouped data (mean/variance)		x	x	x	x	x	x	x	x	x	x	x	x	x	x
Graphs, Tables and Time Series															
– graphical methods	x		x	x	x	x	x	x	x	x	x	x	x	x	x
– tabular interpretation	x		x	x	x	x		i	x	x	i	x	x	i	i
– interpolation	x	x	x	x	x	x		x		x		x		x	x
– index numbers	x		x	x	x			x	x	x	x	x			
– moving averages	x		x	x	x			x	x	x	x	x	x		
– other advanced time series			x		x	x							x	x	
Collection of Data															
– collection of secondary data	x			x	x	x			x	x	x				
– survey methods	x			x	x				x	x					
– collection of internal data	x			x	x	x			x						
– experimentation								x							x
Probability and Probability Distributions															
– simple probability theory		x			x		x		x		x		x	x	x
– normal distribution		x	x	x	x	x	x	x	x	x	i	x	x	x	x
– binomial distribution		x		i			x	x	x		i	x		x	x
– variance of proportions		x						x	x		x	x		x	x
– poisson distribution		x						x						x	x
– "student" t distribution								x						x	x

Continued overleaf

Exhibit A (cont'd)

	King (1913)	Forsyth (1924)	Kelly (1924)	Kent (1924)	Secrist (1925)	Crum & Patton (1925)	Thurstone (1925)	Fisher (1925)	Bowley (1926)	Dittmer (1926)	Elmer (1926)	Camp (1930)	Day (1932)	Davis (1937)	Snedecor (1937)
Correlation (strictly estimation of coefficients)															
– simple correlation	x	x	x	x	x	x	x	x	x	x	x	x	x	x	x
– simple linear regression		x	x	x	x	x	x	x	x			x	x	x	x
– multiple correlation		x	x					x	x			x		x	x
– multiple linear regression		x	x					x	x			x		x	x
– rank order correlation		x				x						x	x	x	
– correlation ratio		x	x					x				x	x	x	
– correlation of time series							x	x			i	x	x	x	
– coefficient of contingency		x						x				x			
– advanced correlation methods		x						x				x		x	
Chi-Square Tests															
– goodness of fit test			x	x	x			x	x			x	x	x	x
– test of independence								x							x
Proability Distribution Tables															
– standardized normal							x	x	x			x		x	x
– "student" t								x						x	x
– chi-square								x	i		i			x	x
– F-distribution															x
Use of Sampling Distribution (i.e., degrees of freedom)								x				x		i	x
Test of Two Means, Two Variances and Paired Means								x			i				x
Use of Significance (rather than probable error)								x							x
Analysis of Variance															
– ANOVA								x							x
– ANOVA applied to regression								x							x
– experimental design								x							x
– analysis of covariance															x
Reliance on Calculus		x	x					x			x				

contingency, rank order correlation) are typically found in the calculus based books.

The Market Research Texts

Exhibit B lists statistics topics in each of ten market research texts published between 1916 and 1937. The Starch (1923) and White (1927) texts focused on advertising research.

As can been seen in Exhibit B, six out of ten authors adequately covered measures of central tendency, but none sufficiently treated dispersion. Wheeler's (1937) discussion of dispersion was judged incomplete since he merely stated its importance without explication of formulae, usage or interpretation. Five out of ten texts covered two or more topics within graphs, tables and time series.

A heavy emphasis was found in these texts on collection of data. Eight of ten authors discussed all of secondary data, survey methods and internal firm data. In addition, three authors discussed experimentation (the two advertising textbook authors, plus Reilly (1929)).

With the exception of Reilly (1929), the statistical content of these books tends is rather limited. Reilly discussed: (1) variance of proportions; (2) accuracy of proportions (i.e., confidence interval construction); and (3) a test of "internal reliability" (i.e., a test of the difference between two proportions). Noteworthy is that Reilly placed the latter two tests in Fisher's sampling theory context relying on a 1 percent significance level.

None of the market research books adequately treated variance, probability, probability distributions, any method of correlation or regression, chi-square tests, two sample tests or analyis of variance. The late inclusion of the F-distribution and ANCOVA in book form by Snedecor (1937) precludes their omission from market research texts as examples to resistance to innovation.

The quotation from Charnes et al. (1985), presented at the beginning of the article, appears substantiated for market research textbooks. The content analysis suggests that basic statistical concepts such as variance and correlation, the latter introduced by Pearson at the turn of the century, were omitted by market research textbook authors. On the other hand, all of the texts analyzed in Exhibit A included discussions of variance and correlation. For this reason, the market research texts can be classified as less sophisticated application texts. This does not imply that market research books lacked redeeming qualities. On the contrary, they are particularly strong in nonstatistical research areas which other texts are weak in. For example, the sections on questionnaire design and the costs versus benefits of research in the market research texts are unparalleled. Nor does the classification of market research texts as less sophisticated imply that authors from other disciplines were any quicker at adopting innovative statistical methods. While Day (1932) did

Exhibit B

CONTENT ANALYSIS OF THE MARKET RESEARCH TEXTS

x represents discussion of topic
i represents incomplete
  discussion of topic

	Shaw (1926)	Copeland (1917)	Duncan (1922)	Starch (1923)	White (1927)	Reed (1929)	Reilly (1929)	White (1931)	Brown (1937)	Wheeler (1937)
Measures of Central Tendency and Dispersion										
– mean	x	x	i	x		x	x			x
– mode	x	x	i	x		x	x			x
– median	x	x	i	x		x	x			x
– weighted mean	x	x		x			x			x
– standard deviation										i
Graphs, Tables and Time Series										
– graphical methods		x	i	i	i				x	x
– tabular interpretation	x	x	i	x			x	x	x	
– index numbers	x	x		x						x
– other advanced time series			x	x		x				i
Collection of Data										
– collection of secondary data	i	x	x	x	x	x	x	x	x	x
– survey methods		i	x	x	x	x	x	x	x	x
– collection of internal data	i	x	x	x	x	x	x	x	x	x
– experimentation			x	x		x		i	i	
Probability and Probability Distributions										
– variance of proportions							x			i
Correlation and Regression										
– simple correlation			i	i	i				i	i
– simple linear regression										i
– rank order correlation			i							
Accuracy of Proportions							x			i
Internal Reliability of Proportions							x		x	i

discuss variance and correlation, he did not adopt Fishers sampling theory, nor did he discuss tests of two statistics, chi-square tests, experimental design or ANOVA.

Two recently published market research books were examined (Aaker and Day 1983 and Churchill 1987) to allow comparisons to be drawn with earlier texts. Both authors covered the two foundations of market research; data collection and data analysis. Approximately 40% and 35% of the Churchill, and Aaker and Day texts are devoted to data collection and related topics, respectively. This points out that data collection is still a backbone of market research methodology. Both texts covered test of two means, correlation, dispersion and chi-square tests. Churchill treated analysis of variance, but only in an appendix. Nonrigorous treatment of advanced methods such as factor analysis and clustering methods were found in both texts.

FACTORS LIMITING ADOPTION OF STATISTICAL METHODS

Sir Ronald Fisher

In 1925 Ronald Fisher published <u>Statistical Methods for Research Workers</u>. He broke away from the mold in which texts of the period were typically cast. Harold Hotelling, the eminent statistician, in a review of the text, stated (1927, p.41):

Most books on statistics consist of pedagogic rehashes of identical material...[This book] summarizes for the non-mathematical reader the author's independent codification of statistical theory and some of his brilliant contributions to the subject.

His "brilliant contributions" included the analysis of variance technique and the latin square and randomized block experimental designs.

Although Fisher's contributions were monumental, he did little to smooth the way for their acceptance. He was well known for a volitile temper which led to "titanic battles" with leading statisticians such as Pearson and Gosset (Tankard 1984, p. 116). These battles often centered around the merits of various methods. Fisher's introduction of degrees of freedom to Pearson's extant chi-square formula provides an example of a topic over which he and Pearson disagreed, in spite of the fact that most statisticians agreed with Fisher. For his book, Fisher developed a new and now widely accepted format for the chi-square distribution. This was because Pearson, <u>Biometrika</u>'s editor at the time, denied Fisher permission to use W.P. Elberton's tables. These tables were previously published in the journal, and hence were under copyright protection.

After 1918, Fisher refused to publish in <u>Biometrika</u>, and some of his most distinguished works appeared in obscure outlets such as the <u>Proceedings of the International Congress of Mathematics, Toronto</u>. He frequently omitted assumptions, constantly failed to reference work done by others (Tankard 1984) and wrote enigmatically. Mantel stated (1976, p. 125):

> Once we had the sense to understand, we could appreciate the preciseness of writing in R.A. Fisher's texts - but then wonder how mysterious it could still be to the novice.

Thus it should not be surprising that many of his ideas became popular after other authors translated them (Tankard 1984). A notable example is Snedecor's (1937) text which contains many of Fisher's ideas.

This discussion illustrates two factors which could have slowed adoption of Fisher's notions by all potential users, not just those in marketing. First, conflicting opinions over an innovation by experts may retard adoption (Gatingnon and Robertson 1985, p. 857). Fisher's "battles" could have slowed the rate at which potential users adopted his ideas. Second, ineffective communication of the existence of an innovation could hamper adoption. Fisher's tendency to publish in obscure outlets and his puzzling writing style could have slowed the adoption of his ideas.

The quote which follows suggests Reilly believed that statisticians were not communicating in a manner which promoted the transfer of statistics to the market research discipline (1929, p. 136):

> True, some statisticians have done notable work in the theory of sampling, but little has been done to adapt this sampling theory to the study of market problems in such a way that the adaptation might be understood and used by one unschooled in higher mathematics.

Reilly's discussion of accuracy and internal reliability of proportions could have been an effort on his part to address this shortcoming.

This discussion helps explain why Fisher's notions were omitted from market research texts, but it does not address the omission of simpler statistical methods. The following two subsections present more encompassing factors which could have delayed the adoption of statistical methods.

Statistics as a Discipline
Three properties of statistics as a discipline could have impeded the adoption of statistical methods: (1) the extent of the educational infrastructure; (2) the properties of statistics as a body of mathematics; and (3) symbolic inconsistency.

First, statistics was a relatively new discipline in American colleges and universities. The courses that existed appear to have focused on descriptive and not inferential statistics. Determining the exact content of each course at various institutions and exactly which institutions were offering which courses is beyond the scope of this research. Some educational trends can be found in the work of Glover (1926) and Walker (1927) however. They discussed the results of a 1925 survey in which 40 out of 125 responding colleges and universities reported offering no statistics courses. Thus, in at least one third of responding institutions, students had no opportunity to be exposed to statistics. In providing a list of what is most needed in market research, Reilly (1929, p. 213) included: "Academic training of men in mathematics and experimental methods."

As for content, King (1926) and Chaddock (1926) proposed similar "ideal" introductory courses. Their suggested courses focused on: (1) interpretation of charts, diagrams and simple statistics (e.g., mean, mode, median); (2) sources of data; (3) problem definition; and (4) unit of analysis. King (1926) felt introductory courses should be titled "Interpretation of Statistics," and objected to the often used misleading title "Elementary Statistical Method."

A one term market research instructor may not have had the time, nor perhaps the ability or student capabilities, for developing skills in advanced statistics. Market research textbook authors, themselves being marketers, and their publishers, were probably aware of these potential deficiencies and may have taken them into account when designing market research texts. An educational infrastructure able to provide a market of sufficient size and sophistication may not have existed.

Second, statistics is a complex body of mathematics and its relative trialability and observability are low because of the required time investment before potential users comprehend techniques. If product trialability and observability are positively related to the speed of diffusion, and complexity is negatively related (Gatingnon and Robertson 1985, p. 862), then the properties of statistics could indeed have slowed the rate at which the notions of the discipline were adopted.

Third, and last, some critics claimed statistics lacked symbolic uniformity, which is still true to some extent today. Walker stated (1927, p. 170):

> [Statistics]...Has not yet secured any considerable uniformity of language, symbolism, and certainly any uniformity of teaching aims.

If technology standardization is associated with more rapid diffusion (Robertson and Gatingnon 1986, p. 5), then a lack of symbolic uniformity could have been a barrier toward absorption of statistical methods. However, the symbolism within the reviewed texts did not appear to be any more inconsistent than that of contemporary texts. On balance, this last factor does not appear to have been a major barrier to diffusion.

Market Research Practices
By the 1920s and 1930s, market researchers were really

addressing a wide range of questions. During the early 1930s, the Norge division of the Borg-Warner Corporation, a maker of electric refridgerators, engaged in competitor analysis (Blood 1935). Across competitors, they assessed consumer buying intentions, brand recognition, volume per dealer and the relative importance of price in consumer purchase decsion-making. The National Trade Journal forecasted annual construction industry sales (Sales Management 1930a). IBM initiated a "Future Demands Department" with the mandate to, "...Discover new needs in the business machine field and locate promising markets, then to build devices to meet specific demands," (Ehret 1929, p. 9). McNeice (1929) demonstrated how the profitability of individual items in a product line could be assessed using internal financial data. The International Silver Company employed a survey to aid management in product design (Dowd 1931). Westinghouse test marketed a new electric iron in Rochester. (White 1930). A year later, interviews of about 1000 product users furnished a product name and suggested directions for advertising copy and merchandising plans.

In addition, in a vein more akin to marketing research rather than market research, marketing processes were researched. How advertising budgets of industrial firms were distributed across various expenditures (e.g., conventions, house organs) was researched (Sales Management 1929). Smith (1934) discussed how consumer's demand for specific brands at point-of-purchase differed across products (e.g., paints versus automobiles) and buying situations (e.g., grocery versus drug stores).

From these examples, it is evident that market research was heavily dependent on the survey method of data collection. Converse (1987), in a history of American survey methods, concluded that business, and marketing in particular, pioneered the field during the 1920s and early 1930s.

Of the concerns of market researchers during this period, two appear predominant. The first relates to the determination of sample sizes. Market researchers relied on an odd variety of quota sampling and experience, as opposed to probability sampling methods. Clark (1929) suggested the scope of the investigation, influential factors (e.g., whether geographical differences exist), quantitative versus qualitative factors and the number of important dependent variables could all be used to help determine the required sample size.

Sample sizes were sometimes calculated by adding observations until estimates of percentages or means stabilized to an acceptable level. This often led, by contemporary standards, to exorbitant sample sizes. For example, the International Silver Company surveyed 15,000 consumers in its study, asking each to select his/her first and second most preferred silverware design among ten alternatives (Dowd 1931). In a study of brand preferences in Milwaukee, 6,700 housewives were surveyed (Sales Management 1936). Blood (1935) suggested 10,000 responses were required before estimates stabilize in consumer studies, while only 250 were required in dealer research.

326

Market researchers of the period tended to rely on what will be called the "eyeball" method (i.e., they focused on obviously large differences among group means or proportions). However, statistical theory states that increasing sample size generally leads to decreasing sampling error. It follows that when the "eyeball" method is used, the likelihood of Type I error decreases as sample size increases. This implies that the relevance of inferential statistics to market research was limited during this period. One could even conclude that inferential statistics was incompatible with the dominant market research methods, leading to the possibility that market research procedures were an obstacle, or a perceived obstacle, to the adoption of techniques.

The second predominant concern revolved around question wording. Market researchers stressed the importance of making questions easy to understand and of not asking misleading or biased questions. Most of the reviewed market research texts discussed question wording (see, for example, Reilly 1929, p. 82; White 1927, p. 62-63). Articles also appeared in the trade press on how to write unbiased questions (see, for example, Franken 1927; Sales Management 1930b).

During the 1920s and early 1930s, the objectives of the American Statistical Association focused on collecting and combining data (Harshbarger 1976). A similar emphasis was found in the reviewed market research texts. The purpose of collecting data is to aid management in marketing decision-making. As shown, market researchers were addressing a wide variety of questions associated with the identification of markets, sales forecasting, product design, product line analysis, new product test marketing and competitor analysis. This suggests that few new basic market research questions have since been identified. The ultimate adoption of inferential statistics could represent a refinement of the decision-making process. The adoption of inferential statistics certainly does not represent any change in market research objectives. This supports Fullerton's (1988, p. 122) contention that the period of marketing since 1930 is, "The era of refinement and formalization."

The skills that market research texts passed along to readers were closely linked to the collection and intrepetation of data. These skills, coupled with a thorough understanding of measures of central tendency, proportions and tabulation, would allow a researcher to correctly answer important, meaningful market-related questions, especially in conjunction with large sample sizes. Therefore, the texts of the period appear to have passed along precisely what was needed. Apparently not required was knowledge of advanced inferential statistics.

As a final note, Reilly (1929) was the first American market research textbook author found in this research to adopt inferential statistics. It is interesting that he applied inferential statistics only to proportions. This is probably more than mere coincidence since the market research texts and articles

examined here used proportions more often than any other summary
measure, including mean and mode, to convey survey results.

SUMMARY AND CONCLUSIONS

This research sought to determine the degree to which known,
readily available statistical methods were not being expounded by
market research textbook authors during the 1915-1937 time period.
A content analysis indicated that market research text authors did
not include much beyond measures of central tendency.

The omission of more complex methods was explained within an
adoption of innovation framework. Three factors were examined.
First, Fisher's battles with other leading statisticians, his
enigmatic writing style and his tendency to publish in obscure
outlets may all have slowed that rate at which his innovations were
adopted.

Second, the teaching of statistics at the university level
appears to have been limited and the introductory courses that were
taught focused on descriptive statistics. An infrastructure able
to provide a market large enough to digest advanced statistics in
market research textbooks may not have existed. Also, the
complexity and lack of observability and trialability that
characterize statistics could be important factors which affected
the adoption rate.

Lastly, market research practices could have precluded the
need for widespread use of inferential statistics. There is
evidence that market researchers relied on large sample sizes and
large differences in estimates thereby alleviating the need for
inferential statistics. The decision-making objective of market
research has changed little over the years and the ultimate
adoption of inferential statistics could merely represent more
efficient decision-making.

REFERENCES

Aaker, David A. and Day, George S. 1983. Market Research. Chicago:
     The Dryden Press.
Bartels, Robert 1976. The History of Marketing Thought. Columbus,
     OH: Grid, Inc., Second Edition.
Blood, Howard 1935. "Comparative Research." Printers' Ink 172
     (August 22) 37+.
Bowley, Arthur L. 1926. Elements of Statistics. London: P.S.
     King and Sons, Ltd., Fifth Edition.
Brown, Lyndon O. 1937. Market Research and Analysis. New York: The
     Ronald Press Company.
Camp, Burton H. 1930. The Mathematical Part of Elementary
     Statistics. New York: D.C. Heath and Company.
Chaddock, Robert E. 1926. "The Function of Statistics in
     Undergraduate Training." Journal of the American Statistical
     Association 21 (March) 1-8.

Charnes, A., Cooper, W.W., Learner, D.B. and Phillips, F.Y. 1985. "Management Science and Marketing Management." Journal of Marketing 49 (Spring) 93-105.

Churchill, Gilbert A. Jr. 1987. Market Research. New York: John Wiley and Sons.

Clark, Stanley I. 1929. "How Many Questionnaire Replies Give an Accurate Answer?" Printers' Ink 148 (July 18) 17-20.

Converse, Jean M. 1987. Survey Research in the United States: Roots and Emergence 1890-1960. Los Angeles: University of California Press.

Copeland, M.T. 1917. Business Statistics. M.T. Copeland (ed.). London: Oxford University Press.

Crum, William L. and Patton, Alson C. 1925. An Introduction to the Methods of Economic Statistics. New York: A.W. Shaw and Company.

Davis, Harold T. 1937. Elements of Statistics with Application to Economic Data. Bloomington, IN: The Principa Press, Inc., Second Edition.

Day, Edmond E. 1932. Statistical Analysis. New York: The Macmillan Company.

Dittmer, Clarence G. 1926. Introduction to Social Statistics. New York: A.W. Shaw Company.

Dowd, Leo 1931. "How International Silver Pre-Tested Product Designs." Sales Management 25 (January 17) 112.

Duncan, C.S. 1922. Commercial Research. New York: The Macmillan Company.

Ehret, Clement 1929. "International Business Machines Inagurates a Future Demand Department." Sales Management 18 (April 6) 9-10.

Elmer, Manual C. 1926. Social Statistics: Statistical Methods Applied to Sociology. Los Angeles: Press of Jesse Ray Miller.

Franken, Richard B. 1927. "How to Get Unprejudiced Market Data." Printers' Ink 139 (April 21) 127-8+.

Fisher, Ronald A. 1925. Statistical Methods for Research Workers. Edinburgh: Oliver and Boyd.

Forsyth, C.H. 1924. An Introduction to the Mathematical Analysis of Statistics. New York: John Wiley and Sons, Inc.

Fullerton, Ronald A. 1988. "How Modern is Modern Marketing? Marketing's Evolution and the Myth of the "Production Era"." Journal of Marketing 52 (January) 198-225.

Gatignnon, Hubert and Robertson, Thomas S. 1985. "A Propositional Inventory for New Diffusion Research." Journal of Consumer Research 11 (March) 849-67.

Glover, James W. 1926. "Statistical Teaching in American Colleges and Universities." Journal of the American Statistical Association 21 (December) 419-24.

Harshbarger, Boyd 1976. "History of the Early Developments of Modern Statistics in America (1920-1944)." in On the History of Statistics and Probability. D.B. Owen (ed.). New York: Marcel Dekker, Inc.

Hotelling, Harold 1927. Book Review of "Statistical Methods for Research Workers." by R.A. Fisher. Journal of the American Statistical Association 22 (September) 411-2.

Kelly, Truman 1924. Statistical Method. New York: The Macmillan Company.

Kent, Frederick C. 1924. <u>Elements of Statistical Method</u>. New York: McGraw-Hill Book Company.

King, Willford I. 1913. <u>The Elements of Statistical Method</u>. New York: The Macmillan Company.

_____ 1926. "Content and Purpose of Training in Elementary and in Advanced Statistics." <u>Journal of the American Statistical Association</u> 21 (December) 430-5.

Mantel, Nathen 1976. "Statistical Techniques for Quasi Experiments." in <u>On the History of Statistics and Probability</u>. D.B. Owen (ed.). New York: Marcel Dekker, Inc.

McNiece, Thomas M. 1929. "Are There Profitless Black Sheep in Your Line of Products?" <u>Sales Management</u> 18 (June 22) 591-2+.

Reed, Virgil L. 1929. <u>Planned Marketing</u>. New York: The Ronald Press Company.

Reilly, W.J. 1929. <u>Marketing Investigations</u>. New York: The Ronald Press Company.

Robertson, Thomas S. and Gatingnon, Hubert 1986. "Competitive Effects of Technology Diffusion." <u>Journal of Marketing</u> 50 (July) 1-12.

<u>Sales Management</u> 1929. "New Survey Shows How Technical Advertising Budget is Spent." 20 (October 5) 20+.

_____ 1930 a. "Building Forecasts Show Seven to Nine Billion Dollars for 1930." 21 (February 8) 246+.

_____ 1930 b. "The ABC's of Casting a Sales Research Questionnaire." 23 (September 20) 430+.

_____ 1936. "4-Year Analysis Shows Changes in Brand Preferences in Milwaulkee." 38 (April 20) 648-9.

Secrist, Horace 1925. <u>An Introduction to Statistical Methods</u>. New York: The Macmillan Company.

Shaw, Arch W. 1916. <u>An Approach to Business Problems</u>. Cambridge, MA: Harvard University Press.

Smith, Everett R. 1934. "Brand Selection at Counter in 36.9% of Sales." <u>Printers' Ink</u> 169 (December 27) 35-6+.

Snedecor, George W. 1937. <u>Statistical Methods Applied to Experiments in Agriculture and Biology</u>. Ames, IO: Collegiate Press.

Starch, Daniel 1923. <u>Principles of Advertising</u>. New York: A.W. Shaw Company.

Tankard, James W. Jr. 1984. <u>The Statistical Pioneers</u>. Cambridge, MA: Schenkman Publishing Company, Inc.

Thurstone, L. 1925. <u>The Fundamentals of Statistics</u>. New York: The Macmillan Company.

Walker, Helen M. 1927. <u>Studies in the History of Statistical Method</u>. Baltimore: The William and Wilkins Company.

Wheeler, Ferdinand C. 1937. <u>The Technique of Marketing Research</u>. New York: McGraw-Hill Book Company, Inc.

White, Percival 1927. <u>Advertising Research</u>. New York: D. Appleton and Company.

_____ 1930. "Don't Plunge Wildly on New Products - Test Your Market." <u>Sales Management</u> 24 (November 8) 225+.

_____ 1931. <u>Marketing Research Technique</u>. New York: Harper and Brothers.

[33]

The Art of Marketing Research: Selections from Paul F. Lazarsfeld's "Shoe Buying in Zurich" (1933)

Ronald A. Fullerton
Southeastern Massachusetts University

The market research studies done in Central Europe by Paul F. Lazarsfeld's Institute for Economic Psychology from 1926–1933 are unheralded classics of market analysis. Prefiguring today's "post-modernist" inquiry, they probe consumers' behavior with astonishing depth, power, and sensitivity. A translation of major sections from one report is presented here with an introductory commentary.

INTRODUCTION

Paul F. Lazarsfeld (1901–1976) was one of the greatest social scientists of this century. Most famous in later life as a sociologist, Lazarsfeld was a major figure in American as well as European marketing thought during the 1930s and 1940s (Blankenship 1942; Converse 1987, especially p. 105; Kassarjian 1989). Presented here are selections from "Shoe Buying in Zurich," a market research report done in 1933 by a team under his direction. It was completed in May of that year, a few months before Lazarsfeld left his native Austria for the United States.[1] Like the other market research studies which Lazarsfeld had directed during the previous several years, this was remarkably advanced for its time, embodying ways of analyzing consumer behavior which retain the power to inspire our investigations today. It is at once a valuable historical document and a classic of market analysis.

"Shoe Buying in Zurich" was the third study of shoe buying conducted by Lazarsfeld's Institute for Economic Psychology (*Wirtschaftspsychologische Forschungsstelle*)

at the University of Vienna; it followed investigations done in Vienna and Berlin. It is based on detailed interviews with 900 respondents in Zurich; the interviews were conducted by university students and recent graduates, possibly under the direction of Hans Zeisel, Lazarsfeld's closest colleague and informal second-in-command (Wagner 1989). While it is not known if Lazarsfeld himself came to Zurich, the study design, questionnaire formulation, and above all the interpretation of results were largely his work: colleagues have unanimously attested to Lazarsfeld's active directing style (Bartos 1986; Jahoda 1983; Wagner 1989; Zeisel 1979). The report is written according to the guidelines which Lazarsfeld promulgated in training sessions for Institute members (Lazarsfeld 1933).

The Zurich shoe study illustrates the innovative approach to marketing research for which Lazarsfeld was rapidly becoming known in both Europe and the United States, and which had enormous influence from the 1930s well into the 1950s. Soon after coming to the United States, he described his approach in the *Harvard Business Review* (Lazarsfeld 1934), marketing journals (1935, 1937a), and in the four chapters he was invited to write for the recently-formed American Marketing Association's handbook on marketing research (Wheeler 1937, Chapters 3, 4, 11, 15). Briefly, Lazarsfeld's approach was to begin with in-depth interviews of hundreds of consumers, using sophisticated questionnaires, then interpret the results with a probing and elegant combination of statistical analysis, the depth psychologies of Freud and others, and experimental psychology. Sometimes other disciplines were utilized as well.

In each of his publications on market research methodology, Lazarsfeld developed his arguments with examples of research done by the Vienna Institute. The shoe studies figured prominently. Decades later he still referred to them with pride (e.g., Lazarsfeld 1960). It is clear that the bulk of Lazarsfeld's published[2] thought on marketing research was developed while he directed market studies in Central Europe.

Journal of the Academy of Marketing Science
Volume 18, Number 4, pages 319-327.
Copyright © 1990 by Academy of Marketing Science.
All rights of reproduction in any form reserved.
ISSN 0092-0703.

THE ART OF MARKETING RESEARCH: FULLERTON
SELECTIONS FROM PAUL F. LAZERSFELD'S "SHOE BUYING IN ZURICH"

The translation which appears below is the first publication in any language of one of these studies, hence a first
look at important work by one of modern marketing's old
masters. More than twenty commercial projects had preceded it, allowing Lazarsfeld and his colleagues to hone
their methods. Intrinsically interesting, the work also has
considerable relevance for today's academics and practitioners. Its fine balance between statistical tables and statements
given by consumers in detailed interviews, shows that the
marriage of the quantitative and the qualitative may be amic-
able as well as fecund. Its searching analysis of consumers'
experiences prefigures the broadened approach towards
which today's "post modernist" consumer researchers appear
to be moving (See Thompson, Locander, and Pollio 1989).
Written at a time when the classical economists' vision of
an omniscient, super-rational, coolly calculating consumer
was taken quite seriously even by practicing businessmen,
this report showed many consumers to be groping in a fog
of half-knowledge, some of them tormented with anxieties
and uncertainties about shoe purchases.

These consumers are *real*. Distant from us in time and
space, they are, to this author, truer-to-life than the desic-
cated specimens who still populate some of our contemporary marketing and consumer behavior literature. "Shoe Buying in Zurich" captures a consumer dilemma which introspection will tell us is by no means extinct today—we know
what we want but are simply unable to judge which product
offering really offers it, hence we grasp at surrogates. On
another note no classical economist could have hit, the report
analyzes the erotic effect of young female salespeople on
male customers, then speculates that a similar effect might
apply to women.

The penetration achieved here was due to Lazarsfeld's
innovations in both questioning and in interpreting results.
He envisioned purchasing as an intricate process occurring
over time, in which personal characteristics, outside influences, and product attributes were all in play. The actual
act of buying was only one part of it. To evoke consumers'
experience of the full process, Lazarsfeld devised "detailed"
questions, that is, searching open-ended queries (Lazarsfeld
1935, 1937a, 1937b). These questions were made as
specific, concrete, and clear as possible, in order to stimulate
consumers' memories (Lazarsfeld 1932). Respondents were
asked about their most recent actual purchase of a product,
then taken back along a time line to past purchases. Questions probed what was done and what happened in each
case, from the first sensation of perceived need through the
complete experience of product usage; further questions
explored what the respondent believed should have ideally
happened in each case (Lazarsfeld 1932; "*Verkaeufer und
Kunde,*" ca. 1933). Interviewers, who were selected from
the cream of university students and graduates,[3] were trained
to press for concrete replies (Wagner, ca. 1932). The
rationale for specific questions was that they elicited far
more from people's memories than general queries would
have. Judging from the replies cited in this and other Institute
reports, respondents certainly did open up. Zurichers report-
edly responded with enthusiasm because they perceived the
shoe buying questions as a positive new manifestation of
democracy (Herzog 1933).

Responses were full and enthusiastic, but were they true?
Could they be a basis on which to orient marketing efforts?
It was a common objection to market research at that time
(especially in Europe) that most people did not remember
accurately, and often did not know what they wanted even
when they did remember. Lazarsfeld's counterargument
(1932, 1933, 1934) was subtle but powerful. Of course it
was impossible to verify the accuracy of people's memories,
he agreed, but accuracy was not the key issue. What really
mattered, however, was possible—to *compare* and *interpret*
remembered experiences, looking for underlying meanings
and patterns. If people did not always know what they really
wanted, or why they made the decisions which they did,
careful analysis of their statements could uncover these
things.

As the author of a recent history of survey research concludes, Lazarsfeld has had few peers as an interpreter of
market research (Converse 1987, p. 137). Comparing his
studies with those reported by Link (1932) being done by
psychologists in the United States at the same time, one is
struck by the vastly greater depth of the Viennese work. In
interpreting consumer experience, Lazarsfeld drew upon a
rich, multi-disciplined conceptual framework; he knew
many of the people, and most of the work which made
1920's Vienna one of the world's great intellectual centers—
Einstein, Freud, and Wittgenstein were only a few of those
active there (See Zeisel 1967).

As the hundreds of thick questionnaires were brought back
from Zurich, Lazarsfeld read and re-read them, discussed
them with Institute colleagues in seminars, discussed them
informally with others, encouraged interviewers to discuss
them, and read them some more (Wagner 1989). Replies
were tabulated, totalled, and analyzed statistically for distributions, correlations, index numbers, and percentages—
all by hand. Cross tabulation tables, among the earliest in
empirical research, were drawn up—again by hand (Bartos
1986). A master of hand tabulation, Lazarsfeld found enormous pleasure and satisfaction in attacking towering stacks
of completed questionnaires (Neurath 1989). It was fortunate
that he did, for the Institute lacked the high speed punched
card counter-sorters some American market researchers used
then (See Wheeler 1937, Chapter 14). It had no adding
machine. Indeed, its only "equipment" was a second-hand
typewriter and shared access to a mimeograph machine.

Eventually Lazarsfeld would have a complete and unified
interpretation, drawn from statistical as well as verbal an
alysis.[4] "Shoe Buying in Zurich" provides several examples
of Lazarsfeld's interpretational virtuosity. Lazarsfeld himself was proudest of finding the inferiority complex among
some shoe buyers. This complex had been identified by the
famous Viennese psychologist Alfred Adler, of whose work
Lazarsfeld was well aware.[5] The idea to apply the inferiority
complex came to Lazarsfeld from an introspective report
given by one of the interviewers in the Vienna shoe study;
he then went through the questionnaires to see if the idea
fit the reply data. Introspection was a favorite technique of
the psychologist Karl Buehler, Lazarsfeld's mentor at the
University of Vienna and nominal head of the Institute.

A second example also drew on work in linguistic analysis
by Buehler and other Viennese thinkers of the time. In

THE ART OF MARKETING RESEARCH:
SELECTIONS FROM PAUL F. LAZERSFELD'S "SHOE BUYING IN ZURICH"

FULLERTON

analyzing respondents' statements about what quality they wanted most in shoes, Lazarsfeld reasoned that the more important would be spoken first: "The respondents each cite *several desired qualities* in their answers. But if one examines the first word in these answers, then the desire for good fit comes more closely to the fore."

The third example appears in the discussion of buyers' reactions to window displays. Comparing stated evaluations of "good" and "bad" displays with actual purchases, Lazarsfeld noticed discrepancies between attitudes and actions— 35% of those queried had bought shoes in stores with displays they judged "bad." U.S. researchers were also detecting and analyzing similar discrepancies in several product markets (Link 1932, pp. 42–45). What distinguishes Lazarsfeld's work is the attempt to probe and to explicate the reasons for the discrepancy. The consumer's evaluation of a display, he decided, was based upon the overall impression which it made; but if in an overall "bad" display there was one shoe which the consumer found appealing, he or she might well purchase it. "In other words," Lazarsfeld explained, "alongside the overall impression made by a display, there are the separate impressions made by *individual shoes*." The client was advised that "The issue of *right* display is to pay heed to the display's double function: conveying an *overall style* while also providing sufficient *selection possibilities*."

Overall, the report evinces a sophisticated understanding of marketing. Segmentation is clearly addressed, as is the distinction between immediate and long-term effects of advertising. The whole report is based on the premise that by probing and analyzing from multiple perspectives it will be possible to identify the consumer's true needs, and eventually for the. client firm to meet those needs.

The Shoe Retailing Scene in Zurich

Reading the full report, it is clear that shoe stores were numerous and appealed to several market segments. There were several chains, some of them manufacturer-owned. The stores were located downtown and in neighborhood shopping districts, where pedestrian traffic was high and window displays easily seen. Shoes must have been relatively more expensive to many people than they had been a few years before, since 1933 was the nadir of the Depression in Western Europe. This may account for the wistful tone so evident in many respondent comments.

A Note on the Translation

The full report has 98 pages in six parts; approximately 28 pages from Parts 2–4 have been translated here. The intent has been to capture the spirit as well as the letter of the original. Lazarsfeld (1933) wanted the Institute's reports to be interesting for clients to read. The German is clear, precise, and often colloquial. Throughout, numerical tables, citations from respondent statements, and short analytical paragraphs are carefully proportioned for a visually enticing text. Underlines are liberally used to highlight key ideas. Within tables, exclamation points are sometimes inserted to emphasize how striking or unexpected a finding is. Bursts

of citations (*Zitate*) convey the effect that consumers are coming forth to speak on this point or that; the citations appear as direct quotations but more likely are actually mixtures of quotations and paraphrased responses to open-ended questions as recorded by interviewers. To heighten the verisimilitude, the consumer responsible for each citation is identified by occupation, socio-economic class, and sometimes by age and sex.[6]

Last, but not least: the client firm liked this and the earlier shoe reports so much that they were reproduced and circulated for its retail managers and salespeople to read.

SHOE BUYING IN ZURICH

An Exploratory Study by the Institute for Economic Psychology, May 1933 (Excerpts translated by Ronald A. Fullerton)

The Right Salesperson

[ABSTRACT] What the customer wants from a shoe salesperson, what are his experiences with the salesperson, what are the main issues of good shoe salesmanship.

General Wants

We employed the following two questions to inform ourselves about the public's opinion regarding shoe salespeople:

What role did the salesperson play in your latest shoe purchase?

What should the salesperson be like (i.e., your wishes and criticisms)?

The answers about experiences with shoe salespeople during the most recent purchase were highly *positive*:

	(%)
Positive	81 (!)
Negative	19
	100

Respondents over 25 (i.e., the "old") talked about salespeople far more than did the young. While each young shopper made an average of 1.1 statements, we heard an average of 2.4 from shoppers over 25. This is doubtless due in part to the latter's greater experience, and in part to the fact that *salespeople* play a *larger role* in their buying.

The frequency of remarks about salespeople is the same for males and females, so that no distinction can be made in this regard.

We consider next buyers' *wants* concerning salespeople, which we will then compare to their actual *experiences* with them. To give a better overview, we group wants concerning salespeople into two large categories, one regarding salespeople's technical, objective, *competence (Sachlichkeit)* and the second dealing with their *social*, personal, qualities and characteristics.

The first category includes all wants of the following nature: the salesperson should "provide alert and rapid service," should be "an expert," should be able to "give advice," and should know to bring out a large selection of shoes for inspection.

We will refer to this group of wants as the desire for an *active* kind of competence, in contrast to the desire for the more *neutral*—restrained—competence which we will explain shortly. First a few examples of the desire for active competence:

A stenotypist from [socioeconomic] class B1[7]: "The salesperson should bring out a *large selection.*"

A commercial artist: "A salesman should *never serve two customers at the same time.* He should find the correct shoe as quickly as possible. He *must* be calm and *competent.*"

A housewife: "The saleslady should be able to *advise* me as to what suits me best. Sometimes a stranger knows better than oneself."

Still others want these traits of competence to be coupled with a certain professional reserve, or *neutrality.* By this is meant that the salesperson should "not want to talk one into something"; that he should explain "not only a shoe's advantages" but also "its disadvantages; and that he "shouldn't take up too much of one's time."

A few examples of such wishes about salesperson behavior:

Housewife: "The saleslady should *not talk too much* in the effort to thrust something upon one—I *know myself exactly what I want.*"

Assistant: "One should *give me what I ask for, not be wanting to convince me that I should wear another kind of shoe.*"

Lawyer: "The saleslady took up *too much of my time,* she was determined to sell me shoes other than those which I had selected. She should comply with my wishes in *a thoroughly businesslike manner.*"

In contrast to these desires emphasizing the salesperson's technical competence, those falling into the second major category of wants express the desire for a certain *social demeanor* on the part of the salesperson: he should be "friendly," "amiable," "accommodating," should "show interest," and should "be able to put himself in the customer's place."

A stenotypist thus wishes: "The saleslady should be *obliging* and should be able to be sympathetically understanding to the clientele."

A university student: "The salesladies *shouldn't stand around looking bored* when one comes into the shop."

An ironer [in a cleaner's]: "In the first place a salesperson should *be friendly*, even when it's not exactly the most expensive shoe that's going to be purchased."

Alongside these wishes for *socially expressive activity* are wishes for socially restrained *neutral behavior*: the salesperson should be "not pushy," "modest," "as inconspicuous as possible". All of the "specific qualities" desired in the salesperson also belong in this group. He should be "sincere," look "neat and well-groomed," and the like.

A university student: "Above all a salesman must be *unobtrusive.*"

A merchant: "The salesman must *look neat,* then one buys more and happily."

A teacher (female): "A saleslady must be able to *give advice in a calm manner,* allowing one time to think things over."

We obtain from our research the following division of wants about the salesperson: he/she should be:

	(%)	(%)
Technically competent		
active	28	
neutral	20	58[8]
Social demeanor		
active	26	
neutral	16	42
		100

The Inferiority Complex of the Shoe Buyer

When we compare buyers' wants with their actual *experiences* during their most recent shoe purchase, the following distribution emerges. Shoe sellers' qualities of competence and the social demeanor are praised by the following percentages of buyers (We have put in parentheses in the right column buyers' wants as reported in the previous section):

Technical competence	75%	(58%)
Social demeanor	25	(42)
	100%	100%

This means that in 42 of 100 cases people want a good "social" experience. But that wish is fulfilled in only 25 of these same 100 cases. Thus the greater part of the shoppers, including those who did make purchases, were *not satisfied* with the salesperson's *willingness to oblige.* Exactly how long and strongly personal resentment against an unsatisfactory salesperson can linger, is shown by the following statement:

"At . . . [name of store] the service was *friendly* and pleasant, though I do believe that they did not give me the correct size. In . . . [name of another store] the following happened to me many years ago: they served a well-dressed lady who came in *after me,*

THE ART OF MARKETING RESEARCH:
SELECTIONS FROM PAUL F. LAZERSFELD'S "SHOE BUYING IN ZURICH"

ahead of me. I can still remember clearly how they let me sit there." (Cloak-room attendant, B1).

Again, a landlady told an anecdote about a salesperson which had occurred some time in the past:

"The following happened to me three years ago: in response to my request to see *a larger selection*, the saleslady replied '*Yes, we have others but they're too expensive for you.*' That was very unpleasant for me."

In our other shoe market investigations [in Berlin and Vienna], we have also found this peculiar frame of mind to surround the shoe salesperson, and have at last concluded that we must speak of a specific shoe buyer *inferiority complex*. The complex is engendered by his/her special situation. We cite the report of a Viennese respondent who is trained in the technique of introspection. The report clearly articulates this remarkable frame of mind:

"I rarely feel so *uncomfortable* as I do when buying shoes. One has the feeling of being *totally exposed* to the shop's people. To begin with, one isn't sure that there may not be a *hole in his sock*. Then one has to sit there for a while with no shoes on, feeling totally undressed and completely at the mercy of the salesperson. Whatever happens, one cannot get away quickly, even if nothing suitable is found, because the shoes have to be put back on again. Often I *buy shoes against* my better judgement and then never go back to that store."

Among respondents who are less accustomed to introspection the disquiet takes the form of *criticism* directed at some trifle or other, in which this singular feeling of insecurity is nevertheless clearly evident.

"I had exactly this experience at . . . [name of store] and at . . . [name of another store], that the girl on duty was immediately and openly *unfriendly and lazy*. Brings out only the bare minimum and when asked about a greater selection says, 'Yes we have more but they'd be too expensive for you.' Her kind *hurts the store so*. (Polisher, female, A1).

"At . . . [name of store] the salesgirl made me *wait a long time*. On Saturdays there should be extra sales help there, because one gets *very annoyed* at having to wait in a shoe store." (Hairdresser, A1).

One observes that, as the last respondent said, people do get annoyed at having to wait in a shoe store. On the other hand, they always react with gratitude when the *astute salesperson* seeks to *ease* the buyer's inferiority complex.

A male university student reported: "The salesgirl was very *pretty*. She stressed that I·*could only wear expensive, distinguished, shoes*. That amused me."

A household helper: "I wanted to know what my feet needed. A salesgirl checked my feet carefully, 'X-rayed them,'[9] and was very concerned and pleasant towards me. I bought then because I did not want to disappoint the nice girl."

The Salesperson as Advisor

The shoe buyer's peculiar psychological situation makes it understandable that the salesperson plays a very special role in shoe retailing. . . . Approximately half of all shoe buyers are regular customers at a specific shop. 15% of these buyers say that they remain loyal because of the store's sales help; while, on the other hand, 13% of those who will not buy in a certain shop any more report that they do so because of unpleasant sales help. A consequence of the salesperson's vital role is that there is a second sore point in shoe buying in which the salesperson is of great importance.

When we ask our shoppers what is the most important quality in shoes, they give answers like these:

"Above all it should be *comfortable*, nice in appearance, and *hold its shape well*." (Boarding house owner, B2).

"The shoe must be *comfortable*, the shape of the heel must please me, and it must be made of *good* material." (Manager, female, B2).

"Above all the shoes should be *comfortable*, that is, they should have the necessary arch support. Also, they should have *sewn casings*." (Household helper, B2).

"The shoe must have a slender shape, be made of soft, flexible, leather, and have medium-height heels." (Household helper, B2).

"With regards to a dancing [i.e., dress] shoe it must above all: 1) fit well, 2) look elegant, and 3) go with one's clothing. Work and sport shoes should: 1) fit comfortably, 2) hold their shape well, and 3) be waterproof." (University coed, B2).

"The shoe should *keep its shape* and make one's foot look beautiful. It should look *elegant* and *interesting*, not like a commonplace thing." (University coed, B2).

"The shoe should *fit* but not *pinch*. It shouldn't be of some fussy color and shouldn't be too expensive." (University student, B2).

"Shoes for daily use should above all be *waterproof*. Sunday shoes should be *light*, beautifully worked, and of a somewhat pointed cut." (Temporary office worker, A1).

"The shoes must correspond to the form of the foot, the leather must *be strong*, and they must *be inexpen-*

THE ART OF MARKETING RESEARCH:
SELECTIONS FROM PAUL F. LAZERSFELD'S "SHOE BUYING IN ZURICH"

FULLERTON

sive, because it doesn't make sense any more to pay a lot." (Doctor, C2).

A statistical overview of these answers shows that they distribute themselves as follows. The emphasis is on:

	Men (%)	Women (%)
Fit	42	36
Appearance and color	31	33
Quality	16	14
Price	7	9
Other	4	8
	100	100

Thus the clearly dominant desire is for shoes to fit well.

How much this is so is shown by the following detail: the respondents each cite *several desired qualities* in their answers. But if one examines the first word in these answers, then the desire for good fit comes more closely to the fore. The answers which the respondents are readiest to give now distribute themselves thus:

	Men (%)	Women (%)
Fit	67	37
Appearance and color	8	33
Quality	15	8
Price	6	1
Other	4	1
	100	100

The priority of fit is also shown by the fact that it above all qualities here is mentioned first in answers.

But there is a truly difficult dilemma connected with this priority of fit: during the purchasing process it is difficult for the shopper him or herself to determine which shoe fits correctly. One only really knows after wearing shoes for a while. In addition, it is also true that people simply do not know the problems of their own feet. As a result, during the purchasing process suitable fit inadvertently takes a back seat to external appearance. This is especially true of women. One sees this clearly in the statistics on respondents' answers to our question, "What was the main reason why you purchased your last pair of shoes?"

We show in parentheses the statistics on the main attributes sought in shoes. The comparison of these [with the main reason for the last purchase] is telling.

	Men (%)		Women (%)	
Fit	22 (!)	(42)	20 (!)	(36)
Appearance and color	44 (!)	(31)	52 (!)	(33)
Quality	15	(16)	13	(14)
Price	12	(7)	10	(9)
Other	7	(4)	5	(8)
	100	100	100	100

In fact, fit drops to scarcely half of the incidence of appearance and color. It appears therefore that buyers who consider proper fit crucial realize that it is difficult to succeed in finding it. They are thus easily inclined to bring to the *foreground*, such *outward manifestations* of the shoe as its appearance and shape. All the more do they wish, however, whether explicitly or implicitly, that the *salesperson would help* them to find shoes which fit well. One could almost say that for the average buyer a kind of "division of authority" is evoked. The buyer *him or herself* attends to the shoe's *appearance*, the *salesperson* attends to its correct *fit*. Quotations of the following type are not at all uncommon:

> "The feeling that the *salesgirl is genuinely interested* in bringing out and recommending a shoe which fits one well—this feeling contributes decisively to one judging a store positively. One doesn't want other, and unwanted, things palmed off on him." (Law student, C2).

> "The shoes at . . . [name of store] did not fit my feet, which are sensitive. They had no foot X-ray machine there. And at . . . [name of another store] there was no good fit." (Housewife, D1).

> "I want to know what my feet need. I would like *better service*, like at . . . [name of store]. At . . . [name of another store] the girl didn't want to show me any more, she was *really curt*." (Servant girl, A1).

> "The saleslady presented a large selection, she understood what I needed and gave *considerable* thought and *effort* to *satisfy me*. Salesladies should be more aware of the needs of heavy customers." (Housewife, D1).

> "*Friendly* but *dumb*. The girl *talked me into a pair* that didn't quite match my feet. I had to bring the shoes back and have them stretched. Originally I had wanted to buy a pair which had fit me exactly."[10]

Particularly in the last quotation it is striking how the customer went against her better knowledge to take shoes which the salesgirl had recommended as suitable.

Here we see an important area for the *training* of the *shoe salesperson*. We are not saying, it should be emphasized, that "the salesperson has to accede to the customers' wishes". After all, these wishes are to a large extent unclear and uncertain. Rather, we believe that it is the job of the salesperson to help the customer first of all by giving a *correct picture* of what his or her feet need. Relevant aids such as the X-ray machine play a major role for our respondents.

In addition, it is certainly important that the salesperson be correctly informed about foot anatomy. . . .

Men and Women

It is interesting that age differences among respondents have no influence upon the proportions reporting positive experiences with salespeople's technical competence on the one hand, and with their social deportment on the other.

THE ART OF MARKETING RESEARCH: FULLERTON
SELECTIONS FROM PAUL F. LAZERSFELD'S "SHOE BUYING IN ZURICH"

Within the reported average of 25% good social experiences, respondents over 25 had 24% and those under had 27%, hence a strong constancy. There appears, however, to be a noticeable difference in attitudes among the *sexes*. The contrast between desired and actual experiences among male shoe buyers is quite different from that found among females. Desires about salespeople are distributed as follows:

	Men (%)	Women (%)	Average (%)
Technical competence	51	62	58
Social demeanor	49	38	42
	100	100	100

Men's socially-related wants are thus somewhat greater than those of women. When we now place the men's desires next to their reported experiences, we get this table:

	Wishes (%)	Good (actual) experience (%)
Technical competence	51	61
Social demeanor	49	39
	100	100

The analogous table for women looks like this:

	Wishes (%)	Good (actual) experience (%)
Technical competence	62	81
Social demeanor	38	19 (!)
	100	100

Thus among men good experience with the personality and social deportment of the salespeople comes very close to what they had hoped for, while among women there is a marked gap. This may well be explained by the fact that most of the salespeople in shoe stores are female, and that their erotic effect upon men swells the percentage of satisfaction. We find this confirmed in some of the statements made by respondents:

A university student: "Ah, . . . [name of store], there's a very *beautiful girl* there."

A merchant: "Next time I'm certainly going to go to . . . [name of store], for there's a *bewitching girl* who waits on you there."

One can surmise that there is an analogous effect of male salespersons upon female customers. This possibility should be tested out.

Window Displays

[ABSTRACT:] The problems connected with window displays will be enumerated . . . It should be noted at the outset that in a study of this scope it is neither *intended* nor *possible* to solve all of the detailed problems of display arrangements.

Displays

The extraordinary importance of shop window displays for shoe retailing hardly needs to be proven. We would like, nevertheless, to show the dramatic statistics which demonstrate this, and have therefore analyzed our research findings to show the reasons, other than habit, for *choosing a shoe store*:

	(%)
Displays	54
Advertising	4
Recommendation and reputation	31
Other (proximity, personal connection, etc.)	11
	100

This means that over half of the reasons for choosing a shoe store have to do with display. . . .

"Good" and "Bad" Displays

Experts are well aware that people's judgments of "good" and "bad" displays are highly relative. This display pleases the one customer but not the other, and so forth—and what makes things still more complicated is the fact that not infrequently one buys in the store with a "bad" display and avoids making his purchases in that with a "good" display.

This tricky and complex situation was revealed through the following technique in our inquiry: we asked people to give a specific *example* of a good display. . . .

We instructed our researchers to, after they had elicited from respondents an example of a store with a good display, ask the respondents if they did in fact make a purchase at the cited store.

In no less than 56% of the cases the answer was "no," so that one can see a pervasive discord between the *theoretical* and the *practical* points of view here.

Perhaps even more telling is the fact that 35% had made a purchase from a store *despite judging its display "bad."*

Such incongruity in no way means that respondents are untrue to their own evaluative beliefs when they cite a store's display as exemplary. Rather, their theoretical position on whether a display is "good" or "bad" is based upon *only one aspect* of the display, namely its style.

In other words, one's characterization of a display as good or bad is dependent upon whether its style is pleasing. This enjoyment in turn is based upon the *overall impression* made by the display, and not upon its details.

At the same time, however, there is a *second aspect* which contributes to a display's impact. This varies somewhat in effect from case to case, but always draws the gaze of the watcher in a totally different way than does the display's style. For alongside the overall impression made by a display, there are the separate impressions made by *individual shoes*; our statistics explicitly confirm the practitioner's experience that the customer's *seeking out* the right shoe in a display is an important element of the buying process.

Thus the issue of the, to use the more appropriate term, "*right*" display is to pay heed to the display's double func-

THE ART OF MARKETING RESEARCH: FULLERTON
SELECTIONS FROM PAUL F. LAZERSFELD'S "SHOE BUYING IN ZURICH"

tion: conveying an *overall style* while also providing sufficient *selection possibilities*. The display problem can only be
solved on a case by case basis, in each case carefully taking
into account the customer segments (*Kaeuferschichten*) for
whom the display is intended. . . .

Unsolved Problems

We noted at the beginning of this section that the solution
to the highly complex display problem was neither intended
nor possible within the confines of this [exploratory] report.
But let us suggest, however briefly, a way in which the
problem could be solved.

As follows logically from all of our prior discussion, it
is first of all a question of analyzing the social structure of
each store's clientele . . . [It requires] having at one's disposal a sufficient number of respondents for each and every
store so that customers can be grouped by their social class,
age, and sex, and so that in each of these groups there are
enough subjects. . . .

The method of investigation which we have employed in
this study does not capture the details of displays' impacts
upon people. The reason for this is, that when one questions
a buyer some time after an actual purchase, he/she can only
recall the broad overall effect of the display. Whether he
was drawn to this side or that of the display; whether he
lingered here or there or, on the other hand, if certain parts
of the display escaped his notice—these are questions which
can only be handled with research methods utilizing *direct
observation* of people looking at displays and their directly
subsequent purchase choices.

This means that extremely detailed observations are necessary, in order to in the first place determine the *visual effectiveness* of various arrangements.

Yet ascertaining visual effectiveness hardly answers all
of the questions involving displays. The greater part of the
investigation must use the following approach. The decisive
question about a display's effect is how much it stimulates
or encourages actual purchases. This, as we term it, "*real
effectiveness*" of a display can only be made clear through
the following method:

1. First, exacting statistics on the sales of shoes which
   are displayed must be compiled (*purchase statistics*).

2. During the time these are being compiled, systematic *variations* in the arrangement of the display must
   be carried out, in order to be able to control for the
   corresponding variations in sales figures.

3. Finally, extremely careful *observations of the act
   of purchase* itself will be used to ascertain the extent
   to which the buyer's verbal formulations in requesting shoes points to a definite effect which the display
   has had.

Only widespread investigation using this methodology
can inform us in detail how displays work. Make no mistake,
it is undeniable that an "experiment" of this type requires
some sacrifices from a retail firm. It is ultimately a question

of commercial rationality, how far one will go in carrying
out such experiments.

Advertising

[ABSTRACT:] What shoe advertising is known in Zurich,
what role is played by posters and [newspaper] ads. . . .

Short and Long-Term Effects

. . . The figures [on reasons for purchase] presented earlier
. . . convey only a tiny fraction of the actual impact of shoe
advertising. The table shows only cases where advertising
led directly to purchase. . . .

Before we explore the details of such [direct impact]
advertising, we want briefly to characterize the other extreme
of . . . shoe advertising—the *general* advertising . . . which
in no way intends to pull the customer directly from in front
of the poster into the store.

The effect of this [long term] advertising is slower to be
realized. As one respondent reported:

> "I looked at the . . . [name of firm's poster] *photo-
> graphs with great pleasure* and in fact did *buy*
> at . . . [name of firm] *a few weeks later*. Just now,
> as [you, the interviewer] were questioning me, it
> occurred to me that, that [purchase] was possibly
> connected with my pleasure in the poster. The [firm]
> name stayed in my mind though I could not re-
> member it exactly."

In this case the respondent was able to reconstruct the
connection in her conscious mind. But in the overwhelming
majority of cases people are naturally not able to do so, and
the effect of such advertising is much less palpable than
that of ways of advertising which propel people directly into
a shoe store.

Direct impact advertising is characterized by the following: in 73% of the cases which we recorded, respondents
said that the price offer made in an advertisement was the
decisive element for them.

> "When I saw that *low price* on a poster, I decided
> at once to try it out." (University student, B1).

> "I once bought on account of a newspaper ad—[for
> a] close out sale—but it was really the impact of
> the *low price* [mentioned in the ad]." (Nurse, B2).

This observation about the impact of price offers corre-
sponds to what we discovered in our research in Berlin.
There too we were able to determine that in *three quarters*
of the cases the *price* is the only part of advertising content
of which is taken note. The remainder of cases are where
specific, and especially welcome, *types of shoe* are noticed.

ACKNOWLEDGMENTS

This research has been supported by the Foundation and
by the College of Business and Industry of Southeastern

THE ART OF MARKETING RESEARCH: FULLERTON
SELECTIONS FROM PAUL F. LAZERSFELD'S "SHOE BUYING IN ZURICH"

Massachusetts University. I also want to acknowledge the help of Professor Paul Neurath, Director of the Lazarsfeld Archive at the University of Vienna, and Professor Guenther Schweiger of the Economic University of Vienna.

NOTES

1. Lazarsfeld came as the recipient of a Rockefeller Fellowship, which was granted him because of the Institute's now-classic study of long-term unemployment (Jahoda, Lazarsfeld, Zeisel 1971/orig. 1933) and also its market research studies. He intended to return to Austria, but the arrest of members of his family (which was active in Socialist politics and Jewish) by a new right-wing government in 1934 persuaded him to remain in the U.S. He founded institutes similar to the Vienna one at the University of Newark and later at Columbia University. See Neurath 1988.
2. Lazarsfeld's publication on market research ceased in 1937. He continued to conduct studies for over twenty years afterwards, often using newer methods—but this will be the subject of another paper.
3. The depressed economic conditions in Central Europe ensured that there were many bright students and otherwise idle graduates eager to work for the inevitably low pay the Institute provided. See Zeisel 1979.
4. The care which went into these studies led to their frequently being delivered late and costing more to produce than the fees charged to clients, according to Lazarsfeld's co-workers Wagner (1989) and Zeisel (1979).
5. Alfred Adler (1870–1937) was a then-famous psychologist who had worked with then broken with Freud. Lazarsfeld's mother Sophie had studied with Adler. His best known work is on the inferiority complex.
6. Socioeconomic class was determined by the interviewers. Four classes were identified for this report: D = rich people; C = upper middle class; B = lower middle class; and A = proletarians. Those sub-labelled "2", e.g. B2, derived their livelihoods from more intellectual activities than those labelled "1". Thus an "A2" female might be a salesgirl, an "A1" a maid. A doctor would be labelled "C2", the owner of a construction firm "C1". Sub-proletarians were not surveyed.
7. Lower middle class, income derived from less intellectual pursuit. See Note 6.
8. Numbers do not add up to 58% in the original—translator.
9. Some shoe stores had X-ray machines in which both buyer and salesperson could see through one's feet. These machines, which were also common in the U.S., were later taken out of use as too hazardous.
10. Respondent's profession and class omitted in original—translator.

REFERENCES

Bartos, Rena. 1986. Hans Ziesel [sic]: Forensic Sociologist," *Journal of Advertising Research* (Feb/Mar): 39–42.
Blankenship, Albert. 1942. "Psychological Difficulties in Measuring Consumer Preference." *Journal of Marketing* 6(4) Part 2: 66–75.
Converse, Jean M. 1987. *Survey Research in the United States: Roots and Emergence, 1890–1960.* Berkeley: University of California Press.
Herzog, Herta. 1933. Speech extolling market research done by the Institute for Economic Psychology. Lazarsfeld Archive, University of Vienna.

Jahoda, Marie. 1983. "The Emergence of Social Psychology in Vienna," *British Journal of Social Psychology* 22: 343–349.
Jahoda, Marie, Paul F. Lazarsfeld, and Hans Zeisel. 1971 [1933]. *Marienthal,* translated by John Reginall and T. Elsaesser. Chicago: Aldine-Atherton.
Kassarjian, Harold. 1989. Book Review, *Journal of Marketing* 53(1): 123–126.
Lazarsfeld, Paul F. 1932. "Neue Wege der Marktforschung," *Mitteilungen der Industrie-und Handelskammer zu Berlin* (October 25). Printed speech. Lazarsfeld Archive, University of Vienna.
———. 1933. "Gutachtenkurs." Parts I–V. July 20–28. Lazarsfeld Archive, University of Vienna.
———. 1934. "The Psychological Aspect of Marketing Research," *Harvard Business Review* 13(1): 54–71.
———. 1935. "The art of Asking WHY in Marketing Research," *National Marketing Review* 1: 32–43.
———. 1937a. "The Use of Detailed Interviews in Market Research," *The Journal of Marketing* 2(1): 3–8.
———. 1937b. Chapters 3, 4, 11, 15 in Ferdinand C. Wheeler et al., eds., *The Technique of Marketing Research.* New York and London: McGraw-Hill.
———. 1960. "Notes of January Seminar Session" (seminar on motivation in marketing and sales, Montreal). Lazarsfeld Archive, University of Vienna.
Link, Henry C. 1932. *The New Psychology of Selling and Advertising.* New York: Macmillan.
Neurath, Paul 1988. "Paul Lazarsfeld und die Anfaenge der modernen psychologischen Markt- und Konsumentenforschung in Wien," *Werbeforschung und Praxis* 33(2): 29–31.
———. 1989. Interviews with the author, June 12th, 14th, 21st.
"Schuhkauf in Zuerich. Eine Probeerhebung der Wirtschaftpsychologische Forschungstelle." 1933. Lazarsfeld Collection, Columbia University Library, Box 34.
Thompson, Craig J, William B. Locander, and Howard R. Pollio. 1989. "Putting Consumer Experience Back into Consumer Research: The Philosophy and Method of Existential-Phenomenology," *Journal of Consumer Research* 16(2): 133–146.
"Verkaeufer und Kunde. Wie der Kunde die Sache sieht" (n.d., ca. 1933). Typed report, Lazarsfeld Collection, Columbia University Library, Box 33.
Wagner, Gertrude. 1989. Interview with the author, June 23rd.
———. (n.d., ca. 1932). "Vortrag bei Prof. Buehler." Lazarsfeld Archive, University of Vienna.
Wheeler, Ferdinand C., Louis Bader, and J. George Frederick, eds. (1937). *The Technique of Marketing Research.* New York and London: McGraw-Hill.
Zeisel, Hans. 1967. "Die Wiener Schule der Motivforschung," presented at WAPOR-ESOMAR Conference. Lazarsfeld Archive, University of Vienna.
———. 1979. "The Vienna Years," in *Qualitative and Quantitative Social Research,* Robert K. Merton, J.S. Coleman, and P.H. Rossi, eds. New York: The Free Press, pp. 11–15.

ABOUT THE AUTHOR

Ronald A. Fullerton's interest in Central European contributions to marketing dates to a Harvard graduate seminar in 1965; his current research is exploring the work of Lazarsfeld and several other pre-World War II Central European scholars of market research and consumer behavior. Professor Fullerton is Associate Professor of Marketing at Southeastern Massachusetts University.

[34]

Excerpt from Hugh S. Hardy (ed.), *The Politz Papers: Science and Truth in Marketing Research*, 1–14.

1

Alfred Politz, the Man

In 1937, Alfred Politz, a 35-year-old native of Berlin, revulsed by the rise of Nazism in Germany, came to America to start a new life. He brought with him a Ph.D. in physics, 8 years of success in marketing and advertising research, a scanty knowledge of the English language, an athlete's body, boundless energy and—perhaps most important—an enormous ego and supreme confidence in himself.

With promised backing from an American businessman, Politz planned to start a company to make and market a well-known German headache remedy known as Spalt Tabletten. (It is still sold in Germany.) As part of his plan to escape Hitler's Germany, he had already marketed the product successfully in Sweden, and was given U.S. rights to the name and the formula by MUCH A.G., his former client.

Politz had been forced to flee Germany with only a small amount of cash and no further access to his considerable assets. When the U.S. Food and Drug Administration decided not to approve the Spalt Tabletten formula, he was left in a somewhat awkward position.

In a 1983 Advertising Age article titled, "He Was Called Everything From Genius to Nut",* columnist and writer Jack J. Honomichl quoted Mr. Politz as saying:

> " 'What to do? I arrived in New York and studied the problem,' Politz wrote in his personal papers long after retiring as a millionaire in 1967 and about a year before his death on November 8, 1982: 'Which profession makes the most money with the least intelligence? The answer was 'advertising'. But my English was not good enough for this field.' "

Honomichl continued:

> "He should have added, 'At least, not right away. . . .' That career choice, seen in retrospect, was momentous. Politz was to become a legend in his own time, a dynamic and controversial personage in the relatively—circa 1950s—unsophisticated field of advertising, research and marketing. Extremely critical of prevailing practices in all three, he especially deplored the lack of 'professionalism' and 'logic'. Although a middle-aged outsider with a heavy accent, he was an iconoclast who would prevail. In fact, there are admirers today who would argue that Alfred Politz had more impact and lasting influence in the fields of marketing/

---

*Later included as Chapter 13 in the book, "Honomichl on Marketing Research", by Jack J. Honomichl, published by National Textbook Company (Crain Books), Lincolnwood, Illinois. 1986.

2   The Politz Papers

advertising/research than William Bernbach, relatively, had in the field of advertising."

THE BEGINNING

Alfred Politz was born in Berlin on July 6, 1902. He was a precocious child with a prodigious mentality which was recognized very early. He wrote his first scientific paper as a teenager. As he himself wrote: "At the age of 15 I thought I had discovered something, and wrote a paper on it. . . . 'The Deduction of Gravity from the Concept of Mass'. I went to the Institute of Physics at Humboldt University in Berlin, which was headed by Gustav Hertz, the son of the discoverer of the Hertzian waves, Dr. Heinrich Rudolph Hertz. The younger Dr. Hertz, who was also an atomic physicist, was so amused by his visitor that at the next faculty meeting he told about the funny boy who thought he had made a major discovery. Max Planck, the German physicist who founded the quantum theory, was present and asked Hertz to contact me in order to arrange a meeting. I visited Max Planck at the university, and he suggested that I should sign up for theoretical physics when I entered university. In 1924 I passed my doctoral examination in Theoretical Physics."

It was a highly improbable beginning for a man who was to become a marketing legend in a new land, but there was never a doubt that Alfred Politz would succeed in some field.

After graduation, the logical next step was to teach and do scientific research, but the death of his father made it essential that he find a source of higher income to support his mother. Thus, outside of regular teaching, he taught evening classes to engineers who wanted to brush up on their math, and wrote short stories. The latter led to his success as a journalist, leading in turn to a position as advertising director of a large and prestigious publishing organization by the name of Rudolph Mosse, which also owned one of the largest advertising agencies in Germany.

Politz soon began to develop his own advertising theories, and challenged the conventional wisdom, circa 1929, by writing an article strongly critical of advertising practices and effectiveness. This article titled, "Advertising Psychology and Technique: Theory and Practice of Modern Advertising", appeared in the German trade magazine *Weltmacht-Reklame,* August 1929. (An English translation of this still-timely article is printed in its entirety as an appendix to this book.) Contacts made with American clients during this period, especially with Kenneth Parker, head of the Parker Pen company, were to prove helpful a decade later when Politz sought U.S. immigrant status.

Early in the 1930s, Politz started his own firm, Politz Werbeberatung, a consultancy which worked on the marketing of pharmaceutical and industrial products. Always an exceptionally active and athletic man, Politz's non-business activities included writing, playing the organ, boxing, and flying gliders. It was while a member of a gliding club that he got his first glimpse of what the National Socialist party was really aiming for.

In Germany in those days such "clubs" were sometimes clandestine training units for what was to become the Luftwaffe, but Politz wanted no part of the military, which he feared would conscript him because of his training in physics.

He was appalled by the rise of Nazism in Germany and, as an outspoken critic, drew the unfavorable attention of the Nazis. When Hitler finally took over, Politz knew he was a marked man and began to make plans for his escape.

Politz became more deeply involved with his pharmaceutical client, MUCH A.G., and began to conduct experimental marketing and advertising programs in Germany and Sweden for its Spalt Tabletten brand. This necessitated frequent business trips to Sweden, where he carefully built business and personal relationships; when he finally decided to forsake Germany, the escape route was through Sweden.

By the mid-1930s, as the Nazis followed every Politz move, Alfred's desire to escape to a freer land grew more intense. He and his fianceé, Martha Bruszat, knew that if they married escape would become almost impossible. They adopted a "moving target" strategy, changing hotels almost daily. The strategy worked, and one day Politz, the businessman, was able to slip safely away to freedom.

NEW BEGINNING IN AMERICA

Alfred Politz arrived in New York in late 1937. He had only a very small income, from his work in Sweden, which ceased when the war started, and life was not easy; U.S. authorities were suspicious of non-Jewish Germans arriving in America. He would have nothing to do with physics, as it could have military applications—and he still had his ailing mother, his fianceé and his academic friends in Germany.

When he failed to obtain FDA approval for his headache tablets, Politz had to find other ways to earn money. At first he taught judo, and with a friend ran a lunch counter in North Bergen, N.J. With an artist friend, he attempted to syndicate a daily newspaper cartoon strip. The principal character, Lord Boastermore, was fashioned after British prime minister Neville Chamberlain, for whom he felt nothing but contempt; the contempt intensified after Munich, which Politz felt had encouraged Hitler and led to a preventable war. During this period he even invented a variable speed automobile transmission, but other developments intervened before he got around to a patent.

Politz continued to struggle, but in the Spring of 1939 the picture brightened when his fianceé was able to leave Germany. Alfred Politz and Martha Bruszat were married in March, 1939 in North Bergen, N.J. To his everlasting sorrow, he was never able to get his mother out of Germany. Before leaving, he had moved her to what he considered a safe location in the eastern part of Germany, and he was haunted by what the Russian occupying troops could, and did, do at the end of the war.

4 The Politz Papers

In 1940, through the intervention of Kenneth Parker and several others, Politz got a job with the Elmo Roper opinion research company. Here, as technical director, he began to question what appeared to him to be fallacious and even dangerous sampling procedures, and developed new theories of his own.

He wrote and gave lectures on his theories at various universities, and several of his articles were published. Compton Advertising was impressed, and hired Politz as their research director. But he promptly ran afoul of the head of research at Procter & Gamble, Compton's biggest client. Years later, Alfred Stanford of Compton wrote, "Alfred's scathing comments on what was passing for 'research' under client aegis led to some fiery confrontations. It was then that Alfred set up his own business, with little money, no prospects, no clients". On the plus side, as Politz liked to say, "There was no one around to fire me".

Stanford retained a close friendship with Politz, and in 1974 wrote, "Surely Alfred is one of the advertising greats, but it always seems to me his greatness was in a larger frame of logic and philosophy . . . Advertising was an exercise machine for a supple and brilliant mind".

GROWTH OF THE LEGEND .

Alfred Politz Research was launched in a tiny Madison Avenue office, with Martha as secretary and receptionist, and Jane Klein, a 1940 mathematics graduate of Bryn Mawr as his assistant. Klein had been his assistant at Roper. On the few occasions when an early client came to visit Politz, one or both of the others had to go for coffee. The company was incorporated four years later, in 1947.

Among the first clients was the Advertising Research Foundation, whose technical director was Dr. Darrell B. Lucas, then a marketing professor at New York University. Lucas had met and been impressed by Politz when the latter was with Roper, and decided to use him for a new Continuing Study of Transportation Advertising. The first stage, a study in Newark, N.J., in April, 1944, was the first commercial application of the Politz-developed "random sampling technique". The first national probability sample of the U.S. population was executed in 1947 for the Can Manufacturer's Association.

Another early client was Mobil Oil, then known as Socony-Vacuum Oil Company. Soon Life magazine became a client, followed by Dupont, United Fruit, the Automobile Manufacturers Association, the Florida Citrus Commission, and others.

Through the 1940s and 1950s, Alfred Politz Research Inc. continued to grow and prosper. Politz's staff grew to 220 to help him service new blue-chip clients (only one per industry), such as Anheuser-Busch, Kimberly-Clark, British American Tobacco Co./Brown and Williamson, Bristol Myers (later Colgate Palmolive), Chrysler, Coca Cola, S.C. Johnson, U.S. Steel and Seagrams.

Media surveys, of course, became an important adjunct to the business. For two decades after the first ARF survey, Politz set the standards and totally dominated the field of advertising media research.

Politz seldom solicited new accounts: they sought him, and became devo- tees. He never had more than ten industrial clients at one time because he did not want to handle single surveys. He considered it essential to establish a continuing relationship with his clients, which meant exclusivity within each client's industry. He liked to work with the man at the top, and came to count among his personal friends some of the biggest names in American marketing: John R. Kimberly, Samuel and Edgar Bronfman, J. Paul Austin, Henry Bris- tol, Herb F. Johnson, Andrew Heiskell, Vernon Bellman and Rosser Reeves.

Politz's clients were at once awed and delighted both by his work and his personality. Engaging and possessing what one client called "a delicious sense of humor," Politz won wide renown and respect from clients, academics, scientists and co-workers alike. Typical is a comment made by Eugene A. Olson, research director of International Cellucotton (later Kimberly-Clark), who made no bones about how his company regarded Politz: "He's way out front—far ahead of the rest of the field with his methods and techniques. We find him extremely stimulating to work with—his findings, and his interpreta- tions of them, really keep us hopping."

Indeed, Politz himself believed this to be his greatest contribution to the field of research—what questions to ask, how to interpret the answers, and then come up with recommendations. While he was acclaimed as the developer of new sampling techniques, Politz himself never took credit for this important development, saying that he was only the first to apply area or probability sampling to commercial research. The methods had been developed, and used, by the Census Bureau and other government agencies in Washington.

Nevertheless, as early as 1945, the American Marketing Association (AMA) awarded Politz a citation for his use of the new sampling technique. The following year, AMA heaped further recognition on him with its award for "Leadership in Marketing." Politz modestly took all this praise in stride, worrying that marketing research was not developing quickly enough into the science he knew it should be. But he was quick to recognize significant progress.

Some years later, Dr. Lucas said:

"He was a champion of fairness in an era of growing abandonment of honesty and fair play: no matter how low the rank of one who sparked a useful idea, Alfred wanted to make sure that the credit was given where deserved. No matter how high the rank of anyone who, through carelessness or ignorance broke from ideal practice, he held that person in unconcealed contempt. As a personality, either at work or play, Alfred displayed a life pattern which would only inspire those fortunate enough to have known him."

A dimension of Politz which helped him establish rapport with clients and their advertising agencies, was his sensitivity to the creative process. According to Rosser Reeves, then Chairman of Ted Bates Advertising,

6   The Politz Papers

"He was the only research man I ever met who understood copy, partly because he fancied himself a writer." In private correspondence some years later, in supporting Mr. Politz's nomination to the Advertising Hall of Fame, Reeves added,
"Alfred had a mind like a knife edge. I stole from him everything I could for my book ('Reality in Advertising'). Consider incisive reasoning like this:
1. Many people say 'My advertisement must get attention.'
2. Therefore, they reason, 'My advertisement must be different.'
Such advertising, as Alfred once pointed out to me, bypasses the product, and when it does, it bypasses the advertising function. It is a classical example of confusing the means with the ends, for if a product is worth paying money *for,* it is worth paying attention *to.* The consumer need not be shocked or entertained into giving it his attention."

ENHANCING THE LEGEND

During the same two decades, Politz also became the dominant figure in advertising media research. He was first exposed to audience surveys when he was in the Roper shop, where he became dissatisfied with the projection of audiences to the population of the U.S. Politz suspected that quota sampling tended to inflate the audience measurement.

By the time he started his own company, Politz had attracted the favorable attention of the Advertising Research Foundation, which hired him to do a controlled recognition survey of the car card audience in Newark, N.J. In early 1944 Politz devised a unique random sampling procedure which removed the selection of respondents from the hands of interviewers. (See Appendix IV). However, his first major ARF-supported audience study was a 1948 "Study of 11 Magazines" in Canada, for Maclean-Hunter with the co-operation of the Canadian Advertising Research Foundation.

That study, along with other work done by Politz, led to a decision by the ARF to approve certain surveys (e.g. those purporting to project national audiences/market shares), ONLY if based on probability samples. Alfred Politz had achieved his first major victory, but his 1949 "Study of Accumulative Audience of Life Magazine" clearly established his pre-eminence in the field. After several years of difficulties with its own research, and unsuccessful attempts to discredit the Politz studies, an executive of Saturday Evening Post asked in frustration: "Do I have to use Politz to gain acceptance for my audience surveys?" Prospective advertisers replied with a resounding "YES".

A testimony to his impact on audience measurement, and on the research profession generally, was a full page ad in Advertising Age 15 years after his retirement. The headline read "Alfred Politz Knew It All The Time", and the ad went on to quote a Politz study done 16 years earlier.

In order to service his major clients, Politz had developed the largest, best-trained staff of field interviewers in the country. However, with only a small number of clients, there were slow periods; so Politz formed National Field Service, a subsidiary which made this resource available to companies and advertising agencies that wanted to design and analyze their own regional or nation-wide surveys. NFS operated quite separately, and may well have carried out the field work on surveys for competitors of the parent company's clients.

And Politz continued to generate heat and controversy, writing and speaking extensively about his ideas and experiences. He never hesitated to express his generally strong views, starting with the inadequacies of quota sampling, extending on to debate the merits (few, in his view) of motivational research, and to openly attack the Advertising Research Foundation, in speeches and in print. He criticized the ARF for carrying on research jobs that he felt belonged to independent research firms.

Servicing the Florida Citrus Commission acquainted Politz with the pleasures of living in Florida, and he vowed to buy a vacation home there "as soon as I could afford it". In 1951, he opened what the Tampa Chamber of Commerce hailed as a branch office of the "famed market researcher" and he bought a lakeside home near Tampa. Later, he acquired a retail hardware supply business and liked to press customers to see how a salesperson could switch them off of nationally advertised brands.

In the late 50s, Politz hired a young Canadian researcher, Hugh Hardy, who was to figure prominently in later developments in the Politz organization. Initially, Hardy was head of experimental marketing, and spent much of his time in Tampa running a new company that made and sold mouthwash throughout Florida. The company, Action Laboratories Corp., was used as a marketing laboratory, testing new marketing and advertising ideas. The conclusions were conveyed to APRI clients and to staff through special seminars. At the end of the experimental period, Hardy returned to New York to head the National Field Service subsidiary.

Already well-advanced, Politz's fame spread further when Martin Mayer's best-selling book, *Madison Avenue, USA,* came out in 1958. Mayer quoted Politz at length, explained his viewpoint on advertising and research, and they became close friends. Mayer once described Politz as:

> "A short, athletic man who could be graphically represented by three triangles (broad forehead to jutting chin, big shoulders to narrow waist, hips to small feet), Politz, at fifty, is one of the most forceful people in advertising. Didactic by temperament, he teaches his clients and their agencies as well as his associates and fellow researchers; when he feels that the lesson is not going well he can become exceedingly scornful. He still speaks a slightly pedantic English with a marked German accent, which adds a perhaps unintentional force to his scorn. Since opening his own office in 1943 he has devoted himself to eliminating the illogic from consumer research, especially in the areas of sampling, questionnaire construction and 'project design'—a term of his own invention expressing his belief that no single survey can be more than one part of an over-all research project."

Jack Honomichl, a later chronicler of the Politz legend, described Politz as "hyperactive", and quoted Andrew Heiskell as saying "Alfred conveyed a sense of enormous energy—as if he were barely able to keep inside his skin." Politz ran to work every day from his penthouse apartment in a chic building on East 54th Street, just a few blocks from his Madison Avenue office. The

8   The Politz Papers

apartment featured a wall mirror, 12 ft. high and 15 ft. long, which enabled him to observe people while he played a huge, white organ. Sometimes he'd take co-workers to the apartment for lunch—steak tartare or cottage cheese and beer—and improvise on the organ while they ate; he gobbled his food and always finished first.

Throughout his life, Alfred Politz was an active, restless and impatient man—both physically and intellectually. He would prefer to run, rather than walk—and his thinking proceeded in great creative leaps, rather than in contemplative daydreams.

His physical impatience seldom expressed itself in frustration or anger, but always in action. His New York office was on the eighth floor of a Madison Avenue building, but Politz was usually too impatient to wait for the elevator. He solved his problem by running up eight long flights of stairs, taking two steps at a time. Lesser athletes who waited for the elevator would find him at his desk when they arrived at the floor—and this was when he was in his late 50s!

It was not unusual for Politz to become restless in staff meetings after a short time, and start to do handstands—after carefully removing loose change from his pockets—to break the monotony. Sometimes before a speech or a major presentation, to ease the tension, he'd walk on his hands.

When he could not hail a taxi in the city, he would run to his appointments. He explained that if he could not find an empty cab, then traffic was very bad and he could move faster on foot anyway.

Until the very last years of his life, Politz pursued a vigorous program of daily exercise—running, doing push-ups, chin-ups, and the like. He did not seem to have any real fitness objective, since fitness was certainly not a problem for him. It was simply an expression of his boundless energy, a pleasure in which he indulged himself. His chess opponents claim he even played chess vigorously.

Politz was a broad-shouldered, usually tanned, and handsome man, always dapperly dressed, often wearing a bow tie. But his relatively short stature (he was about 5'7") bothered him.

Recalled Rosser Reeves, who was a frequent drinking buddy (their favorite watering hole was the bar at the 21 Club), "Alfred greeted me with something like, 'God, I hate you big bastards; if I was as tall as you, I wouldn't have to use my brains [to make a living].' "

Politz, like many creative people, would work intensively in spurts—usually about 18 days, through weekends—and then take a train to his home in Odessa—he wouldn't fly if he could possibly avoid it. He'd often take along a secretary or two and work on the way down to Florida.

At his home in Florida he used a trampoline, and spent hours at physically demanding jobs around his property, usually starting at daybreak. He built a 1,200 foot long path into the middle of a swamp using old railway ties; there he built a platform where he and his guests could enjoy the sights and sounds of this natural setting.

And he would play at water sports, and work in his famous tool shed. The Politz "tool shed" was, in a sense, an externalized representation of the Politz mind. It was a 50' x 100' aluminum structure crammed with power tools and hand tools, lengths of metal and wood, boxes of springs, heavy bolts, magnets and clamps of all sizes, bottles of mercury, and lots of just plain junk. It was never really tidy, but something exciting was always going on there. The roof of the tool shed was used as a landmark by pilots making daylight landings at Tampa airport; the reflection of sunshine from the aluminum roof could not be missed.

It was here that he worked on physical experiments and inventions, the most renowned being an "automatic" sailboat that had a venetian blind-like apparatus in lieu of cloth sails, and an almost-perpetual-motion machine, a huge, ugly, and cumbersome-looking, Rube Goldberg-like device, which, after a gentle shove, ran for almost 24 hours on at least one occasion. In one corner of the shed, there was always a small barrel of cold beer, usually Michelob draft. A small room was stocked with fireworks. No matter what serious business brought one to the shed, fun and diversion were always close at hand.

He liked astronomy and on top of his home in Florida, he had a quite powerful telescope; he spent many evening hours looking at the stars and universe. This interest in the unknown inspired him to write poems and short stories which were often a cross between science fiction and the occult.

FIGHTING THE ESTABLISHMENT

After his respites in Florida, Politz would bound back to Manhattan, often to resume his personal battles with elements of the research establishment.

Most prolonged was his battle against the proponents of motivational research, especially Dr. Ernest Dichter, the Vienna-born champion of what Politz tended to ridicule as a fad. Such "qualitative" research he dismissed in these words:

> "If I say, 'It's warm in here'—that is qualitative statement. If I say, 'It's 78 degrees in here'—that is a quantitative statement. Qualitative statements are just quantitative statements made at a sloppy level of approximation."*

Politz's tendency toward controversy was revealed much earlier. Because of his success in promoting probability sampling, Politz had acquired a reputation as a highly-quotable spokesman for the research industry. In 1948, after the surprise election of Harry Truman as president, reporters sought his views on the polling debacle which had shown Thomas Dewey as almost certain of victory. Politz's reply: "It will help get rid of the charlatans", was resented by the pollsters. In fact, for several years Politz had been very outspoken about the inevitability of such a disaster due to the inadequate sampling methods used by most pollsters and, in speeches only days before the election, he predicted the outcome.

*This subject is covered more fully in Chapter 4.

10 The Politz Papers

In all his years of research, Politz carried out only one national public opinion study—at the specific request of President Dwight D. Eisenhower. This survey was done in a matter of two weeks in anticipation of a meeting with Winston Churchill. It has been said that the Politz contribution had a significant effect on the course of history, and Politz prized a letter to this effect from President Eisenhower.

His most audacious move, in the fall of 1961, was to rent a ballroom in a hotel and invite hundreds of people in the advertising/research community to hear a speech, in which he delivered a scathing denunciation of the Advertising Research Foundation (ARF), capping it with a suggestion that the ARF be dissolved. He argued that the ARF had violated its non-profit function by competing with private research organizations, and in many respects lowered research standards and "contributed to mediocrity" by catering to the lowest common denominator, which was the fate of any committee-run organization.

This naturally caused a furor, but a few months later, Politz went a big step further. He mailed a monograph entitled, "Is Progress in Advertising Research Endangered by the Advertising Research Foundation?" to some 1,500 advertisers, agencies and media representatives. While many agreed with Alfred's impeccable logic in the speech and monograph, they would not say so in public.

Only a very few people ever knew what finally triggered the attack, and Politz himself never chose to reveal the cause. It was that an ARF consultation panel approved two different media study reports, (the first by Politz, the second by a competitor), within the course of a single month; the second report contained a word-for-word copy of the description of methods in the first.

Some veteran research professionals are convinced it was the Politz outburst that led, ultimately, to the transformation of the ARF from the tripartite organization it was (advertisers, agencies and media), to the truly professional and representative organization it is today.

THE GOLDEN YEARS

The 1950s were the golden period for Alfred Politz Research Inc., as the dynamic Politz continued to attract large and prestigious new clients. Clients were enthralled with Politz, and what he was doing for them. Lester R. Frankel, who was vice president of the company from 1951 to 1957, says Politz sometimes gave them Dutch uncle lectures bordering on rudeness. "Yet they loved to come to his presentations, not to hear the study results but to hear Alfred's interpretation of the findings". But by restricting himself to one exclusive client in each industry, Politz put a self-imposed limit on his revenues, which topped out at around $10 million. He could probably have made much more money by handling one-shot surveys, but he chose to leave those as well as international studies to Universal Marketing Research, the successor to National Field Service.

Politz surrounded himself with some of the brightest people in research. He persuaded the already-eminent statistician, Dr. W. Edwards Deming, to

commute from Washington to New York to teach statistics as a professor in
the Graduate School of Business Administration at New York University.
This made it simpler for the two to consult and collaborate on sampling and
other matters, including co-authoring several articles.

Politz was a genius in locating and hiring highly-talented people, which
contributed to his company becoming the glamorous "hot shop" of the period,
renowned for its high professional standards and innovation. He attracted a
number of prominent mathematicians and experimental psychologists, and the
company served as a training ground for many more. His staff members were
fiercely loyal, regarding him as leader, teacher and inspirer. When presented
with some complicated issue, he had the knack of reducing it to simple terms
with an often humorous or pithy analogy. He was tireless and worked hard
himself, but never hesitated to assign credit to any employee who made a
contribution.

The feeling of camaraderie was enhanced by Politz's habit, especially during
periods of intense work, of breaking into the ongoing work with the suggestion
that everyone take off for a cocktail at a nearby bar—with him in the lead.

THE DECLINE OF THE POLITZ ERA

In the late 1950s, Alfred Politz began to think about the day when he could
relinquish some of his responsibilities and spend more time at his beloved
home in Florida. Indeed, his experiments with mouthwash and a hardware
store were, at least in part, manifestations of his still unformulated wishes. Of
course, many of his major clients still insisted on his personal involvement in
their studies, but this blended nicely with his need for continuing recognition.

After Hugh Hardy took over National Field Service, and began to build it
into a sizable firm in its own right, Politz saw an answer to his dilemma.
(Politz and Hardy had become good friends during the mouthwash experiment
in Florida). NFS was incorporated as Universal Marketing Research Inc.,
which became an affiliate rather than a subsidiary, and was moved to Park
and 54th Street. Over the next few years, as a full-service research company,
U.M.R. was built into a significant international operation, with a second
office in Chicago, a wholly-owned subsidiary in Germany, a dozen affiliates
in other countries, and major clients around the world.

Politz professed game plan, understandably disclosed to only a very few
people, called for U.M.R. to continue to grow, domestically as well as internationally, with Hardy as president. Then, at some indeterminate future date,
the companies might be brought together, and Politz could begin to slow
down, as chairman of the two companies or a single merged entity.

The first part of the game plan was pretty much on target in the early
1960s, but the closer it came to realization the less willing he was to accept
a diminishing role for himself. Unfortunately, while his recalcitrance was
understandable, it coincided with other developments that were more troublesome.

12   The Politz Papers

An incipient drinking problem was exacerbated by other little-known health problems, and the combination contributed to deteriorating client relations. The Politz star was beginning to descend, and some long-time clients shifted the balance of study project contacts to Hardy and other senior Politz staff.

As with many another great developer and genius before him, Politz found it difficult to relinquish his lead role, even in the face of severe difficulties. Several clients, acutely aware of the situation, suggested that Hardy set up his own company with the assurance of their support; he declined to do so.

In early 1964 Hardy resigned and returned to his native Canada. Within six months there was a mass exodus; two of APRI's earliest and most senior executives departed to establish a new company, taking with them other senior professional staff members—and a number of important clients.

Later in 1964, A. Edward Miller, who as research director of LIFE magazine had hired Politz to conduct his first major media study, came to APRI as president and chief operating officer; Politz moved up to become chairman. Unfortunately, given the loss of both clients and senior Politz-trained staff, recovery was an uphill battle, and the company was unable to attract significant new commercial clients. For the first time, media studies became the major activity. A "barnburner" study of 11 magazines (discussed in Chapter 7) was carried out in late 1964, and an even more ambitious study was completed in 1966.

The latter study was to be the last of the great Politz media epics; later that year the company was sold to Computer Sciences Corporation. Politz began to spend more of his time in Odessa, and the following year he officially retired and moved to Florida permanently, saying "I thereby gained the time to turn to other problems."

THE FINAL YEARS

There was a certain poetic symmetry to the professional life of Alfred Politz; at age 15 he became a protégé of famed German nuclear physicist Max Planck, and on retirement he returned to scientific matters. In his Florida "laboratory" he had hundreds of magnets, needles, and balances arranged in experimental designs. He challenged the algebra of infinities, and he went into a serious study of the three-dimensional interpretation of visual perception; he did not consider the traditional parallax explanation sufficient. He gave lectures on the subject at various universities, and his proposition was published in 1979 in the Journal of Philosophy and Phenomenological Research at the State University of New York, Buffalo. He resumed work on a "Variomatic Transmission" for automobiles; continuing a project he had been forced to abandon 40 years earlier.

In addition, Politz composed organ music by ear, wrote poetry and sometimes-bizarre short stories, and wrote long "think piece" articles for publications such as *Advertising Age*, some of which were published as late as 1974. And he remained physically active—he was 75 when he applied for a licence to fly hot air balloons.

In February, 1981, throat cancer necessitated the removal of Mr. Politz's larynx. He could not speak, and had to communicate by writing. He could not eat, and had to be fed intravenously. In August, 1982, he suffered a massive stroke and was completely paralyzed; he died in his Florida home on November 8, 1982 at the age of 80.

On December 2, 1982 a memorial service for Alfred Politz was held in the Time-Life Building in New York. It was attended by hundreds of luminaries from the marketing world, as well as the many friends, colleagues and admirers of this remarkable man. Rosser Reeves summed up the feeling this way: "Alfred was one of the best friends I ever had. This great man filled many gaps in my knowledge, and I miss him desperately."

THE LEGACY OF ALFRED POLITZ

This entire book is a legacy to one of the world's greatest marketing research pioneers, but a few summary remarks are called for. Alfred Politz was a genius who started over in mid-life in a strange land, and went on to impact his field as few others have, or probably ever will. He could reduce complex issues to understandable terms by using simple examples and analogies. His speeches and his numerous articles were loaded with them. He brought the order and discipline of the scientist to marketing research, and converted it into a real profession. He made countless friends but, because he was "ruthlessly honest", he also made a few enemies.

Some observers consider the introduction of probability sampling to have been his greatest contribution to research, but Politz himself always downplayed his role. Most of his commercial and industrial clients would agree with his own conclusion that his greatest contribution was the application of logic and experimental design to the research process: What questions to ask, how to interpret the answers, and how to come up with recommendations leading to predictable effects. In doing so, Politz set exceptionally high standards for himself, and these became the standards for the research industry.

It is perhaps unfortunate for the student of marketing research that Alfred Politz had so few clients—apart from media studies, he served only about 30 organizations in all. And since he chose to confine himself to only one client in any given industry, on an exclusive and continuing basis, some of his best work was little-known. For obvious competitive reasons, his clients were reluctant to reveal everything they learned.

In later years Politz was dismayed at what he saw as a serious deterioration of research quality in the late 1960s and 1970s. In a 1976 interview with Rena Bartos, as part of the ARF's "Founding Fathers of Research" series, Politz spoke of researchers not yet having learned the principles of experimental design and the relatively simple process of either eliminating or making effective use of response bias. He also spoke of contemporary researchers paying lip service to the use of probability samples while violating the principles and

14 The Politz Papers

processes in the application.

In the same interview, Politz said research would probably stay on the same level as long as there was no risk to the researcher. He went on to advise students of research to study some mathematical statistics and experimental psychology for their disciplined use of strict scientific rules.

However, perhaps the greatest legacy of Alfred Politz was that his company served as the development or training ground for a great number of professional researchers. His dynamic character and innovative ideas attracted people with already-established reputations as statistical sampling specialists and experimental psychologists. But Politz was the leader, and he created an environment that stimulated such people to new and greater accomplishments.

Young researchers fortunate enough to be hired into such an environment learned quickly and well. As Jack Honomichl wrote: "The Politz company served as the training ground for a small army of survey research and marketing practitioners. For many it was their first—and most exciting—job, the apprenticeship, the stimulus that was to shape a career."

Not everything that came out of the Politz organization was the work of Politz alone, but he engendered the respect and fierce loyalty of both groups by sharing the credit for all accomplishments. And he imbued people with the confidence, and the courage, to make predictive recommendations to clients. In so doing, he helped many people on their way to independent success as researchers or marketing generalists. Most departures were friendly separations, but all who left or were sent on their way departed with the most marketable of all research credentials—they had worked for Alfred Politz.

The influence of Alfred Politz continues to permeate the marketing community; it is unlikely that his performance will ever be equalled.

[35]

Excerpt from Hugh S. Hardy (ed.), *The Politz Papers: Science and Truth in Marketing Research*, 291–301.

10

The Influence of Politz on European Research

by Wolfgang Schaefer

A Personal Note

This is neither an objective nor a complete account, but rather a subjective, personalized and limited one. This is so despite the fact that several colleagues have generously helped me trace Politz's influences on research on this side of the Atlantic.

My personal involvement goes back to 1950, when a group of four German researchers were invited under the Fulbright program to study social science, opinion, and market research operations in the U.S.A. Among the researchers we talked to was Alfred Politz. He ranked among the more impressive people we met. The significance of his contributions to research became evident to me only a few years later.

When in 1954 the Axel Springer Publishing House hired me I remembered the examples of media research I had seen in the U.S.A. Consequently, we made every attempt to keep up with the most advanced research projects. Very kindly and generously, Ed Miller of LIFE, Jack Maloney of Reader's Digest and Don Hobart of Curtis sent copies of their latest pieces of research,— and a cartoon movie on the methodology of the famous "Study of Four Media".

Alfred Politz Research had made practically all of those studies. All of them were milestones,—and miles ahead of what we did. They served as references for our work and as sources of inspiration. This was true of their ingenious design, true of their excellent technical execution, and true of their lucid descriptions.

On business trips to the U.S.A. I met him again in 1959 and 1961; and our discussions led, to my surprise, to Alfred and Hugh Hardy offering me the job setting up a German subsidiary company. This was realized in 1962. Unfortunately, our introductory phase of red figures lasted until 1964, by which time the parent company had gotten into trouble. When I suggested buying half the German company, seeing the financial turning point close by,

Alfred graciously offered me the whole company at a minimal price. Most gratefully, as well as reluctantly, I agreed and started my own business in January 1965.

This personal history of a relatively strong affinity between Alfred Politz and myself may serve to explain the fact that a good proportion of references to his work comes from me.

It must be acknowledged that not all of the Politz research methods were known to, or accepted by, all European researchers. Limited communication was (and still is) the main reason for that. And not everything known was adopted, because of cost considerations, or different requirements, or lack of insight.

Politz's media research had the greatest impact; since such studies were carried out with the express intent of being published, they were easily available. And they were of such an exemplary character that European media researchers made every effort to get hold of them. In contrast, most of the product, advertising and general market research carried out for the clients of Alfred Politz Research was highly confidential, and reports were seldom released. As a consequence, the largest proportion of what follows is devoted to media research.

POLITZ MEDIA RESEARCH AS BENCHMARK

If references in readerships research articles were counted, most likely Politz would come out as world champion by a wide margin.

Recent correspondence with my European colleagues confirmed his influence on their work:

• Jean-Michel Agostini (France), after quoting 5 of his own papers relating to Politz; "Moreover, the Politz studies on cumulative audiences of U.S. magazines, in which he proposed empirical formulas for estimating cumulative audiences beyond the observed number of issues, were for me a source of inspiration in my subsequent works about the development of media models".

• Tom Corlett (U.K.), recalled that for his first talk on readership research (in 1960) "much of the material for this talk was based on Politz's work"; and that "Politz's techniques were indeed an important topic in most of the significant discussions of readership research which took place in Britain in the early 1960s". He then referred to a 1982 article of his (1) where he contrasts the thorough method employed by Politz with stripped-down techniques by other researchers and concluded: "So you will see that at least the memory of his early work remains powerful and relevant in Britain even to-day."

• Wolfgang Ernst (Germany): "Who else would deserve an appreciation more than Alfred Politz—he really has provided important stimuli."

• Harry Henry (U.K.) wrote: "I knew Alfred, had a certain amount of direct contact with him in the late fifties, and respected his line of thinking—primarily because it was so much the same as my own . . ." He went on to refer to his own book on "Motivation Research" in which he had described "the 'British' form of motivation research, following the same general principles of scientifically rigid analysis as Alfred habitually followed" (2).

• Jan D. Noordhoff (Netherlands): "Regarding the Politz Papers, I believe that there is a good reason for recalling somebody whose influence on media research is almost that of a genius. All in all one can say that Politz has had a profound influence on my development and through that on the development of media research in the Netherlands, . . . Nobody can afford to ignore Politz!"

• Friedrich Tennstaedt (Germany): "For me and so for IfD Allensbach, the work by Politz was indispensable for the start of German readership research (1949), but especially fruitful for the further development of methods in the 50s and 60s. Most of all we were impressed by his 'psychology' of questionnaires in conjunction with his clear mathematical-statistical considerations regarding inquiry techniques. In my opinion Politz personified almost perfectly the successful synthesis of psychology and mathematics."

• The importance of media research carried out by Politz can also be gauged by the quotes in relevant books. In her 1962 dissertation Eva-Maria Hess wrote: "Politz is regarded at present to be the most significant readership researcher of the USA . . . The readership surveys by Politz are distinguished by the special care given to their methodological concepts" (3). In her index of names, Politz leads with 14 entries, compared with 8 for the next name. And in her 1981 book, Politz shares first place with one other researcher (4).

• A voluminous Swedish book on mass communication by Jarko Cerha (5) refers to such diverse Politz contributions as the "not-at-homes" concept; the glue-spot technique to ascertain ad-page exposure; the measurement by camera of exposure to transit posters; and his statement on the influences of importance, believability, and uniqueness on advertising effect.

There always was, and still is, a remarkable discrepancy between the general respect for Politz's media studies, and the paucity of equivalent studies carried out in Europe. Why is that so?

There seem to be two major reasons. One was described by Alan Wilson: ". . . the main inhibitor to importing the new Politz techniques into Europe was the imperative of sample size and so of cost. U.S. media had many times the ad revenue of European equivalents, duly reflected in their research budgets."

Probably just as important are different priorities set in America and Europe, as expressed by Harry Henry in 1962 (6):

"We have always regarded it as essential to cover all major press and magazine media at one go. The thinking behind this is that it is less useful to know everything about one magazine . . ."

This second factor can easily be illustrated by comparing how many media were dealt with in American and European studies.

For their own competitive reasons, the publishers of the largest U.S. magazines had decided to use the Politz organization to carry out readership measurements of great precision even though that entailed limiting the number of different publications or media covered. The awesome "Study of the Accumulative Audience of LIFE" dealt with just that one magazine. "A Study of Four Media" encompassed 4 magazines, 1 newspaper supplement, 4 radio and 5 TV programs—a total of 14 individual media.

In contrast, the British had included in their "first true readership survey in 1939: 71 magazines, 22 national and 101 regional newspapers", as Tom Corlett reported. "A further survey with similar coverage followed in 1947; the annual Hulton Readership Surveys (1948-1953) followed a similar pattern—so

294   The Politz Papers

that a tradition of extensive coverage (at least 60-80 publications per survey) was already firmly established in Britain by the early 1950s."

The first German cooperative readership survey in 1954 was patterned after the British studies in methodology and scope; it dealt with 48 magazines (7).

It was not just the excellence of the Politz media studies which constantly kept them in our minds. The very tradition of providing media planners with data on a large (and steadily growing) number of media reinforced this tendency in a peculiar way, as Theodor Harder pointed out in 1961: "The practice of the readership survey including 40-50 objects contains an antimony which consists of this large number of participants exacerbating the requirement for neutrality of the total research design, and at the same time this number is responsible to a large extent for the methodological difficulties to maintain such a neutrality" (8).

No wonder that Harder referred to Politz three times, and suggested following his footsteps—if not in general then in certain areas.

READERSHIP REPETITION & ACCUMULATION

Most readership research in Europe had centered on estimating the readers of one average issue. One was aware of the phenomenon of cumulation, but prior to the early sixties few attempts had been made to incorporate that aspect coincidentally with issue readership.

Politz's "Study of Four Media" had provided readership, audience, and viewership repetition plus cumulation data, by interviewing the same respondents six times in the course of one year. This extreme effort caused admiration only. No one was willing to spend so much time and money finding out something deemed secondary in importance.

But the nagging thought remained that perhaps media planning and research were neglecting an important aspect.

In 1955 and 1959 papers, I had mentioned this task for research and referred to the 1953/54 LIFE study by Politz (9/10). And Theodor Harder had pleaded in his 1961 paper for the inclusion of measurements of reading frequency and readership accumulation, either using the Politz technique or another one.

A little later, a British working party stated, among other requirements: "For all media, problems of cumulation (over media units and over time) need to have careful consideration since coverage (over units and over time) is an essential component of a media plan" (11). They, of course, quoted several Politz studies.

But generally the Politz approach was regarded as too cumbersome and expensive if applied to a large number of publications. And no practical alternative was in sight.

Agostini was the first one to show a way how to solve the problem. He used a simple verbal scale of reading frequency ("regularly/occasionally/never"); and checked the answers with the "Politz technique". The results looked rather promising (12/13).

The Influence of Politz on European Research   295

However, the breakthrough was achieved by Politz alumnus Lester Frankel who proposed asking people how many issues out of 10 they had looked into or read (14). The first European survey based on such a reading frequency scale was carried out in 1964 for "STERN" magazine by the German Politz subsidiary (15/16).

It paved the way for the universal use of this technique in Germany. British researchers adopted the scale method soon afterwards (17). And so did numerous other countries.

READING DAYS

In Germany as elsewhere, the minimal requirement for a "reader" was to have looked into a copy of a publication. With regard to the chances of a given advertisement being exposed and looked at, advertisers and publishers had the strong feeling that the difference between such a reader and one who thoroughly reads a copy is likely to be great.

As early as 1955 we had made an attempt to shed light on this matter by using some kind of reading intensity scale (18). Because of the subjective, not validated, character of this approach, it had no success.

Then came the Politz study on "reading days" for Reader's Digest in 1956 (see Chapter 7, page 180). Its advantages were the simplicity of obtaining such estimates, and its relative objectivity. This led Otmar Ernst and myself to design an experimental study in 1958/59 in which we dealt with reading days plus contacts per day per copy. The results were quite good for our company's radio and tv guide magazine "Hoer Zu" and paved the way for a series of studies on advertising page exposure and the quality of contacts in the next three decades (19).

The German cooperative institution (advertisers, agencies, media) which sponsors yearly media surveys incorporated the "reading days" into their program starting in 1962 (7). And in 1963/64 Odhams Press carried out a study which included "reading days" (20).

QUALITY OF MAGAZINE READERS

The next logical step, after establishing on how many days one copy of a magazine is read, was to determine the "quality" of the readers by demographic and purchasing characteristics. These were present in the Politz Media "Study of Primary and Pass-Along Readers of Four Major Magazines", sponsored by *Reader's Digest*.

In a booklet describing a large number of different measurements of the relationship between readers and publications, the intensity of reading etc., Merbold and Johannsen wrote about this Politz study in some detail (21). Their reason: "This Politz study was dealt with in an elaborate way because it had been of great significance for the later development of the subject of the relationship between readers and publications. This especially with regard to methods since the qualitative methods used appear time and again (up to the

296   The Politz Papers

present) in research."

The subject was chosen for one of the Thomson awards; Agostini won the Gold Medal for his proposal. It was based on the Politz approach but went beyond, improving it in certain respects (22). As a consequence, later surveys everywhere in Europe are likely to have been based on Agostini's suggestions.

ADVERTISING PAGE EXPOSURE

The successful attempts by Alfred Politz Media Studies to go beyond the measurement of simple issue contact had also attracted great attention in Europe.

As explained above, the Springer Publ. House had very early carried out studies researching the intensity of reading of its illustrated TV and radio program magazine, Hoer Zu. Its twofold function as a program guide plus family magazine, and its lengthy stay in the household, contributed to the multiple exposure chances of advertisements.

Consequently, in 1962 they commissioned the Infratest institute to duplicate the "Ad Page Exposure" study Politz had carried out for Curtis' "Saturday Evening Post" (see Chapter 7, Page 211). This included preliminary experiments to obtain indications about the validity of the questioning procedure in Germany. As it turned out, the concept was usable with a few minor modifications (23).

The study was well received. Springer and Infratest researchers went on to design and test substitute techniques for the Politz method and extended measurements into a more qualitative direction (24/see also 7).

We used the original Politz method in two studies (25/26).

The 1963/64 readership study conducted in the U.K. by Odham's Press included 'page exposure' in addition to 'reading days'. In their Technical Appendix to the report on the latter they stated: "This study owes a great deal to the work of Alfred Politz". Prior to the survey they had conducted validation checks using the "glue spot" technique. No further study of this kind in the U.K. is known.

Politz's strict "APX" method limits the number of publications which can be dealt with in one interview. This has caused sponsors and researchers to refrain from its use. But the concept was so attractive that it induced researchers everywhere to look for a substitute method.

The general direction of these attempts was to find scales with which readers could express how many pages or what proportion of a magazine or newspaper they would look at or read.

Jan Noordhoff compiled a documentation of such efforts in Europe up to 1974 in a book with 49 pages of text plus 117 pages of descriptions of relevant studies (26).

Noordhoff's point of departure, headed by the title "Philosophie", were quotes from Alfred Politz's Foreword to the 1957 study on ad page exposure.

In the same vein, Ingeborg Wendt-Maeder began her digest of such studies with this sentence: "From Politz to NINA, in fact from 1958 to 1975" (27).

(NINA was the Dutch approach to ascertain exposures).

The Italian point of departure was the "MPX" study of the American Magazine Publishers Assn., the methods of which were duplicated in their 1985 survey. "In presenting the published results of the Italian MPX study," Liliana Denon wrote, "I introduced the subject of MPX . . . by quoting extensively . . . Politz's studies about advertising page exposure and the value of repetition."

"BLANK PAGE TEST"

In 1958 Politz went one step beyond APX with the 'personal message' studies for Medical Economics, a U.S. medical journal for doctors. They were another way of measuring APX, suited to a publication with only one definable reader per copy that the advertiser cared about. The logic was that remembering a sensational personal message to the individual physician (on a 'blank' page), was equivalent to exposure to the page containing it.

This idea appealed to the "Medical Tribune", a newcomer on the already-crowded Swiss and German markets for medical publications.

In 1968 and 1969 they carried out such "Blank Page Tests" in Switzerland by telephone with an interviewer of their own (28). And in 1969 they commissioned us to conduct the same kind of test in Germany (29).

POSTER RESEARCH

As described in Chapter 7, the Politz researchers had early on (1954) developed the concept of "exposure" as a potentially useful criterion in poster research, and carried out studies realizing that concept.

This was duly noted by British researcher, Brian Copland, in his "review of Poster Research" (30). But the method did not find his favor; note his fine irony: "The trouble about mechanical devices, to which Americans appear to be addicted, is that they measure with increasing accuracy aspects of the situation which are of decreasing importance."

I don't know whether the British ever used such a method. The French Metrobus Publicité did so in 1961, with slight technical deviations. And the German Infratest institute followed suit in 1963/64. Their researchers very carefully considered all aspects in relationship to the Politz "Study of Outside Transit Poster Exposure" of 1959, and carried out a pilot study (31 "Vorstudie"). They succeeded in reducing the interval between exposures from 1 second to 0.5, thereby increasing the accuracy of photographic measurement appreciably. They also combined the measurement by camera with a representative survey to find out people's opportunities to be exposed to outside transit posters.

However, the most precise replication of the Politz technique was in Italy. In 1964 SIRME carried out such a study for the Milan public transport advertising institution (32). They not only credited the Politz organization, they used the original set of Politz cameras, which we loaned them for the purpose.

TESTING OF ADVERTISEMENTS

The testing of print and tv advertisements with the method described in Chapter 6, p. 167 of this book was practiced by the German Politz subsidiary and subsequently my own company for several years.

We eventually discontinued this service because of lack of interest in it. One problem was its relatively high cost.

(One needs carefully matched samples of 150-250 persons to ensure that worthwhile differences are statistically significant; and one additional sample is required to serve as control. Both requirements increase costs beyond those of the more simple types of ad testing.)

This author presented the method and some findings of general interest at international researchers' conferences in 1963 and 1965 (10/33). The reactions by some members of the audiences were gratifying. But neither paper seems to have had any discernable effects on advertising research in Germany or Europe. It is worth noting that an extensive collection of ESOMAR papers on various ad testing methods (34) did not even include a reference to this approach. Curiously, the same case of omission occurred in the ARF's counterpart (35).

This oversight is all the more remarkable for two reasons:

(1) In a paper which has had some impact Timothy Joyce had presented the view: "It is also true that the object of advertising is more that of getting the product recognised and known than the advertising recognised and known. This is a point well made by Politz' parable of the three mirrors" (36). He then went on to retell it (see Chapter 3, page 40).

(2) The Politz company had used this ad testing concept in the famous "Rochester Study" and subsequent research. That study had so frequently been quoted as an outstanding example of how to measure advertising effects that Otmar Ernst of the Springer Publishing House decided to have the report reprinted, together with a translation (37).

PRODUCT RESEARCH AND TESTING

At the 1963 ESOMAR congress at Luzern, Hugh Hardy presented the Politz philosophy of product testing (38), as elucidated in Chapter 3, page 31.

Since this was an international gathering it is probable that some researchers took notice of this philosophy and as a consequence may have carried out their product tests accordingly.

Only one reference to this paper has come to my attention. In his rather critical exposition of motivation research, Gerhard Schmidtchen (40) stated that only now one discovers that the objective quality of a product is important for success in the market in the long run, even though consumers may not be able to distinguish between different qualities in unfair small-scale tests. He then referred to the so-called "excess power of groups" as an explanation why a larger group may have the ability to find differences of quality even though individuals may appear to be quite uncertain. Although this may sound somewhat mythical, he went on, it has a real meaning since consumers by cumulative experiences may gain a certain image of a product's qualities.

Even to-day one can read statements regarding consumers' inability to find differences between different products—based on research folklore and/or inadequate tests. I shall resist the temptation to quote examples. However, a number of large, mostly international manufacturers have carried out tests for two or three decades (if not longer) which are based on large enough groups of consumers who are given the test product for a long enough period of time to get thoroughly acquainted with it before they are asked for their opinions about it. Questionnaires used contain properly worded relevant characteristics; and test participants are asked to indicate on some kind of scale the extent to which the item applies to the product. Then, a quantitative analysis (in the sense of the natural sciences) can be carried out.

The method has proved time and again that even small differences of quality, consistency, taste, flavor etc. are properly reflected by test results.

These successes have, of course, propagated the method. Whether the original impetus came from Politz directly or indirectly will be hard to ascertain; good ideas quite often occur simultaneously to several people. In our own case the direct influence is obvious; and we have had the good fortune to meet clients who accepted this convincing concept.

REFERENCES

1. Corlett, Tom: "Readership Research: Theory and Practice: A Review", Admap, June 1982.
2. Henry, Harry: "Motivation Research", Crosby Lockwood, London, 1958; reprinted by MCB University Press, Bradford, 1986.
3. Hess, Eva-Maria: "Methoden der Leserschaftsforschung", Doctoral Dissertation, Muenchen, 1962.
4. Hess, Eva-Maria: "Leserschaftsforschung in Deutschland—Ziele, Methoden, Techniken", Burda, Offenburg, 1981.
5. Cerha, Jarko: "Selective mass communication", Kungl. Boktryckeriet PA Nordstedt & Soener, Stockholm 1967.
6. Henry, Harry: "Press Audience Measurement in the United Kingdom", AAPOR/WAPOR Conference, 1962.
7. Arbeitsgemeinschaft Leseranalyse: "Die Zeitschriften-Leser 1954", Frankfurt a. M.
   Arbeitsgemeinschaft Leseranalyse: "Leseranalyse 1962", Frankfurt a. M.
8. Harder, Theodor: Memorandum of 1961, quoted in (55), Part 1, pp 267-269.
9. Schaefer, Wolfgang: "Leserschaftsforschung und Insertionwertforschung", in Die Anazeige, Sept. 1959.
10. Schaefer, Wolfgang: "Kann Kommunikationsforschung den Erfolg der Werbung messen?", IMF/BVM Congress, Hamburg, 1963.
11. Market Research Society: "The Advertising Chain up to the Point of Reception", by the Working Party on Intermedia Comparisons, The Market Research Society, London, 1963.

300   The Politz Papers

12. Agostini, Jean-Michel: "Direct Questions on Reading Habits: Are They Really too Unreliable?", ESOMAR, Amsterdam, 1962.

13. Agostini, Jean-Michel: "Towards a Better Estimation of Magazine Audiences by Means of Simpler Techniques", Thomson Award Papers, London 1962.

14. Frankel, Lester R.: "Mass Media: The Process of Communication", BVM/IMF Conference, Hamburg, 1963.

15. Schaefer, Wolfgang: "Zeitschriften-Kumulationswerte", in Die Anzeige, August 1964.

16. Schaefer, Wolfgang: "Scale Measures of Magazine Reading", Journal of Advertising Research, December, 1965.

17. Corlett, Tom, and J. W. Osborne: "The Development of Reading Frequency Scales", Institute of Practitioners in Advertising, London, 1966.

18. Shaefer, Wolfgang: "Von der Quantuplikationveber die Kumulation zum Doppelseitenkontakt" in: "Festschrift fuer Ernst Braunschweig", Arbeitsgemeinschaft Leseranalyse, Frankfurt a. M., 1968.

19. Springer Publ. House: "Appelle-Untersuchung", unpubl. report, 1958.

20. Odhams Press: "A New Measurement Study of Women's Weekly Magazines", London, 1964.

21. Merbold, Claus, and Uwe Johannsen: "Masse der Leser-Blatt-Bindung", Gruner & Jahr Publishing House, Hamburg, 1977.

22. Agostini, Jean-Michel: "Methods of Classifying Magazine and Newspaper Readers According to Readership Derivation and Quality of Readership", Thomson Gold Medal Paper, London 1964.

23. Infratest: "Der Kontaktwert—Ein Weg zur Bestimmung des Insertionswertes von Zeitschriften", Springer Publishing House, Hamburg, 1962.

24. Infratest: "Anzeigen-Kontakt-Chancen in Publikumszeitschriften", Springer Publishing House, Hamburg, 1970.

25. Schaefer-Marktforschung: "Die Nutzungsintensitaet der GONG-Leser", Gong-Verlag, Nuernberg, 1969.
    Schaefer, Wolfgang: "Einige Bemerkungen zu Inhalt und Methoden der Zeitschriften-Leserschafts-Analysen von 1954 und 1955", paper presented to Arbeitsgemeinschaft Leseranalyse, Frankfurt a.M, Dec. 7, 1955.

26. Noordhoff, Jan D.: "Ermittlung von Seitenkontakten—Eine Dokumentation", Arbeitsgemeinschaft Media-Analyse, Frankfurt a.M, 1976.

27. Wendt, Ingeborg and Friedrich: "Vom Leser pro Nummer zur Nutzungswahrscheinlichkeit", Part 2, Arbeitsgemeinschaft Mediaanalyse, Frankfurt a. M., 1983.

28. Medical Tribune: "Blank-Page-Test II", Wiesbaden, 1969.

29. Medical Tribune: "Potentielle Leserschaft einer Anzeigenseite in Medical Tribune" (Ausgabe fuer Deutschland), Wiesbaden 1968 und 1969.

30. Copland, Brian D.: "A Review of Poster Research", Institute of Practitioners in Advertising, London, 1963.

31. Infratest: "Vorstudie" & "Reichweite der Verkehrsmittelwerbung in Duesseldorf", Fachverband Plakatanschlag, Verkehrsmittel- und Grossflaechenwerbung e.V., Duesseldorf, 1963 & '64.

32. S.I.S.A.R.: "Efficacia pubblicitaria dei mezzi di trasporto urbani" carried out by SIRME s.p.A. for Societa Italiana Stampati Affini Reclame, Milano, 1964.

33. Schaefer, Wolfgang: "Should Advertisements be 'Believable' or 'Convincing'?", ESOMAR, Amsterdam, 1965.

34. Broadbent, Simon (ed.): "Market Researchers Look At Advertising", Sigmatext Ltd., London, for ESOMAR, Amsterdam, 1980.

35. Lipstein, Benjamin (ed.): "Copy Research/A Historical Retrospective" Advertising Research Foundation, New York, 1986.

36. Joyce, Timothy: "What do we know about how advertising works?", ESOMAR, Amsterdam, 1967.
37. Springer Publ. House: "The Rochester Study" ("Ein Beitrag zur Bedeutung der Mehrfach-Knotakte"), Hamburg, 1971.
38. Hardy, Hugh S.: "The Illusion of the Image and the Excess Power of Groups", ESOMAR Congress, Amsterdam, 1963.
40. Schmidtchen, Gerhard: "Motivforschung und Soziologie", in "Vortraege zur Marktforschung 13/14", BVM/Bundesverband deutscher Marktforscher e.V., Verlag Hansen & Hansen, Itzehoe, 1965.

OTHER REFERENCES

Agostini, Jean-Michel: "Analysis of Magazine Accumulative Audience" Journal of Advertising Research, December 1962.
Agostini, Jean-Michel: "The Case for Direct Questions on Reading Habits", Journal of Advertising Research, June, 1964.
DIVO: "Leseranalyse", sponsored by Springer Publ. House, Hamburg, 1955.
Heyde, Chr. v.d.: "A Method for Improving the Results of Primary Investigation by Including the Reasons for Non-Response in Sample Design and Weighting", ESOMAR Congress Amsterdam, 1975.
Institut fuer Demoskopie Allensbach: "Experimente zur Leserschaftsforschung 1968", Heinrich Bauer Publ. House, Hamburg. 1968.
Schaefer-Marktforschung: "Leser-analyse fuer die Zeitschrift "Leben und Erziehen", Einhard-Verlag, Aachen, 1965.
Tennstaedt, F.W.R., and J. Hansen: "Validating the recency and through-the-book techniques" & "Frequency of reading Allensbach's point of view", in Harry Henry (ed.): "Readership Research: Theory and Practice", Sigmatext, London, 1981.
Wendt-Maeder, Ingeborg: "The Measurement Of Page Exposure A Matter Of Pragmatic Decisions", NOVUM b.v., Haarlem, 1978.

[36]

Excerpt from Hugh S. Hardy (ed.), *The Politz Papers: Science and Truth in Marketing Research*, 302–6.

11

Epilogue: The Legacy of a Research Legend

by Hugh S. Hardy

Introduction:

In observing the marketing research scene in the years following his retirement in 1967, Alfred Politz was not encouraged by what he saw:

• After succeeding in his long battle to gain acceptance for probability sampling, he saw practitioners paying lip-service to more rigorous techniques without actually using them.

• Having repeatedly demonstrated the advantages of employing experimental design, he saw increased use of such devices as "focus group" sessions and "depth interviews", not as hypothesis-building steps in the process, but as a substitute for quantifying surveys.

• He saw researchers producing longer and more detailed reports, and slipping further in the corporate hierarchy as management, blaming lack of time to read the reports, delegated responsibility downward.

• On the plus side, he felt there was some increase in the amount of "useful" research; at the same time, however, he believed there should have been far more research that could lead to predictions of the consequences of recommended actions.

The book he had started to write was to be his final attempt to influence all levels of the marketing chain—management, marketing directors, advertising people at the client, media and agency levels, as well as marketing research practitioners.

This book has been an attempt to fill the void he left.

The conscientious reader will have gained considerable knowledge about Alfred Politz, his scientist's approach to marketing research, and his contributions to the evolution of the overall marketing function. The reader also will have gleaned practical knowledge about many of the actual methods and procedures that were developed by Politz and are now used by many professional researchers.

The articles and speeches in the book were prepared by Alfred Politz at different times and for different audiences, with the result that there is some unevenness of writing and presentation style, as well as overlap in subject and content. Although we have attempted to diminish repetition and, in some cases, to smooth out his sometimes-pedantic or awkward use of the English language, there is a residue that may have obscured some of the key elements of the Politz philosophy.

The following comments may help put in perspective several of the key elements of Alfred Politz's contribution—and even cause the reader to return to specific sections of the book.

Sampling:

Alfred Politz was not the originator of probability sampling, but it was certainly Politz who brought the techniques into commercial marketing research. He always insisted that the questionnaire and the overall experimental design of a survey were equally as important as the sample. The efficiency and dependability of the questionnaire can be tested on statistical grounds only if the sample test is rigid and unbiased. The researcher must be interested in the sample problem, because it is the means to the end of a good survey.

Importance of the Product & the Relationship to Advertising:

If MARKETING is to be successful, the marketer must know and learn to anticipate consumer needs and wants. He must work diligently to offer products or services that fill those needs and wants before the competition beats him to it.

For ADVERTISING to be effective and increase sales, advertising executives must know everything about the product and how best to communicate the product's key attributes to the consumer in order to stimulate purchase.

Politz suggested that in order for *Research* to be truly useful to marketing and advertising, the researcher must first become an expert on the product and then become an expert on advertising. Only after carefully designed and executed research has been digested and analyzed; only after the researcher understands the synergy of marketing, advertising and research; only then can research assist in the development of better products and more effective advertising. And he insisted that researchers must "get their hands dirty", saying they must avoid ". . . the danger of becoming either sterile technicians or arrogant armchair strategists who sell advice to the fighting forces without ever appearing on the fighting lines".

Alfred Politz considered himself, first and foremost, a marketing man, and he never underestimated the importance, or the intelligence, of the consumer. At the same time, he believed implicitly that the most important ingredient in the marketing mix was the quality of the product. A company must start with a good product and, through "dialogue" with consumers in the form of marketing research, ensure its continuing high quality. Then advertise it honestly and in language consumers can relate to. Good advertising could only rescue a bad product in the very short term. Indeed, good advertising could draw attention to a product's shortcomings, and hasten its demise.

304   The Politz Papers

Observational Powers of Large Groups:

Some observers have had difficulty with the Politz assertion that large numbers of people could "observe" small product differences that no individual could discern. In particular, they were skeptical about the claim that marketing research could sometimes discover product characteristics or shortcomings that were known only to the technical or R & D people and, in some cases, even before these specialists became aware of them. Yet it was true, as was repeatedly demonstrated.

To cite one example, which is an extension of one that was alluded to by Politz in an earlier chapter:

> A major study of motorists was conducted in ten countries in Europe for the Mobil Oil Company. Among many other things, the survey revealed that engine knocking was a significantly greater cause for complaint by motorists in some countries than in others. For example, knocking was a big cause for complaint in Switzerland, but not in the Netherlands. This did not surprise us, as earlier studies in the U.S. had dealt with the consequences of such factors as varying climatic conditions, different road gradients and other driving conditions. We suggested that Mobil might gain a competitive advantage by increasing its octane rating in gasoline sold in the more mountainous parts of Europe. It worked.
>
> And there was an important additional benefit—the head of product research, an engineer who had always been highly skeptical about the value and reliability of marketing research, was both surprised and delighted to find it confirming and supporting his recent recommendation to do just that—and for the same reasons. Marketing research had gained a convert who became an enthusiastic participant in other successful product/marketing innovations.

The Value of Continuity in Research:

Early in his research career, Politz was often frustrated to review the findings of a just-completed survey, and wish he had asked a number of additional questions. This was a major factor in his decision to confine himself to a small number of clients, with whom he could consult on a continuing basis. The benefits of building on previously-developed knowledge are displayed through-out this book.

Continuity of the Politz type is only possible if the buyer of research insists on it, and establishes a virtual partnership with a research supplier. It is probable that very few contemporary research directors actually do this, preferring to do their own design and analysis and buy only the field work and processing. There is nothing inherently wrong with this, provided the research director has the requisite intelligence and experience. In fact, given the dearth of contemporary research suppliers who are prepared to either restrict themselves to a limited number of clients or to stick their necks out and make unequivocal recommendations, the corporate research director is forced to do it himself.

The lesson from Politz is that he should discipline himself to carry out such intelligence-building research, and not look at each study as a new exercise in gathering information.

The Concept of the Controllable Cause:

Politz said the causes behind consumers' actions are infinite, some the result of physical circumstances, while others are of a subjective or even psychological nature. He taught that the problem of the researcher was not to discover the many causes for consumer buying behavior, but to find controllable causes—those on which action can be taken. Effective research recognizes that behind every consumer's act in buying or not buying there can be a multiplicity of causes, and generally not just a single, unique cause. The purpose of the research is to find those causes which can be controlled by the advertiser—to tell the advertiser what to do in order to sell more of his product or service.

This is such a simple and logical concept, one wonders that it was not better understood and used in the development of new products and the re-design of older ones, in the selection of distribution methods, and in advertising. Because they were misdirected by inadequate research, or no research at all, the consequence was that advertisers and their agencies wasted or, at best, under-employed countless millions of dollars.

Experimental Design:

Without doubt the most vital lesson that can be learned from the work of Alfred Politz is the importance of applying experimental design in the early stages of any research. He once wrote, "Hypotheses are hunches formulated with rigor so that experimentation can provide the verdict as to the correctness or incorrectness of the hypotheses". Yes, the sample is important; yes, the quality of the field work is important; yes, you must exercise intelligence in the analysis of the results. But unless you have constructed a questionnaire that will test out hunches and hypotheses that you have thought through in advance, the survey results may be interesting but non-actionable.

Some years ago, after reading the Harvard Business Review article in which Politz had discussed the car accelerator spring/pick up example, a British researcher wrote a book in which he was rather critical of the Politz study, concluding that it was "only by happy chance that the questionnaire included a question that revealed the relationship" between the softness of the spring and the perception of pick-up. This researcher entirely missed the point. Politz was not seeking the "truth" from respondents; he was testing his guess that there was some connection between the two things, and included straight-forward and innocent questions for the express purpose of making the cross reference later. The research design was deceptively simple; only the advance thinking was difficult, and the outcome was profound.

Alfred Politz understood the importance of experimental design, and he employed it successfully in his research work. He shared his views and many of his experiences with everyone who took the time or had the wisdom to

306   The Politz Papers

listen. Certainly he embedded it in the minds of his employees, many of whom honed their already well-developed talents under his tutelage. No one who ever worked for Alfred Politz forgot the lessons he taught them. Many are still at work as professional researchers and others have re-taught the lessons to students from their teaching positions at various universities.

Students of marketing and marketing research, as well as current practitioners, would do well to heed the Politz advice that they include mathematical statistics and experimental psychology in their studies. These provide the knowledge, and the discipline, that will enable the researcher to seek out hypotheses, develop hunches, even fantasize, and then apply scientific rigor to the design of his or her surveys. He has said, "Many people are not aware that a survey operation based on mere interviewing and experimental design can be made so rigid a tool as to often exceed the industrial laboratory in precision".

This, then, is the final legacy of Alfred Politz:
MARKETING RESEARCH, CARRIED OUT BY SINCERE AND DEDICATED PROFESSIONALS, USING RIGOROUS METHODS TO PRODUCE FINDINGS IN WHICH THEY COULD HAVE TOTAL CONFIDENCE, AND WITH THE COURAGE TO MAKE RECOMMENDATIONS AND PREDICT THE OUTCOME, COULD BE ONE OF THE MOST IMPORTANT TOOLS AVAILABLE TO THE MANAGEMENT OF ANY ENTERPRISE.

That this was not more readily recognized by either researchers or management did not diminish its importance or validity. It gave his clients and some other like-minded companies immense competitive advantages, but was a cause of disappointment and sadness to Alfred Politz, the teacher, who so freely shared his knowledge and his wisdom.

Part VI
Consumer Behaviour

[37]

Excerpt from A. Elizabeth Levett, *The Consumer in History*, 17–40.

IV.

Elizabethan England.

The sixteenth century saw something of a revolution in the position of the consumer. The producer was growing steadily wealthier and more apt to produce on a large scale, especially as international

17

THE CONSUMER IN HISTORY.

trade developed, and demand for larger supplies, uniform in quality, stimulated production. But as the producer tends towards capitalism, so the number of wage-earning " consumers " increases, and the basis of consumption is broadened at the bottom of the scale. Again, the accumulation of capital, and the growing tendency to lend it at interest, or to invest it in a company or in some novel enterprise, was very marked, and for the first time seems to make possible a class of " consumers " who are not in any direct degree producers. Formerly such a class could hardly exist, save as pensioners, or on assigned incomes from land. From the sixteenth century onwards it is increasingly common to find men and women living upon invested capital, and, therefore, forming a small specialised group of pure consumers.

The Tudor period is essentially the age of the middle class, and, indeed, of the " middle man " in the economic sense. The question of *distribution* became acute, and it is interesting to notice how great was contemporary wrath with the distributor. Described as " brogger," " bodger," " broker," " forestaller," " regrater "—in a whole vocabulary of abuse—he appears as the villain of all economic troubles. Into his operations a strong element of monopoly, of " cornering," might often enter, but it is usually apparent that he was fulfilling a useful and necessary function, rendered all the more necessary by the difficulties of transport. Tudor England was liable to extremes of want of different commodities in isolated districts, and was unreasonably jealous of those who,

18

THE CONSUMER IN HISTORY.

for a substantial consideration, endeavoured to supply
those districts. The history of the Welsh cattle
drover, for example, is the story of producers who,
by inventing a " middle man," performed a valuable
service to the consumer—the English farmer who
bought Welsh cattle at the fair.

Again, the Tudor period is emphatically the period
of State control and protection of the consumer. The
balance of industries and interests, at which the
mercantile statesmen aimed, was to be ensured by
legislation. The consumer is definitely told what he
may not consume, and he is carefully instructed (by
Act of Parliament in the case of fish), as to what he
ought to consume, but apparently in England the
extreme step was never taken of ordaining how much
of certain monopolised or taxed goods the consumer
must consume. On the whole, however, the interests
of the consumer were protected by the constant
legislation as to food prices and food supply; both
the State and the municipalities kept up an active,
if not always very clear-sighted, supervision of the
question of distribution and the reasonable profits
of the distributor. But what was statesmanlike in
this policy finally broke down in the indiscriminate
granting of monopolies, in which the interest of the
consumer was definitely sacrificed to that of the
privileged producer—not a whole class, but a few
favoured individuals.

With the passing of the Tudor Government, and of
the early Stuart monarchs, we pass into an age in
which the State abdicates its care for the consumer,

19

THE CONSUMER IN HISTORY.

and the only motto in common use seems to have been: " Let the devil take the hindmost." The problem before us, therefore, in modern times is how and when and how far did the consumer decide that he would not be the hindmost.

The ever-recurring complaint of the social historian throughout the centuries was that the foreign merchant, or the capitalist merchant, was importing manufactured goods into England, raising the standard of luxury, creating a vast new army of retailers, and incidentally producing unemployment in the staple English industries. Convincing complaints reach us of the army of pedlars, packmen, itinerant traders and " bodgers," who supplemented and sometimes replaced the periodic fairs by more informal visits to church porches or abbey gates on Sundays. The moralist was annoyed, and the manufacturer, always a trifle too conservative, was alarmed. The economist, looking back, notes chiefly the widening of the basis of consumption. What is much less clear to the student is the vast extension during this period of what we know as the " shop "—the purely retail business on a permanent footing.

In the early Middle Ages the stalls in the market seem to have been more or less permanent structures; rent was regularly paid for them, and sometimes their design was legally laid down. Thus, at Codicote, a *hovel* was held to mean a little hut or building of four posts and a roof, but without walls or ceiling. The " shambles " of a butcher's stall are likewise defined. These stalls were open one, two, or more

20

THE CONSUMER IN HISTORY.

days a week, according to demand, and from the
names of ancient streets we see how various trades
were segregated, and the hovel became a shop, which
is often both workshop and place of distribution.
This change has been effected largely by the consumer, whose demand becomes both more individual
and more capricious. But the shop belonging to a
member of a productive guild is quite unlike the modern
retail shop, since it is primarily a workshop. What
we want to know is when the permanent retailer came
into existence, apart from the guild. When does the
consumer demand a shop which shall be at his disposal
at all hours? When did the village shop of to-day
begin its existence? Was the "truck" or "tommy"
shop of the early nineteenth century something new
in kind? We know the annual fair, the weekly
market, the wandering pedlar, the wealthy guildsman
by numberless descriptions. The permanent retailer
is almost a stranger in social history or in literature,
and as to the "consumer," who brings him into existence, he is equally seldom mentioned. Occasionally,
in following random footsteps about the town, we
meet the shop. The Royal Exchange, built by Sir
Thomas Gresham, formed a quadrangle, the lowest
rooms of which were covered in like a cloister, and
used as shops. But these shops were dark and dank,
and more like warehouses; the "upper pawn," or
first floor, was the scene of fashionable business. The
whole must have resembled the famous arrangement
of the shops in the "Rows" of Chester. At one
shop door a girl talks to the passer-by.

21

THE CONSUMER IN HISTORY.

" Would ye have any fair linen cloth ? Mistress, see what I have, and I will show you the fairest linen cloth in London; if you do not like it, you may leave it; you shall bestow nothing but the looking on, the pain shall be ours to show them you."

Language has changed, but the method of attracting or beguiling the consumer has evidently remained much the same through the centuries. Shopping in the Exchange was a fashionable morning pastime for ladies, rendered the more agreeable by the escort of one or two gentlemen of leisure, or some small boys most uncomfortably smartened and tidied for the occasion. What they bought is not hard to discover; the " London Cries " of the streets teach us how easy it was to fall a victim to the delights of " fine Seville oranges," " Cherry Ripe," a very fine cabinet, a fine scarf, good cambric, or fair bone lace; pins, points, garters, Spanish gloves, or silk ribbons, or " a new book, new come forth." Less fashionable shoppers satisfied humbler needs on hot mutton pies, live periwinkles, fresh herrings, or ripe cowcumbers. Elizabethan England had moved far indeed from the old standards of the self-sufficing household, and the "consumer" is rapidly becoming a power in the land. As yet, however, he hardly recognises his own power, and the State, perhaps, recognises it only too clearly, and is too ready both to limit and to supplement the strength of an efficient economic demand.

22

THE CONSUMER IN HISTORY.

V.

The Seventeenth Century.

The seventeenth century seems somewhat lacking in points towards a history of the consumer. It is the age of associations of merchants on a large scale— the great chartered and regulated companies, and of the re-groupings of the industrial workers into municipal companies—a half-way house between the guild and the trade union. For the first twenty years of the century private monopolies remained the great burden upon the consumer. Regulation of prices survived sporadically, but probably made little effective difference to the cost of living. The abolition of monopolies in 1619 was considerably more important in lowering prices.

But the Puritan tendency to individualism has, perhaps, been unduly emphasised, and, during the Commonwealth period, there were certainly signs that the Government was prepared to consider the needs of the poor consumer. On the whole, however, the Puritan mind was apt to regard consumption as almost a sin in itself, and there is no doubt that the enforced simplicity of life among Puritans and Quakers hastened the accumulation of capital in middle-class hands, while the consumer of this class was reasonably able to protect himself by his capacity to defer or decrease consumption.

The really serious problem of the seventeenth century was, however, financial, and it is only possible to indicate the problem here, without working out its effect upon the consumer. Since the reign of

23

THE CONSUMER IN HISTORY.

Elizabeth, the influx of silver from the New World
had caused a steady rise in prices, with an accompanying rise in the cost of government and in the
cost of living among private citizens. Wages, which
have in them always an element of custom, seldom rise
as quickly as prices, and at this time they were being
artificially kept low by the somewhat irregular assessments of the Justices of the Peace. Taxation, in like
manner, had in it a strong element of custom, and
when the Crown tried to adjust taxation to the need
for a growing revenue, a constitutional crisis was the
result, which ended in the great Civil War. The great
economic problem of the seventeenth century was the
adjustment of social conditions to a change in the
value of money, and there seems to be little doubt
that the poorer consumers, less organised now than
in the Middle Ages, and less capable perhaps of
domestic production, suffered acutely during the
process, in spite of efforts to help them.

Before passing on, however, to the consumer of the
eighteenth century, and his relation to the retail
trader, it may be useful to examine briefly the
resources of the humbler types of consumers, whose
great numbers were ultimately to compensate for the
slenderness of their purse, in determining the lines of
production.

The earlier forms in which wages were paid are
worthy of some notice, since they throw some light
upon the "truck" system of modern times, and they
illustrate one of the most potent influences of the
"consumer" upon economic history. By the four-

THE CONSUMER IN HISTORY.

teenth century it is usual to find a considerable number of regular farm workers who are being paid wages, in addition to the smallholders who owed compulsory labour. Often the regular workers are also smallholders, and the two classes shade into each other insensibly. Wages are found to consist of (*a*) a yearly sum of money, from 2s. to 6s.—that is, the price of a cheap horse or a quarter of wheat; (*b*) a weekly supply of corn, perhaps a bushel a week, which might be worth 10d. or 1s.; (*c*) a remission of rent and services, varying in value from 5s. to 12s. or 15s. per annum; (*d*) certainly some meals " at the lord's table ".; (*e*) some perquisites of timber, or hay, or fruit, or milk and cheese, or the last lamb, or the smallest pig.

It is obviously difficult to estimate the prosperity of a man thus remunerated; it is also evident that his needs as *consumer* are being satisfied in the easiest way, and that so long as quality of product and intensity of desire remained more or less uniform, he would continue to accept the lord's corn rather than seek to purchase in a market some miles away. This elementary form of "truck" survived in some degree in agricultural wages down to recent times, and, though commonly advantageous, has been an important factor in retarding any organisation of consumers in country districts. Demand changes slowly, but when demand changes, organisation will change; if margarine and cinemas are preferable to butter and no cinema, the consumer will begin to do something about it. The organisation of a local milk supply is

25

THE CONSUMER IN HISTORY.

an obvious field for consumers' efforts. The mediæval
town-labourer, while he was an apprentice, lived under
something very like a " truck system," in which it
might be necessary to regulate by contract the quality
of his meals and dress. The remuneration of the
" journeyman," the day-labourer of the guild system,
is a question as yet imperfectly explored and his
manner of living is very obscure. Whether he " lived
in," whether he could or could not marry, how far his
wages were supplemented by payments in kind—
these are questions not easy to answer. Certain it is
that he was the discontented element in the system—
the man whose demand for a better standard of life
would ultimately produce changes.

Throughout the sixteenth and the seventeenth
centuries it seems clear that the assessment of wages
by the Justices of the Peace was tending to keep
wages artificially low, and thus to limit at the base
the wage-earner's capacity as a consumer. The Poor
Law system did something to keep him from dire
need, and in country districts and small towns the
little plot of land usually attached to his cottage,
together with his share of common made him to some
extent a producer on his own behalf as well as for his
employer. It would be difficult to produce a weekly
"household budget" for this period, showing how the
workman's slender wage was spent; but it is clear
that his effective demand as a consumer was too
slight and too irregular to be capable of much organisation. On the other hand, Defoe, at the end of the
century, complains that one of the causes of poverty

26

THE CONSUMER IN HISTORY.

lies in the fact that the English working man " will eat and drink, but especially the latter, three times as much as any sort of foreigners of the same dimensions." But Defoe was rather apt to ascribe to the vices of the poor all the effects of the greed of the rich, though he admits elsewhere that higher wages, by stimulating consumption, would ultimately increase industry and trade and national prosperity. Among all his projects, however, he did not include any association of consumers—possibly because his experience had lain chiefly among the consumers of luxuries.

VI.

The New Shopkeeping.

Defoe's well-known work on " The Compleat Tradesman " gives a remarkable historical picture of the lives of shopkeepers at the beginning of the eighteenth century. The mediæval world had gone; the modern store had not arrived; the City of London must have resembled the country town of our own memories. " Customers appear to have been extraordinarily trying; the arrogance which Defoe describes in fashionable purchasers is almost incredible. Subserviency is the shopkeeper's virtue; a good tradesman must dissemble his rage, even if he is obliged to run upstairs and kick his unoffending family to relieve his feelings. The 'compleat tradesman' at that time lives over his shop and keeps a small group of assistants and apprentices, for whom he provides a kind of family life, conceived on tolerably generous lines of reason-

27

THE CONSUMER IN HISTORY.

able supervision. He reads prayers to them every evening, unless he is so much given up to ostentation as to be unwilling to serve even his Maker. In that case he offers a small salary to the parish reader ! He has a country house for his wife and children, but he sends them away and continues to attend to his business alone. He ought not, if he is to be successful, to ride or hunt, or learn ' to talk dog-language.' A good man of business must take his recreations in his wife's parlour behind the shop. Indeed, a striking feature of Defoe's description is the utter lack of any reasonable recreations or limitation of hours. The master should be accessible from 7 a.m. till 12, and again from 2 p.m. till 9 p.m. The country gentleman's horses, dogs, and gardens are inappropriate; the society man's coffee house, gaming table, balls, or facilities for drinking were pernicious and a waste of time. Politics were impossible. If he wished to put his country first, let him give up business and enlist. His hours were inconsistent with the playhouse."*

The voluminous descriptive literature of the eighteenth century seems to be curiously lacking in descriptions of the small shop of the period. Two of the most detailed modern works—Mrs. George's *London in the Eighteenth Century*, and A.S. Turberville's *Men and Manners* — have been searched almost in vain. Hogarth's delightful little handbill for his sister's millinery shop was the only reward. Plenty of material must exist, some of it in the books of

* "Social and Political Thinkers of the Augustan Age."—ED. HEARNSHAW.

28

THE CONSUMER IN HISTORY.

household accounts kept by careful middle-class
housewives; some of it in the old tradesmen's books
which have been preserved. The history of tradesmen's tokens, by which a scarcity of small coin was
partially remedied, would produce more links. Towards the end of the century the pressing burden of
poverty among the agricultural labourers led to
investigations of their weekly purchases, such as
are to be found in the Rev. David Davies' detailed
work on *The Case of the Labourers in Husbandry* (1795)
or in Eden's *State of the Poor*. But, broadly speaking,
no detailed investigation has ever been made by any
competent historian of the manner in which the
ordinary household supplied its needs during the
eighteenth century. Much might be done, by a very
careful investigation of the cost of living of different
classes, to show how far the extremes of poverty
might have been avoided by some type of consumers'
association. Possibly only a small fraction of the
evil could have been avoided, but the way to far-
reaching changes was pointed out by such early
associations as the Hull Anti-Mill Society, founded
in 1795, which sought to combat the high prices of
food by attacking the cost of production and the
employers' profits. Flour was not a very promising
commodity to deal with in the days of a European
war, but the success of the mill, which survived till
1894, shows how readily the profits of the industrial
revolution might have been differently distributed,
if better leadership and more political freedom had
been available. Conditions in shops such as Defoe

29

THE CONSUMER IN HISTORY.

described had changed but little by the early years of the nineteenth century, for which Robert Owen has left us a vivid description of a shop assistant's life and hours. It might well appear that it is the shopkeeper who first needs protection against the capricious consumer. We have, however, no familiar contemporary description of a shop catering for the poor wage-earner in the eighteenth century, and if we may trust the moralists of the period, it was the gin shop to which wages usually found their way. The sudden outbreak of gin drinking in the early eighteenth century must have had a demoralising effect upon the social habits of thousands of wage-earners.

Throughout the century, however, the type of demand was changing, and the shop changes with it. Domestic industries were dying in all directions; every invention, every development of machinery, meant cheaper goods for sale in shops and less willingness to carry on the traditional household crafts of baking and brewing, spinning and weaving. They disappeared at different rates in different districts, affected by local circumstances, such as the abundance or scarcity of fuel, and of the traditional articles of diet. When the industrial revolution came, bearing off the women into the factories, the change was rapid and unavoidable. For a short time, during the worst abuses of the Poor-law system, large numbers of women were employed in agriculture, more or less permanently, and the household arts underwent another degradation. The corresponding change, the

30

THE CONSUMER IN HISTORY.

evolution of the general village shop, or the small general store in the towns, is an economic change which has never been adequately explored. Before we have realised its appearance as part of the normal village economy, we are confronted with its abuse in the " truck shop." The rise of new centres of specialised industry made necessary the supply of foodstuffs and other indispensable goods, and it might often be to the interest of the employer to organise this supply, and of the workmen to utilise it. It was in this way that Robert Owen gained his experience, at the New Lanark mills, of the purchase and distribution of general stores. But in the hands of unscrupulous employers it is evident that such organisation of supplies might be a fruitful source of oppression and fraud, while the granting of a monopoly right to a single " truck shop " might create a tyranny such as had never entered the wildest dreams of a feudal lord! Perhaps the most vivid picture of the abuses of the system is that contained in Disraeli's novel, *Sybil*—a picture which was based on solid evidence for all but its sketches of personalities. The repeated legislation on the subject shows how essential it was to secure the workman freedom to buy in the cheapest market, and to empower him to receive the whole of his wage in cash and to expend it as he pleased. But difficulties of transport loomed large in the early nineteenth century; the building of railways, for example, meant large temporary settlements of migrant labourers, and the employer's shop or monopoly canteen died hard. In the Welsh valleys

31

THE CONSUMER IN HISTORY.

the system defied the law, and a truck shop was closed in Aberdare as late as 1868.

Cheapness, however, was almost more important than freedom. A benevolent tyrant, such as Owen, might dare to establish a monopoly with some hopes of success, because the benefits he could offer were so substantial; wholesale buying and greater facilities for transport could effect a reduction in prices which might double the purchasing power of wages. An important factor in the situation was the provision of credit for wage-earner. Defoe had seen with his usual acuteness that the most common cause of pauperism was the unforeseen emergency—accident or illness, or unavoidable loss of employment. He had seen, too, that some form of insurance was the only means of preventing the evils of this type of poverty. The loan-funds or "stock" possessed by some parishes also provided to some extent against emergencies. But the "truck shop" was prepared to give the kind of credit which created poverty. Many of the speculative enterprises of the industrial revolution seem to have paid wages when and as they pleased, sometimes not oftener than once a month. Transport of cash was in some districts still difficult and dangerous, and if the manager with the wages was two days late, whole families might be in distress. Credit tickets on the shop were an obvious method of meeting the difficulty, but they only created fresh problems. A wage-earner who was a month in debt to the truck shop, or to his employer's stores, could hardly hope to free himself, and the shackles of monopoly closed

32

THE CONSUMER IN HISTORY.

upon him more tightly. Perhaps the closest parallel of quite modern times lies in the village shops of Ireland, many of which had established a local tyranny only to be combated by co-operative efforts.

In contrast to such perilous forms of credit, we find in some agricultural districts a long-established tradition of leaving part of the weekly wages in a trusted employer's hands until a bi-annual " settling "—a simple form of thrift which adds considerably to the purchasing power of wages.

The development of economic theory, and the closer analysis of economic conceptions, also played its part in the emergence of " the consumer " as a distinct economic force. The distinction between real wages and nominal wages—the distinction between the money rate of wages and their actual purchasing power—could only become clear when certain elementary facts as to currency and prices had been defined and made common knowledge.

VII.

Effects of the Industrial Revolution.

The early part of the nineteenth century saw a serious decline in the wages of many industries; cash wages declined in the competition of machinery; real wages were very seriously and uniformly diminished by the high prices of food, caused largely by the Corn Laws and the multitude of other duties; the rapid fluctuations of prices were almost more disastrous than their rise. The usual acceptance of the " wage-

33

THE CONSUMER IN HISTORY.

fund theory " made it the more difficult to hope for any general rise in wages. All these factors make a background from which it would be reasonable to expect that associations of consumers would emerge. As a matter of fact, however, attention was concentrated upon production. Distress was so acute that radical changes seemed as necessary in economics as in politics. Writers of " Utopias " had usually based their schemes upon some discussion of the amount of labour needed to support life. Sir Thomas More had suggested six hours a day as sufficient to provide for the " good life." Obscure writers of the early nineteenth century were busy asserting that the labour of one man and one horse for 340 days would produce corn enough for fifteen persons for one year; that one acre of land would support two persons; or that two hours' work a day would support a family. Some of these calculations seem a little optimistic in view of both the mediæval and modern practice of smallholders, but they contained an element of truth which made them highly influential.

Hence co-operation in production, with equality in distribution, becomes one of the most popular solutions of the social problem. Robert Owen's belief that human labour is the only natural standard of value, and that labour is the only source of wealth, led to a scheme for a complete change in the foundation of society—a setback in the processes of history, with a general reversion to the self-supporting village community. To produce and to enjoy were to be the ideals of such communities, while the more modern

34

THE CONSUMER IN HISTORY.

desires to trade and to accumulate were to be eliminated from human life.

In all the later phases of his life, however, Robert Owen brought an element of the fantastic into his scheme, which could only secure his own defeat. He seems to have expended all his practical good sense and experience upon his own experiments at New Lanark, and his efforts for the reform of the factory system and the passing of Factory Laws.

Nevertheless, the ideal of co-operative production held the field, however impracticable any individual experiment might seem. It was worked out elaborately by the French Socialists, Fourier and Saint-Simon, and finally by Louis Blanc, who in his " Social Work-shops " (*Les Ateliers Sociaux*) endeavoured to show how co-operative workshops could be set up and financed at first by the State, while gradually becoming independent owners of their own capital. (It is important to notice, in this connection, that Louis Blanc's scheme was not identical with the " National Workshops," set up in the emergency period of 1848, and his ideas were not fairly tested by the revolutionary experiments.) It was probably natural and inevitable that associations of producers should arouse more, and more immediate, interest than associations of consumers. Man thinks of himself as a *creative* animal; it is perhaps one of the great distinctions between him and the lower animals that he is not content with consumption. The consumer is really a mental abstraction like the economic man, and it requires an effort to realise his existence. Pro-

35

THE CONSUMER IN HISTORY.

duction concerns the whole conduct and purpose and
condition of life; consumption seems merely a means to
an end. So at least thinks the normal man or woman—
the citizens of whom the healthy state should be
composed.

Hence it is at first only stern necessity, only the
desire for necessary opposition to tyranny, monopoly,
or gross inefficiency that brings into being the consumers' association. Just as in the Middle Ages the
opposition to the lord's monopoly of mills was the
typical cause of trouble, so in the late eighteenth
century we have the Hull Anti-Mill Society, already
mentioned, created in opposition to the private flour
mills of Hull. This action of " a large number of the
poor inhabitants of Hull " building their own mill,
at a cost of £2,000, raised by subscriptions of 1s. 9d.
a week or less, formed an emphatic protest against
the dearness of food to the consumer. Although it
could do little or nothing to mitigate the effects of
war and of the Corn Laws, it could at least eliminate
individual monopolistic policy; the wicked miller of
mediæval legend was at least curbed in his activities by
resolute combination. The movement grew very slowly;
a second mill was started in Hull in 1801, and others
followed at Whitby and elsewhere, partly as a protest
against adulteration. That the enterprise was financially
sound is evident from the fact we have noticed of the
survival of the original mill for nearly 100 years. The
Rochdale Pioneers Cooperative Society was soon
constrained to add a flour mill to its other activities.

36

THE CONSUMER IN HISTORY.

VIII.
Consumer and Producer.

This is not, however, the place to write the history of the origin of co-operation. That has been done by Mrs. Sidney Webb. All that has been aimed at here is an attempt, in looking back over history, to isolate " the consumer," and to show when and where he becomes sufficiently articulate to organise himself, with a view to increasing his *spending* power, rather than his earning power. Yet, if Mrs. Webb proves anything, she seems to prove that it is this side of economic life which is organised with most difficulty. Producers are slow to realise themselves as consumers; when once they have done so they begin to see that their consumption involves someone else's production, and that they cannot, in so far as they are a body with ideals beyond that of mere quantity, ignore the conditions of production. Hence the consumers' association, which wants cheap boots or cheap cocoa or cheap fruit, may be driven back to production— to owning its own factories and farms and plantations. The growth is slow and gradual, and many forces tell against the union of the two classes, but the moral of the experiment is very significant. Neither consumer nor producer can ignore the other. Even within the bounds of one society their interests may be opposed. And the relationship is far more complex than a question of wage. It has its bearing upon the whole national organisation of industry, and, as has been shown by Mr. Leonard Woolf, also upon international questions. Not only is the relationship

37

THE CONSUMER IN HISTORY.

between producer and consumer complicated by
almost all the social and political problems of the
world, but the consumer himself is not at unity with
himself. It was not only Marie Antoinette who
believed that cake could be substituted for bread.
Men genuinely desire, after certain elementary needs
are satisfied, to consume different objects. The opium
smoker, and the prohibitionist, and the distiller of
" potheen " have all to be fitted into a world which,
if possible, shall be at peace. There are those of us
who genuinely do not want artificial silk to oust the
older cottons and linens which used to satisfy us.
But an industrial world organised for production can
pay no heed to minority groups among consumers.
Nor can associations of consumers organised on a
large scale. The way seems to be open to large
numbers of small co-operative groups, organised for
the provision of specialised services or commodities,
and controlled by managers who have the outlook
of artists.

Under modern methods of production large minorities remain dissatisfied, suffering poor workmanship
and crude colours when they both could and would
pay reasonable sums for good quality. It would be
an interesting experiment if certain great firms would
reserve part of the advertising space so ably filled
by " Callisthenes " and similar ladies, for a series of
articles by well-known professional men and women
who would explain " *How and where the modern shop
or store fails me.*" We would suggest that half a dozen
of our favourite contributors to *Punch* be invited to

38

THE CONSUMER IN HISTORY.

begin. Candid remarks by the consumer, which now never get beyond the ears of the shop assistant, might often result in an association of consumers, or at least in a different orientation of production. It is not true to say that the consumer can indicate his choice by his purchases. Those of us who are occupied in production, or in purely intellectual work, can often only spend a few minutes each day as consumers, and we save time by accepting the unsatisfactory object.

It is because I believe any reasonable economic future, for those who desire the " good life " rather than the maximum wealth, must lie with numerous and varied groups of consumers, that I would advocate more historical study of the whole subject.

The great difficulty of writing even a few pages under the title " The Consumer in History " is that the preliminary spade work has not been done. " The purchaser " has not been studied with the same minuteness as the producer. We do not know who purchased the goods made by the guild-brethren. We cannot easily follow a piece of cloth beyond the market-place or the Cloth Hall, into the very hands of the consumer. In many cases the original material does not exist for this study. But much could be done by a re-orientation of interest. Historians are already busy trying to trace in detail the consumption of English wool as a raw material. How did it find its way to the weaver ? How far and where was there any home consumption of the professionally manufactured woollen cloth ? Who bought the first

39

THE CONSUMER IN HISTORY.

cottons ? When and why were they preferred to
linens ? In the case of a specialised industry, the
mediæval English silk weavers and embroideresses,
it is possible to give an almost exact answer to such
questions, but this is rare. Again, there is, I believe,
no detailed study of " the shop " in Tudor times or
in the seventeenth century, yet there must be much
literary and a little statistical evidence available.
Eighteenth century household accounts and tradesmen's books, as already suggested, would go far to
supply a detailed picture, but nothing of the kind is
to be found in the " social histories " which multiply
so rapidly.

There are here at least half a dozen themes for
research students in search of a " subject "; some of
them might make readable books. In any case the
search would necessarily discover many elementary
associations of consumers, and would illuminate the
motives of such associations. That is, perhaps, the
great desideratum. If the future lies with co-operation, it must be an infinitely varied co-operation.

Let me end with a memory, which is also an allegory.

Some years ago an idealistic but unwise journalist
sat talking with a wise and idealistic writer in journals.
Said the wise man to the unwise: " Why, John, to
hear you talk one would almost think that production
was a sin in itself."

One of these two is now a member of His Majesty's
Government; it is, perhaps, safer to leave the reader
to discover which.

40

[38]

Desire - Induced, Innate, Insatiable?

Kathleen M. Rassuli and Stanley C. Hollander

An explosion of interest in consumption has occurred among American and European historians. While social historians have paid the most attention to consumption a broad array including economic, communications and intellectual historians have taken up this issue. These authors have varying views of the nature of changes in consumption and of the dimensions and causes of these changes. This article attempts to summarize the historians' views.

"O reason not the need: our basest beggars
Are in the poorest thing superfluous.
Allow not nature more than nature needs,
Man's life is cheap as beast's. Thou art a lady;
If only to go warm were gorgeous,
Why, nature needs not what thou gorgeous wear'st,
Which scarcely keeps thee warm. But, for true need—"
King Lear, Act II, Scene iv
William Shakespeare, 1605

The desire to purchase and consume goods above some minimum level traditionally has been frowned on by moral and social critics, and even those less intent on criticism at least consider certain types of consumption superfluous. The moral debate on consumption will, no doubt, continue to rage. However, many historians believe that for good or ill the Western world is in the midst of, not merely high levels of consumption, but actually a "culture of consumption" (Fox and Lears 1983; McKendrick, Brewer and Plumb 1982; Horowitz 1985; Leach 1984; Hollitz 1981; Potter 1954). Likewise, marketers, who are viewed variously either as one of the causes of that culture or as having exacerbated it, continue to be at the heart of the controversy which surrounds the topic (Potter 1954; Ewen 1976; also see Pollay 1986).

Kathleen M. Rassuli is Lecturer in the Division of Business and Economics, Indiana-Purdue University, Fort Wayne, Indiana. Stanley C. Hollander is Professor of Marketing, Michigan State University, East Lansing, Michigan.

What are the roots of this culture of consumption? How, when and why did it evolve? What has been and what will be the role and impact of marketing? The notion that these questions are of great historical import is beginning to be recognized by a wide variety of historians, including intellectual and social historians as well as economic, anthropological, and communications scholars with historical orientations. The answers to such questions help to explain modern society. The same questions are also of great relevance to marketers at both a macro and micro level because they contribute to the evaluation of marketing and to the prediction of its future role. Indeed, marketers and consumer behaviorists must ask whether the desire for more goods and services is induced, innate, and/or insatiable?

Historians and historically oriented writers assign America's entrance into a "culture of consumption" to various points, ranging from the 1920s to mid-nineteenth century and even earlier. Horowitz (1985, p. 187) notes that modern scholarship tends to affirm an early rather than a late date for the birth and growth of the consumer culture. Many writers also see that consumption culture as having been preceded, in the eighteenth and nineteenth centuries, by major expansions of consumptive activity and interest both abroad and in the United States. In this review of the literature we note what these historians tell us about the development of that culture.

Since we are not trying to write a history of the history of consumption, we have tended to rely on modern sources and generally have not reproduced the extensive reference trails that underlie most of the books and articles we do cite. But one of the results of this work is awareness of a vast bibliographic asset generally untapped by marketing scholars.

The term "culture of consumption" seems to include several elements which can be listed in order of increasing significance:

• People (or some very substantial segment of the population) consume at a level substantially above that of crude, survival-level subsistence.

• People obtain goods and services for consumption through exchange rather than self-production.

• Consumption is seen as an acceptable and appropriate activity.

• People, in fact, tend to judge others and perhaps themselves in terms of their consuming lifestyles.

Notwithstanding the relative importance of the questions raised by the history of consumption, to date consumer behavior textbooks have had little to say on the subject. Some textbook authors neglect the topic of history completely. Others follow the generally accepted "evolution of the marketing concept." One example of this latter approach is Markin (1969, p. 4). He notes,

> During the early 1950's the U.S. economy began to witness a profound and fundamental alteration. Suddenly business firms began to realize that we are moving into an era of widespread affluence. Consumers, too, began to realize that [quoting Britt] "no matter how little money [they] might have, [they] are 'millionaires' compared to most people in the world." . . . So born of necessity

> and ingenuity, and nurtured by practitioners and by economic reality, the marketing concept began to be widely accepted and implemented. [Last two brackets appear in the original.]

Assael (1984) also approaches the history of consumption through the conventional textbook model of the development of the marketing concept; i.e., a production economy until 1930, a sales promotion economy until 1950 and then a marketing economy. A notable exception is McNeal (1982), who devotes a small but well-written section to the history of consumption. In the context of development, Zaltman and Wallendorf (1983) also touch on some historical factors in consumer behavior. On the whole, however, aside from the exceptions mentioned, attention to historical detail is scant. The Association for Consumer Research Singapore conference (Tan and Sheth 1985) on history is a step toward rectification of this shortcoming.

Besides exhibiting considerable chronological shortsightedness and probable inaccuracy, the prevailing view also tends to focus on changes in consumer affluence and firms' production capabilities, perhaps to the exclusion of other factors. Moreover, while consumer researchers generally concede that variables such as culture, society, and social class are important in understanding consumers, there is little integration of these variables in buyer decision models.

Historical work in no way contradicts veteran marketing teacher George Burton Hotchkiss' now-forgotten .1938 assertion that buyers' markets, conditions in which supply outruns *effective* demand, constitute historical normalcy. Since many historians emphasize the early role of advertising and marketing in creating the consumption society, their work does in many instances contrast with a view, prevalent among modern marketers, that we lived in a society characterized by insufficient goods to meet eager markets until about 1930, or possibly 1920, when aggressive selling suddenly became necessary to move great surpluses (for contrary views see Fullerton 1985 and Hollander, forthcoming). The historians do expand marketing perspectives on consumption, perhaps revise prevailing thoughts on how present consumption levels were reached, and provide additional illustration for both existing and new consumer behavior theory.

THE LITERATURE

Robert Lynd may have been guilty of some exaggeration, but not of gross error, in his 1934 statement that the literature virtually ignored the ultimate consumer; that a good university library of 600,000 volumes might contain 10 on the consumer of which seven or eight would have been written by advertising or marketing people intent on exploitation. Horowitz (1978, p. 388) believes that the lack of attention to the consumer is "especially glaring" in light of the importance of consumption to our society. Furthermore, Blumin (1985, pp. 318, 330-334) finds us still woefully lacking good retrospective consumption studies. Certainly, we are all aware of how both the technical consumer behavior and the consumerist publications have increased in recent decades. Lately historians, especially social historians and national culture specialists, and more recently economic historians (Stuard 1985) have demonstrated a similar increase of interest in consumption. In the following sections our aim is to describe some of the approaches and insights that the historically oriented have added to the study of consumption. We do not presume to claim that this is a definitive statement on the history of consumption, only that it is an introduction to the topic.

The individual authors who addressed the culture of consumption by no means can be considered a cohesive group. Included in their ranks are historians, sociologists, political scientists, communications specialists, and anthropologists. Each from his or her own perspective lists a variety of causes and enabling mechanisms which contributed to the development of the consumption culture of which, they believe, we are a part. The varied nature of their arguments defy a neat classification scheme; to classify them is, perhaps, to oversimplify their theses. Nevertheless, some similarities do come to the fore.

Although a few writers (Bell 1978; Schudson 1984) suggest societies or epochs with little interest in consumption (mainly remote ones), most of the literature we have encountered accepts the idea of fairly strong desires for goods and services. However, the effective strength of that desire in the marketplace is seen as a function of not only the spending power consumers have but also such factors as

orientation of the prevailing ethos toward austerity or hedonism (Hollitz 1981; Fox and Lears 1983; Linden 1979; Vichert 1971), the degree of mobility prevailing in class relations (Gilboy 1932; Potter 1954; Lears 1985), and the extent of the marketing effort being exerted upon the consumers (McMahon 1972; Ewen 1976; Potter 1954). In other words, although the desire to consume may seem always strong, the historians would argue that it is even stronger, or more precisely, has stronger expression, under some circumstances than others. In the words of Braudel (1981), *"Mutatis mutandis* then, one could argue that there is always a potential consumer society" (p. 177).

The circumstances or forces to which historians ascribe the blossoming of consumer societies are shown in Exhibit 1. The main divisions in the exhibit are between external facilitating factors, socioenvironmental factors, and internal motivational factors.

Forces that one might describe as "ecotechnological" occupy the first section of the exhibit. The first of these forces essentially results from the activities of businesses, such as marketing and advertising, supply factors, technology, and innovation. The second major category, "socioenvironmental" forces, refers to broad sociological changes which historians believe to be necessary to support a consumer society. Demographic forces are included in this category as well. The third major division includes the set of factors, innate within the individual, which are believed to foster the growth of a consumer society. Included here are the desire to show and emulate and desires to use goods to communicate status, tastes or other attributes, and to use goods to demonstrate or establish affiliation.

The complex arguments put forth by historians generally cannot be classified under a single heading. Almost all of the historians include two or more of the factors in their historical arguments; many include all of the factors to some extent. Potentially, historical work can enrich our understanding of consumption behavior by shedding light on the relationship between psychology, sociology, and technology as they impinge upon consumers' behavior. However, the inter-relatedness of factors results in a pedagogical problem, and the material covered in the sections to follow will not closely resemble headings in Exhibit 1.

EXHIBIT 1

ASCRIBED FACTORS WHICH INFLUENCE THE DEVELOPMENT OF CONSUMER SOCIETY[a]

I.   External Facilitating Factors

   A.   Technical
      1.   Supply of Goods and Services
      2.   Growth of Production Capabilities
      3.   Growth of Mass Marketing Institutions
      4.   Growth of Communications and Transportation Technologies
      5.   Growth of Advertising Media
      6.   Innovation

   B.   Economic Factors
      1.   Increased Wealth and Purchasing Power
      2.   Increased Diffusion of Wealth and Purchasing Power
      3.   Growth of Marketing and Promotion
         a.   Capitalistic Manipulation of Consumers

II. External Socioenvironmental Factors

   A.   Physical Environment
      1.   Population Density—Urbanization
         a.   Decline of Self-sufficiency
         b.   Urban Anonymity
      2.   Geographic Mobility

   B.   Changes in Societal (Collective) Values
      1.   Protestant Reformation
      2.   Rise of Materialism
      3.   Decline of Sumptuary Laws
      4.   The Nature or Absence of Class Structure
      5.   The Myth of Progress

III. Internal Motivational Factors

   A.   Desire for Possessions

   B.   Desire for Status
      1.   Desire to Show Status
      2.   Desire to Emulate People of Status

   C.   Desire for Affiliation and to Communicate Affiliation
      1.   Reference and Aspirational Groups
      2.   Opinion Leadership

   D.   Perceptions of Abundance

[a]This list should not be considered exhaustive; rather it reflects factors which were mentioned by the authors under review here.

In the remainder of this section, the historians' arguments have been classified on the basis of *relative* emphasis placed on one factor or another. In some cases, two or more of the factors listed in Exhibit 1 always occur in tandem. Therefore, they are presented together. Moreover, depending upon the cited authors' perspective, the elements of Exhibit 1 are seen as either causal factors or merely enabling mechanisms. With the exception of fashion history, most of the works discussed herein relate to the *level*, as opposed to the *type*, of consumption.

Marketing/Advertising

Many discussions of advertising and marketing are paradoxical. Generally, speaking, critics, even scholarly and restrained critics such as Potter (1954), see advertising as a highly powerful force that shapes consumer wants and actions. In contrast, defenders such as Borden (1942) and Schudson (1984) point to advertising's weakness and its inability "to make people buy anything that they wouldn't want." Schudson (whose writing follows a rich but complex process of building and then attacking various evaluative propositions) ridicules this argument, but adopts it and holds that both historical example and advertiser tactics show that advertising expenditures follow rather than induce sales results.

Some terminological and conceptual difficulties tend to cloud that debate. The defenders often define "advertising" literally, and then argue that magazine or television presentations are far more economical ways of reaching mass markets than the use of salesmen (Borden 1942). True enough, but the critics often seem to be using "advertising" as a shorthand for all demand stimulation. That is, the critics are, or would be, equally disturbed by the use of large salesforces. We will generally use the broad definition here (see Horowitz 1985; Pollay 1986).

Both sides tend to stipulate that newspaper classified advertising and most retail advertising, especially supermarket price lists, are information and help improve market efficiency. None seem to wonder whether those supermarket lists are actually used as price guides or mainly serve image-building purposes.

The greatest weakness of the debate is the failure of the two sides to meet on common ground. The critics see advertising and marketing as selling not only items but also as selling the general idea of consumption. They hold that advertising in some way shapes media. Wilson (1983) describes mid-nineteenth century American magazines as elitist, depending on voluntarily-submitted manuscripts, and edited for the gentle reader. After 1880, however, they became carefully crafted packages of articles and stories, either commissioned or staff-produced, that would appeal to a broad audience and deliver the circulation advertisers wanted. More importantly, according to the critics, advertising proclaims the virtues of spending, using, and displaying and thus fosters materialism. It affects not only the pattern but the level of consumption.

The defenders can make strong cases by showing instances in which advertising failed to sell products that were not "right," that did not fit consumer tastes or needs. (The media and the agencies do tend to talk more about successes when they promote themselves to potential advertisers.) But the question of promotion's effect on the level of consumption is much less easily researched and it is harder to claim that the massive expenditures are without overall effect.

In a major work McKendrick, Brewer and Plumb (1982) provide a nonjudgmental, but perhaps implicitly approving, description of the role of marketing in evoking consumer demand in eighteenth-century England. They thus place the consumer revolution about a century before the dates most historians assign to the emergence of the American culture of consumption.

McKendrick, who contributed the chapters on the commercialization of the economy, offers a multi-causal explanation for the expansion of demand among all classes of society in eighteenth-century England. Increased supply, income and urbanization played roles. So did the "density" of society; i.e., a class structure composed of many ambiguously defined layers in close contact and blending into each other. This encouraged emulation and fashion "trickle-down." New attitudes toward consumption were important. But all of this was energized by the two major elements of the marketing system: promotion and distribution. Clever promoters, like Josiah Wedgwood (who is treated here as an example rather than as a deviant—his usual place in British economic history), proved to be a master fashion publicist. Wedgwood was also an extremely skilled merchandiser with a keen sense of stratified tastes. These promoters generated enormous interest in their wares. And a complex retailing and distribution system furthered that interest at the local level and also assured the supply that converted consumer interest into actual sales volume. To McKendrick et al., demand did not just exist. Although their value judgments seem different, they agree with the critics in assigning a crucial role to marketing.

Although another British writer (Fraser 1981) also accepts a multiplicity of causes for consumption increases between 1850 and 1914, he seems more interested in what happened rather than why it happened. His work is particularly interesting in three respects: he is more concerned with working people than with the aristocracy, he provides richly detailed descriptions of food, clothing, housing and "luxury" consumption, and he is much concerned with the marketing mechanism that served consumption. In the last named category he deals with developments in credit and transportation as well as in the retail structure.

Daniel Boorstin (1973) is interested in the way in which goods and consumption came to play new roles in American life, and he credits much to the role of business, and especially marketing, in affecting that transformation. As noted earlier, such views are in accord with the proposition that American business became actively market- and marketing-oriented much earlier than is typically indicated in modern marketing textbooks.

Retail Department Stores

Although McKendrick et al. and Fraser discuss the activities of specialist retailers in increasing consumption, others such as Boorstin (1973) and Barth (1980) give pride of place to the late nineteenth century department store.

Urban department stores emerged and blossomed in the mid- to late 1800s and flourished until 1940 or 1950, although the industry went through a severe shakeout in the 1920s and in the Great Depression. Those stores are often seen as occupying a pivotal role in expanding the culture of consumption. "Palaces of consumption; schools for a new culture of buying" (Porter 1979, p. 203) "did more than any other institution to bring fashion to multitudes of people" (Leach 1984, p. 328) and democratized desire (Barth 1980).

The stores did this in many ways; the vast assortments of goods themselves were enticing and they were often enhanced by attractive displays and skilled promotion. Store atmosphere frequently applied a strong sense of gentility to mass merchandising, and this, combined with the momentum generated by the presence of numerous other people engaged in the same activity, legitimized consumption buying. The relative anonymity of the customer, the physical separation of salesclerk and customer in many departments, the consequent ease of terminating a transaction, the impression (and to a lesser degree the reality) of fixed prices, the availability of return and guarantee safeguards, and conveniences in buying made department stores much more congenial than small, snobbish specialty stores for the timorous and the unsophisticated. The department store prices also were often lower.

But department stores, while important mechanisms, were not prime movers. Necessary conditions for their growth were urban population concentrations with sufficient purchasing power to support large-scale enterprise, a condition which in turn was reinforced by the growth of intraurban transportation systems; a supply of goods varied enough to fill those large establishments; and a culture itself receptive to the assignment of a large population sector to the role of shoppers. Traditional department stores developed in North America, Western Europe, Australia, Hong Kong and some other parts of Asia, but had only very limited success in Southern Europe and much of Latin America.

There is some question as to whether department store influence spread below the middle class. As noted, Barth (1980) talks of democratization, and Leach (1984, p. 327) says: "For the first time women of nearly any economic bracket could choose from a spectrum of mass produced, increasingly streamlined everyday wear and sportswear." Schudson (1984), in contrast, believes that the stores more democratized envy than consumption and Porter (1979) sees them as primarily catering to a middle class from professional, ownership, and managerial circles. But she does discuss the existence of basement stores. Both the marketing and the social historians' fascination with the "marble palace" stores also seems to have obscured attention to the cheaper, sleazier department stores.

Supply Characteristics

The notion of supply-side causes has been well documented. In fact, many believe that the supply orientation has been over-emphasized in economic and social history (Foley 1893; Gilboy 1932; Fullerton 1985). Still, most writers would agree that increasing production capabilities and improved technology provided some impetus to the development of a mass consumption society. Many authors surveyed mention one or both of those two factors as a cause or mechanism. However, Atwan, McQuade and Wright (1979) place the most emphasis on technology and innovation. In their upbeat (although undocumented) chapter on invention, they attribute a pivotal role to inventors in the development of a consumer society. They argue that mass production became a cause of new and continued invention and how advertising had the positive and necessary role of informing Americans of new inventions. Foley (1893) and Adam Smith (Rosenberg 1968) also believed advanced productive skills were critical elements.

Although Braudel (1981, vol. 1, p. 324) believes innovation to be a source of progress, he would take exception to arguments of entrepreneurial/innovation determinism (1981, vol. 2, p. 575) in the development of modern civilization. He characterizes the history of inventions as a "misleading hall of mirrors" (1981, vol. 1, p. 435). In Braudel's judgment the necessities of the market led to capitalist innovations. By way of example, he feels the steam engine, which was invented long before the industrial revolution, was launched by the revolution instead of the reverse (ibid., p. 435).

Abundance and Emulation/Show

Beyond increased production, abundance itself is seen as having played a developmental role. The arguments for abundance go beyond the mere notion of Say's Law—supply creates its own demand—and tend to appear in connection with arguments about individuals' desire to show or emulate (Foley 1893; Potter 1954; Rosenberg 1968). While the existence of more goods is part of the notion of abundance, by "abundance" we do not simply mean the availability of any specific object. Nor are we referring to a lush tropical paradise in which fruit drops, neatly washed, peeled, and sliced into the mouths of the inhabitants. Rather, we are referring to a mind-set, a materialism, an interest in getting and spending that results from the *perception* of possibilities for acquiring large sets of desirable goods and services, and the perception that others are generally also so engaged. To some extent innate desires are coupled with the favorable circumstances and perception of abundance. An early proponent of this belief, according to Rosenberg (1969), was Adam Smith. Rosenberg attempts to show that Smith considered consumer taste in his theory of economic growth. Although not completely comfortable with the notion of increased consumption, proportedly Smith did believe it had positive consequences. He felt that the "progress of opulence" was a result of the desire of the rich to "gratify the most childish vanity" in conjunction with the availability of new commodities ("great objects of ambition

and emulation") (Rosenberg 1968, p. 365, 368; also see Spiegel 1971, p. 230, p. 237-238). As Roseberg points out, Smith's discussion of demand factors, in *The Wealth of Nations*, is not well developed. Nevertheless, he shows that Smith believed that the mechanisms which aided the progress toward a consumption society were the growth of agricultural surpluses fired by the desire of the land-owning class to pursue "rank and distinction," exposure to foreign luxuries through trades and the growth of manufacturers.

Over a century later, Foley characterized fashion as the "coefficient" of demand (1893, p. 462). She felt that diversity in consumption resulted from the availability of goods (through trade and production) and several human factors. In regard to the latter, Foley refers to the "cosmic law of rhythm," a law of variety in wants, as an innate human characteristic. To strengthen her point she refers back to authors from earlier centuries. In particular, Foley quotes the Limberg chronicler from 1380: "'At this time the fashion in raiment was so changed, that he who last year was a master-tailor became in a twelve month a laborer'" (Foley 1893, p. 465). Moreover, consumption was also affected by what she calls a "nexus of social factors" which include love of distinction, imitation, and an effort toward equalization (Foley 1893, p. 461). More contemporaneously, Potter (1954) could be included with Foley and Smith. He felt that economic abundance in natural resources and American ingenuity in using them, along with a desire to show, imitate, and emulate were the reasons America had moved from a production to a consumption society. Potter adds something of a twist to the notion of show. He believes that the American character results from the unusually high competition in the U.S. But he also argues competition only occurs when competitors have opportunities to win records. Thus, consumption is a result of the need to show one's success in competition (Potter 1954, p. 60). Mobility, both geographical and social, is viewed as a mechanism which helps produce the illusion of classlessness needed in a consumer society. Classlessness (or ambiguity about individual's classification) is important to this connection since rigid stratification would vitiate any attempt to gain status through consumption. If individuals can move, even very temporarily as on holiday, into situations in which they perceive themselves as able to take on the attributes and status of superordinate classes, then a class structure may encourage rather than discourage ostentatious consumption (McKendrick, Brewer and Plumb 1982).

Beginning from similar causal factors Smith, Foley and Potter each enumerate what they believe to be the consequences of the consumer orientation. Smith believed that unknowingly, in an effort to satisfy their own desires, the landowners brought about the demise of the feudal system. The reason was that landowners no longer used surpluses to care for tenants and therefore eroded their power base. (This was part of his principle of an invisible hand which helped advance the interests of society. See Spiegel 1971, p. 238.) Moreover, changing tastes led to an accelerated growth of output which resulted in an increase in capital stock, and therefore, led to economic growth (Rosenberg 1968). Foley felt that fashion led to incessant small vibrations in industry but also, to the extent that conformity resulted, production was simplified and costs were reduced (1893, p. 469). Potter (1954) felt that advertising, the "institution of abundance," came into existence to educate consumers. While he did feel that abundance leads to an apparent equalization of classes and is conducive to democracy, its institution (advertising) leads to mindlessness, the perpetuation of current attitudes and materialistic virtues and the creation of demand (Potter 1954, p. 188). He felt that the consumer learns to "like what he gets" instead of getting what he likes (ibid., p. 188).

Emulation and Urbanization/Mobility

As stated earlier, none of the cited authors' positions are totally distinct from one another. Several authors argue that the dual forces of urbanization and the desire to emulate or show have worked to bring about our mass consumption society. An early advocate of this argument is John Rae (1834: 1905 reprint). Although not particularly concerned with history, Rae draws on numerous historical examples back to antiquity in order to make his argument that consumption is the result of an innate human desire to be conspicuous. In his appendix "Of Luxury," in *The Sociological Theory of Capital*, Rae argues that luxuries only contribute to

man's desire to show (Rae labels this "vanity") and as such "All luxuries occasion a loss to society, in proportion to their amount" (Rae 1834, p. 273). As evidence of the historical tendency toward vanity the author notes that Cleopatra once had a pearl dissolved so she could drink it. Rae then cites Pliny, who showed that this practice was also a fashion in Rome at the time. Further, Pliny tells us of the jewels Caligula's wife wore when visiting friends were worth 40 million sesterces (Rae estimated this to be "upwards of two hundred thousand pounds sterling," 1834, p. 259). He believed that this desire for conspicuous consumption could be found in all cultures and at all times. To this end he gives examples from ancient historians' descriptions of Babylonian and other Asiatic monarchs, from the desire of the American "savages" for trinkets and feathers, and from the writings of missionaries about the Chinese. Nevertheless, in modern times (i.e., the 1800s), it was the spread of towns which led to a desire to distinguish oneself and also the anonymity of the city which made it possible to "pass oneself off" as a member of a different class.

The theme of conspicuous consumption and urbanization runs through the work of others as well. Gilboy (1932) saw what could be labeled as a circular relationship between the introduction of new wants, an increase in demand, a change in the nature of demand for different classes and inter-class mobility. Certainly, new goods must be available for the upper class to try. Then with a shift in real income and with the opportunity to imitate the upper class, the high level of consumption (necessary for the industrial revolution) would follow. Potter (1954) also felt that social and geographical mobility were necessary to create an illusion of classlessness. And recently, Lears (1985, p. 460), while arguing against the conspicuous consumption thesis, believes that the reason "commodity vendors" (marketers) have assumed such a powerful role in society is because of technology and urbanization. Both of these forces create a "sense of unreality" in the population, which gives way to the role of marketing and advertising to exacerbate and then offers relief in the form of products (Lears 1985, p. 461). It is the "market relations in urban settings, which created an impersonal status drama where social identities could be chosen and discarded and the older rigid sense of 'character' could slip away . . ." (Lears 1985, p. 460-461). Interestingly, while Lears would take issue with those who argue that consumption is conspicuous, his supporting arguments are similar, for instance, to those of Rae.

In *The Structures of Everyday Life*, Braudel (1981) touches on the concept of luxury. He prefaces his discussion by stating that the meaning of luxury is context-specific. Braudel argues that luxury as opposed to production is a driving force in society and that luxury represents an "eternal class struggle." He takes exception, however, to the notion (which he attributes to Sombart) that the luxury of "princely courts" laid the foundation for modern capitalism. Braudel to some extent would probably agree with Rae (1834), but adds historical depth to the notion of luxury. Before the industrial revolution, luxury was not a sign of growth, rather a limit to growth. To Braudel, during that period conspicuous and wasteful consumption were signs of an economy failing to find a "meaningful use for its accumulated capital" (1981, vol. 1, p. 186).

Emulation and Show

We have already used these terms several times and their meaning is probably self-evident. But, to be explicit, emulation involves the desire to copy some respected other(s)—a superordinate class, fashion leaders, or others. It involves probably, at the micro level, an ability to fantasize oneself absorbing some of the status of the model; at the macro level it requires a certain classlessness, ambiguity, fluidity, or anonymity (often associated with urbanization) that facilitates such fantasies. "Show" refers to the desire of people to use their consumption as status communications. It may be Veblenesque or it may involve reverse snobbishness, but it transmits a message. In connection with emulation and show in fashion theory, McCracken (1985) interestingly recommends more attention to intermediate classes' attempts to discard what subordinate ones adopt as well as to copy what superordinate ones select.

While emulation and show apply to far more than fashion goods, and there are many other explanations for fashion change, we discuss fashion theory here since those two forces loom so large in so many fashion discussions.

Fashion Theory

Ideas about fashion changes are of interest for the following reasons: (1) consumer interest, or acquiescence in, fashion change probably increases total consumption; (2) scholarly writing on fashion is generally explicitly or implicitly historical (see bibliographies in Solomon 1985); and (3) fashion theorizing illustrates and adds to theories of consumption. To elaborate on the last point Braudel (1981), for instance, believes frivolousness in fashion is related to a willingness in society to break with tradition, and to a society's openness to innovation and growth. Further, fashion was an important impetus to world trade (1981, vol. 1, pp. 323-324).

Fashion theories may attribute style change to the power of a few individual consumers or suppliers (e.g., Robinson 1963; Ansbach 1967; Nunn 1984, among the avowed historical writers), to aspects of human nature such as desires for novelty, modesty, and erotic expression (C. Flugel 1930 cited by Bell 1978, another historian), and to important political or environmental events. Bell (1978) attacks these theories on both conceptual and empirical grounds. Another view, not discussed by Bell, holds that fashion moves through consistently repetitive cycles (Robinson 1975). Bell makes two points which contradict the inevitability or automaticity of fashion cycles: (1) that fashion change is really mainly a post-medieval Western European phenomenon, and (2) that men's fashions, once highly sumptuous and volatile, have long remained sober and stable. Braudel's (1981) work agrees with that of Bell. Braudel feels that fashion in the sense of "keeping up with the times" began in 1700; up to 1300 he feels there was no change at all from Roman times (p. 315). But designer tendencies to draw upon past sources fit well into Sproles' (1985) eclectic model.

Bell's own theory, inspired by but deviating from Veblen (1899), is a "trickle-down" one; i.e., emulative in our terminology, emphasizing the importance of Conspicuous Consumption and Conspicuous Leisure. Goods are also viewed as communicators, but the imitative process is conducted by classes struggling for position, rather than by individuals. Men wore ornate, nonfunctional clothing when leisure, and military, and athletic prowess were the only respectable attributes of the dominant (aristocratic) males. Fashionable male clothing became much more sober and functional (although not suitable for manual labor) after the Reformation and Industrial Revolution made commercial and administrative acumen meritorious. Elaborate display was then centralized on the nonworking females as vicarious consumers for the heads of their households.

Trickle-down theories have been rejected in recent years by marketing writers and sociologists who either have noted apparently eccentric empirical behavior (the atypical adoption and rejection pattern for the "sack" dress in the 1960s) or have not accepted a simple pyramidical view of society. King's (1963) argument that fashion moved laterally from opinion leaders to followers within each class is one of many attacks on trickle-down. Apparently working independently of Bell, McCracken (1985) attempts to rehabilitate the theory, but leaves it in very loose form. He argues that super- and subordinate may be a matter not of class, but of assigned racial, occupational, gender, age or other rankings. The borrowings are not necessarily of entire styles, but rather of badges and symbols. Thus, he says that currently female professionals have tried to appropriate the "tailored look" or badge of authority of male professionals. But among other problems with this thesis, there is a great danger in using current perceptions of current fashion situation as a basis for generalization, as Bell himself points out. Bell further cautions against his own conclusion that we have become much less fashion-conscious than our predecessors. Perhaps the most promising approach for the long run has been taken by Sproles (1985), whose diagrammatic model includes parts of most prevailing theories but at present provides no basis for predicting what sources and vectors will be influential in any particular situation.

Goods As Communicators

The notion of conspicuous consumption has also been rejected in favor of a more complex thesis of goods as communicators. Here "communication" is not used in the narrow sense of communicating wealth or status (Rae 1834; Veblen 1899), or of communicating success (Potter 1954). The function of goods is viewed as that of communicating belongingness to a group (especially Douglas and Isherwood 1978;

Leiss, Kline and Jhally 1985; Nunn 1984; Ames 1980; Scheflen 1972). According to Boorstin (1973, p. 89-90), "Now men were affiliated less by what they believed than by what they consumed." Goods are a communication system which help to build social relationships; groups are formed around products (Douglas and Isherwood 1978; Leiss, Kline and Jhally 1985). This, of course, raises the old issue of whether Ford and Chevy owners differ from one another. Further, Douglas and Isherwood (1978), for instance, believe that patterns of consumption reflect the person's need to acquire and control information. In terms of mechanisms to aid this process the rituals of society are organized around goods, according to Douglas and Isherwood (1978), and according to Leiss, Kline and Jhally (1985, p. 8) as traditional groups have given way to collectives organized around products, marketing and advertising have attempted to provide messages about goods-people relationships.

The Intellectual and Ideological Roots of Consumption

Key to understanding the growth of the consumer society, in the opinion of several authors, are the ideological changes which preceded mass consumption (Vichert 1971; Leiss 1974; Linden 1979; Hollitz 1981). Clearly, the history of the evolution of ethical philosophy is beyond the scope and intent of this study. Nevertheless, in the literature under review, some historians argue that the history of ideological change provides the foundation for the consumer society. In fact, many of the cited authors use intellectual developments as the pivotal point from which to condemn what they see as the evils of consumption. A recent work by Horowitz (1985) argues that critics as well as supporters of consumption can be traced back to common intellectual lineages, either conservative or liberal. And in his view most turn of the century critics were conservative, while new critics are generally liberals.

Linden (1979) presents a somewhat exotic version of the long-term "battle of reason over nature." According to Linden, tool-making, monotheism, domestication of agriculture, "desanctification" of religion, "extrasomatic intelligence" (i.e., libraries and universities), the Puritan religion's sanction of work and America's break with English traditions *should* have led to the ultimate triumph of reason over nature. However, in the consumer society, according to Linden, reason has taken the form of the myth of progress; this myth is controlling society (1979, p. 114). Thus the author is able to conclude that most of the negative aspects of our society—deteriorating health, environmental destruction, crime, etc.—are the consequences of consumption.

Leiss (1974) makes a similar argument about our "imperialism" over nature. He invokes Judaeo-Christian thought and modern thinkers such as Francis Bacon and John Hobbes. All are shown to have sanctioned man's conquest of nature and to have provided a basis for the "infinite expansion of wants" (Leiss 1974, p. 30). Leiss believes that now "'Economic progress'. . . has become . . . the underlying social 'cement'. . .'" (1974, p. 31).

Hollitz (1981) has a shorter time horizon than Linden and Leiss. He concentrates on the time between 1890 and 1920, when he believes the consumer society came into being. The notion of progress plays an important role in his theory. However, Hollitz takes a detached perspective and simply discusses the intellectual tug-of-war between the old "gospel of saving" (defended by the conservative moralists) and the new "gospel of consumption" (Hollitz 1981). He provides examples from all types of written material (from scholarly journals to popular magazines) to support his thesis. Presidents Theodore Roosevelt and Calvin Coolidge, as well as prominent social reformers, are shown to have contributed to the debate. Labor leader George Gunton (a vocal proponent of fewer hours and higher salaries to allow more mass consumption; also see Horowitz 1977, 1980) and his mentor Ira Steward are viewed as participants in the debate.

In essence, Hollitz argues that American faith in material progress—and the realization that consumer demand was the key to this progress—led to the increased levels of consumption we find in the consumer society. Of course, this realization was accompanied by and tandem with the broad macro-level changes of increased productivity and new methods of mass distribution and selling. He credits the depressions between 1890 and 1920 with disposing of Say's law notions and showing manufacturers their dependence on the consumers. Further, advertising is considered to be a major stimulant.

Advertising is accorded a central position in Lear's essay (in Fox and Lears 1983). But advertising's acceptability is linked to a therapeutic philosophy that arose out of the secularization of Protestantism. Instead of emphasis on next-world salvation, this philosophy ennobled self-fulfillment and was interpreted to sanction instant gratification. The idea that one could be healthier, and therefore it was a positive duty to become healthier, was compatible with patent medicine advertising and soon extended to other consumption realms. Fox, Lears and the other contributors see goods and services taking on new meanings in the consumer culture.

In sum, these authors believe that a number of mental steps were necessary before the collective of Western civilization would be prepared to be vigorous consumers. Interestingly, some of the debate and inner tension mentioned by Hollitz and Leiss can be seen in the writings of Smith and Rae discussed earlier. Perhaps the limit has been discussed by Larabee (1960, p. 66). He retells a tale, "The Midas Touch" (Frederik Pohl), of a hypothetical society where people have a consumption quota and the privileged class is so because it has the right *not to consume*.

Two points can be made about the preceding discussion. First, the line between history and historiography becomes blurred when works of the various authors are considered. The arguments of the historians tend to support their own beliefs about consumption. To some extent all authors discussed in this review, not just those in this section, show signs of their own values in their choice of the factors they believe to be most important in bringing the rise of the consumer society. Horowitz (1985) follows the changing ideologies of both the critics and supporters of high levels of consumption. There may also be room for a similar effort on historians' beliefs.

Secondly, the extent to which actual consumption practices have been influenced by the intellectual and ideological debate is not at all clear. Consumers have long gone their own way in using goods and quantities for which they have been scolded by the moralists. Yet the prevailing attitude of members of society in some epochs does seem to have been more conducive to consumption than in others.

Although he does not deal directly with consumption but is concerned with capitalism in general, Braudel (1981) has touched upon this debate. He does not draw a final conclusion on the question of the importance of ideological change. However, Braudel mainly dismisses arguments such as "capitalism equals rationalism" and "puritanism equals capitalism" (vol. 2, pp. 566-577) which recur in the works of authors discussed in this section. To Braudel, rationalism, as it is used in economics, belongs to the noncapitalistic sector of western economies—what Braudel calls the market economy. Capitalism to Braudel is the "'irrational' behavior of speculation" (ibid., p. 577). On the subject of puritanism, Braudel's view is that the Protestant Reformation enabled Northern Europe to unite and thereby develop trade networks. Thus Northern Europe was better able to compete with the more-established Catholic south (especially Italy). Moreover, the Catholic counterrevolution, which followed, led to more flexible societies that were more favorable to the expansion of capitalism. Thus, from the perspective of this review, Braudel's work helps to tie ideological change to other macrosocietal factors.

Consumerism and Consumer Education

Consumerism is somewhat peripheral to our major theme, since it affects suppliers and the market as much as it affects consumers. Formal consumer education (domestic science or household management classes) may also be unimportant, in contrast to the total socialization to which potential homemakers have been subjected. Yet both do operate to modify consumption behavior and both have been studied historically. In fact, Hollitz (1981) argues that it was the New Housekeeping movement (the application of scientific management to the home) which ultimately helped to reconcile the thrift versus consumption debate and helped legitimize the wife's new role as consumer. That is, wise expenditure became synonymous with "real" thrift. The extent to which this phenomenon extended beyond the movements' organizers (and below the upper middle class) is not obvious.

If the term "consumerist" is defined very broadly, then some consumerists such as the nineteenth century Utopians have sought a reorganization of prevailing values. The consumer cooperative movement in the early years

of the century had a leadership that was entranced with the somewhat mystical concept of "The Co-operative Commonwealth," although the Rochdale pioneers were, of course, much more pragmatic and materialistic. Some early twentieth century consumerism (The National Consumer League) like modern boycotters sought to use consumer power to effect social changes such as improvements in labor conditions. But in the main the consumer movement has shared the marketing fraternity's basic materialism. It has mainly tried to increase the quantity/quality of goods and services that consumers receive for their dollars; it has not asked: "Why bother?" This view has been echoed in consumer education's prime attention to "better buymanship," i.e., the maximization of household acquisition (Creighton 1976; Herrmann 1982; Schudson 1984). Consumerism and consumer education thus dealt mainly with the pattern rather than the level of consumption and its legitimacy; this is to the dismay of Holsworth (1980) who argues that this is the ultimate failing of Ralph Nader.

Other Explanatory Factors

The New Left. A group of New Left historians see the contemporary consumer culture as part of a conscious plot (Ewen 1976; Brown 1973, pp. 151-159 and sources cited therein).[1] The exploiting class uses the workers' desire for an ever-increasing bundle of goods and services as a disciplinary device to keep the labor force at its tasks. The material rewards that flow from this drudgery are the opiate that insures docility while the sheer volume of purchases (and hence sales) swells the exploiters' profits. This contemporary orientation contrasts with an earlier Puritan-like emphasis upon abstinence and frugality, combined with hard work, advocated during the years of capital formation.

Muir (1927, p. 67), a nonradical British visitor to the U.S. in the 1920s, felt that many prominent American businessmen had come to adopt a "high wages will permit mass buying" philosophy in the early 1920s, even though many exceptions to this attitude existed and more pragmatic economic factors (e.g., restricted immigration) helped explain the wage level.

[1]We have not actually run across the use of the term "conspiracy," but how would you interpret "overarching," "hierarchical," "bureaucratic," "quasi-totalitarian apparatus of manipulative consumption?"

There is no doubt in our minds that worker acquisitiveness and materialism are highly compatible with contemporary capitalism. In fact, one of the most interesting and forgotten episodes in the history of marketing-related economic thought was the ultimate co-opting by the Rockefellers of the prominent radical labor reformer Gunton (discussed earlier), who argued that a shorter workweek would greatly increase worker spending. For many years one of the platitudes of marketing rhetoric was that Soviet communism could be destroyed if a sufficient number of Russian workers were exposed to copies of the Sears Roebuck catalog. So while businesspeople may occasionally see worker spending as improvident or pretentious, they generally like both the sales volume and the socioeconomic effects. But that is quite different from seeing such an attitude as part of a self-conscious scheme. Although exceptions can be cited, most notably in programs of building up worker debt at mill-town company stores, most employers do not actively try to inculcate lavish spending habits among their own employees. Instead they tend to engage in market cultivation, not for spending in general (although that may be a by-product), but for their own particular products and brands. Such behavior can more easily be explained on traditional, businesslike profit-seeking grounds than by conspiracy theory.

Retention of Nominal Autonomy. Even non-institutionalized consumers may lose or transfer some of their selection and buying power and activity to people outside the family circle. This happens, for example, when a physician specifies the medicines to be purchased at the pharmacy or a professor selects the text to be obtained from the bookstore. Nineteenth century rural Britons asked local shopkeepers and haulers to buy for them in London (Fraser 1981) and colonial planters expected similar service from their homeland agents. During the late nineteenth century and up to World War II, a number of American women set up as independent professional shoppers to buy clothes and household goods for remote or timorous upper middle class consumers. Buying club "package" and subscription purchase plans substitute one big purchase for many little ones.

Although such arrangements seem to offer considerable convenience and are consistent with a general trend to contract out many once

familial functions (e.g., child rearing), they have achieved only very limited acceptance. The record suggests that consumers generally have been receptive when constrained by severe knowledge or power inferiority (e.g., prescriptive medicines), when drastically separated from the market, or when offered a very substantial price advantage (Hollander 1974).

Moreover, consumers participating in such arrangements often retain significant discretion—the power to give the purchasing agent specifications—and rights of rejection as formalized in negative option book plans. Apparently, even though the consumer may be susceptible to only partially perceived external influence in buying, the record suggests a strong desire for a feeling of being in control.

Limitations and Unexamined Issues

Since this is a review of others' works, it is subject to two sets of limitations: those of the authors reviewed and our own. In addition to the usual ones of possible misinterpretation and inadequate analysis, the limitations of this work include those attributable to the historians (such as class orientation, excessive emphasis on a long-run perspective and the failure to use the marketing literature) and our own omissions.

Class Orientation. Although there is a substantial volume of literature on labor and working class history (Neufeld, Leab and Swanson 1983), historians interested in consumption generally have paid much more attention to the more fortunate classes. Much of the historical literature emphasizes upper, and possibly upper middle, class consumption; there are some notable exceptions (especially Fraser 1981; also McKendrick et al. 1984; Braudel 1981; Cohen 1980). Three factors produce this somewhat snobbish orientation.

1. The historical profession, somewhat like those of genealogy and biography, is not devoid of researchers with elitist and patrician tastes. Adburgham (1964) frankly subtitles her book on British retailing, "Where and How the Well-Dressed English-woman Bought Her Clothes."

2. The wealthy and the powerful are the most likely to generate data from which historians can reconstruct past expenditures. It was

the large landowners, not the urban artisans, who sent written and sometimes preservable instructions to their city agents and country stewards for the purchase of household and personal goods. Probate inventories (estate tax calculations) do exist for some individuals of very modest means, but even the tax collector would be more interested in the great mansion than the mean shanty.

3. The well-to-do obviously could assume more, both in quantity and variety, than the poor.[2] The greater discretionary nature of upper class consumption evokes a wider range of historical questions. Blumin (1985) cites studies that tend to show nineteenth-century married urban blue-collar workers tied pretty much to a subsistence plane of living unless resident working children supplemented the household income. But he also notes that British worker visitors to the U.S. felt that their American counterparts enjoyed a much richer material lifestyle.

To talk of discretion under such working class circumstances may be tantamount to saying the worker had a choice between shivering in a shabby blue shirt or a shabby gray one. Nevertheless, there is good evidence that many urban and rural workers did enjoy some measure of discretionary spending power. This discretion had at least two dimensions. One was the power to balance the purchase of one desirable but nonessential item, say a grandfather's clock, against the acquisition of some other furniture or nonfurniture item. The second, after brands began to proliferate in the late nineteenth century, was to choose between Brand A and Brand B of the same product. By 1898, 2,583 major national advertisers, many of them in the packaged goods field, were using American magazines and newspapers (Sherman 1900, p. 23), an indication of substantial brand competition. We have noted how the historians' fascination with the upper classes may have given us a distorted picture of the nature of the early department stores. It may have obscured our understanding of other marketing phenomena as well.

[2]However, at times threatened social elites find themselves unable to compete with rising bourgoisie in expenditure. This situation has lead variously to sumptuary legislation, and in less autocratic societies, to advocacy of a dignified and quite comfortable "simplicity" (see Leverette 1983 for an interesting example).

Cohen (1980) does deal with working class tastes. She points out that many workers did live in sub-standard housing, and that many struggled with overwork (boarders, home labor, child labor, etc.) and sub-standard diet in order to buy housing. Middle class reformers urged this as a way to make labor "more dependable" and to siphon off immigrant remittances that encouraged further immigration; but workers were fulfilling their own traditional community values. Working class tastes were not simply lagged reflections of middle class taste but again reflected traditional value. As long as they regarded the home as a haven from outsiders, and only admitted closest friends and family, the kitchen was appropriate entertainment space. As they accultured, they began to create parlors. But the furnishings were different—overcrowded, heavy, plush. Cohen's argument that this was not a lagged interpretation of middle class Victorian taste is not entirely convincing. Furthermore, while a limited number of authors have dealt with the working class, it appears that nobody we have encountered has read and analyzed advertising in working class magazines (or magazines aimed at a lower educational level).

Long-Run Perspective. The materials reviewed here have been concerned primarily with explaining or describing long-run changes in consumption. Thus, with the exception of some of the fashion history (notably Bell 1978), the reviewed literature has not said much about ideas, tastes, and product or service offerings that proved transitory or abortive. Some additional attention to what might have happened, but did not, could be instructive.

Consumer Behavior Technology and Terminology. In general, there is a failure to use consumer behavior literature. Lears appears to be the most knowledgeable but he still draws on the economics literature. And most authors have used economic instead of marketing literature. Douglas and Isherwood acknowledge the existence of information generated by marketing research ("for its limited purposes") but do not use it.

Terminology and Definitions. We have mainly taken the historians' arguments at their face value, accepting their definitions of terms. However, certainly there are heated debates, within the various disciplines, as to the definition of, for example, the "industrial revolution" or the "progressive era."

Omitted Literature. In addition, we have not discussed the histories of specific commodity or service categories. Much interesting and insightful work has been done on changes in America's preference for, and attributions of meaning to, foods, spectator and participant sports, reading materials, medical therapies, housing, clothing and automobiles—to mention only a few.

Nor have we explored what historians have said about *where* people shop, except from our notes on a few of the many discussions of the rise of what is now usually called the "conventional downtown department store." Further examination of reports of the locations and the institutions from which consumers obtained their supplies could shed light on such issues as consumer propensity to travel for goods and services, consumers' loyalty to particular sellers and types of sellers (the prevalence of Gregory Stone's 1954 "ethical consumer," whose choice was guided by some sense of moral obligation external to the transaction), and the sources of many social frictions between sellers and consumers (the well-known marginal position of the trader in peasant societies). Even vendor- and system-oriented histories of mail order selling, for example, such as Fuller (1964), Emmet and Jeuck (1950), Smalley and Sturdivant (1973), D. Cohen (1940) might tell us much about consumer responsiveness to innovation. Study of shopping sources could be especially interesting in view of the relatively novel "new right" historical idea that the persistence and extent of black markets is essentially a manifestation of opposition to the intrusion of government into economic affairs.

Finally, we have not looked at ethnohistory to see how, and at what pace, various immigrant groups have both assimilated and enriched mainstream American consumption preferences.

Unresolved Questions and Research Opportunities

In addition to research in the unexamined literature mentioned above, there are a number of issues which have not been addressed here and must be left for the future.

Individualism. First, an interesting question is what historians believe happened to the balance between individuality and conformity. Most modern marketers would probably argue that there is a high degree of individualism in consumption today. The historians are likely to say that what individualism exists is relatively superficial—that mass consumption has bureaucratized and regulated our consumption (see Fox and Lears 1983).

Personal versus Vicarious Consumption. Also, only a limited number of sources discuss the balance between personal and vicarious consumption through spouses and children (Veblen 1899, Bell 1978 on the consuming role of the wife, and McKendrick et al. 1982 on the commercialization of childhood).

Change Mechanism. Third, with the possible exception of the fashion literature, there is a lack of a good explanation of the change process. This is not so much in the sense of diffusion. Rather, how are consumption norms (standards of taste) formed? Why, in our society, is it unacceptable to pin a $20 bill to one's necktie, but acceptable to wear one with a designer symbol that indicates it costs $20 more than its intrinsic worth?

Other Consumption Societies? A great deal of emphasis has been placed on the arrival of the era of mass consumption. However, one might question whether societies before the industrial revolution were so unenthusiastic about consumption as Schudson (1984) argues. Somewhat sketchy evidence exists in the archeological literature that prehistoric peoples buried consumption-related materials with their dead—which implies a concern with consumption. Pfeiffer (1982, p. 65-67) describes a burial site 20,000 to 25,000 years old near Moscow. The occupants were wearing garments decorated with 8,000 tiny ivory beads, along with rings and bracelets. At the same site darts, daggers, and spears made from mammoth tusks were found. Still earlier, 60,000 years ago, in Neanderthal graves, "side scrapers and other flint tools, some in mint condition" were found, as well as charred animal bones, "indicating that chunks of roasted meat were buried together with the body" (Pfeiffer 1982, p. 100). Certainly evidence exists that the Etruscans buried their dead with consumption instruments (cloths, ornaments, cooking utensils, etc.), and that the Egyptians did the same for their nobility and royalty. The extravagant and degenerate luxury and consumption in the later years of Rome and Athens are well known (see Rae 1834). Further, the medieval prevalence and

ubiquity of sumptuary legislation certainly indicates strong consumption urges (see Hollander
1984; Nunn 1984). Douglas and Isherwood
(1978, p. 134) describe the consumption goods
of a tribe of American Indians, the Yurok, as an
example of "unfettered individualism and
enormous discriminations of wealth."

Although some historical evidence suggests
that consumption was an important aspect of
life even in preindustrial times, the question of
how important still remains.

How Central is Our Own Consumption? Even
now, one might wonder whether we really
identify ourselves as consumers. Most people
still describe themselves to strangers in terms of
their occupations, "I am Jones, a banker"
rather than 'I am Jones, a consumer." Moreover, the recommended modern substitute for
housewife is "homemaker" not "homeuser."

It is true that many conversations among
strangers thrown into social togetherness situations (say table mates on cruise ships or at some
resorts where people share tables) may center
around consumption and particularly food
preferences. This would seem to reinforce
Daniel Boorstin's (1973) point about there being
"consumption communities" or shared ties
between people who use the same products.
But maybe it also means just the opposite—that
while people have commonality of experience
in all consuming some sort of breakfast, so that
they are able to talk more or less meaningfully
about it, they would have great difficulty in
sharing insights into details of their respective
professions. Discussion of breakfast does not
involve the revelations of intimacy involved in
discussing family matters or the emotional
dangers of discussing religion or politics. After
all, we discuss weather in what Herbert Simon
has called "phatic communication"—making
social noises to indicate recognition of other
people—but we normally do not identify ourselves primarily as weather experiencers.

All of the above notwithstanding, we do
have big consumption. But what, if any, are the
limits? Why are there any nonforced savings?
And what of voluntary early retirement? While
it does involve an exchange of a "production"
role for one of consumption, it also means
sacrificing potential higher future consumption
power. Fullerton (1984) cites sources (Sombart,
Weber) who report medieval employer complaints that peasants and laborers would accept

only sufficient work to support a subsistence
plane of living. This seems to indicate that the
workers were disinterested in the extra consumption that could have been feasible with
extra income. Of course such complaints must
be examined carefully, whether as part of historical evidence or in studies of the LDCs, to
determine what the marginal tradeoffs were.
Employers who do not have to expend the
energy and workers who do may have different
ideas of what constitutes the appropriate leisure-
consumption tradeoff curve. The point is not to
deny the existence of the change that historians
discuss, but rather to find the bounds on the
change.

A Micro-, Mezzo-, Macro-View. In lectures
Phillip Kotler has suggested the usefulness of a
tripartite analysis of marketing activity: micro
as the transaction and firm realm, mezzo (as in
mezzo-soprano) as the industry realm, and
macro as the overall economy realm.[3] We have
here concentrated on what historians have said
about macroconsumption, although some of the
evidence, such as McKendrick's (1982), was
drawn from micro and mezzo experiences. We
have also pointed out that research and review
of the literature in the latter two realms would
provide useful insights. Based upon experience and some exposure to that literature, we
might offer some tentative impressions.

We certainly can find considerable evidence
of consumer acceptance and popularization of
particular products and industries without any
highly concentrated advertising and marketing
effort. Borden (1942) cites several mezzo examples, such as the growth of demand for medical services and leafy vegetables. We can remember after World War II when consumers stood in
line outside apparel shops in hopes of being able
to purchase the newly-introduced nylon stock-
ings and the DuPont Company advertised
cautionary remarks to *reduce* consumer expectations. In other instances, the record is very
mixed. Schudson (1984) claims cigarette smok-
ing became popular among men prior to its
promotion; Bernays (1928) describes a subtle
campaign based upon free publicity to popularize the same practice among women. The
question of why Ford was so much more successful than other early (and earlier) automobile

---

[3]We do not, at this time, advocate the establishment of a
Journal of MezzoMarketing.

manufacturers is subject to various answers, but production skills must claim substantial credit. Chandler (1962), however, has shown how General Motors used marketing to take the leadership away from Ford. Similarly, again drawing on Chandler, it seems that large-scale packaged goods manufacturers, other process type consumer goods industries, and the manufacturers of complex consumer appliances (e.g., sewing machines) needed considerable marketing skill to induce adequate consumption. Thus, with regard to the pattern if not the level of consumption, business (marketing and promotional) activity is often a necessary, even if not a sufficient, condition for the alteration of consumption. (Of course, the popularization of a particular item or type of item in a high-level economy may, through the media, serve as a demonstration that creates a desire for the same item(s) in poorer markets.)

To jump from those micro and mezzo categories to the macro, from the pattern to the level of consumption, is an act of faith. Nevertheless, we have a suspicion that some of those products that have been popularized by promotion (e.g., packaged foods and health and beauty aids, consumer appliances and automobiles) loom so large in the national consumption budget that their promotion has probably expanded total consumption.

Other Macro Questions. Some other important macro questions have also been overlooked. For instance, what have been the implications of industry-restrictive practices or even of popularly accepted gossipy allegations, warranted or unwarranted, that industry deliberately withholds superior products (such as the alleged keeping of the ballpoint pen or long-burning light bulbs off the market)?[4] Manipulative consumption, such as in company stores, and forced or mandated consumption (Larson and Wasserstrom 1983) have not been considered herein. Restrictions on consumption by age, gender or race provide room for future research. For instance, sumptuary laws (Hollander 1984) for women and costume differences for married versus unmarried men or women, as well as occupational dress codes, all could provide additional insights into consumption.

---

[4] A very tangential personal experience with the development of the ball point pen has led one of the authors to believe that the allegations of deliberate suppression are incorrect. An amusing, but apparently correct, account appears in Thomas Whiteside (1954) *The Relaxed Sell*.

Another area for future research is cross-cultural comparison. The material covered in the present work includes historians from both sides of the Atlantic. There is some indication of variations in the timing, speed, rate, and extent of the adaptation of various western societies to mass consumption.

Finally, studies of the type that we have examined here could have implications for a broader and deeper question than the ones so far summarized. In an essay on Karl Polanyi, a social historian often cited by marketing scholars who was actually highly critical of the market economy, Block and Somers (1984, p. 77) cite Marxist criticism of Polanyi as a "circularist." That is a derogatory term for one who puts emphasis on other conditions, such as market arrangements, rather than production as the prime force in society. Obviously individual consumption (the desire for goods and services and its satisfaction) is not the only significant aspect of economic society or even its only possible objective, although the latter of course is the basis for Adam Smith's whole system. Nevertheless, detailed study of many societies, something Polanyi urged, and specifically examination of consumption stimuli and behavior in a large number of precapitalist and noncapitalist environments, could help in measuring the strength of fundamental economic forces.

CONCLUSIONS AND MACROMARKETING IMPLICATIONS

The review presented in this article falls short of providing a definitive answer to the question posed—that is, is desire innate, induced, and/or insatiable? Nevertheless, some of the general impressions presented can be useful to marketers interested in consumption. The literature reviewed deals with groups of people and not individuals and thus sheds light on some of the broad, macro aspects of consumption, as yet not widely discussed or recognized in marketing. Most historians see a multifactored set of causes that resulted in our culture of consumption. From this perspective, we begin to understand the synergy between innate impulses, macro influences, and social and intellectual dynamics involved in the change. Most authors, regardless of their intellectual base, see a historical trend toward more consumption, with perhaps minor ups and downs. Although we have expressed some doubts about the centrality of consumption, the record demonstrates how much consumption has grown over the years. It also demonstrates that the consumption urge and actual above-subsistence consumption are not historically something new. Moreover, it is more than likely that a "conspiracy" (New Left theory) was not necessary to bring society to its present consumption culture. Nevertheless, organized marketing has both facilitated and stimulated increased consumption.

Although the historians have not yet told us of the degree to which the urge to engage in large-scale consumption is inextricably imbedded within us, they certainly show us that consumption is a strongly imbedded element of our culture and, apparently, our personalities. This suggests that, although somewhat fluctuating numbers of ascetics may be found in our society, notions of "voluntary simplicity" and "less is better" are not likely to radically change consumption styles. These notions seem mainly transitory ascetic vogues that are likely to affect individual product designs and some individuals' inventories, but not basic outlooks. Much more cataclysmic environmental changes would be required for such a change. Alderson's (1957) prediction of a retreat from superfluity seems unlikely.

Similarly, the historians and the data we have examined do not deal with highly self-conscious attempts to modify adverse economic conditions by increasing or reducing consumption through exhortation. The "You Auto Buy" and the "WIN—Whip Inflation Now" efforts of recent decades are examples. Although marketing and promotion do seem capable of affecting attitudes and propensities, we think they normally work much more subtly than those efforts at sloganeering. The complexity of the factors affecting consumption suggest that such campaigns are likely to be ineffective except perhaps in times of widely and deeply perceived national emergency. As marketing students, we know that these campaigns may have adverse effects through suggesting to consumers the individual wisdom (even if social disasterousness) of hoarding either cash or goods.

The mixture of causal factors and enabling measures cited by historians indicates that the growth of consumption must be best explained by a fairly complex model of interrelationships.

No one factor is sufficient. Some elements may be necessary, such as the supply of goods and services and the propensity to consume, but they are result as well as cause. Within that system, we think marketing and advertising play a role. They do follow consumption, as the advertising defenders maintain. But it seems impossible for advertising and marketing to constantly proclaim the joys of consumption without reinforcing materialistic values. And one should note, as McKendrick et al. (1982) do, that the often overlooked physical distribution side of marketing clearly changes the supply that is available for consumption. Many of the writers have shown that an important role for distribution agencies, particularly retailers, is stimulating consumption. We wonder whether stimulating consumption is a possible suitable and profitable role for such agencies in a modern marketing society or whether that function is best performed by other media.

From the perspective of economic development, historical work implies that our own industrial development is the result of a concatenation of causal factors. As noted earlier, some authors believe that the supply-side causes of the consumption society have been over-emphasized. According to Mukerji (1983) the anthropological view, in general, looks at goods as communicators and the economic view tends to see goods as objects of supply and demand (that is, the objects of production). Taken together, the historical work reviewed here facilitates a more rounded view of the development of the consumer society. Perhaps the complexity of interrelationships has broad implications for our approach to development. Certainly, attitude toward consumption may be an overlooked cultural value with implications for cross-cultural studies, for understanding and defining social welfare, and for the "marketing" of marketing.

That most marketers have not drawn upon history is not surprising. To some extent choice of information sources depends upon one's horizon—so that in attempting to make managerial decisions contemporary literature may be more helpful than history. However, two consequences can result from marketers' familiarization with history. First, the history of consumption can benefit from our more extensive studies of consumer behavior; to date little of marketing literature has been integrated into the historical literature. Second, and perhaps more importantly, marketers can benefit from the synergistic outlook on consumption behavior which historians have to offer. By including both ecotechnological and socioenvironmental and motivational factors, the historical literature provides input into the relationship between psychology and sociology, between society, its technology, and its individuals. This broadened perspective may help to infuse the marketing and consumer behavior literature with a fresh outlook. Belk and Hirschman (see Belk 1984) have also called for a new perspective. The major long-run question is whether, and if so, which, external and internal forces could create a different society or change ours. The answer to this question has implications for our future as well as for our approach to developing countries which we hope to aid and from which we hope to benefit.

REFERENCES

Adburgham, Alison (1964), *Shops and Shopping 1800-1914*, London: George Allen and Unwin Ltd.

Alderson, Wroe (1957), *Marketing Behavior and Executive Action*, Homewood, IL: Richard D. Irwin, Inc.

Ames, Kenneth L. (1980), "Material Culture as Non Verbal Communication: A Historic Case Study," *Journal of American Culture*, 3 (Winter), 619-641.

Ansbach, Kaylene (1967), *The Why of Fashion*, Ames: Iowa State University Press.

Assael, Henry (1984), *Consumer Behavior and Marketing Action*, 2nd edition, Boston: Kent Publishing Company.

Atwan, Robert, Donald McQuade, and John W. Wright (1979), *Edsels, Luckies, & Frigidaires Advertising the American Way*, New York: Dell Publishing Company.

Barth, Gunter (1980), *City People*, New York: Oxford University Press.

Belasco, Warren J. (1984), "'Lite' Economics: Less Food, More Profit," *Radical History Review*, 28-30, 254-278.

Belk, Russell W. (1984), "Manifesto for a Consumer Behavior of Consumer Behavior," *1984 AMA Winter Educators' Conference: Scientific Method in Marketing*, Paul F. Anderson and Michael J. Ryan, eds., Chicago: American Marketing Association, pp. 163-167.

Bell, Quentin (1978), *On Human Finery*, 2nd edition, New York: Schocken.

Bernays, Edward J. (1928), "Manipulating Public Opinion," *American Journal of Sociology*, 33 (May), 958-971.

Block, Fred and Margaret T. Somers (1984), "Beyond the Economistic Fallacy: The Historic Social Science of Karl Polanyi," in *Vision and Method in Historical Sociology*, Theda Skocpol, ed., Cambridge: Cambridge University Press, pp. 47-84.

Blumin, Stuart M. (1985), "The Hypothesis of Middle-Class Formation in Nineteenth-Century America," *The American Historical Review*, 90 (April), 299-338.

Boorstin, Daniel J. (1973), *The Americans: The Democratic Experience*, New York: Random House.

Borden, Neil (1942), *The Economic Effects of Advertising*, Chicago: Richard D. Irwin.

Braudel, Fernand (1981), *Civilization and Capitalism, Fifteenth-Eighteenth Century*, translated from the French by Sian Reynolds, Volume 1, "The Structures of Everyday Life," and Volume 2, "The Wheels of Commerce," New York: Harper and Row.

Brown, Bruce (1973), *Marx, Freud and the Critique of Everyday Life*, New York: Monthly Review Press.

Chandler, Alfred Dupont (1962), *Strategy and Structures*, Cambridge: M.I.T. Press.

Cohen, David L. (1940), *The Good Old Days*, New York: Simon and Schuster.

Cohen, Lizabeth A. (1980), "Embellishing a Life of Labor: An Interpretation of the Material Culture of American Working Class Homes, 1885-1915," *Journal of American Culture*, 3 (Winter), 752-775.

Creighton, Lucy Black (1976), *Pretenders to the Throne*, Lexington: Lexington Books.

Douglas, Mary and Baron Isherwood (1978), *The World of Goods*, Harmondsworth, Middlesex, England: Penguin Books Ltd.

Emmet, Boris and John E. Jeuck (1950), *Catalogues and Counters*, Chicago: University of Chicago Press.

Ewen, Stuart (1976), *Captains of Consciousness*, New York: McGraw-Hill Book Company.

Flugel, John C. (1930), *The Psychology of Clothes*, London: Hogarth Press.

Foley, Caroline A. (1893), "Fashion," *Economic Journal*, 458-474.

Fox, Richard Wrightman and T. J. Jackson Lears, eds. (1983), *The Culture of Consumption*, New York: Pantheon Books.

Fraser, W. Hamish (1981), *The Coming of the Mass Market, 1850-1914*, Hamdon: Archon Books.

Friedman, Monroe (1985), "Consumer Boycotts in the United States, 1970-1980: Contemporary Events in Historical Perspective," *Journal of Consumer Research*, 19 (Summer), 96-117.

Fuller, Wayne E. (1964), *RFD*, Bloomington: Indiana University Press.

Fullerton, Ronald A. (1984), "Capitalism and the Shaping of Modern Western Marketing: Marketing As a World-Historical Force," presented to the Ninth Macromarketing Seminar, Vancouver, British Columbia.

————— (1985), "Marketing in the Long Run," Stanley C. Hollander and Terrence A. Nevitt, eds., East Lansing: Department of Marketing and Transportation, Michigan State University.

Gilboy, Elizabeth W. (1932), "Demand as a Factor in the Industrial Revolution," in *Facts and Factors in Economics History*, A. H. Cole, ed., New York: Russell & Russell.

Gilmartin, Sister J. (1970), "An Historical Analysis of the Growth of National Consumer Movement in the United States From 1947 to 1967," unpublished Ph.D. dissertation, Georgetown University.

Goldsmith, Raymond W. (1955), *A Study of Savings in the United States*, Volume I, Princeton, NJ: Princeton University Press.

Herrmann, Robert O. (1982), "The Historical Development of the Content of Consumer Education: An Examination of Selected High School Text Books, 1938-1978," *Journal of Consumer Affairs*, 16 (Winter), 195-223.

The Historical Statistics of the United States: Colonial Times to 1970, Bicentennial Edition (1975), U.S. Bureau of the Census, Washington, DC: U.S. Government Printing Office.

Hollander, Stanley C. (1971), "She 'Shops for or With You:' Notes on the Theory of the Consumer Purchasing Surrogate," in *New Essays in Marketing Theory*, George Fisk, ed., Boston: Allyn & Bacon, pp. 218-240.

————— (1972-1973), "Consumerism and Retailing: A Historical Perspective," *Journal of Retailing*, 48 (Winter), 6-21.

————— (1974), "Buyer-Helping Businesses and Some Not-So-Helpful Ones," *MSU Business Topics*, 52-68.

———— (1984), "Sumptuary Legislation: Demarketing by Edict," *Journal of Macromarketing* (Spring), 4-16.

———— (Forthcoming), "The Marketing Concept: A Deja View," in *Marketing Management Technology and Social Process*, George Fisk, ed., New York: Praeger.

Hollitz, John Erwin (1981), "The Challenge of Abundance: Reactions to the Development of a Consumer Economy, 1890-1920," unpublished Ph.D. dissertation, University of Wisconsin-Madison.

Holsworth, Robert D. (1980), *Public Interest Liberalism and the Crisis of Affluence*, Boston: G. K. Hall and Company.

Horowitz, Daniel (1977), "George Gunton and the Emergence of a Theory of Mass Consumption in the United States," in *Humanitas Essays in Honor of Ralph Ross*, Quincy Howe, Jr., ed., Claremont, CA: Scripps College.

———— (1978), "Consumption, Capitalism, and Culture," *Reviews in American History* (September), 388-393.

———— (1980), "Consumption and Its Discontents: Simon N. Patten, Thorstein Veblen, and George Gunton," *Journal of American History*, 67 (September), 301-317.

———— (1985), *The Morality of Spending: Attitudes Toward the Consumer Society in America 1875-1940*, Baltimore: The Johns Hopkins University Press.

Hotchkiss, George B. (1938), *Milestones of Marketing*, New York: MacMillan Company.

Hoyt, Elizabeth Ellis (1968), *Primitive Trade Its Psychology and Economics* (first published in 1926), New York: Augustus M. Kelley Publishers.

Kallen, Horace M. (1936), *The Decline and Rise of the Consumer*, New York: D. Appleton-Century Company.

Kiernan, Thomas (1985), *The Road to Colossus*, New York: William Morrow and Company, Inc.

King, Charles W. (1963), "Fashion Adoption: A Rebuttal to the 'Trickle Down' Theory," in *Toward Scientific Marketing*, Stephen A. Greyser, ed., Chicago: American Marketing Association, pp. 108-125.

Kleinberg, S. J. (1979), "Success and the Working Class, (at the turn of the century)," *Journal of American Culture*, 2 (Spring), 123-138.

Larrabee, Eric (1960), "After Abundance, What?" *Horizon* (July), 66-72.

Larson, Brooke and Robert Wasserstrom (1983), "Coerced Consumption in Colonial Bolivia and Guatemala," *Radical History Review*, 27, 49-78.

Leach, William R. (1984), "Transformations in a Culture of Consumption: Women and Department Stores (1890-1925)," *Journal of American History*, 71 (September), 319-342.

Lears, T. J. Jackson (1985), "Beyond Veblen: Remapping Consumer Culture in Twentieth Century America," in *Marketing in the Long Run*, S. C. Hollander and T. Nevitt, eds., East Lansing: Department of Marketing and Transportation, Michigan State University.

Leiss, William (1974), "The Imperialism of Human Needs," *The North American Review* (Winter), 27-34.

Leiss, William, Stephen Kline, and Sut Jhally (1985), "The Evolution of Cultural Frames for Goods in the Twentieth Century," in *Marketing in the Long Run*, S. C. Hollander and T. Nevitt, eds., East Lansing: Department of Marketing and Transportation, Michigan State University.

Leverette, William E., Jr. (1983), "Simple Living and the Patrician Academic: The Case of William James," *Journal of American Culture*, 6 (Winter), 36-43.

Linden, Eugene (1979), *Affluence and Discontent*, New York: A Seaver Book/Viking Press.

Lynd, Robert (1934), "Introduction," *Annals of the American Academy of Political and Social Science*, 173 (May), viii-xiv.

Markin, Rom J. (1969), *The Psychology of Consumer Behavior*, Englewood Cliffs, NJ: Prentice-Hall, Inc.

Mason, Roger S. (1981), *Conspicuous Consumption*, New York: St. Martin's Press.

McCracken, Grant D. (1985), "The Trickle-Down Theory

Rehabilitated," in *The Psychology of Fashion*, Michael R. Solomon, ed., Lexington, MA: Lexington Books.

McKendrick, Neil, John Brewer and J. H. Plumb (1982), *The Birth of a Consumer Society*, Bloomington: Indiana University Press.

McMahon, A. Michal (1972), "An American Courtship: Psychologists and Advertising Theory in the Progressive Era," *American Studies*, 13, 5-18.

McNeal, James U. (1982), *Consumer Behavior An Integrative Approach*, Boston: Little, Brown and Company.

Muir, Ramsey (1927), *America the Golden*, London: Williams and Northgate.

Mukerji, Chambre (1983), *From Graven Images: Patterns of Materialism*, New York: Columbia University Press.

National Consumers Committee for Research and Education (1982), *Consumer Activists: They Made a Difference*, Mount Vernon, NY: Consumers Union Foundation.

Neufeld, Maurice F., Daniel J. Leab, and Dorothy Swanson (1983), *American Working Class History: A Representative Bibliography*, New York: Bowker.

Nunn, Joan (1984), *Fashion in Costume 1200-1980*, New York: Schocken Books.

Nystrom, Paul (1928), *The Economics of Fashion*, New York: Ronald.

Ostreicher, Richard (1981), "From Artisan to Consumer: Images of Workers 1840-1920," *Journal of American Culture*, 4 (Spring), 47-64.

Pfeiffer, John E. (1982), *The Creative Explosion*, New York: Harper and Row Publishers.

Pollay, Richard (1986), "The Distorted Mirror: Reflections on the Unintended Consequences of Advertising," *Journal of Marketing*, 50 (April), 18-36.

Pope, Daniel (1983), *The Making of Modern Advertising*, New York: Basic Books.

Porter, Susan Benson (1979), "Palace of Consumption and Machine for Selling: The American Department Store, 1880-1940," *Radical History Review*, 21 (Fall), 199-221.

Potter, David M. (1954), *People of Plenty*, Chicago: The University of Chicago Press.

Rae, John (1834, 1905), *The Sociological Theory of Capital*, New York: The MacMillan Company. Originally published under the title of *The New Principles of Political Economy*, Boston: Hilliard, Gray.

Rathje, William L. (1984), "The Garbage Decade," *American Behavioral Scientist*, 28 (September/October), 9-29.

Robinson, Dwight E. (1960), "The Styling and Transmission of Fashions Historically Considered," *Journal of Economic History*, XX.

———— (1963), "The Importance of Fashions in Taste to Business History: An Introductory Essay," *Business History Review*, 37, 5-36.

———— (1975), "Style Changes: Cyclical, Inexorable and Foreseeable," *Harvard Business Review*, 53 (November-December), 121-131.

Rosenberg, Nathan (1968), "Adam Smith, Consumer Tastes, and Economic Growth," *Journal of Political Economy*, 76 (May-June), 361-374.

Rubin, Joan Shelley (1985), "Self, Culture, and Self-Culture in Modern America: The Early History of the Book-of-the-Month Club," *Journal of American History*, 71 (March), 782-806.

Scheflen, Albert E. (1972), *Body Language and the Social Order: Communication as Social Control*, Englewood Cliffs, NJ: Prentice-Hall.

Schudson, Michael (1984), *Advertising, the Uneasy Persuasion*, New York: Basic Books.

Schulter, David Benjamin (1979), "Morality from Consumption: The Theory of Consumer Market Conduct in American Sociological Thought: 1894-1901," unpublished Ph.D. dissertation, Brandeis University.

Shammas, Carole (1982), "Consumer Behavior in Colonial America," *Social Science History*, 6 (Winter), 67-86.

Sherman, Stanley (1900), "Advertising in the United States," *Journal of the American Statistical Association*, VII (December), 120-162.

Smalley, Orange and Frederick D. Sturdivant (1973), *The Credit Merchants*, Carbondale: Southern Illinois University Press.

Solomon, Michael R. (1985), ed., *The Psychology of Fashion*, Lexington, MA: Lexington Books.

Spiegel, Henry William (1971), *The Growth of Economic Thought*, Englewood Cliffs, NJ: Prentice-Hall, Inc.

Sproles, George (1985), "Behavioral Science Theories of Fashion," in *The Psychology of Fashion*, Michael R. Solomon, ed., Lexington, MA: Lexington Books.

Stone, Gregory (1954), "City Shoppers and Urban Identification," *American Journal of Sociology* (July), 36-45.

Stuard, Susan Mosher (1985), "Medieval Workshop: Toward a Theory of Consumption and Economic Change," *Journal of Economic History*, 45 (June), 447-451.

Tan, Chin Tiong and Jagdish N. Sheth (1985), "Historical Perspectives in Consumer Research: National and International Perspectives," *Proceedings*, Association for Consumer Research, International Meeting, Singapore (July 18-20).

Veblen, Thorstein (1899), *The Theory of the Leisure Class*, New York: MacMillan.

Vichert, Gordon (1971), "The Theory of Conspicuous Consumption in the 18th Century," in *The Varied Pattern: Studies in the 18th Century*, Peter Hughes and David Williams, eds., Toronto: A. M. Hakkert, Ltd.

Williams, Rosalind H. (1982), *Dream Worlds: Mass Consumption in Late Nineteenth Century France*, Berkeley: University of California Press.

Wilson, Christopher (1983), "The Rhetoric of Consumption," in *The Culture of Consumption*, Richard W. Fox and T. J. Jackson Lears, eds., New York: Pantheon Books, pp. 39-64.

Winstanley, Michael J. (1983), *The Shopkeeper's World 1820-1914*, Manchester, England: Manchester University Press.

Whiteside, Thomas (1954), *The Relaxed Sell*, New York: Oxford University Press.

Zaltman, Gerald and Melanie Wallendorf (1983), *Consumer Behavior: Basic Findings and Management Implications*, New York: Wiley.

[39]

Excerpt from Terence Nevett and Ronald A. Fullerton (eds), *Historical Perspectives in Marketing: Essays in Honor of Stanley C. Hollander*, 9–33.

2

Parallel Development of Marketing and Consumer Behavior: A Historical Perspective

Jagdish N. Sheth
Barbara L. Gross

Introduction

The history of consumer behavior with respect to substantive focus, research methodology, and influence from external disciplines has largely paralleled the history of marketing thought. The focus of marketing has historically been directed toward the market, with an emphasis on understanding the needs and behavior of consumers. As a result, the study of consumer behavior has been closely aligned with the study of marketing. Although traditionally an area of inquiry within the larger discipline of marketing, consumer behavior began in the 1960s to emerge as a subdiscipline, and is currently showing signs of becoming a discipline distinct from marketing. Four eras of marketing thought and research may be identified, each associated with different "schools of thought" and each influencing the focus of consumer behavior research.[1]

The first era of marketing's history was dominated by the classical schools of marketing thought. These schools of thought emerged in the early 1900s, as marketing divorced itself from the founding discipline of economics. The classical schools focused on aggregate market behavior and borrowed from such social science disciplines as economics and sociology. The second era of marketing thought was dominated by the managerial marketing schools. Emerging in the early 1950s, the managerial schools shifted the focus of marketing to individual behavior, yet continued the tradition of borrowing from the social sciences. The third era of marketing thought has been dominated by the behavioral marketing schools, emerging in the 1960s and continuing to influence marketing research today. The behavioral marketing schools have borrowed from the behavioral sciences, including several branches of psychology, in an effort to gain greater insight into individual behavior. Finally, the fourth era of marketing thought is associated with what we have termed the adaptive marketing schools, and is currently emerg-

10 • *Historical Perspectives in Marketing*

ing. The adaptive schools are shifting the focus of marketing back to aggregate market behavior and borrowing from the social sciences as well as from the behavioral sciences.

It appears that each era of marketing thought has motivated interest in specific areas of consumer behavior. Further, each era has influenced the preferred research methodologies applied to consumer behavior. Figure 2–1 provides a summary of the specific schools of marketing thought associated with each era, and identifies emphases in consumer behavior that parallel the emphases of the marketing schools. The consumer behavior emphases identified as paralleling the adaptive marketing schools represent predictions for the future of consumer research.

Classical Marketing Schools and Parallel Consumer Behavior

The emergence of marketing as an independent discipline, divorced from the founding field of economics, has been eloquently documented by Bartels (1962). Three schools of thought were identified as emerging in the early 1900s. These have come to be known as the classical schools of marketing thought, and are specifically referred to as the commodity school, the functional school, and the institutional school. Additionally, we include the regional school as contributing to the first era. All four schools emphasized descriptive research focusing on aggregate market behavior, and borrowed heavily from the social sciences. Specifically, they were influenced most by demand theory in microeconomics, including concepts of consumer surplus and monopolistic competition (e.g., Marshall 1890; Chamberlin 1933); and by theories of spatial markets, trading areas, and rural versus nonrural market definitions in economic geography and economic demography (e.g., Marshall 1890; Ohlin 1933).

The commodity school has been the most enduring of the classical schools of thought. Writers identified with the commodity school have focused on the objects of market transactions as the central subject matter of marketing, and have attempted to differentiate various classes of products on the basis of their physical characteristics and associated consumer buying behavior. The focus of the commodity approach was originally on manufactured products and agricultural commodities, with the relevance of the commodity school to services not recognized until later.

The commodity school is perhaps most identified with the work of Copeland (1923), who generated the still popular convenience goods, shopping goods, specialty goods trichotomy. Even earlier, however, Parlin (1912) identified a threefold classification of goods as convenience goods, shopping goods, and emergency goods. Several subsequent writers (e.g., Holton 1958,

MARKETING AND CONSUMER BEHAVIOR FOCUS ON:

	AGGREGATE MARKET BEHAVIOR	INDIVIDUAL BEHAVIOR
SOCIAL SCIENCES	**Era One** <u>Classical Marketing</u> 1900-1950 a. Commodity School b. Functional School c. Institutional School d. Regional School <u>Parallel Consumer Behavior</u> 1930-1970 a. Consumption Economics b. Retail Patronage	**Era Two** <u>Managerial Marketing</u> 1950-1975 a. Managerial School b. Systemic and Exchange School <u>Parallel Consumer Behavior</u> 1960-1975 a. Opinion Leadership and Diffusion of Innovation b. Brand Loyalty c. Family Life Cycle d. Demographics and Socioeconomics
BEHAVIORAL SCIENCES	**Era Four** <u>Adaptive Marketing</u> 1975-Present a. Macromarketing School b. Strategic Planning School <u>Parallel Consumer Behavior</u> 1980-Present a. Cross-cultural Consumer Behavior b. Retaining Existing Customers c. Consumer Perception of Competition d. Behavior Modification and Focus on Behavior	**Era Three** <u>Behavioral Marketing</u> 1965-Present a. Organizational Dynamics School b. Consumerism School c. Buyer Behavior School <u>Parallel Consumer Behavior</u> 1960-Present a. Consumer Buying Behavior b. Motivation Research c. Personality d. Psychographics e. Attitudes f. Information Processing g. Involvement

(Row labels at left: **SOCIAL SCIENCES** and **MARKETING AND CONSUMER BEHAVIOR RELIANCE ON:** for the top portion; **BEHAVIORAL SCIENCES** for the bottom portion.)

Figure 2-1

1959; Luck 1959; Bucklin 1963; Kaish 1967) attempted to refine the Cope-land classification by providing more precise definitions. In contrast, Aspinwall (1958) provided an independent classification based on the color spectrum (red, orange, and yellow goods). His classification was specified in terms of replacement rate, gross margin, degree of adjustment, time of consumption, and searching time.

12 • *Historical Perspectives in Marketing*

In contrast with the other classical schools, the commodity perspective continues to hold the interest of contemporary marketing researchers. Most notably, Holbrook and Howard (1977) recently expanded the Copeland classification to include a fourth category termed preference goods. Enis and Roering (1980) and Murphy and Enis (1986) adopted and refined this classification, demonstrating its relevance to services and ideas as well as goods. They also distinguished between the consumer perspective and the marketer perspective in defining the four types of products, and related the classification to marketing strategy.

Emerging concurrent with the commodity school, the functional school promoted a focus on marketing activities or functions as the central subject matter of marketing. Shaw (1912), generally acknowledged as the founder of the functional approach, identified marketing functions performed by middlemen to include sharing the risk; transporting the goods; financing the operations; selling; and assembling, assorting, and reshipping. While not intending to provide an exhaustive list of marketing functions, Shaw's early contribution aroused the interest of other authors who sought to provide more conclusive classifications relevant to all marketing organizations (rather than just middlemen). This resulted in a number of alternative classifications (e.g., Weld 1917; Cherington 1920) and an unfortunate lack of unanimity.

By the mid-1930s, Ryan (1935) reported that at least twenty-six books and articles had been published that dealt with marketing functions, and that fifty-two distinct functions had been proposed by various authors. The lack of consensus among authors advocating the functional approach led Fullbrook (1940) to admonish that most authors had failed to recognize the distinction between the pervasive and inherent functional requirements of the marketing process (appropriately regarded as functions) and the specific activities involved in the performance of marketing functions (not appropriately regarded as functions). McGarry (1950), holding a similar view, proposed a classification consisting of the contactual function, the merchandising function, the pricing function, the propaganda function, the physical distribution function, and the termination function. Central to McGarry's classification was the idea that marketing functions may be accomplished via a variety of specific activities.

The functional school has received little attention since McGarry's contribution. However, a relatively recent article by Lewis and Erickson (1969) attempted to integrate the functional approach with the systems perspective, and identified two major functions of marketing as obtaining demand and servicing demand.

The third school of thought, the institutional school, emerged concurrent with the commodity and functional schools, focusing on the agents or organizations that perform marketing functions. The early stimulus for the institutional school was the belief among consumers that middlemen add excessive costs to products without a concomitant addition of value. Thus, early authors evaluated the roles of marketing intermediaries to determine whether the economic contributions of these organizations could justify their existence. Often regarded as the founder of the institutional school, Weld (1916) argued that middlemen such as wholesalers and retailers provide essential value added services by fostering time, place, and possession utilities (an approach also taken by Butler 1923). Further, Weld argued that marketing efficiency is enhanced through functional specialization, analogous to the efficiency achieved through production specialization. Other early authors seeking to justify the role of marketing middlemen (e.g., Breyer 1934) emphasized the role of middlemen in overcoming the various obstacles and resistances to the exchange of goods.

With these early authors having offered cogent justification for the existence of marketing intermediaries, subsequent contributors to the institutional school largely focused on the structure and evolution of distribution channel systems. As examples, Converse and Huegy (1940) discussed the potential benefits and risks associated with vertical integration, Balderston (1964) sought to provide a normative approach to optimal channel design, and McCammon (1965) identified various types of centrally coordinated channel systems and suggested reasons for their emergence. Both Bucklin (1965) and Mallen (1973) proposed theories to explain and predict the inclusion of intermediaries in channels of distribution. Bucklin introduced the principles of postponement and speculation to explain the creation of intermediate inventories between producers and consumers, and hence the use of indirect versus direct channels. Mallen proposed the concept of functional spin-off, hypothesizing that marketers will choose between performing functions themselves and subcontracting (spinning off) to functional specialists so as to minimize the overall cost of performing marketing functions.

Finally, the regional school viewed marketing as economic activity designed to bridge geographic or spatial gaps between buyers and sellers. The regional school is less well known than the commodity, functional, and institutional schools, and is often overlooked in discussions of schools of marketing thought. However, it is another early school that emphasized aggregate market behavior and borrowed from the social sciences.

Emerging somewhat later than the other classical schools, the origins of the regional school may be traced to the writings of Reilly (1931) and Converse (1943, 1949). These authors developed mathematical formulas termed "laws of retail gravitation" for determining the boundaries of retail trading areas and for predicting where consumers are most likely to shop. Their early work was continued by Huff (1962, 1964), and subsequent authors also examined wholesaler and manufacturer trading areas (Vaile, Grether, and Cox 1952; Revzan 1961; Goldstucker 1965). Grether (1950, 1983), a proponent of the regional approach for nearly half a century, enriched the

14 • *Historical Perspectives in Marketing*

contribution of the regional school substantially by using the regional perspective to analyze interregional trade (i.e., predict the flow of goods and resources among geographic regions varying in resource abundance).

As the classical schools dominated marketing thought prior to World War II, their reliance on social science disciplines, focus on aggregate markets, and use of research methodologies appropriate to the study of aggregate markets influenced the early study of consumer behavior. Early consumer researchers largely focused on consumption economics and retail patronage. Researchers focusing on consumption economics examined such issues as aggregate consumer demand and standards of living (e.g., Waite 1928; Zimmerman 1936; Wyand 1937; Norris 1941); household budgeting (e.g., Katona and Mueller 1953, 1956; Foote 1961); and the phenomena of conspicious consumption and consumption of necessities versus luxuries (Katona 1953; Katona, Strumpel, and Zahn 1971). Additionally, the focus of consumption economics contributed to early work on reference group influence as a determinant of consumer behavior (e.g., Bourne 1957; Stafford 1966). Researchers focusing on retail patronage examined such concepts as self-service (Robinson and May 1956); retail gravitation (Reilly 1931; Huff 1962); and the wheel of retailing (Hollander 1960). Research methodologies favored by early consumer researchers included case studies, market surveys, and analysis of census data. As demonstrated by Bartels (1962) and by Lockley (1974), interest in conducting consumer research studies and in examining market research methodology proliferated during this period.

Managerial Marketing Schools and Parallel Consumer Behavior

The classical schools, with their emphasis on describing aggregate market behavior, gave way to the managerial marketing schools, with their emphasis on controlling individual behavior in the marketplace. These schools, referred to specifically as the managerial school and the systemic and exchange school, emerged in the 1950s in the midst of the unprecedented economic boom following World War II. Due to enhanced production capability and a proliferation of new product introductions, it was found that the supply of products exceeded the demand in most markets. Thus, it was desired to control market behavior for the benefit of producers.

The managerial school of thought advocated a managerial approach to marketing, maintaining that the market can be managed for the benefit of the marketer (e.g., Howard 1957; Kelley and Lazer 1958). Pioneering authors generated such well-known and enduring concepts as the marketing mix (Borden 1964); product differentiation and market segmentation (Smith

1956); the product life cycle (Levitt 1965; Smallwood 1973); and the marketing concept (McKitterick 1957; Keith 1960; Levitt 1960). Additionally, considerable emphasis was given to generating concepts and theories relevant to specific elements of the marketing mix. Early examples included the concepts of skimming and penetration pricing introduced by Dean (1950), the hierarchy of effects model of advertising developed by Lavidge and Steiner (1961), and the "need satisfaction theory of personal selling" advocated by Cash and Crissy (1958). Each of these areas and concepts continues to generate substantial research today.

The systemic and exchange school emerged in the late 1950s, advocating that marketing must be viewed as a system and that marketing exchanges or transactions are the central focus of marketing activity. The launching of the systemic and exchange perspective has been dually credited to McInnes (1964) and to Alderson (1957, 1965; Alderson and Martin 1965). McInnes (1964) proposed that markets result when the makers and users of products seek to satisfy their needs and wants through exchange. Alderson and Martin (1965) proposed the "law of exchange" to explain why two parties decide to enter into a transaction. Subsequently, others such as Kotler (1972a) and Hunt (1976) gave more explicit focus to the exchange perspective by arguing that transactions or exchanges should be considered the central subject matter of marketing. Bagozzi (1974, 1975, 1978, 1979) refined and elaborated on the concept of exchange, attempting to develop a theory of exchange to serve as the foundation of marketing thought and practice.

Although the managerial schools, like the classical schools, relied on the social sciences, authors associated with this era were generally influenced by more recently developed concepts and research methodologies. To illustrate, scholars associated with the managerial schools eagerly borrowed concepts and methods from the emerging field of managerial economics (e.g., Dean 1951). This branch of economics focused on the theory of the firm, rather than on demand theory, and contributed such influential concepts as monopolistic competition and product differentiation. The managerial schools were also influenced by research in communications on opinion leadership (Katz and Lazarsfeld 1955; Katz 1957); research in rural sociology and economic anthropology on diffusion of innovation (Rogers 1962); and research in sociology on social stratification and household structure (Loomis 1936; Warner and Lunt 1941; Glick 1947; Kahl 1953).

Accompanying the shift in emphasis within marketing was a similar shift in emphasis within consumer behavior. Rather than focusing on aggregate market behavior, consumer researchers began to focus on individual consumers or households as the unit of analysis. Like marketing as a whole, however, consumer behavior continued to borrow from the social sciences. As a result, research emerged on such topics as opinion leadership and diffusion of innovation (Silk 1966; Arndt 1967; Bass 1969; Myers and Rob-

16 • *Historical Perspectives in Marketing*

ertson 1972); brand loyalty (Cunningham 1956; Frank 1962; Harary and Lipstein 1962; Kuehn 1962); life-cycle stages of households (Wells and Gubar 1966; Murphy and Staples 1979; Gilly and Enis 1982); and market segmentation based on demographics and socioeconomic status (Martineau 1958; Coleman 1960; Levy 1966; Wasson 1969; Sheth 1977). Preferred research methodology included developing stochastic and other operations research models with longitudinal panel data (to predict brand loyalty), and developing econometric models with cross-sectional data (to measure the impact of demographic and socioeconomic variables on buying behavior).

Behavioral Marketing Schools and Parallel Consumer Behavior

As the focus of research shifted away from aggregate markets and toward individual behavior, the marketing discipline observed that the behavioral sciences could contribute much to marketing's understanding of individual behavior in the marketplace. Thus, marketing scholars searched the literatures of various branches of psychology for concepts and research techniques to facilitate this understanding. In contrast with the other eras discussed in this paper, consumer behavior rather than marketing is credited with initiating the shift in perspective. Thus, during this era, rather than marketing leading consumer behavior, the study of consumer behavior led and influenced the study of marketing. At least three identifiable schools of thought emerged. These may be referred to as the organizational dynamics school, the consumerism school, and the buyer behavioral school (focusing on organizational buying behavior as well as on consumer behavior).

Authors associated with the behavioral marketing schools have been influenced by economic psychology, with its emphasis on customer expectations (Katona 1951, 1953); by clinical psychology, with its emphasis on subconscious motivation (Hall and Lindzey 1957); by organizational behavior, with its emphasis on power, conflict, and bounded rationality (March and Simon 1958; French and Raven 1959; Emerson 1962; Pondy 1967); and by social psychology, with its emphasis on the desire for cognitive consistency (Festinger 1957; Heider 1958). Consistent throughout these behavioral science disciplines is the finding that it is often perception, rather than objective reality, that drives human behavior. Thus, marketers concluded that much behavior relevant to marketing (e.g., among competitors, customers, and channel members) is driven by individual perception.

The emergence of the organizational dynamics school, with its emphasis on the behavior of distribution channel members, is generally credited to the work of Stern (1969), and particularly to his early papers on the topics of power and conflict in channels of distribution (Beier and Stern 1969; Stern and Gorman 1969; Rosenberg and Stern 1971; El-Ansary and Stern 1972). However, the behavioral approach to investigating interorganizational relationships in marketing may be traced to even earlier work by such authors as Ridgeway (1957) and Mallen (1963). Largely receiving impetus from Stern's work, a number of authors since the early 1970s have investigated the impact of power (Hunt and Nevin 1974; Lusch 1976; Etgar 1976; Frazier 1983b); conflict (Etgar 1979; Brown and Day 1981; Eliashberg and Michie 1984); and various influence strategies (Angelmar and Stern 1978; Frazier and Summers 1984; Frazier and Sheth 1985) on channel performance and relationships. Additionally, a number of authors have endeavored to develop general models of interorganizational relations (Robicheaux and El-Ansary 1975–1976; Stern and Reve 1980; Achrol, Reve, and Stern 1983; Frazier 1983a). The political economy perspective introduced by Stern and Reve (1980) and Achrol, Reve, and Stern (1983) has provided a framework for integrating the economic focus of the institutional school with the behavioral focus of the organizational dynamics school.

The consumerism school emerged in the late 1960s in response to the growing consumerism movement in the United States. Consumerism, as a social movement, focused on issues of consumer welfare, sought to correct the perceived imbalance of power between buyers and sellers, and criticized specific firms and industries as being guilty of negligence or malpractice (Beem 1973; Kotler 1972b). Concerned with the implications of consumerists' criticisms for marketing practice (Drucker 1969), a substantial amount of research effort has been devoted to investigating such issues as deceptive advertising (Jacoby and Small 1975; Gardner 1976; Armstrong, Gurol, and Russ 1979); the provision of product information (Day 1976; Resnik and Stern 1977; Houston and Rothschild 1980); marketplace treatment of disadvantaged consumers (Kassarjian 1969; Ashby 1973; Andreasen 1975); and consumer satisfaction, dissatisfaction, and complaining behavior (Day 1977; Hunt 1977; Day and Hunt 1979; Oliver 1980; Churchill and Surprenant 1982; Oliver and Bearden 1983).

As in other eras, the shift in emphasis associated with the behavioral marketing schools was paralleled by a similar shift in consumer behavior. As mentioned previously, however, the shift in emphasis within consumer behavior actually preceded and influenced the shift in marketing. Since its emergence in the early 1960s, the buyer behavior school has contributed the bulk of research to date on consumer behavior and organizational buying behavior.

As it became accepted that buying behavior is psychologically driven, the focus of consumer behavior turned toward examining the inner world of the individual buyer (Bauer 1960; Dichter 1964; Howard and Sheth 1969). Concepts borrowed from social, cognitive, and organizational psychology were used as building blocks in developing comprehensive models of consumer and organizational buying behavior (Andreasen 1965; Nicosia 1966; Howard and Sheth 1969; Engel, Kollat, and Blackwell 1968; Webster and Wind 1972; Sheth 1973); and concepts borrowed from clinical psychology served as the bases of motivation research, personality research, and psychographic research (Evans 1959; Dichter 1964; Kassarjian 1971; Wells and Tigert 1971; Wells 1975). Psychological approaches to the study of attitude (Rosenberg 1956; Katz 1960; Fishbein 1967; Fishbein and Ajzen 1975) influenced attitude research in consumer behavior (Wilkie and Pessemier 1973; Sheth 1974a; Mazis, Ahtola, and Klippel 1975; Lutz 1977; Locander and Spivey 1978); and research on information processing and involvement in cognitive psychology (Krugman 1965; McGuire 1976) influenced the study of consumer information processing and high- and low-involvement choice behavior (Bettman 1979; Olshavsky and Granbois 1979; Antil 1984). Further, research methodologies appropriate to the study of individual psychological phenomena were borrowed by consumer researchers from the behavioral sciences. Such methodologies included laboratory experimentation; focus group interviewing, depth interviewing, and projective techniques (used in motivation research); and cross-sectional mail and telephone survey techniques (used in attitude and psychographic research).

It should be noted that the behavioral marketing schools have been largely responsible for increasing the scientific sophistication of the marketing discipline, with the buyer behavior school in particular deserving much of the credit. Further, with a strong theoretical and methodological base available from the behavioral sciences, the emergence of the buyer behavior school propelled the status of consumer behavior to that of a subdiscipline with adequate maturity to assert considerable independence from marketing. The growing independence of consumer behavior has been evidenced by the establishment of a separate association for the study of consumer behavior (the Association for Consumer Research) and an interdisciplinary journal devoted to consumer research (the *Journal of Consumer Research*).

Adaptive Marketing Schools and Parallel Consumer Behavior

Most recently, marketing has begun to shift its emphasis back to the study of aggregate market behavior. Substantial attention has recently been focused on opportunities and threats generated by such environmental forces as regulation, technology, and global competition. This has resulted in the emergence of the adaptive marketing concept, derived from management thinking which maintains that it is more effective to adapt the organization to fit environmental realities than to attempt to adapt the environment to fit the organization (Toffler 1985). Schools of thought identified with this era are the macromarketing school and the strategic planning school. Researchers associated with these schools of thought have continued to borrow from the behavioral sciences, but have also borrowed concepts from the social sciences relevant to the study of environmental contingencies. Such concepts include environmental scanning (Steiner 1979), stakeholder analysis (Freeman 1984), and competitive analysis (Porter 1980, 1985).

The macromarketing school emerged in the 1970s in response to the growing interest across business disciplines in the impact of business on society and in the impact of societal forces on business. Regarding marketing as a social institution, the macromarketing school is associated with work that examines the effects of marketing on society, examines the effects of societal forces on marketing, adopts the perspective of society, and/or studies marketing systems at the societal level (Hunt and Burnett 1982). While other schools of thought (particularly the managerial school) have recognized that environmental factors influence marketing, they have generally regarded these factors as uncontrollable (McCarthy 1960). Thus, these schools of thought have afforded little research attention to environmental factors. In contrast, the macromarketing school has sought to give in-depth attention to societal forces, analyzing their impact on marketing as well as marketing's impact on them. While the macromarketing perspective may be traced to early writings by Holloway and Hancock (1964) and Fisk (1967), the macromarketing school did not emerge in full force until the latter 1970s. The development of macromarketing as a school of thought has largely followed from the University of Colorado's organization of the first in a continuing series of macromarketing seminars (Slater 1977), and from the founding of the *Journal of Macromarketing*.

The strategic planning school is currently emerging as the newest school of marketing thought (Sheth and Gardner 1982). Authors associated with this perspective emphasize the importance of analyzing environmental dynamics and of proactively adapting the organization to the environment. Many contributions of the strategic planning school have come from consulting firms and their clients. Such contributions include produce portfolio models developed by General Electric and the Boston Consulting Group; experience curve models developed by the Boston Consulting Group; and the Profit Impact of Marketing Strategies (PIMS) program, initiated by General Electric and currently under the management of the Strategic Planning Institute. Further, a substantial number of marketing researchers have recently advocated strategic planning and environmental management perspectives in their writings (e.g., Abell 1978; Montgomery and Weinberg 1979; Anderson 1982; Cook 1983; Henderson 1983; Sheth and Frazier 1983; Wind and Robertson 1983; Zeithaml and Zeithaml 1984; Day 1986). The Spring 1983 issue of the *Journal of Marketing* was devoted to articles on marketing strategy (Cunningham and Robertson 1983); and an increasing

20 • *Historical Perspectives in Marketing*

number of marketing texts are being written from a strategic planning perspective (e.g., Luck and Ferrell 1979; Jain 1981; Cravens 1982).

As the environmental forces fostering the adaptive marketing perspective become more pronounced, we predict that at least four areas of consumer research will emerge or escalate in importance. First, as markets have become increasingly global (Levitt 1983), a growing emphasis has been placed on international marketing. This has fostered a concomitant interest in cross-cultural consumer behavior and increased research on culture as an influence on consumption and buying behavior (Sheth and Sethi 1977; Plummer 1977; Green et al. 1983; Belk 1984a; Sherry 1986). We predict that this interest and emphasis will increase as globalization continues.

Second, with maturing markets and intensified competition, the emphasis of marketing appears to be shifting away from the acquisition of new customers and toward the retention of existing customers (Albrecht and Zemke 1985; Desatnick 1987). Thus, we predict that the focus of consumer research will shift as well. For example, interest in consumer satisfaction and dissatisfaction may be expected to increase. In particular, more in-depth research on complaining behavior, word-of-mouth communication, and other consumer responses to dissatisfaction is anticipated (Richins 1983; Resnik and Harmon 1983; Bearden and Mason 1984; Folkes 1984).

Third, with maturing markets, interest in the competitive environment has intensified (Kotler 1980). Thus, we predict that interest will be fostered in consumer perceptions of marketing competition. The need for research on this topic has already become apparent as marketing has sought to take a customer-oriented approach in its efforts to define product markets and analyze market structure (Day, Shocker, and Srivastava 1979; Srivastava, Alpert, and Shocker 1984). Additionally, with much competitive effort currently directed toward psychological positioning (Ries and Trout 1981), consumer researchers may be expected to aid marketers in evaluating their positioning strategies. Insights relevant to marketing may be provided by examining such phenomena as comparison shopping, consumer perceptions of competitive advertising, and consumer perceptions of competitive pricing.

Finally, with the accelerated pace of competitive and technological change, a recent trend in marketing practice has been to use behavior modification strategies rather than persuasion strategies in attempting to influence consumers (Markin 1977; Nord and Peter 1980). Traditional persuasion strategies endeavor to first effect attitudinal change, with behavioral change following. In contrast, behavior modification strategies endeavor to first effect behavioral change, with attitudinal change following. In light of this trend, we predict that the future emphasis of consumer research will be less on the study of perceptions, cognitions, and attitudes, and more on the study of actual behavior and behavior modification techniques. Early focus on behavior modification has included research on foot-in-the-door techniques (e.g., Scott 1977; Hansen and Robinson 1980) and research on the effectiveness of incentives in stimulating purchase and repeat purchase behavior (e.g., Scott 1976). Additionally, some recent work has taken a classical conditioning perspective (Gorn 1982; Allen and Madden 1985; Bierley, McSweeney, and Vannieuwkerk 1985). Evidence of a growing interest in actual consumption behavior is provided by several recent calls for research on consumption experience (Jacoby 1978; Sheth 1982; Holbrook and Hirschman 1982; Belk 1984b; Holbrook 1985; Sheth 1985); and by the current interest in naturalistic inquiry (Hirschman 1986).

Along with these forecasts, however, we also predict that as the adaptive perspective gains support in marketing, consumer behavior may be faced with a serious dilemma. As an integral part of marketing, the subdiscipline of consumer behavior will undoubtedly wish to continue to investigate issues relevant to marketing's needs. This will necessitate an emphasis on aggregate consumer behavior and increased borrowing from the social sciences (Kollat, Blackwell, and Engel 1972; Sheth 1974b; Nicosia and Mayer 1976; Engel 1981; Kassarjian 1982; Sheth 1982; Zielinski and Robertson 1982). However, we expect that many consumer researchers will be reluctant to abandon their emphasis on individual behavior and the scientific traditions gleaned from the behavioral sciences. Prior to specializing in consumer behavior, many consumer researchers received their scientific training in psychology. As a result, they are most skilled in investigating individual behavior. Further, influenced by the behavioral sciences, the field of consumer behavior has embraced logical positivism as its dominant scientific philosophy. Many consumer researchers therefore regard the alternative philosophical approaches and research methodologies embraced by the social sciences as lacking in scientific rigor.

Given these traditions, it is not certain that consumer behavior will automatically follow marketing as it has in the past. It is perhaps more probable that consumer research will become polarized. While marketing will almost certainly continue to study consumer behavior from its own perspectives and investigate topics relevant to its own needs, the science of consumer behavior may emerge as an independent discipline continuing to focus on individual consumer behavior.

Notes

1. Although there currently exists considerable controversy as to what is appropriately considered a "school of thought" (as opposed to a theory or paradigm), we have chosen to avoid this debate. Instead, we have followed the tradition of Bartels (1962) in referring to the various approaches to the study of marketing as schools of thought.

22 • *Historical Perspectives in Marketing*

References

Abell, Derek F. 1978. "Strategic Windows." *Journal of Marketing* 42 (July). 21–26.

Achrol, Ravi Singh, Torger Reve, and Louis W. Stern. 1983. "The Environment of Marketing Channel Dyads: A Framework for Comparative Analysis." *Journal of Marketing* 47 (Fall). 55–67.

Albrecht, Karl, and Ron Zemke. 1985. *Service America!: Doing Business in the New Economy.* Homewood, Ill. Dow Jones-Irwin.

Alderson, Wroe. 1957. *Marketing Behavior and Executive Action: A Functionalist Approach to Marketing Theory.* Homewood, Ill.: Richard D. Irwin.

———. 1965. *Dynamic Marketing Behavior: A Functionalist Theory of Marketing.* Homewood, Ill.: Richard D. Irwin.

Alderson, Wroe, and Miles W. Martin. 1965. "Toward a Formal Theory of Transactions and Transvections." *Journal of Marketing Research* 2 (May). 117–127.

Allen, Chris T., and Thomas J. Madden. 1985. "A Closer Look at Classical Conditioning." *Journal of Consumer Research* 12 (December). 301–315.

Anderson, Paul F. 1982. "Marketing, Strategic Planning and the Theory of the Firm." *Journal of Marketing* 46 (Spring). 15–26.

Andreasen, Alan R. 1965. "Attitudes and Customer Behavior: A Decision Model." In Lee E. Preston, ed., *Research Program in Marketing: New Research in Marketing.* Berkeley: Institute of Business and Economic Research, University of California. 1–16.

———. 1975. *The Disadvantaged Consumer.* New York: The Free Press.

Angelmar, Reinhard, and Louis W. Stern. 1978. "Development of a Content Analytic System for Analysis of Bargaining Communication in Marketing." *Journal of Marketing Research* 15 (February). 93–102.

Antil, John H. 1984. "Conceptualization and Operationalization of Involvement." In Thomas C. Kinnear, ed., *Advances in Consumer Research.* Provo Utah: Association for Consumer Research. 11:203–209.

Armstrong, Gary M., Metin N. Gurol, and Frederick A. Russ. 1979. "Detecting and Correcting Deceptive Advertising." *Journal of Consumer Research* 6 (December). 237–246.

Arndt, Johan. 1967. *Word of Mouth Advertising: A Review of the Literature.* New York: Advertising Research Foundation.

Ashby, Harold J., Jr. 1973. "The Black Consumer." In William T. Kennedy, ed., *New Consumerism: Selected Readings.* Columbus, Ohio: Grid. 149–176.

Aspinwall, Leo. 1958. "The Characteristics of Goods and Parallel Systems Theories." In Eugene J. Kelley and William Lazer, eds., *Managerial Marketing: Perspectives and Viewpoints.* Homewood, Ill.: Richard D. Irwin. 434–450.

Bagozzi, Richard P. 1974. "Marketing as an Organized Behavioral System of Exchange." *Journal of Marketing* 38 (October). 77–81.

———. 1975. "Marketing as Exchange." *Journal of Marketing* 39 (October). 32–39.

———. 1978. "Marketing as Exchange: A Theory of Transactions in the Marketplace." *American Behavioral Scientist* 21 (March/April). 535–556.

———. 1979. "Toward a Formal Theory of Marketing Exchanges." In O. C. Ferrell,

Stephen W. Brown, and Charles W. Lamb, Jr. eds., *Conceptual and Theoretical Developments in Marketing*. Chicago: American Marketing Association. 431–447.

Balderston, F. E. 1964. "Design of Marketing Channels." In Reavis Cox, Wroe Alderson, and Stanley J. Shapiro, eds., *Theory in Marketing*. Homewood, Ill.: Richard D. Irwin. 176–189.

Bartels, Robert. 1962. *The Development of Marketing Thought*. Homewood, Ill.: Richard D. Irwin.

Bass, Frank M. 1969. "A New Product Growth Model for Consumer Durables." *Management Science* 15 (January). 215–227.

Bauer, Raymond A. 1960. "Consumer Behavior as Risk Taking." In Robert S. Hancock, ed., *Dynamic Marketing for a Changing World: Proceedings of the 43rd National Conference of the American Marketing Association*. Chicago: American Marketing Association. 389–398.

Bearden, William O., and J. Barry Mason. 1984. "An Investigation of Influences on Consumer Complaint Reports." In Thomas C. Kinnear, ed., *Advances in Consumer Research*. Provo, Utah: Association for Consumer Research. 11:490–495.

Beem, Eugene R. 1973. "The Beginnings of the Consumer Movement." In William T. Kelley, ed., *New Consumerism: Selected Readings*. Columbus, Ohio: Grid. 13–25.

Beier, Frederick J., and Louis W. Stern. 1969. "Power in the Channel of Distribution." In Louis W. Stern, ed., *Distribution Channels: Behavioral Dimensions*. Boston: Houghton Mifflin. 92–116.

Belk, Russell W. 1984. "Cultural and Historical Differences in Concepts of Self and Their Effects on Attitudes Toward Having and Giving." In Thomas C. Kinnear, ed., *Advances in Consumer Research*. Provo, Utah: Association for Consumer Research. 11:754–760.

———. 1984. "Manifesto for a Consumer Behavior of Consumer Behavior." In Paul F. Anderson and Michael J. Ryan, ed., *1984 AMA Winter Educators' Conference: Scientific Method in Marketing*. Chicago: American Marketing Association. 163–167.

Bettman, James R. 1979. *An Information Processing Theory of Consumer Choice*. Reading, Mass.: Addison-Wesley.

Bierley, Calvin, Frances K. McSweeney, and Renee Vannieuwkerk. 1985. "Classical Conditioning of Preferences for Stimuli." *Journal of Consumer Research* 12 (December). 316–323.

Borden, Neil H. 1964. "The Concept of the Marketing Mix." *Journal of Advertising Research* 4 (June). 2–7.

Bourne, Francis S. 1957. "Group Influence in Marketing and Public Relations." In Rensis Likert and Samuel P. Hayes, Jr., eds. *Some Applications of Behavioural Research*. Paris: Unesco. 207–257.

Breyer, Ralph F. 1934. *The Marketing Institution*. New York: McGraw-Hill.

Brown, James R., and Ralph L. Day. 1981. "Measures of Manifest Conflict in Distribution Channels." *Journal of Marketing Research* 18 (August). 263–274.

Bucklin, Louis P. 1963. "Retail Strategy and the Classification of Consumer Goods." *Journal of Marketing* 27 (January). 50–55.

24 • *Historical Perspectives in Marketing*

————. 1965. "Postponement, Speculation and the Structure of Distribution Channels." *Journal of Marketing Research* 2 (February). 26–31.

Butler, Ralph Starr. 1923. *Marketing and Merchandising.* New York: Alexander Hamilton Institute.

Cash, Harold C., and W. J. E. Crissy. 1958. *A Point of View for Salesmen.* Vol. 1 of *The Psychology of Selling.* New York: Personnel Development Associates.

Chamberlin, Edward Hastings. 1933. *The Theory of Monopolistic Competition.* Cambridge, Mass.: Harvard University Press.

Cherington, Paul T. 1920. *The Elements of Marketing.* New York: Macmillan.

Churchill, Gilbert A., Jr., and Carol Surprenant. 1982. "An Investigation Into the Determinants of Consumer Satisfaction." *Journal of Marketing Research* 19 (November). 491–504.

Coleman, Richard P. 1960. "The Significance of Social Stratification in Selling." In Martin L. Bell, ed., *Marketing: A Maturing Discipline.* Chicago: American Marketing Association. 171–184.

Converse, Paul D. 1943. *A Study of Retail Trade Areas in East Central Illinois.* Urbana: University of Illinois Press.

————. 1949. "New Laws of Retail Gravitation." *Journal of Marketing* 14 (October). 379–384.

Converse, Paul D., and Harvey W. Huegy. 1940. *Elements of Marketing.* Englewood Cliffs, N.J.: Prentice-Hall.

Cook, Victor J., Jr. 1983. "Marketing Strategy and Differential Advantage." *Journal of Marketing* 47 (Spring). 68–75.

Copeland, Melvin T. 1923. "Relation of Consumers' Buying Habits to Marketing Methods." *Harvard Business Review* 1 (April). 282–289.

Cravens, David W. 1982. *Strategic Marketing.* Homewood, Ill.: Richard D. Irwin.

Cunningham, Ross M. 1956. "Brand Loyalty—What, Where, How Much?" *Harvard Business Review* 34 (January-February). 116–128.

Cunningham, William H., and Thomas S. Robertson. 1983. "From the Editor." *Journal of Marketing* 47 (Spring): 5–6.

Day, George S. 1976. "Assessing the Effects of Information Disclosure Requirements." *Journal of Marketing* 40 (April). 42–52.

————. 1986. *Analysis for Strategic Market Decisions.* St. Paul, Minn.: West Publishing Company.

Day, George S., Allan D. Shocker, and Rajendra K. Srivastava. 1979. "Customer-Oriented Approaches to Identifying Product Markets." *Journal of Marketing* 43 (Fall). 8–19.

Day, Ralph L., ed. 1977. *Consumer Satisfaction, Dissatisfaction and Complaining Behavior.* Bloomington/Indianapolis: Department of Marketing, School of Business, Indiana University.

Day, Ralph L., and H. Keith Hunt, eds. 1979. *Refining Concepts and Measures of Consumer Satisfaction and Complaining Behavior.* Bloomington/Indianapolis: Department of Marketing, School of Business, Indiana University.

Dean, Joel. 1950. "Pricing Policies for New Products." *Harvard Business Review* 28 (November). 45–53.

————. 1951. *Managerial Economics.* Englewood Cliffs, N.J.: Prentice-Hall.

Desatnick, Robert L. 1987. *Managing to Keep the Customer*. San Francisco: Jossey-Bass Publishers.

Dichter, Ernest. 1964. *Handbook of Consumer Motivations: The Psychology of the World of Objects*. New York: McGraw-Hill.

Drucker, Peter. 1969. "The Shame of Marketing." *Marketing/Communications* 297 (August). 60–64.

El-Ansary, Adel I., and Louis W. Stern. 1972. "Power Measurement in the Distribution Channel." *Journal of Marketing Research* 9 (February). 47–52.

Eliashberg, Jehoshua, and Donald A. Michie. 1984. "Multiple Business Goals Sets as Determinants of Marketing Channel Conflict: An Empirical Study." *Journal of Marketing Research* 21 (February). 75–88.

Emerson, Richard M. 1962. "Power-Dependence Relations." *American Sociological Review* 27 (February). 31–41.

Engel, James F. 1981. "The Discipline of Consumer Research: Permanent Adolesence or Maturity?" In Kent B. Monroe, ed., *Advances in Consumer Research*. Vol. 8. Ann Arbor, Mich.: Association for Consumer Research.

Engel, James F., David T. Kollat, and Roger D. Blackwell. 1968. *Consumer Behavior*. New York: Holt, Rinehart and Winston.

Enis, Ben M., and Kenneth J. Roering. 1980. "Product Classification Taxonomies: Synthesis and Consumer Implications." In Charles W. Lamb, Jr. and Patrick M. Dunne, eds., *Theoretical Developments in Marketing*. Chicago: American Marketing Association. 186–189.

Etgar, Michael. 1976. "Channel Domination and Countervailing Power in Distributive Channels." *Journal of Marketing Research* 13 (August). 254–262.

———. 1979. "Sources and Types of Intrachannel Conflict." *Journal of Retailing* 55 (Spring). 61–78.

Evans, Franklin B. 1959. "Psychological and Objective Factors in the Prediction of Brand Choice: Ford Versus Chevrolet." *Journal of Business* 32 (October). 340–369.

Festinger, Leon. 1957. *A Theory of Cognitive Dissonance*. New York: Row, Peterson and Company.

Fishbein, Martin, ed. 1967. *Readings in Attitude Theory and Measurement*. New York: John Wiley & Sons.

Fishbein, Martin, and Icek Ajzen. 1975. *Belief, Attitude, Intention, and Behavior: An Introduction to Theory and Research*. Reading, Mass.: Addison-Wesley.

Fisk, George. 1967. *Marketing Systems: An Introductory Analysis*. New York: Harper & Row.

Folkes, Valerie S. 1984. "Consumer Reactions to Product Failure: An Attributional Approach." *Journal of Consumer Research* 10 (March). 398–409.

Foote, Nelson N., ed. 1961. *Household Decision-Making*. Vol. 4 of *Consumer Behavior*. New York: New York University Press.

Frank, Ronald E. 1962. "Brand Choice as a Probability Process." *Journal of Business* 35 (January). 43–56.

Frazier, Gary L. 1983a. "Interorganizational Exchange Behavior in Marketing Channels: A Broadened Perspective." *Journal of Marketing* 47 (Fall). 68–78.

26 • *Historical Perspectives in Marketing*

———. 1983b. "On the Measurement of Interfirm Power in Channels of Distribution." *Journal of Marketing Research* 20 (May). 158–166.

Frazier, Gary L., and Jagdish N. Sheth. 1985. "An Attitude-Behavior Framework for Distribution Channel Management." *Journal of Marketing* 49 (Summer). 38–48.

Frazier, Gary L., and John O. Summers. 1984. "Interfirm Influence Strategies and Their Application Within Distribution Channels." *Journal of Marketing* 48 (Summer). 43–55.

Freeman, R. Edward. 1984. *Strategic Management: A Stakeholder Approach*. Boston: Pitman Publishing.

French, John R. P., Jr., and Bertram Raven. 1959. "The Bases of Social Power." In Dorwin Cartwright, ed., *Studies in Social Power*. Ann Arbor: Research Center for Group Dynamics, Institute for Social Research, University of Michigan. 150–167.

Fullbrook, Earl S. 1940. "The Functional Concept in Marketing." *Journal of Marketing* 4 (January). 229–237.

Gardner, David M. 1976. "Deception in Advertising: A Receiver Oriented Approach to Understanding." *Journal of Advertising* 5 (Fall). 5–11, 19.

Gilly, Mary C., and Ben M. Enis. 1982. "Recycling the Family Life Cycle: A Proposal for Redefinition." In Andrew A. Mitchell, ed., *Advances in Consumer Research*, Vol. 9. Ann Arbor, Mich.: Association for Consumer Research.

Glick, Paul C. 1947. "The Family Cycle." *American Sociological Review* 12 (February). 164–174.

Goldstucker, Jac. 1965. "Trading Areas." In George Schwarzt, ed., *Science in Marketing*. New York: John Wiley & Sons. 281–320.

Gorn, Gerald J. 1982. "The Effects of Music in Advertising on Choice Behavior: A Classical Conditioning Approach." *Journal of Marketing* 46 (Winter). 94–101.

Green, Robert T., Jean-Paul Leonardi, Jean-Louis Chandon, Isabella C. M. Cunningham, Bronis Verhage, and Alain Strazzieri. 1983. "Societal Development and Family Purchasing Roles: A Cross-National Study." *Journal of Consumer Research* 9 (March). 436–442.

Grether, E. T. 1950. "A Theoretical Approach to the Analysis of Marketing." In Reavis Cox and Wroe Alderson, eds., *Theory in Marketing: Selected Essays*. Chicago: Richard D. Irwin. 113–123.

———. 1983. "Regional-Spatial Analysis in Marketing." *Journal of Marketing* 47 (Fall). 36–43.

Hall, Calvin S., and Gardner Lindzey. 1957. "Freud's Psychoanalytic Theory." In *Theories of Personality*. New York: John Wiley & Sons. 29–75.

Hansen, Robert A., and Larry M. Robinson. 1980. "Testing the Effectiveness of Alternative Foot-in-the-Door Manipulations." *Journal of Marketing Research* 17 (August). 359–364.

Harary, Frank, and Benjamin Lipstein. 1962. "The Dynamics of Brand Loyalty: A Markovian Approach." *Operations Research* 10 (January-February). 19–40.

Heider, Fritz. 1958. *The Psychology of Interpersonal Relations*. New York: John Wiley & Sons.

Henderson, Bruce D. 1983. "The Anatomy of Competition." *Journal of Marketing* 47 (Spring). 7–11.

Hirschman, Elizabeth C. 1986. "Humanistic Inquiry in Marketing Research: Philosophy, Method, and Criteria." *Journal of Marketing Research* 23 (August). 237–249.

Holbrook, Morris B. 1985. "Why Business is Bad for Consumer Research: The Three Bears Revisited." In Elizabeth C. Hirschman and Morris B. Holbrook, eds., *Advances in Consumer Research*, Vol. 12. Provo, Utah: Association for Consumer Research.

Holbrook, Morris B., and Elizabeth C. Hirschman. 1982. "The Experiential Aspects of Consumption: Consumer Fantasies, Feelings, and Fun." *Journal of Consumer Research* 9 (September). 132–140.

Holbrook, Morris B., and John A. Howard. 1977. "Frequently Purchased Nondurable Goods and Services." In Robert Ferber, ed., *Selected Aspects of Consumer Behavior: A Summary from the Perspective of Different Disciplines*. Washington, D.C.: National Science Foundation, Directorate for Research Applications, Research Applied to National Needs.

Hollander, Stanley C. 1960. "The Wheel of Retailing." *Journal of Marketing* 25 (July). 37–42.

Holloway, Robert J., and Robert S. Hancock, eds. 1964. *The Environment of Marketing Behavior: Selections from the Literature*. New York: John Wiley & Sons.

Holton, Richard H. 1958. "The Distinction Between Convenience Goods, Shopping Goods, and Specialty Goods." *Journal of Marketing* 23 (July). 53–56.

———. 1959. "What is Really Meant by 'Specialty' Goods?" *Journal of Marketing* 24 (July). 64–66.

Houston, Michael J., and Michael L. Rothschild. 1980. "Policy-Related Experiments on Information Provision: A Normative Model and Explication." *Journal of Marketing Research* 17 (November). 432–449.

Howard, John A. 1957. *Marketing Management: Analysis and Decision*. Homewood, Ill.: Richard D. Irwin.

Howard, John A., and Jagdish N. Sheth. 1969. *The Theory of Buyer Behavior*. New York: John Wiley & Sons.

Huff, David L. 1962. *Determination of Intra-Urban Retail Trade Areas*. Los Angeles: Real Estate Research Program, Graduate School of Business Administration, Division of Research, University of California, Los Angeles.

Huff, David L. 1964. "Defining and Estimating a Trading Area." *Journal of Marketing* 28 (July). 34–38.

Hunt, H. Keith, ed. 1977. *Conceptualization and Measurement of Consumer Satisfaction and Dissatisfaction: Proceedings of Conference Conducted by Marketing Science Institute with Support of National Science Foundation*. Cambridge, Mass.: Marketing Science Institute.

Hunt, Shelby D. 1976. "The Nature and Scope of Marketing." *Journal of Marketing* 40 (July). 17–28.

Hunt, Shelby D., and John J. Burnett. 1982. "The Macromarketing/Micromarketing Dichotomy: A Taxonomical Model." *Journal of Marketing* 46 (Summer). 11–26.

28 • *Historical Perspectives in Marketing*

Hunt, Shelby D., and John R. Nevin. 1974. "Power in a Channel of Distribution: Sources and Consequences." *Journal of Marketing Research* 11 (May). 186–193.

Jacoby, Jacob. 1978. "Consumer Research: A State of the Art Review." *Journal of Marketing* 42 (April). 87–96.

Jacoby, Jacob, and Constance Small. 1975. "The FDA Approach to Defining Misleading Advertising." *Journal of Marketing* 39 (October). 65–68.

Jain, Subhash C. 1981. *Marketing Planning and Strategy.* Cincinnati, Ohio: South-Western Publishing Company.

Kahl, Joseph A. 1953. *The American Class Structure.* New York: Rinehart & Company.

Kaish, Stanley. 1967. "Cognitive Dissonance and the Classification of Consumer Goods." *Journal of Marketing* 31 (October). 28–31.

Kassarjian, Harold H. 1969. "The Negro and American Advertising, 1946–1965." *Journal of Marketing Research* 6 (February). 29–39.

———. 1971. "Personality and Consumer Behavior: A Review." *Journal of Marketing Research* 8 (November). 409–418.

———. 1982. "The Development of Consumer Behavior Theory." In Andrew A. Mitchell, ed., *Advances in Consumer Research.* Ann Arbor, Mich.: Association for Consumer Research. 9:20–22.

Katona, George. 1951. *Psychological Analysis of Economic Behavior.* New York: McGraw-Hill.

———. 1953. "Rational Behavior and Economic Behavior." *Psychological Review* 60 (September). 307–318.

Katona, George, and Eva Mueller. 1953. *Consumer Attitudes and Demand. 1950–1952.* Ann Arbor: Survey Research Center, Institute for Social Research, University of Michigan.

———. 1956. *Consumer Expectations, 1953–1956.* Ann Arbor: Survey Research Center, Institute for Social Research, University of Michigan.

Katona, George, Burkhard Strumpel, and Ernest Zahn. 1971. *Aspirations and Affluence.* New York: McGraw-Hill.

Katz, Daniel. 1960. "The Functional Approach to the Study of Attitudes." *Public Opinion Quarterly* 24 (Summer). 163–204.

Katz, Elihu. 1957. "The Two-Step Flow of Communication: An Up-to-Date Report on an Hypothesis." *Public Opinion Quarterly* 21 (Spring). 61–78.

Katz, Elihu, and Paul F. Lazarsfeld. 1955. *Personal Influence: The Part Played by People in the Flow of Mass Communications.* Glencoe, Ill.: The Free Press.

Keith, Robert J. 1960. "The Marketing Revolution." *Journal of Marketing* 24 (January). 35–38.

Kelley, Eugene J., and William Lazer, eds. 1958. *Managerial Marketing: Perspectives and Viewpoints.* Homewood, Ill.: Richard D. Irwin.

Kollat, David T., Roger D. Blackwell, and James F. Engel. 1972. "The Current Status of Consumer Behavior Research: Developments During the 1968–1972 Period." In M. Venkatesan, ed., *Proceedings 3rd Annual Conference of the Association for Consumer Research.* College Park, Md.: Association for Consumer Research. 576–585.

Kotler, Philip. 1972a. "A Generic Concept of Marketing." *Journal of Marketing* 36 (April). 46–54.

————. 1972b. "What Consumerism Means for Marketers." *Harvard Business Review* 50 (May-June). 48–57.

————. 1980. *Marketing Management: Analysis, Planning, and Control.* Fourth ed. Englewood Cliffs, N.J.: Prentice-Hall.

Krugman, Herbert E. 1965. "The Impact of Television Advertising: Learning Without Involvement." *Public Opinion Quarterly* 29 (Fall). 349–356.

Kuehn, Alfred A. 1962. "Consumer Brand Choice as a Learning Process." *Journal of Advertising Research* 2 (December). 10–17.

Lavidge, Robert J., and Gary A. Steiner. 1961. "A Model for Predictive Measurements of Advertising Effectiveness." *Journal of Marketing* 25 (October). 59–62.

Levitt, Theodore. 1960. "Marketing Myopia." *Harvard Business Review* 38 (July/August). 45–56.

————. 1965. "Exploit the Product Life Cycle." *Harvard Business Review* 43 (November/December). 81–94.

————. 1983. "The Globalization of Markets." *Harvard Business Review* 61 (May-June). 92–102.

Levy, Sidney J. 1966. "Social Class and Consumer Behavior." In Joseph W. Newman, ed., *On Knowing the Consumer.* New York: John Wiley & Sons. 146–160.

Lewis, Richard J., and Leo G. Erickson. 1969. "Marketing Functions and Marketing Systems: A Synthesis." *Journal of Marketing* 33 (July). 10–14.

Locander, William B., and W. Austin Spivey. 1978. "A Functional Approach to Attitude Measurement." *Journal of Marketing Research* 15 (November). 576–587.

Lockley, Lawrence C. 1974. "History and Development of Marketing Research." Chap. 1 in Robert Ferber, ed., *Handbook of Marketing Research.* New York: McGraw-Hill.

Loomis, Charles P. 1936. "The Study of the Life Cycle of Families." *Rural Sociology* 1 (June). 180–199.

Luck, David J. 1959. "On the Nature of Specialty Goods." *Journal of Marketing* 24 (July). 61–64.

Luck, David J., and O. C. Ferrell. 1979. *Marketing Strategy and Plans: Systematic Marketing Management.* Englewood Cliffs, N.J.: Prentice-Hall.

Lusch, Robert F. 1976. "Sources of Power: Their Impact on Intrachannel Conflict." *Journal of Marketing Research* 13 (November). 382–390.

Lutz, Richard J. 1977. "An Experimental Investigation of Causal Relations Among Cognitions, Affect, and Behavioral Intention." *Journal of Consumer Research* 3 (March). 197–208.

McCammon, Bert C., Jr. 1965. "The Emergence and Growth of Contractually Integrated Channels in the American Economy." In Peter D. Bennett, ed., *Marketing and Economic Development (The 50th Anniversary International Symposium of Marketing and Allied Disciplines).* Chicago: American Marketing Association. 496–515.

McCarthy, E. Jerome. 1960. *Basic Marketing: A Managerial Approach.* Homewood, Ill.: Richard D. Irwin.

30 • *Historical Perspectives in Marketing*

McGarry, Edmund D. 1950. "Some Functions of Marketing Reconsidered." In Reavis Cox and Wroe Alderson, eds., *Theory in Marketing*. Chicago: Richard D. Irwin. 263–279.

McGuire, William J. 1976. "Some Internal Psychological Factors Influencing Consumer Choice." *Journal of Consumer Research* 2 (March). 302–319.

McInnes, William. 1964. "A Conceptual Approach to Marketing." In Reavis Cox, Wroe Alderson, and Stanley J. Shapiro, eds., *Theory in Marketing*. Homewood, Ill.: Richard D. Irwin. 51–67.

McKitterick, John B. 1957. "What is the Marketing Management Concept?" In Frank M. Bass, ed., *The Frontiers of Marketing Thought and Science*. Chicago: American Marketing Association. 71–82.

Mallen, Bruce. 1963. "A Theory of Retailer-Supplier Conflict, Control, and Cooperation." *Journal of Retailing* 39 (Summer). 24–32, 51.

———. 1973. "Functional Spin-Off: A Key to Anticipating Change in Distribution Structure." *Journal of Marketing* 37 (July). 18–25.

March, James G., and Herbert A. Simon. 1958. *Organizations*. New York: John Wiley & Sons.

Markin, Rom J. 1977. "Motivation in Buyer Behavior Theory: From Mechanism to Cognition." In Arch G. Woodside, Jagdish N. Sheth, and Peter D. Bennett, eds., *Consumer and Industrial Buying Behavior*. New York: Elsevier North-Holland, Inc. 37–48.

Marshall, Alfred. 1890. *Principles of Economics*. London: Macmillan.

Martineau, Pierre. 1958. "Social Classes and Spending Behavior." *Journal of Marketing* 23 (October). 121–130.

Mazis, Michael B., Olli T. Ahtola, and R. Eugene Klippel. 1975. "A Comparison of Four Multi-Attribute Models in the Prediction of Consumer Attitudes." *Journal of Consumer Research* 2 (June). 38–52.

Montgomery, David B., and Charles B. Weinberg. 1979. "Toward Strategic Intelligence Systems." *Journal of Marketing* 43 (Fall). 41–52.

Murphy, Patrick E., and Ben M. Enis. 1986. "Classifying Products Strategically." *Journal of Marketing* 50 (July). 24–42.

Murphy, Patrick E., and William A. Staples. 1979. "A Modernized Family Life Cycle." *Journal of Consumer Research* 6 (June). 12–22.

Myers, James H., and Thomas S. Robertson. 1972. "Dimensions of Opinion Leadership." *Journal of Marketing Research* 9 (February). 41–46.

Nicosia, Francesco M. 1966. *Consumer Decision Processes: Marketing and Advertising Implications*. Englewood Cliffs, N.J.: Prentice-Hall.

Nicosia, Francesco M., and Robert N. Mayer. 1976. "Toward a Sociology of Consumption." *Journal of Consumer Research* 3 (September). 65–75.

Nord, Walter R., and J. Paul Peter. 1980. "A Behavior Modification Perspective on Marketing." *Journal of Marketing* 44 (Spring). 36–47.

Norris, Ruby Turner. 1941. *The Theory of Consumer's Demand*. New Haven, Conn.: Yale University Press.

Ohlin, Bertil. 1933. *Interregional and International Trade*. Cambridge, Mass.: Harvard University Press.

Oliver, Richard L. 1980. "A Cognitive Model of the Antecedents and Consequences of Satisfaction Decisions." *Journal of Marketing Research* 17 (November). 460–469.

Oliver, Richard L., and William O. Bearden. 1983. "The Role of Involvement in Satisfaction Processes." In Richard P. Bagozzi and Alice M. Tybout, eds., *Advances in Consumer Research*. Ann Arbor, Mich.: Association for Consumer Research. 10:250–255.

Olshavsky, Richard W., and Donald H. Granbois. 1979. "Consumer Decision Making—Fact or Fiction?" *Journal of Consumer Research* 6 (September). 93–100.

Parlin, Charles Coolidge. 1912. *Merchandising and Textiles*. 5–6.

Plummer, Joseph T. 1977. "Consumer Focus in Cross-National Research." *Journal of Advertising* 6 (Spring). 5–15.

Pondy, Louis R. 1967. "Organizational Conflict: Concepts and Models." *Administrative Science Quarterly* 12 (September). 296–320.

Porter, Michael E. 1980. *Competitive Strategy: Techniques for Analyzing Industries and Competitors*. New York: The Free Press.

———. 1985. *Competitive Advantage: Creating and Sustaining Superior Performance*. New York: The Free Press.

Reilly, William J. 1931. *The Law of Retail Gravitation*. Austin: The University of Texas.

Resnik, Alan J., and Robert R. Harmon. 1983. "Consumer Complaints and Managerial Response: A Holistic Approach." *Journal of Marketing* 47 (Winter). 86–97.

Resnik, Alan J., and Bruce L. Stern. 1977. "An Analysis of Information Content in Television Advertising." *Journal of Marketing* 41 (January). 50–53.

Revzan, David A. 1961. *Wholesaling in Marketing Organization*. New York: John Wiley & Sons.

Richins, Marsha L. 1983. "Negative Word-of-Mouth by Dissatisfied Consumers: A Pilot Study." *Journal of Marketing* 47 (Winter). 68–78.

Ridgeway, Valentine F. 1957. "Administration of Manufacturer-Dealer Systems." *Administrative Science Quarterly* 1 (March). 464–483.

Ries, Al, and Jack Trout. 1981. *Positioning: The Battle for Your Mind*. New York: McGraw-Hill.

Robicheaux, Robert A., and Adel I. El-Ansary. 1975–76. "A General Model for Understanding Channel Member Behavior." *Journal of Retailing* 52 (Winter). 13–30, 93–94.

Robinson, Lawrence R., and Eleanor G. May. 1956. *Self-Service in Variety Stores*. Boston: Harvard University, Graduate School of Business Administration, Division of Research.

Rogers, Everett M. 1962. *Diffusion of Innovations*. New York: The Free Press of Glencoe.

Rosenberg, Larry J., and Louis W. Stern. 1971. "Conflict Measurement in the Distribution Channel." *Journal of Marketing Research* 8 (November). 437–442.

Rosenberg, Milton J. 1956. "Cognitive Structure and Attitudinal Affect." *Journal of Abnormal and Social Psychology* 53 (November). 367–372.

Ryan, Franklin W. 1935. "Functional Elements of Market Distribution." *Harvard Business Review* 13 (January). 205–224.

32 • *Historical Perspectives in Marketing*

Scott, Carol A. 1976. "The Effects of Trial and Incentives on Repeat Purchase Behavior." *Journal of Marketing Research* 13 (August). 263–269.

———. 1977. "Modifying Socially Conscious Behavior: The Foot-in-the-Door Technique." *Journal of Consumer Research* 4 (December). 156–164.

Shaw, A. W. 1912. "Some Problems in Market Distribution." *Quarterly Journal of Economics* 26 (August). 703–765.

Sherry, John F., Jr. 1986. "The Cultural Perspective in Consumer Research." In Richard J. Lutz, ed., *Advances in Consumer Research*. Provo, Utah: Association for Consumer Research. 13:573–575.

Sheth, Jagdish N. 1973. "A Model of Industrial Buyer Behavior." *Journal of Marketing* 37 (October). 50–56.

———. 1974a. "A Field Study of Attitude Structure and Attitude-Behavior Relationship." In Jagdish N. Sheth, ed., *Models of Buyer Behavior: Conceptual, Quantitative, and Empirical*. New York: Harper & Row. 242–268.

———. 1974b. "The Next Decade of Buyer Behavior Theory and Research." In Jagdish N. Sheth, ed., *Models of Buyer Behavior: Conceptual, Quantitative, and Empirical*. New York: Harper & Row. 391–406.

———. 1977. "Demographics in Consumer Behavior." *Journal of Business Research* 5 (June). 129–138.

———. "Consumer Behavior: Surpluses and Shortages." In Andrew A. Mitchell, ed., *Advances in Consumer Research,* Ann Arbor, Mich.: Association for Consumer Research. 9:13–16.

———. 1975. "Presidential Address: Broadening the Horizons of ACR and Consumer Behavior." In Elizabeth C. Hirschman and Morris B. Holbrook, eds., *Advances in Consumer Research,* Provo, Utah: Association for Consumer Research. 12:1–2.

Sheth, Jagdish N., and Gary L. Frazier. 1983. "A Margin-Return Model for Strategic Market Planning." *Journal of Marketing* 47 (Spring). 100–109.

Sheth, Jagdish N., and David M. Gardner. 1982. "History of Marketing Thought: An Update." In Ronald F. Bush and Shelby D. Hunt, eds., *Marketing Theory: Philosophy of Science Perspectives*. Chicago: American Marketing Association. 52–58.

Sheth, Jagdish N., and S. Prakash Sethi. 1977. "A Theory of Cross-Cultural Buyer Behavior." In Arch G. Woodside, Jagdish N. Sheth, and Peter D. Bennett, eds., *Consumer and Industrial Buying Behavior*. New York: Elsevier North-Holland. 369–386.

Silk, Alvin J. 1966. "Overlap Among Self-Designated Opinion Leaders: A Study of Selected Dental Products and Services." *Journal of Marketing Research* 3 (August). 255–259.

Slater, Charles C., ed. 1977. *Macro-Marketing: Distributive Processes from a Societal Perspective*. Boulder: Marketing Division, Graduate School of Business Administration, University of Colorado.

Smallwood, John E. 1973. "The Product Life Cycle: A Key to Strategic Marketing Planning." *MSU Business Topics* 21 (Winter). 29–35.

Smith, Wendell R. 1956. "Product Differentiation and Market Segmentation as Alternative Marketing Strategies." *Journal of Marketing* 21 (July). 3–8.

Srivastava, Rajendra K., Mark I. Alpert, and Allan D. Shocker. 1984. "A Customer-Oriented Approach for Determining Market Structures." *Journal of Marketing* 48 (Spring). 32–45.

Stafford, James E. 1966. "Effects of Group Influence on Consumer Brand Preferences." *Journal of Marketing Research* 3 (February). 68–75.

Steiner, George A. 1979. *Strategic Planning: What Every Manager Must Know.* New York: The Free Press.

Stern, Louis W., ed. 1969. *Distribution Channels: Behavioral Dimensions.* Boston: Houghton Mifflin.

Stern, Louis W., and Ronald H. Gorman. 1969. "Conflict in Distribution Channels: An Exploration." In Louis W. Stern, ed., *Distribution Channels: Behavioral Dimensions.* Boston: Houghton Mifflin. 156–175.

Stern, Louis W., and Torger Reve. 1980. "Distribution Channels as Political Economies: A Framework for Comparative Analysis." *Journal of Marketing* 44 (Summer). 52–64.

Toffler, Alvin. 1985. *The Adaptive Corporation.* New York: McGraw-Hill.

Vaile, Roland S., E. T. Grether, and Reavis Cox. 1952. *Marketing in the American Economy.* New York: The Ronald Press Company.

Waite, Warren C. 1928. *Economics of Consumption.* New York: McGraw-Hill.

Warner, W. Lloyd, and Paul S. Lunt. 1941. *The Social Life of a Modern Community.* New Haven, Conn.: Yale University Press.

Wasson, Chester R. 1969. "Is It Time to Quit Thinking About Income Classes?" *Journal of Marketing* 33 (April). 54–57.

Webster, Frederick E., Jr., and Yoram Wind. 1972. "A General Model for Understanding Organizational Buying Behavior." *Journal of Marketing* 36 (April). 12–19.

Weld, L. D. H. 1916. *The Marketing of Farm Products.* New York: Macmillan.

———. 1917. "Marketing Functions and Mercantile Organization." *American Economic Review* 2 (June). 306–318.

Wells, William D. 1975. "Psychographics: A Critical Review." *Journal of Marketing Research* 12 (May). 196–213.

Wells, William D., and George Gubar. 1966. "Life Cycle Concept in Marketing Research." *Journal of Marketing Research* 3 (November). 355–363.

Wells, William D., and Douglas J. Tigert. 1971. "Activities, Interests and Opinions." *Journal of Advertising Research* 11 (August). 27–35.

Wilkie, William L., and Edgar A. Pessemier. 1973. "Issues in Marketing's Use of Multi-Attribute Attitude Models." *Journal of Marketing Research* 10 (November). 428–441.

Wind, Yoram, and Thomas S. Robertson. 1983. "Marketing Strategy: New Directions for Theory and Research." *Journal of Marketing* 47 (Spring). 12–25.

Wyand, Charles S. 1937. *The Economics of Consumption.* New York: Macmillan.

Zeithaml, Carl P., and Valarie A. Zeithaml. 1984. "Environmental Management: Revising the Marketing Perspective." *Journal of Marketing* 48 (Spring). 46–53.

Zielinski, Joan, and Thomas S. Robertson. 1982. "Consumer Behavior Theory: Excesses and Limitations." In Andrew A. Mitchell, ed., *Advances in Consumer Research,* Ann Arbor, Mich.: Association for Consumer Research. 9:8–12.

Zimmerman, Carle C. 1936. *Consumption and Standards of Living.* New York: D. Van Nostrand Company.

[40]

Economics, Psychology, and the Literature of the Subdiscipline of Consumer Behavior

Robert A. Mittelstaedt

University of Nebraska, Lincoln

This paper traces the development of the subdiscipline of marketing known as "consumer behavior" and its literature which grew during the 1950s and 1960s and at an increasing rate during the 1970s. In spite of marketing's roots in economics, it came to rely more heavily on psychology as a source for conceptual borrowing. It is suggested that this may have resulted from greater congruity between marketing scholars and psychologists with respect to research purposes and philosophies of science.

INTRODUCTION

Although marketing scholars have always been interested in the behavior of consumers, the institutionalization of that interest is relatively recent. This paper is about the development of consumer behavior as a subdiscipline of marketing and, in particular, its intellectual ties to economics and psychology. It begins with a brief history of the institutions of the subdiscipline, from the research conferences of the 1950s, through the development of journals and textbooks, to the appearance of the Association for Consumer Research and maturation of the field. In a later section, the focus shifts to the development of the subdiscipline's literature. Traced as a developing body of books and papers by marketing scholars, the field grew during the 1950s and 1960s and at an increasing rate during the early 1970s.

In spite of marketing's roots in economics, psychology soon became the discipline from which the new field came to borrow most heavily. In the final section, it will be suggested that this resulted from greater congruity between marketing scholars and psychologists with respect to their research purposes and philosophies of science.

Journal of the Academy of Marketing Science
Volume 18, Number 4, pages 303-311.
Copyright © 1990 by Academy of Marketing Science.
All rights of reproduction in any form reserved.
ISSN 0092-0703.

THE INSTITUTIONS OF CONSUMER BEHAVIOR

The process of institutionalization appears to have followed a pattern described by Ziman (1984), who claims that the development of an academic specialty follows a pattern of four stages.

At first the emerging specialty is only observable as a nodal point in the network of citations. Then scientists whose research is associated with this co-citation cluster organize little research conferences to discuss their common interest, or are commissioned to write articles for a special issue of a primary journal drawing attention to progress in this particular problem area. An "invisible college" begins to condense out, in the form, say, of a semi-official association held together by further conferences, the regular exchange of pre-prints and re-prints and the publication of an informal "newsletter." In due course, the association develops into a regular learned society, whose newsletter has become a reputable primary journal. A hierarchy of authority is soon set up to preside over conferences, edit journals, allocate resources, and confer recognition on members of the new discipline (p. 94).

Among the first "little research conferences" was the initial meeting of the Committee for Research on Consumer Attitudes and Behavior in 1952. Eventually, this group held five conferences, reported in four volumes of proceedings, with papers by scholars from many disciplines (Clark 1955a, b; 1958; Foote 1961). Other notable conferences were held at Stanford University in October 1964 and Purdue University in July, 1966. The Stanford conference, reported in a volume of papers edited by Newman (1966), included 22 attendees selected "because they were known for their advanced research and thinking about consumer behavior, and because they represented different orientations" (p. 4). The proceedings of the Purdue conference (Bass, King, and Pessemier 1967) contained the work of 20 "leading scholars [who] were commissioned to write papers in the areas of their research specialization covering diverse contributions of the behavioral and quantitative sciences to Marketing" (p. i).

The American Marketing Association (AMA) was cognizant of the growing importance of the study of consumer behavior; the *Journal of Marketing* (JM) carried many "consumer behavior" articles during the 1950s and early 1960s. Further, in recognition of the importance of "motivational research" in the 1950s, the AMA sponsored a volume (Ferber and Wales 1958) to bring together, in the words of its President, D. Maynard Phelps, "a carefully selected group of articles on motivational research" chosen so that "readers can more easily secure a sound, well-balanced, critical view of the present status of motivation research and, particularly, in reference to market behavior" (p. v).

In 1964, the AMA began publishing the *Journal of Marketing Research* (JMR), providing a new outlet for those doing research in the field. The apparent intention of the JMR was to provide a forum for methodological articles. As William R. Davidson, then AMA President, wrote in the first issue, "The objective . . . is to publish articles in the field of marketing research, defining this field in the broadest sense as the application of problem-solving methods and techniques to the solution of marketing problems" (Davidson 1964, p. 9). However, there were hints that the new journal might serve other intellectual needs; Davidson went on to speak of the "significant strides . . . being made in the application of quantitative methods and behavioral science approaches to marketing problems" (p. 9).

During the same period, the appearance of the "managerial approach" in the teaching of marketing specifically raised the question, "Why do people choose particular products and brands?" and textbooks began to reflect this focus. Two of the first marketing texts organized around the "four Ps" reflected this interest. Howard's first edition of *Marketing Management* (1957) contained a chapter (5) called "Demand Analysis—Consumer Behavior" which was subdivided into sections called "The Buyer as Individual," "The Influence of Other People," and "The Influence of Social Stratification." In the second edition (1963b), this discussion was greatly expanded and revised to include much more behavioral material and explicit models of "extensive problem solving," "limited problem solving," and "automatic response behavior." The first edition of McCarthy's *Basic Marketing: A Managerial Approach* (1960) contained a section of six chapters on the consumer including two with considerable behavioral content, "Consumers: How They Behave" and "Consumers: How They Buy."

For the growing number of courses in consumer behavior Bliss' *Marketing and the Behavioral Sciences* (1963) presented a collection of 34 readings from economics, psychology and sociology intended as a text for "upper-level undergraduate and first-year graduate courses" (p. vii). Bliss noted that "The purpose of the book is to bring together a group of studies from these diverse areas in the belief that they can contribute to a better understanding of the field of inquiry which marketing people consider their own" (p. vii). In 1967, Myers and Reynolds published the first text with the words "consumer behavior" in its title. The market was soon dominated by Engel, Kollat, and Blackwell (1968).

At about the same time, the "invisible college" of researchers interested in consumer behavior was becoming more visible. In the summer of 1969, a group of scholars met in Columbus, Ohio, at the invitation of James Engel. Besides presenting papers, the group laid plans for a 1970 meeting in Amherst, Massachusetts, where the Association for Consumer Research (ACR) was formed. The organization's second president, Robert Pratt recalled:

> My first knowledge of interest in forming an Association was contained in a letter from Jim Engel dated September 16, 1969, in which he stated in part: "those in attendance unanimously agreed that we need a new organization cutting across the lines of various disciplines and organizations which are currently involved in or concerned with consumer behavior research. The organization is intended to bring in people from psychology, economics, all phases of industry, home economics, and other areas" (1971, p. 4).

From the initial meeting of 40 in Columbus, the new organization grew to 100 in its first full year of operation, 1971. Two hundred more joined in 1972 and by the end of 1973, membership was nearing 500 (Stafford 1973). Whatever its founders' intentions, ACR's membership was dominated by marketing academicians. In a 1973 membership survey 61 of 96 respondents were in marketing departments of academic institutions (Wells 1973). The 1977 membership survey showed about 60% of members were marketing academics with about 14% in other academic fields (Kernan 1977).

Meanwhile, the Association continued its annual conferences. Proceedings volumes started with the 1971 meeting; in 1973 they were renamed as *Advances in Consumer Research*. It should be noted that proceedings continue to make up an important segment of the literature of the field; a recent analysis of the citations in the *Journal of Consumer Research* shows that proceedings account for about 24% of all citations, compared to less than 3% in other academic fields (Leong 1989). In 1971, interest in founding a journal dedicated to consumer behavior began to coalesce (Kassarjian and Bettman 1984) and, in 1974, ACR joined with seven other scholarly organizations to start the *Journal of Consumer Research* (JCR).

As the 1970s neared their end, the subdiscipline was reaching maturity. As one sign, the rate of increase in publication was slowing down (Helgeson et al. 1984). Further, the new subdiscipline was starting to have a self-conscious history. Gardner's (1977) "Presidential Address" at ACR's 1976 Annual Conference looked to the beginnings of the field and spoke of Katona, Howard, Holloway, Bliss, and Nicosia as its "pioneers." At the 1980 Conference, the first Fellow in Consumer Behavior awards were made to John Howard and James Engel.

LITERATURE OF CONSUMER BEHAVIOR

This section looks at the development of the literature of consumer behavior within marketing. Discussed first are its

growth and content, in particular its intellectual roots in
economics and psychology. Each of those disciplines had
its own literature of consumer behavior and, later in the
section, these are examined.

Growth of the Body of Literature

The growth of the literature of a scientific discipline seems
to follow the pattern of an innovation (Crane 1972). Helgeson et al. (1984) examined the growth of the literature of
consumer behavior between 1950 and 1981. Although they
did not fit a logistic curve to their data, they show that about
10 articles and proceedings papers per year were published
in the 1950s, about 20 per year in the 1960s, and about 175
per year in the 1970s (p. 451). Beginning in 1971, the
volume of consumer behavior literature grew at an accelerating rate for several years. Of course, this period coincided
with the introduction of the ACR *Proceedings* and JCR.

As another indication of growth, the 141 papers listed in
the Holloway, Mittelstaedt, and Venkatesan bibliography
(the Appendix describes the bibiliographies used in this
study) approximate the entire *empirical* literature of the field
in 1970. By comparison, the program of ACR's 1988 Annual
Meeting listed 181 papers, while 53 articles, "Comments,"
"Rejoinders," and pieces called "Research in Brief" were
published that year in JCR.

Thus, the growth pattern of the literature of consumer
behavior resembles that of an innovation with the period of
rapid growth coinciding with the formation of ACR. As
Crane (1972) has argued, periods of rapid growth are common to the literatures of most research areas. In her words,

> Periods of exponential growth can occur because
> research are as, although generally small, are capa-
> ble of being expanded at relatively short notice if
> scientists with secondary and tertiary commitments
> to an area decide to shift their research priorities.
> In other words, if a particular field becomes espe-
> cially attractive, a pool of scientists somewhat on
> the periphery can be rapidly assimilated. In addition,
> new scientists are continually being trained who are
> relatively free of previous commitments and thus
> available to exploit promising areas (p. 24).

Table 1 shows the process by displaying the overlap of
authorship of among "consumer behavior articles" (see Appendix for definition) in JM (1958–1963) and JMR (1964–
1969), papers presented at ACR (1969–1975) and the Purdue
conference (1966), and attendance at the Stanford conference (1964). In Table 1 these are arranged in an approximate
time sequence. Looking at the first line, of the people who
authored or co-authored consumer behavior articles in JM
during the years 1958 through 1963: one participated in the
Stanford Conference; 6 authored or co-authored a paper at
the Purdue Conference; 16 published in JMR; 8 authored
or co-authored a paper given at an ACR meeting; 81 appear
only as authors of JM articles.

Based on Table 1, two observations seem merited. First, to
the extent they were present in the previous literature, the
people who participated in ACR during its formative years

TABLE 1
Authors and Participants in Common Among Several Conferences and Journals[a]

	JM	Stanford Conference	Purdue Conference	JMR	ACR
Journal of Marketing (1958–1963)	81	1	6	16	8
Stanford Conference (1964)		15	2	3	2
Purdue Conference (1966)			6	6	4
Journal of Marketing Research (1964–1969)				159	45
Association for Consumer Research (1969–1975)					327

[a]See Appendix for definitions.

tended to have published in JMR. Second, and more important, a considerable number of new people were drawn into
the field by the formation of ACR; of the 327 who presented
papers at ACR, 268 had not previously published (during
the years represented in Table 1) in JM nor in JMR, nor
had they participated in the Stanford or Purdue conferences.

Changes in the Content of the Literature

From the 1950s through the mid-1970s many changes
occurred in the content of the literature. Three related themes
are evident: (1) a "micro" approach, i.e., a focus on the
purchase behavior of individual consumers, (2) increased
and changing concerns with methodology, and (3) the rise
of conceptual borrowing from psychology and the decreasing
reliance on economics.

As for the micro approach, Alderson had been urging the
study of individual and household decision processes during
the 1950s (1952; 1957). During the 1960s, this movement
became embodied in at least five influential books. After
claiming that "At this time, there is no really useful theory of
buyer behavior, even of the most rudimentary sort," (p. 69)
Howard's *Marketing: Executive and Buyer Behavior* (1963a)
devoted about three fifths of its pages to an examination of
individual buying behavior from the perspectives of
economics, psychology, social psychology, and sociology.
Nicosia's *Consumer Decision Processes* (1966) grew out of
the work of the Consumer Behavior Program at Berkeley.
Drawing on the literatures of marketing, economics, and
the behavioral sciences, its author developed a process model

to predict and explain the purchase behavior of a consumer. This same focus carried on into the first textbooks that were beginning to shape the field. Myers and Reynold's *Consumer Behavior and Marketing Management* (1967) drew almost exclusively on the literature of psychology and social psychology. Engel, Kollat, and Blackwell's *Consumer Behavior* (1968) followed Nicosia's lead, using a behavioral model of the individual consumer's decision process as the organizational scheme of their text. Finally, Howard and Sheth's *The Theory of Buyer Behavior* (1969), while broadening the concept of "consumer" to include the industrial buyer, retained the focus on predicting and explaining the choices of the individual decision maker.

The effect of this trend in the research literature can be seen in the content analysis of Helgeson et al. (1984). The general topics of "internal factors" (e.g., attitudes, information processing) and "purchase processes" (e.g., choice, information search) make up over half of the literature.

Early on, methodological concerns were less strong than they came to be; the majority of articles published in the 1950s were non-empirical and, of the empirical minority, most were descriptive. Beginning late in that decade, these proportions began to change; non-empirical papers declined to about 30% of the literature while descriptive studies nearly disappeared (Helgeson et al. 1984).

By the 1960s, the increased emphasis on hypothesis-testing research led to a focus on the experimental method. JMR's first issue contained an article in which Holloway described the work done in the behavioral laboratory he had established in 1962 (Holloway and White 1964). This paper laid the groundwork for a stream of papers which were published by him and his students in JMR over the next several years. The experimental method dominated the empirical literature of consumer behavior for the rest of the decade, accounting for as much as 45% of the literature in the period 1964 to 1968 (Helgeson et al. 1984). This reinforced the micro focus; as used in the laboratory (as contrasted with the field) the experimental method is suited only to study the behavior of individuals or very small groups. Of course, new topics meant new methodologies; the shift in topics toward the "internal factors," as noted above, was paralleled by an increasing use of multivariate statistics during the 1970s.

In addition to the changes in topics and methodologies, there were changes in the patterns of conceptual borrowing, as indicated by the citations of the developing body of literature. First, there appears to have been an increase in conceptual borrowing in general. Second, although their initial positions were roughly equal, psychology gradually came to replace economics as the discipline from which more borrowing was done.

Initially, borrowing appears to have been rather modest. As one indicator, an examination was made of the references cited in the eleven articles published in JM between 1950 and 1959 that also appeared in two or more of the bibliographies of Bristol (1956), Nicosia (1966), Myers and Reynolds (1967), and Kassarjian and Robertson (1968). In general, all JM articles of this period have few references and, of those, a relatively larger proportion are to books and monographs than to journals, a style noted by Goldman

(1979). Taking that into account, the eleven articles contain a total of 62 references, 29 of which are in one article by Alderson, while three articles contain no references. In the aggregate, there are no citations to any articles in economic journals and only one citation of an article in a psychological journal. In a later period, of the 28 articles published in JM in the period 1960–1965 and classified in the Index as "Consumer Analysis," 4 contain no reference, 7 cite at least one psychological work, while 5 cite at least one work from economics. (See Appendix for definitions.)

Turning to the first years of JMR, a sample of 20 consumer behavior articles (see Appendix for index categories used) was drawn from its first six volumes (1964–1969). Each article had at least one citation to a publication other than the JM, JMR, or AMA Proceedings; the average was 23. Eight articles cited at least one psychological work; 6 cited at least one economics work.

The literature developing in the papers presented at ACR was more psychological in its focus. According to the first Index (Kassarjian and Orsini 1980), 32 people authored or co-authored 6 or more papers at the first ten conferences. In the years 1971–1975, they presented 108 papers (papers for the years 1969 and 1970 were unpublished.) These 108 papers average 11 citations to literatures other than the JM, JMR, AMA Proceedings, or the JCR or ACR Proceedings. Seventy six cited at least one psychological work; only 10 cited any economic work (6 if Ferber's works are classified as "marketing"). However, it must be noted that this remained a marketing literature; 30 of these 32 authors were marketing academics and 87 of their papers cite at least one marketing source, for an average of 6.

The trend toward greater reliance on the psychological literature continued in the JCR. Leong's (1989) citation analysis of Volumes 1, 4, 7, 11, and 14 of JCR shows an increasing number of references to JCR itself. Using his data, and excluding the references to JCR, the proportion of citations from psychology journals stayed almost constant between the two volumes published in the 1970s and the three published in the 1980s (i.e., 32.8% and 32.6%, respectively). A parallel comparison of citations from economics journals shows 10.0% for those published in the 1970s and 5.7% for the 1980s (calculated from Table 1, Leong 1989). Goldman's (1979) citation analysis of JM and JMR between 1968 and 1976 showed similar results. He found a tendency toward greater reliance on marketing sources for referencing in both journals and a decline in the relative importance of economics citations from a level of 8–9% in 1968 to about 4–5% in 1976.

In summary, the period from 1950 to 1975 saw the institutionalization of consumer behavior as a subdiscipline in marketing. The literature began to grow during the mid-1960s and more rapidly during the 1970s. The formation of the ACR was pivotal. Although formed as a separate organization, its members and the literature which they generated retained a marketing focus. This literature became increasingly empirical and came to rely more on psychology than economics for its conceptual foundations.

Before discussing some reasons for these developments, attention should be given to the literatures of economics and psychology and, in particular, their own areas of "consumer behavior." The developments in those fields during the same decades are the subject of the next section.

The Consumer Behavior Literatures of Economics and Psychology

Of the many changes underway in economics in the 1950s and 1960s, four are of special interest. First, the neoclassic approach to consumer choice, and its attendant interest in utility theory, had been resuscitated by Hicks (1939) and Samuelson (1947). Houthakker (1950) had made it amenable to econometric techniques. Brown and Deaton's (1972) review of this literature shows 34 pieces published before 1930, 18 in the 1930s, 15 in the 1940s, with 65 published in the 1950s and 112 between 1960 and 1971. Much of this was empirical work, albeit with aggregated data, on the demand (including income and price elasticities) for various products, e.g., automobiles, meat.

Second, Stigler (1961) had focused attention on the role of information in determining the behavior of all actors in the market, and especially the search behavior of consumers. In addition to empirical research on prices (e.g., Jung 1960), this approach led to conceptual extensions to such issues as product quality (Ackerloff 1970) and advertising (Nelson 1974).

Third, in a widely cited review article in the *American Economic Review* (AER), Ferber (1962) surveyed empirical research on household behavior (p. 48). His review covers 170 items, 51 of which are articles from economic journals. The centrality of the topic to the discipline of economics is evidenced by the fact that 43 of the 51 articles had been published in the "core" journals of the field (as defined by Eagley 1975).

Fourth, there was a modest increase in the sort of empirical studies that would be of direct interest to marketers. The *Index of Economic Journals* for the years 1950–1959 shows five articles published in economics journals (JM, which was covered by the *Index*, was excluded from these counts) which are categorized as "Consumer Motivation, Brand Preference." All of these appeared in the *Journal of Farm Economics* (JFE). It is difficult to generalize about their content except to say that the word "preference" appears in the titles of three of the articles. During the period 1960–1968, the number of articles in the same category rose to 17. Of these 6 were in the JFE and 2 were econometric studies appearing in "core" journals.

As for psychology, 35 articles from psychology journals were cited in the *Annual Review of Psychology* (ARP) during the 1950s. Of these, most concerned three topics: communications effects, attitudes toward products and sellers, and consumers' ability to discriminate product differences. Nearly all appeared in the *Journal of Applied Psychology* (JAP).

During the 1960s this literature, most of it empirical, continued to grow at about the same rate. Combining the three ARP articles of the decade with the relevant entries from the Jacoby review (1975), at least 45 articles were published in psychology journals during the 1960s. Characterizing them as a group becomes more difficult; old themes continued while new ones such as attitudes and social influ-

TABLE 2
Citations by Authors of JMR Articles and Authorship of ACR Papers

	Authored or co-authored ⟵ ACR paper ⟶	
Citations in JMR article	Yes	No
Cited both Economics and Psychology works[a]	2	1
Cited only Psychology works	20	35
Cited only Economics works	4	16
Cited neither Economics nor Psychology works	10	26

[a]See Appendix for definitions.

ences emerged, along with an increased interest in methodology, especially measurement issues. Again, most appeared in JAP.

The behavior of consumers is a central conceptual issue for microeconomic theory. By contrast, the behavior of consumers is an "applied" area for psychologists. Perhaps for that reason, the two literatures were quite separate during this period.

That the economics and psychology literatures were separate entities can be shown by looking at co-citations. Ferber's AER review (1962) of "household decision making" cited 170 items. Of these, only four are cited in any of the ARP reviews. Further, comparing all the items covered in the ARP bibliographies for the two decades with the Brown and Deaton review, there are no common citations.

As a consequence of this separation, marketing scholars were induced to choose between the two. In spite of the talk of "economic psychology" and the work of such people as Katona, the marketing scholar who would borrow from both fields needed to be familiar with the literatures of two very distinct disciplines.

One result can be seen in the papers presented in the first years of ACR; those familiar with the literature of psychology came to the fore. Table 2 describes the writings of the 114 marketing academics who authored or co-authored consumer behavior articles in JMR during the years 1964–1969. As before, the separation of the two literatures is evident; only three people cited works from both psychology and economics. Looking at the second line, it indicates that, of the 55 who cited at least one psychology work in their JMR article, 20 authored or co-authored a paper at ACR during the years 1969–1975. If citing a literature indicates some familiarity with it, it appears that those with some background in psychology were more likely to be authoring ACR pieces.

SUMMARY AND CONCLUSIONS

In spite of a shared interest in the behavior of consumers by scholars in marketing, psychology, and economics, the study of consumer behavior became institutionalized as a subdiscipline in marketing as scholars in that field created their own, new literature. It began with roughly equal ties to economics and psychology but came to rely much more heavily on psychology. This phenomenon appears to go back at least to the late 1950s and early 1960s—a period crucial to the development of the subdiscipline of consumer behavior.

This final section offers some observations on the reasons for the particular path taken in the consumer behavior literature. It first discusses the congruence, or lack thereof, between marketing, economics, and psychology with respect to each discipline's approach to research, and then their objectives for studying consumer behavior. By way of a conclusion, the familiar issue of the "rational economic man" is discussed and related to differences among the disciplines' philosophies of science.

Approaches to Research

A field which borrows its conceptual frameworks and methodological tools faces a peculiar "assimilation" problem. Without broaching the subject of whether or not marketing is a science, there is little doubt that it has been a conceptual borrower from other fields. As Bartels (1988) points out, marketing people have tended to look at borrowed concepts as "tools." Further, as he shows, there has been a long tradition of empirical research in marketing. In other words, it is a common pattern for marketing scholars to borrow concepts from other disciplines and use them in their research to explain the phenomena with which they are concerned. By contrast, the focus in economics and academic (as contrasted to clinical) psychology has been on developing theories and viewing research as a means to test them. Thus, the discipline of marketing needed its own consumer behavior literature.

Congruity of Objectives

The lack of congruity in approaches to research is related to differences in objectives between the fields of inquiry. Although this might be described as an issue of "level of aggregation," it is useful to consider the differences between the three fields with respect to the explanandum of consumer behavior theory.

In the neoclassical formulation of economic theory, the behavior of individual consumers is not the explanandum but, rather, a major input into a systematic examination of more aggregative outcomes. As MacFayden (1986) puts it,

> Social scientists from other disciplines should not be misled by the term microeconomics, since its primary focus is upon aggregates; in particular, while the neoclassical analytical model derives from hypothesized behaviour of individuals, the empirical and policy analysis focuses almost exclusively on the behaviour of groups of people, particularly as expressed in levels of price and total production and/or consumption in economic markets (p. 29).

By contrast, psychology is concerned with the prediction, explanation, and control of individual behavior. Among

marketing scholars there were differences about explicit dependent variables (e.g., attitude formation, attitude change, the initial purchase act, repurchase, etc.). However, as noted earlier, there was general agreement that consumer behavior was about the behavior of individuals or, at least, aggregates no larger than a household. In this sense, the objectives of psychology were more compatible with the objectives being sought by marketing scholars.

Congruity of Philosophies of Science

Much has been said and written about the appropriateness of the "rational economic man" as a model of consumer behavior. Instead of reviewing that long standing discussion, this final section examines the differing concepts of "rationality" in marketing, economics, and psychology during the period and the philosophies of science which accompany them.

By the early 1960s, marketing practice and, to some extent, the marketing literature had been influenced by three models of consumer behavior. First, the Behaviorism of the pre-World War II era depicted the consumer as a non-rational being whose behavior consists of responses to stimuli as shaped by the person's history of reinforcements (Mittelstaedt and Madden 1980). While never an especially popular approach in the consumer behavior literature of the 1950s and 1960s, one variant, the Hullian learning model, was at the heart of Howard's (1963a) original model of consumer behavior. Second, by the 1950s, marketing practice and thought were greatly influenced by "motivational research." Based on Psychoanalytic Theory, this approach pictured the consumer as an irrational being who purchased products for their symbolic value in some idiosyncratic psychodrama, rather than for the utilitarian purposes assumed by economic theory (Mittelstaedt and Madden 1980). However, by the end of the decade, many marketing scholars and practitioners were moving away from this view (cf. Alderson 1958; Politz 1958; Levitt 1960). Coming to the fore were various models from social psychology, most notably Reference Group Theory. To the extent these models relied on some form of "conformity" as their central explanatory mechanism, they pictured the behavior of any one consumer as non-rational in the sense that it would be determined by that person's perceptions of the behavior of other people (Mittelstaedt and Madden 1980). In short, by the mid-1960s, marketing practice and theory had been influenced by a variety of behavioral approaches which rejected, in one way or another, the concept of "rational" behavior.

Meanwhile, other changes were occurring in economics and psychology. Within the discipline of economics, the concept of the "rational economic man" had always had its critics. Clarkson (1963) argues that the debate between competing theories of utility and demand has been, at root, a philosophical one over the criteria to be used in judging the empirical validity of microeconomic theory. In his words,

> On the one side it has been held that the truth value of the micro-theories should depend on the empirical reality of their assumptions. Other economists were of the opinion that it did not matter whether these

assumptions were descriptively realistic or not since at best they had to consist of abstractions from actual behavior (p. 84).

Because of disciplinary differences, putting labels on these views may only engender confusion so they are referred to here as the "first view" and the "second view."

Clearly, the first view includes the institutional economists; writers from Veblen to Galbraith have been highly critical, if not contemptuous, of the rational economic man model. By the late 1950s, the second view, embraced by the neoclassical school, was in ascendancy. Friedman (1953) put the matter in very strong terms:

> The relevant question to ask about the "assumptions" of a theory is not whether they are descriptively "realistic," for they never are, but whether they are sufficiently good approximations for the purpose at hand. This question can be answered only by seeing whether the theory works, which means it yields sufficiently accurate predictions (p. 15).

Like economics, psychology had never been a monolithic discipline, and the same dispute over the empirical reality of assumptions divided the field. By the 1950s Behaviorism, which held to the second view, was still dominant in American psychology (Hilgard 1987, Chapter 7). However, as Bindara (1985) shows, the 1940s and 1950s had set loose a set of forces which would lead to the displacement of Behaviorism by more cognitive approaches. This shift, which Hilgard (1987) calls the "cognitive revolution," took psychology toward a philosophy much like the first view (Manicas and Secord 1983).

As noted previously, during the 1950s Alderson (1952; 1957) had been making a strong case for considering consumer behavior as "problem solving" and this view grew in popularity, coming to fruition in the Engel, Kollat, and Blackwell model which formed the organizing structure of their widely used textbook (1968). Thus, during the 1960s, the view of consumer behavior that was gradually being accepted by marketing scholars emphasized the necessity for realistic assumptions. At the same time, a form of microeconomic theory at odds with this view was in ascendancy in economics, while Cognitive Theory, and its implicit realism, was coming to the fore in psychology. In the end, it proved to be the more persuasive.

Of course, there is more than a little irony in all of this. While the problem solving approach did not view the consumer as, strictly speaking, rational, it was a far cry from the models of various forms of nonrationality which characterized the Behaviorist, Motivational Research, and Reference Group theories. By the late 1960s, research utilizing an "information processing" approach began to appear in the literature. Like the problem solving approach, this meta-model viewed consumer behavior as goal seeking and added elaboration to the actual decision making processes. At the crucial time in the development of the subdiscipline of consumer behavior, marketing scholars explicitly or implicitly rejected the model of rational economic man and embraced a psychological model which pictured consumers as goal seeking, problem solving, information processing persons.

APPENDIX

This appendix describes several bibliographies of the consumer behavior literature which were available for this study. They are covered in chronological order.

Bristol (1955) assembled an annotated bibliography for Clark's (1955b) second volume of proceedings of the New York University Conferences on Consumer Behavior. It contains 132 items classified into eight categories: attributes, social influences, motivation, methodology, indifference curves, utility measurement, the consumption function, and "general."

Shartle (1950), Bellows (1951), Harrell (1953), Kendall (1956), Katzell (1957), Ferguson (1958), and Giller (1960) each reviewed "industrial psychology" for the *Annual Review of Psychology* (ARP). Each review includes some items of what was later called "consumer psychology," although many of the items which they covered were more methodological than substantive. Guest (1962) wrote the first review article on "Consumer Psychology" for ARP. Because Giller's (1960) review had preceded it by only two years, Guest's review covers only about 18 months. Later reviews are by Twedt (1965), Perloff (1968), Jacoby (1976), and Kassarjian (1982). In general, the reviews of the ARP do not overlap; each author tries to review the field since the previous review.

Ferber (1962) surveyed "the main empirical research of recent years on household behavior" (p. 48). His review covers 170 items and is divided into five sections: (1) theories of spending, or saving, behavior; (2) influence of variables other than income on spending and saving; (3) determinants of asset holding; (4) determinants of specific expenditures; and (5) decision processes.

Nicosia (1966) contains a reference list of 474 published and 58 unpublished items. Nicosia made a conscious attempt to include items from marketing, economics, psychology and sociology.

Kassarjian and Robertson's (1968) readings book contains 43 papers organized into categories (e.g., perception, social influences, etc.) and taken from a wide variety of sources. The reference lists of all articles were aggregated into a "master" reference list containing 819 items.

Holloway, Mittelstaedt, and Venkatesan (1971) searched 30 journals and conference proceedings' series published between 1960 and 1968 for all empirical articles which fell into their predetermined set of categories (e.g., attitudes, personal influence, deliberation, brand loyalty). Since many conference papers were later published as journal articles and, in a few instances, published in more than one journal, this unpublished list contains only one entry per study. There are a total of 141 entries from 26 sources.

Brown and Deaton (1972) reviewed "models of consumer behaviour." Their bibliography contains 244 items. The review is divided into five sections, "Brief History and Introduction," "The Theory of Consumer Behaviour and its Relevance to Demand Analysis," "The Analysis of Household Budgets," "Complete Systems of Demand Equations," and "Attempts to Construct Models for Durable Goods."

As for classifying items as "psychological" or "economic," journal items are classified according to the *Union*

ECONOMICS, PSYCHOLOGY, AND THE LITERATURE OF THE
SUBDISCIPLINE OF CONSUMER BEHAVIOR

Serials Catalog. Books, monographs and other items were classified "psychological" if they had been authored by any of the 108 recipients of the American Psychological Association's "Awards for Distinguished Scientific Contributions." Added to that list was Martin Fishbein. Books, monographs and other items were classified "economic" if they were authored by any Fellow of the American Economic Association or Nobel Laureate in Economics. Although the works of Robert Ferber and George Katona are considered by many to be "marketing," they were included among the economists. The works of Herbert Simon which were encountered seemed to be more clearly "psychological" than "economic" and were so classified. With one exception noted in the text, the classifications of Fishbein, Ferber, Katona and Simon did not affect any counts.

"Consumer behavior" articles from the JM were those which appeared in that journal's Index under the headings "Buying and Purchasing," "Consumer Analysis," and "Research and Research Techniques." Those classified as "consumer behavior" in the JMR are those which appeared in that journal's Index under the headings "Attitude and Opinion Measurement," "Brand Loyalty and Preference Studies," and "Consumer and Market Area Research."

ACKNOWLEDGMENTS

A substantially different version of this paper was presented at a joint session of the Fourth Conference on Historical Research in Marketing and Marketing Thought and the Annual Conference of the Economic and Business History Society, and was published as: "Economics and the Subdiscipline of Consumer Behavior in Marketing," in *Marketing History: The Emerging Discipline*, Terence Nevett, Kathleen R. Whitney and Stanley C. Hollander, eds. (East Lansing: Department of Marketing and Transportation Administration, Graduate School of Business Administration, Michigan State University). The author thanks Professor Raymond Benton, Jr., of Loyola University of Chicago for organizing that joint session and encouraging the development of this paper.

REFERENCES

Akerlof, George A. 1970. "The Market for 'Lemons:' Quality Uncertainty and the Market Mechanism." *Quarterly Journal of Economics* 84 (August): 488–500.

Alderson, Wroe. 1952. "Psychology for Marketing and Economics." *Journal of Marketing* 17 (October): 119–135.

———. 1957. *Marketing Behavior and Executive Action*. Homewood, IL: Richard D. Irwin.

———. 1958. "Advertising Strategy and Theories of Motivation." In: *Motivation and Market Behavior*. Robert Ferger and Hugh G. Wales, eds. Homewood, IL: Richard D. Irwin.

American Economic Association. 1961, 1962. *Index of Economic Journals*, Vols. I–V. Homewood, IL: Richard D. Irwin.

Bass, Frank M., Charles W. King, and Edgar A. Pessemier, eds. 1968. *Applications of the Sciences in Marketing Management*. New York: John Wiley and Sons.

Bartels, Robert. 1988. *The History of Marketing Thought*. Columbus, OH: Publishing Horizons.

Bellows, Roger M. 1951. "Industrial Psychology." In: *Annual Review of Psychology*, Vol. 2. Calvin P. Stone and Donald W. Taylor, eds. Palo Alto, CA: Annual Reviews.

Bindra, Dalbir. 1984. "Cognition: Its Origin and Future in Psychology." In *Annals of Theoretical Psychology*, Vol. I. Joseph R. Royce and Leendert P. Mos, eds. New York: Plenum.

Bliss, Perry 1963. *Marketing and the Behavioral Sciences*. Boston: Allyn and Bacon.

Bristol, Ralph B., Jr. 1955. "Bibliography of Consumer Behavior." In: *Consumer Behavior, Volume I: The Dynamics of Consumer Reaction*. Lincoln H. Clark, ed. New York: New York University Press.

Brown, Alan, and Angus Deaton. 1972. "Surveys in Applied Economics: Models of Consumer Behaviour." *The Economic Journal* 82 (December): 1145–1235.

Clark, Lincoln H., ed. 1955a. *Consumer Behavior, Volume I: The Dynamics of Consumer Reaction*. New York: New York University Press.

———. 1955b. *Consumer Behavior, Volume II: The Life Cycle and Consumer Behavior*. New York: New York University Press.

———. 1958. *Consumer Behavior: Research on Consumer Reactions*. New York: Harper and Brothers.

Clarkson, Geoffrey P.E. 1963. *The Theory of Consumer Demand: A Critical Appraisal*. Englewood Cliffs, NJ: Prentice-Hall.

Crane, Diana. 1972. *Invisible Colleges: Diffusion of Knowledge in Scientific Communities*. Chicago: University of Chicago Press.

Davidson, William R. 1964. "Introducing the Journal of Marketing Research." *Journal of Marketing Research* 1 (February): 9–10.

Eagly, Robert V. 1975. "Economics Journals as a Communications Network." *Journal of Economic Literature* 13 (September): 878–888.

Engle, James F., David T. Kollat, and Roger D. Blackwell. 1968. *Consumer Behavior*. New York: Holt, Rinehart and Winston.

Ferber, Robert. 1962. "Research on Household Behavior." *American Economic Review* 52 (March): 19–63.

Ferber, Robert, and Hugh G. Wales, eds. 1958. *Motivation and Market Behavior*. Homewood, IL: Richard D. Irwin.

Ferguson, Leonard W. 1958. "Industrial Psychology." In: *Annual Review of Psychology*, Vol. 9. Paul R. Farnsworth and Quinn McNemar, eds. Palo Alto, CA: Annual Reviews.

Foote, Nelson N., ed. 1961. *Household Decision Making: Consumer Behavior*, Volume IV. New York: New York University Press.

Friedman, Milton. 1953. *Essays in Positive Economics*. Chicago: University of Chicago Press.

Gardner, David. 1977. "Presidential Address." In: *Advances in Consumer Research*, Vol. IV. William D. Perreault, ed. Atlanta, GA: Association for Consumer Research.

Giller, B. von Haller. 1960. "Industrial Psychology." In: *Annual Review of Psychology*, Vol. 11. Paul R. Farnsworth and Quinn McNemar, eds. Palo Alto, CA: Annual Reviews.

Goldman, Arieh. 1979. "Publishing Activity in Marketing as an Indicator of Its Structure and Disciplinary Boundaries." *Journal of Marketing Research* 16 (November): 485–494.

Guest, Lester. 1962. "Consumer Analysis." In: *Annual Review of Psychology*, Vol. 13. Paul R. Farnsworth, Olga McNemar, and Quinn McNemar, eds. Palo Alto, CA: Annual Reviews.

Harrell, Thomas W. 1953. "Industrial Psychology." In: *Annual Review of Psychology*, Vol. 4. Calvin P. Stone and Donald W. Taylor, eds. Palo Alto, CA: Annual Reviews.

Helgeson, James C., Alan E. Kluge, John Mager, and Cheri Taylor. 1984. "Trends in Consumer Behavior Literature: A Content Analysis." *Journal of Consumer Research* 10 (March): 449–454.

Hicks, J. R. 1939. *Value and Capital*. Oxford: Oxford University Press.

Hilgard, Ernest R. 1987. *Psychology in America: A Historical Survey*. San Diego: Harcourt Brace Jovanovich.

Holloway, Robert J., Robert A. Mittelstaedt, and M. Venkatesan, eds. 1971. *Consumer Behavior: Contemporary Research in Action*. Boston: Houghton Mifflin.

Holloway, Robert J., and Todd White. 1964. "Advancing the Experimental Method in Marketing." *Journal of Marketing Research* 1 (February): 25–29.

Houthakker, H. S. 1950. "Revealed Preference and the Utility Function." *Economica* 17 (May): 159–174.

Howard, John A. 1957. *Marketing Management: Analysis and Decision*. Homewood, IL: Richard D. Irwin.

ECONOMICS, PSYCHOLOGY, AND THE LITERATURE OF THE
SUBDISCIPLINE OF CONSUMER BEHAVIOR

———. 1963a. *Marketing: Executive and Buyer Behavior*. New York: Columbia University Press.

———. 1963b. *Marketing Management: Analysis and Planning*, Revised Edition. Homewood, IL: Richard D. Irwin.

Howard, John A., and Sheth, Jagdish N. 1969. *The Theory of Buyer Behavior*. New York: John Wiley & Sons.

Jacoby, Jacob. 1976. "Consumer Psychology: An Octennium." In: *Annual Review of Psychology*, Vol. 27. Palo Alto, CA: Annual Reviews.

Kassarjian, Harold H. 1982. "Consumer Psychology." In: *Annual Review of Psychology*, Vol. 33. Mark R. Rosenzweig and Lyman W. Porter, eds. Palo Alto, CA: Annual Reviews.

Kassarjian, Harold H., and Joseph L. Orsini, eds. 1980. *Index, Association of Consumer Research Proceedings, 1970–1979*. Ann Arbor, MI: Association for Consumer Research.

Kassarjian, Harold H., and Thomas S. Robertson, eds. 1968. *Perspectives in Consumer Behavior*. Glenview, IL: Scott, Foresman.

Katzell, Raymond A. 1957. "Industrial Psychology." In: *Annual Review of Psychology*, Vol. 8. Paul R. Farnsworth and Quinn McNemar, eds. Palo Alto, CA: Annual Reviews.

Kendall, William E. 1956. "Industrial Psychology." In: *Annual Review of Psychology*, Vol. 7. Paul R. Farnsworth and Quinn McNemar, eds. Palo Alto, CA: Annual Reviews.

Kernan, Jerome. 1977. "Membership Survey." *ACR Newsletter* 7 (June): 11–13.

Leong, Siew Meng. 1989. "A Citation Analysis of the Journal of Consumer Research." *Journal of Consumer Research* 15 (March): 492–497.

Levitt, Theodore. 1960. "M–R Snake Dance." *Harvard Business Review* 38 (November–December): 76–84.

McCarthy, E. Jerome. 1960. *Basic Marketing: A Managerial Approach*. Homewood, IL: Richard D. Irwin.

MacFayden, Alan J. 1986. "Rational Economic Man; An Introduction Survey." In: *Economic Psychology: Intersections in Theory and Application*. Alan J. MacFayden and W. Heather, eds. Amsterdam: North Holland.

Manicas, Peter T., and Paul F. Secord. 1983. "Implications for Psychology of the New Philosophy of Science." *American Psychologist* 38 (April): 3 99–413.

Mittelstaedt, Robert A., and C. Stanley Madden. 1980. "Lay Psychology, Marketing Practices and Public Policy." In: *Macromarketing: Evolution of Thought, Proceedings of the Fourth Macromarketing Seminar*. George Fisk, Robert Nason, and Phillip D. White, eds. Boulder, CO: Business Research Division, Graduate School of Business Administration, University of Colorado.

Myers, James H., and William H. Reynolds. 1967. *Consumer Behavior and Marketing Management*. Boston: Houghton Mifflin.

Nelson, Phillip. 1974. "Advertising as Information." *Journal of Political Economy* 82 (July–August): 729–754.

Newman, Joseph W., ed. 1966. *On Knowing the Consumer*. New York: John W. Wiley & Sons.

Nicosia, Francesco M. 1966. *Consumer Decision Processes: Marketing and Advertising Implications*. Englewood Cliffs, NJ: Prentice-Hall.

Perloff, Robert. 1968. "Consumer Analysis." In: *Annual Review of Psychology*, Vol. 19. Paul R. Farnsworth, Mark R. Rosenzweig, and Judith T. Polefka, eds. Palo Alto, CA: Annual Reviews.

Politz, Alfred. 1958. "Motivation Research—Opportunity or Dilemma?" In: *Motivation and Market Behavior*. Robert Ferber and Hugh G. Wales, eds. Homewood, IL : Richard D. Irwin.

Pratt, Robert. 1971. "Presidential Address." In: *Proceedings of the Second Annual Conference*. David Gardner, ed. College Park, MD: Association for Consumer Research.

Samuelson, Paul A. 1947. *Foundations of Economic Analysis*. Cambridge, MA: Harvard University Press.

Shartle, Carroll L. 1950. "Industrial Psychology." In: *Annual Review of Psychology*, Vol. 1. Calvin P. Stone and Donald W. Taylor, eds. Palo Alto, CA: Annual Reviews.

Stafford, James. 1973. "Membership Committee Report." *ACR Newsletter* 3 (December): 3.

Twedt, Dik Warren. 1965. "Consumer Psychology." In: *Annual Review of Psychology*, Vol. 16. Paul R. Farnsworth, Olga McNemar, and Quinn McNemar, eds. Palo Alto, CA: Annual Reviews.

Wells, William. 1973. "Summary of 1973 Membership Survey." *ACR Newsletter* 3 (December): 12.

Ziman, John 1984. An Introduction to Science Studies: The Philosophical and Social Aspects of Science and Technology. Cambridge: Cambridge University Press.

ABOUT THE AUTHOR

Robert A. Mittelstaedt is Nathan Gold Distinguished Professor of Marketing at the University of Nebraska, Lincoln. He received his M.A. in economics at the University of Arizona and his Ph.D. in marketing, with a minor in psychology, at the University of Minnesota.

[41]

Excerpt from William T. Kelley (ed.), *New Consumerism: Selected Readings*, 13–25.

THE BEGINNINGS OF THE CONSUMER MOVEMENT

2

EUGENE R. BEEM

The Consumer Movement Defined

The expression, the *Consumer Movement*, may be used provisionally in either of two ways. In its more inclusive sense, the term refers historically to the efforts of individuals and groups, acting more or less in concert, to solve consumer problems. In this sense, the Consumer Movement refers to activities from the earliest time to the present, and includes the organized activities of consumers themselves, and of other groups and individuals such as teachers, writers, private business, and government agencies that have worked in the consumer interest. In a second sense, the Consumer Movement refers more particularly to the great burst of activities in behalf of consumers that began in the 1930's and has continued at an accelerated pace.

The present chapter reviews the earlier attempts to help solve consumer problems. Chapter 3 describes the Consumer Movement beginning with the 1930's when the pianissimo of consumer discontent swelled into an anvil chorus.

Consumers' Cooperatives

Consumers' cooperatives were an early effort by consumers to solve their buying problems without outside help. "Consumer cooperation is merely an attempt to substitute joint efforts of consumers in supplying their needs for those of private enterprise."[1] Consumers must inevitably perform, in part, certain of the marketing functions, such as storage of goods, some types of risk bearing (spoilage, for example), and, as a rule, transportation of goods from store to household. Consumer cooperation is but an extension beyond the normal sphere of consumer activity.[2] Because of its substitution of mutual benefit for profit gain, a consumer cooperative has no incentive to charge exorbitant prices, to misrepresent goods, or to hold back information concerning quality.

Credit for establishing the principles of modern consumer cooperation is usually given to the Equitable Pioneers Cooperative Society, which was formed in 1844 by 28 poor weavers in Rochdale, England. The Rochdale pioneers laid down basic rules to assure democratic control as well as sound financial and market practices. In addition to the provision that the "co-op" be collectively owned by its members, there were the following requirements:

14   The Beginnings Of The Consumer Movement

1. Open membership.
2. One vote per member regardless of the amount the member invests in the co-op enterprise.
3. A limited return on the capital invested by members.
4. Sales at market prices to avoid price wars with private business.
5. Patronage refunds paid out of net income at the end of the year in proportion to each member's volume of purchases.
6. Sales for cash only.
7. The establishment of reserve funds to be used for expansion and for promotion of cooperative education.

An early effort to apply the Rochdale principles in the United States started in a buying club set up by a Philadelphia labor union in 1862. The co-op failed after four years, but it aroused an interest in the Rochdale methods in the United States. Depression after the Civil War in the Agricultural West led the National Grange and later the Farmers' Alliance to try their hand at cooperative organization — for the purpose of marketing as well as purchasing. After the panic of 1873, two labor groups, the Sovereigns of Industry and the Knights of Labor, encouraged their members to establish cooperatives. Most of the union-sponsored co-ops passed out of existence before 1900, but many of the farm co-ops with their dual role of marketing and purchasing were solidly implanted. Failing co-ops were often the victims of inexperienced management and inadequate capital.

Co-ops sprang up again during the period of rising prices accompanying and following World War I. In 1916, the Cooperative League appeared as a clearing house of information on how to run co-ops, and as a promotional agency. Co-ops in the credit field, called credit unions, became popular in this era. The merchant philanthropist, Edward A. Filene, played an important role in their development. A few co-op petroleum associations also sprouted, mainly in the Middle West. The latter continued to expand during the 1920's, but the co-op movement as a whole made only moderate progress. By 1929, there were 1,476 retail distributive associations including stores, petroleum associations, and a few miscellaneous organizations, such as creameries and bakeries doing a business of approximately $63,000,000 a year, and 85 service associations in such fields as laundries, restaurants, housing, burial, and room and board associations doing a business of about $1,500,000. There were also nine wholesale associations servicing co-op stores which did a business of about $11,000,000, and 974 credit unions doing a business of about $54,000,000.[3] There was little in these statistics over which private business had cause for concern.

Other Self-Help
In addition to the consumer cooperatives several other organizations appeared, in the century preceding the 1930's, whose interests were devoted primarily to the problem of improving the

technique of consumption. The most significant was the American Home Economics Association, founded in 1908 under the leadership of Mrs. Ellen H. Richards (1842-1911), instructor of sanitary chemistry at the Massachusetts Institute of Technology. The A.H.E.A. grew from a series of nine summer conferences held at Lake Placid beginning in 1899, to bring together those interested in promoting better consuming habits. The emphasis at first was on the wiser use of purchased goods. During World War I, the Association became interested in the standardization of consumer goods and in more informative labeling to simplify the complexity of buying. A textile committee was set up in 1919 to secure the cooperation of business in promoting this end. The committee also worked with the National Bureau of Standards to perfect performance tests for judging textiles. In 1927, the Association appointed a standing committee on the standardization of consumer goods, and in 1928, became a member of the American Standards Association, an organization of business and other groups seeking to promote standards for industrial goods. Since the beginning the A.H.E.A. has published the *Journal of Home Economics* to keep its members posted on developments in the field of consumption, and has appeared before congressional committees to testify on issues related to the consumer interest. The membership in the association has never been large, but it has been drawn primarily from the influential ranks of home economics teachers.

Pressure Groups for the Consumer Interest

Another consumer organization was the Chicago Housewives League, started in 1910 with the establishment of study groups to accomplish wiser buying techniques. A campaign to "read your labels" was the first step undertaken in self-help. A few similar organizations in other cities were set up. In a small way, these associations attempted to represent consumers before legislatures. One of the two witnesses appearing on behalf of consumers at the 1921 tariff hearings on the Fordney-McCumber Bill was a representative of a housewives' league. After World War I, some of the leagues organized buyers' strikes in protest against the mounting cost of living. Spontaneous consumer organizations sprang up throughout the country during this inflationary period. They are remembered for their parades, meat strikes, and rent strikes. There was talk of a nation-wide middle class union to represent consumers' interests, but all of this died with the price drops in 1920-1921 and the prosperity which followed.

Organizations with primary interests in labor conditions, social affairs, or civic matters occasionally turned their attention to consumer problems. The National Consumers' League, founded by Florence Kelley in 1899 to organize consumer boycotts against enterprisers who exploited their laborers, occasionally broadened its scope to include matters of more direct concern to consumers. For

16   The Beginnings Of The Consumer Movement

example, the League actively supported the drive for pure foods and drugs which culminated in the 1906 Act. The General Federation of Women's Clubs fought hard for the same cause. The Federation was holding its biennial convention at St. Louis in 1904 at the same time Dr. Harvey W. Wiley was displaying his spectacular exhibit of adulterated foods and injurious drugs at the St. Louis World's Fair. The club women were so impressed with Dr. Wiley's exhibit that they appointed a national committee to educate their members all over the country on the importance of food and drug legislation. They distributed leaflets, made speeches, and submitted petitions. When the bill was held up in committee, the clubs organized a telegram campaign, flooding Washington congressmen with demands for immediate action. The federation deserved no small measure of credit for the eventual passage of the act.

Pioneers in Consumer Education

Some individual authors and educators are important as antecedents of the Consumer Movement because of the stimulus which they exerted on the development of consumer education and consumption theory. Perhaps Benjamin Franklin keynoted the whole development of consumer education by popularizing his slogan, "a penny saved is a penny earned." The home economists, however, were the first to become actively interested in consumer problems. The founder of this movement was Benjamin Thompson (Count Rumford) who made some of the earliest researches into cooking, heating, and other matters of domestic concern near the close of the 18th century. The first course in household arts appears to be that offered by Mrs. Emma Willard in the Troy Female Seminary in 1821. The first texts in home economics were Catherine E. Beecher's *Treatise on Domestic Economy* (1841) and her *Domestic Receipt Book* (1842). Edward L. Youmans, a chemist, published *Household Science* in 1857, a scientific study of food, air, heat, and light from the standpoint of the consumer. Many public school and college teachers were offering courses in domestic science by the end of the 19th century. From their ranks came the home economists who, under the leadership of Mrs. Ellen H. Richards, established the American Home Economics Association in 1908.

With few exceptions, economists, beginning with Adam Smith, have paid lip service to consumption as the sole end of production, and then have proceeded to neglect the subject or treat it as an afterthought or as incidental to a fuller understanding of production. The first prominent American economist who made consumption a primary interest was Simon N. Patten, who published his *Consumption of Wealth* in 1888. He is remembered for his pioneer efforts to establish a theory of consumption, although this theory is best left to the obscurity in which it now reposes. Patten also proposed that consumer education be taught to school children — not as domestic science, but as a general program of economic education.

Herbert J. Davenport, in his *Outlines of Elementary Economics* (1898), and even more so in his teaching, used a consumer approach to economics subject matter. "The schools," he wrote, "should teach us how to use the wealth which we may later gain . . . Education must indeed be a preparation for life, but a preparation in the art of living it . . . "[4]

Considerable impetus toward broadening the scope of economics to include consumer education resulted from the writings of America's Thorstein Veblen, and England's John A. Hobson. Veblen's widely-read *Theory of the Leisure Class* (1899) ridiculed the futility and irrationality of consumer choices. His *Theory of Business Enterprise* (1904), *Engineers and the Price System* (1921), and *Absentee Ownership* (1923) made vituperative attacks upon the wastes of salesmanship and advertising. Hobson decried the overemphasis in economics texts on production, urging in *Work and Wealth* (1914) that economists give equal consideration to consumption.

Wesley C. Mitchell's paper on "The Backward Art of Spending Money", read at the 1912 meetings of the American Economics Association, aroused the interests of many economists in consumer problems.

Five important books appeared in the 1920's, which tried to integrate consumption into the economics curriculum. Benjamin Andrews' *Family Economics* (1923), Hazel Kyrk's *Theory of Consumption* (1923), Elizabeth Hoyt's *The Consumption of Wealth* (1928), Warren C. Waite's *Economics of Consumption* (1928) and Paul Nystrom's *Economic Principles of Consumption* (1929) became textbooks or collateral reading for college courses in the economics of consumption. Dr. Nystrom's text was intended primarily as a guide for producers, rather than education or counsel for consumers.

Specialists in education were pioneers in the effort to integrate consumer education with the regular curricula of the public schools. An early leader in this effort to base the teaching of subjects such as mathematics, business, and general science upon real life problems was Frederick G. Bonser. This movement, which began about 1910, received a great stimulus from Henry Harap's *Education of the Consumer* (1924). Dr. Harap offered quantitative evidence of present habits of purchasing such products as food, housing, fuel, and clothing, and contrasted these habits with what he considered efficient practice. Conclusions from these comparisons were presented as objectives of consumer education. A wealth of suggestions was made for integrating this study material with the regular curriculum.

The Muckrakers

Some of the muckrakers of the Progressive Era called dramatic attention to the problems of the consumer through their vicious exposes of monopoly, graft and corruption. The popular magazines, *Ladies Home Journal* and *Colliers Weekly*, were especially vehement

18   The Beginnings Of The Consumer Movement

in their condemnation of patent medicine frauds. Upton Sinclair, in his best-seller, *The Jungle* (1905), ruined the appetites of many a meat eater with his revealing decription of the filth and fraud in the meat packing industry.[5]

Dr. Harvey W. Wiley

The leader in a 26-year crusade for a Federal Pure Food and Drugs Law was Dr. Harvey W. Wiley, chief of the Bureau of Chemistry in the Department of Agriculture. Through his speeches, writings, exhibits of injurious and adulterated foods and drugs, and his famous "poison squad," he helped to arouse the public indignation which eventually forced Congress to take action. Prior to the 1906 Act almost 200 pure food and drug bills had been introduced into either the House or the Senate, but each one had been killed by the organized opposition of the affected business interests. Dr. Wiley continued as chief of the Bureau of Chemistry until 1912. By then the continued pressure from vested interests upon the chief executive and the Department of Agriculture had resulted in so restricting Dr. Wiley's authority that effective administration of the Pure Food and Drug Law was impossible. He resigned from his government office in disgust and began another vigorous crusade, preaching, with publications and from the rostrum, the ineffectiveness of current food and drug protection. His protesting voice was an impetus toward the expanding Consumer Movement.[6]

Help from Private Business

Alarmed by the widespread criticism of advertising during the Progressive Era, the Associated Advertising Clubs of the World organized a National Vigilance Committee in 1911 to protest abuses in their trade. They adopted "truth in advertising" as a slogan and tried through moral suasion to raise the standards of advertisers. *Printers Ink* contributed a model statute to outlaw misleading and fraudulent advertising, and with the aid of local Vigilance Committees throughout the country, campaigned successfully for its passage in many states. The Vigilance Committees soon changed their name to Better Business Bureaus and expanded their purpose to include the purging of dishonest business practices of all types.

The Hughes life insurance investigation in 1906 led to "house-cleaning" in that industry. Under the inspiring leadership of Dr. Solomon S. Huebner, a program of insurance education was inaugurated in colleges and universities, and a "Chartered Life Underwriter" designation was established for salesmen in 1927. The "C.L.U." program, administered by the American College of Life Underwriters, and still in effect, involves the establishment of educational standards for insurance agents in such fields as insurance principles, economics, finance, American government, social problems, investments, trusts and taxes, and business law. The purpose is to raise the competence of agents in the counselling of consumers as to their life insurance needs. Rigorous examinations are drawn up in the fields noted, and the agent who passes the examinations and has served three years in the industry is awarded the "C.L.U." degree.

Another business group which contributed significantly to the consumer interest in this period was the American Medical Association. Its publications exposed the worthless nostrums and quackery of the Patent Medicine venders.[7]

Caveat Emptor

One of the earliest efforts by organized government to protect consumers against fraud was the adoption of a uniform system of weights and measures and its enforcement by state and municipal governments. The so-called English system of weights and measures, which dates from a law passed in England in 1266, was adopted by the English colonists who migrated to America. With few exceptions, to be noted presently, little else was done by governmental units specifically to aid or protect consumers until the 1930's. The prevalent doctrine, derived from the intensely individualistic Roman law, was *caveat emptor* (let the buyer beware).[8] The problem of developing the vast potential wealth of the American continent was considered paramount. Producers were aided with grants, subsidies, tariff protection, and the dissemination of information on markets and scientific production, while consumers were left to shift for themselves. The philosophy was that of the Scotchman who bought only one spur for his horse, figuring if one half would go, the other half would go too. If only production could be steadily increased, the gains would trickle down to all of the consumers. Recognition that the "invisible hand" which had protected consumers in Adam Smith's day was no longer adequate dawned slowly among legislators. The oil, which made Smith's economic system function smoothly, was the presence of competition and enlightened consumers. The weakening of these checks against business abuse in the late 19th and 20th centuries threw the consumer open to flagrant exploitation.

The first notable exception at the federal level to this policy of *caveat emptor* was the Pure Food and Drug Act of 1906, which made it unlawful to manufacture in any territory or the District of Columbia, or to transmit between states adulterated or misbranded foods or drugs. The bill excluded advertising and cosmetics, however, and required only that drugs and their derivatives be identified on the label in a non-misleading manner. As previously noted, the pprotection which this law provided was weakened by curbing the authority of Dr. Wiley through executive edict. A few of the states had food and drug legislation before the turn of the century, and many more followed the federal lead after 1906.

20   The Beginnings Of The Consumer Movement

As noted earlier, a number of states passed "truth in advertising" laws following 1911. There are, however, relatively few instances in which these state laws have been used to curb advertising abuses, noble though their intent may have been. What improvements there were up to 1929 resulted primarily from the pressure of honest business interests.

Consumers were protected to some extent by federal meat inspection (when interstate commerce was involved) after legislation was passed shortly before 1900. The real motive, it has been alleged, was not to protect consumers but to meet a prerequisite for getting American meat into foreign ports.[9] By 1929, some of the states and municipalities were also providing for meat inspection, and some of the municipalities were inspecting milk and grading it according to butter fat content.

In addition to the limited protection provided through sumptuary laws, a trickle of information was available to consumers through the research activities of various echelons of government. As far back as 1847, the Patent Office in its annual report added some data on proper nutrition. In later reports farm houses and the consumption of milk were discussed. When the Department of Agriculture was established in the federal government in 1862, a Bureau of Home Economics was included to take over the work in the household arts which the Patent Office had begun. In 1894, an Office of Human Nutrition Investigations was added to the Agriculture Department and $10,000 was appropriated for this work. The Smith-Lever Act in 1914 provided for a rural extension service, through the Agriculture Department, which brought training in home management to a limited number of housewives in rural areas.

Some of the states had agriculture departments which furnished comparable services to consumers who took the trouble to use them. In the early 1870's, the land grant colleges in Iowa, Kansas, and Illinois were giving instruction in the household arts. Some of the public colleges and universities followed this lead in later years. The state which furnished the most aid to consumers appears to be North Dakota. Its laboratories were testing consumer goods and publicizing the information on comparative qualities *according to brand names* by the 1920's.

No illusion is held that the foregoing discussion of the government aid to consumers prior to the 1930's is a complete one. No mention has been made, for example, of laws such as the Sherman Act and the Federal Trade Act or the laws to regulate the rates and service of railroads and public utilities, or the Public Health Services in the field of promoting sanitation (except insofar as the latter relate to food inspection). To some extent, these provisions protected consumers in their buying, but the intent was to serve a much broader purpose. This survey has been directed at the question, "What did government agencies in the United States do specifically to further the consumer interest in the years preceding the 1930's?" The paucity of aid was even greater than what is indicated in the foregoing discussion, for very often consumer activities were financed by the meagerest scrapings from the budget barrel, or were administered through groups controlled by producer interests.

The "Guinea Pig" Books

Many consumers who were unaware of their plight, or who passively accepted the labyrinth into which they had been drawn by the complex factors discussed in Chapter IV were jarred out of their complacency by a book which appeared in 1927 entitled *Your Money's Worth*. Written by Stuard Chase and Frederick J. Schlink, this publication was termed by Robert S. Lynd "the *Uncle Tom's Cabin* of the consumer movement." *Business Week* summed up the impact of *Your Money's Worth:*

> Simon Legree and Eliza — crossing-the-ice in Harriet Beecher Stowe's classic may have roused grandma's crusading zeal back in 1852, but grandma's desire to do something about it pales into insignificance alongside mother's when Mr. Chase (who had been on the staff of the Federal Trade Commission) and Mr. Schlink (who had been with the National Bureau of Standards) first told her that the soap which made her so popular at the dance was made with "a little creosol, a common and cheap disinfectant recommended by the government for disinfecting cars, barns and chicken yards;" that the Journal of the American Medical Association had said that $495 worth of Listerine had the antiseptic action of a cent's worth of corrosive sublimate and that its effect was mainly to "cover one smell with another;" . . . that the best and safest mouthwash was a little warm water with salt.[10]

The theme of the book is that the consumer is like Alice in a Wonderland. The market place is a veritable "wilderness in which we consumers wander without chart or compass".[11]

> We buy not for the value of the product to meet our specific needs but because the story told on every billboard, every newspaper and magazine page, every shop window, every sky sign, every other letter we receive — is a pleasing, stimulating and romantic story . . . But whether or not it is a fairy story we do not know save through the bitter and wasteful process of trial and error.[12]

Your Money's Worth was offered as a "Book of the Month" selection and became a best seller with estimated sales of 100,000 copies.[13]

The success of *Your Money's Worth* led to a wave of books debunking advertising and portraying the plight of the consumer. Mr. Schlink collaborated with Arthur Kallet in 1933, to turn out *100,000,000 Guinea Pigs*, the most popular consumer book ever written with estimated sales of over 250,000 copies.[14] The readers are told that they and their fellow Americans are "guinea pigs" because they offer themselves for experimental testing by purchasing all sorts of pernicious and doubtful products. Citing a wealth of illustrations, the book bitterly indicts commercial interests, the inadequacy of the 1906 Food and Drug Law, and the deficiencies of the Agricultural Department officials who were currently administering the law. The authors conclude with a challenge to the consumers to—

> Give your congressmen and senators, and your state legislators no rest until they sit in judgment on the work of the National Food and Drug Administration and the local health and food control authorities.
> Above all let your voice be heard loudly and often, in protest against the indifference, ignorance, and avarice responsible for the uncontrolled adulteration and misrepresentation of foods, drugs, and cosmetics. [15]

The "guinea pig" metaphor caught the public imagination, and soon became the appelation for a whole group of debunking books.

The third largest seller among the "guinea pig" books was *Skin Deep* by Mary C. Phillips, the wife of Mr. Schlink.[16] Mary Phillips placed under the microscope soaps, lipsticks, rouges, cold creams, hair dyes, fat reducers, and other beauty aids, and concluded that many women were wasting their money and endangering their health with these preparations. She urged women everywhere to work for stringent laws governing the sale of cosmetics and fat-reducing nostrums.

Other debunking books, although not reaching the popularity of the big three, were nevertheless important in stimulating interest in consumer problems during the 1930's. Another book by Mr. Schlink, *Eat, Drink and Be Wary* (1934), exposed food adulteration and dietary deficiencies.[17] Our Master's Voice: Advertising, by James Rorty, (1934) was a confession of the abuses in this trade by a former advertising copy-writer. He maintained that advertising cost was—

> The tax which business levies on the consumer to support the machinery of its super-government — the daily and periodical press, the radio, the apparatus of advertising. . . By this super-government the economic, social, ethical, and cultural patterns of the population are shaped and controlled into serviceable conformity to the profit-motivated interests of business.[18]

Counterfeit, by Arthur Kallet (1935), pictured the consumer as duped by manufacturers, advertisers and retailers of many well-known brands of commercial products. He found a paucity of avenues over which consumers could escape.[19] *Partners in Plunder*, by Joseph B. Matthews and Ruth E. Shallcross (1935), paraded some 750 cases by the reader to illustrate the authors' contention that consumer exploitation was a by-product of the profit system as it was then operating.[20] Mr. Matthews' *Guinea Pigs No More* (1936) continued the expose of business mal-practices, but concluded with a constructive plan for organizing consumer resistance to such evils through passage of a bill (given in the book) creating a Federal Department of the Consumer. Through consumer education and organization Mr. Matthews contended that U.S. capitalism could be converted from business dictatorship to consumer dictatorship. [21]

A final "guinea pig" book, important in arousing consumers, was Ruth de Forest Lamb's *American Chamber of Horrors* (1936). Miss Lamb, a member of the staff of the Food and Drug Administration, wrote the book in a crusade for federal legislation controlling the sale and advertising of cosmetics and for more effective food and drug legislation. Miss Lamb ranked with the most effective of the debunkers, as the following passage shows:

> It is all too true that a pretty young woman was blinded by an eyelash dye. It is also true that scores of others suffering from paralysis and impared vision have been sent to hospitals for long expensive treatment as the result of using a rat poison to banish superfluous hair. A prominent business man really was killed by radium-charged drinking water that dissolved the bones of his skull instead of curing the ailment for which it was advertised. Three sisters, one after another, rubbed horse liniment on their cough-racked chests in the pathetic belief that it would cure them — and died of tuberculosis. At this very moment, men and women all over the country are literally burning their tissues to death in trying to reduce their weight with deadly dinitrophenol. [22]

These "guinea pig" books set afire the accumulation of consumer discontent which had been piling up in previous decades, and led directly to the establishment and rapid growth of consumer financed testing and rating agencies. They aroused, from apathy, numerous individual consumers, women's clubs, religious associations, civic groups, labor unions, and educational agencies which set their sights on an attempt to solve the serious problems of the consumer.

QUESTIONS FOR REVIEW

1. What is meant by the "consumer movement"?
2. Why were consumer cooperatives given as an early effort to help the consumer? Why did they fail to do so?
3. Would the extension of producer and consumer cooperatives be the answer to better consumer protection now? Why or why not?
4. Many early pioneers in consumerism pinned their hopes on better education for the consumer in buying? Do you think this was a good idea? Where did it fall down?
5. What is "muck raking"; Who were the "muckrakers"? Why did these early critics seem to originate from the literary area rather than from the professional social scientists of the time?

24 The Beginnings Of The Consumer Movement

6. Evaluate the contribution of Dr. Harvey W. Wiley to the first round of consumerism in America.

7. What is meant by "caveat emptor"? What made this doctrine increasingly inappropriate during the 20th Century?

8. What were the "guinea pig books"? What influence did they have on the consumer movement of the 1930's?

FOOTNOTES

1. Harold H. Maynard and Theodore N. Beckman, *Principles of Marketing* (New York, Ronald Press Co., 1946) p. 211.

2. The difference between the consumer cooperative and the profit-seeking business is set forth clearly by Donald F. Blanknertz, "Consumer Actions and Consumer Nonprofit Cooperation," in *Theory in Marketing,* edited by Reavis Cox and Wroe Alderson (Chicago, Richard D. Irwin Co., 1950), pp. 163-177.

3. Bulletin # 531, *U.S. Bureau of Labor Statistics* (February, 1931), p. 6.

4. Herbert J. Davenport, *Outlines of Elementary Economics* (New York, MacMIllan Co., 1898) p. 280.

5. The following passage from *The Jungle* describes the ingredients which it is alleged the Chicago meatpackers customarily put into their sausage:

> It was the custom . . . whenever meat was so spoiled that it could not be used for anything else . . . to chop it up into sausage . . . There would come all the way back from Europe meat that had been rejected, and that was moldy and white — it would be dosed with borax and glycerine, and dumped into the hoppers, and made over again for home consumption. There would be meat that had tumbled out on the floor, in the dirt and sawdust, where the workers had tramped and spit uncounted billions of consumption germs. There would be meat stored in great piles in rooms; and the water from leaky roofs would drip over it, and thousands of rats would race about on it. It was too dark in these storage places to see well, but a man could run his hand over these piles of meat and sweep off handfuls of the dried dung of rats. These rats were nuisances, and the packers would put poisoned bread out for them; they would die, and then rats, bread, and meat would be shoveled into carts, and the man who did the shoveling would not trouble to lift out a rat even when he saw one — there were things that went into the sausage in comparison with which a poisoned rat was a tidbit. . . Upton Sinclair, *The Jungle* (New York, The Viking Press, 1946, reprinted from the original manuscript, copyrighted 1905) p. 134-135. When this book was first published, President Theodore Roosevelt sent two commissioners to Chicago to investigate stockyard conditions. The commissioners then turned in a report which sustained Sinclair's charges. They told the author later that the only point on which they could get no proof was his statement that men had fallen into the lard vats and gone out to the world as pure leaf lard. (p. 1x author's preface to 1946 edition).

6. See Harvey W. Wiley, *An Autobiography* (Indianapolis, Bobbs-Morill Co., 1930) and Harvey W. Wiley, *History of the Crime Against the Pure Food Law* (Washington, D.C., H. W. Wiley, 1929).

7. See Arthur J. Cramp, *Nostrums and Quackery* (Chicago, American Association, Bureau of Investigation, three volumes published 1911, 1921, 1936).

8. While the exploited consumer had the power under common law to sue the producer who utilized fraud and misrepresentation, this legal protection was an empty shell inasmuch as suits would, as a rule, be more costly and time consuming than consumers could afford, and in addition, might easily be lost by the inability of the consumer to prove intent to defraud or misrepresent.

9. Robert S. Lynd, "The Consumer Becomes a 'Problem,' " *Annals of the American Academy* (May, 1934), p. 2.

10. "The Consumer Movement," *Business Week* (April 22, 1939), p. 40.

11. Stuart Chase and Frederick J. Schlink, *Your Money's Worth* (New York, MacMillan Co., 1927), p. 254.

12. *Ibid.*

13. R. A. Robinson, *Advertising the Consumer Movement* (Crowell Publishing Co., 1937), p. 22.

14. R. A. Robinson, *op. cit.*, p. 22.

15. Arthur Kallet and Frederick J. Schlink, *100,000,000 Guinea Pigs* (New York, The Vanguard Press, 1933) pp. 302-303.

16. Mary C. Phillips, *Skin Deep* (New York, The Vanguard Press, 1934).

17. Frederick J. Schlink, *Eat, Drink and Be Wary* (New York, Covici-Friede Co., 1935).

18. James Rorty, *Our Master's Voice: Advertising* (New York, John Day Co., 1934), p. 30.

19. Arthur Kallet, *Counterfeit — Not your Money But What It Buys* (New York, Vanguard Press, 1935).

20. Joseph B. Matthews and Ruth E. Shallcross, *Partners in Plunder* (New York, Covici-Friede Press, 1935).

21. Joseph B. Matthews, *Guinea Pigs No More* (New York, Covici-Friede, Inc., 1936).

22. Ruth de Forest Lamb, *American Chamber of Horrors* (New York, Farrar and Rinehart, 1936) p. 4.

[42]

Excerpt from William T. Kelley (ed.), *New Consumerism: Selected Readings*, 27–45.

THE CONSUMER MOVEMENT, 1930 TO WORLD WAR II

3

EUGENE BEEM

Consumer Revolt in the 1930's

The propaganda of the "guinea pig" books was the most important reason for the awakened interest in consumer problems in the 1930's, but there were other factors also playing a part. Perhaps the major reason so many consumers reacted strongly to the disclosures of the "guinea pig" books was the simultaneous onslaught of the Great Depression. A whole generation of Americans had grown up in an era of rapidly increasing national product and living standards. The typical individual likened himself to the heroes of the Horatio Alger novels who rose from "rags to riches." The prospect of rapid gains from his producer interest left little inclination to dwell upon the less dramatic gains which might be possible by furthering his consumer interest. The Great Depression shattered, for many, this notion that one's producer role alone would suffice to gain him a high standard of living. The shrinking money incomes of the 1930's made more people tractable to the notion that living standards could best be increased, or maintained by the wiser use of existing income, and by protective consumer legislation rather than through expanded earnings.

The depression also aroused resentment against business enterprise for its failure to keep the economy operating at a high productive level. Consumers, unable to understand the paradox of intense wants alongside idle plants and manpower, were ready to accept the indictments of the "guinea pig" authors. The widespread attitude of cynicism, which was a legacy of the post World War I years, likewise helped to put consumers in a receptive mood for this literature.

Other reasons, too, played a part in bringing the Consumer Movement to fruition in the 1930's. Increased leisure afforded housewives by the time-saving mechanical inventions of the 20th century, and by a reduction in the size of families, gave them more time to devote to problems of wiser consumption. The steady growth of literacy and the higher level of average sophistication, resulting from widening dissemination of college and secondary school education, facilitated the comprehension of consumer problems and cooperation toward their solution.

The possibility of more scientific consumption was a final factor which stimulated the Consumer Movement in the 1930's. Wesley C. Mitchell told his economics colleagues, at the 1912 American Economic Association Convention, "progress in the arts of consumption ... waits upon progress in science."[1] Considerable

28   The Consumer Movement, 1930 To World War II

progress in the scientific testing of consumer goods had been made
by 1929. General Motors had a proving ground for testing its own
and its competitors' products. Sears-Roebuck and Macy's, among
other retail stores, had laboratories for testing the merits of goods
before selling them to customers. Good Housekeeping had a
laboratory where the products of its advertisers were subjected to
analysis as a check on the accuracy of advertising claims. The
Educational Buyers' Association had an arrangement with the
Engineering Department of the University of Chicago, whereby
competing brands of supplies bought by E.B.A. members were tested
and reported upon. The Hospital Bureau of Standards and Supplies
was testing and reporting on competing brands of supplies for its
member hospitals. The U.S. Testing Company and the Electrical
Testing Laboratories were testing a wide range of products for
manufacturers and large scale buyers on a *fee* basis. The American
Medical Association was testing proprietary drugs and certain food
products. Perhaps the most comprehensive testing agency was the
National Bureau of Standards, whose secret reports to government
purchasing agents on the merits of competing goods were said to be
saving the American taxpayer $100,000,000 a year.[2]

Commenting upon the development of scientific product testing
procedures, Chase and Schlink wrote:

> It is evident that the United States contains today a series
> of outposts which are doing sound work in the direction
> of substituting the scientific method for rule of thumb.
> The outstanding difficulties with the exhibit are lack of
> coordination, and a failure to pass on results to the
> consumer in a form he can use ... In the accumulated
> research of these outposts, sufficient technical
> information is now on file to deflate and destroy the
> great majority of selling games; the bulk of poetic
> advertising; the massed magic of salesmanship.[3]

The developments in the scientific testing of consumer goods opened
a new vista to consumers — the possibility of a way out of the maze
of conflicting quality claims by the testing and rating of competing
product brands. They made feasible the establishment of the
product rating agencies which have been described as the "dynamos
of the Consumer Movement."[4]

The Consumer Movement was an inevitable development, made
thus by the magnitude of the plight into which a highly developed
and complex economy had plunged the consumer. The forces
discussed above reacted interdependently to bring consumer
problems to a vivid focus in the 1930's, and to awaken an urge by
millions of consumers for immediate corrective action.

Participating Groups

The groups, which have been active in the Consumer Movement,
may be classified into those whose interest in consumer problems

was a sideline to a broader purpose, and into those whose primary purpose was the alleviation of the consumers' plight. Quantitatively, the former type of organization has been more important than the latter. This type included such groups as the women's clubs, labor unions, settlement houses, religious organizations, educational bodies, some government agencies and certain private business interests. Those groups with a primary concern for consumer problems included the product rating agencies, consumer cooperatives, The American Home Economics Association, consumer committees and councils, and national associations formed to coordinate and represent politically the consumer interest of individuals and all of the previously mentioned groups of both types.

The remainder of this chapter will describe briefly the activities of these various organizations with the exception of the product rating agencies which will be treated in later chapters.[5]

Organizations with Secondary Consumer Interests

(1) WOMEN'S CLUBS. Many of the women's clubs have played a major part in the Consumer Movement. Organizations with civic, political, and multifold purposes having an aggregate membership of over five million have had study programs in their individual chapters on consumer problems, and have supported legislation to protect and further the consumer interest. Their interest has been sporadic rather than persistent, but was particularly forceful in the decade, 1937-1946. Among the major organizations which emphasized consumer programs were the American Association of University Women, the National League of Woman Voters, the General Federation of Women's Clubs, and the Y.W.C.A. Thirteen national women's groups united in support of the Federal Food, Drug and Cosmetic Act enacted in 1938. Various clubs have urged the enactment of such measures as increased appropriations for federal agencies engaged in consumer protection, compulsory grade labeling of canned foods, a Federal Department of the Consumer, and the repeal of the Miller-Tydings Act.

(2) LABOR UNIONS. Labor unions have shown a steadily increasing concern for the consumer interest. Since the 1930's the International Ladies Garment Workers Union has included lectures and courses on consumer problems in its welfare program for members. During World War II years many unions established consumer information centers in their meeting halls to distribute government pamphlets and materials on price control, rationing, and efficient consumption. Some unions held informational meetings at which problems of conservation and wise buying were discussed. Representatives of both the C.I.O. and the A.F. of L. participated in a committee of The American Standards Association which aimed to promote minimum standards for consumer goods. The A.F. of L., the C.I.O., and several of the national unions composing these organizations urged their union members to join consumer

cooperatives, and helped their local unions to establish consumer cooperatives where no existing ones prevailed. Of the non-farm cooperatives reporting to the Bureau of Labor Statistics in 1947, 31 percent said that half or more of their members belonged to unions.[6]

Over 150 union newspapers now publish a syndicated column by Consumers Union entitled, *Your Dollar.* This release, which appears monthly, digests the four leading product ratings contained in the current issue of *Consumer Reports.*

(3) MISCELLANEOUS GROUPS. Miscellaneous groups have intermittently sponsored consumer programs. The Federal Council of Churches has distributed literature and aided churches in establishing consumer cooperatives, the National Congress of Parents and Teachers has encouraged consumer study programs in its local chapters and has supported legislation in the consumer interest. The National Federation of Settlements has organized mothers' clubs which have studied better buymanship techniques and have supported local and national legislation for consumer protection.

An insight into the nature of the study programs, sponsored by the several dozen organizations which have approached consumer problems as a sideline, was provided by an analysis of consumer meetings reported in the press. Among 4,141 meetings between 1940 and 1946, the most popular topics (excluding those which related primarily to the war effort) were: 1) commodity buying information, 2) consumer education, 3) the care and use of consumer goods, 4) the Consumer Movement in general, and 5) health and nutrition.[7]

(4) EDUCATIONAL INSTITUTIONS. Educational institutions have been one of the most significant elements contributing to the Consumer Movement. At the high school level a great upsurge of courses in consumer economics began in the middle 1930's. At the same time, a consumer approach began to win increasing favor in such courses as social studies, economics, sociology, arithmetic, and natural science. A poll of high schools enrolling 300 or more pupils by Dr. Thomas Briggs for the National Association of Secondary School Principals in 1946, showed that 26 percent of the schools responding were offering separate courses in consumer education, exclusive of home economics.[8] Consumer education was being taught as a part of one or more other courses by 87 percent of the schools replying.[9] In 1942, the National Education Study" which led to the publication of 11 text pamphlets, averaging about 100 pages each, on such topics as "Learning to Use Advertising," "Money Management," "Consumer Credit," "Buying Insurance," and "Effective Shopping." The units were suitable for use in either a separate consumer course, or in a consumer approach to other subjects of the secondary school curriculum. About 500,000 copies of these pamphlets were in use during 1949 in more than 2,000 schools.[10] At least one state, Wisconsin, made instruction in consumer cooperatives compulsory in all public high schools.

Public school systems have also furnished teaching personnel and sometimes facilities for adult education in consumption. Evening school classes of this type — most of them paralleling the home economics courses of the secondary schools — had an enrollment of about 326,800 adults in 4,000 adult centers and 500 schools during 1940-1941.[11]

A phenomenal increase in the number of courses in consumer economics has occurred at the college level during the last 20 years. Unfortunately the latest study of such courses appears to be that completed before World War II by Alpheus Marshall. He found 920 separate courses, exclusive of home economics, being given in 451 colleges and universities. His survey covered the catalogue offerings of 1,249 of the 1,709 institutions of higher learning in the United States and outlying territories, in 1939.[12]

A substantial increase in the number and enrollment of these courses has taken place since 1941. A trend may be developing toward the use of a consumer approach in the introductory economics course at the college level. Paul Samuelson's *Economics, An Introductory Analysis* (1948) lays great emphasis upon the importance of the consumption function in maintaining an economy of full employment. His text includes material on problems of personal finance. Leland Gordon's *Elementary Economics* (1950) orients the whole subject matter of economics around the consumer. His goal is to teach consumers how their economic system acts or fails to act to meet their needs. Elizabeth Hoyt's *The Income of Society* (1950) is a more standard treatment of principles, but contains a wealth of material on consumer living standards, buying motives, and consumption problems. A text, *Economics, Experience and Analysis* (1950) by Broadus Mitchell and others, contains three chapters on using the national income.

From 1937 to 1941, the Institute for Consumer Education at Stephens College, Columbia, Missouri, acted as a clearing house for gathering, organizing and testing consumer education materials. The Institute was financed by a generous grant from the Alfred P. Sloan Foundation, and was headed by Professor John M. Cassels. A monthly newsletter, *Consumer Education*, and occasional pamphlets and books kept educators informed of the latest developments in the consumer field. The three national conferences, which were held from 1939 to 1941, brought together several hundred consumer educators, club leaders, government workers, labor representatives, and scientific workers, and gave a stimulus and a coordination to the Consumer Movement as a whole.

(5) BUSINESS AGENCIES. The early reaction of private business interests to the Consumer Movement has been characterized as "watching, wishing, and witching."[13] The "watching" involved a careful analysis of the objectives of the movement by retailing interests and the advertising trade journals in particular. The "wishing" was the conclusion that there was no Consumer Movement at all — only professional agitators. The "witching" was an attempt to smear the movement as subversive. Demands for honest advertising, grade labeling, and consumer cooperatives were termed "doctrines of Moscow." Women's clubs were "transmission belts." By 1941, a significant number of business leaders had recognized as

legitimate many of the demands of the Consumer Movement, and
were attempting to meet them. The activities of these progressive
business groups have furthered consumer education and protected
the consumer in his buying.

The Better Business Bureaus have been the most important
business agency in the Consumer Movement. Their program of fraud
fighting and consumer protection has increased significantly in the
last 20 years. In 1937, the National Better Business Bureau began the
publication of a "Facts You Should Know" series for consumer
education. Pamphlets on 25 subjects have been published on such
topics as "Buying Used Cars", "Cosmetics", "Health Cures",
"Jewelry", "Securities", and "Advertising". About 680,000 "Fact"
booklets are distributed in a typical year.[14]

In addition, 91 local Bureaus reached consumers through radio
programs, newspaper advertising, news items, pamphlets and posters.
Since 1942, the National Bureau has sponsored the Consumer
Education Study of the National Association of Secondary School
Principals, which has been discussed previously. Each of 64 American
Business Firms has contributed $6,000 through the National Bureau
toward the support of this program. The financing does not appear
to have affected the objectivity of the pamphlets.

Another business-sponsored organization which furthered the
consumer interest was the National Consumer-Retailer Council.
Established in 1937, its purpose was "to promote cooperation
between consumers and retailers to the end that problems of mutual
concern could be solved in a way advantageous to both".[15]

Consumer members are the American Home Economics
Association and the National Board of Young Women's Christian
Associations. Seven trade associations of retailers are members of
associate members in addition to the National Better Business
Bureau. An outstanding project of the Council has been its work in
encouraging informative labeling and advertising. Its Sales Promotion
Package Program offers complete instruction to retailers on what
information should be included in advertising and labeling specific
products, such as men's shirts. Guidance is given in planning
programs to educate sales personnel and customers in the value of
such informative selling. The Council also distributes a series of
pamphlets informing consumers how to get the most for their money
in purchasing vegetables, bathing suits, dry cleaning service, and the
like. A transcribed radio program, entitled "Keys to Wise Buying,"
furnishes buying tips to consumers over 22 stations reaching 30
states. The *NCRC News* covers developments in the Consumer
Movement, and is distributed to consumers — primarily teachers — in
2,473 communities throughout the country.

A few business groups have simplified the buying problems of
consumers by their promotion of consumer good standards on an
industry-wide basis. Consumer standards are specific criteria by
which quality, quantity, performance, or terminology may be
judged, or to which they conform. Standards enable a meeting of
minds between seller and buyer. Where standards prevail, a can of

corn labeled "A", size "38" in a topcoat, or a certification by the American Gas Association on the label of a gas stove, provides in each case an understandable basis for consumer selection.

Standardization of consumer goods by individual firms has been practiced for many decades. All this means is that merchandise under a given brand is uniform in quality, that size "7" hats of a particular manufacturer have the same dimensions, that "Fancy" as a particular canner's label for a certain type of peas denotes a uniform quality for *that* canner. Such standards are of limited aid to the consumer when competing firms use different standards. The developments in consumer good standards, which have been a part of the Consumer Movement, were, formerly, on an industry-wide rather than on an individual firm basis.

Foremost among business agencies which have promoted consumer standards is the American Standards Association. The A.S.A., established in 1918, is a clearing house for coordinating the standardization work of private business and governmental agencies. Its membership at present includes more than 100 national, technical, and trade organizations. Several hundred other national organizations are cooperating in A.S.A. standardization work. The primary interest of the A.S.A. has always been in the standardization of producer goods and industrial production methods, but in 1936, an Advisory Committee on Ultimate Consumer Goods organized to coordinate and direct standardization work on consumer goods in particular. The membership of this committee embraces trade associations representing consumers such as the American Association of University Women, Congress of Industrial Organization, American Federation of Labor, American Home Economics Association and Consumers Union. Among the standardizing projects which have been studied are body measurements for children, quality and labeling of bedding and upholstery, shoes, sheets and sheeting, boys' clothing, hosiery, household refrigerators, silver-plated tableware, waterproof and water repellant fabrics, color permanence, and performance criteria for rayon fabrics. Only a few of the 1,124 standards approved, up to July, 1949, by the American Standards Association are in the field of consumer standards. One reason for this is the necessity for support from a consensus of industrial members concerned before promulgation of standards may be undertaken. This limitation is not so serious with industrial goods in which members profit directly from the standards adopted. In the field of consumer standards, producer gains are less direct, and are by no means certain to be shared by all producing units.

A number of commercial agencies grant a seal of approval for use in labeling products which are found to meet specific standards as to safety or quality. The American Gas Association has developed 36 sets of national standards for various gas appliances designed to insure their safety in use. The seal of approval which is granted to manufacturers who conform to the A.G.A. standards is found on more than 95 percent of the gas burning equipment being marketed.[16] Underwriters' Laboratories, Inc. has 150 different sets of standards designed to insure the safety of such products as electrical cords, fuses, fans, lamps, flat irons, radios and television sets, heating appliances, roof-covering materials, electric blankets, and toys. The U.L. seal of approval is displayed on more than 475,000 products manufactured by over 7,500 producers.[17] Fabrics which meet certain tests for shrinkage, color fastness, or tensile strength may exhibit approval seals of the American Institute of Laundering, the Better Fabrics Testing Bureau, or the U.S. Testing Company. The Electrical Testing Laboratories issue a Certification Tag for lamps which meet the specifications of the Illuminating Engineering Society.[18]

The American Medical Association and the American Dental Association have pursued programs to enlighten and protect the consumer. The A.M.A.'s Council of Foods and Nutrition, which had its origin in 1929, makes a systematic analysis of food advertising and labeling, and awards a seal of acceptance to foods which are advertised and labeled informatively and honestly, and which meet the Council's standards for safety and nutrition.[18a] Pamphlets on foods, nostrums, and quackery are distributed to interested consumers. The A.M.A.'s Council of Pharmacy and Chemistry publishes the names of "acceptable" proprietary drugs. A monthly magazine, *Hygeia*, contains material on health education, which is written for the understanding of the layman. The American Dental Association supplies interested consumers with information on dental products such as toothpastes and powders, denture cleaners and mouth washes.

At one time the Association pubslihed a list of "accepted" dentifrices which included those meeting standards of safety plus honest and informative advertising labeling. Such products were permitted to carry the A.D.A. seal of acceptance on their label. In 1950 a new policy was adopted restricting acceptance to dentifrices which demonstrated ability to *prevent* tooth decay. As of July, 1950, no product had qualified for the new standard of acceptance. Dentifrices containing urea and ammonium salts, fluorides, and chlorophyll derivatives were under study by the A.D.A. Council on Dental Therapeutics, but test results were inconclusive.[19]

The focusing point for a large amount of business activity in the Consumer Movement is the Committee on Consumer Relations in Advertising, financed by the American Association of Advertising Agencies and leading advertising media.

The Committee was organized in 1940 for the primary purpose of interpreting the Consumer Movement for advertising interests, and interpreting advertising for the Consumer Movement. A continuing study of consumer meetings in the United States, as reported in the press, was made between 1940 and 1946, and a study of consumer attitudes toward advertising was undertaken in 1946.

The *Consumer News Digest* is a monthly bulletin which reports objectively the important developments in the Consumer Movement. It is mailed without charge to interested producers and consumers. A series of seven pamphlets entitled The *Consumer-Buyer and Distribution*, has been published for use in consumer education studies of adult groups. Catalogues of business-sponsored educational materials and films are published for the guidance of teachers of consumer education. About 250 sources of pamphlets and leaflets are given, and over 1,000 motion pictures and film strips are described. Many of these materials are primarily promotional in nature, but a number offer very objective and valuable aid to consumers.

The Household Finance Corporation has an outstanding consumer education program which originated in 1932. Its series of Better Buymanship pamphlets offer counsel in budgeting and in buying food, clothing, home furnishings, health, and other commodities and services. About 1,000,000 of these booklets are distributed every year at $.05 each to homemakers, schools, adult education groups, women's clubs, and libraries. Charts and filmstrips are furnished to teachers of consumer education.

The "Chartered Life Underwriter" program of the American College of Life Underwriters, which was discussed in the preceding chapter, has grown steadily in stature. In 1950, about 17 percent of all life insurance agents either had a "C.L.U." degree, or were studying for the degree.[20]

(6) GOVERNMENT AGENCIES. A considerable increase in the incidental consumer activities of federal government departments has taken place in the last 20 years. Consumers won *de facto* recognition from the federal government in the 1930's when consumer representatives were placed in several governmental agencies. In the National Recovery Administration a Consumer Advisory Board participated with a Labor Advisory Board and an Industry Advisory Board in approving Industry Codes designed to put the economy back on its feet. The primary significance of the C.A.B. was a beginning of consumer representation in the government, for the Board lacked the well organized constituency which supported the Industry advisors, and was woefully weak.[21]

Advisory Consumer Counsels were provided in the Agricultural Adjustment Administration (1933) and in the National Bituminous Coal Commission (1937). The effectiveness of both in guarding the consumer interest against abuse in the planning programs of those producer-dominated agencies was slight. The A.A.A. Counsel published a *Consumers' Guide*, which campaigned for compulsory grade labeling and consumer cooperatives, and published a wealth of home economics material. Both Counsels and the *Guide* were discontinued.

During the World War II period the Office of Price Administration contained consumer representation in an advisory capacity. The consumer unit encouraged, and to some extent, coordinated the work of the consumer committees on the local Defense Councils which were established in all parts of the nation. The only consumer representation in the federal government as of June, 1950, was the

36   The Consumer Movement, 1930 To World War II

Consumer Advisory Committee to the President's Council of Economic Advisors.

The Committee includes 25 individuals representing consumer, church, educational, negro, welfare, and women's organizations. The significance of this representation is minimal since consumers are only an advisory group to an advisory group for the President, who in turn can merely advise and recommend legislation to Congress. Consumers have been consistently thwarted in their attempt to secure *de jure* recognition in the President's cabinet with a Department of the Consumer which would parallel the type of representation accorded labor, business, and agricultural interests.

Various departments of the federal government have contributed to consumer protection against exploitation and to consumer education in general. Prior to 1938, the Federal Trade Commission could take action to halt deceptive or unfair business conduct *only* when injury to one or more competitors resulted. The Wheeler-Lea amendment to the Federal Trade Act in that year gave the F.T.C. power to initiate action to protect consumers specifically against fraudulent and misleading advertising of foods, drugs, devices, or cosmetics. The F.T.C. made up an exhibit of its work on behalf of consumers which it displayed during 1947, and part of 1948. The display included examples of articles falsely advertised, against which the F.T.C. had acted. A few of the items included suntan lotaion advertised as destroying germs, moth spray which attracts rather than repels moths, and "Pure Raspberry Preserves" found to be a complete fake except for the seeds.

The F.T.C. shares with the Anti-Trust Division of the Justice Department the responsibility of ferreting out monopolistic abuses. The F.T.C. also conducts trade practice conferences at which agreements are established standardizing labeling terminology, promulgating standards of identity, and guarding against consumer deception of other types. The agency also administers the Wool Labeling Act, which became effective in 1941, requiring producers to state the wool content of garments on the label, including the percent of re-processed or re-used wool. The Anti-Trust Division of the Justice Department in the immediate years before World War II, and since the end of that war, has crusaded vigorously against monopolistic restraints such as those in the building trades, which have been especially abusive of the consumer interest.

The Food and Drug Administration and the Office of Education in the Federal Security Agency of the Interior Department have increased in significance for the consumer in the last two decades. Some of the worst defects of the 1906 Food and Drug Act were corrected in the Food, Drug, and Cosmetic Act of 1938. For example, cosmetics and mechanical health devices were brought under control, and more information concerning ingredients and quality of foods and drugs was required. Enforcement provisions were also strengthened. The U.S. Office of Education has distributed bibliographies of readings on consumer economics and has published suggestions for teaching methods in home economics.

The Bureau of Human Nutrition and Home Economics of the Department of Agriculture is devoted to research on homemakers' problems and the dissemination of its findings. The Bureau is currently distributing at a minimum price, about five million copies a year of its 100 or more different bulletins. Advice is offered on such subjects as "Meat for Thrifty Meals," "Money-saving main dishes," "Slip covers for furniture," and "Housecleaning management and methods." The Extension Service of the Department of Agriculture is reaching more than 3,000,000 rural homemakers a year in its program of general consumer education. A great increase in the use of the Department of Agriculture's voluntary food grading plans has taken place in the last 20 years. Although a large part of this grading is used only in wholesale marketing, a steadily growing volume of graded food products is available in consumer markets.[22]

The Board of Governors of the Federal Reserve System has carried on a continuing study of the spending patterns of various income groups since 1946.

The Bureau of Labor Statistics of the Department of Labor studies living standards and reports on living costs. Progress reports are made on consumer cooperatives in the United States and abroad, and information on the establishing and managing of cooperatives is distributed.

From 1935 to 1938, a Consumer Project Division in the Labor Department undertook research on consumer standards and related problems. The Division was the outgrowth of work which was previously being done by the Consumer Advisory Board of the N.R.A.

The National Bureau of Standards of the Commerce Department has cooperated with consumer groups and others in the standardization and simplification of consumer goods. The Department of Commerce contributes to the consumer interest in a second way — through the distribution of educational pamphlets on such subjects as "Care and Repair of the House," and "Safety for the Household."

An increasing concern for the welfare of consumers has also developed at the level of state and local government in ways which parallel to a varying extent, and supplement the activities of the federal agencies discussed above.

Organizations with Primary Consumer Interests

(1) CONSUMER COOPERATIVES. Among organizations dedicated primarily to alleviating consumer problems, consumer cooperatives were, and still are, of major importance. Kenneth Dameron estimated that 0.37 percent of all retail business in the United States was done by co-ops in 1929.[23] *Business Week* estimated that co-ops handled slightly more than one percent of retail sales in 1939, and slightly more than two percent of the $129 billion of retail sales in 1949.[24] The total number of retail

distributive associations grew from 1,476 in 1929, to 3,985 in 1947, and the number of service co-ops in fields such as housing, burial, room and board associations, hospital and health associations, and cold storage lockers grew during the same years from 85 to 793. The number of credit unions increased almost tenfold from 974 to 9,040. The number of wholesale associations servicing co-op stores jumped from 8 to 36.[25]

An indication of the growing significance of consumer cooperatives has been the establishment of the National Tax Equality Association by certain business interests to protest the alleged tax favoritism accorded consumer cooperatives. The net receipts of consumer cooperatives, which are paid out in patronage refunds to members, are exempted from the corporate income tax. The increasing interest of labor unions in consumer cooperatives and the promotional activities of governmental agencies for co-ops have already been recounted. The campaign of the National Tax Equality Association has led the Cooperative League to establish a Washington Office and a Congressional lobby. This lobby not only campaigns for the cooperative cause but also testifies, for what it considers the consumer interest, at hearings on various types of questions affecting consumers.

(2) AMERICAN HOME ECONOMICS ASSOCIATION. Membership in the A.H.E.A. increased from 10,000 in 1929 to 19,345 as of April 30, 1949,[26] and the scope of consumer activities increased significantly. The organization participated actively in the work of the National Consumer-Retailer Council, and the Advisory Committee on Ultimate Consumer Goods of the American Standards Association. From 1936 to 1948, the *Consumer Education Service* was published as a monthly bulletin to report progress in standardization, grade labeling, consumer protective legislation, and other aspects of the Consumer Movement. Occasionally, representatives have testified at Congressional hearings on legislation affecting consumers. The Association has repeatedly urged larger appropriations for the Bureau of Human Nutrition and Home Economics of the Agricultural Department, with which it cooperates in numerous research programs. The "Consumer Speaks Project", initiated in 1946, serves as an information channel between the manufacturer and the consumer. Discussion groups are held throughout the country to determine the qualities women want in various commodities. The votes of the women are tabulated, and standards and specifications are drawn up to express for manufacturers the technical points stressed by the homemakers. Up to June, 1948, 3,942 groups representing 100,000 consumers in 40 states had participated in projects for such products as pots and pans, refrigerators, washing machines, irons, ironing boards, cotton and rayon blouses, and house dresses.[27] The A.H.E.A. reports great interest in these reports on the part of manufacturers.

(3) CONSUMER COMMITTEES AND COUNCILS. During the N.R.A. period about 200 local consumer councils were established

throughout the nation to provide support and a sounding board for the Consumer Advisory Board. A number of the councils continued after the demise of the N.R.A., providing a meeting place for discussing the mutual problems of producers and consumers, and representing the consumer interest before city councils and state legislatures. During the life of the O.P.A. these veteran councils and many additional consumer committees, which were affiliated with local defense councils, attempted to educate consumers in conservation habits, and tried to secure vigorous enforcement of the price and rationing controls. Some consumer groups such as the one in Newark, New Jersey, established consumer information centers in prominent locations to advise consumers on buying problems, and to receive and check complaints of OPA violations.

A leading consumer council is that in Cincinnati, Ohio, which includes 63 cooperating organizations and many individual members. The conference represents consumers at legislative hearings, publishes a monthly bulletin on wise buying, and presents frequent radio programs. An average of 200 attend the monthly meetings.

The St. Louis Consumer Federation conducted a three-day milk strike in 1948, in protest against high milk prices. In 1947, the New York City Consumers Council held a mock trial to denounce the rising cost of living. The Washington, D.C. Committee for Consumer Protection called a meat strike in October, 1946, About 37,000 housewives signed pledges not to pay more than 60 cents per pound for any cut of meat, and many of them set up picket lines in front of butcher shops and groceries.

(4) NATIONAL CONSUMER ORGANIZATIONS. Several attempts were made to coordinate the activities of groups with a primary or secondary consumer interest through a national organization, but most of the efforts have proved abortive. The latest effort was the National Association of Consumers, established following the dissolution of the OPA around a nucleus of groups and individuals which were active in fighting for the maintenance of price controls. Miss Helen Hall, head of the Henry Street Settlement House in New York City, and a veteran leader in the Consumer Movement, was chairman of the N.A.C. Its long range objectives were:

1. To promote the organization and education of consumers.
2. To gain consumer representation in agencies of government — city, state and federal.
3. To secure recognition of consumer interests in programs of business, agriculture, and labor designed to shape and direct the American economy.
4. To gain official consumer representation in the United Nations and its constituent councils and commissions which deal with consumer welfare.[28]

With respect to day-to-day activities, the N.A.C. spoke for consumers at legislative hearings in Washington. The chairperson, Miss Hall, was a member of the Consumer Advisory Council to the President's

40   The Consumer Movement, 1930 To World War II

Council of Economic Advisors. A representative acted in an advisory capacity to the United States Delegation at the United Nations Food and Agriculture Organization meetings. Consumers received aid in establishing local chapters of the N.A.C. in their own respective communities. Finally, a four-page paper, *Consumers on the March*, kept members informed on pending legislation and its significance for the consumer, and on other information of interest to consumers. The membership in January, 1950 included 3,000 group and individual members in 960 communities throughout the nation. Like

FIGURE 2
THE CONSUMER MOVEMENT — 2nd Round

GOAL: "To further the consumer interest"

METHODS: (indicated in diagram below)

A Few Groups Would Add	Some Groups Would Add	General Agreement On Proposals Listed Below	Some Groups Oppose	A Few Groups Oppose
A program of evolutionary socialism or a program leading to a "cooperative commonwealth"	Extension of welfare state. Promotion of consumer co-ops.	Programs of consumer education (including product testing). Protective legislation against fraud and misrepresentation. More effective anti-monopoly legislation. More factual buying information. Standardization of consumer goods. Compulsory grade labeling. Federal Dep't. of the Consumer. Consumer political pressure groups.	Compulsory grade labeling.	Federal Dep't. of Consumer. Consumer political pressure groups.

PARTICIPATING GROUPS:

Consumer Rating Agencies
Consumer Cooperatives
Consumer Committees and Councils
Educational Groups
Settlement Houses

Women's Clubs
Government Agencies
Professional Associations
Religious Groups
Labor Unions
Certain Business Groups.

the national consumer groups which preceded it, the N.A.C.'s chief problem was obtaining financial support to carry on its ambitious program.

A second national consumer group was the Consumer Clearing House, composed of group representatives having a primary or a secondary consumer interest. Under the direction of Miss Caroline Ware, the representatives met for the purpose of exchanging information on consumer issues and planning action. The Clearing House, itself, did not act as a body, but rather recommended action, and provided a means for the member groups to cooperate in programs when they wished to do so.

A Panoramic View of the Consumer Movement

The previous pages have presented a piecemeal view of the Consumer Movement during the 1930's and 1940's, describing briefly the major participating groups with the exception of the rating agencies. The central goal of all participants was to further the consumer interest, but there was a divergence of opinion as to the best way of accomplishing this objective.

The Consumer Movement has been likened to Stephen Leacock's horseman who "jumped on his horse and rode in all directions". Table I shows those methods upon which there is general agreement with a brief indication of the expanded aims of the left wing groups and the restricted proposals of the right wing. Bitter feeling exists between some of the leftist and rightist groups because of their opposing economic philosophies.

The Consumer Movement of these two decades appeared to be predominantly a revolt by a minority of the middle and upper income groups. A study made in 1940 by Dr. George Gallup (parts of which are summarized in Table II) showed that only about 12 percent of the lower income families had even heard of the Consumer Movement. About 32 percent of the middle income group had heard of the Movement, and about 48 percent of the upper income group were aware of the Movement. Among the upper income group, 15 percent had attended meetings for the purpose of discussing what products consumers should or should not buy. Among the middle income group, 10 percent had attended such meetings, while among the lower income group only 4 percent had done so. The same poll showed that the middle and upper income groups were more critical of advertising than the lower income groups, and were more interested in compulsory grade labeling. Subscribers to the services of the consumer rating agencies were likewise concentrated in the middle and upper income groups.

During the period of post-war recovery and unexampled affluence of the 1950's and 1960's, the consumer movement, so vigorously founded in the early 1900's and revived in the 1930's, may be said to have "run down". True, it was never really missing from the American scene during this time. For example, the consumer rating

42 The Consumer Movement, 1930 To World War II

TABLE II
PUBLIC OPINION POLL ON CONSUMER MOVEMENT, 1940*

Response to Question: "Have you heard of the Consumer Movement?"

All income groups:	yes — 27%	no — 73%
Upper income group:	yes — 48	no — 52
Middle income group:	yes — 32	no — 68
Lower income group:	yes — 12	no — 88

Response to Question: "Have you ever attended a lecture or meeting held for the purpose of discussing what products consumers should or should not buy?"

All income groups:	yes — 9%	no — 91%
Upper income group:	yes — 15	no — 85
Middle income group:	yes — 10	no — 90
Lower income group:	yes — 4	no — 96

Response to Question: "Have you any criticisms of advertising?"

All income groups:	yes — 41%	no — 59%
Upper income group:	yes — 56	no — 44
Middle income group:	yes — 47	no — 53
Lower income group:	yes — 30	no — 70

Response to Question: "Are you in favor of having ABC grade labeling made compulsory by the government?" (Asked only of those interested in grade labeling)

All income groups:	yes — 48%	no — 52%
Upper income group:	yes — 60	no — 40
Middle income group:	yes — 54	no — 46
Lower income group:	yes — 39	no — 61

* "Survey of Public's Buying Habits," Ballot 703 C, *A.I.P.O.*, Sept. 29, 1940, pp. 16, 27, 29, 31.

agencies, such as the Consumers Union, continued to grow and flourish; the circulation of *Consumer Reports* grew from about 100,000 just after World War II to more than one million in 1963 (covering about two percent of the nation's families).[29] But, it is fair to say that a substantial hiatus developed in these two decades. As many have noted, the typical American was much more interested in earning money effectively than spending it wisely. Few in the "good old days" of Eisenhower and Johnson perceived that the consumer was not spending very wisely, nor that he needed protection from the rising tide of those "quick buck artists" who were out to exploit him (and not all of this number were counted amongst the "fly-by-night" outfits).

In this affluent, self-satisfied sky a brilliant new rocket rose and exploded, shattering the complacency, and launching a new round of consumerism that made the previous two rounds seem pale by comparison. In the next section we examine the origins of this bright new force, Ralph Nader, and examine his influence, try to apprise whether the third round will be a flash-in-the-pan, as many say, or will become a permanent part of life in our time.

QUESTIONS FOR DISCUSSION

1. Why did the Great Depression, 1930-1939, stimulate the second round of consumerism so strongly?

2. How much protection to the consumer was afforded by the establishment of testing laboratories for products by mass merchandisers such as Sears, Roebuck and Macy's? How about the Good Housekeeping seal of approval?

3. Would it have been a good thing to open up to the public the results of tests on goods done by the National Bureau of Standards? Why, in your opinion, were these valuable reports not released for general dissemination to the public?

4. What influence did the following organizations have during the second round of consumerism:
    (a) Women's clubs
    (b) Educational institutions
    (c) Labor unions
    (d) Better Business Bureaus
    (e) Trade associations and professional societies

5. A number of people were appointed to governmental agencies during the 1930's to represent the interests of the consumers, e.g., NRA, Coal Board, etc. Why did the author feel that their influence was "weak"?

6. It looks as though a great many government agencies in the 1930's were carrying on education and protection programs for the consumers. Why were these less than successful?

7. Why did consumer cooperatives fail to develop very well in the 1930's and 1940's? Were they well adopted to the American marketing environment?

8. Why in your opinion did the consumer movement "run down" in the 1950's and 1960's? What or who revived it?

FOOTNOTES

1. Wesley C. Mitchell, "The Backward Art of Spending Money," *American Economic Review* (1912, Vol. 2), p. 275.

44   The Consumer Movement, 1930 To World War II

2. Stuart Chase and Frederick J. Schlink, *Your Money's Worth* (New York, MacMillan Co., 1927), p. 5.

3. *Ibid.*, p. 238.

4. "The Consumer Movement", *Business Week* (April 22, 1939), p. 41.

5. The descriptive material in this chapter has been obtained from the following sources, in particular, in addition to those cited in later footnotes:
   a. Personal interviews with representatives of many organizations discussed.
   b. Helen Sorenson, *The Consumer Movement* (New York, Harper & Bros., 1941).
   c. Werner K. Gabler, *Labeling the Consumer Movement* (Washington, D.C., American Retail Federation, 1939).
   d. "The Consumer Movement — Some New Trends," *Consumer Education Service* (March-April, 1947).
   e. Caroline F. Ware, *Consumer Goes to War* (New York, Funk Co., 1942).
   f. Helen Hall, "Consumer Protection," *Social Work Year Book* (1949), pp. 142-150.

6. "Consumer Cooperatives: Operations in 1947" *Bulletin #948, Bureau of Labor Statistics* (1947), p. 8.

7. Kenneth Dameron, "Consumer Meeting Agenda, A study in Consumer Interests," (April, 1948), p. 102.

8. Thomas Briggs, "Consumer Education in 1946-47" *Bulletin of the Department of Secondary School Principals* (May, 1947), p. 137.

9. *Ibid.*

10. *Consumer News Digest,* (October, 1949), p. 3, (June, 1949), p. 3.

11. Esther C. Franklin, in *Consumer Education,* edited by James E. Mandenhall and Henry Harap (New York, Appleton-Century Co., 1943), p. 210. The author knows of no later statistics, but a great increase in this type of training appeared during the war years.

12. Alpheus Marshall, "920 Courses in Consumption Economics," *The Educational Record* (January, 1941), p. 27-38.

13. Donald E. Montgomery, Talk to American Association of Advertising Agencies in May, 1940.

14. *Facts You Should Know About Your Better Business Bureau* (no date) p. 13.

15. From the masthead of the *NCRC* News.

16. Jessie Coles, *Standards and Labels for Consumer Goods* (New York, Ronald Press, 1949), p. 493.

17. *Ibid.*, p. 490.

18. The reader who wishes more than this cursory examination of the present status of consumer standards is referred to Part VII in Jessie Coles' *Standards and Labels, op. cit.*

18a. The American Medical Association ceased granting seals of acceptance in the late 1950's. It still carries on the evaluative studies described. The American Dental Association still grants such seals, e.g., see Crest toothpaste.

19. "Revised Procedure for the Evaluation of Dental Products," *Journal of the American Dental Association* (June, 1948), pp. 489-495.

20. Information supplied by Davis W. Gregg, President, American College of Life Underwriters.

21. William N. Loucks, "Price Fixing: The Consumer Faces Monopoly", *Annals of the American Academy* (May, 1934), pp. 113-124.

22. Coles, *op. cit.*, Chapter 22.

23. Kenneth Dameron, *Consumer Problems in Wartime* (New York, McGraw-Hill, Co., 1944), p. 358.

24. "Co-op Growth Faces Hurdles", *Business Week* (December 10, 1949), p. 48.

25. "Consumer Cooperatives: Operations in 1947", *B.L.S. Bulletin #948* (U.S. Department of Labor, 1947), p. 2.

26. Keturah E. Baldwin, *The AHEA Saga* (Washington, A.H.E.A., 1949), p. 101.

27. *Ibid.*, p. 50.

28. *Consumers on the March* (May, 1947), p. 3.

29. Edward L. Brink and William T. Kelley, *The Management of Promotion* (New York: Prentice-Hall, Inc., 1963), p. 358.

Name Index

Shapiro, S. 44, 66, 86, 88–9, 96, 98–9, 105, 129, 131, 151
Shartle, C. L. 567
Shaw, A. W. 6, 10–11, 15, 18, 34, 50–52, 440, 539
Shaw, E. 68
Shawver, D. L. 93
Sherbini, A. A. 95, 108, 109
Sherman, C. B. 291
Sherman, S. 528
Sherry, J. F. 151
Sherry, J. F. Jr 547
Sheth, J. N. 48, 67–8, 89, 138, 141–2, 147, 150, 168, 516, 543–8, 564
Shimaguchi, M. 91
Shipchandler, Z. E. 96
Shiskin, B. 419, 425
Shocker, A. D. 547
Shoemaker, F. F. 89
Shyrock, L. R. 398
Sidgwick, H. 60
Silk, A. 66
Silverman, W. 89
Simcoe, J. G. 215–16
Simmel, G. 157–8
Simon, H. 530, 543, 568
Simpson, R. 365, 380
Sinclair, U. 575
Slater, C. 93, 107, 112, 546
Sloan, A. P. 587
Sloan, H. S. 56
Small, C. 544
Smalley, D. 67
Smalley, O. A. 119, 130, 529
Smallwood, J. E. 542
Smelser, N. J. 93, 99
Smith, A. 59, 521–2, 525, 531, 573, 576
Smith, D. 211
Smith, E. R. 444
Smith, G. L. 66
Smith, W. R. 541
Snedecor, G. W. 436–9, 442
Soldner, H. 99
Solomon, M. R. 523
Sombart, W. 523, 530
Somers, M. T. 531
Sommers, M. S. 86
Sparling, S. E. 6, 15, 46–7, 52
Spiegel, H. W. 521–2
Spivey, W. A. 545
Sproles, G. 523–4
Srivastava, R. K. 547
Stafford, J. E. 541, 562

Stalin, J. 231, 237
Stanford, A. 461
Staples, W. A. 543
Starch, D. 13, 202, 439–40
Steelman, J. R. 415
Steiner, G. A. 542, 546
Stern, L. 66–7, 168, 543–4
Stevens, W. H. S. 10
Steward, I. 525
Stigler, G. 565
Stockton, R. C. 405
Stone, G. 529
Stone, L. 156
Story, R. 407
Stowe, H. B. 578
Strong, E. K. 201–2
Strong, R. 156
Strumpel, B. 541
Stuard, S. M. 517
Sturdivant, F. D. 529
Summers, J. O. 544
Surprenant, C. 544
Swanson, D. 527

Taft, W. H. 310
Taimni, K. K. 109
Tan, C. T. 516
Taney, R. 342, 345, 352–3
Tankard, J. W. 441–2
Tarbell, I. M. 7
Taussig, F. W. 6, 12, 45, 48–9, 52–3, 61
Tawney, R. H. 228
Taylor, A. D. 47
Taylor, F. M. 5
Taylor, F. W. 49–50
Taylor, H. C. 6–7, 13, 46–8, 52
Tebbel, J. 25
Tennstaedt, F. 474
Terpstra, V. 95, 98
Teune, H. 88
Thakara, A. M. 53
Thompson, B. 573
Thompson, C. B. 50
Thompson, C. J. 450
Thompson, E. P. 158
Thomson, J. R. 108
Thorelli, H. B. 87, 91, 94
Thorndike, E. L. 201
Thornton, R. T. 398
Thurstone, L. 436–8
Thwing, C. F. 45
Tigert, D. J. 87, 545
Toffler, A. 545
Torrens, R. 59, 61

QM LIBRARY
(MILE END)